JOSEPH F. SMITH

BRIGHAM YOUNG UNIVERSITY
Church History Symposium

JOSEPH F. SMITH

REFLECTIONS on the MAN and His TIMES

EDITED BY

CRAIG K. MANSCILL, BRIAN D. REEVES, GUY L. DORIUS, AND J. B. HAWS

RELIGIOUS STUDIES CENTER
BRIGHAM YOUNG UNIVERSITY

DESERET BOOK

Published by the Religious Studies Center, Brigham Young University, Provo, Utah, in cooperation with Deseret Book Company, Salt Lake City.
http://rsc.byu.edu

Printed in the United States of America by Sheridan Books, Inc.

ISBN 978-0-8425-2847-4
Retail US $31.99

Front cover painting, Albert E. Salzbrenner, © Intellectual Reserve, Inc.
Cover design by Carmen Cole.
Interior design by Juliana G. Cox.

Library of Congress Cataloging-in-Publication Data

Brigham Young University Church History Symposium (2012 : Salt Lake City, Utah; Provo, Utah), author.
Joseph F. Smith : reflections on the man and his times / edited by Craig K. Manscill and Brian D. Reeves.
pages cm
Includes bibliographical references and index.
ISBN 978-0-8425-2847-4 (hard cover : alk. paper) 1. Smith, Joseph F. (Joseph Fielding), 1838-1918. 2. Church of Jesus Christ of Latter-day Saints--Doctrines. 3. Church of Jesus Christ of Latter-day Saints--History. 4. Church of Jesus Christ of Latter-day Saints--Management. 5. Church of Jesus Christ of Latter-day Saints--Presidents--Biography. 6. Mormon Church--Presidents--Biography. I. Manscill, Craig K., editor of compilation. II. Reeves, Brian D., 1959- editor of compilation. III. Title.

BX8611.B725 2012
289.3092--dc23
[B]

2013036706

Contents

Preface ix
Craig K. Manscill

Keynote Addresses

1. Joseph F. Smith and the Importance of Family 2
Elder M. Russell Ballard

2. Doctrinal Contributions of Joseph F. Smith 17
Joseph Fielding McConkie

Early Years

3. Triumphs of the Young Joseph F. Smith 37
Nathaniel R. Ricks

4. Joseph F. Smith's 1864 Mission to Hawaii: Leading a Reformation 52
Eric Marlowe and Isileli Kongaika

Family and Friends

5. "A Modern Patriarchal Family": The Wives of Joseph F. Smith in the *Relief Society Magazine*, 1915–19 74
Lisa Olsen Tait

6. The Fathering Practices of Joseph F. Smith 96
Mark D. Ogletree

7. Letters from Joseph F. Smith to His Adopted Son Edward Arthur Smith 114
Kevin Folkman

8. Joseph F. Smith's Encouragement of His Brother, Patriarch John Smith 133
J. B. Haws

9. Personal Glimpses of Joseph F. Smith: Adolescent to Prophet 159
David M. Whitchurch

10. "My Dear Charlie": The Friendship of Joseph F. Smith and Charles W. Nibley 181
Matthew C. Godfrey

Theology

11. Joseph F. Smith on Priesthood and Church Government 199
Craig James Ostler

12. Development of the Understanding of the Postmortal Spirit World 221
Joseph Stuart

13. "The Last of the Old School": Joseph F. Smith and Latter-day Saint Liturgy 233
Jonathan A. Stapley

Church Administration

14. The Apostolic Succession of Joseph F. Smith 249
Patrick A. Bishop

15. Joseph F. Smith's Succession to the Presidency 265
Dennis B. Horne

16. Joseph F. Smith and the Hawaiian Temple 279
Richard J. Dowse

17. "We Shall Have Temples Built": Joseph F. Smith and a New Era of Temple Building 303
Gary L. Boatright Jr.

18. Joseph F. Smith and the Great Mormon Building Boom 320
W. Ray Luce

19. Joseph F. Smith and the Origins of the Church Historic Sites Program 342
Jennifer L. Lund

20. Excavating Early Mormon History: The 1878 History Fact-Finding Mission of Apostles Joseph F. Smith and Orson Pratt 359
Reid L. Neilson and Mitchell K. Schaefer

21. "A Godsend for the Salvation of Modern Israel": The Creation of the Seminary Program 379
Brett D. Dowdle and Casey Paul Griffiths

22. Joseph F. Smith and the Shaping of the Modern Church Educational System 401
Scott C. Esplin

23. Church Programs in Transition 418
Richard O. Cowan

24. Joseph F. Smith and the First World War: 434
Eventual Support and Latter-day Saint Chaplains
Kenneth L. Alford

Public Perceptions

25. Joseph F. Smith's Beard and the Public Image of the Latter-day Saints 457
Justin R. Bray

26. The Tongues of the Saints: 470
The Azusa Street Revival and the Changing Definition of Tongues
Matthew R. Davies

27. Index 486

Craig K. Manscill

Preface

In 2012 a symposium was jointly sponsored by the Brigham Young University Department of Church History and Doctrine, the LDS Church History Department, and the BYU Religious Studies Center. It was held over two days, Friday, March 3, at the LDS Conference Center in Salt Lake City, and Saturday, March 4, in Provo at BYU's Conference Center. Keynote speakers were great-grandsons of Joseph F. Smith: Elder M. Russell Ballard of the Quorum of the Twelve Apostles, and Joseph F. McConkie, an emeritus professor from BYU Religious Education. In addition, more than thirty scholars made presentations on topics relating to Joseph F. Smith and his times. Many of the authors have refined their presentations for inclusion in this volume, and we gladly share them with you.

The symposium focused on Joseph F. Smith, the sixth President of The Church of Jesus Christ of Latter-day Saints, and his times. He served for fifty-two years as a General Authority of the Church, as a member of the Quorum of the Twelve Apostles, and as a counselor to four Church Presidents, and for seventeen of those years, as the President of the Church. On October 17, 1901, a week after the death of President Lorenzo Snow, Joseph F. Smith was ordained and set apart as the new President of the Church. He served as President until 1918. He was the last Church President who personally knew Joseph Smith Jr., his uncle.

Church membership nearly doubled during Joseph F. Smith's administration, from 278,645 members in 1901 to 495,962 members in 1918. Though the majority of members still lived in the western United States, President Smith felt a strong connection with members in many nations. He visited Europe in 1906, the first President of the Church to do so while in office, returned there in 1910, and made visits to Saints in Canada and the Hawaiian Islands. He and his counselors encouraged members to be loyal to their governments, to be good citizens, and to remain in their native lands and strengthen local congregations. Church members were no longer encouraged to gather to Utah. Church leaders had counseled earlier generations of Saints to gather to Zion, to geographically separate themselves from the world in order to forge unity and grow in a center of spiritual strength. President Smith emphasized for subsequent generations the importance of living peaceably in the midst of the world while maintaining the legacy of unity and spiritual strength made possible through priesthood ordinances.

Joseph F. Smith spoke and wrote at great length about the incomparable power of the priesthood and strove to help all members understand its significance. At the time he was sustained as Church President, meeting schedules and lessons varied from ward to ward. He sought to unify auxiliary organizations and standardize curriculum. The general boards of the Sunday School, Mutual Improvement Association (for youth), and Primary began publishing uniform courses of study. To address the challenge of increasing leisure time for youth, the Boy Scout program was adopted for young men and a new Beehive program was developed for young women. The Relief Society, which had been encouraging stakes to write lessons for sisters since 1902, began publishing uniform lessons in 1914 and special messages for visiting teachers in 1916. These innovations became part of the new *Relief Society Magazine* to assist Mormon women in looking after one another's spiritual and emotional well-being. For President Smith, it was vital that the auxiliaries work in harmony with the priesthood to teach the gospel and strengthen fellowship among Church members.

Joseph F. Smith sought to comprehend and teach the expansive truths of the gospel of Jesus Christ. He expounded Latter-day Saint doctrine through his letters, writings in Church magazines, and sermons. He and his counselors in the First Presidency took pains to clarify essential doctrines. In "The Origin of Man" (November 1909)[1] and "The Father and the Son: A Doctrinal Exposition by the First Presidency and the Twelve" (June 1916)[2], they taught the true nature of our association with Heavenly Father and Jesus Christ. Joseph F. Smith delivered hundreds of gospel discourses to help Saints understand and live the teachings of Jesus Christ. His close friend Charles W. Nibley declared, "As a preacher of righteousness who would compare with him? He was the greatest that I ever heard—strong, powerful, clear, appealing. It was marvelous how the words of living light and fire flowed from him."[3]

During the symposium, presenters taught that Joseph F. Smith had a challenging life, losing both of his parents before the age of fourteen, but he remained faithful and left a lasting legacy for the Church. He fought to protect the doctrines of the gospel, even against his fiercest critics. He served three missions for the Church: one as a young man in the Sandwich Islands (now known as Hawaii), another in the British Isles, and one more back in the Sandwich Islands to help reclaim members who had strayed from the Church through the influence of apostate Walter Murray Gibson. Joseph F. Smith was very devoted to his family, despite being a fully engaged Church leader; he had six wives (one later divorced), five adopted children, and forty-three biological children. He was blessed to have many mentors and friends, including Brigham Young, John Smith (his half brother), and Charles W. Nibley.

Joseph F. Smith is remembered not only for his long beard, but also for his lasting influence on the Church. He clarified the order of the priesthood and its offices, clarified Church practices and rituals, presided over an upswing in the construction of temples and other Church buildings, acquired Church historic sites and historical information, and fostered improvements in Church education which led to the modern Church Educational System.

During the last few months of his life, President Smith felt particularly close to the Spirit. On October 3, 1918, as he pondered the scriptures and reflected on the Savior's great atoning sacrifice for the redemption of the world, he received a marvelous manifestation concerning the Savior's visit to the dead after his Crucifixion. The revelation later called "the Vision of the Redemption of the Dead" and canonized as Doctrine and Covenants 138, is a fitting capstone to the life of this prophet who untiringly preached the importance of bringing to all of God's children the knowledge of the plan of life and salvation.

Acknowledgments

The editors gratefully acknowledge our colleagues who helped to plan and carry out the symposium, especially Matthew J. Grow, Brent R. Nordgren, and Linda Godfrey. We also thank the many individuals who helped with logistics, performed music, and served as session moderators. We appreciate the publishing team's efforts in producing this volume, including Joany O. Pinegar, Brent R. Nordgren, Devan Jensen, Austin Ballard, Aleesha Bass, Carmen Cole, Juliana G. Cox, Rachel Ishoy, and McKenna Johnson.

Notes

1. "The Origin of Man, by the First Presidency of the Church," *Improvement Era,* November 1909, 75–81.
2. "The Father and the Son: A Doctrinal Exposition by the First Presidency and the Twelve," *Improvement Era,* August 1916, 934–42.
3. *Gospel Doctrine: Selections from the Sermons and Writings of Joseph F. Smith*, 5th ed. (Salt Lake City: Deseret Book, 1939), 406.

Keynote Addresses

Elder M. Russell Ballard

1

Joseph F. Smith and the Importance of Family

I am grateful and humbled at the invitation to speak to you at this year's symposium. We are reviewing the life and teachings of a great man, the sixth President of the Church, President Joseph F. Smith. After looking at the list of subjects and those who will teach of his remarkable accomplishments, I have wondered what I can say to add to our understanding of the life of this very choice son of God.

In my office are the sculpted busts of the Prophet Joseph, his brother Hyrum, and Hyrum's youngest son, Joseph F. Smith. Joseph F. Smith is my mother's grandfather. His son Hyrum Mack Smith is my grandfather. As I look at the faces of these mighty prophets, I think I hear them saying, "Russell, get going! Do more; work a little harder while you still have time."

I pray that we will have the Spirit of the Lord to be with us as I share my thoughts about the remarkable life of Joseph F. Smith, which was molded by the hand of God. He served for seventeen years as prophet and President of the Church of Jesus Christ of Latter-day Saints. Because he was the last President of the Church to have personally known the Prophet Joseph Smith,

---

Elder M. Russell Ballard is a member of the Quorum of the Twelve Apostles.

his life—spanning the years from Nauvoo to November of 1918 in the Salt Lake Valley—has been chronicled time and time again. The more I have read about him, the more I am amazed at how he did all that he did in his eighty years of life.

I acknowledge that much of what I say you may have read or heard before. Some I will take from his own words and some from what others have written. My thoughts are centered on the importance of family as lived and taught by Joseph F. Smith.

As I have pondered over what I would say, it became clear to me that to really come to know President Joseph F. Smith, we need to know about his forefathers from whom he received the faithful, believing blood that flowed through his veins.

President Brigham Young declared the following in 1859:

> It was decreed in the councils of eternity, long before the foundations of the earth were laid, that [the Prophet Joseph Smith] should be the man, in the last dispensation of this world, to bring forth the word of God to the people and receive the fulness of the keys and power of the Priesthood of the Son of God. The Lord had his eyes upon him, and upon his father, and upon his father's father, and upon their progenitors clear back to Abraham, and from Abraham to the flood, from the flood to Enoch and from Enoch to Adam. He has watched that family and that blood as it has circulated from its fountain to the birth of that man. He was foreordained in eternity to preside over this last dispensation.[1]

Additionally, we know from the Book of Mormon that it was revealed to the prophet Lehi that Joseph the son of Jacob, who was sold to merchants on their way to Egypt, saw the day of this final dispensation and spoke of a choice seer to be raised up: "And his name shall be called after me; and it shall be after the name of his father. And he shall be like unto me; for the thing, which the Lord shall bring forth by his hand, by the power of the Lord shall bring my people unto salvation" (2 Nephi 3:15).

In the year of 1638, Robert Smith, a sturdy yeoman of England, immigrated to the New World, the land of promise. He settled in Essex County, Massachusetts, and afterwards married Mary French. Thus the beginning of the believing blood, as prophesied by Joseph of old, was anchored in the United States of America. Robert and Mary had a son they named Samuel, who also had a son he named

Samuel. The second Samuel's son was Asael Smith, who married Mary Duty. Their son Joseph Smith Sr. was born July 12, 1771.[2] It was Joseph and Hyrum's grandfather Asael who made this statement: "It has been borne in upon my soul that one of my descendants will promulgate a work to revolutionize the world of religious faith."[3]

There is no question in my mind that our Father in Heaven influenced Lucy Mack to marry Joseph Smith Sr. so they could become the parents of Joseph, his brother Hyrum, and their siblings. I include Hyrum also as a prophet, who stood valiantly at the side of Joseph and who is the father of Joseph F. Smith. I do not have time to detail all of their history, but Hyrum and his wife Mary Fielding demonstrated in their lives an absolute devotion and unwavering conviction that Jesus Christ is the Son of God and that through the Prophet Joseph Smith the fullness of his gospel was once again restored to the earth.

This brief ancestral sketch would not be complete without pointing out that Lucy Mack, the daughter of Solomon Mack, is the mother that the Lord had his eye upon from the beginning.

John Lathrop, Lucy's fourth-great-grandfather, was one of the brave reformers of Christendom in England. His is a story all of its own, but for my purpose in establishing why Joseph F. Smith became such a great spiritual giant and powerful Church leader, you only need to know that John Lathrop strongly believed in the Bible and the right of all people to have their own copy. After several years in prison for teaching what he believed, he was banished from England. He and his children and some of his followers settled in Massachusetts. It is amazing to know that many of his posterity were members of the Church in Nauvoo, and even more are members today.

The Lord moved Joseph and Lucy Mack step by step, failure by failure, to a plot of ground in Palmyra, New York. The story of their family struggle in establishing a homestead in Palmyra is a story that we are all familiar with. But to me, moving the Smiths to Palmyra was a fulfillment of their destiny.

This believing blood of the Smiths and the Macks flowed through the veins of their children. Surely the Lord was preparing the Prophet's family to recognize the truth and accept the responsibility of supporting Joseph in his call to restore to the earth the fullness of the gospel of Jesus Christ.

I wish we could talk more about the many powerful examples of faith manifested by our sweet but feisty Lucy Mack Smith. Her faith performed miracles.

How grateful we are that when Joseph Smith returned to his home after his experience in the sacred grove and his "mother inquired what the matter was, [Joseph] replied, 'Never mind, all is well—I am well enough off. . . . I have learned for myself that Presbyterianism is not true'" (Joseph Smith—History 1:20).

Also, how grateful we are for the believing blood of Father Smith when in 1823, after having been tutored through the night by Moroni, Joseph went to work in the field with him but was unable to continue. He was sent back to the house. As he attempted to cross the fence out of the field, he fell to the ground. Once again, Moroni appeared to him and, as the Prophet explained, "commanded me to go to my father and tell him of the vision and commandments which I had received. I obeyed; I returned to my father in the field, and rehearsed the whole matter to him. He replied to me that it was of God, and told me to go and do as commanded by the messenger" (Joseph Smith—History 1:48–50). I shudder to think what could have happened had Joseph's parents questioned him and cast doubt on his instructions from God.

Now, why is it important to understand at least this much about the believing faith and trust in God of the forefathers of Joseph F. Smith? It is because of the faithful heritage he was raised in that he was so susceptible to the promptings of the Spirit, through which he gained an unwavering testimony, which I quote:

> As a child I knew the Prophet Joseph Smith. As a child I have listened to him preach the gospel that God had committed to his charge and care. As a child I was familiar in his home, in his household, as I was familiar under my own father's roof. I have retained the witness of the Spirit that I was imbued with, as a child, and that I received from my sainted mother, the firm belief that Joseph Smith was a prophet of God; that he was inspired as no other man in this generation, or for centuries before, had been inspired; that he had been chosen of God to lay the foundations of God's Kingdom.[4]

We do not understand all of the reasons things happen in our lives, but it has always been impressive to me to know that Parley P. Pratt, under extreme personal hardship, accepted the call of Joseph Smith to go on a mission to Ontario, Canada. There he found and baptized John Taylor, Joseph Fielding, and his sisters Mary and Mercy Fielding. We remember that Hyrum returned home from a mission after his beloved wife Jerusha died, leaving him with five living children, including a baby, and no mother for them. Shortly thereafter, heaven sent

Mary Fielding to become Hyrum's wife to help him care for his family. Together they had two additional children, the oldest a boy they named Joseph Fielding, after the Prophet Joseph and Mary's brother Joseph Fielding. The little girl was named Martha Ann.

Mary Fielding, with the background of a schoolteacher from England, certainly taught the children the basic skills of reading and writing, but more importantly, she instilled in them faith and trust in God. Volumes have been written about this good, faithful woman—a woman who also had believing blood that was now mingled with that of Hyrum's, to flow through the veins of their only son, Joseph F. Smith.

Joseph F. Smith is a hero to me. His life is a legacy of faith we would all do well to emulate. There are so many wonderful childhood stories about this special little boy. My heart is touched in reading his account of a homecoming:

> My mother was anticipating the return of my father from somewhere for he and Joseph the prophet had been in concealment away from the mob, and I was looking for them. I went out on the bank of the river close to the old printing office. I sat on the bank of the river, and presently I saw a skiff starting out from the other side of the river. The river there is a mile wide. They rowed on across the stream until they landed close to where I stood. Out of that little skiff the Prophet and my father alighted and walked up the hill. I joined the hand of my father and we went home to my mother, to my father's home. Then both went into the house and sat down; they chatted and talked with each other and while my father was changing his clothes—I suppose his collar and cuffs and something of that kind, probably—Joseph the prophet sat there. He took me on his knee and trotted me a little and then he looked at me a little more carefully and finally he said, "Hyrum, what is the matter with Joseph here?"
>
> "Well," he says, "I don't know; what do you think is the matter?"
>
> "Why, he looks as though he had not a drop of blood in him."
>
> "Oh," Father says, "that is because he has been living on milk only," for up to that time—I was between five and six years of age—I had never eaten a thing harder than milk; I was living on it. I do not know whether that had the effect of making me white or pale, but that was the condition I was in, and that was the remark the Prophet made. I never forgot it.[5]

Joseph F. personally knew the leaders that we all reverence so much. He knew them, and they knew him from his childhood.

Drawing of Hyrum Smith, undated, copy in George Edward Anderson photograph collection, Harold B. Lee Library, Brigham Young University.

To me there is no more tender scene in our Church history than that of Hyrum's last embrace of young Joseph F. President Smith recounted that experience while on a visit to Nauvoo with Charles and Preston Nibley. Of that visit in 1906, Preston Nibley wrote: "He pointed out to us the place in the road where he had stood as he watched his father and 'Uncle Joseph' ride away to Carthage on that fateful day in June, 1844. 'This is the exact spot,' he said, 'where I stood when the brethren came riding up on their way to Carthage. Without getting off his horse father leaned over in his saddle and picked me up off the ground. He kissed me good-bye and put me down again, and I saw him ride away.'"[6] On that same trip, the brethren visited Carthage Jail. This was the first time President Smith had been to the jail. The person in charge pointed to the floor and said, "That stain is the blood of Hyrum Smith." "[President] Smith walked over and sat on the bed. He put his hands over his face and convulsively wept, until Brother Nibley could see the tears dripping through his fingers. He then said, "Charlie, take me out of here!"[7]

President Smith also spoke of seeing his father and Uncle Joseph as they were lying in their coffins following the Martyrdom: "I remember the night of the murder when one of the brethren came from Carthage and knocked on our window after dark and called to my mother, 'Sister Smith, your husband has been killed.'" He remembered his mother's scream on hearing this dreadful news, and her moans and cries throughout the night. He pointed out the room in the old home of the Prophet Joseph where the bodies of the martyrs lay in their coffins, after they had been brought from Carthage and dressed for burial: "I remember my mother lifting me up to look upon [them]."[8]

From Dan Jones's diary we learn more about the sorrowful scene in Nauvoo, everyone sad, all the stores closed:

> [When] I reached the house of the late Joseph Smith . . . [Hyrum and Joseph] lay in their coffins side by side, majestic men as they . . . labored together, shoulder to shoulder, to build the kingdom of Immanuel; eternal love bound them steadfastly to each other and to their God until death; and now, my eyes beheld the blood of the two godly martyrs mingling in one pool in the middle of the floor, their elderly mother, godly and sorrowful, . . . a hand on each one of her sons, . . . her heart nearly broken by the excruciating agony and the indescribable grief. At the head of the deceased sat the dear wife of each one and around their father stood four of Joseph's little children and six of Hyrum's children crying out intermittently, "My dear father. . . . Oh, my father." And from the hearts of the mothers, "My husband killed," and the grey-haired mother groaning pitifully, "Oh, my sons, my sons."[9]

Still, Mother Lucy Mack Smith reported that even in the midst of so much grief and despair there was comfort, and even peace. As she cried in agony, "My God, my God, why hast thou forsaken this family?" she reported hearing a voice reply, "I have taken them unto myself, that they might have rest." Then, as she looked upon the mortal remains of her two sons, she said, "I seemed almost to hear them say, 'Mother, weep not for us, we have overcome the world by love; we carried to them the gospel, that their souls might be saved; they slew us for our testimony, and thus placed us beyond their power; their ascendancy is for a moment, ours is an eternal triumph.'"[10]

The memory of the death of a beloved father and an adored uncle at such a tender age must have returned many times to Joseph F.'s mind, anchoring him to the eternal spirit of man. He said, "I was instructed to believe in the divinity of the mission of Jesus Christ. . . . I was taught it from my father, from the Prophet Joseph Smith, through my mother . . . and all my boyhood days and all my years in the world I have clung to that belief."[11]

Persecution persisted, as we all know, and at age eight Joseph F. Smith had the responsibility of driving one of the family's ox teams from Nauvoo across Iowa to Winter Quarters. At age nine he drove this team the rest of the way to the Salt Lake Valley, arriving in Salt Lake September 23, 1848. We could spend all night strengthening our own faith by observing the spiritual experiences on their journey west. How God blessed that family!

The strength of Mary Fielding Smith is a symposium of its own, but for this occasion, with great tribute and reverence I express my love to Mary Fielding Smith, a mother and teacher worthy of our Heavenly Father's love and total and complete acceptance. After two months of illness, she died at fifty-one years of age, leaving behind her two young children. Joseph F. was just thirteen, and he describes himself in a note to a childhood friend: "I was almost like a comet, a fiery meteor without attraction of gravitation to keep me balanced or guide me."[12] This was evident in an incident at school two years later during the winter of 1853–54. The schoolmaster took out a leather strap to punish Joseph's sister Martha Ann over some small infraction. "Don't whip her with that," Joseph cried. "At that he came at me and was going to whip me, but instead of whipping me, I licked him, good and plenty."[13]

This incident both ended Joseph's short formal education and launched his long ecclesiastical career. His aunt Mercy, whom he loved, along with the leadership of the Church—President Brigham Young, President Heber C. Kimball, and Elder George A. Smith—were watching out for him. I can almost hear them wondering, "What should we do with Hyrum's boy, Joseph?" In the next general conference he was called, at age fifteen, to serve a mission in Hawaii.

Toward the end of his life, Joseph F. said this of his journey to his mission in Hawaii: "I lay there and looked up at the stars, rather a homesick youth, realizing for the first time in my life that I was just about to cut loose entirely from all the associations that I loved and honored and revered in all the world; to go out into the world—I knew not where, nor did I know the circumstances in which I would be placed."[14]

He also said, "My four years mission to the Sandwich Islands restored my equilibrium and fixed the laws and metes and bounds which have governed my subsequent life."[15]

Nothing was very easy for Joseph F. Smith. He faced test after test, all of which prepared him for the many responsibilities he would have in Church leadership. The legacy that he left with the Saints of Hawaii would again take far more time than we have tonight. However, there is another most tender experience from his life that demonstrates his great love for his dear friends of the islands:

Charles W. Nibley, who was perhaps President Smith's closest friend and was the Presiding Bishop of the Church, describes the reunion of President Smith with his beloved Hawaiian mama. Holding a few bananas as a gift, a frail ninety-year-old blind woman approached calling "Iosepa, Iosepa."

> Instantly, when he saw her, he ran to her and clasped her in his arms, hugged her and kissed her over and over again, patting her on the head and saying, "Mama, mama, my dear old mama!"
>
> And with tears streaming down his cheeks, he turned to me and said, "Charlie, she nursed me when I was a boy, sick and without anyone to care for me. She took me in and was a mother to me."[16]

Ten years ago, President Eyring, who was then Commissioner of Education, and I were invited to launch the *Iosepa*, named in honor of President Joseph F. Smith. This canoe was built by the students of BYU–Hawaii. We signed our names on the inside of the hull before launching it off to its adventures in the sea. I have thought since then that the mission to Hawaii as a boy launched President Joseph F. Smith into a lifetime of service, including five missions for the Church, either as a missionary or as a mission president, for a total of thirteen years, and as a defender of the Saints, standing side by side with Porter Rockwell and very likely my father's grandfather, Henry Ballard, when they intercepted Johnston's army. He served fifty-two years in the presiding councils of the Church as a member of the Quorum of the Twelve Apostles, a counselor in the First Presidency, and as President of the Church. He also presided over the stake in Davis County. As President of the Church, he also presided over the Salt Lake Temple, the Sunday School, and the Young Men's Mutual Improvement Association.

His management of financial affairs freed the Church from a million dollars of bond debt. He began the acquisition of historical sites and, with his missionary zeal, developed visitors' centers and an information center on Temple Square. He authorized the construction of the Church Administration Building and the Hotel Utah. He was a practical visionary, a builder, a fearless missionary and a witness of the Restoration. As a gospel teacher, he made the plan of salvation clear and understandable to all who read his discourses. He introduced family home evenings as the place where the gospel is best taught.

He moved the Church forward under extreme difficulties and faced brutal personal attacks, including those by the United States Congress. He was physically

Joseph F. Smith portrait, oil on canvas, 1915. The October 2, 1915, edition of the Deseret Evening News *indicates: "Mr. Salzbrenner the artist . . . came from Dresden, Germany, studied many years under the noted artist Hoffman and also under the sculptor Schilling. This is the second portrait he has painted of Pres. Smith." Courtesy of Church History Library.*

strong and loved sports, including golf—to which I can relate—preferring to participate rather than just observe.

With all that President Joseph F. Smith accomplished in his ministry of building up and moving The Church of Jesus Christ of Latter-day Saints forward, there was nothing more important and precious to him than his love for his wives and his forty-eight children, five of whom were adopted. He repeatedly taught that "the family organization lies at the basis of all true government."[17]

He lived by what he taught. Here are just a few examples that give an insight into his constant teaching and concern for home and family:

> There can be no genuine happiness separate and apart from the home, and every effort made to sanctify and preserve its influence is uplifting to those who toil and sacrifice for its establishment. Men and women often seek to substitute some other life for that of the home; they would make themselves believe that the home means restraint; that the highest liberty is the fullest opportunity to move about at will. There is no happiness without service, and there is no service greater than that which converts the home into a divine institution, and which promotes and preserves family life.
>
> The home is what needs reforming. Try today, and tomorrow, to make a change in your home by praying twice a day with your family; call on your children and your wife to pray with you. Ask a blessing upon every meal you eat. Spend ten minutes in reading a chapter from the words of the Lord in the Bible, the Book of Mormon, the Doctrine and Covenants, before you retire, or before you go to your daily toil. Feed your spiritual selves at home, as well as in public places. Let love, and peace, and the Spirit of the Lord, kindness, charity, sacrifice for others, abound in your families. . . . Let our meetings, schools and organizations, instead of being our only or leading teachers, be supplements to our teachings.
>
> Let the parents in Zion give their children something to do that they may be taught the arts of industry, and equipped to carry responsibility when it is thrust upon them. Train them in some useful vocation that their living may be assured when they commence in life for themselves. Remember, the Lord has said that "the idler shall not eat the bread of the laborer," but all in Zion should be industrious. Neither should they be given to loud laughter, light and foolish

> speeches, worldly pride and lustful desires, for these are not only unbecoming, but grievous sins in the sight of the Lord.[18]

Joseph F.'s love for his children is reflected in these tender words at the death of his firstborn child, three-year-old Mercy Josephine, whom he affectionately referred to as "Dodo":

> I am desolate, my home seems desolate and almost dreary. . . . My own sweet Dodo is gone! I can scarcely believe it and my heart asks, *can it be*? I look in vain, I listen, no sound, I wander through the rooms, all are vacant, lonely, desolate, deserted. I look down the garden walk, peer around the house, look here and there for a glimpse of a little golden, sunny head and rosy cheeks, but no, alas, no pattering little footsteps. No beaming little black eyes sparkling with love for papa; no sweet little enquiring voice, . . . no soft dimpled hands clasping me around the neck, no sweet rosy lips returning in childish innocence my fond embrace and kisses, but a vacant little chair.[19]

Reflecting on his father's love for family, his son, my grandfather Hyrum Mack Smith, said:

> He always has been very conscientious in the care and protection that he bestowed upon his wives and his children, and religiously endeavored to instruct them in the ways of truth and righteousness. He has taught his children from their infancy to be truthful and honest, to be virtuous and chaste, to be kind and just, and merciful, to be temperate and sober, and obedient . . . There was no favoritism, no injustice, no partiality shown . . . He loved them all with a love akin to the love of God for His children.[20]

I talked to Florence Jacobsen, a granddaughter of President Smith who was seven years old when her grandpapa died. Florence was nearly ninety-nine, but with clear voice and recollection, she told me of the times her family would enter the Beehive House from State Street, climb the stairs to the second floor where Grandpapa would greet them from his chair, "Come in, my darlings." He would tell them to look in the drawer where he always kept candy for the children. He would kiss each family member, and Florence recalled how good his beard smelled because it was always so clean. He generally dressed in light suits, sometimes white ones. He was neat in his appearance.

My mother also often talked about sitting on his lap and how his beard tickled her face when he kissed her. Oh, how the children loved their grandpapa!

As I mentioned earlier, Joseph F. Smith sought understanding and knowledge about the great plan of happiness, especially as it pertains to eternal life. His unwavering love for his father and his mother, I believe, focused his thoughts about eternity. Perhaps some of the most important conference addresses ever given by a General Authority are those of President Smith in April 1916 and October 1918. The last thirty months of his life represent an era of unusual spiritual enlightenment. From his words, the heavens seemed to be very close and his view of spiritual realities were expressed clearly, for as he said on October 4, 1918, "I will not, I dare not, attempt to enter upon many things that are resting upon my mind this morning, and I shall postpone until some future time, the Lord being willing, my attempt to tell you some of the things that are in my mind, and that dwell in my heart. I have not lived alone these last five months. I have dwelt in the spirit of prayer, of supplication, of faith, and of determination; and I have had my communication with the Spirit of the Lord continuously."[21]

According to the President's son Joseph Fielding Smith, the prophet was here expressing the fact that during the past half year he had been the recipient of numerous manifestations, some of which he had shared with his son both before and after the conference. One of these manifestations, the vision of the redemption of the dead, had been received just the day before, on October 3, and was recorded immediately following the close of the conference.[22]

President Smith died just a few weeks following that general conference of October 1918. Only a graveside service at the Salt Lake City Cemetery was held because of the flu epidemic. Those who attended did so wearing masks. Sister Jacobson was there, as was my mother, who was almost fifteen years old.

General conference in April was postponed to June 1919. President Grant instructed that the sermons were to express love and appreciation for President Joseph F. Smith. Speaker after speaker told of the love they had for their dear prophet and president. No words spoken that conference were more significant than those of Melvin J. Ballard, newly called member of the Twelve, called to fill the vacancy left at the death of President Joseph F. Smith. I quote:

> I recall my early recollections of President Smith with a good deal of pleasure—because I admired him, he was to me my ideal, I tried in my life, as I became

> acquainted with him, to be as he was. I knew as a child, for the Lord revealed it unto me, that President Smith would some day preside over this Church; and in connection with that I saw many things that President Smith would do; and when, last October he stood before the congregations of the Saints, feeble and weak as he was, my soul was filled with great sorrow, because I knew that all that the Lord had for President Smith to do had been done. That which I saw as a child was fulfilled, finished, completed. And yet there was a feeling of great regret that we should soon have to part with him and let him go on to the work which the Father has prepared him to do in that realm where he is now.
>
> It was my privilege, I presume, to deliver the last public address that President Smith ever listened to, being the last speaker of the last Conference of the Church. And I recall, as I had concluded, he grasped my hand and pressed it and gave me a blessing that I shall not forget, for my whole soul was thrilled with his blessing and with his love.
>
> I bear witness that he was a man who loved the souls of the children of men in the world—not only those who belong to the Church; for no man has done more, than he, looking toward the establishment of the work of the Lord among the nations of the earth.[23]

So the Church said farewell for a season to the man and the prophet of God who bridged the days of Nauvoo in the nineteenth century to the Salt Lake Valley in the twentieth century. No leader has been more beloved as an Apostle and President of the Church by members and strangers alike. Nor has his family forgotten him. Every year near his birthday, we come together in a family home evening, filling the Monument Park Stake Center with his posterity. All come to remember him and to strengthen our resolve to live as he expects all of us to do.

In September of 1983, I stood by the bedside of my mother shortly before she passed away. Having suffered with Alzheimer's for several years, she did not recognize her family. She could not speak to us. While I held her hand and softly talked to her, she opened her eyes and said, "Papa, Grandpapa."

I asked, "Mother, are your father and grandfather here?"

"Yes," she said, pointing up, "Right there."

Joseph F. Smith's "darlings" were never far from his thoughts, and with his son Hyrum Mack they watched over their family here on earth from the heavens above, anticipating the joy of being joined forever as family.

May God bless us with increased faith in the Lord Jesus Christ. May we strive always to keep His commandments so all that has been taught and promised by President Joseph F. Smith may come to pass in our own lives and the lives of our families.

Notes

1. *Discourses of Brigham Young*, ed. John A. Widtsoe (Salt Lake City: Deseret Book, 1954), 108; see also *Journal of Discourses*, 26 vols. (London: Latter-day Saints' Book Depot, 1854–86), 7:289–90.
2. *Church History in the Fulness of Times* (Salt Lake City: The Church of Jesus Christ of Latter-day Saints, 2003), 15–17.
3. Quoted in Daniel H. Ludlow, *A Companion to Your Study of the Book of Mormon* (Salt Lake City: Deseret Book, 1976), 2.
4. Craig K. Manscill, "Life of Joseph F. Smith," *The Presidents of the Church: The Lives and Teachings of the Modern Prophets*, ed. Craig K. Manscill, Robert C. Freeman, and Dennis A. Wright (Springville, UT: Cedar Fort, 2008), 150.
5. Joseph F. Smith, "Boyhood Recollections of President Smith," *Utah Genealogical and Historical Magazine*, April 1916, 57.
6. Preston Nibley, *Presidents of the Church* (Salt Lake City: Deseret Book, 1974), 183.
7. Blaine Yorgason, *From Orphaned Boy to Prophet of God: The Story of Joseph F. Smith* (Ogden, UT: Living Scriptures, 2001), 356.
8. Preston Nibley, *Presidents of the Church* (Salt Lake City: Deseret Book, 1974), 183.
9. Dan Jones, "The Martyrdom of Joseph Smith and His Brother Hyrum," *BYU Studies* 24, no. 1 (Winter 1984): 93.
10. Lucy Mack Smith, *History of Joseph Smith by His Mother*, ed. Preston Nibley (Salt Lake City: Deseret Book, 1853), 324–25.
11. Manscill, "Life of Joseph F. Smith," 150; *Gospel Doctrine: Selections from the Sermons and Writings of Joseph F. Smith*, comp. John A. Widtsoe (Salt Lake City: Deseret Book, 1919), 494.
12. Manscill, "Life of Joseph F. Smith," 152.
13. Francis M. Gibbons, *Joseph F. Smith: Patriarch and Preacher, Prophet of God* (Salt Lake City: Deseret Book, 1984), 26–28.
14. F. W. Otterstrom, "A Journey to the South," *Improvement Era*, December 1917, 106.
15. *Teachings of Presidents of the Church: Joseph F. Smith* (Salt Lake City: The Church of Jesus Christ of Latter-day Saints, 1998), xv.
16. Charles W. Nibley, "Reminiscences," in *Gospel Doctrine*, 519.
17. *Teachings . . . Joseph F. Smith*, 385.
18. *Gospel Doctrine*, 296–301.
19. Arthur R. Bassett, "Joseph F. Smith: Families and Generation Gaps," *New Era*, January 1972, 43.
20. Hyrum Mack Smith, in Conference Report, April 1911, 26–27.
21. Joseph F. Smith, in Conference Report, October 1918, 2.
22. Joseph Fielding Smith, *Life of Joseph F. Smith: The Sixth President of the Church of Jesus Christ of Latter-day Saints* (Salt Lake City: Deseret Book, 1938), 466.
23. Melvin J. Ballard, in Conference Report, June 1919, 68.

Joseph Fielding McConkie

2

Doctrinal Contributions of Joseph F. Smith

It is of doctrine and of a great doctrinal teacher that I speak. President Joseph F. Smith brought much by way of understanding to the revelations given to the Latter-day Saint people and then added to them one of the greatest revelations about Christ and his redemptive ministry ever entrusted to those of the household of faith.

Dubbed the "fighting apostle,"[1] he knew no neutrality where the principles of the gospel were concerned. He had no fear of offending the devil or of disturbing the comfortable. The real Joseph F. Smith cannot be found within the perimeters of a gospel designed to appease those of shallow faith or excuse the need for faith and courage.

He did not suppose that the God of truth could be served in ignorance of the truth. If we learn nothing else from Joseph F. Smith's life's ministry, let us learn that true faith can only be seeded in true doctrine and that the purer the doctrine, the purer the fruits that it will bear.

He served as a special witness of Christ for over half a century. In doing so, he personified the verity that we know Christ and his Father only to the extent

---

Joseph Fielding McConkie (1941–2013) was a professor emeritus of ancient scripture at Brigham Young University.

that we are like them (see John 17:3; 2 Peter 1:1–11). He was the living fulfillment of the promise of the Savior that if a man or woman would do his will, they "would know of the doctrine" (John 7:17).

Describing Joseph F. Smith, Charles Nibley—the Presiding Bishop under President Smith—said that the principles of the gospel "were so thoroughly imbued and indoctrinated in him that they were a part of his very being."[2] Elder Stephen L. Richards, of the Quorum of the Twelve, said, "He so embodied in his life the great principles which I hold dear that he gave them a significance and a meaning and a tangibility that they could have had in no other way."[3]

Elder John A. Widtsoe, who had a profound regard for President Smith and who compiled extracts from his sermons in the book *Gospel Doctrine*,[4] said, "President Smith's sermons and writings breathe the true spirit of the Gospel, are sound as gold in tenet and precept, and express the will of the Master in every word."[5]

One measure of how well you stand for the truth is in who opposes you. As my father so often told his children, "It is as important to have the right enemies as it is to have the right friends." During the course of one week in June 1907, the *Salt Lake Tribune* described President Joseph F. Smith with the following epithets: greedy, lawbreaker, lecher, immoral, ruthless, sordid, viperous, insane, wicked, withered limb, apostate, outcast, traitor, anarchist, rebel, and atheist.[6]

In 1911, when national magazines waged an anti-Mormon crusade, *Cosmopolitan* raked over the old anti-Mormon charge of blood atonement, declaring that, given the power, Mormonism would "re-repeat the Mountain Meadows Massacre in every corner of the land." It described Joseph F. Smith as "furtive," "lurking," and "sly," likening him to a cat that would attack only when one's back was turned.[7]

McClure's added that he was "a man of violent passions; one could easily imagine him torturing heretics or burning witches to advance the kingdom of God."[8] *Everybody's* described him as "a religious fanatic of small and bitter mind" who was, they declared, "the ultimate insane fanatic."[9]

This paper highlights several key moments that illustrate how Joseph F. Smith, while presiding over the Church (1901–18), faced and handled challenges to the doctrines of the Restoration with authoritative statements that illuminated the views of the Church on vital doctrines.

Are Mormons Christians? (1907)

During the period that President Joseph F. Smith presided over the Church, the fire of hatred toward the Church was fanned to fever pitch. In an "Address to the World,"[10] read at the 1907 general conference of the Church, President Smith declared, "Never were our principles or our purposes more widely misrepresented, more seriously misunderstood. Our doctrines are distorted, the sacred ordinances of our religion ridiculed, our Christianity questioned, our history falsified, our character traduced, and our course of conduct as a people reprobated and condemned."[11]

From the beginning of time, Satan and his minions have hated God and his people. We cannot suppose that this will ever change. Nor would we expect arguments against the Church to change, because the truths of salvation do not change.

Some have suggested that hatred of our pioneer forefathers represented a national disdain for polygamy, but it should be remembered that as a people we had been driven from New York to Ohio and from Ohio to Missouri and from Missouri to Illinois and from Illinois outside the boundaries of the United States before polygamy became public.

The real culprit is revelation—revelation given to us as Latter-day Saints—and as long as we believe in a God who is speaking in current times and as long as we are willing to listen to what he has to say, we will be hated by the world. Consider these extracts from this official declaration:

> The religion of this people is pure Christianity. Its creed is expressive of the practical life. Its theology is based on the doctrines of the Redeemer.
>
> If it be true Christianity to accept Jesus Christ in person and his mission as divine; to revere him as the Son of God, the crucified and risen Lord, through whom alone mankind can attain salvation; to accept his teachings as a guide, to adopt as a standard and observe as a law the ethical code he promulgated; to comply with the requirements proscribed by him as essential to membership in his Church, namely, faith, repentance, baptism by immersion for the remission of sins, and the laying on of hands for the gift of the Holy Ghost, if this be Christianity, then we are Christians, and the Church of Jesus Christ of Latter-day Saints is a Christian church.[12]

A number of articles of faith were announced stating what the Latter-day Saints believed in and what they did not believe in. They included the following:

> We hold that man is verily the child of God, formed in his image, endowed with divine attributes, and possessing power to rise from the gross desires of earth to the ennobling aspirations of heaven.[13]
>
> We deny the existence of arbitrary power in the Church; and this because its government is moral government purely, and its forces are applied through kindness, reason, and persuasion. Government by consent of the governed is the rule of the Church.[14]
>
> In answer to the charge of disloyalty, founded upon alleged secret obligations against our government, we declare to all men that there is nothing treasonable or disloyal in any ordinance, ceremony, or ritual of the Church.[15]
>
> We do not believe it just to mingle religious influence with civil government, whereby one religious society is fostered and another proscribed in its spiritual privileges, and the individual rights of its members, as citizens, denied.[16]

The declaration reaffirmed our belief in the principle of revelation and affirmed that God continues to reveal himself to mortals, as in ancient times; it rejected all arguments that such a belief precludes our being loyal citizens to this country or to any earthly government.

> We refuse to be bound by interpretations which others place upon our beliefs; or by what they allege must be the practical consequences of our doctrine.
>
> We deny that either our belief in divine revelation, or our anticipation of the coming kingdom of God, weakens in any degree the genuineness of our allegiance to our country.[17]

The congregation voted to accept this declaration as binding on them as scripture.[18] The relevance of this declaration, made over one hundred years ago, to our current circumstances is quite striking. Indeed, many members of the Church might feel the same sentiments expressed in the declaration are just as relevant today as they were when President Smith first read them.

Higher Criticism and Darwinism

The new century brought with it new challenges to the faith, not just of Latter-day Saints but of all Bible believers. Marching under the banner of science, biblical higher criticism and Darwinism joined together in an assault on biblical literalism and the reality of revelation.

Higher criticism is the study of authorship, dates of writing, and meaning of the books of the Bible, using the techniques or findings of archaeology, literary criticism, and comparative religion.[19] When this approach is not balanced with faith, it becomes the study of revelation by those who deny the principle of revelation.

While the theory of evolution, or Darwinism, has itself evolved over the years, it then asserted and still maintains today (1) that the various forms of life on earth (including humans) share a common pedigree or ancestry, (2) that biological variations arise and are passed down to subsequent generations by hereditary transmission, and (3) that the mechanism driving the differentiation of the various kinds of life is natural selection.

As with the higher critics, Darwinism, in its purest secular form, eschews the idea of revelation and of a god in whose image and likeness we were created. It announces no purpose in the existence of man, no hope of eternal life, and certainly does not embrace the idea that humanity may become as God is. It was concepts such as these that prompted President Smith to prophetically clarify some of the truths that Darwinism brought into question.

Human Origins (1909)

In 1909, while some in the world celebrated the hundredth birthday of Charles Darwin and honored his contributions to the world of science, the Church issued an official declaration known as "The Origin of Man."[20] Elder Orson F. Whitney was the wordsmith,[21] but the First Presidency and Quorum of the Twelve sat in council frequently to assure that it properly reflected their faith and those truths that had been revealed on the matter.

James E. Talmage, noted scientist and former president of the University of Utah, who would be called to the apostleship two years later; John A. Widtsoe, also a noted scientist and president of Utah State, who would be called to the apostleship twelve years later; and George H. Brimhall, the president of Brigham

Young University, were invited into some of those councils to make whatever suggestions they had.[22]

The document reads in part as follows:

> "God created man in his own image, in the image of God created he him; male and female created he them" (Genesis 1:27). In these plain and pointed words the inspired author of the Book of Genesis made known to the world the truth concerning the origin of the human family. Moses, the prophet-historian—"learned," as we are told, "in all the wisdom of the Egyptians" (Acts 7:22)—when making this important announcement was not voicing a mere opinion, a theory derived from his researches into the occult lore of that ancient people. He was speaking as the mouthpiece of God, and his solemn declaration was for all time and for all people.

Moses taught that man had both a spirit and a temporal creation. If therefore we can ascertain the form of the Father of our spirits we will be able to discover the form of the original man.

> Adam, our first progenitor, "the first man" (Moses 1:34), was, like Christ, a preexistent spirit, and like Christ he took upon him an appropriate body, the body of a man, and so became a "living soul"(Genesis 2:7). . . . All men existed in the spirit before any man existed in the flesh and that all who have inhabited the earth since Adam have taken bodies and become souls in like manner.
>
> It is held by some that Adam was not the first man upon this earth, and that the original human being was a development from lower orders of the animal creation. These, however, are the theories of men. The word of the Lord declared that Adam was "the first man of all men" (Moses 1:34), and we are therefore in duty bound to regard him as the primal parent of our race. . . .
>
> The Church of Jesus Christ of Latter-day Saints, basing its belief on divine revelation, ancient and modern, proclaims man to be the direct and lineal offspring of Deity. . . . [God] formed every plant that grows, and every animal that breathes, each after its own kind, spiritually and temporally—"that which is spiritual being in the likeness of that which is temporal, and that which is temporal in the likeness of that which is spiritual" (D&C 77:2). He made the tadpole and the ape, the lion and the elephant, but He did not make them in His own image, nor endow them with Godlike reason and

> intelligence. Nevertheless, the whole animal creation will be perfected and perpetuated in the Hereafter, each class in its "distinct order or sphere," and will enjoy "eternal felicity." That fact has been made plain in this dispensation (D&C 77:3).[23]

I have learned over the years that people see in this document what they are prepared to see, but I do not know how our language could allow for a more expressive and enlightening statement than the declaration that people are the *"direct and lineal offspring of Deity."*

Brigham Young University (1911)

Like the ash of a volcanic eruption, higher criticism and Darwinian evolution descended on the faculty and student body of Brigham Young University as its most learned and popular professors took up the cause of this new enlightenment.

Three members of the faculty either ignored or didn't understand the 1909 statement of the First Presidency and became particularly zealous advocates of both higher criticism and Darwinism. The First Presidency became involved in the matter and assigned Horace Cummings, commissioner of Church Schools (1905–20), to learn more about the situation in Provo. According to Cummings's report to the First Presidency, their classroom lectures included such expressions as the following:

The Bible is "a collection of myths, folk-lore, dramas, literary productions, history and some inspiration."[24]

The story of Adam and Eve, the Flood, the confusion of tongues, the parting of the Red Sea, and the temptations of Christ were cited as classic examples of the mythical nature of the Bible and why it should not be taken literally.

While the Bible was not to be trusted as being literal, the theory of evolution was treated as a demonstrated law in their classes, giving those who stand in its light a new center of gravity by which they could then reinterpret all other gospel principles.

Thus it was reasoned that all truths change and evolve. Nothing is fixed or reliable. And since these newly found "truths" applied to the Bible, they must apply in like manner to the revelations of the Restoration. Visions and revelations were spoken of as mere mental suggestions. In their classrooms, the objective reality of the First Vision was open to question, as would be any account of angels restoring priesthood keys or authority.[25]

The zeal of these professors and their professed loyalty to so-called academic integrity caused the First Presidency to call for their resignation following which many in the student body protested using an avowed anti-Mormon newspaper to air their displeasure.[26]

Discerning Truth

The evolution of the word *science* captures the story that was unfolding. In Webster's 1828 dictionary, *science* is defined as "the comprehension or understanding of truth."[27] With the passage of years, the nature of the word changed so that it now describes various branches of study; the focus has shifted to the process rather than the end result.

"All truth," declared Joseph F. Smith in the 1906 First Presidency Christmas Message, "from whatever source it seems to emanate, in science, in art, in philosophy, in theology, in discovery or invention, which promotes happiness and elevates mankind, is from the Father of light who sent his Son Jesus Christ of Nazareth, into the world to uplift his sons and daughters and bring them out of darkness, ignorance and sin into communion with him and obedience to his laws."[28]

A few years later President Smith taught, "We believe in righteousness. We believe in all truth, no matter to what subject it may refer. No sect or religious denomination in the world possesses a single principle of truth that we do not accept or that we will reject. We are willing to receive all truth, from whatever source it may come; for truth will stand, truth will endure."[29]

President Smith told college students that they could use the theories of men as a temporary scaffolding for research purposes. "It is," he said, "when these theories are settled upon as basic truths that trouble appears, and the searcher stands in grave danger of being led hopelessly from the right way. . . . The religion of the Latter-day Saints is not hostile to any truth, nor to scientific search for truth. 'That which is demonstrated, we accept with joy,' said the First Presidency in their Christmas greeting to the Saints, 'but vain philosophy, human theory and mere speculations of men, we do not accept, nor do we adopt anything contrary to divine revelation or to good, common sense.'"[30]

He noted that the professors who had been dismissed from Brigham Young University were of the settled opinion that when religion found itself at odds with science, it required modification on the part of religion, not science. "The Church, on the contrary," President Smith said, "holds to the definite authority of divine revelation which must be the standard; and that, as so-called 'science' has changed from age to age in its deductions, and as divine revelation is truth, and must abide forever, views as to the lesser should conform to the positive statements of the greater; and, further, that in institutions founded by the Church for the teaching of theology, as well as other branches of education, its instructors must be in harmony in their teachings with its principles and doctrines."[31]

The gospel of Jesus Christ embraces all truth and all light. Since all people have been born with the Light of Christ, we each can and should be a source of truth. Upon hearing or learning truth we embrace it as part of the everlasting gospel. Using the principles taught by President Smith as our guide, we can discern the light of heaven from its counterfeits with the following principles:

1. "That which doth not edify is not of God, and is darkness" (D&C 50:23)—the basic question being, does the idea or theory involved exalt or debase humankind?

2. Is the idea or theory being espoused in harmony with divine truths already revealed? (D&C 52:15–19). Truth cannot contradict itself, nor can it be in a constant state of flux. The God of heaven does not need to be redefined with each passing generation.

3. Common sense and reason form a part of the gospel; they are as the Aaronic Priesthood is to the Melchizedek Priesthood. If they have the light of heaven in them, they will always sustain and conform to the higher order of things.

Everything that embraces the Light of Christ—be it true science, true philosophy, or true religion—must comply with these principles.

Figurative or Literal

The greater the spiritual truth, the greater the opposition will be to it. An effective way to oppose spiritual truths is to declare that which is literal to be figurative and that which is figurative to be literal. Thus one can profess belief in the words of scripture while taking all meaning from them. Nowhere is this more evident than in truths that deal with the nature of God and our relationship to him. God said people were created in his image and likeness (see Genesis 1:27). Latter-day Saints believe it. Satan and his minions say to so believe is blasphemy.

When I served as a mission president, a minister in the Church of Scotland asked me to come and talk to him. I accepted his invitation. He insisted that we limit our discussion to the Bible. I bore him a testimony of the Bible like he had never heard before in which I told him about all the Bible characters who appeared to the Prophet Joseph Smith. I told him that Adam was one of them.[32]

He told me that my testimony could not be true because Adam was simply a myth, a way for primitive man to give explanation to that which they could not otherwise understand.

I told him that if Adam was a myth, then the Fall was a myth, and if the Fall was a myth, the Atonement was a myth. This being the week before Easter, I asked what he would be preaching next Sunday.

He sat silent. I was simply repeating what I had been taught by my grandfather Joseph Fielding Smith, and I have always assumed that he was taught the same thing by his father.[33] It is what the Book of Mormon teaches, and they were students of the Book of Mormon (see Mormon 9:12).

My minister friend had spent twenty years teaching theology classes at a Scottish university and had lost himself in the kind of thing that comes from the higher critics. For these scholars, when a literal reading of scripture did not harmonize with science, it was designated as figurative.

Eternal Progression

Among some of our faith, it is argued that the Fall was the result of natural law and thus that mastery of universal laws constituted the path to exaltation. Advocates of this notion then reached out and defined eternal progression as involving both men and God in the endless search for knowledge that they might live in harmony with law.[34]

This is a doctrine that never set well with the family from which I come. Joseph Smith did not like it; my second-great-grandfather Hyrum Smith did not like it; my grandfather Joseph Fielding Smith Jr. did not like it; and my father, Bruce R. McConkie, did not like it.[35] Modern revelation declares that "all kingdoms have a law given; and there are many kingdoms; for there is no space in the which there is no kingdom; and there is no kingdom in which there is no space, either a greater or a lesser kingdom. And unto every kingdom is given a law; and unto every law there are certain bounds also and conditions." Continuing, the revelation states that God "comprehendeth all things, and all things are before him, and all things are round about him; and he is above all things, and in all things, and is through all things, and is round about all things; and all things are by him, and of him, even God, forever and ever" (D&C 88:36–42).

This revelation clearly states that God is the creator of all law, not its servant or its partner. Our God is not, as Joseph F. Smith put it, "a congeries of laws floating like a fog through the universe."[36]

Divine Sonship of Christ (1915)

The God of whom President Joseph F. Smith testified was a personal being, the actual and literal parent of our spirits. Developing this theme at a stake conference in the Box Elder Stake in Brigham City in January 1915, he said, "The Savior Jesus Christ, begotten of God, was in the likeness of his Father, resembling him so nearly that He said on one occasion that 'He that hath seen me has seen the Father.'" Directing himself particularly to the Primary children, President Smith said:

> I see a little boy. He has hair, he has eyes and he has a face which resembles his father's, and when he grows up we say that we cannot tell him from his father, so perfect is resemblance between the boy and his father. . . . Jesus Christ was created just like his Father; had the same features; same frame, same kind of body and was so like Him when you saw him you saw an exact likeness or similitude of His Father.
>
> You all know that your fathers are indeed your fathers and that your mothers are indeed your mothers—you all know that don't you? You cannot deny it. Now, we are told in scriptures that Jesus Christ is the only begotten Son of God in the flesh. Well, now for the benefit of the older ones, how are children begotten? I answer just as Jesus Christ was begotten of his father. The Christian denominations believe that Christ was begotten not of God but of the spirit that overshadowed his mother. This is nonsense. . . .
>
> Now, little boys and girls, when you are confronted by infidels in the world who know nothing of how Christ was begotten, you can say he was born just as

the infidel was begotten and born, so was Christ begotten by his Father, who is also our Father—the Father of our spirits—and he was born of his mother Mary.

The difference between Jesus Christ and other men is this: Our fathers in the flesh are mortal men, who are subject unto death; but the Father of Jesus Christ in the flesh is the God of Heaven. Therefore Jesus, as he declared, received the power of life from his Father and was never subject unto death but had life in himself as his father had life in himself. Because of this power he overcame death and the grave and became master of the resurrection and the means of salvation to us all. . . .

Now, my little friends, I will repeat again in words as simple as I can, and you talk to your parents about it, that God, the Eternal Father is literally the father of Jesus Christ.[37]

The Father and the Son (1916)

In the nineteenth century and early twentieth century, the leaders and teachers of the Church used Jehovah, Elohim, Lord, God, and other titles interchangeably to describe the Father and the Son. Additionally, the accepted canon of the Latter-day Saints rarely differentiates the titles of the Father and the Son. In an effort to help members better understand the Godhead and their roles, and to avoid confusion with scriptural texts referring to Christ as our father, President Smith issued a document titled *Doctrinal Exposition on the Father and the Son* from the First Presidency in 1916.[38] In the exposition, four different senses in which the word *father* is used in reference to Deity are given:[39]

1. *"Father" as a literal parent.* God the Father is the literal father of our spirits and of the Lord Jesus Christ in the flesh.

2. *"Father" as creator.* Christ under the direction of the Father created the heavens and the earth and thus is referred to as "Father."

3. *Jesus Christ the "father" of those who abide in his gospel.* Those who are born again are adopted as the sons and daughters of Christ.

4. *Jesus Christ the "father" by divine investiture of authority.* Christ, who perfectly represents the Father, speaks in the first person for him.[40]

Vision of the Redemption of the Dead (1918)

At the October 1918 general conference, President Smith declared that he had received several divine communications during the previous months. One of these, concerning the Savior's visit to the spirits of the dead while his body was in the tomb, he had received the previous day.

At the conclusion of the conference, he dictated this revelation to his son Joseph Fielding Smith Jr., and it was then submitted to the counselors in the First Presidency, the Council of the Twelve, and the Patriarch, and unanimously accepted by them. President Smith passed away two weeks later.[41]

In 1978 the revelatory experience was added to the Pearl of Great Price along with Joseph Smith's vision of the celestial kingdom. Shortly thereafter these two revelations were taken out of the Pearl of Great Price and given their present places in Doctrine and Covenants 137 and 138.

On a personal note, as a young man I had the opportunity to attend some institute classes at the University of Utah taught by my father. In one of those classes, he presented the vision of the redemption of the dead and discoursed on it using as his text the book *Gospel Doctrine,* where the vision is recorded. In the course of that class, he told us that the day would come when this vision would be added to our canon of scripture. I understood that to be a prophetic statement.

It was about twelve years later that he as a member of the Scripture Committee made the recommendation that this revelation and Joseph Smith's vision of the celestial kingdom be added to our canon of scripture. When he made that recommendation he had already ordered these revelations in verse form.

I had an interesting visit with him about that. The revelation follows the pattern of such revelations as the one shown to Nephi by the angel of the Lord in 1 Nephi 11–14, which consists of a series of different visions with no particular concern for a chronological sequence.

We see the same thing in Joseph Smith's vision of the degrees of glory, which starts with the celestial kingdom and then moves to the fate of the sons of perdition, then to the terrestrial kingdom, the telestial kingdom, and back to the celestial kingdom.

Our discussion centered around the fact that people were combining the second part of the vision of the redemption of the dead, which refers to those living in our dispensation, and placing them in the spirit world at the time of

Christ. Dad spoke of this as an unfortunate misunderstanding. I asked him if he had considered dividing the vision into two separate sections, which would help separate these events. He thought about that for a moment and said, "No, but I wish I had thought of it at the time."

In the first part of this revelation, the Lord teaches those there assembled "the doctrine of the resurrection and the redemption of mankind from the fall, and from individual sins on conditions of repentance" (D&C 138:19). Next, mission calls are extended with further instruction as to the message they are to take to those they taught. The third and final part of the revelation deals with the place of temples in making the ordinances of salvation available to those who embrace the gospel in the spirit world.

While Joseph Smith's revelation on the degrees of glory (D&C 76) is the greatest revelation ever given on the nature of the worlds to come, the vision of the redemption of the dead (D&C 138) is without peer in what it reveals about the world of disembodied spirits.

Describing the righteous in paradise we read the following:

> I beheld that they were filled with joy and gladness, and were rejoicing together because *the day of their deliverance was at hand.*
>
> They were assembled awaiting the advent of the Son of God into the spirit world, to declare their *redemption from the bands of death.*
>
> Their sleeping dust was to be restored unto its perfect frame, bone to his bone, and the sinews and the flesh upon them, the spirit and the body to be united never again to be divided, that they might receive a fulness of joy.
>
> While this vast multitude waited and conversed, *rejoicing in the hour of their deliverance from the chains of death,* the Son of God appeared, declaring *liberty to the captives* who had been faithful;
>
> And there he preached to them the everlasting gospel, the doctrine of the resurrection and the redemption of mankind from the fall, and from individual sins on conditions of repentance.
>
> But unto the wicked he did not go, and among the ungodly and the unrepentant who had defiled themselves while in the flesh, his voice was not raised;
>
> Neither did the rebellious who rejected the testimonies and the warnings of the ancient prophets behold his presence, nor look upon his face.

> Where these were, darkness reigned, but among the righteous there was peace;
>
> And the *saints* rejoiced in their redemption, and bowed the knee and acknowledged the Son of God as *their Redeemer and Deliverer from death and the chains of hell.* (D&C 138:15–23; emphasis added)

Again, it would be hard to imagine language that was more plain and expressive than that in this revelation, teaching us that everyone in the spirit world is in spirit prison. Many members of the Church are surprised to be told this.

Among the great truths we learn from this revelation are the following:

1. At death the just or the righteous go to paradise—as have the righteous before them—to await the day of their deliverance. Paradise is in spirit prison. There the righteous dead look upon the long absence of their spirits from their bodies as a bondage. To understand this is to have a greater appreciation for and understanding of the Atonement of Christ.

2. The Lord's house is a house of order in which no one arrogates to themselves the right to minister the gospel. This must be done under the authority of the priesthood. All who properly represent the Lord must be called by the Lord to do so. This principle is as true in the spirit world as it is in mortality (see D&C 84:19). The righteous dead from the time of Adam to the time of the visitation of Christ could not teach the gospel to those in darkness until they were properly called and commissioned by Christ himself.

3. In like manner, "the faithful elders of this dispensation, when they part from mortal life, continue their labors in the preaching of the gospel of repentance and redemption, through the sacrifice of the Only Begotten Son of God, among those who are in darkness and under the bondage of sin" (D&C 138:57).

Conclusions

By the latter decades of the first century AD, the meridian Church was losing its identity, eschewing the principles upon which it was founded and becoming acceptable to the world by embracing the beliefs and practices of the world.

Mormonism, so-called, found itself in a position to do a similar thing as the world transitioned from the nineteenth to the twentieth century. During this period, a people maligned and persecuted on the one hand and deluged with the faithless learning of the wise on the other, found their identity, retrenched themselves in the doctrines of the Restoration, and continued to build the Church and kingdom of God under the inspired leadership of President Joseph F. Smith.

He was the last of our prophets to have personally known the Prophet Joseph Smith. He was blessed as an infant by Joseph Smith Sr.,[42] and as a boy in Nauvoo he had the spirit of that place and the events surrounding the death of his own father and the Prophet deeply riveted upon his soul.

In the teaching of the revelations of the Restoration, he was without peer. His was the courage born of truth and the unwavering and uncompromising testimony that comes from pure knowledge.

He defended the foundational doctrines of the Church—the Creation, Fall, and Atonement—as actual and literal at a time when they were being assailed by many of the so-called higher critics and theories of science. With eloquence and fervor he testified of God and his Son Jesus Christ and our place in the heavenly family.

At the same time he threw open the doors of the Church to truth from wherever it might come. "No sect or religious denomination in the world possesses a single principle of truth that we do not accept or that we will reject," he declared.[43]

He was no less bold in defending the Church against its critics. To contend against Mormonism, he said, was to contend against the Bible; it was to contend against God, Christ, and all that was true. No one, he affirmed, "could prevail against 'Mormonism' on scriptural ground. . . . Why? Because we believe the scripture; we are established upon the scriptures of divine truth; we are built upon the foundation of apostles and prophets, Jesus Christ himself being the chief cornerstone."[44]

Of the Church's critics he said:

> They cannot uproot us nor overturn us by the scriptures; it can't be done. . . . The moment that men attempt to fight this Church they fight God, they fight the principles of His gospel and His truth, they fight faith in God, faith in Jesus Christ, faith in righteousness, faith in the resurrection of the Lord Jesus Christ, faith in every principle that exalts and uplifts and ameliorates the condition

> of man in the world. If they undertake to fight us they fight these principles, because we have espoused these principles. They are our principles, and they are not principles of error, of injustice, or unvirtue, or ungodliness. We do not espouse any such doctrines.[45]

His was a sure voice in a time of tempest that steadied the good ship *Zion* through the storms of the day, teaching with eloquence and power those principles upon which the fulfillment of our destiny must rest.

Notes

1. Joseph Fielding Smith, *Life of Joseph F. Smith* (Salt Lake City: Deseret News, 1938), 440.
2. Charles Nibley, in Conference Report, April 1919, 63.
3. Stephen L. Richards, in Conference Report, April 1919, 54.
4. Alan K. Parrish, "Joseph F. Smith and John A. Widtsoe: Reaching the Young Men Through the *Improvement Era*," in *Times of Transition*, ed. Thomas G. Alexander (Joseph Fielding Smith Institute for Latter-day Saints History, Brigham Young University, 2003), 33–42.
5. *Gospel Doctrine: Sermons and Writings of President Joseph F. Smith* (Salt Lake City: Deseret Book, 1919), vi.
6. *Salt Lake Tribune*, June 5–11, 1907.
7. *Cosmopolitan*, March 1911, 111 16; 696 97.
8. *McClure's*, January 1911, 259.
9. *Everybody's*, July 1911, 209–22.
10. Joseph F. Smith, in Conference Report, April 4, 1907, 9; See also Journal History, April 5, 1907. The following is recorded in the Journal History at a council meeting of the First Presidency and the Council of the Twelve and a few Presidents of the Seventy held on January 3, 1907, in Salt Lake City, Utah.

    > "President [Joseph F.] Smith called attention of the Council to the palpable falsehoods and misrepresentations against the Church contained in the printed speeches of Senators [Julius C.] Burrows and [Fred T.] DuBois, made on the floor of the Senate of the United States, and he felt it was due to the Church that a complete answer in refutation thereto be prepared and published.
    >
    > This was fully concurred in by the Council, and a committee was appointed to prepare the answer, composed of Bro[ther]s. [Orson F.] Whitney, [David O.] McKay, [B. H.] Roberts, [James E.] Talmage, Nephi [L.] Morris, Joseph F[ielding] Smith Jr., F[ranklin] S. Richards, LeGrand Young and Richard W. Young." Richard E. Turley Jr., ed., *Selected Collections from the Archives of The Church of Jesus Christ of Latter-day Saints* (Provo, UT: Brigham Young University Press, 2002), vol. 2, DVD 27.

11. Apparently because of its length this document was not included in the Conference Report. To read the document in full, see James R. Clark, comp., *Messages of the First Presidency*, 6 vols (Salt Lake City: Bookcraft, 1970), 4:143–55 or Smith, *Life of Joseph F. Smith*, 382–94.
12. Smith, *Life of Joseph F. Smith*, 382–83.

13. Smith, *Life of Joseph F. Smith*, 382–83.
14. Smith, *Life of Joseph F. Smith*, 387.
15. Smith, *Life of Joseph F. Smith*, 391.
16. Smith, *Life of Joseph F. Smith*, 393.
17. Smith, *Life of Joseph F. Smith*, 393.
18. In Conference Report, April 1907, 9.
19. "One of the most far-reaching activities of the modern mind," said Will Durrant, "has been the 'Higher Criticism' of the Bible—the mounting attack upon its authenticity and veracity, countered by the heroic attempt to save the historical foundations of Christian faith; the results may in time prove as revolutionary as Christianity itself." *Caesar and Christ* (New York: Simon and Schuster, 1944), 553.
20. First Presidency, "Editor's Table: The Origin of Man," *Improvement Era*, November 1909, 75–81.
21. On September 24, 1909, George F. Gibbs wrote to James E. Talmage as follows: "The presidency invite you to meet them at their office at 10 o'clock on Monday morning, 27th inst. They desire you to sit with them and the apostles listening to an article by Elder Orson F. Whitney on the origin of man, considered from a Church standpoint." *Minutes of the Apostles of The Church of Jesus Christ of Latter-day Saints, 1900–1909* (Salt Lake City: n.p., 2010), 552.
22. The information on each of these three men comes from their personal journals.
23. First Presidency, "Editor's Table: The Origin of Man," 75–81.
24. Horace H. Cummings, report of investigations of the theological teaching at Brigham Young University, 21 January 1911, 7.
25. Ernest L. Wilkinson, *Brigham Young University: The First One Hundred Years*, 4 vols. (Provo, UT: Brigham Young University Press, 1975), 1:420, 423.
26. Thomas G. Alexander, *Mormonism in Transition: A History of the Latter-day Saints, 1890–1930* (Urbana: University of Illinois Press, 1996), 172.
27. Noah Webster, *American Dictionary of the English Language* (1828), s.v. "science."
28. First Presidency, "Editor's Table: First Presidency Christmas Message," *Improvement Era*, January 1906, 248.
29. In Conference Report, April 1909, 7.
30. Joseph F. Smith, "Editor's Table: Theory and Divine Revelation," *Improvement Era*, April 1911, 548, 550; Smith, *Gospel Doctrine*, 39.
31. Smith, "Editor's Table: Theory and Divine Revelation," 548–51.
32. On this matter we have the testimony of President John Taylor, in *Journal of Discourses* (London: Latter-day Saints' Book Depot, 1854–86), 18:326; Orson Pratt, in *Journal of* Discourses, 9:41; and Zebedee Coltrin, in *The Teachings of Joseph Smith*, ed. Larry E. Dahl and Donald Q. Cannon (Salt Lake City, Bookcraft, 1997), 18.
33. Joseph Fielding Smith, *Doctrines of Salvation*, comp., Bruce R. McConkie, 3 vols. (Salt Lake City: Deseret Book, 1954–56), 1:120.
34. Thomas G. Alexander, *Mormonism in Transition*, 279.
35. For Joseph Smith see the *Lectures on Faith* (Salt Lake City: Deseret Book, 1985), 4:11; for Joseph Fielding Smith and Hyrum Smith, see *Doctrines of Salvation*, 1:5–10; for Bruce R. McConkie, *Mormon Doctrine* (Salt Lake City: Bookcraft, 1966), 238–39.
36. Joseph F. Smith, in Conference Report, April 1907, 39.
37. James R. Clark, "Box Elder Talk," in *Messages of the First Presidency*, 4:328–32.

38. Both President Smith and his counselor Charles W. Penrose addressed the matter in the April conference of the same year.
39. *Messages of the First Presidency,* 5:26–34.
40. This document can be found in full in James E. Talmage, *The Articles of Faith,* 465–73.
41. We would assume that President Smith's tenure as the President of the Salt Lake Temple from 1898 to 1911 played an important part in preparing him to receive this vision. Also the premature deaths of many of his children, including Hyrum Mack, who was a member of the Quorum of the Twelve, and his wife who died the previous month (September 1918), combined to make President Smith keenly interested in the nature of the spirit world.
42. Joseph F. Smith received a name and father's blessing under the hands of his grandfather Joseph Smith Sr. He was named after the Prophet and after Mary Fielding's brother Joseph Fielding. See *Life of Joseph F. Smith,* p. 446. See also *Pioneer Women of Faith & Fortitude,* 4 vols. (Salt Lake City: International Society, Daughters of Utah Pioneers, 1998), 1:96.

    "Phoebe Morton Angell was spoken of as 'Mother Angell' because of her service as a midwife and nurse among early pioneers. She attended Mary Fielding Smith when Joseph F. Smith was born, Nov 13, 1838. This was in Far West, Missouri while his father Hyrum Smith, was in jail because of his religious convictions. Hyrum's father had sent word to his son that he was the father of a baby boy and asked Hyrum what the child's name should be. Hyrum sent back that when the baby was eight days of age, his grandfather was to bless him and give him the name of Joseph Fielding Smith. This was done and it was Mother Angell who dressed the baby for the occasion and placed him in his grandfather's arms to receive his blessing. She tended the mother until she was well." *Heart Throbs of the West,* 12 vols. (Salt Lake City: International Society, Daughters of Utah Pioneers, 1939–51), 3:123.
43. Joseph F. Smith, in Conference Report, April 1907, 7.
44. Joseph F. Smith, in Conference Report, October 1910, 128.
45. Joseph F. Smith, in Conference Report, October 1910, 128–29.

Early Years

Nathaniel R. Ricks

3

Triumphs of the Young Joseph F. Smith

"Surely, this man who presides over the Church, and whose life is an open book, has been prepared for his labor."

—*John A. Widtsoe*[1]

At the 1984 Sidney B. Sperry Symposium on the Doctrine and Covenants, Robert L. Millet gave a presentation on the process that led Joseph F. Smith to receive the revelation now found in Doctrine and Covenants 138. Brother Millet catalogued a number of events throughout President Smith's life that prepared him for his role as a revelator, among them his "frequent confrontation with death," especially in losing members of his immediate family, his decades of Church service, and his prolific writings and sermons on spiritual subjects. Brother Millet surmised, "He was foreordained to serve the Lord in the leading councils of the Church, and he spent the last fifty years of his life realizing that election, actively involved as a legal administrator in the kingdom."[2] This perspective coincides with conclusions I have made after several years of examining Joseph F. Smith's Sandwich Islands and British mission diaries. His youth

---

Nathaniel R. Ricks teaches history at Endeavor Hall and Pikes Peak Community College.

provided spiritually grounding experiences and planted the seeds of character traits notable in his presidential years. Rather than solely the transcending of a difficult and dismal past, we see in his early life examples of how the Lord prepared Joseph F. Smith for the leader he would become—and how young Joseph F. began the process of triumphing over his weaknesses.

Foundational Experiences

A number of Joseph F. Smith biographers have noted the challenges inherent in the death of Joseph F.'s mother, Mary Fielding Smith.[3] Orphaned at thirteen years of age, young Joseph F. certainly struggled to overcome the loss of his sole living parent. (His father, Hyrum Smith, had been murdered alongside Joseph Smith Jr. in 1844.) Yet during the summer prior to Mary Fielding Smith's death, Joseph F. experienced two spiritually foundational events: his baptism and his patriarchal blessing. His testimony of the transformation inherent in baptism has been quoted often (most recently by Bishop Keith B. McMullin in the priesthood session of the October 2011 general conference),[4] yet his patriarchal blessing, bestowed at the hands of his great-uncle, offered counsel, promises, and preparation that have heretofore eluded biographers. On June 25, 1852, barely a month after his baptism, Church Patriarch John Smith (1781–1854) placed his hands upon Joseph F. Smith's head and issued a number of promises that are enlightening, considering Joseph F.'s later life.[5]

Among other things, Joseph F. was promised that he would enjoy a "fullness . . . of the everlasting priesthood," which would "reveal unto [him] all the hidden mysteries of the Redeemer's kingdom." We could well consider this a foretelling of the later vision of the redemption of the dead and possibly even his setting apart as Church President, holding all keys of the priesthood.[6] Joseph F. was told that he, like others of the lineage of Ephraim, was called to "push the [Lord's] people together from the ends of the earth and from the Isles afar off," and was promised that he would baptize captains and sailors while "lead[ing] thousands to Zion." Throughout his missions he placed special emphasis on recording the names of captains of vessels on which he traveled,[7] especially while leading many British Saints to Utah in his role as emigration agent. He was promised a large posterity: "They shall spread upon the Mountains so numerous that they cannot be numbered."[8] His role as a Church leader was foretold with two phrases: "Your name shall be had in honorable remembrance among the saints forever"—certainly the constant retelling of stories from his life fulfills this specifically—and "The mantle of thy father shall be upon thee." Hyrum Smith had served as Church Patriarch, which office eventually rested on his oldest son, Joseph F.'s half brother John; Hyrum also jointly held the Presidency of the Church with Joseph Smith Jr. following Oliver Cowdery's apostasy, in a position usually called "assistant president" of the Church (see D&C 124:94–95). Joseph F. assuming the mantle of his father could thus possibly refer to his destiny to lead the Church, though other explanations of the mantle could apply as well. Hyrum had received this promise of the Lord in 1829: "Seek not for riches but for wisdom; and, behold, the mysteries of God shall be unfolded unto you. . . . I will impart unto you of my Spirit, which shall enlighten your mind, which shall fill your soul with joy; and then shall ye know . . . all things whatsoever you desire of me" (D&C 11:7, 13–14). Perhaps, then, the promise of inheriting his father's mantle could be a reinforcement of the idea that Joseph F. would be a revealer of truth.

One last phrase from the patriarchal blessing merits discussion. Before the blessing's end, Patriarch Smith promised his great-nephew, "You shall live to take vengence [*sic*] on those that have slain your Father." This seemed a most interesting and dark promise: is this meant to imply that the thirteen-year-old Joseph F. would be able to exact vengeance on the mob that killed Joseph and Hyrum? Perhaps not, for the emphasis on vengeance may be referring to justice and closure rather than retribution. Those who killed Joseph and Hyrum at the Carthage Jail in June 1844 made it a dark place, a place of infamy for the Church. When the Church, under President Joseph F. Smith's direction, purchased the jail in 1903, the process of transforming the place from one of darkness and despair to one of reverent memory began. What more fitting vengeance than that thousands of Church members and investigators visit the site of the Martyrdom annually, ensuring that Joseph and Hyrum's deaths will not go unremembered and that the work of the Restoration will not go unnoticed? Carthage was just the first such historic site to be purchased: the Joseph Smith birthplace in Sharon, Vermont, and the Smith family homestead and Sacred Grove followed within a few years.[9]

Joseph F.'s baptism and patriarchal blessing illustrate that the Lord was mindful of both the young boy and the trials he would soon endure. Following this spiritual outpouring, Joseph F.'s mother died. He entered a challenging eighteen months, yet he had been granted a degree of preparation for his life.

Carthage Jail. © Intellectual Reserve, Inc.

Similar preparatory events—and further opportunities for growth—came while Joseph F. served his missions to the Sandwich Islands (1854–57) and the British Isles (1860–63).[10] During these two missions, Joseph F. Smith left behind a rich record of diaries and letters that portray him as a young man who prevailed in difficult circumstances.

Biographers have noted both spiritual "mountaintop experiences" and "valleys of discouragement and doubt" during Joseph F.'s first two missions.[11] Far from being a reluctant or ill-prepared emissary of the restored gospel, however (as some have hinted that his first call to serve was intended solely to get him out of trouble), Joseph F. threw himself into the work wholeheartedly.[12] (One could well point out that he had been fortified for his work with the receipt of his endowment, assumedly on the same day he was set apart as a missionary.[13]) Indeed, shortly after arriving in the Sandwich Islands, he wrote to Apostle George A. Smith, his father's cousin, "I know that the work in which I am ingaged [*sic*] is the worke of the living and true god, and I am reddy [*sic*] to bare my testimony of the same, at any time ore at any place ore in whatsoever circumstances I may be placed. and hope and pray that I ever may prove faithful in serving the lord my god. I am happy to say that I am reddy to go through thick and thin for this cause in which I am ingaged, and truly hope and pray that that [*sic*] I may prove prove [*sic*] faithful to the end."[14] During the two missions he served between 1854 and 1863, Joseph F. began to develop a number of qualities that later became hallmarks of his time in the Church presidency, indicating not only the continuing presence of the Lord's preparatory hand, but also the deliberate effort Joseph F. placed on triumphing over his weaknesses and obstacles. Among the qualities evident in the records of these two missions are Joseph F.'s intellectual development, his ability to defend the Church, his dedication to family and friends, his love for the Saints, and his spiritual aptitude.

Intellectual Development

First, Joseph F. grew in his knowledge of the world and its ways. Though his formal education had been meager, the Lord provided opportunities for Joseph F. to educate himself enough throughout his life, as one tributary wrote, to have "read widely, spoken with men of many minds, and . . . thought deeply. Of broad and generous sympathies with everything that is noble and good, he has acquired a culture, which none dares question."[15] There is ample evidence of this intellectual preparation throughout Joseph F.'s missions. During his first mission, he seemed to be reading constantly—at least, his diaries convey that idea. Not only did he study religion, but "Joseph F. read voraciously in history, philosophy, poetry, the classics, current events, virtually anything he could acquire. He regularly perused the LDS-oriented newspapers *Deseret News* and *Western Standard*, reading each issue in its entirety whenever he received copies by mail. Other publications he occasionally came across included the *Mormon, London News, New York Weekly Times, Harper's Magazine*, and *Zion's Watchman*."[16] On his British mission he continued to read as much as he could.[17] "As a direct result of the print culture of which he eagerly partook, Joseph F. gained an enlarged vocabulary, a broader knowledge of the world, and a greater appreciation of his own LDS culture."[18]

He also grew through his own writing—of letters, diary entries, mission reports, and even occasional lines of doggerel. Consider, for example, the ludicrous letter Joseph F. drafted to Joseph C. Rich, fellow missionary and son of Apostle Charles C. Rich, while in Britain:

> Humbly deprecatingly and appologetically imploring your Extreeam leniency and benevolent paliation of my unpardenable inadvertancy in procrastinating to such an incorrigable extention, my feeble essay to expaciate in acknowledgement of your eloquential acrafampthical but brief, curt, communication of the 13th inst.
>
> I assume an unnormal and sedentary position to inchovate my allocutionary and Chirographical elaborations to you. Perhaps I ought to perpetrate essoine for arrata prior to farther procedure, but feeling sanguin your knowledge of the inamplitude of my escritoir will elicit from your high-toned benevolence, sentiments of alleviation anti-animadversion and non-annui, I greatfully avoid the exigency of the case.[19]

Numerous pages of Joseph F.'s diaries were devoted to new vocabulary words, verb conjugations, inspirational poetry, and handwriting practice. Additionally, Joseph F. meticulously catalogued the natural wonders, curiosities, and historically significant events he observed while on his missions. In the Sandwich Islands these included the 1856 eruption of Mauna Loa on the Island of Hawaii; tours of sacrificial temples, lava tubes, and live volcanoes; and news received of disasters at sea and scandals in the Hawaiian royal family.[20] While in Britain, Joseph F. noted marriages and deaths in the British royal family, industrial tragedies, news of the American Civil War, and other sundry happenings.[21] Traveling through New York City in July 1863, Joseph F. described the fear and chaos of the riots that broke out in response to the Union's imposition of conscription during the Civil War.[22] And numerous times in his diaries Joseph F. described the plays, circuses, grand estates, curiosity displays, zoological menageries, and architectural wonders he observed while in Europe.[23] Each mission expanded his vision of the world, providing the foundational experiences that would help him one day lead an increasingly global church.

Defender of the Faith

The second attribute in which Joseph F. was prepared was a fiery commitment to the defense of Mormonism. He regularly studied the history of the Church and availed himself of opportunities to argue against the Church's critics. While on the island of Moloka'i in 1857, Joseph F. spent an entire evening in heated repartee with Samuel Gelston Dwight, a Presbyterian minister. By Joseph F.'s own account, "Some fiew [*sic*] gesticulations and feats of the strength of the Lungs [were] performed," lasting until midnight. "I told [Dwight] he was bigoted, that [refusing to read a tract defending plural marriage] was not 'proving all things and holding fast to the good,' and that he who judges a matter before he heareth, is not wise. I told him a person who would do so was not a man, 'what is he then?' said Mr Dwight. a 'monkey,' said I."[24] Joseph F.'s own first cousin, Josephine Smith, incurred a tirade of testimony when she criticized the Utah Mormons in a letter; Joseph F. replied, "Do you not know that Mormonism is the foundation upon which I have built? The Life of my soul, the sweetest morsel of my existance, the highth of my pride and ambition? *it is!* . . . —hear it ye worlds!—I KNOW IT IS TRUE!"[25] Additional heated exchanges took place in Britain: with Joseph F.'s uncle James Fielding, with distant family, and with relatives of Church members.[26] In each encounter, Joseph F. was challenged in several ways: first, in his reasoning and explanation of the gospel, and second, in controlling his temper. Joseph F. acknowledged the nature of his temper; when confronted by a distant cousin's husband, who was ignorant of his beliefs, Joseph F. recorded, "I never was so insulted and managed my rather unmanageable temper well."[27] While he eventually gained a reputation as a "fiery radical" during his years in the apostleship,[28] these early preparatory experiences help to illustrate why, by the time he reached the presidency, he could answer the criticisms and questions of the most powerful men and media outlets in America without batting an eye.[29]

Family Man and Faithful Friend

Biographers have often focused on the loneliness that attended Joseph F. following the loss of his mother; however, a close examination of his letters and diaries clearly illustrates a third attribute of triumphal preparation: that Joseph F. began early in his life to build an extensive network of kinship and friendship; a network that would expand throughout his life to include hundreds of immediate and extended family members, in addition to the countless individuals who regarded Joseph F. as a friend. In addition to writing to dozens of friends and family members in California and Utah, Joseph F. regarded his fellow Sandwich Islands missionaries with the highest esteem, rejoicing in the time they spent together both at mission conferences and in the field.[30] He also found joy in his relationships with his siblings. Joseph F. exchanged numerous letters with his half brother, John Smith (who became Presiding Patriarch of the Church while Joseph F. was away), his half sister Sarah Griffin and her husband, Charles, and his sister Martha Ann Smith, who married William J. Harris in 1857. Joseph F. also regularly followed developments in the efforts to help his half sister Lovina emigrate to Utah from the east.[31]

Church leaders and other mentors at home provided friendship, direction, and counsel. Joseph F. exchanged letters with Apostles George A. Smith (his father's first cousin) and Heber C. Kimball (whom Mary Fielding Smith had married before the exodus to Utah); he was familiar with Brigham Young, who occasionally read the young missionary's letters, and he cherished the stanzas of poetry written to him by Eliza R. Snow.[32] Additionally, one of his most lasting relationships had its inception during this time: he began corresponding with George Q. Cannon, who was running the Latter-day Saint newspaper *Western Standard* and publishing religious literature (including the Hawaiian-language Book of Mormon) in California at the time. They would later serve together in the First Presidency for more than twenty years.

Joseph F. especially felt love and praise in the words of two of his mother's siblings, Joseph Fielding and Mercy R. Thompson. Fielding wrote to his nephew in early 1857: "I have rejoiced to behold the Grace of God which has been manifested in your Communications generally . . . and I can truly say that your Success in your Mission has been and is [a] Matter of much rejoicing with myself and my Family." Thompson wrote to Joseph F. a few months later: "I cannot help having something like a Mother's feelings [toward you] for I have but one on Earth who seems any [d]earer to me than yourself [i.e. Mary Jane Thompson, her daughter], and I do not hesitate to say that I believe you have not many who feel more deeply interested in your welfare than myself."[33] Joseph F. continued developing relationships as a British missionary, adding his own spouse to the myriad missionaries, Church leaders, and family members he strove to love. While it would not be until later that he met one of his most devoted friends, Charles Nibley, the seeds were planted on Joseph F.'s British mission for one of his and Nibley's favorite pastimes: the game of checkers. Joseph F. bought a checkerboard in October 1860 and developed this talent by playing—time and time again—against British Saints, fellow missionaries, and traveling companions.[34]

One could argue that the loss of his family and his early separation from loved ones led him to surround himself with many friends and a large posterity. At the very least, we see evidence that the Lord placed many people in his path; people that could both buoy him up in challenging times and have their lives blessed by associating with him.

Love for the Saints

A fourth, and closely related, attribute of triumph is evident in Joseph F.'s development of an immense love for members of the Church, first in his mission fields and later throughout the Church. Edward H. Anderson noted at the close of Joseph F.'s life that he had been "ever anxious for the welfare" of Church members and that "even in the midst of the cares, burdens and anxieties of his active life weighing heavily upon him, he was never known to be too busy to give counsel, experience, testimony, helpful ideas, [and] sympathetic consideration to workers or members of the Church who called upon him."[35] He cultivated this "sympathetic consideration" first in the Sandwich Islands and British Isles, where he spent the better part of nine years serving others and being served by them in turn. His diaries are replete with touching stories of service, such as the time when Church member Jonathan Napela gave Joseph F. the shoes from his own feet, and the many instances of small gifts given to Joseph F. by poor sisters among the British Saints.[36] Equally compelling is the love Joseph F. reciprocated. When leaving the Saints on Maui in 1856, Joseph F. recorded, "I then arose and attempted to speak, but was over come with tears for the first time [and] the saints joined me in a brief and hearty show of tears; . . . we shuck [shook] hands with some before whom we had often stood to proclaim our message, as we suppose now for the last time."[37]

His heart ached for individuals facing severe trials, like the Englishman whose wife was labeled insane and incarcerated, leaving five children.[38] And yet he began to learn that those most in need of his help were unrepentant sinners. He developed a reputation as a powerful counselor and speaker, a "preacher of righteousness."[39] He realized during his missionary years that withholding chastisement could be more detrimental to Church members than injuring their pride. He often berated members who left the Church or spurned its teachings and had to bridle his passion to avoid speaking himself hoarse. Joseph F. was cautioned by his brother John (who had received reports on Joseph F.'s preaching style from their distant cousin,

Silas S. Smith), "When you preach dont hollow [holler] so loud and do take care of your lungs [just] because you are young dont think you can stand every thing and cannot be wore out."[40] Certainly, Joseph F. expended immense effort in learning the principles of the gospel and communicating them to the Saints whom he loved so deeply, growing that love throughout his life.

Revealer of Truth

Lastly, Joseph F. began early in life to develop his spiritual ears, evidence of preparation for his role as a revelator. In 1856, while reflecting with melancholy on prior commemorations of the 24th of July, he concluded "I must content myself and obey the voice of the good sheepherd [*sic*] that said 'he that loveth his Father, his Mother his friends his lands &c, more than he loveth me he is not worthy of me,' I pray his spirit to be with me, that [I] may for ever listen to his voice, and the world let go where it will."[41] Joseph F. had numerous spiritual experiences on his missions, experiences that would strengthen his testimony of the restored gospel and of the Lord's watchful care. For example, at a Sabbath meeting on the island of Hawaii, during a season of loss and depression for the young missionary, Joseph F. recorded that he "was made to rejoice, for the spirit bore testimony to [him] of the work of the Lord."[42] In myriad other diary entries, he documented the presence of the Holy Ghost in his own activities and in the midst of the Saints.[43]

It was as a missionary that Joseph F. learned to rely on dreams as a source of inspiration, comfort, and counsel from the Lord. The story of his so-called "dream of manhood" has been quoted many times (and incorrectly remembered as occurring on Joseph F.'s mission to the Sandwich Islands),[44] but an earlier dream from his Hawaiian mission provided similar inspiration during a discouraging season. After reflecting on the abject poverty of the Hawaiian Islanders, and his own poverty following a terrible fire in 1856, he dreamt that Brigham Young met him outside the "old Tithing store" at the corner of South Temple and Main Street in Salt Lake City, surprised to find the young missionary home already. "You are going back a gain [*sic*] in the morning, are you not?" asked Brother Brigham. Joseph F. replied, "yess [*sic*] if you want me to." With that, Brigham refused to shake hands and went off. Joseph F. concluded, "I have not finished my mission yet," and woke the next morning recommitted to the work.[45]

Numerous dreams followed. Some seemed sources of counsel; others filled him with a sense of foreboding.[46] By the time he received the vision of the redemption of the dead that would be later canonized as Doctrine and Covenants 138, Joseph F. would be well acquainted with the revelatory medium of dreams. The proximity to the spirit which made possible his 1918 vision was indeed developed over a lifetime.

Conclusion

I have not intended this list of preparatory categories and principles to be comprehensive. Certainly we could note Joseph F.'s early experiences in Church leadership, fiscal responsibility, musicality, organization, or other areas. At any rate, his life is exemplary of that which we hope is taking place in our own lives: over time, he became something that the Lord prepared him to become—and that he *chose* to become. A story is often recounted of the time period following his mother's death: he wrote to Samuel L. Adams in 1888 that he (Joseph F.) had been like "a comet or a fiery meteor, without attraction or gravitation to keep [him] balanced or guide [him] within reasonable bounds."[47] While Joseph F. certainly meant this simile to illustrate his self-destructive capacity, we could note that he truly did become a comet, a meteor—a shining light for many whom he influenced—once he realized the potential the Lord saw in him. He found guidance within the bounds of the gospel, within the bounds of the preparatory experiences the Lord provided him in his early life and beyond.

Notes

The title of this paper is loosely based on Scott Kenney's "Before the Beard: Trials of the Young Joseph F. Smith," *Sunstone* 120 (November 2001): 20–42. The author would like to thank David Grua and Ben Park for their feedback in the writing process.

1. John A. Widtsoe, "An Appreciation," in *Gospel Doctrine: Selections from the Sermons and Writings of Joseph F. Smith* (Salt Lake City: Deseret News, 1919), 644–45.
2. Robert L. Millet, "The Vision of the Redemption of the Dead," in *Hearken, O Ye People: Discourses on the Doctrine and Covenants* (Sandy, UT: Randall Book, 1984), 253.
3. Scott G. Kenney, "Before the Beard: Trials of the Young Joseph F. Smith," *Sunstone* 20 (November 2001): 23, 25; Richard Neitzel Holzapfel and R. Q. Shupe, *Joseph F. Smith: Portrait of a Prophet* (Salt Lake City: Deseret Book, 2000), 20–21; Francis M. Gibbons, *Joseph F. Smith: Patriarch and Preacher, Prophet of God* (Salt Lake City: Deseret Book,

1984), 26–27; and *Teachings of the Presidents of the Church* (Salt Lake City: Intellectual Reserve, 1998), xv.

4. Keith B. McMullin, "The Power of the Aaronic Priesthood," *Ensign*, November 2011, 48. The original reflection on baptism is given by Joseph F. Smith, in Conference Report, April 1898, 65–66.
5. Patriarchal Blessing of Joseph F. Smith, 1852, holograph, L. Tom Perry Special Collections, Harold B. Lee Library, Brigham Young University, Provo, UT. John Smith was a brother of Joseph Smith Sr. and thus Joseph F.'s great-uncle. He served as Patriarch of the Church from 1847–54, and in ten years as local and Church Patriarch he issued 5,560 blessings. See Irene M. Bates and E. Gary Smith, *Lost Legacy: The Mormon Office of Presiding Patriarch* (Urbana: University of Illinois, 1996), 115–18.
6. As Robert Millet ably phrased it, the vision "confirms and expands upon earlier prophetic insights concerning work for the dead; it also introduces doctrinal truths not had in the Church before October of 1918." See Millet, "Vision," 259–63.
7. Joseph F. Smith, diary, April 17, 1856; April 21, 1857; May 5, 1857; and July 11, 1857, in *"My Candid Opinion": The Sandwich Islands Diaries of Joseph F. Smith, 1856–1857*, ed. Nathaniel R. Ricks (Salt Lake City: The Smith-Pettit Foundation, 2011), 25, 94, 99, and 112; and Joseph F. Smith, diary, July 27, 1860; May 14, 1862; September 1, 1862; May 14, 1863; and July 2, 1863, Joseph F. Smith Papers, Church History Library, The Church of Jesus Christ of Latter-day Saints, Salt Lake City.
8. His five wives (excluding Levira Annette Clark Smith, who divorced him without children in 1867) bore him forty-three children (and an additional five were adopted). Shortly before his death, he spoke to his gathered progeny: "When I look around me and see my boys and girls, whom the Lord has given to me . . . I have reached the treasure of my life, the whole substance that makes life worth living. I have a family I am proud of, every individual member of it I love." Joseph Fielding Smith, *Life of Joseph F. Smith, Sixth President of the Church of Jesus Christ of Latter-day Saints* (Salt Lake City: Deseret News, 1938), 477–78; see also 487–90.
9. See Edgar T. Lyon, "How Authentic Are Mormon Historic Sites in Vermont and New York?," *BYU Studies* 9, no. 3 (1969): 341–50.
10. While most biographers have discussed each of these missions, few have utilized Joseph F.'s own words in analyzing the positive changes each mission brought about in his life. Gibbons devotes two chapters to the Sandwich Islands mission and portions of an additional two chapters to the British mission, though he mostly includes stories taken from Joseph Fielding Smith's biography of Joseph F., which did not rely on Joseph F.'s diaries (see Gibbons, *Joseph F. Smith*, 26–44 and 47–64; and Joseph Fielding Smith, *Life of Joseph F. Smith*, 164–92, 196–205). Holtzapfel and Shupe spend less than five pages on the Sandwich Islands mission and a mere three paragraphs on the British mission, citing only five total Joseph F. Smith diary entries (*Portrait of a Prophet*, 21–26, 29–31). Kenney's 2001 article does refer to the Joseph F. diaries, though it is confined primarily to discussing hardships faced by Joseph F. during the Sandwich Islands mission and the development of marital troubles between Joseph F. and his first wife, Levira, during the British mission. Kenney, "Before the Beard," 25–30.
11. Gibbons, *Joseph F. Smith*, 40; see also Kenney, "Before the Beard," 25–30; and Holzapfel and Shupe, *Portrait of a Prophet*, 21–26, 29–31.

12. See Kenney, "Before the Beard," 23; Holtzapfel and Shupe, *Portrait of a Prophet*, 20–21; and Charles W. Nibley, "Reminiscences," in *Gospel Doctrine*, 655–56.
13. Joseph Fielding Smith, *Life of Joseph F. Smith*, 164; and Gibbons, *Joseph F. Smith*, 27.
14. Joseph F. Smith to George A. Smith, October 20, 1854, correspondence, George A. Smith Papers, Church History Library.
15. Widtsoe, "An Appreciation," 650–51. On Joseph F.'s formal education, see Kenney, "Before the Beard," 23–25. Joseph F. is sometimes regarded as an anti-intellectual, based on his role in both the First Presidency's proclamation "On the Origin of Man" (1909) and the so-called "BYU Crisis" of 1908–11, when he supported Brigham Young University's disciplining of several popular professors who had taught evolution and "higher biblical criticism." Yet, as this section elucidates, he strove to learn as much as he could about the world around him, interpreting it through the lens of faith. See Thomas M. Martin, Duane E. Jeffery, and Randy L. Bennett, "'Christ Is Scientist of This Earth': President Joseph F. Smith's Attitudes and Policies toward Science," in Thomas G. Alexander, ed., *Times of Transition: Proceedings of the 2000 Symposium of the Joseph Fielding Smith Institute for Latter-day Saint History of Brigham Young University* (Provo, UT: Joseph Fielding Smith Institute for Latter-day Saint History, 2003), 75–81; and Richard Sherlock, "Campus in Crisis: BYU, 1911," *Sunstone* 13 (January–February 1979): 10–19.
16. "*My Candid Opinion*," xiv.
17. Dozens of references to his reading various works appear in the British mission diaries. See Joseph F. Smith, diary, 1860–63, Joseph F. Smith Papers, Church History Library.
18. "*My Candid Opinion*," xiv–xv.
19. Joseph F. Smith, draft of letter to J. C. Rich, July 27, 1861, Joseph F. Smith Papers, Church History Library.
20. Joseph F. Smith, diary, May 20, 1856; April 19 and 29, 1856; August 22, 1856; December 25, 1856; and February 14, 1857, in "*My Candid Opinion*," 31, 26, 27, 50, 70, 81.
21. See examples in Joseph F. Smith, diary, December 16, 1861; March 10, 1863; January 27, 1862; and September 27, 1862, Joseph F. Smith Papers, Church History Library.
22. Joseph F. Smith, diary, July 13–18, 1863, Joseph F. Smith Papers, Church History Library.
23. See examples in Joseph F. Smith, diary, October 20, 1862; April 15, 1863; January 26, 1862; October 3, 1861; and August 29, 1862, Joseph F. Smith Papers, Church History Library.
24. See Joseph F. Smith, diary, June 29, 1857, in "*My Candid Opinion*," 109–10.
25. Josephine was a daughter of Don Carlos Smith and had relocated to California during the Mormon exodus. She remained estranged from the Church, though she would stay in touch with Joseph F. throughout their lives. See Josephine Smith to Joseph F. Smith, July 22, 1857, correspondence; and Joseph F. Smith to Josephine Smith, September 1, 1857, correspondence, Joseph F. Smith Papers, Church History Library, emphasis in original. See also "*My Candid Opinion*," 122n15.
26. Joseph F. Smith, diary, April 23–25, 1862, and December 22, 1860, Joseph F. Smith Papers, Church History Library.
27. Joseph F. Smith, diary, April 23, 1862, Joseph F. Smith Papers, Church History Library.
28. See Nibley, "Reminiscences," in *Gospel Doctrine*, 658.
29. See *Proceedings Before the Committee on Privileges and Elections of the United States Senate in the Matter of the Protests against the Right of Hon. Reed Smoot, a Senator From the State of Utah,*

to Hold His Seat, 4 vols. (Washington, DC: Government Printing Office, 1904), 1:80–389; see also John P. Livingstone, "Prophet under Fire: President Joseph F. Smith Handles the Media," in Alexander, *Times of Transition*, 43–54.

30. See, for example, Joseph F. Smith, diary, August 11, 1856; December 17, 1856; April 8, 1857; and October 4, 1857, in *"My Candid Opinion,"* 48, 69, 90, 131.
31. See *"My Candid Opinion,"* 49n67, 75n27, 122n14.
32. See *"My Candid Opinion,"* 75n27; and Eliza R. Snow, "Lines address'd to Elder Joseph Smith, Missionary to the Sandwich Island[s]," July 20, 1855, Joseph F. Smith Papers, Church History Library. The fact that the poem was not destroyed in the 1856 fire that took most of Joseph F.'s letters and personal effects indicates that he valued the poem enough to keep it with him rather than store it in his trunk at the mission headquarters on Lanai.
33. Joseph Fielding Smith to Joseph F. Smith, January 6, 1857, correspondence; and Mercy R. Thompson to Joseph F. Smith, May 3, 1857, correspondence, Joseph F. Smith Papers, Church History Library.
34. See examples in Joseph F. Smith, diary, October 25, 1860; November 9, 1860; February 4, 1861; and July 1, 1863, Joseph F. Smith Papers, Church History Library.
35. Edward H. Anderson, "Last of the Old School of Veteran Leaders," in *Gospel Doctrine*, 684.
36. See Joseph F. Smith, diary, March 1, 1856, in *"My Candid Opinion,"* 13; and Joseph F. Smith diary, November 29, 1860; August 17, 1861; December 26, 1861; and February 25, 1862, Joseph F. Smith Papers, Church History Library.
37. Joseph F. Smith, diary, March 30, 1856, in *"My Candid Opinion,"* 20. See another tender moment in Joseph F. Smith, diary, September 29, 1857, in *"My Candid Opinion,"* 129.
38. Joseph F. Smith, diary, September 2, 1860, Joseph F. Smith Papers, Church History Library.
39. See *Gospel Doctrine*, vi; and Nibley, "Reminiscences," in *Gospel Doctrine*, 661.
40. See examples of chastisement in Joseph F. Smith, diary, July 27, 1856, and January 26 and 27, 1857, in *"My Candid Opinion,"* 45–46 and 76; and Joseph F. Smith, diary, February 24, 1861, Joseph F. Smith Papers, Church History Library. On Joseph F.'s preaching style, see John Smith to Joseph F. Smith, November 3, 1856, Joseph F. Smith Papers, Church History Library.
41. Joseph F. Smith, diary, July 24, 1856, in *"My Candid Opinion,"* 45.
42. Joseph F. Smith, diary, June 26, 1856, Joseph F. Smith Papers, MS 1325, box 1, folder 3, Church History Library.
43. See numerous examples from the Sandwich Islands mission in Joseph F. Smith, diary, January 27, 1856; February 8 and 24, 1856; March 6, 9, and 19, 1856; April 8, 1856; May 25, 1856; June 1, 8, and 29, 1856; July 23, 1856; August 7, 10, 30, and 31, 1856; September 6, 14, and 21, 1856; October 19, 1856; December 7, 1856; January 18, 1857; February 1, 1857; March 15, 1857; April 19 and 28, 1857; May 3, 1857; and August 9 and 23, 1857, in *"My Candid Opinion,"* 9, 10, 13–15, 17, 22, 32–34, 40, 45, 47, 48, 52–55, 61, 67, 75, 77, 86, 93, 96, 97, 118, 121. Additional examples from the British mission can be found in Joseph F. Smith, diary, September 9, 1860; January 6, 1861; November 10, 1861; December 15, 1861; May 25, 1862; June 29, 1862; and October 7, 1862, Joseph F. Smith Papers, Church History Library.
44. The original dream took place during Joseph F.'s British mission; see Joseph F. Smith, diary, January 13, 1862, Joseph F. Smith Papers, Church History Library.

45. Joseph F. Smith, diary, July 5, 1856, in *"My Candid Opinion,"* 41.
46. See, for example, Joseph F. Smith, diary, June 6, 1856, in *"My Candid Opinion,"* 34; and Joseph F. Smith, diary, December 22, 1860; January 23, 1863; and April 27, 1863, Joseph F. Smith Papers, Church History Library.
47. Joseph F. Smith to Samuel L. Adams, May 11, 1888, quoted in Kenney, "Before the Beard," 23.

Eric Marlowe and Isileli Kongaika

4

Joseph F. Smith's 1864 Mission to Hawaii:

Leading a Reformation

At age twenty-five, Joseph F. Smith was part of two of the more recognizable events in Hawaiian Church history: the drowning of Lorenzo Snow and the excommunication of Walter Murray Gibson. However, these are only two incidents in a unique eight-month mission Joseph F. served to the Hawaiian Islands (then the Sandwich Islands) in 1864.[1]

Missionary work in Hawaii began in 1850, and in just a few years membership exceeded four thousand.[2] In 1854, coinciding with the beginning of Joseph F.'s first mission to Hawaii (1854–57) at age fifteen, the Church was able to procure use of land on the island of Lanai as "a place of gathering" for the Hawaiian Saints.[3] Yet, despite such early promise, a year later membership seemed to plateau and would eventually decline by more than 25 percent in the years following the recall of missionaries from Hawaii in 1858 because of the Utah War.[4] From the spring of 1858 until the arrival of Walter Murray Gibson in the summer of 1861, native members were responsible for the leadership of the Church in the Hawaiian Islands.

Eric Marlowe is an assistant professor and Isileli Kongaika is an associate professor at Brigham Young University–Hawaii.

The life of Walter Murray Gibson and his time as a member of the Church are rather astonishing. It appears Captain Gibson, most noted for voyages to the East Indies, had an obsession to build an island empire with him as king. Apparently he saw an opportunity to accelerate his plan as a Church member and later took advantage of the unassuming Saints in Hawaii and used the "gathering place" of Lanai as the beginning of this empire.[5] Tensions were high between the US government and the Church in 1856 when Gibson—though not yet a Church member—hatched a plan to relocate the Church from Utah to New Guinea. Though Gibson's proposal failed, his attempts led him to Utah, where he eventually joined the Church in 1860. In 1861, Gibson convinced Brigham Young to call him on a mission to Japan and Malaysia, and while en route he visited the Saints in Hawaii. Noticing a void in leadership, Gibson stepped in, eventually establishing himself as "Supreme Leader" with the island of Lanai as headquarters for his intended island kingdom. Over time, however, some native members questioned Gibson's assertions of absolute authority over the Church. In a letter to former Hawaiian missionary Alma L. Smith, some native Hawaiian Saints queried, "The matter that we wish to write to you about is concerning our Prophet living here, Walter M. Gibson. Is it true that he is our leader? He says that Brigham Young has no authority over . . . the Pacific and Indian Oceans."[6] These native Saints also questioned

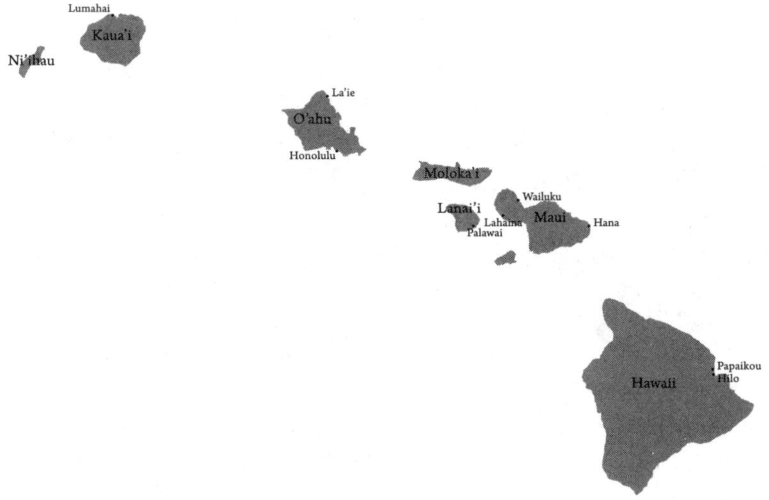

Map of the Hawaiian Islands, identifying places related to Joseph F. Smith's 1864 mission.

Gibson's right to ordain Twelve Apostles and a Quorum of Seventy, his practice of taking payment for conferring priesthood offices, and his claim that he alone owned the Lanai property, though it had been purchased mainly through the donations of Church members.[7] Gibson's deeds eventually reached President Brigham Young, who, on January 18, 1864, assigned Apostles Ezra Taft Benson and Lorenzo Snow and called former Hawaiian missionaries Joseph F. Smith (age twenty-five), William W. Cluff (age thirty-two), and Alma L. Smith (age thirty-three) to "go to the islands and set the churches in order and do what is necessary."[8] Furthermore, Brigham Young directed that Joseph F. was "to preside over the Islands after the Twelve [Snow and Benson] returned."[9]

Joseph F. had returned from a three-year mission to Great Britain only months before this call, and at the time was attending to his ailing wife, Levira, with whom he had spent more years apart than together due to missionary service. Though it was a challenging time,[10] Joseph F. did not vacillate in accepting this new assignment. While setting Joseph F. apart, Brigham Young pronounced that Joseph F. would "see things as they are, and understand the mind of the Lord, that you may know the hearts of men, and their feelings towards you, and towards the brethren." President Young delineated, "We . . . set you apart to take the charge of this mission when the Apostles shall return from the Islands." And perhaps acknowledging Joseph F.'s relatively young age of twenty-five, President Young declared that he would "be equal to any that lives upon the earth . . . [and] have knowledge and wisdom beyond [his] years."[11] On Wednesday, March 2,[12] almost seven years after returning from his first mission to Hawaii, Joseph F. was going back to assist Elders Benson and Snow with the Gibson affair; he would then lead the Hawaiian Mission.

The group arrived in Honolulu (on the island of Oahu) Sunday morning, March 27. Though not their final destination, Joseph F. and William W. Cluff disembarked.[13] William recounted:

> It being Sunday and about the usual hour for meeting, we decided to go to the meeting house. On entering we took seats near the entrance, finding several natives already there. The presence of two white men soon attracted their attention; they looked at us, then at each other, and presently we heard them say in a subdued voice: "Ka ha ha, O losepa a me Wiliama, ka." (Why, it is really Joseph and William, sure). Observing that they had recognized us, we

> went forward and saluted them with "Aloha Oukou." They were very pleased to see us, and welcomed us back warmly, saying they had often prayed for our return to them. The news of our arrival quickly spread. Many soon gathered and we held meeting with them, and they greatly rejoiced. After the meeting we returned to the vessel, accompanied by a number of the Saints.[14]

Setting sail from Honolulu, the group later anchored offshore of Lahaina (on the island of Maui),[15] and Thursday morning, March 31, all but Joseph F. attempted to go ashore in a small boat. In his journal Joseph F. wrote, "This morning Bro. Benson, Snow, Cluff and A. L. Smith started ashore in the schooner's boat, which was upset in the surf, and Bro. Snow was drowned but brought to with the greatest difficulty, when I came on shore, I found them, . . . Bro. Snow nicely recovering."[16] Though Joseph F. offers some basic facts, it is William Cluff's detailed account of this incident that has become the main source of retelling this story.[17] Cluff describes the capsizing of the small boat, and the ensuing search for Elder Snow which eventually yielded his seemingly lifeless body from the water. Tense efforts involving powerful prayer and inspired actions followed. Among other things, Elder Cluff was impressed to put his mouth over Elder Snow's and breathe for him, "imitating, as far as possible, the natural process of breathing."[18] After what Elder Cluff estimated to be an hour, Elder Snow regained consciousness. Regarding Joseph F., Cluff briefly describes him as remaining on the boat due to "some misgivings," his "great anxiety" observing the event, and his deep rejoicing that all were alive.[19] However, a later sketch of Joseph F.'s life published in 1901 offers further insight into this incident and into Joseph F.'s character. According to this account, based on his familiarity with the harbor, a dilapidated boat, and dangerous waves, Joseph F. "refused to go ashore, and tried to prevail upon the others to abandon the attempt until a better boat could be obtained." The author continues:

> So persistent, however, were some of the brethren, that he [Joseph F.] was chided for his waywardness, and one of the Apostles even told him: "Young man, you would better obey counsel."[20] But he reiterated his impression of danger, refusing positively to land in that boat, and again offering to go alone for a better boat. But the brethren persisted, whereupon he asked they leave their satchels with their clothes and valuables on the anchored ship with him. . . .
>
> The incident illustrates two predominating traits in his [Joseph F.'s] character: When he is convinced of the truth, he is not afraid to express himself in its favor to

> any man on earth. When he does express himself, it is often with such earnestness and vigor that there is danger of his giving offense.[21]

Furthermore, in 1919, referring to this incident, President Heber J. Grant said:

> At that particular time the Lord revealed to him [Lorenzo Snow] the fact that the young man Joseph F. Smith, who had refused to get off the vessel . . . would someday be the Prophet of God. Answering Lorenzo Snow who was in charge of the company, he said: "If you by the authority of the Priesthood of God, which you hold, tell me to get into that boat and attempt to land, I will do so, but unless you command me in the authority of the Priesthood, I will not do so, because it is not safe. . . ." They laughed at the young man Joseph F. Smith, but he said, "The boat will capsize." The others got into the boat, and it did capsize; and but for the blessings of the Lord in resuscitating Lorenzo Snow he would not have lived, because he was drowned upon that occasion. It was revealed to him, then and there, that the boy, with the courage of his convictions, with the iron will to be laughed at and scorned as lacking courage to go in that boat, and who stayed on that vessel, would yet be the Prophet of God. Lorenzo Snow told me this upon more than one occasion, long years before Joseph F. Smith came to the presidency of the Church.[22]

Upon Apostle Snow's recovery, and exactly one month after leaving Salt Lake City, the group took a small boat sixteen miles to the island of Lanai,[23] where on April 3 they met Walter Murray Gibson, the presuming leader. In a letter to George Q. Cannon, Joseph F. described some of the conditions and events of the next few days:

> On arriving at Palawai [the Church colony on island of Lanai], we found Capt. Gibson snugly settled in a small village of some fifty grass houses, very neatly arranged and surrounded by some forty or more families of the most faithful members of the Church.
>
> We found he had ordained Twelve Apostles, High Priests, Seventies, Elders, Bishops, and "Priestesses of the Temple." All of whom had to pay a certain sum corresponding to the various degrees of honor bestowed upon them. . . . Gibson had bought the District of Palawai (six thousand acres) by the donations of the saints, assuring them he was doing it all for them, or the Church. He persuaded them to give all they had to the "Church" and made it a test of fellowship, many

> could not bear it and were excommunicated, while the faithful remained and became wholly dependent on him for both food and clothing.
>
> Brother Benson and Snow required him to sign the land over to the church, as it was deeded to him and his heirs. This he flatly refused to do, informing them he should take this own course, that he had not been sent here by the church, had received no counsel from President Young, had acted upon his own responsibility in what he had done, and he was not beholden to the Church.
>
> He also told them he should ask no counsel of them, but would pursue his own course for the future. He should treat us as friends so long as we treated him as such. Whenever he had an opportunity, he declared he should use his influence to keep the natives in his power . . . that they should receive no benefit from the land they had bought only as they would become subject to him, it is useless to say more. He was cut off from the Church.[24]

Further understanding of Joseph F.'s actions and role during the encounter with Gibson can be gleaned from Cluff's description of events.[25] After the group received a "cool and very formal"[26] reception from Gibson and most of the native Saints, Elders Snow and Benson spent the next two days working with Gibson in hopes of him seeing the condition he was in. During this time, Joseph F., William Cluff, and Alma Smith made a tour of the valley with Mr. Gibson's daughter as their guide. Having served on the island of Lanai during his previous mission to Hawaii, Joseph F. was familiar with the challenges and setbacks this island had presented the Saints as a "gathering place."[27] Therefore, when observing the temporal developments, it is likely Joseph F. agreed with Cluff that "many improvements had been made since our last visit, that were praiseworthy, and reflected great credit on Mr. Gibson."[28] However, they were dismayed by the spiritual conditions they observed. For example, Cluff explains that Gibson "had succeeded in surrounding his own person and residence with such a halo of sacredness in the minds of the natives, that they always entered his house on their hands and knees. . . . It was the old customary way, in which the natives had been in the habit of paying respect to their kings, and the custom had been revived by Mr. Gibson, in order to increase his personal prestige."[29] The three missionaries observed "a large rock, the top several feet above the ground. Mr. Gibson had a chamber cut into this rock, in which he had deposited a Book of Mormon, and other things, and called it the corner stone of a great temple, which would be erected there."[30]

The young elders also noticed Gibson was "organizing and drilling all male members in military tactics."[31] When Apostle Snow later asked Gibson about this, "he replied with pomp and self-pride: 'Why, as soon as they are thoroughly drilled, I will purchase a vessel, man it with these drilled men, and go to one of the other groups of islands and take possession. Leave there some of my veterans, to hold possession, take on some raw recruits and go to another group and do the same, and so continue until I have subjugated all the islands in the Pacific Ocean. Then organize one great Polynesian empire.'"[32]

A conference was convened on April 6th in which Gibson, disregarding the Apostles, spoke first, addressing the congregation as follows:

> My dear red-skinned brethren, sisters and friends, I presume you are all wondering, and anxious to know why these strangers have come so suddenly among us, without giving us any notice. . . .
>
> These strangers may say they are your friends, but let me remind you how, when they lived here, years ago, they lived upon your very scanty substance. . . . Did I not come here and find you without a father, poor, and discouraged? Did I not gather you together here, and make all these improvements that you today enjoy?
>
> Now, you, my red-skinned friends, must decide who your friend and father is; whether it is these strangers, or I, who have done so much for you.[33]

Elder Benson then requested that Joseph F. speak. Elder Cluff observed:

> On arising [Joseph F.] said: "I am pleased, after an absence of over seven years, to return and meet with you again. I have often thought of you and I know that all of the elders who have labored among you have remembered and prayed for you. Many of them send their kind love."
>
> This met a hearty response—Ae Aloha Elakiu. He then reviewed our labors among them; referred to the labors of Pukuniahi (Elder George Q. Cannon),[34] and how the Lord poured out His Holy Spirit upon that nation, and thousands of them received the Gospel and had a testimony of the divine mission of Joseph Smith.
>
> "You know how you rejoiced in that knowledge then," he continued, "and we have come back now to bear the same testimony."[35]

After reminding them that it was the missionary efforts of Elder Cannon and others that had established the gospel among them (1850–58), Joseph F. asked the congregation by what right Mr. Gibson (among them 1861–64) called himself the father of the people and those who originally establish them in the gospel strangers.[36] Of Joseph F.'s words, Elder Cluff recorded, "It seemed impossible for any man to speak with greater power and demonstration of the Spirit. . . . The spirit and power that accompanied Brother Smith's remarks astonished the Saints and opened their eyes. They began to see how they had been imposed upon."[37] However, Cluff also noted, "While addressing the Saints . . . Elder Smith enjoyed a great flow of the Holy Spirit and spoke with much power; . . . yet we could see that Gibson had a great influence over many of them."[38] Later that afternoon Elders Benson and Snow spoke to the Saints with Joseph F. as their interpreter.

The following day a priesthood meeting was held in which Gibson was called on to answer the charges of exceeding his authority (i.e., ordaining Apostles and seventies, attempting to build a temple, assuming leadership over the Church in Hawaii), as well as selling priesthood offices, deeding land acquired by member donations to his own name, introducing pagan superstitions, and trying to establish an independent kingdom in the Pacific Isles. Gibson repeated the speech he made the day before, then held up some letters of appointment given him by President Young and said, "Here is my authority, which I received direct from President Brigham Young. I don't hold myself accountable to these men!"[39] After reviewing Gibson's past actions, Elder Benson motioned that his course be disapproved; however, all but one of the native elders voted against the motion. Elder Snow then prophesied that Gibson would see the time when no Saints would remain with him,[40] and Joseph F. emphasized Gibson's audacity to think he could ordain Apostles and high priests for money. "The Apostles informed Mr. Gibson and the Saints that, when they left the islands for home, Elder Joseph F. Smith would be left in charge of the mission. That all those who wished to be considered in good standing in the Church should leave Lanai and return to their homes on the other islands, where the branches would be reorganized and set in order by the brethren who would be left for that purpose."[41] The next day, upon returning to Lahaina, a council was held and Gibson was cut off from the Church.[42]

Leaving William Cluff and Alma Smith on the island of Maui, Joseph F. accompanied Elders Benson and Snow to Honolulu. In the days awaiting the Apostles' departure, Joseph F. "started, alone around Oahu, rode nearly 40 miles. Held meeting at Laie, and travelled 30 miles to Waihapai and held meeting in the evening."[43] He returned to Honolulu on Saturday, April 16, the same day Elder Cluff arrived from Lahaina. On Sunday, April 17, a conference was held in Honolulu at which Elder Joseph F. Smith was unanimously sustained as president of the Hawaiian Mission, with Elders William W. Cluff and Alma L. Smith as his assistants. On Monday the Apostles embarked on their return home.[44]

The task before the newly sustained twenty-five-year-old mission president was daunting. Church membership at one time had exceeded four thousand, but at this point active membership was likely less than five hundred.[45] In his own words, Joseph F. wrote, "There has been a very great falling away!"[46] Gibson had introduced objectionable practices in the lives of previously faithful members. Furthermore, members had donated land, livestock, and crops—even sold their chapels—to finance Gibson's personal purchase of Lanai and now had nothing to show for it. What's more, Elder Benson had instructed the Hawaiian Saints on Lanai to return to their previous homes and communities, yet some no longer had homes or the means to make a new start, and others may have felt too ashamed to return.[47] Many of the Hawaiian Saints were disillusioned, bitter, or both. The challenge facing Joseph F. was formidable.

Two directives from Elders Benson and Snow to Joseph F. and his companions seem clear: foremost, they were to reorganize and set in order the branches of the Church; at the same time, they were to identify a new "gathering place" for the Hawaiian Saints.[48] Though some Saints still hoped to recover Lanai, over the next six months Joseph F. and his companions actively pursued the identification and purchase of another location.[49] Missionary correspondence indicates sites were considered in Hana, island of Maui;[50] Lumahai, island of Kauai;[51] and Brigham Young even approved the purchases of Papaikou,[52] just north of Hilo on the island of Hawaii, but the sale fell through. As Joseph F. explained just weeks prior to his departure:

> We have made every enquiry and exertion to obtain information in regard to land that would be suitable for a gathering place . . . but have not yet succeeded. . . . There is scarcely a man or woman in the Church but mourns the loss of his or her property. . . . The natives have been trying to recover Lanai, but . . . I am of opinion it will cost as much as it is worth to regain it.

> . . . To obtain a tolerable gathering place on any of the inhabited Islands, will cost no less than from $7,000–$14,000.[53]

Just months after Joseph F.'s departure in October, the Church purchased Laie Plantation (about six thousand acres) on the island of Oahu for $14,000.[54] Joseph F. was familiar with Laie and apparently endorsed its purchase,[55] and William Cluff received a spiritual manifestation endorsing Laie,[56] but the final task of identification and purchase fell to Elders Francis Hammond and George Nebeker, who arrived later that year.[57]

Now considering their directive to set in order the branches of the Church upon the departure of the Apostles, Joseph F. and William Cluff set out around the island of Oahu to visit all the branches,[58] and Alma Smith continued doing the same on Maui. Describing their efforts on Oahu, Joseph F. wrote, "Brother Cluff and I have just returned from a tour around this Island. We have organized 6 Branches, each Branch numbering from 25 to 50 persons all feeling well, but [out of 400 that were in the Church when we served here before] there are not above 20. . . . Some have gone to other islands, many have apostatized, and many have died."[59] Regarding his labors on Maui, Alma Smith observed: "The saints [are] in a very low and sunken condition, both spiritually and temporally. There were no meetings held on the island, no family prayers attended to. They said the reason for this was that Gibson had not only instructed, but actually forbid them to hold meetings, preach the gospel, read the scriptures, or attend to family prayers, etc."[60] These conditions and the casual approach of many members to the gospel often frustrated Joseph F. and his companions. At one point Joseph wrote, "They have been preached to for forty years, and they are degenerating every year! . . . We cannot even see that the Gospel has benefited them one iota!"[61]

After visiting all the branches on Oahu, Joseph F. and William Cluff traveled to the island of Kauai to visit their branches. They returned to Oahu and on June 10, warmly welcomed new missionaries John R. Young (age twenty-seven)[62] and Benjamin Cluff (age thirty-four).[63] It was decided that John Young should visit Gibson on Lanai and, if possible, recover some Church belongings, then join Alma Smith on Maui.[64] Benjamin Cluff was sent to the north side of Oahu to learn the language. Not long after, Elders Young and Smith were sent to regulate Church affairs on the island of Hawaii. In a letter dated July 5, Joseph F. explained, "It is not quite three months since Elders Benson and Snow left us.

Since then we have been very busy traveling from place to place, organizing branches and regulating affairs to the best of our understanding. So far I think we have succeeded as well as could have been expected under the circumstances."[65] Shortly after this letter, William Cluff returned to oversee Church affairs on Kauai and Joseph F. went to Maui.[66] Indicative of Joseph F.'s character is John R. Young's account of Alma and his return from Hawaii to Maui: "[We] landed on [August] 6th at Malia. Here we met President Joseph F. Smith, who in those days, as now, was always active, and thoughtful for others. He met us on the beach with horses, and a hearty welcome."[67]

Notably, during their efforts to set in order the branches of the Church, they began to selectively rebaptize some members. For example, John R. Young recorded:

> On Sunday, August 14, 1864, a conference was held at Wailuku, with sixty members present. . . .
>
> President Joseph F. Smith testified that the Saints, in following Mr. Gibson's teaching, had departed from the Gospel of Jesus Christ, and had become darkened in their minds. "As soon as you manifest works meet for repentance," said he, "we will let you renew your covenants by baptism, and then we will place upon you the responsibility of preaching the Gospel to this nation."
>
> [The next day] I had the pleasure of accompanying President Smith on a visit. . . . After dinner, we rode up to the mountain, following a deep canyon, until we came to a beautiful orange grove. . . . The native brethren asked President Smith to rebaptize them. The request was granted, and I went into the water, a pure mountain stream, and baptized Kanahunahupu, George Raymond, and Kapule, three intelligent and staunch defenders of the Gospel. We next confirmed and blessed them.[68]

Rebaptism would seem unusual today; however, in 1856–57 (seven years prior to this mission) Church leaders initiated rebaptism as part of a rejuvenation movement to rekindle faith and testimony throughout the Church. This rebaptism symbolized both forgiveness of sin and a recommitment to obey commandments.[69] This movement, known today as the "Mormon Reformation of 1856–57," would have been well understood by Joseph F.,[70] and circumstances in the Islands at that time evidently appeared appropriate to him for such measures.

Apparently, only a limited number of rebaptisms occurred in the months prior to an island-wide conference held in Honolulu, October 1–3, 1864. With about two hundred members in attendance, Joseph F. explained in his opening remarks, "We have met to be instructed and encouraged in this great work, and to inaugurate a reformation . . . restoring the confidence and love of the Saints to the truth." He went on to say, "We have felt that you were living under a broken covenant, and should have commenced this reformation long since. . . . We are now going to commence a reformation, and we want those only to be re-baptized who are willing to repent and forsake their sins."[71] Elder William Cluff bore testimony to what had been said, then added, "We have not been hasty in this reformation; we have been pleading with you for several months. We want you now to choose 'whom ye will serve.'"[72]

Later in the same meeting, Elder Jonathan H. Napela, a pioneer among native Hawaiian Saints and one who had followed Gibson, explained, "We have sinned ignorantly. We were deceived and led away by Gibson's cunning words, and thereby have broken the sacred covenants we had made, but we are now undeceived, therefore let us renew our covenants and be faithful. I know this work is of God, that Joseph Smith and Brigham Young are prophets of God. . . . I do know it is true."[73] At the conclusion of the meeting, President Joseph F. Smith read the names of fifty persons selected to be rebaptized that evening. The next day sixty-three more names were read and later rebaptized.[74]

In a letter written a few days after this conference, J. W. H. Kou, a native Church leader who had also followed Gibson for a time, explained the effect of this rebaptism: "While we followed Gibson, the covenant of the Gospel was broken, and we were baptized again. So, my family and I are committed to obey the voice of the servants of God."[75]

This conference was the culmination of six months' effort to reorganize the branches and revitalize the members, and Joseph F. was pleased so many had participated. Furthermore, at this conference much of the leadership responsibility was shifted to the native members, and Alma L. Smith was designated as mission president, with Benjamin Cluff to assist. Feeling matters were sufficiently arranged, Joseph F., William Cluff, and John R. Young boarded a ship to San Francisco en route for home just over a week later.[76]

Sometime after the Gibson incident, a New York newspaper, the *Sun*, reported, "We believe the Mormon leaders unanimously attribute to him [Gibson] the fact that their people no longer have a foothold in the dominion of Kamehameha [Hawaiian Islands], or indeed, we believe, anywhere in the whole Pacific."[77] This, however, was not true. As the Honolulu conference of October 1864 shows, Joseph F. and his fellow missionaries had laid a solid foundation from which the Church would again rise and flourish in Hawaii.

One more incident from Joseph F.'s 1864 mission that occurred in San Francisco during his return from Hawaii to Salt Lake City deserves mention. "Now comes the temper," wrote John R. Young, prefacing his account of the following occurrence:

> There were living in San Francisco quite a number of relatives by marriage to the Smith family, and some of them were wealthy. They held a family reunion and invited Joseph to attend. He asked me to accompany him, which I did. We met them, . . . some twenty all told; six or eight strong, healthy looking men. A few stories were told, then the conversation drifted into personal experiences and present home conditions. They pitied Joseph and offered to deed him a good home if he would cut loose from the "Utah Mormons" and stay with them, *his true friends*. He declined, and said if they would excuse him he would bid them good night. All rose up, and then the storm broke. Their spokesman said in substance, "Joseph, we are disappointed in you; we thought you were a Smith, but any man who will come and go at the command of Brigham Young, the man who connived at the murder of your father and Uncle Joseph, has not a drop of Smith's blood in his veins." Joseph: "Do I understand you to say that Brigham Young connived at the murder of the Prophet Joseph Smith?" "Yes, and I can prove the assertion." Then there leaped from Joseph's lips the strongest expression that ever I heard come from them. "You are a damned infernal liar! Joseph Smith never had a truer friend than Brigham Young." To me, how grand he looked. He seemed to expand until he towered head and shoulders above his opponents. While their faces scowled with anger, yet like the tempest tossed waves of the ocean, whose fury had been spent at the foot of the boulder, they recede, leaving the beach cleaner and whiter than before the storm.
>
> How I loved that man's manliness; he not a Smith? The very tension of the rigid muscles proclaimed him the embodiment of the chivalrous Macks and Smiths.[78]

Certainly the cumulative experience of this eight-month mission to Hawaii helped mold the character and expand the leadership ability of Joseph F. Smith. Over a month and a half of tutelage and close association with two Apostles, responsibility for the Church in Hawaii, disillusionment and apostasy among members, loss of a "gathering place," financial setbacks to Church and members, re-establishment of Church organization, leadership and programs, and more would have enlightened, stretched, and strengthened him in unlikely ways for a twenty-five-year-old. George Q. Cannon, a man deeply regarded by Joseph F., and arguably one of the most influential missionaries to the Hawaiian Islands, acknowledged the confidence so many had in young Joseph F. this way: "Gibson must be a precious scoundrel. . . . I feel, however, that you will be able to counteract all this; it may be slowly, yet surely; and to build up a feeling of confidence that will stand the severest tests. The labor will be a severe and heavy one and will require patient perseverance, but, when accomplished, it will bring an abundant reward."[79] True to such confidence, as blessed by Brigham Young when set apart for this mission, young Joseph F. exhibited "knowledge and wisdom beyond [his] years."[80]

Notes

1. Prior to 1864, Joseph F. had served a mission to Hawaii (1854–57, ages fifteen to nineteen); served in the Echo Canyon campaign of the Utah War (1857, age nineteen); married Levira A. Smith (1859, age twenty-one); and served a mission to Great Britain (1860–63, ages twenty-two to twenty-five). See Church Educational System, *Presidents of the Church Student Manual* (Religion 345) (Salt Lake City: The Church of Jesus Christ of Latter-day Saints, 2003), 94.
2. See R. Lanier Britsch, *Moramona: The Mormons in Hawaii* (Laie, HI: The Institute for Polynesian Studies, 1989), 44. See also Nathaniel R. Ricks, *"My Candid Opinion": The Sandwich Islands Diaries of Joseph F. Smith, 1856–1857* (Salt Lake City: Smith-Pettit Foundation, 2011), 3; hereafter cited as *Sandwich Islands Diaries*.
3. See Fred E. Woods, "The Palawi Pioneers on the Island of Lanai: The First Hawaiian Latter-day Saint Gathering Place (1854–1864)," *Mormon Historical Studies* 5, no. 2 (Fall 2004): 3–35.
4. See Britsch, *Moramona*, 44, 49. According to Britsch, membership went from more than 4,650 in 1855 to 3,067 members of record in April 1858.
5. See Britsch, *Moramona*, 50–58. Referring to the settlement of Saints on Lanai, Gibson wrote, "I could make a glorious little kingdom out of this," and later explained, "I view him [the Hawaiian] and treat him as an interesting yet feeble younger brother, a subject of an ocean empire. . . . Who or what shall I fear when I am King." Britsch, *Moramona*, 54–55.
6. Letter to Alma L. Smith, July 23, 1863, CR 1234, 1, box 29, folder 12, Church History Library, Salt Lake City.
7. Letter to Alma L. Smith, July 23, 1863.
8. Journal History of the Church of Jesus Christ of Latter-day Saints, January 18, 1864, vol. 178, Church History Library, The Church of Jesus Christ of Latter-day Saints, Salt Lake City. Elder Wilford Woodruff wrote: "Met with Pres. Young and several of the Twelve . . . [he] informed us he had a letter from brethren on the Sandwich Islands which was read informing us that Capt. Gibson had ordained on the island a quorum of Twelve Apostles and Seventies and Bishops

and High Priests. He charged $100 for ordaining the Twelve, $40 for each of the Seventies, $50 for a bishop and $25 for a bishop's councillor, and he had claimed all the island to himself and said that Brigham Young had no dominion over those islands and all his conduct is accordingly. He has taken possession of the island and takes from the saints all that they raise. ... After reading the letter he said that he wanted two of the Twelve to take several of the young brethren, who had been over there before, and go to the islands and set the churches in order and do what is necessary" (original spelling preserved).

9. In Journal History, January 24, 1864, vol. 178; Elder Wilford Woodruff wrote: "I met with Prests. Brigham Young and Eleven of the Twelve Apostles. ... Pres Young appointed Ezra T. Benson and Lorenzo Snow to the Pacific Islands. He also appointed Joseph F. Smith to go with them to preside over the Islands after the Twelve returned. He also appointed Wm w. Cluff John r. Young and Alma L. Smith to go as missionaries to the Islands. He said Joseph F. Smith and Cluff might take their wives with them, if they wished." *History of the Church*, 45.

10. In a letter to George Q. Cannon, Joseph F. explained his circumstances upon receiving his call to Hawaii in 1864: "When I reached home [from mission to Great Brittan] about the 1st of October, 1863, I found my wife very low; long and severe illness had racked her whole nervous system, and had reduced her to a mere shadow of her former self. ... I gladly turned my whole attention towards doing what lay in my power to revive her drooping spirits and to renew hope and life, but she soon became so low that by many she was given up. ... At last a change came for the better, and slowly ... she improved in health and her reason gradually came back. ... I began to make my calculations for the spring. ... [Then] Word came from the valley that, Walter M. Gibson, was not conducting affairs in a proper manner on the Sandwich Islands, and President Young concluded to send two of the Twelve to straighten up matters, and brothers. W. W. Cluff, A. L. Smith, and myself, were selected to accompany them as interpreters. Consequently in a few weeks, we ... were on our way to the Sandwich Islands." Journal History, May 4, 1864, vol. 180.

11. Blessing given by Brigham Young to Joseph F. Smith, February 29, 1864: "Brother Joseph F. Smith, we lay our hands upon your head in the name of the Lord Jesus Christ of Nazareth, and we set you apart to a mission to the Sandwich Islands in the Pacific Ocean, to go there in company with Bro Benson, Snow, Smith and with Br William W. Cluff, your companions, and we ask our father in heaven to bestow on you the light of truth to that degree that your heart will be lifted up on high, that you may see things as they are, and understand the mind of the Lord, that you may know the hearts of men, and their feelings towards you, and towards the brethren, that you may understand the good and the evil. And we pray our father in heaven to protect you, to inspire your heart, and to give you great power and wisdom to accomplish this mission, for we dedicate you, and set you apart to take the charge of this mission when the Apostles shall return from the Islands. And we pray that you may have wisdom to counsel your brethren, to guide and direct, and to dictate, to have knowledge and wisdom in financial matters, and in all the spiritual kingdom of God upon the earth; all of which shall be given you according to the mind of the Lord and the necessities that are upon you, and that you are under to know and understand things pertaining to the kingdom of God upon the earth, that you shall be equal to any that lives upon the earth, that your name shall be had among the nations of the earth for good and for evil. We pray that your knowledge may increase greatly upon you, so that your labors will become easy, and your judgment and understanding may

be clear, to be an helpmate to your brethren in all things to the building up of the kingdom of God on the earth. Go in safety and in peace, and all the blessings your heart can desire in righteousness we seal on you, and say unto you go thy way rejoicing; we understand the labors you have had, and passed through, what has been upon you while you have been traveling from place to place, although young you have traveled and seen much, therefore, your wisdom shall be great, and your knowledge shall reach to the heavens. May you have knowledge and wisdom beyond your years, and visions by day and dreams by night, to show you the designs of the wicked against you, and the dangers that are spread on your path, and you shall escape, and overcome every obstruction and evil that may lay in your pathway, and you shall accomplish a great and good work on the earth, to which we ordain you and set you apart in the name of Jesus Christ, Amen." MS 1325, box 50, folder 21, Church History Library. See also Journal History, February 29, 1864, vol. 178.

12. Joseph F. Smith, journal, MS 1325, box 2, folder 3, Church History Library.
13. William and Joseph F. were well acquainted. Years before, they had served several months as mission companions in Hawaii and had maintained correspondence for some time thereafter.
14. The Cluff Family, *The Cluff Family Journal* (Provo, UT: Cluff Family Reunion, 1899–1904), 227. See also Joseph F. Smith, journal (MS 1325, box 2, folder 3, Church History Library).
15. Joseph F. Smith, journal, March 29–30, MS 1325, box 2, folder 3, Church History Library.
16. Joseph F. Smith, journal, March 31, MS 1325, box 2, folder 3, Church History Library.
17. See William W. Cluff, *Fragments of Experience* (Salt Lake City: Juvenile Instructor Office, 1882), 6: 63–68. See also *Cluff Family Journal*, 227–29. Note, most published accounts of Lorenzo Snow's near drowning appear to quote or paraphrase these two accounts by William W. Cluff (i.e., Eliza R. Snow, *Biography and Family Record of Lorenzo Snow* [Salt Lake City: Deseret News, 1884]; Orson F. Whitney, *Lives of Our Leaders: Character Sketches of Living Presidents and Apostles of The Church of Jesus Christ of Latter-day Saints*, Lorenzo Snow [Salt Lake City, Deseret News, 1901], 9–28; Joseph Fielding Smith, *Life of Joseph F. Smith, Sixth President of The Church of Jesus Christ of Latter-day Saints* [Salt Lake City: Deseret Book, 1969]; and Francis Gibbons, *Joseph F. Smith: Patriarch and Preacher, Prophet of God* [Salt Lake City: Deseret Book, 1984]).
18. Cluff, *Fragments of Experience*, 66.
19. Cluff, *Fragments of Experience*, 68. See also *Cluff Family Journal*, 245.
20. This was likely Elder Benson. In 1901 Joseph F. wrote, "Being familiar with the coast at that point, I had declined to enter the ship's boat with the rest, or to disembark while the waves were running high. Brothers Cluff and Smith were equally averse to going in that boat, but yielded to Brother Benson's persuasions." James R. Clark, "Joseph F. Smith, First Presidency," introduction, notes, and index to *Messages of the First Presidency of the Church of Jesus Christ of Latter-day Saints, 1833–1964* (Salt Lake City: Bookcraft, 1901–15), 4:21.
21. Deseret News, *Lives of Our Leaders: Character Sketches of Living Presidents and Apostles of The Church of Jesus Christ of Latter-day Saints* (Salt Lake City: Deseret News, 1901), 58–59. See also *Gospel Doctrine: Selections from the Sermons and Writings of Joseph F. Smith*, comp. John A. Widtsoe (Salt Lake City: Deseret Book, 1977), 534–36.
22. Heber J. Grant, "Inspiration and Integrity of the Prophets," *Improvement Era*, August 1919, 848.
23. William W. Cluff recounts the following experience as they crossed over to Lanai: "When about half way across the channel, we ran into a large school of whales, some of them

swimming with their backs out of water while others were sporting around us, some spouting and others throwing up their great flukes. One of them, a monster whale, came swimming toward us on the starboard side, his back three feet above the surface. He was fully sixty feet in length; to all appearance, he would strike our boat in the center. When within a few yards of us he lowered himself in the water and passed under the boat. Apparently his back was not more than a foot below the keel; had it struck him he would, no doubt, have thrown up his flukes and cut our boat in two or thrown it high into the air. In either case we should have been in a worse dilemma, than when we were capsized in the surf, as we were eight miles from land. A most providential escape." *Cluff Family Journal*, 245.

24. Joseph F. to George Q. Cannon, May 4, 1864, correspondence, Journal History, History of Brigham Young, May 4, 1864, vol. 180.
25. Cluff, *Fragments of Experience*, 69–74; and *Cluff Family Journal*, 245–50.
26. Elder Benson referred to Gibson's reaction as "more surprised than rejoiced at seeing us" in R. Lanier Britsch, *Unto the Islands of the Sea: A History of the Latter-day Saints in the Pacific* (Salt Lake City: Deseret Book, 1986), 122.
27. See Fred E. Woods, "The Palawai Pioneers on the Island of Lanai: The First Hawaiian Latter-day Saint Gathering Place 1854–1864," *Mormon Historical Studies* 5, no. 2 (Fall 2004): 21–22. See also Ricks, *Sandwich Islands Diaries*, 115–31. Due to multiple crop failures and other setbacks faced by the saints on Lanai, in 1857, it was deemed advisable to select a more suitable "gathering place" on another island.
28. Cluff, *Fragments of Experience*, 69.
29. Cluff, *Fragments of Experience*, 70. See also *Cluff Family Journal*, 245–50.
30. Cluff, *Fragments of Experience*, 69–70. See also *Cluff Family Journal*, 245–50.
31. *Cluff Family Journal*, 246.
32. *Cluff Family Journal*, 246.
33. Cluff, *Fragments of Experience*, 71.
34. George Q. Cannon was among the first missionaries to preach the Gospel to the native Hawaiians, and he was deeply respected and loved by them.
35. *Cluff Family Journal*, 247.
36. *Cluff Family Journal*, 247–48.
37. Cluff, *Fragments of Experience*, 71–72 .
38. *Cluff Family Journal*, 248.
39. Cluff, *Fragments of Experience*, 72.
40. Britsch explains that Gibson stayed "on Lanai with those Saints who would remain with him. His influence had been strong among them, but when it was learned that he had been officially cut off from the Church, the people of Lanai left him very quickly. In October 1864, only six months later, it was reported that there were only fourteen members of the Church still living under Gibson's direction on Lanai. These people requested to be cut off from the Church in October 1864, and their request was granted." Britsch, *Islands of the Sea*, 123.
41. Cluff, *Fragments of Experience*, 73.
42. Gibson, aware of his fate, wrote a letter to Brigham Young stating, "I cannot forget my love and regard for your person, although you have dealt precipitately and harshly with me. . . . I think and feel, that though my spirit has not responded to your call, and we are now in different channels, that yet my course, will never lead me into an attitude that will be hostile to you, or

the work you direct." CR 1234-1, reel 40, box 29, folder 19, Church History Library. Though Gibson was excommunicated, he maintained a civil, if not courteous, relationship with the Church thereafter. Britsch, *The Mormons in Hawaii*, 58.

43. Joseph F. Smith, journal, January 24, 1864–April 25, 1864, also April 14–15, MS 1325, box 2, folder 3, Church History Library.

44. *Cluff Family Journal*, 249. See also Joseph F. Smith, journal, January 24, 1864–April 25, 1864; see also April 16–18. MS 1325, box 2, folder 3, Church History Library.

45. The authors of this article base this estimate on letter correspondence, between April and October 1864 that indicate rather small gatherings of Saints as the missionaries travel throughout the Islands to reestablish the Church. Further substantiating a rather small number, only two hundred people attend the Islands-wide conference held six months later in Honolulu.

46. Journal History, vol. 181, July–August 1864, Extracts from a letter by Joseph F. Smith printed in *Deseret Weekly News*, August 31, 1864, 385.

47. Margaret Bock explained, "It was not considered desirable to leave them under his [Gibson's] influence. Another area was sought for a gathering place and also for headquarters for the reestablishment of the Church. The natives were disillusioned and had scattered throughout the islands, some to their former homes; others were social outcasts; and others were still too ashamed and depressed to try to make places for themselves in the communities. The Church felt responsible in trying to reorganize their members who had been misled by the fanciful Gibson." Margaret Bock, "The Church of Jesus Christ of Latter-day Saints in the Hawaiian Islands" (master's thesis, University of Hawaii, 1941), chapter 3.

48. William Cluff recorded, "As Mr. Gibson had succeeded in obtaining a personal title to the land leased for that purpose, on the island of Lanai, brothers Benson and Snow advised the Elders who remained, to notice in their travels what appeared to them the best places for this purpose, that, when the time came for it, a good selection might be made." *Fragments of Experience*, 74.

49. Britsch explained: "One might wonder whether the Church attempted to recover the lands it had purchased on Lanai. Although the native Saints did make a half-hearted attempt to do so, the missionaries made no legal effort to win back the land. The reason for this was twofold. First, Joseph F. Smith, who was in Hawaii earlier when the decision had been made to look for a new gathering place, would have had to institute such litigation, but he did not believe that Lanai was worth fighting for. His feelings about the matter had apparently not changed since 1857. Second, Elder Smith was convinced that the costs of a court battle would be greater than the value of the land. Thus Gibson was left alone to do as he desired with the Palawai plantation. He had difficulty accomplishing much there after the Saints left because his subservient laborers could not be replaced from another source" Britsch, *Islands of the Sea*, 123.

50. Alma L. Smith to Joseph F. and William Cluff, May 3, 1864: "Went to Hana [island of Maui]. . . . Ascertained what information I could about that 600 acres of land in Hana, it belongs to a Mr Steele at Makawao but the prospects concerning it was anything but flattering." MS 1325, box 9, folder 24, Church History Library. Alma L. Smith to Joseph F., June 22, 1864: "I took particular pains to go and see Mr Steele of Makawao about that land at Hana, he says that he once wanted to sell it, price 1000 dollar, but has since changed his mind and will not sell it. So there is the 'end of that.'" MS 1325, box 9, folder 24, Church History Library.

51. William W. Cluff to Joseph F., August 6, 1864: "I have examined the land at Lumahai [island of Kauai] and I think it will be as good a place for our purpose as any we can find. If you do not succeed in getting that piece on Hawaii we might try and get this." MS 1325, box 9, folder 22, Church History Library.
52. Joseph F. to Brigham Young, August 30, 1864: "Our friend Haalelea, has offered us a large tract of land on Hawaii [Papaikou] for $3,000. Bros Alma L. & John R. called and saw it, and were well pleased with it. Quite a number of the saints are eager to buy it, but to raise the money will be no small task at present, I assure you." CR1234/1, box 42, folder 10, reel 55, Church History Library. Brigham Young to Joseph F. October 17, 1864: "If it be as good and suitable as you describe for a plantation and place of settlement for the Saints, you had better close for it, at the price you state, and advise me when you have done so and draw on me for the amount." MS 1325, box 9, folder 25, and MS 1325, box 9, folder 25, Church History Library. However, in a letter to Joseph F., September 1, 1864, J. W. H. Kou, a native member, likely sent to negotiate the purchase, writes, "It will not be purchased; it was rejected." MS 1325, box 9, folder 23, Church History Library, translated by Kamoa'e Walk, Kapi'olani Akhay, Noelani Nomiyama, and Leonahenahe Aina.
53. Journal History, July–August 1864, vol. 181, Honolulu, Oahu, extracts from a letter by Joseph F. Smith, printed in *Deseret News Weekly*, August 31, 1864, 385.
54. Riley M. Moffat, Fred E. Woods, Jeffrey N. Walker, *Gathering to Laie* (Laie, HI: The Jonathan Napela Center for Hawaiian and Pacific Islands Studies, 2011), 24.
55. See Smith, *Messages of the First Presidency*, 21.
56. Moffat, Woods, and Walker, *Gathering to Laie*, 23–24.
57. Moffat, Woods, and Walker, *Gathering to Laie*, 24–25.
58. Joseph F. Smith, journal, January 24, 1864–April 25, 1864, MS 1325, box 2, folder 3, Church History Library.
59. Journal History, May 4, 1864, vol. 180, History of Brigham Young, letter from Joseph F. Smith to George Q. Cannon. See also Journal History, May 20, 1864, vol. 180, letter from Joseph F. Smith to his cousin David Taylor, published in *Deseret News*, August 17, 1864, 366.
60. Alma L. Smith to Brigham Young, April 29, 1864, correspondence, CR 1234-1, reel 41, box 30, folder 5, Church History Library; see also Journal History, April 29, 1864, 179, published in *Deseret News*, June 22, 1864, 305.
61. Journal History, July 5, 1864, 181. Joseph F. appears to be referencing Protestant missionaries who arrived in Hawaii approximately forty years prior. At the time he wrote this, Latter-day Saint missionaries had only been in Hawaii for fourteen years. Joseph F.'s frustration generally arose from recognition that despite the missionaries' best efforts to assist native members both spiritually and temporally, many native members would retain their old religious traditions and remain in poor living conditions.
62. John R. Young had previously served in the Hawaiian Islands and spoke fluent Hawaiian. He was Brigham Young's nephew.
63. Benjamin Cluff is William W. Cluff's older brother. Unlike the other missionaries, he had not previously served in Hawaii and did not yet speak Hawaiian.
64. Regarding his attempt to recover some Church belongings from Gibson, John R. Young writes, "I crossed to Lanai in a whale boat. I stayed a week with Mr. Gibson. He surrendered to me five hundred Books of Mormon, his temple clothes, and a watch that my father had given

to him. I recrossed the channel to Maui . . . and found Elder A. L. Smith anxious to learn the success of my mission." *Memoirs of John R. Young, Utah Pioneer, 1847* (Salt Lake City: Deseret News, 1920), 132.

65. Journal History, July–August 1864, vol. 181, extracts from a letter by Joseph F. Smith printed in *Deseret News Weekly,* August 31, 1864, 385.
66. Journal History, July–August 1864, vol. 181, extracts from a letter by Joseph F. Smith printed in *Deseret News Weekly,* August 31, 1864, 385.
67. *Memoirs of John R. Young,* 137.
68. *Memoirs of John R. Young,* 138. Another recorded incident of rebaptism is found in a letter from William Cluff (then on island of Kauai) to Joseph F. dated July 22: "I found Bro Brown well and feeling good. . . . I re-baptized him last evening." February 18, 1864–November 2, 1864, MS 1325, box 9, folder 22, Church History Library.
69. Paul H. Peterson, "Reformation (LDS) of 1856–1857," in *Encyclopedia of Mormonism,* ed. Daniel H. Ludlow (New York: Macmillan, 1992), 3:1197–98.
70. Joseph F. mentions this movement of rebaptism in his personal journal and correspondence during his first mission to Hawaii. See Ricks, *Sandwich Island Diaries;* see also letters from Joseph F. Smith to Martha Ann Smith Harris, in *My Dear Sister: Letters between Joseph F. Smith and His Sister Martha Ann,* ed. Richard Neitzel Holzapfel and David M. Whitchurch (Provo, UT: Religious Studies Center; Salt Lake City: Deseret Book, forthcoming).
71. Joseph F. shared his intent to conduct a reformation/rebaptism among the Hawaiian members with Brigham Young; however, it appears Joseph F. did so of his own initiative because President Young's endorsement of the approach comes in a letter dated October 17, 1864—almost two weeks after Joseph F. had done so in the Honolulu conference. In the letter Brigham Young said, "Your [letter] of August 30th . . . was perused with interest. So far as advised, your course and the counsels of yourself and the Elders to the people in relation to re baptism and the renewing of their covenants and the other matters mentioned in your letter meet my mind, and, if adopted, and carried out by the people in the proper Spirit, cannot fail to be attended with beneficial results." July 28, 1864–November 13, 1864, MS 1325, box 9, folder 25, Church History Library.
72. Journal History, September–October 1864, vol. 182; Minutes of a Conference, held in Honolulu, Sandwich Islands, October 1st, 2nd, and 3rd, 1864; "Sandwich Islands Mission," *Deseret News,* November 30, 1864, 67. See also Andrew Jenson, *History of the Hawaiian Mission of the Church of Jesus Christ of Latter-day Saints,* Special Collections, Brigham Young University–Hawaii, Laie, HI.
73. Journal History, September–October 1864, vol. 182; Minutes of a Conference, held in Honolulu, Sandwich Islands, October 1st, 2nd and 3rd, 1864; "Sandwich Islands Mission," *Deseret News,* November 30, 1864, 67. See also Jenson, *History of the Hawaiian Mission.*
74. Journal History, September–October 1864, vol. 182; Minutes of a Conference, held in Honolulu, Sandwich Islands, October 1st, 2nd, and 3rd, 1864; "Sandwich Islands Mission," *Deseret News,* November 30, 1864, 67. See also Jenson, *History of the Hawaiian Mission.* Notably, in the conference minutes, Joseph F. reported "fourteen persons as still adhering to Gibson, and who wished to be dropped from the church; motioned and seconded that they be cut off from the church; carried unanimously." Thus in six months Elder Snow's prophecy that not one of the Saints would remain with Gibson appeared fulfilled. Cluff, *Fragments of Experience,* 73.

75. October 7, 1864, MS 16877; J. W. H. Kou's report of 1864 visit of Joseph F. Smith, E. Benson, and L. Snow to Hawaii, translated by Kamoa'e Walk, Kapi'olani Akhay, Noelani Nomiyama, and Leonahenahe Aina.
76. The departure of Joseph F. after only six months labor may seem precipitous. However, in a letter to Joseph F. and the other missionaries dated July 28, 1864, Brigham Young stated: "I now write to inform you that the management of the mission and the length of the stay of either or all of you, upon the Islands is hereby left entirely to your own judgments guided by the dictates of the Spirit to you. It seems to me that you will be able to leave the affairs of the mission in the hands of the native brethren as advantageously as the present circumstances will permit, giving them such organization, counsel and, instructions as may be most fitting to their condition, which will release you to the performance of duties where the spheres of your usefulness will be much more enlarged. . . . Should you conclude that Elders John R. Young and Benjamin Cluff can be instrumental in doing good by tarrying a while after the rest of you leave, all right; and should you decide it best for all of you to return together, that will also be equally right, for the matter as before stated is left with yourselves under the dictates of the Spirit to you." July 28, 1864, MS 1325, box 9, folder 25, Church History Library. In a letter to George A. Smith dated August 30, 1864, Joseph F. explains, "I believe the best thing that can be done, is to shift as much of the load upon them [the native members] as possible, and require them to act for themselves. As soon after our October conference as possible some of us will make the best of our way home." CR1234/1, box 42, folder 10, reel 55, Church History Library.
77. Thomas G. Thrum, *The Shepherd Saint of Lanai: Rich "Primacy" Revelations, Gathered from Various Sources and Produced in Historical Shape for the First Time in the "Saturday Press", Dec. 24, 1881 to Jan. 14, 1882* (Honolulu: Thos. G. Thrum, 1882), http://www.archive.org/stream/shepherdsaintofl00unse#page/n0/mode/2up, p. 40.
78. *Memoirs of John R. Young*, 279–80.
79. George Q. Cannon to Joseph F. Smith, August 9, 1864, correspondence, MS 1325, box 9, folder 22, Church History Library.
80. MS 1325, box 50, folder 21, Church History Library; see also Journal History, February 29, 1864, vol. 178.

Family and Friends

Lisa Olsen Tait

5

"A Modern Patriarchal Family":

The Wives of Joseph F. Smith in the *Relief Society Magazine*, 1915–19

Joseph F. Smith's devotion to his families is legendary. "I love them with an imperishable love," he wrote of his wives in one letter. "I honor them as the Mothers of my children! I cherish them as the dearest partners of my greatest joys, the sweetest, best ministers to my earthly pleasures and happiness."[1] Recollections of various grandchildren repeatedly emphasized their awareness of his great love and enjoyment of them, his personal attention to each individual, and his secret pocket of candies for his "babies." "He had the marvelous ability of making every member of his entire family feel as though he loved him or her the most," said one granddaughter.[2] President Smith's close friend Charles W. Nibley eulogized his family as his "greatest work of all": "Here is the work of a man indeed! Nay, is it not more like the work of a God?" he exclaimed.[3]

Bishop Nibley's tribute appeared in the January 1919 issue of the *Relief Society Magazine* as part of a lengthy feature article memorializing Joseph F. Smith upon his death. This article took a significant turn when, after briefly recounting President Smith's leadership in church and community, author Susa Young Gates abruptly shifted gears, removing the focus from the prophet himself.

Lisa Olsen Tait is a historian and writer in the LDS Church History Department.

She declared, "President Smith himself would be loath to see this article appear in the leading women's *Magazine*, in the Church, without due affectionate notice given to the women who have helped to mold his own character and that of his children."[4] Following were six pages of text and photographs profiling his five wives and their families.

Since its founding in 1915, the *Relief Society Magazine* had frequently given face and voice to the wives of Joseph F. Smith. They were featured not only for their relationship to him but also for being accomplished women in their own right. Today these remarkable women are largely unknown, and even in biographies of Joseph F. Smith they are mentioned only in passing.[5] Yet we cannot hope to fully understand President Smith's life without a complete picture of his families—"his greatest work" and the context in which he lived on the most personal level. Even more, these women—Julina, Sarah, Edna, Alice, and Mary—deserve recognition as individuals whose life experiences were at once unique and representative of many other LDS women of their generation.

This article presents a preliminary step toward a complete study of the Joseph F. Smith families by examining the portrayals of Joseph F. Smith and his wives in the *Relief Society Magazine* from its inception in 1915 to his death in 1918. This approach enables us to give an introduction to each woman while also highlighting how President Smith's family was portrayed publicly. Moreover, it raises some interesting questions concerning the dynamics of this large plural family—and also concerning the place of plural marriage in the LDS Church almost three decades after the Manifesto. In order to probe at those questions, I will first consider what *is* said in these accounts and then consider what is *not* said.

It must be acknowledged that the portrayals of the Smith wives and families in the *Relief Society Magazine* were written primarily for public consumption in an official Church publication and therefore present only a partial and idealized view. There are two important responses to those concerns. First, by all accounts, the Smith families seem to have achieved a high level of love and unity, and the effusive, affectionate accounts of the participants and contemporary observers should not be discounted, regardless of the venue in which they appeared. Certainly, as I will discuss below, there must have been more complex dynamics under the surface; in hindsight we will never be able to fully separate idealization from genuine feeling. However, these facts do not render the genuine feeling invalid. Second, the fact that this was the image of plural marriage that the participants themselves and the editor of the *Relief Society Magazine* wanted to portray, at this particular point in time, is significant and deserves examination for what it tells us about how Latter-day Saints were thinking about plural marriage as the end of that era came to a decisive close. In any case, I hope that this necessarily brief treatment will suggest fruitful avenues of inquiry for future research.

The Smith Families in 1915

By way of overview, we should take note of the status of the Smith families in January 1915 as the magazine began publication. There were five wives at that time (in order of marriage): Julina Lambson, Sarah Ellen Richards, Edna Lambson, Alice Kimball, and Mary Schwartz. Of President Smith's forty-eight children, thirty-six were living; nineteen were married and had produced over seventy grandchildren (see appendix).[6] The wives ranged in age from forty-nine to sixty-five years of age; the oldest living child was Mary Sophronia (forty-five years old) and the youngest was Royal Grant (eight years old). Joseph F. Smith was seventy-six years old; he and Julina had been married for forty-eight years. (His first marriage and subsequent divorce is discussed below.) President Smith maintained close relations with all of his families and took his wives on various trips and excursions in turn. Each wife had her own home in downtown Salt Lake City—Julina in the Beehive House; Sarah, Edna, and Alice in adjoining lots on 300 West; and Mary just a few blocks away on North Temple.[7] Mary also had a farm in Taylorsville.

"Each is a queen in her own right," Susa Young Gates declared of the Smith wives in her "Memoriam" article four years later. "They have been and are as faithful and fond wives, as true and wise mothers as ever lived upon the earth." While President Smith deserved great credit for the "remarkable family" he had fathered, she continued, "it must be said that the five noble and high-principled 'mothers of his children'—as he loved to call them—deserve and should receive equal share in the credit for the beneficent training and careful nurture given to their families."[8] She then proceeded to profile each woman in turn.

Julina Lambson Smith: "At the Head of Her Husband's Kingdom"

Julina Smith, wrote Susa Young Gates, was "amply qualified by her own native housewifely and social abilities, her broad sympathy and just understanding of the sacred principle of celestial marriage, to stand at the head of her great husband's kingdom."[9] Honored as the first wife of President Smith, she had given her life to creating one of the most remarkable and successful families in Mormondom, entering into a unique partnership with him and four other women in building what she once called "a modern patriarchal family."[10] As the second counselor to general Relief Society president Emmeline B. Wells, moreover, Julina was recognized as a leader and public worker. In her own mind, Sister Smith saw the domestic and public aspects of her life as mutually reinforcing, and in her published comments she encouraged other LDS women to take the same perspective.

Julina Lambson was born in 1849 to Alfred Lambson and Melissa Jane Bigler, pioneers of 1847.[11] In 1866, at age seventeen, Julina married Joseph F. Smith, who was then twenty-seven years old. At the time, as I will discuss below, he was already married to his cousin Levira, but Julina entered willingly into the role of plural wife. "He is the only man I have ever seen that I could love as a husband," she told her mother.[12] Julina gave birth to eleven children and adopted two others, immersing herself in her chosen life. After taking a course in obstetrics in the mid-1870s, she added frequent service as a midwife to her family responsibilities. Managing the ever-growing household with her sister-wives during the frequent absences of their husband, Julina also accompanied him to the Sandwich Islands (Hawaii) in 1885 when he was exiled to avoid prosecution by antipolygamy forces. When Joseph took up residence in the Beehive House after becoming President of the Church in 1901, Julina moved there and served as a sort of "First Lady" to the Church while increasing her public work with her acceptance of the call to the Relief Society presidency in 1910.

In the *Relief Society Magazine*, Julina Smith expressed her devotion to motherhood repeatedly. "A woman who would make a success of her life must endeavor to make her home an altar of peace, love and companionship," she wrote in the first issue. "Her husband should rest confident in her gentle solicitude, and her children trust in her unfailing wisdom. Such an ideal does not imply wealth, education nor brilliant gifts. Faith, affection, fidelity, industry, and above all, integrity, constitute the requirements for such a happy woman's life and success."[13]

Her public addresses also stress these themes. While other Relief Society leaders of the day discussed their participation in national women's organizations and in charitable and educational efforts, Julina's comments at Relief Society conferences showed her to be primarily concerned with home and family and with teaching the younger generation. At the April 1915 conference, for example, Sister

Julina and Joseph Smith on their golden wedding anniversary, May 5, 1916, an event highlighted in the Relief Society Magazine. *"Sister Smith wore a golden wedding gown of white satin, beautifully made by one of our own sisters and modestly decorated with laces and flowers. She was not handsomer on her wedding day than she was on this happy occasion." Courtesy of Church History Library.*

Smith "urged with great force the careful training of children religiously and morally. To this problem every mother should bend her best efforts because of the sacredness of the duty laid upon her as a parent."[14]

Two aspects of Julina's public work received particular notice in the *Relief Society Magazine*. She served as supervisor of the Wedding and Burial Clothes Department, overseeing the production and sale of temple and burial clothing to members of the Church, a work that had grown "steadily and surely" under Sister Smith's leadership.[15] Julina was also recognized in the magazine for her work as a midwife. "It has always been a joy to me to place a tiny one for the first time in its mother's arms, for then I felt again the thrills that I have felt in looking into the baby faces of my own," she recalled.[16] A profile of "Ye Ancient and Honorable Order of Midwifery" celebrating early Mormon women mentioned both Julina and her sister Edna—"the two splendid sisters, and wives of Joseph F. Smith"—in this capacity.[17]

It was, of course, those "baby faces of [her] own" that consumed most of Julina Smith's life, and her voice came through most forcefully in the *Relief Society Magazine* in her nostalgic recollections of her unusual family experience. The first—appearing in the fifth issue of the *Magazine*—was her "Loving Tribute" to her sister-wife Sarah after Sarah's death in March 1915. This piece is remarkable for its deeply affectionate tone. "'Not dead but sleeping,' and sweet is thy memory to me, Aunt Sarah," Julina began, "as are the recollections of our associations through the 48 years that we have journeyed together always sharing each other's joys, loves and sorrows."[18] In speaking of her family, Julina always used the first-person plural—"we" and "our family" in a way that clearly included more than herself and her husband.

Julina wrote tenderly of her husband's subsequent two marriages—events that, in another situation or for another woman, could have caused great heartache. Continuing to address Sarah directly, Julina recalled:

> Mere girls, we were, when we started life together.
>
> I the mother of one little one, when two years after my marriage 'Papa' brought you home his wife. . . .
>
> A few years together, Joseph, you and I, and then again our family was increased, the home made larger and Aunt Edna came, to make a triangle of happiness with our husband as the center controlling bond of love.

The picture painted by this recollection is one of three young women raising their families cooperatively as they all lived together in the same house, known as the Homestead. She then describes some of their "happiest hours" in vivid detail:

> My large dining-room was always the personal property and common gathering place of all. Even now I can hear the laughter of our children as they played about us before being kissed, and tucked in their beds. There, too, I can see the evening picture of three tired but happy mothers, often busy with kneeless stockings, seatless trousers or other articles of clothing needing buttons or stitches; or with, perhaps, something good to read or ideas to exchange.

It is notable that this "triangle" of love and happiness includes the husband only by implication—his presence seems to have been felt mostly in his absence, and the bonds between the three women were perhaps primary. "As often as possible our papa was with us," Julina wrote, "but oftener we three were alone, for we were the wives of a soldier of the truth whose armor was always on."[19] Julina's portrayal suggests that this modern "patriarchal" family may have been in fact, on a daily basis, more of a matriarchy—something that was undoubtedly true in other polygamous households. This is not to say that the women and children did not love their husband and father and defer to him when he was there, but it suggests the complexity of the emotional ties and daily dynamics in the family.

By any standard, Julina Smith's descriptions of her life as a plural wife are remarkable. She is confident and unapologetic, affectionate and effusive; she comes across as totally and unhesitatingly dedicated to the life she has chosen, and her love for the people in that life is unequivocal. At the same time, as I will discuss below, she leaves much unsaid. We should also note that, of the Smith wives, hers is the only voice that appears directly in the magazine. While this fact is certainly due in large part to her position in the Relief Society, it nonetheless highlights her undisputed position as "first" wife of Joseph F. Smith and "first lady" of Mormondom.

Sarah Ellen Richards Smith: "A Quiet Power"

"I am grateful beyond my power to express that 'papa' has 'Aunt Sarah' 'over there' to comfort and take care of him now," Julina Smith is reported to have said when she looked into her husband's coffin.[20] Sarah Ellen Richards Smith had been gone for over three years when Joseph F. Smith died in November 1918. She was nonetheless included in Gates's memorial tribute to the women in his life, her death

Sarah Ellen Richards Smith (1850–1915) was the only one of Joseph F. Smith's wives to precede him in death. "So easy, so guileless so cheerful is her deportment that her company is eagerly sought by those who know her best," her husband wrote. "Her cheery laugh and her determined optimism make her world a very beautiful place to live in." 1910 portrait, courtesy of Church History Library.

having created a parallel scene of grief that left "a whole family in tears and deep mourning at her departure."[21] Sarah was remembered as "beautiful, courteous and extremely intelligent." "All her life was guided by high principle, and no mean or ignoble word or act marred the gentle standard of her fine character," Gates wrote."[22]

Sarah Ellen Richards, a daughter of President Willard Richards and Sarah Longstroth, was born in Salt Lake City in 1850. She married Joseph F. Smith in March 1868; as recounted in the Smith family history, President Brigham Young had counseled Joseph to take another wife, and Joseph and Julina together selected Sarah as their choice.[23] Immediately after their marriage, the newlyweds went to Provo, where Joseph had been assigned by Brigham Young to resolve some local problems. This also gave them a few months together for a honeymoon. Sarah eventually bore eleven children, five of whom preceded her in death. Sarah's life, like Julina's, was immersed in her family and household. She served in her ward Relief Society and was one of the founding officers of the Daughters of the Utah Pioneers. She also did much genealogy and temple work on behalf of her ancestors. She seems to have had delicate health, which likely served to curtail her public activities. Sarah loved to sew and took up much of that sort of work in the household; she was also known for being very particular about cleanliness and order.[24]

On the occasion of her death in 1915, the magazine carried as its lead article a memorial article in which the voices of both Joseph and Julina were featured, paying tribute to Sarah in poignant and loving terms. "The character of Sister Sarah E. Smith is at once strong and well controlled," her husband wrote. "There is a quiet power about her spirit that manifests itself to all who come into her presence. But with that power she unites the gentle tact of a true woman." Joseph characterized her as "guileless" and "cheerful," with a "cheery laugh" and "determined optimism" that make her world "a very beautiful place to live in."

No greater tribute could be paid, Joseph continued, than "to name the simple fact that out of all her honored husband's family there could be found no single wife or child who had aught but loving words of praise and esteem for their beloved 'Aunt Sarah.' What greater proof of true loveliness could be adduced? . . . This tribute would be incomplete if there was no mention made of the tender consideration which this good wife accords to her busy and burdened companion," Joseph concluded. "'The heart of her husband doth safely trust in her.'"[25] Such a tribute from any husband would be high praise indeed, but it is followed by the equally loving pen-sketch from Julina discussed above. "Your place is vacant now, Aunt Sarah" Julina wrote, "but memory is sweet. Our love has grown stronger with the passing years and today I feel your absence as keenly as if you were my own sister—my own flesh and blood."[26]

Sarah's voice is not included in this profile, or anywhere else in the magazine, making her seem more quiet than perhaps she actually was, but clearly the impression conveyed in these tributes, as well as the "Memoriam" profile, is of a strong but gentle woman who was known for her loving nature and her sterling character. Whereas Julina was noted for her domesticity and leadership, Sarah stood as an example of the individual virtues LDS women aspired to develop.

Edna Lambson Smith: A "Most Unique and Faithful Living Woman"

Edna Lambson was born in 1851, the younger sister of Julina. Still in her midteens when her older sister married, Edna spent much time at her sister's home. At age fifteen, she was healed of a "severe and almost fatal illness" after a dramatic night during which her brother-in-law and future husband, Joseph F. Smith, administered to her continuously for several hours. Having been counseled by Brigham Young to take another wife, Joseph was sealed to nineteen-year-old

Edna Lambson and Joseph F. Smith, early 1900s. Edna's simple but pretty dress and her direct, confident expression seem to reflect her energetic, no-nonsense personality. "Comely, nervously active in all her movements, and gifted with piercing eyes, she is sometimes abrupt and vigorous in her expressions," wrote Susa Young Gates. Courtesy of Church History Library.

Edna on New Year's Day, 1871. According to family history, this decision was made in a family council in which Edna was deemed a natural choice for a plural wife "since she was there most of the time anyway."[27] Edna bore ten children, five boys and five girls, six of whom preceded their father in death—most painfully, perhaps, Hyrum Mack, the eldest son in the family and an apostle, whose death in January 1918 seemed to precipitate his father's decline. With the death of her son, Edna also became the Smith wife to lose more of her children than any other.

In speaking of Edna, Gates emphasized her position as matron of the Salt Lake Temple, reporting that the sister workers in the temple "love her for the sterling virtues which buttress her character with unyielding fortitude and strength"; in return for their dedication, Sister Smith "mothers them all." Edna was described as being "like a lightning flash, instant in speech, strenuous in activity" but also "an ardent lover of deep spiritual truths" who reads the scriptures as her "diversion" (in other words, her hobby). "The sister workers in the temple who know her best give quick and willing service under her swift, directing hand," Gates reported.[28]

Temple work was a subject close to Susa Young Gates's heart, and it received much emphasis in the *Relief Society Magazine* during her editorship. One feature article on this subject gave extended attention to Edna's work in the temple. While the war was turning the world's attention to the "generous and tenderly sympathetic labors" of women such as Clara Barton, Gates asserted, Latter-day Saints should remember "that we have women amongst us, consecrated women, who have not only reared large families and ministered in the Relief Society, but also have labored as priestesses in the temples of the living God, and thus brought hope and cheer to the helpless, imprisoned spirits behind the veil." Among those, Edna Smith was "the most unique and faithful living woman associated with temple work."[29]

As recounted in this piece, Edna began her service at the age of twenty-two in the Endowment House, first working in the kitchen and then becoming an ordinance worker. When the Salt Lake Temple was dedicated in 1893, she was set apart as an ordinance worker, and in 1910 she was called to be the matron of the temple—"in charge of the sister workers," as Gates put it. In addition to her ordinance work, Edna was assigned to be in charge of "maintaining cleanliness"; in that capacity, she had "accomplished marvels in the regulation and inner arrangements of the temple." She was also asked in 1916 to assist the president of the Logan temple in recommending major renovations and improvements to that building.[30]

In addition to Edna's labors in the temple, she served on the General Board of the Primary and was a leader in the Daughters of Utah Pioneers. She was also credited with inspiring a Churchwide fundraising movement in 1915 that raised over $30,000 for "destitute families and orphan children of the war" in Europe—money that was distributed by her son Hyrum and his wife, Ida, while he served as president of the European Mission.[31]

Along with Edna's public labors, Gates described her personality in vivid terms:

> Sister Smith is a woman of deep, spiritual insight, with an abounding love of the higher things of the kingdom. She is a natural student and possesses a keen mind. Comely, nervously active in all her movements, and gifted with piercing eyes, she is sometimes abrupt and vigorous in her expressions and with her quick word of counsel; but those who know her best forget the thrust of the two-edged sword in contemplating the mercy of the wound, which was made only that righteousness might increase and obedience be enforced.

"Those who come closest to her," Gates concluded, "love her for her integrity, her genuineness, her nobililty, and her pure, upright spirit."[32]

Edna Smith's success in motherhood was also mentioned. When her son Hyrum Mack died, the magazine's eulogy honored Edna's influence in his life: "From his youth up his mother followed his every footstep, taught him the principles of the gospel, inculcated the fear of the Lord in his soul, and helped him to overcome all youthful temptations, turning errors into experience and making of conquered temptation a bent circle of protection for the future guidance of his own children."[33]

Of all the wives of Joseph F. Smith, Edna Lambson's presence in the *Relief Society Magazine* was most visibly connected to her public work. While portrayals of Julina placed her public work alongside, or even subordinate to, her domestic role, it was just the opposite for Edna. She was honored as a mother, to be sure, but whenever she was mentioned in the magazine it was primarily as a woman whose energies were turned outward, beyond her home. Nonetheless, Edna's public work was consecrated work, and her depictions in the magazine served to remind LDS women of their own potential to make important contributions to the community.

Alice Kimball Smith and Mary Taylor Schwartz Smith: "Well-Known Women"

Taken together, Julina, Sarah, and Edna represented three distinct but interrelated points on the family "triangle"; based on their portrayals in the *Relief Society Magazine,* we might perceive that those women formed the central axis of the family. However, there were two other wives: Alice Kimball and Mary Schwartz. In her memorial article, Susa Young Gates asserted that all of President Smith's wives were "well-known women in this community."[34] In the magazine, however, this was not necessarily the case: Alice and Mary were barely mentioned. Because they received so much less mention than the other three, I will consider them together here.

Alice Kimball was described in the memorial article as "a lovely, sensitive, highly spiritualized character." She had inherited "keen, incisive humor," "dignity," and "seeric gifts" from her father, Heber C. Kimball, and she was "devoted to her home and its constant needs." Nonetheless, Alice had served publicly as general treasurer of the YLMIA and had "traveled much" in that capacity, always "lifting up her eloquent and appealing voice" to bear testimony of the gospel. She and her family were "prostrated with the influenza plague" when Joseph died, preventing Alice from being at his deathbed; only through her "indomitable courage and will" was she able to come, "stricken and pallid," to the funeral.[35]

Other than a brief allusion to her name in a previous sketch by Julina, this is the only mention of Alice in the *Relief Society Magazine*. She was born in 1858 to Heber C. Kimball and Ann Alice Gheen. Alice was a twin; her brother Andrew Kimball was a stake president in Arizona and father of future Church president Spencer W. Kimball. Alice had been married previously, to a man with an alcohol problem. She bore him three children before finally seeking a divorce. According to Smith family tradition, President John Taylor advised Joseph F. Smith to marry Alice in order to provide for her and her children.[36] Alice was sealed to President Smith in December 1883. He adopted the three children from her first marriage, and they had four more children together, making her the mother of seven. Her youngest child was eighteen years old the year of his father's death.

A biographical sketch in Gates's *History of the YLMIA* mentions some of Alice's talents. She had "the skill of the housewife and the rarer artistic handling of the needle, which can make old garments look like new, and can fashion the

Alice Kimball Smith, fourth wife of President Joseph F. Smith, ca. 1880. Alice's elaborate hat reflects the love of beauty and refined sense of style for which she was known. "Her heart is ever a-quiver with the suppressed emotions of a keenly sensitive spirit; and when she is forced to appear before an audience, she forgets self and remembers only God and the eager girls who are listening to her moving appeals," wrote Susa Young Gates, describing Alice's work in the YLMIA. Courtesy of Church History Library.

new into robes of grace and beauty," Gates reported. "She is her own seamstress, and does not shrink even from the difficult art of tailoring her own outer garments." Alice was also gifted "with the love of art in all its manifold expressions," though she had never found opportunity for "proper cultivation" of that love. Upon becoming treasurer of the YLMIA in 1905, she felt that she did not know enough to fulfill that position to the highest standards, so she took a course in bookkeeping.[37] "She is a most devoted wife and fond mother, giving her wealth of passionate service without personal regard, or at times without self-protection," Gates wrote in the *Relief Society Magazine*, suggesting that Alice had at times sacrificed her health in performing that service.[38]

Mary Taylor Schwartz Smith was profiled in the "Memoriam" article as a "loyal and devoted wife" who bequeathed to her children "the quick intelligence" and the "love of literary and educational pursuits" that she herself inherited "from

Mary Taylor Schwartz Smith with her husband and sons, December 1896. Mary spent several years in Idaho in the 1890s; on her return to Utah, she purchased a farm where she could teach her five sons to work. "She has bequeathed to her children the quick intelligence, the love of literary and educational pursuits, which she, too, inherited from a superior ancestry. She has not disdained, however, to take up a farm and to lead her sons by precept and example to love Mother Earth in all her changing bestowals," Susa Young Gates observed. Courtesy of Church History Library.

superior ancestry." Gates declared that Mary had raised five "stalwart and exemplary boys" and commended Mary for raising those boys on a farm, leading her sons "by precept and example" in engaging in "homely toil" that had "dignified their ideals" and "solidifed their natural gifts."[39] (For some reason, she did not mention Mary's daughter, Agnes, who was twenty-one years old at the time of Joseph's death.) Beyond this article, Mary is pictured in the photograph taken of the group that attended the International Genealogical Congress in San Francisco in 1915,[40] and her name is mentioned in Julina's Golden Wedding sketch.[41] Otherwise, she does not appear in the *Relief Society Magazine*.

Mary Taylor Schwartz was born in 1865 to Agnes Taylor, sister of President John Taylor, and William Schwartz, a German convert and miller. Mary's mother was asked to become the official housekeeper at President Taylor's residence, the Gardo House, in 1881, and Mary accompanied her as an assistant. Mary was the "official ironer" for President Taylor, since she was the only one who could do his shirts to his liking. She was also included in the social circle of the Taylor children and enjoyed her youthful activities.[42]

Mary was married to Joseph F. Smith—again, according to Smith family tradition, at the urging of President John Taylor—in January 1884, but her marriage could not become public knowledge for several years afterwards due to the antipolygamy prosecutions initiated by the Edmunds Act. More than once, she had to evade the federal marshals (and other would-be suitors who did not know she was married). President Smith went to Hawaii in 1885; Mary visited briefly in 1887 before he was recalled to Utah. She studied obstetrics and nursing under Salt Lake physicians Margaret Roberts and Mattie Hughes Cannon. Her first child was born in 1888, and over the next eighteen years she bore six sons and one daughter to Joseph F. Smith. She also lived for some years in Idaho, where she went to "make a home or a place of refuge for the family in case of need"—in other words, because of continued threats of antipolygamy prosecution. After returning to Utah, she eventually purchased a farm in Taylorsville, southwest of Salt Lake City, as a place for her boys to learn to work.[43]

Mary was a noted beauty. "She was tall and stately," one biographer wrote, "and as the maidens of the Bible history was often described, of a comely appearance and fair to look upon." She was known for her love of learning—she was one of the first Utah subscribers to the *Encyclopedia Brittanica*—and she served as a leader in the Primary and the Relief Society. "The principal trait or characteristic in this daughter of the pioneers, is loyal courage. . . . She will do what is right, no matter what the consequences may be."[44]

Clearly, both Alice and Mary were in fact "well-known women" in the LDS community by the time of their husband's death. Because their public work was conducted under the auspices of other auxiliaries (the YLMIA for Alice, the Primary for Mary), it may not be surprising that they were not mentioned in the *Relief Society Magazine*. Even so, this would not explain why they received so little attention in the personal and familial profiles. This brings us to the subject of what is *not* said about the Smith wives in the magazine.

"From a Triangle to a Star": What Is *Not* Said

As we have seen, the *Relief Society Magazine* contained several interesting depictions of Joseph F. Smith's wives. The net result is a remarkable portrait of a large, loving family—unusual, perhaps, in its composition, but founded upon the same principles of love and womanly service that all LDS women were encouraged to adopt in their own lives. While certainly composed for public consumption and intended to present an ideal image, there is no reason to doubt that these portrayals were true and sincere. At the same time, it seems important to consider some of the things that are *not* said—because those things can also give us greater insight into the families of Joseph F. Smith and even into the development of the Church under his administration.

The first and perhaps most complete silence concerns Joseph's first wife, Levira, to whom he had already been married for seven years when Julina entered the household in 1866. By that time, the relationship was already strained due to his lengthy absences and Levira's poor health; after another turbulent period, Joseph and Levira were divorced sometime in 1868–69.[45] Perceptive readers of the *Relief Society Magazine* would have known of Levira's existence; she is mentioned in a genealogical chart published in conjunction with a profile of Mary Fielding Smith (Joseph's mother) in the March 1916 issue. This brief notice, however, is presented somewhat deceptively. It reads, "Joseph Fielding Smith m[arried]. (firstly) 5th Apr., 1859, Levira A. Smith. . . . She d[ied]. and he m[arried]. (secondly) 5th May, 1866, Julina Lambson."[46] Technically, it was correct that Levira had died, but that event occurred in 1888, not before Joseph's marriage to Julina, as the wording here implies, and no mention is made of the divorce.

Julina makes absolutely no mention of this painful chapter in their lives, which is understandable on many levels, especially given that she was essentially a Victorian woman, raised with the reticent norms of that era. But she is almost equally silent about Alice and Mary. In her tribute to Sarah, Julina obliquely mentions the other two wives, but in a way that one would have to already know the story in order to catch the reference. "The family triangle was changed into a star," she wrote. Having referred to herself, Sarah, and Edna, as a "triangle" in a previous paragraph, this image introduces two more "points" to the family scheme.[47] Later, in her golden wedding sketch, Julina mentions Alice and Mary by name, but only in passing.[48] Given her openness about Sarah and Edna, this reticence cannot be attributed to a general reluctance to mention plural marriage and therefore seems all the more notable.

It is tempting to speculate about the reasons for this silence on Julina's part. Why are the last two wives not mentioned when she speaks so lovingly of the other two? One obvious possibility is that she did not like or get along with Alice and Mary, and indeed there are hints in the family recollections that the first three wives were not too happy when their husband married these younger women, over a decade after his marriage to Edna.[49] However, those same accounts, as well as the comments in the magazine and other sources, insist that all of the families loved each other and got along well. It seems more likely that any difficulty with the new marriages on the part of the three wives could more likely be attributed to two causes. First is the fact that, as Julina's tributes make clear, the three original women had formed a very close bond with each other and had worked out a harmonious, efficient system for running their joint household. Bringing new women into the picture—especially a divorced mother of three and a young, relatively inexperienced girl—would have presented a severe emotional and logistical disruption to the tightly knit family.

Another, more important reason may have been the timing of the last two marriages—December 1883 and January 1884, in the wake of the Edmunds Act and the intensification of the national crusade against plural marriage. While Joseph F. Smith would have been a wanted man regardless because of his position and his previous plural marriages, at least the case could be made that the first three wives were married at a time when the legal standing of plural marriage was still unsettled and its practice was relatively uncontested. No such thing could be said in 1884, and these new marriages may have seemed a terrible risk and further complication in the face of escalating uncertainty. If that was the case, the existing wives' hesitation probably had nothing to do with Alice or Mary personally but with the situation more generally.

These ideas are, admittedly, speculative and do not fully explain why Julina would have been so quiet about Alice and Mary when she was so vocal about Sarah and Edna, especially since she was writing two decades after her husband had been pardoned, when plural marriage was all but a thing of the past. Taking a broader view and reading between the lines a bit, what we do learn from the portrayals of Joseph F. Smith and his wives in the *Relief Society Magazine* is that he essentially had two sets of families—the original three, with Julina, Sarah, and Edna, which were very tightly knit and well established, and the last two, with Alice and Mary, which were perhaps more complicated than those in the original group. By all accounts, the women learned to love and respect each other. Nonetheless, it is certain that Alice and Mary had a very different experience, at least in the first decade of their marriages, than the other women had had.

For one thing, they had to hide their marriages. Sometimes they had to hide themselves. The results of this situation are clear enough in the record of their children: neither gave birth to a child by Joseph F. Smith until years after their marriage (see appendix). Moreover, both women had to be more independent from the beginning. Alice already had a house of her own and had been a single mother for some time; she may not have been any more comfortable "intruding" on the original families than they were in rearranging their lives. Mary bore her first child in 1888 in the old homestead where the three original families lived, with Julina as midwife, but she did not live there permanently; she went through a series of living arrangments after her marriage and then spent years in Idaho, far removed from the rest of the family. In fact, upon her return to Utah, she purchased a farm in Taylorsville and again spent much of her time at a distance from the rest.

For Alice and Mary, then, marriage to Joseph F. Smith was never marked by the idyllic communal household and cooperative childrearing that had bonded the first wives so closely together, and they entered into plural marriage at a highly stressful and dangerous time. Even if there was no animosity or conflict between any of the wives, it was inevitable that these two women would have a much different experience than their sister-wives, and it is probably this dynamic that the seeming lack of notice in the *Relief Society Magazine*, especially Julina's reminiscences, captures.

Looking beyond the specific matter of Joseph F. Smith's wives and families, modern readers may find the open, celebratory discussion of plural marriage in the *Relief Society Magazine*—the official publication of a Church auxiliary organization—almost thirty years after the Manifesto, a bit surprising. We speak today of President Woodruff's 1890 announcement as the decisive end to plural marriage. What these depictions remind us is that the demise of plural marriage was a process, not an event. This fact would have been all too familiar to the many readers of the *Relief Society Magazine* who were themselves still living with the vestiges of plural families past. As they undoubtedly realized, plural marriage died in theory long before it died in practice. The Manifesto is best thought of as the starting point in a long course of transformation—a painful, uncertain, and gradual progression away from one of the founding ideals of the community.

By the time of the *Relief Society Magazine*, the Church had firmly and decisively broken with its polygamous past. That break, and the subsequent passage of time, had created a space in which plural marriage could be openly discussed and even idealized as part of celebrating the heroic pioneer past. Nonetheless, those discussions—as illustrated by the treatment of the Joseph F. Smith families—served as a reminder that the demise of plural marriage had to be worked out not only on an institutional, political, and theoretical level, but also in the individual lives of thousands of families. Hence, there is much said, but also much left unsaid. While the *Relief Society Magazine* shows no inclination to return to the practices of the past, it nonetheless notes that past and honors those, like Joseph F. Smith and his families, who sacrificed so much for the sake of their faith.

Notes

1. Joseph Fielding Smith, *Life of Joseph F. Smith, Sixth President of the Church of Jesus Christ of Latter-day Saints* (Salt Lake City: Deseret News, 1938), 452.
2. Imogene Kesler Linford, "When I Was Baptized," Joseph F. Smith Family Association website; http://www.josephfsmith.org/node/85 (accessed December 5, 2012).
3. "In Memoriam: President Joseph F. Smith," *Relief Society Magazine*, January 1919, 12.
4. "In Memoriam," 5.
5. The one readily accessible recent treatment of Julina Lambson Smith mentions plural marriage only briefly and does not give the names of her sister-wives. See Leonard J. Arrington, Susan Arrington Madsen, and Emily Madsen Jones, *Mothers of the Prophets*, revised edition, (Salt Lake City: Deseret Book, 2009), 159–76.
6. This number includes five adopted children: two adopted by Joseph and Julina and the three children from Alice Kimball's first marriage, whom Joseph adopted when he married her.

Life of Joseph F. Smith, 487–90; Susa Young Gates, "Mothers in Israel: Mary Fielding Smith, Wife of the Patriarch Hyrum Smith," *Relief Society Magazine*, March 1916, 142–46. To reconcile the few discrepancies between these listings, I consulted Joseph F. Smith Family Genealogical Committee, *The Descendants of Joseph F. Smith (1838–1918)* (Provo, UT: J. Grant Stevenson, 1976), Church History Library, The Church of Jesus Christ of Latter-day Saints, Salt Lake City.

7. Photographs of the Smith homes are published in Richard Neitzel Holzapfel and R. Q. Shupe, *Joseph F. Smith: Portrait of a Prophet* (Salt Lake City: Deseret Book, 2000), 134–35. This book also contains lovely portraits of all the Smith families, some of which are still held in private collections.
8. "In Memoriam," 5.
9. "In Memoriam," 6.
10. "A Priceless Golden Wedding," *Relief Society Magazine*, July 1916, 373.
11. Unless otherwise cited, biographical information about Julina Smith and the other wives is taken from *The Descendants of Joseph F. Smith*, cited in note 6 above. Another version of this information is available in Karol G. Chase, "The Wives and Children of Joseph F. Smith," http://josephfsmith.org/node/44 (accessed January 10, 2013). Chase's compilation incorporates and expands upon a similar account located in the Church History Library, an untitled, unattributed typescript written as if in first person by each wife.
12. *Mothers of the Prophets*, 166.
13. "From the General Board of the Relief Society," *Relief Society Magazine*, January 1915, 5.
14. Amy Brown Lyman, "The April Conference," *Relief Society Magazine*, June 1915, 263.
15. "The Historical Office of the First Presidency. And the New Relief Society Department Headquarters," *Relief Society Magazine*, November 1917, 608–10. The Wedding and Burial Clothes Department should be seen as a forerunner to Beehive Clothing; this is an area where further research is needed.
16. "A Priceless Golden Wedding," 370.
17. "Ye Ancient and Honorable Order of Midwifery," *Relief Society Magazine*, August 1915, 348.
18. Julina Lambson Smith, "A Loving Tribute to Sarah Ellen Richards Smith," *Relief Society Magazine*, May 1915, 215.
19. Smith, "A Loving Tribute," 215.
20. "In Memoriam," 6.
21. "In Memoriam," 8.
22. "In Memoriam," 8.
23. "How Joseph F. Smith Chose His Wives," in *The Descendants of Joseph F. Smith*, 1.
24. "Sarah Ellen Richards Smith," *Relief Society Magazine*, May 1915, 211–14.
25. "Sarah Ellen Richards Smith," 213–14.
26. Smith, "A Loving Tribute," 216.
27. "How Joseph F. Smith Chose His Wives,"1.
28. "In Memoriam," 8.
29. "A Friend of the Helpless Dead," *Relief Society Magazine*, September 1917, 483.
30. "Friend of the Helpless Dead," 484–85.
31. "Daughters of Zion: Mrs. Ida Bowman Smith," *Relief Society Magazine*, October 1916, 543–44.
32. "Friend of the Helpless Dead," 485.

33. Susa Young Gates, "The Passing of Apostle Hyrum M. Smith," *Relief Society Magazine,* March 1918, 125.
34. "In Memoriam," 5.
35. "In Memoriam," 8, 10.
36. I have found no mention of the name of Alice's first husband in any of the available sources, though the family biography refers to him as "the son of a great pioneer" (*The Descendants of Joseph F. Smith,* 112). Clearly, further research is warranted on this subject.
37. Susa Young Gates, *History of the Young Ladies' Mutual Improvement Association* (Salt Lake City: Deseret News, 1911), 297.
38. "In Memoriam," 10.
39. "In Memoriam," 10.
40. Susa Young Gates, "International Genealogical Congress at the Panama-Pacific Exposition," *Relief Society Magazine,* September 1915, 396 (frontispiece). Mary is seated next to her husband on the front row and is identified as "Mary T. Smith" in the caption.
41. "A Priceless Golden Wedding," 370.
42. Unless otherwise cited, biographical information about Mary Schwartz Smith is taken from *The Descendants of Joseph F. Smith,* 137–39.
43. "Mary Taylor Schwartz Smith," *The Descendants of Joseph F. Smith,* 138.
44. Elizabeth Roundy, "Mary Taylor Schwartz Smith," in Ja[me]s T. Jakeman, *Daughters of the Utah Pioneers and Their Mothers* (Western Album, n.d.), n.p. This volume, probably published in 1916, was a gift book or album containing biographical information and photographs of over four hundred women. It is available online; http://archive.org/stream/albumdaughtersof00byujake#page/n7/mode/2up.
45. Though he does not give an exact date for the divorce, the essential source on this sad episode is Scott G. Kenney, "Before the Beard: Trials of the Young Joseph F. Smith," *Sunstone,* November 2001, 20–42. Available online; https://www.sunstonemagazine.com/wp-content/uploads/sbi/articles/120-20-43.pdf.
46. Gates, "Mothers in Israel," 142.
47. "Sarah Ellen Richards Smith," 215.
48. "A Priceless Golden Wedding," 370.
49. "How Joseph F. Smith Chose His Wives" says that when Joseph married Alice "the three wives were unhappy that they had no choice in the matter this time, but concluded to support their husband in this as in all else" (p. 1). Joseph F. Smith entered into these last two marriages at the urging of President John Taylor.

Mark D. Ogletree

6

The Fathering Practices of Joseph F. Smith

"The richest of all my earthly joys is my precious children."

—*Joseph F. Smith*[1]

Fathers are crucial to the healthy development of their children. Family scholars have documented that a father's involvement in his child's life influences three key outcomes: economic security, educational attainment, and delinquency avoidance.[2] From a gospel perspective, a loving, caring, involved father can affect his children positively in every aspect of their lives, especially spiritually. The impact of a strong father in the lives of his children is immeasurable.

The prophet Joseph F. Smith was an exceptional father and served as a patriarchal role model to the entire Church. Because of his love and kindness, Joseph F. was able to impact his children in many critical areas of their lives. In describing Joseph F. Smith as a father, the following areas will be considered: how he managed demands on his time and schedule, how he showed love and

---

Mark D. Ogletree is an associate professor of Church history and doctrine at Brigham Young University.

care towards his wives and children, how he served as a surrogate father to many other children, and how he taught the gospel in his home.

Father Time

Joseph F. Smith was extremely busy. During his entire tenure as a father, he was also a member of the Quorum of the Twelve Apostles, where he served until he died. While an Apostle, he was nearly always a member of the First Presidency. Furthermore, during his prime fathering years, he was a member of the territorial House of Representatives, a full-time missionary, a city councilman, the Church Historian, and a recorder at the Endowment House. What little time he had left was divided between his family and his farm.

A day in the life of Joseph F. Smith typically began at four-thirty or five in the morning, when he performed his farm chores. Soon after, he was often found in the Endowment House doing ordinance work. He spent his afternoons attending to his Church administrative duties. When he was able to get out from behind his desk, he often spoke at funerals and administered to the sick. His position on the city council or in the territorial legislature occupied much of his time during the later afternoons and early evenings.

When Joseph F. had free evenings, he often stayed home or took one of his wives to the theater.[3] He also enjoyed spending time with his children. He made the rounds each night, tucking his children into bed.[4] "He took a personal interest in each child, devoting the time necessary to train and counsel within the limits of his crowded schedule."[5]

He frequently had to perform more farm chores before retiring to bed. In fact, he spent many of his weekends and other spare moments in maintaining his farm. Because of his many responsibilities, Joseph F. had a difficult time keeping up with his farm duties. He lamented once in his journal, "At home, mostly at work about home. I have no one to do anything about my place but myself. My wives have their children to take care of, all of them being small, . . . my oldest boy being 7 years of age. I am not in circumstances to hire help. I am compelled therefore to 'pitch in' . . . both morning and evening after the usual labors of the day."[6]

As an Apostle and member of the First Presidency, many of Joseph F.'s weekends were occupied with stake conference assignments and other ecclesiastical duties. Nevertheless, he understood the need to balance his heavy work schedule with recreation and cultural activities, a practice that was crucial for his

President Joseph F. Smith in his thirties, the prime of his fatherhood. Photo by C. W. Carter, circa 1874, courtesy of Church History Library.

own sanity. Historian Francis M. Gibbons reported, "[Joseph] was fond of skating, and during the cold winter months occasionally indulged in this sport. His favorite exercise, however, was walking, and he frequently took long walks that not only were physically invigorating but also had a mentally soothing effect."[7] Joseph F. also enjoyed plays, concerts, music, and drama and was fond "of a good story or a humorous joke."[8]

He spent a healthy dose of time with his children, but it was often in work-related efforts, such as fixing up the home or the farm. Joseph believed deeply in the principle of work and industry. Not only was he a tireless worker, but he taught his children the value of work. He declared, "Labor is the key to the true happiness of the physical and spiritual being. If a man possesses millions [of dollars], his children should still be taught how to labor with their hands; boys and girls should receive a home training which will fit them to cope with the practical, daily affairs of family life."[9]

For example, on Saturday, May 18, 1872, Joseph F. recorded: "Making a fence at home. Painted and nailed up 215 pickets, six nails in each. Three rail picket fence. Edward assisting me."[10] Edward was one of Joseph's adopted children and was somewhat older than his siblings. Therefore, Joseph and Edward did many things together, and Joseph relied heavily on him to help with the farm.[11] One of the ways that Joseph F. connected with his children and spent time with them was by working with them. In August 1879, Joseph F. recorded in his journal, "Doing my chores at home. Pulled a large quantity of weeds out of my garden, my children helping me."[12] The next month, Joseph recorded that he got up early to feed and milk his cows. "I also gathered a couple of buckets of apples for the cows—the children also gathered some for the cows."[13] Joseph F.'s children also helped him to mend fences, paint barns, and fix up the home. However, he often tried to balance work with play. Work always came first, but playing seemed just as important.

For example, on the same day when Joseph and his children harvested apples, they later went to Lake Point on the Great Salt Lake (which is about twenty miles west of the present-day Salt Lake City International Airport). Joseph F. took his wives Sarah and Julina and seven of their children. The family played in the lake, went out to eat, and rode the train back into Salt Lake City. As the family settled in for a relaxing evening, Joseph rushed off to a city council gathering, only to have the meeting adjourn shortly after he arrived.[14]

The family also enjoyed swimming at Blackrock,[15] a beach resort on the Great Salt Lake complete with a refreshment stand, picnic bowery, and bath and shower houses.[16] On Friday, August 25, 1871, Joseph F. reported that his family, as well as the Richards family, loaded up their wagons and headed out to Blackrock. They had a picnic there, which included melons, fruit, and wine. "The girls all had baths except Julina who was not well."[17]

Another form of family recreation was frequenting the warm springs north of Salt Lake City, which were often compared to the pool of Siloam and known for their "healing" qualities. Joseph F., his wives, and his children would often picnic at the warm springs, soak in the pools, take baths or showers, and then drive home in their carriage. The Smiths often invited other families to accompany them. When Hyrum Mack Smith turned eight years old, Joseph F. baptized and confirmed him at the spring.[18]

The Smith family also enjoyed other activities. Joseph F. often took his wives and children on carriage or buggy rides.[19] Besides riding out to the springs, they would sometimes travel to Fuller's Hill, which was a pleasure garden, complete with rides and amusements. Other times, when they didn't want to travel so far, Joseph F. drove the family to the town drug store for soda water.[20] Joseph F. also enjoyed taking his children to the fair and to the circus when it came to town. In May 1873, he recorded that he took "Julina and my two little girls to the circus, the children were very much pleased with the animals and birds."[21] Joseph F. especially enjoyed being with his children outdoors. They swam in the summer, as previously noted, and in the winter he loved to sled and "frolic" in the snow with his "babies."[22]

Joseph F. Smith was an "intentional" father who found ways to make time for his family. He enjoyed working, playing, and having fun with them. In this way, he helped build lasting memories in the lives of his children. The enjoyable times the family had together also strengthened them as they forged through many trials and obstacles. Contemporary fathers who are extremely busy can learn much from Joseph F. Smith and his priorities.

Patriarchal Love, Care, and Concern

Joseph F. lost his father at age five and his mother at age thirteen. Joseph's heart must have ached for parental love—especially since he was robbed of it at such a young age. He was very grateful for surrogate fathers like Brigham Young and George A. Smith, who each took Joseph F. under their wing. They literally helped

Fuller's Hill Pleasure Garden was a place of recreation the Smith family frequented (1887). © 2008 Utah State Historical Society.

save Joseph F. in many ways, and he grieved bitterly when these "giants of men" passed away.

Perhaps by overcompensating, or at least by concentrating on what he lost as a child, Joseph F. Smith was a father who was demonstrative in paternal affection and care. He never wanted his children to doubt his love and allegiance for them. Moreover, he was also in tune with their needs. He demonstrated love to his offspring physically, verbally, and emotionally. He taught parents that

> if you can only convince your children that you love them, that your soul goes out to them for their good, that you are their truest friend, they, in turn, will place confidence in you and will love you and seek to do your bidding and to carry out your wishes with your love. But if you are selfish, unkindly to them, and if they are not confident that they have your entire affection, they will be selfish, and will not care whether they please you or carry out your wishes or not, and the result will be that they will grow wayward, thoughtless, and careless.[23]

Joseph F. gave nicknames to each of his children. He often referred to his eldest daughter, Mercy Josephine, as "Jodo"[24] or "Dodo."[25] His son Joseph Richards was known as "Joseph R.,"[26] while Hyrum was known as "Hyrum M."[27] Donnette was most often called "Donnie,"[28] while Mary Sophronia was referred to as "Mamie."[29] Joseph F. called his children by these endearing nicknames well into adulthood. In fact, he often referred to his children as his "babies," regardless of how old they were.

Another way Joseph F. expressed his love to his children was by purchasing things for them. How he loved to buy things for his children! One Christmas he wept openly when he saw Christmas treasures in store windows downtown, knowing that he did not have the funds to purchase the bare minimum for his "babies." He reported, "I wanted something to please them, and to mark the Christmas day from all other days but not a cent to do it with! I walked up and down Main Street, looking into the shop windows . . . everywhere—and then slunk out of sight of humanity and sat down and wept like a child until my poured-out grief relieved my aching heart; and after awhile returned home, as empty as when I left, and played with my children, grateful and happy . . . for them."[30]

It broke Joseph's heart that he could not give his children the kind of Christmas he felt they deserved.[31] Once Joseph was able to obtain a steady cash flow, his journal became saturated with accounts of purchasing his children clothing, gloves,[32] hats,[33] skates,[34] knives,[35] boots,[36] sleds,[37] and whatever else they may have needed. He especially loved buying his children toys,[38] nuts, and candy.[39] Joseph's son Samuel remembered that it was customary for his father to kiss and hug his children when he came home from work; however, the added bonus was the licorice[40] he shared from his pocket![41]

One of the ways Joseph demonstrated love to his family was by giving gifts. Not only did he enjoy purchasing gifts for his children, but his wives were often the recipients of wonderful gifts. On his missions, it was common for him to send clothing, silverware, or other home decor to his wives via mail. Since Joseph F.'s childhood was deprived of material possessions and even some of the basic necessities, it was imperative for him to put food on the table and meet the basic financial needs of his children. He enjoyed being able to provide material goods for his family—things that he often lacked as a child.

Joseph also showed love towards his children by hugging and kissing them. He was not shy when it came to expressing physical love to his children. On June 27, 1918 (about five months prior to his death), at the dedication of a monument in the Salt Lake City Cemetery to honor his father, Hyrum Smith, Joseph F.

spoke thus: "I am rich; the Lord has given me great riches in children and in children's children. . . . I want you to just take a look here at a little flock of my grandchildren—right here, every one of them. I love them. I know them all. I never meet them but what I kiss them, just as I do my own children."[42]

This habit of showing constant physical affection is exemplified in one of Joseph's last memories of his father occurred in June of 1844. Before Hyrum left for Carthage Jail, he gathered his family and prayed with them. He bid each of his loved ones goodbye except for Joseph F., who was out playing. When Hyrum was about to ride away, he saw Joseph F. in the street. He rode over, picked Joseph up, hugged and kissed him, and then charged him to be a good boy while he was away.[43] That was the last time Joseph F. Smith saw his father alive; it was a memory engraved into the core of his heart.

Physical affection became important in the life of Joseph F. Since he had lost his father as a boy and his mother as a teenager, he "lavished upon his children all the love and affection of which he was capable. His feelings were shown not only by his words but by his looks and actions."[44] It was customary for him to kiss each of his children, no matter how old they were, or in the case of his grandchildren, no matter how dirty they were.[45] Most certainly, Joseph F. missed this kind of physical affection from his own parents, and he wanted his children to know that they were loved.

One of Joseph F.'s sons, Samuel, recalled a time he was serving in the armed forces during World War I. Once he came home on leave to visit his sick father, he surprised Joseph F. by entering the back door of the Beehive house. As Samuel approached, he noticed that his father was standing in his bathrobe with a cane in his hand. Samuel said that "when he saw me, he forgot about the cane and hurried over to me. He took me in his arms, hugging and kissing me, saying 'My boy, my boy.'"[46] Joseph F. didn't need to say much; Samuel understood how much his father loved him.

Joseph F. and his wives adopted several children and raised them as their own. One such daughter was named Marjorie. As a little girl, Marjorie was extremely afraid of thunder and lightning. Once, during a very terrible storm, Marjorie was crying and whimpering. Joseph F. got up, put on his robe, and came into Marjorie's room, where he tenderly comforted her. Then, he invited Marjorie to put her robe and slippers on, and then they walked out onto the veranda, attached to the second story of the Beehive House. Marjorie then recalled, "He held my hand, and that gave me a feeling of security and strength. Still, when the sky would light up, I would tremble. Father explained to me what lightning meant and what made the noise. Then he said, 'See, it will bring the rain that will make everything so beautiful. You must not be afraid.' From that day to this I have never been frightened of a thunderstorm."[47]

On one occasion, Joseph F.'s son Willard was playing in the road in front of the Beehive House. A bully approached Willard, roughed him up, and then shoved his face into the mud, nearly suffocating him. This was in February, and it was very near Valentine's Day. Willard decided to write a valentine card to the bully, including every evil word that he could think of. But Willard inadvertently sent the Valentine card that was intended for the bully to one of his uncles. The wise uncle, of course, passed the note to Willard's father. One morning after family prayer, Joseph F. followed his routine by kissing each one of his children, except for Willard. Instead, he told his son, "I will see you in my office."

Feeling rebuked, Willard went into this father's office and waited patiently as Joseph F. wrote for a while at his desk. Joseph F. then opened a large Bible and said, "Come close, Willard. What does that say?" Willard read, "Swear not at all." Then Joseph F. turned to another passage and asked Willard to read it. Willard reported, "It says, 'Forgive seventy times seven.'" Joseph F. agreed with his son, and then had him read a third scripture, and then a fourth, and then several more. This process of teaching from the scriptures went on for approximately twenty minutes. Finally, Joseph F. said, "Come here, Son." He then embraced Willard and kissed him and that was the end of the lesson. Willard later said that he "never used a bad word again." Joseph had won his son over with love. The lesson of forgiveness and the legacy of physical affection continued through the generations. As a father, Willard R. Smith continued the tradition of kissing his children on the lips, no matter how young or old they were.[48] Arguably, the following statement on child discipline by President Joseph F. Smith is one of the most incredible declarations given on the topic. He said:

> If you wish your children to be taught in the principles of the gospel, if you wish them to love the truth and understand it, if you wish them to be obedient to and united with you, love them! And prove to them that you do love them by your every word or act to them. . . . When you speak or talk to them, do it not in anger, do it not harshly, in a condemning spirit. Speak to them kindly; get them

> down and weep with them if necessary and get them to shed tears with you if possible. Soften their hearts; get them to feel tenderly toward you. Use no lash and no violence. . . . Approach them with reason . . . with persuasion and love unfeigned. With these means, if you cannot gain your boys and your girls . . . there will be no means left in the world by which you can win them yourselves. But, get them to feel as you feel, have interest in the things in which you take interest, to love the gospel as you love it, to love one another as you love them; to love their parents as the parents love the children. You can't do it any other way. You can't do it by unkindness; you cannot do it by driving; our children are like we are; we couldn't be driven; we can't be driven now. . . .
>
> You can't force your boys, nor your girls into heaven. You may force them to hell, by using harsh means in the efforts to make them good, when you yourselves are not as good as you should be. . . . You can only correct your children by love, in kindness, by love unfeigned, by persuasion, and reason.[49]

Joseph appears to have lived exactly how he taught when it came to child discipline. He did not force his children to be good. Instead, he taught them, he wept with them, and he loved them.

Another demonstration of Joseph F.'s love and affection occurred when his children were sick or injured. It seemed that Joseph had a sixth sense when it came to detecting when his children were in trouble. On one occasion, Joseph F. felt extremely depressed and anxious about their well-being. At the time, he was far away from home on Church business. He later learned by letter that the reason for his depression was that "one of his beloved little ones at home lay cold in death."[50] Another time, while laboring in Scotland in April 1874, Joseph felt some anxiety about his children. He tried to pass his worries off, but could not do it. He learned a little while later that several of his children had scarlet fever. He wrote in his journal, "I have felt some worried about my children Being [*sic*] sick, but I must leave them in the hands of the Lord."[51]

Since several of Joseph F.'s children died young, and childhood disease was prevalent, his worry for their health and well-being often consumed him. His journals are replete with accounts of his children's sicknesses. When they were unwell, Joseph F. was deeply involved in their treatment and care. When Mercy Josephine was sick, he wrote, "Waited on my little daughter all day."[52] Although this was an isolated incident, it was a common practice of his to be up and down all night with his sick little ones.[53] He would hold his children, comfort them, and medically treat them. Because many childhood sicknesses in his day were respiratory related, Joseph did not feel comfortable sleeping.[54] He wanted to make sure his "chicks" were breathing free and easy. Therefore, he would stay up into the early hours of the morning—many times not going to bed until three or four in the morning. Often he would only sleep for an hour or two, and then begin his workday.[55] Charles W. Nibley, Joseph F.'s close friend, observed, "I have visited his home when one of his little children was down sick. I have seen him come home from his work at night tired, as he naturally would be, and yet he would walk the floor for hours with that little one in his arms, petting it and loving it, encouraging it in every way with such tenderness and such a soul of pity and love as not one mother in a thousand would show."[56]

Another testament of Joseph's love for his children is found in letters he wrote them while he was away on Church business. On July 3, 1875, he wrote his wife Sarah, "One of the severest trials of my mission is being deprived of the society of my family and the innocent prattle of my little babes."[57] He missed his family so much that he often stared at photographs of his children. Occasionally, Joseph F. would talk to the photographs. He wrote to Julina, "When I get time I take my Album and talk to all my babies and call them all the little names I can think of. . . . Please keep my weaknesses over my babies to yourselves."[58]

On March 30, 1875, while serving as a missionary in England, Joseph wrote to his daughter, six-year-old Mary Sophronia, whom he often called "Mamie." In the letter, Joseph F. explained why he had been away for such a long time. He also attempted to teach her a few principles, as well as assess her learning. The letter reads as follows:

> I am going to write you a letter. I know you will be pleased to get a letter from your Papa. You have wondered many times, no doubt, why I stay away from home so long. You must not think it is because I want to stay away from you, and from your little brothers and sisters; but it is because I am on a mission. I am trying to do what the Lord wants me to do. By and by I will return home. But not until I have filled my mission. You will understand better what a mission is when you get older. I want you to be a real good girl. You must mind your Mamma and Aunties, and be so good to all your little brothers and sisters. I wonder if you know all your letters? How many can you count? You are over

> five years old now. Do you know when you were born? Can you sing any pretty songs? Can you speak some nice pieces? When Mamma writes you must answer me these questions. From your affectionate Papa.[59]

In another letter, he invited Mamie to "pray to the Lord to keep us all from harm until we meet again."[60] He then reassured her that "Papa prays for all my little children morning & night & always."[61] For Joseph F., one of the best ways to stay connected to his children was to view their pictures often, write them letters, and pray for them constantly. He also taught his children to be compassionate brothers and sisters, to help around the home, and how to love the gospel of Jesus Christ. In August 1875, he wrote to his son Hyrum Mack:

> You must be a good boy. Take good care of Alvin, and little brother Richards, and little sister Donnie, and never let anybody hurt them. Papa wants his little men to grow up great and good men. Good Latter-day Saints and true to their fathers. Who was the Savior of Mankind? Jesus Christ, the Son of God. Who was one of the greatest Prophets that ever lived and one of the best, and greatest men that ever lived? Your grand uncle, Joseph Smith. And President Brigham Young is another Prophet of God and good man.[62]

Joseph F. Smith was a kind and affectionate father. When he was away from his children, he missed them terribly. When he was with them, he cared for them and nurtured them as well as any mother could do. Modern fathers can strengthen their relationships with their own children by following the example Joseph F. Smith demonstrated in terms of love and affection.

Surrogate Father

Joseph F. Smith was not only committed to his own family, but to all children, male and female, Mormon and non-Mormon. He treated all children with love and kindness. He adopted several children and took them under his wing. He looked out for children in his neighborhood, bought them candy,[63] and occasionally babysat them.[64] Joseph F. also treated his grandchildren as if they were his own children and loved spending time with them.

Once he held a party for all of his grandchildren. He asked his daughters to take care of the details, such as food and entertainment. However, he was surprised when he walked into his dining room and found his adult children seated at the table with their spouses. "Where are the grandchildren?" he asked. The aged patriarch was told that his grandchildren would be eating in another room—the same room they were playing in. Joseph then told the adults, "No. They are to eat in here. You may eat in there."[65] Joseph F.'s grandchildren knew of his love for them, and they never questioned his loyalty.

Charles W. Nibley, the Presiding Bishop of the Church, remembered that "[Joseph F.'s] love for children was unbounded." Bishop Nibley recounted a trip the two of them took to St. George, Utah. Many little children were paraded before President Smith, who adored them. It was Bishop Nibley's responsibility to get the company going to the next settlement, but it was difficult to pull President Smith away from the children. "He wanted to shake hands and talk with every one of them."[66]

Once, President Smith was riding in a train car that was hot and uncomfortable. Across from him sat a mother with three small children, one of whom was an infant. The children were hot, tired, and upset, the baby was crying, and the mother was exhausted. President Smith approached the mother and asked if he could take the baby and try to get it to sleep. "This he did and rocked the infant in his own arms, crooning to it and gained its confidence while it tangled its hands in his beard, until it fell asleep."[67]

Because of Joseph F.'s love for all children, he could not stand it when they were abused or mistreated. Nothing disturbed Joseph F. more than to see a child maltreated or neglected by its parents.[68] Once President Smith attended a stake conference and the meeting hall was completely full. With the quarters quite crowded, a large, strong woman came near the front of the meeting room and abruptly jerked a small child from her seat. The woman then took the seat for herself, leaving the small girl standing in the aisle. President Smith directed someone to bring the child to him, and he then invited her to sit by his side on the stand. When it was President Smith's turn to speak, he powerfully taught the congregation, including the woman who took the child's seat, the proper way to respect children and how they should be treated. He explained that "little children were as much entitled to seats in the congregations of the Saints as grown people, especially when they came early and obtained them."[69]

Perhaps because of his own experiences as an orphan, Joseph F. especially looked out for those children or youth who seemed to need help or attention. A teenage girl who was not a member of the Church traveled to Salt Lake City and took a job in a downtown hotel. She didn't like her job and decided to quit, leaving with a total of twenty-five cents. She was a stranger in Salt Lake City and had nowhere to go for food or shelter. She walked up the street until she came to the Eagle Gate, where she stopped and observed people going about their work. Everyone seemed so happy, and yet this girl was miserable and in great distress. No one spoke to or noticed her. She was ready to burst into tears when the door of the Beehive house opened and President Joseph F. Smith walked out. He walked past the distressed girl, took a few more steps, and then turned around. He approached her and said, "What is the matter, my girl? You seem to be in trouble." The girl reported that President Smith listened to her as her own father would have. Then he said, "Well, daughter, come with me." He took the girl to his home, presented her to his wife, and said, "Here is a poor, friendless girl. Take care of her until she gets a good place to work." The girl reported that she was taken to the house of President Smith and was treated with much kindness. In time, she found a better situation and moved on with her life. However, she stated, "No, I shall never forget President Joseph F. Smith."[70] Modern fathers would do well to follow Joseph F.'s example of reaching out to all children—not merely their own offspring.

Gospel Teacher

The gospel of Jesus Christ was the centerpiece of Joseph F. Smith's life. He viewed everything through the gospel lens. His next greatest priority was his family. In fact, the gospel and his family were all that really mattered to him. He wrote to his wife Edna, "I have nothing to live for but my family and the Kingdom of God, as pertaining to this mortal life."[71]

Joseph F. felt that teaching the gospel in his home was one of his chief duties. He taught, "Not one child in a hundred would go astray, if the home environment, example and training, were in harmony with the truth of the gospel of Christ. . . . Fathers and mothers, you are largely to blame for the infidelity and indifference of your children. You can remedy the evil by earnest worship, example, training and discipline, in the home."[72]

He lived what he taught, especially when it came to practicing his religion in the home. One of his daughters, Edith, remembered that the family "would kneel down always in the morning or in the evening and have our family prayer. Many times I actually thought that the Lord was right in the house because of the way Father would talk to him and express his feelings. He was talking to his

Heavenly Father, and we felt it keenly. Often as a little girl I wanted to open my eyes during the prayer to see which direction the Lord was in because Father was talking to him and we knew it."[73]

Not only was it obvious to his children that he had a close relationship with his Heavenly Father, but it was just as apparent that Joseph F. practiced the principles he knew to be true. There was a time in Joseph F.'s life when he was severely ridiculed in the local media. Many things said about him were downright slanderous. Some of these stories and allegations trickled into the schools, where some of his children heard them. Edith came home from school one day, extremely frustrated about the lies being told about her father. Joseph F. looked at her with a smile and said, "Baby, don't get upset. They are not hurting me one bit; they are only hurting themselves. Don't you know, Baby, that when someone tells a lie they are only hurting themselves more than anyone else?" Years later, Edith reflected, "That was a lesson I have never forgotten."[74]

Joseph F. Smith was a powerful gospel teacher. He was also an astute scholar and historian. His children benefited tremendously from his wealth of knowledge and powerful teaching. Joseph Fielding Smith said of his father:

> He spent [part of his home time] instructing his children in the principles of the gospel. They one and all rejoiced in his presence and were grateful for the wonderful words of counsel and instruction which he imparted on these occasions in the midst of anxiety. They have never forgotten what they were taught, and the impressions have remained with them and will likely to do so forever. . . . My father was the most tenderhearted man I ever knew. . . . Among my fondest memories are the hours I have spent by his side discussing principles of the gospel and receiving instruction as only he could give it. In this way the foundation for my own knowledge was laid in truth.[75]

Joseph F. Smith constantly lobbied parents to teach their children the gospel of Jesus Christ in their homes. In the April 1912 general conference he stated, "It is the duty of Latter-day Saints to teach their children the truth, to bring them up in the way they should go, to teach them the first principles of the gospel . . . that they may walk in the light as Christ is in the light."[76]

One of the favored memories of Joseph Fielding Smith was studying the gospel with his father. In fact, when Joseph Fielding turned eight years of age, Joseph F. was hard-pressed for money. Nevertheless, he managed to scrape some funds together and purchased for his son a defective copy of the Book of Mormon.[77] After Joseph Fielding's baptism, Joseph F. presented him with the book, accompanied by the invitation to read it. Joseph Fielding went to work and commenced reading. By the time he was ten, he had read the Book of Mormon twice.[78] He became one of the greatest doctrinal scholars of the Book of Mormon in our dispensation. His love affair for the truth began at the knee of his father. Contemporary fathers can become the spiritual leaders in their homes by following the course Joseph F. Smith laid out. Joseph F. not only taught the gospel to his children—but also lived the teachings of the Savior daily.

Notes

1. Quoted in Joseph Fielding Smith, *The Life of Joseph F. Smith, Sixth President of the Church of Jesus Christ of Latter-day Saints* (Salt Lake City: Deseret Book, 1969), 449.
2. K. M. Harris, F. F. Furstenberg, and J. K. Marmer, "Paternal Involvement with Adolescents in Intact Families: The Influence of Fathers Over the Life Course," *Demography* 35, no. 2 (May 1998): 201–16.
3. Joseph F. Smith (hereafter referred to as JFS), diary, January 1, 1874 to January 27, 1874, box 3, folder 6, L. Tom Perry Special Collections, Harold B. Lee Library, Brigham Young University, Provo, UT.
4. Smith, *Sixth President of the Church*, 441–22.
5. Francis M. Gibbons, *Joseph F. Smith: Patriarch and Preacher, Prophet of God* (Salt Lake City: Deseret Book, 1984), 191
6. JFS, diary, August 25, 1879 to September 13, 1879, box 3, folder 11.
7. Gibbons, *Patriarch and Preacher*, 99.
8. Smith, *Sixth President of the Church*, 443.
9. *Gospel Doctrine: Selections from the Sermons and Writings of Joseph F. Smith*, comp. John A. Widtsoe (Salt Lake City: Deseret Book, 1949), 527.
10. JFS, diary, May 7, 1872 to May 26, 1872, box 3, folder 2.
11. JFS, diary, November 2, 9, 28, and 30, and December 14, 1872, box 3, folder 2.
12. JFS, diary, August 21, 1879, box 3, folder 11.
13. JFS, diary, August 25 and September 3, 1879, box 3, folder 11.
14. JFS, diary, September 3, 1879, box 3, folder 11.
15. JFS, diary, August 25 and September 9, box 3, folder 1.
16. Tommy W. Case, "Black Rock," *TWC Transcribing;* http://www.twc-transcribing.com /greatsaltlake/BlackRockSunsetBeach/Blackrock000.htm.
17. JFS, diary, August 25, 1851, box 3, folder 1.
18. JFS, diary, March 21, 1880, box 4, folder 1.
19. JFS, diary, March 19, 1880, box 4, folder 1.
20. JFS, diary, June 22, 1872, box 3, folder 2.
21. JFS, diary, August 8, 1872, and May 29, 1873, box 3, folder 3.
22. JFS, diary, January 1, 1879, box 3, folder 11.

23. Smith, *Gospel Doctrine*, 388.
24. JFS, diary, June 7 and 8, 1870, box 2, folder 6.
25. Joseph F. Smith Letterpress Copybooks (1875–1917), January 22, 1875 to January 28, 1875, box 30, folder 1, Special Collections, Brigham Young University, 28–51.
26. JFS, diary, December 9, 1873, and July 24, 1879, box 3, folder 5, and box 3, folder 11, respectively.
27. JFS, diary, November 12 and July 15, 1879, box 3, folder 11; Joseph F. Smith Letterpress Copybooks, letter to Hyrum M., August 21, 1875, box 30, folder 2, 138.
28. JFS, diary, February 1 and March 12, 1874, and January 20, 1879, box 3, folder 6, respectively.
29. JFS, diary, March 12, 1874, and March 26, 1880, box 3, folder 6, and box 4, folder 1, respectively.
30. Arthur R. Bassett, "Joseph F. Smith: Families and Generation Gaps," *New Era*, January 1972, 40.
31. Emerson Roy West, *Latter-Day Prophets* (American Fork, UT: Covenant Communications, 1999), 63.
32. JFS, diary, March 25 and 29; April 9, 16 and 30; and June 4, 1874; box 3, folder 6.
33. JFS, diary, May 9, 1879, box 3, folder 11.
34. JFS, diary, December 24, 1879, box 2, folder 5.
35. JFS, diary, May 19, 1879, box 3, folder 11.
36. JFS, diary, November 12, 1879, box 3, folder 11.
37. JFS, diary, December 23, 1879, box 3, folder 11.
38. JFS, diary, December 24, 1869, box 2, folder 5.
39. JFS, diary, December 24, 1869; November 13 (memoranda entry) and December 31, 1873; and March 20, 1880; box 4, folder 1; box 3, folder 3; and box 2, folder 5, respectively.
40. Joseph's granddaughter Amelia Smith McConkie recalled that when he would return home from the Church offices, his grandchildren always waited for his greeting. But it wasn't just hugs and kisses he would bring. He also would have a pocket full of candy that he would distribute to them. Amelia Smith McConkie, "Grandpa Joseph F. Smith," *Ensign*, September 1993, 12–14.
41. Norman S. Bosworth, "Remembering Joseph F. Smith: Loving Father, Devoted Prophet," *Ensign*, June 1983, 21–22.
42. "Fathers in the Home," in *Teachings of Presidents of the Church: Joseph F. Smith* (Salt Lake City: The Church of Jesus Christ of Latter-day Saints, 2011), 381.
43. Don C. Corbett, *Mary Fielding Smith: Daughter of Britain* (Salt Lake City: Deseret Book, 1966), 164.
44. Gibbons, *Patriarch and Preacher*, 88.
45. Smith, *Sixth President of the Church*, 476.
46. Bosworth, "Remembering Joseph F. Smith," 21–22.
47. Bosworth, "Remembering Joseph F. Smith," 21–22.
48. Truman G. Madsen, *Presidents of the Church* (Salt Lake City: Deseret Book, 2004), 159–60.
49. Joseph F. Smith, *Gospel Doctrine*, 316–17.
50. Smith, *Sixth President of the Church*, 280–81.
51. JFS, diary, April 28, 1874, box 3, folder 6.
52. JFS, diary, June 4, 1874, box 2, folder 6.
53. JFS, diary, April 19, 21, 22, 23, 24, and 26, 1879, box 3, folder 11.
54. JFS, diary, December 11, 12, and 14, 1879, box 3, folder 11.
55. JFS, diary, May 29–30, 1879, box 3, folder 11.

56. Preston Nibley, *Presidents of the Church* (Salt Lake City: Deseret Book, 1974), 213.
57. Joseph F. Smith Letterpress Copybooks, letter to Sarah, July 3, 1875, box 30, folder 1, 421.
58. Joseph F. Smith Letterpress Copybooks, letter to Julina, January 7, 1875, box 30, folder 1, 6–7.
59. Joseph F. Smith Letterpress Copybooks, letter to Mary Sophronia, March 30, 1875, box 30, folder 1, 240.
60. Joseph F. Smith Letterpress Copybooks, letter to "Mamie" (Mary Sophronia), August 21, 1875, box 30, folder 2, 136.
61. Joseph F. Smith Letterpress Copybooks, Letter to "Mamie," August 21, 1875, 136.
62. Joseph F. Smith Letterpress Copybooks, letter to Hyrum M., August 21, 1875, box 30, folder 2, 138.
63. JFS, diary, March 19, 20, and 29; 1879, box 3, folder 11; President Smith seemed to have a fond affection for neighborhood child Harry Lipton. On March 19, 1879, he bought Harry ten cents worth of candy; on March 20, 1879, he sent a doctor to see Harry when he was sick.
64. JFS, diary, October 31, 1864, to May 21st, 1877, box 2, folder 4.
65. Amelia Smith McConkie, "Grandpa Joseph F. Smith," *Ensign*, September 1993, 12–14.
66. Charles W. Nibley, "Reminiscences," in *Gospel Doctrine*, 523.
67. Joseph Fielding Smith, *The Life of Joseph F. Smith* (American Fork, UT: Grandin Press, 2010), 511.
68. Smith, *Life of Joseph F. Smith*, 511.
69. Smith, *Life of Joseph F. Smith*, 511.
70. As cited in Smith, *Sixth President of the Church*, 183–84.
71. Joseph F. Smith Letterpress Copybooks, letter to Edna, February 6, 1875, box 30, folder 1, 110
72. Smith, *Gospel Doctrine*, 302.
73. Bosworth, "Remembering Joseph F. Smith," 21–22.
74. Bosworth, "Remembering Joseph F. Smith," 21–22.
75. Joseph Fielding Smith, cited in Joseph Fielding Smith Jr. and John J. Stewart, *Life of Joseph Fielding Smith* (Salt Lake City: Deseret Book, 1972), 40.
76. Smith, *Gospel Doctrine*, 291.
77. Joseph Fielding Smith noted that the book was reduced in price because some of the pages were out of sequence. See Smith and Stewart, *Life of Joseph Fielding Smith*, 57.
78. Smith and Stewart, *Life of Joseph Fielding Smith*, 57.

Kevin Folkman

7

Letters from Joseph F. Smith to His Adopted Son Edward Arthur Smith

Sometime in the mid-1940s, LaVon Lyons Moore saw a piece of paper blowing around in her grandmother's backyard. As she picked up the paper to throw it in the trash, she realized it was a letter written on First Presidency stationery from Joseph F. Smith to her late grandfather Edward Arthur Smith. A quick scramble recovered at least twenty-five letters to Edward, Joseph's adopted son, but many more were lost to a fire in a backyard fireplace. Edward's widow, Cytha Ellen "Ella" Smith, was apparently feeding the fire without thought to the value of the letters in her possession.[1]

From these letters, we learn that Edward and his adopted father sustained a frequent and regular correspondence throughout their lives. The surviving letters from Joseph F. Smith show an affectionate and concerned father and offer glimpses into his personal, professional, and religious life. Joseph wrote about parental concerns, shared family news, and discussed with Edward many of his own struggles as a father and Church leader. More importantly, Joseph F. Smith took great interest in building young Edward's character and responsibilities to

---

Kevin Folkman is an independent researcher and historian living in Redmond, Washington.

his family and his church. The correspondence ended only when Edward died an early death in Raymond, Alberta, Canada, in 1911.

For this article, I have reviewed the contents of these letters and selected the most frequently referenced topics, which cover education and personal development, the importance of work, family health issues, and religious doctrine and instruction. I will also place these letters in the context of the life of Joseph F. Smith and the larger events that shaped the lives of both men.

Biographical Information

While serving as a missionary in England, Joseph F. Smith met the family of an impoverished coal miner and his wife. One of the children was a boy, Edward Arthur Thorpe, born in 1858 in Brampton, Derbyshire, England.[2] The family gave Edward up to be adopted by Joseph. Little has been known in the Church at large about Edward Arthur Smith, and he is barely acknowledged in the current biographies of Joseph F. Smith.[3] Edward was the first of five children that Joseph F. Smith adopted in addition to the forty-three children born to him by five of his six wives.[4]

Edward would have been the oldest child in the Smith's households, only ten years younger than his adoptive mother, Julina Lambson.[5] Edward's biological mother may have joined the Church, but died sometime in early 1863, and Edward's father was absent and not taking care of Edward and an older sister. The family histories, while differing on the actual date and circumstances of Edward's arrival in the Smith home, indicate that Edward Arthur was eleven years of age at the time. However, Joseph F. Smith's journals give the date as 1863, which would put Edward's age at four. Joseph wrote to his first wife, Levira, shortly before departing from England in 1863 that he had received a "gift" of an orphaned four-year-old boy.[6] Additional entries mention Joseph purchasing a hat for Edward in 1865 and there is also a letter from 1869.[7] Edward's whereabouts from 1863 to 1869 are still unclear. It is known that some of his childhood and adolescent years were spent living with the Smith's close relatives, Frank and Rhoda Knowlton of Farmington, Davis County, Utah.

While living with the Knowlton family, Edward became acquainted with Ella Smith, the daughter of neighbors Thomas Sasson Smith and his second wife, Amanda Hollingshead. Edward and Ella were married by Joseph F. Smith in the Endowment House on March 3, 1881, and began their family in Farmington.[8] By 1884, Edward and Ella, with two daughters, had moved to Sand Creek, Fremont

County, Idaho, near present-day St. Anthony. Edward worked both as a farmer and a carpenter, served in several Church leadership positions, and added seven more daughters and one son to their family.[9] In 1902, encouraged by Ella's brothers, Edward took his family to Raymond, Alberta, Canada, to homestead new land. He continued to farm and to work as a carpenter. There, he and Ella had their eleventh child, a son, who died at four months of age in 1904. Edward suffered some unidentified accident or illness in 1909 and died two years later in 1911.

Books and Education

Joseph F. Smith did not have much formal education. As a result of his own struggles, he tried to impress on Edward the importance of schooling and continuous study throughout life. The oldest existing letter from Joseph to Edward stressed this theme. The letter was sent February 11, 1879, while Edward was living and working with the Knowlton family, and was addressed "My Dear Boy." Joseph noted sending several books, including *A Voice of Warning* and *Key to Theology*. "You will see that I have had them many years," he writes. "I have taken great care of them." These books seem to be the volumes by Parley P. Pratt from Joseph's own personal library. "I hope you will prize them for my sake," he continued, "as well as for their intrinsic worth." After a few bits of family news, he closed with the admonition to grow into "a useful, faithful, and upright man."[10]

This theme for Edward of educating and bettering himself is repeated often throughout the letters. A year later, on February 8, 1880, Joseph wrote in response to a letter from Edward. "Don't you think it would be a good idea for you to come to the city for a while and go to school? You ought to try and improve your mind all that you can." He asked if Edward had read the books he sent a year earlier, then closed with the phrase, "I am your father and friend."[11] On November 30 of that same year, he advised Edward "to read, write, and spell correctly," then underlined this phrase: "<u>But books are good friends to keep by you & to consult often.</u>"[12] The formal education that Joseph desired for his son did not come about. Within a year Edward married Ella, and providing for a family precluded any more school.

Some twelve years later, on July 28, 1892, Joseph wrote and lamented that Edward had not better educated himself. "I wish you had better improved your chances at school." Joseph likely had regrets about his own schooling. When a schoolmaster threatened to whip fifteen-year-old Joseph's sister, Martha Ann, Joseph instead "licked him, good and plenty," as Joseph recounted to his close friend Charles W. Nibley. The fight ended Joseph's formal schooling.[13] Joseph continued in his letter to Edward that more school would have been "a great advantage." Perhaps Joseph F. Smith regretted the early end of his own formal education and knew the difficulty of continued self-education. He did not want Edward to brood about it though and recommended that Edward get on with his life. In the same 1892 letter, Joseph explained, "But it is wise to remember that the grist will not be ground by the water which has passed the mill."[14]

Joseph never gave up on encouraging Edward to do as he had done, which was to strive to learn as much as he could throughout his life. "Improve your leisure moments in study; . . . give your children all the chances to learn."[15] Books were frequent gifts, both from Joseph and from Edward's adopted siblings.[16] Joseph, whose own spelling was occasionally less than perfect, wanted to help Edward with his. "I would like to give you a few short lessons in spelling, and may do so next time."[17]

This personal encouragement of Edward towards more formal education appears to be somewhat contrasting to some of Joseph F. Smith's publicly stated views. For example, in the April 1903 general conference, Joseph encouraged training in agriculture and vocations over books. "We need manual training schools instead of so much book learning. . . . If we would devote more money and time, more energy and attention to teaching our children manual labor in our schools than we do, it would be a better thing for the rising generation."[18] This emphasis on vocational training and home industries became a frequent sermon theme of the public Joseph F. Smith during his tenure as an Apostle and later as President of the Church. Much of this, perhaps, is a reflection of those times. It is not inconceivable to imagine a father wanting a certain type of education for his own son, but maintaining a different attitude towards the needs of the Church as a whole. The Church throughout the nineteenth century in Utah promoted a separation from "the world" and what Brigham Young viewed as corrupting Gentile influences. Only after the First Manifesto of 1890, which called for an end to polygamy, did the Church and its members begin to see interaction with the rest of the nation and greater world as something to be encouraged rather than avoided. President Smith's tenure as Church President marked a transition from the insular society, favored by Young and others, to a fuller integration with American culture and society at large.

Joseph F. Smith still may have preferred a slower transition than he often observed. In the *Improvement Era* in 1903, Joseph wrote the following: "I have often thought of the undesirableness of the young men of our community seeking for light employments, and lucrative positions, without regard to manual and mechanical skill, and knowledge and ability in agriculture."[19]

It should be pointed out that the schooling Joseph desired for Edward does not equate to a present-day public-school education. Joseph had a deep mistrust of secular schooling, preferring a primary education that gave as equal an emphasis to religion as to reading and writing. In 1915, at a general conference session, he resisted the introduction of publicly funded high schools, over which the church had no control. "We are having forced upon the people high schools throughout every part of the land. I believe that we are running education mad . . . to teach the learning or education of the world. God is not in it. . . . If we will have our children properly taught in principles of righteousness, morality and religion, we have to establish Church schools or institutions of education of our own."[20]

Perhaps the model of education that Joseph desired for his sons can be seen with the examples of Edward's adopted brothers, Joseph Fielding and Hyrum Mack Smith. Both of these men served as Apostles. Joseph Fielding Smith became, arguably, the Church's preeminent scriptural scholar in his time, with a number of books published on Church history and doctrine.[21] Joseph Fielding completed school through the LDS College and received what we today would consider a high school education. Similarly, Hyrum attended the Deseret College, supplemented with a large amount of religious instruction.[22]

Work and Economy

Life in the late-nineteenth-century Intermountain West for most people revolved around the hard work of survival. Mormon colonization was still under way, and subsistence farming was the norm for most families. Outside the handful of Wasatch Front cities, land had to be cleared, roads and irrigation canals built, and homes constructed from scratch.[23] The theme of working, knowing how to make a living off the land, and providing for a family was often mentioned by Joseph in his letters to Edward. Joseph wrote about the difficulty of providing for his large family with multiple households. Gardens and livestock for food and farm work were a frequent topic. In 1880, Joseph inventoried his livestock assets as "two horses, three cows, and a calf at home now, and I hardly know what to do with them." He also inquired about some cedar posts to build some sheds on his urban property in Salt Lake City.[24]

After Edward's marriage and move to Idaho, Joseph and Edward often discussed crops and the prospects of the harvest. In 1892, Joseph responded to an optimistic letter regarding Edward's Idaho farm, writing, "I hope your good prospects this year for raising your bread will be all you expect." As for himself, Joseph observed, "I never see an idle day or moment scarcely," even with Joseph's other sons getting old enough to help about the property.[25] Later that year, he described to Edward that he had gathered some seventy-five tons of hay from thirty acres of land and noted that his livestock holdings had grown to include five horses, a colt, seven cows, and two calves at his various residences with wives Julina, Sarah, and Edna. He also commiserated with Edward's loss of some wheat to an early frost and hoped that enough could be saved to get Edward's family through until the next harvest.[26]

Despite all the emphasis on work and self-sufficiency, Joseph and other members of his family frequently discussed the challenges of raising a family as large as Joseph's. Joseph and Julina's daughter Donnette wrote in November 1893 that Mother Julina was sending Edward a "Christmas box or bundle, money is scarce but we will try to send something if it is not much."[27]

On December 7, 1903, Joseph wrote Edward concerning a number of financial issues. At this time, Joseph appeared to be doing well enough that he was able to send a check for three hundred dollars. Edward, with some of Ella's brothers, had moved to Raymond, Alberta, Canada, to homestead. Homesteading required a house to be built to establish a claim, and Edward, with son-in-law Thomas Lyons, built a home. The check was to cover the first three hundred dollars towards the cost of lumber and other materials, with Edward to satisfy the rest of the bill. Joseph noted, "My taxes this year have reached nearly $900, and it has been a very heavy pull upon me." Joseph closed with an admonition: "Be sure and pay every dollar of your debts you can, and keep out of debt."[28]

A follow-up letter that Joseph wrote in February of 1904 indicated, "I am glad you were able to get into your house before the coldest of the winter came."[29] Edward, who made his living both as a carpenter and a farmer, had built homes for several of his neighbors as well as his own. He also took jobs from time to time helping to build railroad grades, an opera house in Raymond, and other carpentry jobs.[30]

In addition to Church duties he performed in the Historian's Office, Joseph also served in the territorial legislature as an Apostle, and in several missions, which made him a very busy man.[31] He occasionally mentioned that work had kept him from replying to letters as promptly as he would have liked, and on one occasion, he apologized and expressed his regrets when Edward and Ella were in Salt Lake City for April conference and Joseph was too busy to see them.[32]

There are less direct references in the letters to the difficulties affecting Joseph. In a letter from July 1884, Joseph wrote expressing his concern over Edward's loss of some horses and unspecified "property." He reminded Edward that however much fun "camping out" must be for Edward's young family in warm weather, "it is hard on women and children. And it is certainly not much easier on men." Whatever the specific loss involved, it had left Edward, his wife, and two daughters under three years of age without a home on a new farm in Idaho. After apologizing for his own inability to help Edward make a new start, Joseph said, "This is perhaps about the most difficult time of my life. The children are all small and dependent. They bring nothing in, but cost their keep and clothes and their schooling. . . . I started with nothing and have held my own well, and have gained a little steadily, but have not gathered riches."[33]

The time that Joseph is referring to is a time of antipolygamy persecution and related legal troubles. Joseph, if not actually in formal hiding in 1884, was avoiding public appearances to keep the federal marshals at bay. They were seeking him not only to prosecute him for his own cohabitation with plural wives, but also as the Apostle directly responsible for the records and marriages in the Endowment House. Hoping to use these records as evidence and Joseph as a witness, federal officers made Joseph a wanted man.[34]

A year later, Joseph noted the delays in mail being forwarded to him. "I have not been home for several months, and am now a long way from there." This letter, one of the few not written on First Presidency stationery, was written from Hawaii. Joseph had gone there with Julina and their newest baby under assumed names, hiding from federal officers. Whatever joy Joseph had in returning to his beloved Hawaiian Islands would have been tempered by the knowledge of the circumstances that had forced the travel. He told Edward to send any letters to the First Presidency office in Salt Lake City for forwarding. Joseph may have feared that mail might be intercepted; no mention of his location is given in this letter other than to being "again a missionary in a foreign land." He mentioned the expense of the travel to avoid prosecution had cost him seven hundred dollars in the previous six months. There were about thirty members of the family dependent on him and "but little except my own income to sustain them."[35] The threat of prosecution for polygamy ended in 1890 with the First Manifesto but left Joseph with five families to continue to provide for. He expressed his concern in October 1892, noting that while he and Julina were back in their old home in Salt Lake City, "The government will not allow me to live with the others, altho[ugh] I may provide for them and visit the children."[36]

Health and Hope

Struggles to provide a living were not the only issues of concern for families in the late nineteenth and early twentieth centuries. Minor illnesses and diseases, which are often disregarded in our day of modern medicine, were serious issues. Preventing and treating infectious disease still overwhelmed medical practitioners in the Mountain West. Nationally, infant mortality rates were high, ranging from 175 to 215 deaths per 1,000 live births in the last half of the nineteenth century, and the life expectancy of someone born in the same period hovered around forty-five years of age.[37] As would be expected, the Smith family's personal letters frequently discussed health, sickness, and occasional deaths. These issues were never far from any of the correspondents' thoughts.

Colds and coughs were frequently mentioned,[38] and a particularly illness-free winter was noted for its happy exception to the rule.[39] Other letters expressed serious concerns for family members, and some read like a catalog of health crises and illnesses. In 1896, Joseph wrote, "Joseph R. Aunt Sarah's oldest boy, now about 23, had to undergo an operation for appendicitis; . . . for 3 weeks we all had a hard pull of it."[40] The winter of 1897 again saw serious illness. "Little Ruth, Aunt Ednas youngest . . . was taken very sick just after Christmas with measles and bronchitis combined, and we have had a very serious time with her. . . . Your mother has had a heavy cold and cough a great part of the winter. . . . And several of the little ones have been quite sorely troubled with coughs, sore throats, [etc.]. . . . One of the little ones at the old home has the measles."[41] Ruth, in fact, lived just over another year, dying at age four in March 1898 from scarlet fever, the eighth and last of Joseph's offspring to die in childhood.[42]

Such losses certainly made Joseph more sensitive to the loss of Edward and Ella's eleventh child, Lester Ray, born in August 1903, who succumbed to illness in January 1904. Joseph sent his sympathy and shared some of his own perspective of loss, along with encouraging the eternal perspective of their shared religion. "I also received the . . . sad news of the death of the baby, in which sad loss you and El have my most sincere sympathy. There are worse things than the death of pure innocent little babies."[43] Joseph was not trying to minimize the loss; it was an experience Joseph had been through himself. Of the eight child deaths in the families of Joseph F. Smith and his wives, four died before their first birthday. Four more died under the age of five. While Joseph's family's losses were only half the average rate for infant mortality in the United States at the time, these statistics would have been small comfort for Joseph and his wives. Very few fathers of the time would have had to endure losing four infants and four more children in early childhood.

Joseph made mention of these losses, and the pain that it caused him, in his journals and in letters to other family members. In a letter written to his sister Martha Ann two months after the death of Julina's daughter Mercy Josephine, he wrote: "The weather is very oppressive, and the atmosphere sultry and merky [*sic*], as tho' impregnated with smoke. Much as it was on the days memorable as the 27th, of June 1844. And the 21st. and 22nd of Sept. 1852—the day of fathers death, and the death and burial of Mother, I recollect them distinctly. It is two months to the day since my own sweet babe joined her grand father and mother in the spirit world, leaving in my hearts affections a void and broken space that time nor earth can ever fill. I mourn the earthly loss of the brightest, purest, dearest, treasure God ever gave me."[44]

In a similar vein, he had written to wives Julina and Edna on the passing of Julina's eldest child, Mercy:

> O God only knows how much I loved my girl, and she the light and the joy of my heart. The morning before she died, after being up with her all night, for I watched her every night, I said to her, "My little pet did not sleep all night." She shook her head and replied, "I'll sleep today, papa." Oh! how those little words shot through my heart. I knew though I would not believe, it was another voice, that it meant the sleep of death and she did sleep. And, Oh! the light of my heart went out. The image of heaven graven in my soul almost departed. . . . Thou wert a heavenly gift directly to my heart of hearts.[45]

As discouraging as the deaths of eight of his children must have been, they led Joseph F. Smith to ponder the mysteries of immortality. This ultimately led to his vision of the redemption of the dead, received shortly before Joseph's death in 1918 and now canonized as Doctrine and Covenants section 138. In 1898, following the death of Edna's daughter Ruth, he recorded a precursor to the 1918 revelation: "O my soul! I see my own sweet mother's arms extended welcoming to her embrace the ransomed glorious spirit of my own sweet babe! O my God! For this glorious vision, I thank Thee! And there too are gathered to my Father's mansion all my darling lovely ones; not in infantile helplessness, but in all the power and glory and majesty of sanctified spirits! Full of intelligence, of joy and grace, and truth."[46]

Doctrine and Lived Religion

Joseph F. Smith was ordained an Apostle by Brigham Young in 1866. He was involved in preaching and Church leadership from the time that Edward came into his home. Joseph did not neglect instructing his son in regards to matters of doctrine and living his religion. As a Church leader, Joseph F. Smith presented a firm and certain vision of how to live the gospel. Elder John A. Widtsoe, in describing Joseph, called him a "fighting apostle," referring to the often strident and unyielding tone of his public sermons. "His loyalty is such," Elder Widtsoe continued, "and his convictions are so firmly established, that evil may not be spoken about truth without arousing the lion within him, . . . never to give quarter to evil or untruth or injustice."[47]

The admonitions to Edward, though firm, were often simple, such as the reminder in 1884, "I pray for you, pray for yourselves. . . . Stick to duty & be industrious."[48] Shortly after the birth of Edward and Ella's first daughter, Joseph wrote, "Continue to do right and live your religion."[49]

Others letters reflected on the maturing of Edward in both church and family responsibilities. In an 1894 letter to Edward, then living and farming in Sand Creek, Idaho, he addressed church service. "I am glad you are faithful to your duties in the church. And I wish you had ample information and other qualifications to make you efficient in your labors."[50] Edward had been called to serve as the superintendent of the Sunday School in the Parker Ward of the Bannock Idaho Stake in 1893, and later in January of 1894 was called to be a "techer [teacher] and councler [bishop's counselor]" in that same ward. He also appeared to be acting as a clerk in some respects, as his personal journal and account book records items relating to the Parker Ward, including baptisms, fast offerings, priesthood ordinations, and the like. Other pages describe personal records of income, accounts with merchants, and material costs.[51]

In the same 1894 letter, Joseph lamented that some of his other sons—names not specified—were not as obedient as Joseph desired, apparently in regards to both church attendance and education. "Some of the children now feel very much as you did when a boy, as though it was too much of a task to attend Sunday Schools, Improvement meetings, Sunday meetings and go to school. Several of the little boys like to play better than to study. And if they do not take care they will feel the need and regret their neglect when they get older."[52]

In 1896, Joseph included some advice to Edward, related to a recent call to be presiding elder or bishop while still living in the Sand Creek area. "I hope you will always do honor to the appellation of 'Bishop'. You know what Paul said to Timothy about a Bishop. (See 1 Timothy 3:1–7:) ("a bishop then must be blameless, the husband of one wife. i.e., he should not be a single man, for in those days plural marriage was common.) vigilant, sober, of good behavior, given to hospitality, apt to teach"—[etc.], [etc.]. The Apostle Paul put upon Bishops a very high estimate."[53]

In the same letter he also asked if Edward had received a couple of books, sent to Edward in the hands of a mutual friend. The books included *The Compendium*—presumably a copy of the book by the same name by Franklin D. Richards and James A. Little—and the *Ready Reference*—perhaps the scriptural reference work produced by missionaries in Great Britain, later edited and revised by James E. Talmage in 1917. These were part of an effort to continue Edward's education and growth in the gospel as Joseph had always encouraged.

Some references to doctrine are more direct and consistent with Joseph F. Smith's unequivocal public speaking profile. For example, in 1897, he wrote to Edward, "Partaking of the Sacrament is not breaking fast. The only way to break fast is to eat food with the intention to satisfy hunger or gratify the apetite [*sic*]. Partaking of the Sacrament is an ordinance, and it may be partaken of both in Sunday School and in regular Sacrament meeting without affecting the fast at all."[54]

A stronger statement is made to Edward in a letter that appears to be from 1881(part of the date is illegible) while Edward was working at a logging or mining camp in Wyoming. Reading this letter, it is obvious to see the concern that Joseph as a father had for his son and new wife living in rough circumstances with questionable coworkers. Three of the four paragraphs in the letter deal directly with the problems that Joseph saw in Edward's current situation.

> Now my boy, it will be far better for you to keep away as much as possible from the sort of company you mention. Still, you have no need to swear nor drink nor desecrate the Sabbath because others may do so. These may be considered the smaller crimes, but never the less they are crimes. Anything that violates the laws of God—or natures laws is a crime both against God and his law.
>
> Of course I need not tell you that to steal, or kill, or commit adultry [*sic*] or whordom [*sic*] is most abominable in the sight of God. Remember your covenants, made in the House of the Lord, and the penalties attaching to the violations of those covenants. Remember that you have a wife, and that you have become a man, that you are no longer a boy, and your friends all expect you to be manly and honorable and good. . . .
>
> You have your fortune to make a name to establish, your character to build up, and your home to procure. The road to these lies through industry and economy.

The letter is signed for emphasis "Your best friend [etc.] Jos. F. Smith."[55] These admonitions were in keeping with Joseph's view. Some sins were certainly more egregious than others, but all sins were to be equally abhorred. At a conference of the Granite Stake in 1917, Joseph emphasized that "determined, premeditated and deliberate wrong in man or woman, in the world—truth will not tolerate it. We can not forgive that kind or class of crime and wickedness."[56]

On another occasion, he preached, "True repentance is not only sorrow for sins, and humble penitence and contrition before God, but it involves the necessity of turning away from them, a discontinuance of all evil practices and deeds, a thorough reformation of life, a vital change from evil to good."[57] One could choose right or wrong, but never be neutral, and it was the duty of fathers to teach their children that principle.[58]

Joseph, however, could be accommodating when the circumstances required. Such a test came in connection with a large family gathering in January of 1904, on the occasion of the 104th anniversary of his father's, Hyrum Smith's, birth. Among the two hundred or so family members present was Frederick M. Smith, oldest son and counselor to Joseph Smith III, president of the Reorganized LDS (RLDS) Church. Relations between Joseph F. Smith and his cousins, sons of the Prophet Joseph Smith and leaders in the RLDS Church, had long been strained, with polygamy as a central issue. Joseph F. Smith's mother, the widow of the Prophet's brother Hyrum Smith, had come west with her children, following Brigham Young and the Quorum of the Twelve after the expulsion from Nauvoo. Joseph Smith's widow, Emma, remained in Nauvoo with her children, rejecting Young's claim to leadership of the Church and the practice of polygamy that had created such great conflict in her marriage. The subsequent establishment of the RLDS Church, the eventual elevation of Emma's son Joseph Smith III to its presidency, and the RLDS rejection of polygamy and Joseph Smith's participation in the practice, created a schism in the extended Smith family. What should have been a bond through a shared sense of loss instead developed into conflicting claims of truth and a deep doctrinal chasm.[59] Joseph F. Smith had angered Frederick's uncle Alexander, youngest son of Joseph Smith Jr., during an 1883 visit to Salt Lake City. Alexander was speaking to a congregation where his cousin Joseph F. was in the audience. Joseph requested permission to address the gathering, which Alexander granted. Alexander wrote to a friend of what happened next. Joseph bore "his testimony to Polig[polygamy] and charged his father and my father with being Polig's [polygamists] and with lying in their published testimony against it. . . . [I] was heartily ashamed of him to stand before that immense congregation and proclaim his father *a liar*."[60] It was an awkward moment for both men, to be sure, with each promoting competing narratives of their fathers' legacies.

For Frederick Smith's 1904 visit to Salt Lake City, Joseph took a more conciliatory stance. Joseph wrote to Edward of the events:

> "Fred. M. Smith, the oldest son and counselor of my cousin Joseph Smith, of the Re-organized Ch. He is still visiting with us. He is about 30 years of age, is married and has one child. We have not mentioned any of the differences of our views on religion, so that his visit may be as pleasant as possible. Last evening he attended a brilliant gathering of M.I.A. workers at Sister McClunes, and this afternoon he has been visiting with Cousin Clarissa Smith Williams, with your Mother and Aunts Sarah and Edna L. He has nothing to do but to enjoy himself if he will. I cannot guess what he will say about us when he returns home."[61]

Again, it must have been an awkward visit; polygamy was no longer being practiced overtly, yet here was Frederick Smith visiting his cousin Clarissa with three of the wives of Joseph F. Smith.

Final Years

Edward appears to have heeded much of Joseph's advice over the years. His descendants remember him as a hardworking and industrious man, yet circumstances denied him from ever being firmly established. He and his family got by, but they did not prosper or accumulate property or wealth. He remained faithful in the LDS Church and served in leadership positions, though never at the same levels as his father.

Farming in southeastern Idaho was not easy, as several of these letters describe. By 1902, with prospects not improving, Edward and his family, which also included his oldest daughter, Julina, and her husband, Tom Lyons, decided to move to Canada to take advantage of lands available for homesteading in southern Alberta. Ella already had brothers in the area, who reported fertile land and a growing population. On July 3, 1902, Edward and Tom staked out claims and went to work as carpenters, building homes for others and erecting buildings in nearby Raymond, Alberta, and the surrounding area. They also worked constructing the railroad between Lethbridge and Raymond and built homes and dry farms for themselves, first in Magrath, then later closer to Raymond.[62]

In 1909, Edward was involved in an accident, the details of which are not currently known. He lost the use of his legs, later his upper body, and became a complete invalid. Ella wrote to Joseph, prompting a reply written July 20, 1909, to Edward: "I received a letter from Ella, Signed 'Mrs. E. A. Smith,' in which she speaks of your illness and consequent necessities. I should have answered it at once, but I have been so pressed with my work, and so much troubled over Serious Sickness at home, that it seemed as tho' I could not get a moment to write." After describing the illnesses and health issues at home, Joseph continued: "We hope you will soon be better and again recover your health. Ella did not say what ailed you. What is the matter?" After promising some help, he closes the letter: "We all hope and pray that you will soon be better and all right. With love to all, I am [etc.] Jos. F. Smith."[63]

On November 18, 1909, Julina finally completed a letter to "Edward and 'Ell,'" a task she had been unable to accomplish while tending to her own sick children and helping with the children of Joseph's other wives. Julina had also been involved in helping Aunt Alice, another of Joseph's wives, who had been in the hospital during this time. "I was very much grieved," she writes, "to hear of the condition of Edward. I wish something could be done to help him. . . . The children often say to me Mama I think you ought to write to Edward." Julina closes the letter with hopeful expressions that underscore the seriousness of Edward's condition. "I hope Edward will be better by the time we hear from you again. The Doctors do not always know. Hoping to hear from you soon I remain ever Mama JLS. Love to all."[64]

It is unknown whether the doctors referred to were local to Raymond or specialists sent by Joseph to consult on the case as indicated by a letter from one of Edward's daughters.[65] On July 17, 1911, Edward finally succumbed to the combination of illness and injury. Julina wrote to Ella eleven days later, expressing her grief:

> We received the news of Edward's death, which was quite unexpected as we did not think of his going so soon. I was making preparations to come up there in August, after Papa's return home, to visit you. My house has been full of visitors for a long time, and I was unable to get away for his burial. I am here alone looking after company. . . . I am very sorry that I could not come to help you in your time of need. We expect Papa home next week. I sent him word of Edward's death. The girls will be home from the Canyon tomorrow night. I have had thirteen visitors staying here while they have been gone and have had almost more than I could do as I have been suffering with rheumatism in my ankles and it has been hard for me to get around.
>
> Write and let us know what the funeral expenses were and how you are fixed.
>
> Papa will write you as soon as he returns home.
>
> Praying the Lord to bless and comfort you in your berievement [*sic*], I am, Lovingly your mother, Julina L. Smith.[66]

Conclusions

Joseph F. Smith's family was unusually large, even by standards of nineteenth-century plural marriage. With forty-three children, five wives, and multiple households, the addition of five more adopted children was not a trivial undertaking. Edward was the first to be adopted, but also the oldest of all of Joseph F. Smith's children, taken in while Joseph was serving a foreign mission and sent back to Utah to an unsuspecting and childless first wife, Levira.[67] Edward's treatment by his father seems typical of Joseph F. Smith's relationship to all of his children, regardless of which wife they called mother or whether they were biological or adopted.

From these letters, we can see that Joseph F. and Julina Smith took great interest in Edward's family and welfare throughout Edward's life, even as Edward moved away to Idaho and Canada, far from the close family circle in northern Utah. Concerned parental advice is mixed with family news and shared struggles and continued to emphasize living Joseph F. Smith's expected standards for church activity and commitment to a gospel-centered life. Largely unknown outside of his direct descendants, Edward Arthur Smith can now be recognized as a regular member of the Smith family. Saved from a backyard bonfire, these letters show that Joseph's 1880 admonition for Edward to grow into a "useful, faithful, and upright man," coupled with Joseph's continuing support and encouragement through struggles and challenges, resulted in a life that fulfilled the expectations of Edward's remarkable father.

Notes

1. Cytha Ellen Smith is variously referred to as Cytha, Ellen, or Ella. As Ella is the most common usage in these letters, I have chosen to use Ella to identify Edward Arthur Smith's wife in this article, except where source documents use another name. Family History of Edward Arthur Smith and His Descendants, no author listed, assembled and privately distributed to family members by various grandchildren and great-grandchildren of Edward Arthur Smith, copy in my possession, three pages, n.p., n.d. (hereafter EAS family history).
2. As with much of Edward Arthur Smith's beginnings, even his birth date is in dispute. All of the family genealogy lists his birth date as November 1, 1858. However, in a copy of Edward's personal journal and account book, he lists in his own handwriting a birth date of November 1, 1859. Edward Arthur Smith, journal and account book, n.p., n.d., copy in my possession, 137.
3. Joseph Fielding Smith, who authored a biography of his father Joseph F. Smith, makes no mention of Edward Arthur, except in a listing of all family members in the appendix; Joseph Fielding Smith, *Life of Joseph F. Smith* (Salt Lake City: Deseret News, 1938), 477. Biographer Francis Gibbons makes one reference to Edward in his book *Joseph F. Smith: Patriarch and Preacher, Prophet of God* (Salt Lake City: Deseret Book, 1988), 87.
4. Smith, *Life of Joseph F. Smith*, 487–90. The others were Marjorie Virginia, Alice May, Heber Chase, and Charles Coulson Smith.
5. Exactly how young Edward came to the Smith family is uncertain. Family tradition tells that Joseph brought him home from one of his missions to England; however, Joseph F. served his first mission to Great Britain in 1860 to 1863, prior to his marriage to Julina, and next served as President of the European Mission in Liverpool during parts of 1874 and 1875. Joseph and Julina's daughter Donnette Smith Kessler related in a letter that her father met the family while in England in 1868, but admits that family information does not agree. Joseph F. notes in a journal entry dated January 20, 1870, "Edward was very sick tonight, vomiting severely.

I think he has the mumps," indicating that Edward was resident in Joseph and Julina's home early in 1870. Joseph F. Smith, journal, in *Selected Collections of the Archives of the Church of Jesus Christ of Latter-day Saints*, ed. Richard E. Turley Jr., 2 vols., DVD (Provo, UT: BYU Press, 2002). Donnette also indicated that Edward may have been brought from England by her "uncle" William W. Burton, also a relative of the Smith family, but Joseph's journal entries indicate that Edward boarded an America-bound ship in 1863 with a family by the name of Cook. Donnette Smith Kessler to Wilburta Moore, June 7, 1955, correspondence; EAS family history; Joseph F. Smith, journal, May 4, 25, 26, and 29, 1863, Church History Library, The Church of Jesus Christ of Latter-day Saints, Salt Lake City.

6. Joseph F. Smith and Levira Annette Clark Smith, May 13, 1863, correspondence, Joseph F. Smith papers, Church History Library, The Church of Jesus Christ of Latter-day Saints, Salt Lake City.
7. Joseph F. Smith autobiographical writings and notebooks, April 9, 1865, Church History Library.
8. Edward A. Smith, journal, 137–38.
9. Edward A. Smith, journal, 137–38.
10. Joseph F. Smith (hereafter "JFS") to Edward Arthur Smith (hereafter "EAS"), correspondence, February 11, 1879, Church History Library.
11. JFS to EAS, February 8, 1880, correspondence.
12. JFS to EAS, November 30, 1880, correspondence.
13. Gibbons, *Joseph F. Smith*, 26–27.
14. JFS to EAS, July 28, 1892, correspondence.
15. JFS to EAS, October 19, 1892, correspondence.
16. JFS to EAS, December 14, 1893, correspondence; also JFS to EAS, April 17, 1896, correspondence.
17. JFS to EAS, March 28, 1894, correspondence.
18. Joseph F. Smith, *Gospel Doctrine: Selections from the Sermons and Writings of Joseph F. Smith* (Salt Lake City: Deseret Book, 1977), 347.
19. Smith, *Gospel Doctrine*, 343.
20. Joseph F. Smith, in Conference Report, October 1915, 6.
21. Gary James Bergera, review of *Joseph Fielding Smith: Gospel Scholar, Prophet of God*, in *Journal of Mormon History* 19, no. 2 (Fall 1993): 157–60.
22. Authoritative information about the education of Hyrum Mack Smith and Joseph Fielding Smith has proved elusive. Most of what is known is from undocumented family histories and anecdotal comments.
23. See, for example, Leonard J. Arrington, *Great Basin Kingdom: An Economic History of the Latter Day Saints, 1830–1900* (Lincoln: University of Nebraska Press, 1966), particularly chapter 7, "A Decade of Growth: Planning for Self-Sufficiency."
24. JFS to EAS, February 8, 1880, correspondence.
25. JFS to EAS, July 28, 1892, correspondence.
26. JFS to EAS, October 19, 1892, correspondence.
27. Donnette Smith to EAS, November 26, 1893, correspondence.
28. JFS to EAS, December 7, 1903, correspondence and JFS to EAS, October 16, 1903, correspondence.

29. JFS to EAS, February 12, 1904, correspondence.
30. EAS family history.
31. JFS to EAS, February 11, 1879, correspondence.
32. JFS to EAS, April 17, 1896, correspondence.
33. JFS to EAS, July 14, 1884, correspondence.
34. Gibbons, *Joseph F. Smith*, 137–51.
35. JFS to EAS, April 27, 1885, correspondence; Gibbons, *Joseph F. Smith*, 137–51.
36. JFS to EAS, October 19, 1892, correspondence.
37. Michael Haines, "Fertility and Mortality in the United States," *The Cambridge Economic History of the United States* (Cambridge: Cambridge University Press, 2000), 178.
38. JFS to EAS, February 11, 1879, correspondence; JFS to EAS, February 10, 1894, correspondence; JFS to EAS, March 28, 1894, correspondence.
39. JFS to EAS, February 8, 1880, correspondence.
40. JFS to EAS, April 17, 1896, correspondence.
41. JFS to EAS, January 30, 1897, correspondence.
42. Smith, *Life of Joseph F. Smith*, 487–90; JFS to EAS, December 7, 1898, correspondence.
43. JFS to EAS, February 12, 1904, correspondence.
44. JFS to Martha Ann Smith Harris, August 6, 1870, correspondence, quoted in David M. Whitchurch, "The Pedagogy of a Church Leader: Lessons Learned from Joseph F. Smith's 1854–1916 Letters to His Sister, Martha Ann Smith Harris," *Religious Educator* 2, no. 2 (2001): 97.
45. Smith, *Life of Joseph F. Smith*, 456–57.
46. Smith, *Life of Joseph F. Smith*,463.
47. Smith, *Gospel Doctrine*, 511.
48. JFS to EAS, July 14, 1884, correspondence.
49. JFS to EAS, September 19, 1882, correspondence.
50. JFS to EAS, March 28, 1894, correspondence.
51. Edward A. Smith, journal, 250–61.
52. JFS to EAS, March 28, 1894, correspondence.
53. JFS to EAS, April 17, 1896, correspondence.
54. JFS to EAS, January 30, 1897, correspondence.
55. JFS to EAS, August 7, 188[number illegible], correspondence.
56. Smith, *Gospel Doctrine*, 214.
57. Smith, *Gospel Doctrine*, 100.
58. Smith, *Gospel Doctrine*, 287–88.
59. Linda King Newell and Valeen Tippetts Avery, *Mormon Enigma: Emma Hale Smith* (Garden City: Doubleday, 1984), 280–95; Gibbons, *Joseph F. Smith*, 91–92.
60. Ronald E. Romig, "Alexander H. Smith: Remembering a Son of Joseph and Emma Smith," *Journal of Mormon History* 37, no. 2 (Spring 2011): 37.
61. JFS to EAS, February 12, 1904, correspondence.
62. EAS family history; Edna Smith Patrick, *Brief Histories of the Family of President Joseph F. Smith and Julina L. Smith*, booklet, n.p., n.d., Edna Smith Patrick collection, 1–4.
63. JFS to EAS, July 20, 1909, correspondence.
64. Julina L. Smith to EAS, November 18, 1909, correspondence.

65. Edna Smith Patrick, *Brief Histories*, 3; Florence Adelia Smith Anderson, May 25, 1967, correspondence.
66. Julina L. Smith to Cytha Ellen Smith, July 28, 1911, correspondence.
67. Joseph includes Edward as an unusual "gift" pressed upon him just prior to his departure from England in 1863 in a letter to Levira. The ultimate relationship of Levira and Edward is not known; in all correspondence, Joseph F. Smith refers to his second wife, Julina, as Edward's mother, a sentiment echoed in the handful of Julina's letters to Edward and his family. For Joseph's letter to Levira informing her of Edward's adoption, see correspondence, JFS to Levira, May 13, 1863 (n. 6).

J. B. Haws

8

Joseph F. Smith's Encouragement of His Brother, Patriarch John Smith

A good argument could be made that no General Authority in the history of the Church has served as long in a presiding position and is yet as almost entirely forgotten as John Smith. He was the Church's Presiding Patriarch for fifty-six years; he gave over twenty thousand patriarchal blessings; he was sustained in general conference as a prophet, seer, and revelator; and yet, in some recent histories, it is occasionally difficult to even find John's name listed among Hyrum Smith's children.[1]

Part of this anonymity stems undoubtedly from the fact that there has not been an active Patriarch to the Church since 1979, when Eldred G. Smith (John Smith's great-grandson) was given emeritus status.[2] The passage of the thirty-plus years since then has made that office and its history more and more obscure. Part of this anonymity also stems from the reality that more attention is directed to John Smith's younger brother, Joseph F. Smith—and to be sure, no one would say that such attention is misdirected, considering Joseph F. Smith's pivotal importance in Latter-day Saint history and thinking. Yet there is also a sense that part of John Smith's anonymity reflects, as a handful of historians have recently suggested, a

---

J. B. Haws is an assistant professor of Church history and doctrine at Brigham Young University.

legacy of ambivalence and even discomfort about the Presiding Patriarch's proper place in the Church's hierarchy in general, and John Smith's role in that office in particular.[3] (He was, after all, publicly chastised by the prophet during general conference!) This paper seeks to address both that anonymity and that ambivalence.

Of course, for Latter-day Saints living at the turn of the twentieth century, Patriarch John Smith and his relation to President Joseph F. Smith were well known—and invited obvious comparisons to an earlier prophet and patriarch. In February 1902, for example, Elder Rudger Clawson had just visited the Oneida (Idaho) Stake conference, and he was giving a report of the visit to his fellow Apostles in their weekly Thursday temple meeting with the First Presidency. Elder Clawson reported that he saw the following written "on a blackboard in the room where the conference was assembled":

Coincidence

	1844	
Joseph Smith Prophet	(brothers)	Hyrum Smith Patriarch
Brigham Young President of the Twelve Apostles		
	1902	
Joseph F. Smith Prophet	(brothers)	John Smith Patriarch
Brigham Young [Jr.] President of the Twelve Apostles[4]		

While the parallels of these younger brothers/older brothers prompted the chalkboard diagram in Idaho, the contention here is that perhaps a better model for understanding President Joseph F. Smith's relationship with his older brother John might be in the way that Joseph Smith Jr. treated Joseph Smith Sr.'s calling as Patriarch—Joseph Smith Jr. sought to elevate the office and office holder. There are important things to be considered here not only about an oft-forgotten John Smith but also about Joseph F. Smith's attitude toward his brother and his brother's office—and these considerations have broader implications related to the order of the Church.

A Biography of Peaks and Valleys

Long before sharing the stand at general conference, the two brothers shared heartbreak. John Smith was Hyrum's oldest son, the third child born to Hyrum and his

Taken from the introductory pages of Matthias F. Cowley, Prophets and Patriarchs of the Church of Jesus Christ of Latter-day Saints *(Chattanooga, TN: Ben E. Rich, 1902).*

first wife, Jerusha.[5] John was barely five when his mother died; six when his new stepmother, Mary Fielding Smith, gave birth to his younger brother Joseph F.; eleven when his father was killed. As a young teenager, he nursed Colonel Thomas L. Kane for two weeks when Colonel Kane was sick at Winter Quarters. On the night of his sixteenth birthday—September 22, 1848—John Smith "drove five wagons down Big Mountain." In fact, "it was dark long before he got to camp with the last wagon. On the way one wheel of his wagon ran into a tree which was about fifteen inches through. He had to lie on his back and chop the tree down with a dull ax before he could go any further."[6]

Hyrum Smith's Children

Hyrum married Jerusha Barden on November 2, 1826. Their children are: • Lovina Smith Walker, 1827–76 • Mary Smith, 1829–32 • John Smith, 1832–1911 • Hyrum Smith, 1834–41 • Jerusha Smith Peirce, 1836–1912 • Sarah Smith Griffin, 1837–76 Jerusha Barden Smith died on October 13, 1837, eleven days after Sarah was born.	Hyrum married Mary Fielding on December 24, 1837. Their children are: • Joseph F. Smith, 1838–1918 • Martha Ann Smith Harris, 1841–1923 Mary Fielding Smith died on September 21, 1852.

After arriving in Utah, John helped in building the family's home, and then managed the family's farm in Sugarhouse. In the spring of 1850, he "was enrolled in a company of horsemen, called the Battalion of Life Guards organized for the purpose of standing guard . . . to protect from the marauding Indians, who were hostile at the time. For about ten years he was compelled to keep on hand a saddle horse and other equipment for that purpose."[7]

September 21, 1852—the day before John's twentieth birthday—Mary Fielding Smith passed away after a two-month illness. For Joseph F. (six years younger than John), his mother's death was, understandably, a crushing blow.[8] John's own writings also hint at how difficult this loss was for him. It is obvious that he did not think of Mary as a stepmother; in his handwritten autobiography, he originally wrote that September 21 was the day of "the death of my mother," and then there appears, as an insertion added above the text, the word "step."[9] An even stronger indicator is found in a letter that John sent to his missionary brother in 1856, in which he refers to "the death of our mother."[10]

Mary's death meant that John was thus left "to provide for a family of eight" by virtue of his station as the oldest son, but also because "Brother Brigham preached a surmon and he at that time appointed [John] gardian [*sic*] over the family."[11]

Three years later, in 1855, President Brigham Young expanded that familial appointment. As the oldest male descendant of Joseph Smith Sr. in the Church, it was John Smith's right and responsibility to fill the office of Church Patriarch. John became the Church's fifth Patriarch and the fourth in the line of Joseph Smith Sr.[12] Brigham Young anticipated that some in the Church might have thought that the twenty-two-year-old John was too young; President Young's feeling was that "[John] can seal up a Patriarchal blessing upon the heads of the people better than any old man in the church." President Jedediah M. Grant likewise expressed confidence in John, saying that he "would rather have a young man to fill this office than an old man who is filled with the leaven of sectarianism." Significantly, Brigham Young said, in ordaining John, that he was conferring on John the "keys" which John's father, Hyrum, "would have conferred . . . on [him] if he had been alive."[13]

Patriarchs of The Church of Jesus Christ of Latter-day Saints

1. **Joseph Smith Sr.**—1833–40
2. **Hyrum Smith**—1841–44
3. William Smith—1845

   *Asael Smith (brother to Joseph Smith Sr.), unofficial Patriarch, 1845–46
4. John Smith$_1$ (brother to Joseph Smith Sr.)—1847–54
5. **John Smith$_2$** (son of Hyrum Smith)—1855–1911
6. **Hyrum Gibbs Smith** (grandson of John Smith$_2$)—1912–32

   *Nicholas G. Smith (son of John Henry Smith [Apostle], who was the son of George A. Smith [Apostle], who was the son of John Smith$_1$), unofficial Patriarch, 1932–37

   *George F. Richards (Apostle), Acting Patriarch, 1937–42
7. Joseph F. Smith II (son of Hyrum Mack Smith [apostle], who was the son of President Joseph F. Smith, who was the son of Hyrum Smith)—1942–46
8. **Eldred G. Smith** (son of Hyrum Gibbs Smith)—1947–79

   In October 1979, Eldred G. Smith was designated Patriarch Emeritus.

Bold typeface indicates the Joseph Smith Sr.–Hyrum Smith–John Smith line. Based on "Appendix B" in Irene M. Bates and E. Gary Smith, Lost Legacy: The Mormon Office of Presiding Patriarch *(Urbana and Chicago: University of Illinois Press, 1996).*

After serving more than seven years as Patriarch, John was called on a mission to Denmark in 1862. He became fluent in Danish—on one occasion he wrote that he went seventeen days without speaking English except to show the locals what English sounded like, or to pray when non-Danish speakers were present.[14] He also was a lifelong attendee at reunions and celebrations of the Scandinavian Saints in Utah. He cared for his missionary comrades when they were ill. On the return trip, he was elected president of the company of Saints on the ship *Monarch of the Sea* and then captain of a returning wagon train.[15]

Yet, despite what would seem to be a commendable record of service typical of Church leaders in those pioneer times, in October 1875, after two decades as Patriarch to the Church, the First Presidency and the Twelve voted to remove John Smith from office and replace him with his brother, Joseph F. As Wilford Woodruff recorded in his journal, that decision was tabled only after Joseph F. and John together pled with Brigham Young to give John an additional six months of probation.[16] He never was removed from office, yet over the years John Smith was admonished by Church leaders in public and in private settings.

In 1871, for example, Joseph F. Smith, then a young Apostle, recorded in his diary an account of a Kaysville, Utah, conference where he "said a few words about patriarchal blessings, and admonished John to forsake his follies, the people might seek him for blessings rather than he seek the people to bless them." Then, in the hours following that admonition, Joseph F. "wrote for [John]" as he "blessed six persons."[17] In an even stronger show of disapproval, President Wilford Woodruff rebuked Patriarch Smith from the pulpit of an 1894 general conference, suggesting that either John Smith change his ways or else he had "better resign."[18]

In terms of John's personal morality and rectitude, three basic issues popped up in these periodic complaints about John's fitness to serve: first, John's closeness to his Smith cousins in the Reorganized Latter Day Saint movement; second, his inconsistent commitment to the actual practice of plural marriage; and third, his delayed personal adherence to the proscriptions of the Word of Wisdom. So troubling were these issues to John's brother that in 1883, Joseph F. Smith told his colleagues in the Quorum of the Twelve and the First Presidency that he did not feel that John was worthy to be included in their Salt Lake School of the Prophets meetings—and he wondered if that should also be taken as a sign that John was not worthy to continue as Patriarch either.[19]

His Brother's Presidency— The Implications of Greater Prominence

Considering all of this uncertainty (and even displeasure) surrounding Elder John Smith, what is to be made of the fact that on October 17, 1901, President Joseph F. Smith invited his brother not only to attend the first weekly meeting of the Twelve over which Joseph F. now presided (after the death of President Lorenzo Snow) but also to act as voice in setting apart Joseph F. Smith as President of the Church? This was an unprecedented ordination in the history of the Presidents of the Church.[20] What is to be made of the fact that John Smith would thereafter be a regular participant in those weekly temple meetings? Or that, beginning in general conference in October 1902, John Smith's name, as Church Patriarch, would be included in the group sustained as "prophets, seers, and revelators"?[21] Or in the fact that one month after becoming Church President, Joseph F. Smith instructed that Patriarch John Smith was to be included in the General Authority schedule to visit the Church's stakes?[22]

Only two decades after questioning his brother's fitness for his presiding role—and only two decades after decisively excluding his brother from a meeting of the First Presidency and the Twelve—Joseph F. Smith repeatedly instituted measures to enlarge his brother's hierarchical and public profile. What does this apparent about-face signal?

The first suggestion here is that this seemed to signal something different in Joseph F. Smith's mind than it did in the minds of some of his brethren in the Twelve. To some of the Apostles, these overtures to increase the stature of the Church Patriarch raised potentially confusing issues about the order of succession. The full story is larger than the confines of this paper, and it has been treated thoroughly in other places, most notably in Irene Bates and Gary Smith's book, *Lost Legacy,* and in Michael Quinn's *The Mormon Hierarchy.* In a November 1901 special conference, when President Smith proposed that the Patriarch be sustained in general conference before the Twelve, or even before the First Presidency, some of his colleagues worried that this would muddle the issue of seniority and authority.[23] It is understandable that there were periodic back-and-forths as to whether the Church's Patriarch was a presiding patriarch—over a quorum of patriarchs, for example—or simply the Patriarch to the Church. In 1979, when Elder Eldred G. Smith (the last Church Patriarch and John Smith's great-grandson) was given emeritus status, his title had been Patriarch to the Church. But during Joseph F. Smith's administration (and at various times in earlier administrations), John Smith was clearly identified as the Presiding Patriarch.[24] Without question, there are broader issues involved in the inherent conflicts between what could seem like parallel lines of authority, when one line is hereditary and lineal and the other is based on selection and seniority. It is a conflict, as Irene Bates and Gary Smith have written, between "familial charisma" and organizational or "office charisma."[25] One needed only to raise the specter of a William Smith to highlight the difficulty in placing too much authority in a hereditary office.

Joseph F. Smith apparently did not push his proposal to change the sustaining order; the only change to the sustaining, as mentioned earlier, was to include the Patriarch in the group sustained as "prophets, seers, and revelators."[26] Importantly, there is reasonable evidence to suggest that succession was not President Smith's intention at all. When he discussed apostolic succession, he never included the office of Patriarch in that discussion.[27] When he proposed in the November 1901 special conference that the Patriarch be given priority when Church authorities were sustained, he explicitly stated that he wanted to follow "the law of the Church in relation to the *presentation* of the authorities of the Holy Priesthood as they were established in the Church [D&C 124:123–24], and from which I feel that we have no right to depart."[28] And he clearly authorized the Twelve with selecting and commissioning John Smith's successor in 1911, a strong signal of the Apostles' preeminence, for it was the "duty of the Twelve to look after these evangelical matters."[29]

Therefore, the proposition here (and this is admittedly a proposition based on a particular reading of the sources) is that President Joseph F. Smith's approach to his brother and his brother's office seems to represent a concrete application of President Smith's understanding of, and teachings about, the patriarchal order of the priesthood. Looking at it this way, his attention to the Church Patriarch shows ties to the past as well as implications for the future: it harked back to patriarchal precedents in his own family line, and it also suggested principles that have manifested themselves even in the Church's most recent handbook. For President Joseph F. Smith, the stature of a patriarch—whether the Patriarch to the Church or the patriarch in the home—was uniquely important, and because of that, it called for a unique type of deference and honor. Instead of being concerned with the Patriarch's place in the order of apostolic seniority, it seems that Joseph F. Smith's approach is better understood as a recognition that the hereditary nature of the office of Church Patriarch, this father to the Church, deserved respect precisely because it was different than other Church offices.

Only four months after becoming Church President, Joseph F. Smith wrote this: "The patriarchal order is of divine origin and will continue throughout time and eternity." He then spoke about the presiding authority that a father held in his own home, even if Apostles or stake presidents or bishops were also visiting in that home.[30] Significantly, in his discussion of different priesthood offices in the Church, President Smith explained that, first and foremost, patriarchs "are fathers."[31] This ties these teachings together: "This patriarchal order has its divine spirit and purpose, and those who disregard it under one pretext or another are out of harmony with the spirit of God's laws as they are ordained for recognition in the home. It is not merely a question of who is perhaps the best qualified. Neither is it wholly a question of who is living the most worthy life. It is a question largely of law and order, and its importance is seen often from the fact that the authority remains and is respected long after a man is really unworthy to exercise it."[32]

Now, obviously, this could be pushed too far. Worthiness did matter to President Smith, and when John Smith passed away in 1911, Joseph F. Smith instructed the Apostles "to go and talk personally with John's family, not with a view to selecting any one member of his family unless it be ascertained that he is worthy to act; and should it be found that neither of John's sons is capable and worthy for this position, it may be possible, President Smith said, that one of his grandsons may be found worthy and capable."[33] Indeed, Hyrum Gibbs Smith, John's grandson, was ordained the next Presiding Patriarch of the Church instead of John's oldest son (and Hyrum Gibbs Smith's father), Hyrum Fisher Smith.[34]

Reorganite Relatives, Plural Marriage, the Word of Wisdom, and Reticence

There are good reasons for modern readers to be cautious about assuming too quickly that John was not essentially living a "worthy" life, based on the standards of the day. Because of those standards, the worthiness questions that swirled around John Smith—Reorganite relatives, plural marriage, Word of Wisdom—deserve further comment, especially since by 1901, and because of various circumstances, those questions seemed to be largely resolved—or at least less troublesome. Finally, and even more significant here, it also seems that some of John Smith's General Authority colleagues complained most of all that John was not really a *Presiding* Patriarch—that is, he did not actively magnify a leadership role. It is in response to that deficiency that Joseph F. Smith's actions perhaps make the most sense.

First, the concern about the cousins of the Reorganization: In 1864, Joseph F. wrote to his brother in Denmark and informed him that some at home called him a "Josephite." John replied that it was "no new thing" because his wife Hellen "wrote the same" six months earlier. But what is most interesting about John's response letter is that the discussion of his being a Josephite is preceded by John's pleas for Joseph F. to help their brother-in-law, Lorin Walker; both John and Joseph F. feared Lorin was leaning toward the Reorganized Church. Lorin was the husband of John's older sister Lovina, and the Walkers had stayed first in Illinois until 1856, and then Florence, Nebraska, until 1860, so they had experienced a greater exposure to much of the Reorganization movement. What is most striking about this letter is what John wrote to Joseph about helping Lorin: "I beleave him to be an honets man but he lacks firmness or resolution. . . . If I were where I could see him . . . every month or two I could keep him straight, I hope you will take hime by the hand and talk with him. . . . I should very much dislik to have them go away now I have been to the trouble of getting them up there."[35] Lorin and Lovina did stay in Utah—and with the LDS Church.

There is no question that John maintained lifelong relationships with his Illinois cousins—and such bonds would seem, in many ways, only natural and expected. He was just six weeks older than Joseph Smith III; both were thirteen when John left Nauvoo. But those close family ties were also strained by the diverging trajectories of post-Martyrdom Mormonism—the subsequent competition for the loyalty of the Saints meant that those ties were subjected to an "aiding and abetting the enemy" type of scrutiny.[36]

The strength of John's language in various pieces of correspondence with his relatives says much about the strength of his convictions, convictions that he expressed soon after the exodus from Nauvoo. Joseph Smith III sent a letter to his cousin John in the spring of 1848. From the text of Joseph III's letter, it can be inferred that John had recently written to Joseph III, trying to persuade him to join their imminent westward march. Apparently, John had suggested that Joseph

III was being unduly influenced by other people because Joseph III lashed out at the thought that he "would condisend [*sic*] to be dictated by any person what [he] shall write and what [he] shall not write." Joseph III also revealed that John expected "largely upon helping to roll on the great work in the track of [their] fathers," and had obviously pled with his cousin and friend to join that work. Even in that earliest letter, Joseph III brought up the issue of plural marriage (he called it "spiritual wifery") and adamantly denied that either of their fathers "upheld such doctrines in public or practised them in private."[37] It is apparent that even for these teenaged boys, there was no mistaking the chief issue that divided their respective interpretations of their fathers' religion. John chose to go west.

Another vignette in this ongoing discussion took place in 1860. John, while in the East to help bring Lovina's family to Utah, visited Nauvoo and all of his relatives. This visit took place just a few months before Joseph III was appointed president of the Reorganization, and John was on the westward trail when he received word that the appointment was going to take place. In no uncertain terms, he sent a letter back to Nauvoo, urging his cousin to disassociate himself with a group that John feared would "make a tool of [Joseph] to carry out there schemes that they may get gain." He plainly stated, "As for my part I cannot sanction any such thing."[38] The letter reached Joseph after the action had already been taken, and therefore did not have its desired effect. But the letter did (and does) have the effect of speaking to John's loyalties and sympathies.

After that 1860 visit, John wrote about Nauvoo in a letter to his brother, since Joseph F., on his way to England, was planning to pass through that city. This brief note provides the interesting insight that John considered "the Prophet's family . . . basically still Mormons except for their rejection of polygamy."[39]

Any lingering doubts about John's commitment to the "Utah" church go unsupported in his mission correspondence. In no fewer than four consecutive letters to his brother Joseph F., John mentioned their cousin Solomon Mack in New Hampshire. Since Joseph F. would return home from England before John would return from Denmark, John requested that Joseph "go and see him when you get to New York," or at least "write to cousin Mack and punch him."[40] John wished he could "tak [*sic*] the business in my own hands . . . and bundle them up and push off in a hurry" on the return trip to Salt Lake City.[41] The concern evident in his repeated inquiries about this branch of the family gives a journal entry at the end of John's mission an even greater air of sadness: "I received a letter from Solomon Mack and his wife. . . . He wished he could go with me to Zion but his wife did not wish to go to Zion. She said that she had here [*sic*] reasons but would not tell them."[42]

Similar attention was given to the cousins in Colchester, Illinois. John had visited them sometime before his mission, and wrote to his brother that he wished Joseph F. would try and take their cousin "Don CS Millikin home with you next summer." In a very telling passage, John confided that he is "afraid that Cousin Joseph will get him to be baptised in there church if someone does not interfear."[43] Clearly, as Irene Bates and Gary Smith write, John's "friendship with his Reorganized Church cousins . . . did not alter John's commitment to the Utah church."[44]

John Smith had cast his lot for good with Brigham Young and his successors. Yet giving his loyalty to the so-called "Brighamite" Church with its principle of plural marriage did not, of course, mean that practicing that principle would come easily for him—and there are indications that it did not. In 1883, Joseph F. Smith complained to his apostolic colleagues that one of his concerns with his older brother's behavior was that John "'lived entirely with one [wife],'' even though he had married a second wife in 1857 at the encouragement of Brigham Young.[45] John's first wife, Hellen, wrote to Joseph F. about the inner turmoil she confronted when John married Nancy Melissa Lemmon. She said, "Dear Joseph it was a trial to me but thank the Lord it is over with. . . . I care not how many he gits now, the ice is broke as the old saing is, the more the greater glory."[46]

The understandable emotional toll this marriage took on Hellen is evident in a letter she wrote to John three months after his second marriage: "Talk about me apostatizing, God forgive me for I am a later day saint, but the Lord knows that I am know polygamist, and with the help of the Lord I will have nothing to do with it, can you understand that." In these and other letters, Hellen's strong will comes through, as does her love and loyalty to her husband, despite the difficulties of plural marriage. The poignant ups-and-downs that must have been a part of daily life come through too, in a letter from John replying to Hellen's suggestion that he "get two more wives when [he gets] home," but "on [her] terms." John's telling reply was, "I know that your generous hart is ever ready to do me good but for the present allow me to say that I have wives enough."[47] John and his second wife, Melissa, had one son, but that son died when he was only nine years old—and Melissa did receive financial support from the living allowance that came to John Smith because he was a General Authority.[48] With the hindsight that history affords, there is something to be admired even in these apparently halting efforts to live one's faith in the face of moments of heart-rending anguish—and there is something to be said in the fact that John, and Hellen, still devoted their lives to his service in the Church. And it seems likely that because of the Manifesto of 1890, the complexities of John's commitment to plural marriage largely, and circumstantially, faded into the background.

The most glaring of John's "follies," at least in terms of public notice, was his apparent laxness toward the standards of the Word of Wisdom. Today it would be unthinkable for a Church authority to drink a morning coffee or enjoy a little tobacco, but the attitudes of both Church members and Church leaders were significantly different in the nineteenth century. Some of the Patriarch's General Authority contemporaries were famous for struggling with these difficult habits.[49] Even Joseph F. Smith, who on occasion reprimanded his brother for his failings in this area, reported that on an August 1872 weekend camping trip in Big Cottonwood Canyon, everyone "attended to our prayers, & only violated t 'wofw' by drinking coffee."[50] This was a time when it seems that the establishment of this principle developed in a line-upon-line way, showing still that the Word of Wisdom was "adapted to the capacity of the weak and the weakest of all saints" (D&C 89:3).

Yet, in the later years of the nineteenth century and the first of the twentieth, the Word of Wisdom took on a greater urgency as a test of faithfulness; in fact, John's brother would do much to accelerate that change.[51] In that same 1883 setting where Joseph F. worried about John's halfhearted practice of plural marriage, Joseph F. also mentioned John's Word of Wisdom problems as a source of concern. When President Wilford Woodruff publicly chastised Patriarch Smith at that 1894 general conference, he specifically addressed John's "tobacco and smoking" and "liquor habits." President Woodruff, from the pulpit, said that if John thought "those things are of greater value then the Holy Spirit," then "[he] better resign."[52]

Again, historical hindsight allows for a degree of sympathy for someone caught between the rock of personal addiction and the hard place of a transition toward stricter Church norms. Early in Joseph F. Smith's administration, he "urged stake presidents and others to refuse recommends to flagrant violators, but to be somewhat liberal with old men who used tobacco and old ladies who drank tea."[53] This case-by-case leniency meant that the Word of Wisdom was progressing toward—but still not yet—a hard-and-fast standard for temple recommends.[54]

Nevertheless, it is obvious that in John Smith's case, some of his brethren in Church leadership became periodically (and publicly) impatient with him. As strongly worded as President Woodruff's reprimand had been, Joseph F. had suggested no less in the 1883 meeting with the Twelve and the First Presidency and various stake leaders of the Church. He at that time had "asked the brethren to use their influence that Bro. John might become a man."[55] John's reputation did occasionally suffer; John even wrote to Joseph F. in the late 1880s to defend himself against rumors that he (John) had been barred from the temple.[56]

Still, with all of this in mind, and based on the memory of Brigham Young Jr., President Brigham Young had apparently *another* reason altogether for seeking to replace John in 1875. Heber J. Grant remembered this conversation: "Brigham Young [Jr.] said that if his father had had his way that Joseph F. Smith would have been the Patriarch of the Church, but that brother Joseph F. had begged that the office be given to his brother and had almost refused to have it when his [Brigham Young Jr.'s] father wanted him to take the place. He knew that his father had felt strongly that Brother Joseph F. Smith should be the Patriarch. He felt that the Patriarch should be a man who could stand with the First Presidency of the Church and meet and counsel with them."[57]

President Brigham Young wanted a man who "could stand with the First Presidency" and the Quorum of the Twelve as presiding authorities, someone who could "counsel with them." John Smith did not seem to be that man. By all accounts, John Smith was not suited by disposition to preside. By his own admission, he shied away from public speaking, even demurring repeatedly when Brigham Young tried to have him say the benediction at conference.[58] (When Joseph F. and John Smith traveled together to a conference in Kaysville in 1871, Joseph F. recorded, revealingly, that he spoke for fifty-five minutes, and then John spoke for five!)[59] He worried about the work involved in keeping a record of all the Church's patriarchs as part of a suggestion that he oversee a quorum of patriarchs.[60] John Smith certainly was no William Smith—trying to grab more power—but neither was he an "Uncle" John Smith, his immediate predecessor, who served as president of the Salt Lake Stake, as well as an assistant counselor to the First Presidency.[61] That reality seems to have motivated Brigham Young's desire to have Joseph F. in the office.

But based on his refusal to accept Brigham Young's proposal, as well as his subsequent words and actions, it seems reasonable to assert that in the particular case of this specific office, Joseph F. Smith was attuned to something else. It seems that Joseph F.'s attention to the stature of the Patriarch (both the position itself and the brother who occupied that position) is better understood as a recognition that the hereditary nature of this office, this father to the Church, deserved respect precisely because it was different than other Church offices—and that it indeed was a question of *order* in this case, rather than, just as he had said about patriarchs in the home, a question of who is best qualified.

Order mattered deeply to President Smith. In the November 1901 special conference that was convened to sustain his new First Presidency, he said, "I do not know of any more perfect organization than exists in the Church of Jesus Christ of Latter-day Saints today. We have not always carried out strictly the order of the Priesthood; we have varied from it to some extent; but we hope in due time that, by the promptings of the Holy Spirit, we will be led up into the exact channel and course that the Lord has marked out for us to pursue, and adhere strictly to the order that He has established." With that prelude, he then read from what is now Doctrine and Covenants 124:123–24 and mentioned specifically the office of Church Patriarch: "It may be considered strange that the Lord should give [in D&C 124:124] first of all the Patriarch; yet I do not know any law, any revelation or any commandment from God to the contrary."[62]

And this is perhaps the point: Joseph F. Smith's efforts to respect that order, that familial right,[63] seemed to bear fruit in the life of his brother. John's grandson remembered that in his grandfather's later years, he did give up tobacco.[64] And while John may not have been naturally comfortable with the "presiding" half of his Presiding Patriarch calling, he in fact did more actively participate in leadership and administrative and training functions during his brother's administration.[65]

This says something important about Joseph F. Smith too. After all, Joseph F. Smith was a man who, as a teenage missionary, wrote to John about John's new patriarchal responsibilities and prayed that John would be as honored and respected as their father. Joseph F. Smith was a man who used double exclamation points when he first heard that his brother had given patriarchal blessings. This was a man who, as an Apostle, encouraged his brother and then scribed for him. This was a man who interceded on his brother's behalf before President Brigham Young. This was a man who asked his Church colleagues to help make "a man" of his brother. Importantly, this was a man who trusted his brother to give a patriarchal blessing to his own son, Joseph Fielding Smith. And this was a man who asked his brother to serve as voice to set him apart and ordain him to the highest office in the Church.[66]

Looking Backward and Forward

As mentioned earlier, in this spirit, Joseph F. Smith seemed to be both responding to precedent and setting precedent. There is much to commend historian Richard Bushman's analysis of Joseph Smith Jr.'s desire to honor his father with the office and calling of patriarch—especially in the gesture of having his father sit in the most elevated seat in the Kirtland Temple pulpits, a seat even above that of the Prophet. The Prophet Joseph said of his father, "Blessed of the Lord is my father, for he shall stand in the midst of his posterity and shall be comforted by their blessings when he is old and bowed down with years, and he shall be called a prince over them." Professor Bushman portrays this as an almost redemptive moment, since "like Adam [Joseph Smith Sr.], would assemble his children—his one undoubted accomplishment." This made "priesthood . . . a father's legacy to his son, counting for more than lands and herds."[67]

In the case of Joseph F. and John Smith, it seems that there are echoes of something that Joseph Smith Sr. said in blessing his sons. First to Hyrum, "Thou hast always stood by thy father, and reached forth the helping hand to lift him up, when he was in affliction, and though he has been out of the way through wine, thou has never forsaken him, nor laughed him to scorn." Then to Joseph, "Thou has stood by thy father, and like Shem, would have covered his nakedness, rather than see him exposed to shame."[68] This family legacy of honoring a patriarch seemed to have passed to Joseph F. Smith.

On the other hand, in terms of setting a precedent that is relevant in the modern Church, consider that in a 2010 Church worldwide leadership training meeting convened to introduce thoroughly revised handbooks, Elder Quentin L. Cook drew special attention to new instructions about the priesthood participation of fathers:

> Elder Oaks has said that these handbooks focus on the salvation of the children of God and the strengthening of their families. Under that focus, I call attention to some important changes that affect fathers performing priesthood ordinances and blessings. Please turn to chapter 20, section 20.1.2, which sets forth the general principle. It reads:

> "Only a Melchizedek Priesthood holder who is worthy to hold a temple recommend may act as voice in confirming a person a member of the Church, conferring the Melchizedek Priesthood, ordaining a person to an office in that priesthood, or setting apart a person to serve in a Church calling."
>
> Now note carefully the next two paragraphs:
>
> "As guided by the Spirit and the instructions in the next paragraph, bishops and stake presidents have discretion to allow priesthood holders who are not fully temple worthy to perform or participate in some ordinances and blessings. However, presiding officers should not allow such participation if a priesthood holder has unresolved serious sins.
>
> "A bishop may allow a father who holds the Melchizedek Priesthood to name and bless his children even if the father is not fully temple worthy. Likewise, a bishop may allow a father who is a priest or Melchizedek Priesthood holder to baptize his children or to ordain his sons to offices in the Aaronic Priesthood. A Melchizedek Priesthood holder in similar circumstances may be allowed to stand in the circle for the confirmation of his children, for the conferral of the Melchizedek Priesthood on his sons, or for the setting apart of his wife or children. However, he may not act as voice."
>
> Note the two important principles at work in these sections: First, recognition of the eternally significant role of fathers, and second, the discernment that must be righteously exercised by bishops and stake presidents.[69]

The suggestion here is that in these contemporary instructions there can be heard echoes, too, but this time of President Joseph F. Smith's voice, that the "patriarchal order has its divine spirit and purpose, and those who disregard it under one pretext or another are out of harmony with the spirit of God's laws as they are ordained for recognition in the home. It is not merely a question of who is perhaps the best qualified. Neither is it wholly a question of who is living the most worthy life. It is a question largely of law and order, and its importance is seen often from the fact that the authority remains and is respected long after a man is really unworthy to exercise it."[70] Similar sentiments seem to resound in President Smith's plea that his colleagues use their influence to motivate and inspire his brother to rise to the measure of his calling.

In the end, that is perhaps the most important chapter in this story, for while the "presiding" aspect may not have been part of John Smith's natural disposition, contemporaries witnessed that the "patriarch" aspect—that of a spiritual father or a prophet—indeed *was* part of his nature. One of his twenty thousand blessings is worth mentioning here. In this particular blessing, he told a young man, "The Lord has a work for thee to do, in which thou shalt see much of the world, assist in gathering scattered Israel and also labor in the ministry. It shall be thy lot to sit in council with thy brethren and preside among the people and exhort the Saints to faithfulness." That young man was a thirteen-year-old David Oman McKay.[71]

Elder James E. Talmage eulogized Patriarch Smith this way: "He was a patriarch in manner and life as well as in calling."[72] In reporting John's death, the *Salt Lake Tribune*—a paper not known for heaping praise upon the Church—memorialized Hyrum's oldest son by saying that "perhaps no man has been so widely known and loved by so many generations among members of the church. Few central figures in spiritual affairs of Mormonism have received such universal esteem and tribute."[73]

To contemporaries, Joseph F. Smith's wish for his brother expressed more than a half-century earlier—that he be "honored and respected as our father was"—had been realized. It is hoped that in some small measure, this paper would find approval in that vein as well.

Notes

1. For John Smith's biography, see Irene M. Bates and E. Gary Smith, "Continuing the Tradition," in *Lost Legacy: The Mormon Office of Presiding Patriarch* (Urbana and Chicago: University of Illinois Press, 1996), 123–50; see also Andrew Jenson, "John Smith," in *Latter-day Saint Biographical Encyclopedia*, 4 vols. (Salt Lake City: Andrew Jenson Historical Company, 1901–20), 1:183–86, 3:780. For examples of John's relative anonymity in recent works dealing with Latter-day Saint history, see Church Educational System, *Church History in the Fulness of Times (Religion 341–43)* (Salt Lake City: The Church of Jesus Christ of Latter-day Saints, 2000), 76, where John Smith is listed as Hyrum's son in a chart that illustrates Asael Smith's posterity, but he is not referenced in the index. Leonard J. Arrington, Susan Arrington Madsen, and Emily Madsen Jones, in their discussion of Mary Fielding Smith in the revised edition of their book *Mothers of the Prophets* (Salt Lake City: Bookcraft, 2000), do list John as part of the family, and mention his call as Patriarch, but leave out his name from their index (there is, in the index, a reference to Mary's "stepchildren"). The book's summary of John Smith's life after Mary Fielding Smith's death makes the mistake (an understandable one, considering the shared name) of saying that John was ordained Church Patriarch upon the death of his grandfather in 1854. In reality, John's grandfather was Joseph Smith Sr., who died in 1840. John Smith succeeded his

great-uncle (Joseph Smith Sr.'s brother John) as Patriarch. A common approach in biographies of John Smith's family members is to simply state that Hyrum had five living children at the time of his marriage to Mary Fielding rather than listing the children by name; see examples of this in *Teachings of Presidents of the Church: Joseph F. Smith* (Salt Lake City: The Church of Jesus Christ of Latter-day Saints, 1998), xi–xii, and Richard Neitzel Holzapfel and R. Q. Shupe, *Joseph F. Smith: Portrait of a Prophet* (Salt Lake City: Deseret Book, 2000), 14. One last example is the epilogue of a fictionalized biography of John's older sister, Lovina. It relates that she and her husband, Lorin Walker, emigrated west in 1856 with the help of Lorin's brother William, but fails to mention that the Walkers actually stayed in Florence, Nebraska until 1860, when John Smith came with the supplies to bring them to Utah. See Becky Paget, *The Belle of Nauvoo* (American Fork, UT: Covenant Communications, 1994), 189.

2. See Conference Report, October 1979, 25, for the statement read by President N. Eldon Tanner announcing the emeritus designation.
3. Along with Bates and Smith, *Lost Legacy*, 123–50, see also D. Michael Quinn, *The Mormon Hierarchy: Extensions of Power* (Salt Lake City: Signature Books, 1997), 116–31.
4. Stan Larson, ed., *A Ministry of Meetings: The Apostolic Diaries of Rudger Clawson* (Salt Lake City: Signature Books, 1993), 393.
5. Hyrum and Jerusha's children were Lovina (1827–76), Mary (1829–32), John (1832–1911), Hyrum (1834–41), Jerusha (1836–1912), and Sarah (1837–76). Family group sheets are included in Jerry C. Roundy, *Copies of a Biography and a History from Ralph Gibbs Smith concerning a Great Grandmother and a Grandfather* (Provo, UT: reprinted by Earl H. Peirce, 1999), Church History Library, Salt Lake City. The reprint includes an introduction, additional related text, photographs, and commentary.
6. Ralph Gibbs Smith, *A Biography of Patriarch John Smith* (1976), included in *Copies of a Biography and a History from Ralph Gibbs Smith*, 6. Ralph Gibbs Smith was John Smith's grandson. It is apparent that Ralph Smith relied on his grandfather's autobiography for much of his account. Compare John Smith, *Autobiography* (1885), Accn 1567, Special Collections, J. Willard Marriott Library, University of Utah, Salt Lake City, 5.
7. *Biography of Patriarch John Smith*, 6–7; spelling standardized. Compare John Smith, *Autobiography*, 5.
8. Joseph F. wrote in 1888, "After my mother's death there followed 18 months—from Sept 21st, 1852 to April, 1854 of perilous times for me." Joseph F. Smith to Samuel L. Adams, May 11, 1888; cited in *Teachings of Presidents of the Church: Joseph F. Smith* (Salt Lake City: The Church of Jesus Christ of Latter-day Saints, 1998), xv. One biographer noted that young Joseph was "so shaken that he fainted & suffered from shock to the extent that some feared for his life." Scott G. Kenney's notes, in Scott G. Kenney Collection, UU_Ms0587, box 5, folder 1, Special Collections, J. Willard Marriott Library.
9. John Smith, *Autobiography*, 6.
10. John Smith to Joseph F. Smith, January 31, 1856, in the John Smith Papers, Vault MSS 803, box 1, folder 30, L. Tom Perry Special Collections, Harold B. Lee Library, Brigham Young University, Provo, UT.
11. John Smith, *Autobiography*, 6; John Smith to Joseph F. Smith, January 31, 1856; original spelling retained throughout. Apart from the Smith children, an older man, George Mills, and an older woman, Hannah Grinnels, were also included in the household (and perhaps

another older woman as well—see Jenson, *Latter-day Saint Biographical Encyclopedia*, 185). Joseph F. Smith mentions that George Mills was "blind and deriped," and that the woman was "an old lady, whom we called 'Aunty' Hannah Grinnels." See Joseph F. Smith diary, November 13, 1860, Joseph F. Smith Papers, MS 1325, box 1, folder 11, Church History Library, The Church of Jesus Christ of Latter-day Saints, Salt Lake City; included on the two-volume DVD set *Selected Collections from the Archives of The Church of Jesus Christ of Latter-day Saints*, ed. Richard E. Turley Jr. Apparently, Hannah Grinnels had helped tend the children ever since Jerusha Smith's death, and the family had taken care of George Mills, "an old British soldier," since their days in Kirtland. See Arrington, Madsen, and Jones, *Mothers of the Prophets*, 98–99.

12. Joseph Smith Sr. was the Church's first Patriarch. He was followed in that office by his sons Hyrum and William, and then his brother John. Occasionally, Joseph Sr.'s brother Asael (or Asahel) is listed as an "unofficial patriarch" or "fourth patriarch" for the years 1845–46. See Jenson, *Latter-day Saint Biographical Encyclopedia*, 1:182, where he noted that "as his [Asael's] health was poor, he is not known to have taken any active part in the office of presiding Patriarch"; see also the helpful chart in appendix B of Bates and Smith, *Lost Legacy*, 235.
13. Quoted in Bates and Smith, *Lost Legacy*, 128, 125. John's name was presented for a vote of the Quorum of the Twelve in July 1854, but he wasn't set apart as Patriarch until February 1855. See *Wilford Woodruff's Journal, 1833–1898,* 7 vols., ed. Scott Kenney (Midvale, UT: Signature Books, 1983), 4:283
14. John Smith to Joseph F. Smith, August 7, 1863, in the John Smith Papers, Vault MSS 803, box 1, folder 30, L. Tom Perry Special Collections,.
15. See Bates and Smith, *Lost Legacy*, 128; Jenson, *Latter-day Saint Biographical Encyclopedia*, 1:186; John Smith, *Autobiography*, 10–12.
16. *Wilford Woodruff's Journal*, October 9, 1875, 7:249–50: "Last evening the 12 met at Presidet Youngs and after Discussing the Subjet of the Presidency & Twelve voted to drop John Smith from the Patriarchal Office & put in his place Joseph F Smith but during the day John & Joseph F had Seen Presidet Brigham and pled vary hard to try John another six month to see if he would magnify his calling any better than he had done in the past."
17. Joseph F. Smith, diary, September 17, 1871, Joseph F. Smith Papers, MS 1325, box 3, folder 1, Church History Library; included on the *Selected Collections* DVDs.
18. Wilford Woodruff, in an October 1894 general conference address, as cited in Bates and Smith, *Lost Legacy*, 139.
19. See Bates and Smith, *Lost Legacy*, 134–35.
20. See Larson, *Ministry of Meetings*, 337.
21. See Conference Report, October 1902, 83. For a thorough discussion of changes in the way the Patriarch's name was presented and sustained over the years, see Quinn, *Mormon Hierarchy*, 116–31.
22. See Larson, *Ministry of Meetings*, 358.
23. See the comments of President Joseph F. Smith at a November 10, 1901, "Special Conference" called by the First Presidency, in Conference Report, October 1901, 71, where, after reading from what is now Doctrine and Covenants 124:123–24 ("Verily, I now say unto you, I now give unto you the officers belonging to my Priesthood. . . . First, I give unto you Hyrum Smith to be a patriarch unto you"), he added, "It may be considered strange that the Lord should give first of all the Patriarch; yet I do not know any law, any revelation or any commandment from God

to the contrary. . . . At the same time we well know that this order has not been strictly followed from the day we came into these valleys until now—and we will not make any change at present. But we will first take it into consideration; we will pray over it, we will get the mind of the Spirit of God upon it, as upon other subjects, and be united before we take any action different to that which has been done." That last comment about unity seems especially significant, considering concerns raised by several apostles. See Elder Rudger Clawson's record of the June 1902 discussion of the Twelve about this issue in Larson, *Ministry of Meetings*, 457–58. Elder Clawson first recorded his own feelings (in third person): "And besides, the Lord has brought the apostles still closer [to] the Presidency by designating them, prophets, seers, and revelators. Not so in the case of the patriarch. He [Elder Clawson] viewed the present arrangement as being just right."; and then the feelings of President Brigham Young Jr.: "Pres. Young said that when Pres. [Joseph F.] Smith, the head, indicated what is right in this matter we would be ready to sustain him. Nevertheless, if he desires our views upon the subject, we will give them. Said, 'If I were John Smith, I would work where I am until the Lord calls me to stand before the Twelve. By urging his own claims, he only hurts himself and lessens rather than strengthens his influence.' When the matter comes up and Pres. Smith indicates what is right, let us accept the decision and be one." Apparently President Smith never did push this issue, and instead the only change made was to include the Patriarch in the list of prophets, seers, and revelators in the next general conference (held in October 1902).

24. See D. Michael Quinn's important and extensivelymreferenced treatment of changes to the Patriarch's role and position in the larger context of evolving Church government in chapter 4 of his *The Mormon Hierarchy: Extensions of Power*, 116–31. John Smith was explicitly sustained as "presiding Patriarch" in the November 1901 special conference called by President Joseph F. Smith and his new First Presidency, though the Conference Report for the previous conferences that year only list him as "Patriarch to the Church" (compare, for example, in Conference Report, April 1901, 44, and in Conference Report, October 1901, 62, 80). Contemporaries referred to, and understood, the office to be a presiding one, even after John Smith's death. For one example, see John A. Widtsoe, *Rational Theology*, reprint ed. (Salt Lake City: Signature Books, 1997), 100: "The Patriarchs of the Church possess the sealing and blessing powers and receive instructions from the Presiding Patriarch." *Rational Theology* was originally published in 1915 as a priesthood manual.

25. See Bates and Smith, "Introduction," *Lost Legacy*, 5–10.

26. See note 24 above. Quinn notes, in *The Mormon Hierarchy: Extensions of Power*, 123, that "this was the first time since Hyrum Smith in 1841 that a patriarch was given such a title."

27. See his discussion of succession in the (note the date) May 1902 *Improvement Era*, included in Joseph F. Smith, *Gospel Doctrine: Selections from the Sermons and Writings of Joseph F. Smith* (Salt Lake City: Deseret Book, 1986), 175: "When he [the President of the Church] dies, the calling of his counselors ends, and the responsibility of Presidency falls upon the quorum of Twelve Apostles, because they hold the Holy Melchizedek Priesthood and are the next quorum in authority."

28. President Joseph F. Smith at the November 10, 1901 "Special Conference" called by the First Presidency, in Conference Report, October 1901, 71; emphasis added.

29. See *Minutes of the Apostles of The Church of Jesus Christ of Latter-day Saints*, 4 vols. (Salt Lake City: Privately Published, 2010), L. Tom Perry Special Collections, Harold B. Lee Library,

Brigham Young University, Provo, UT, 4:98, for a record of this December 7, 1911 meeting: "President Smith, referring to the subject of the calling of Patriarchs, said he would like President Lyman and any of the brethren of the Apostles he might wish to have associated with him, to take up the question of a successor to the presiding patriarch, John Smith; and he would like them to go and talk personally with John's family, not with a view to selecting any one member of his family unless it be ascertained that he is worthy to act; and should it be found that neither of John's sons is capable and worthy for this position, it may [be] possible, President Smith said, that one of his grandsons may be found worthy and capable. As it is the duty of the Twelve to look after these evangelical matters, the President said he would like President Lyman and the Twelve to consider the matter of a successor to the Presiding Patriarch."

30. Joseph F. Smith, *Gospel Doctrine,* 287.
31. Joseph F. Smith, *Gospel Doctrine,* 181.
32. Joseph F. Smith, *Gospel Doctrine,* 287.
33. *Minutes of the Apostles of The Church of Jesus Christ of Latter-day Saints,* 4:98.
34. For a discussion of the circumstances surrounding this ordination, see Bates and Smith, *Lost Legacy,* 151–58.
35. John Smith to Joseph F. Smith, January 2, 1864, in the John Smith Papers, Vault MSS 803, Box 1, Folder 30, L. Tom Perry Special Collections; spelling in original.
36. See Bates and Smith, *Lost Legacy,* 131.
37. Joseph Smith III to John Smith, March 21, 1848, in John Smith Papers, Vault MSS 803, box 2, folder 43, L. Tom Perry Special Collections. It is possible that a crossed-out word in Joseph Smith III's letter, immediately preceding the phrase "spiritual wifery" might be "Brighamism," so that the sentence could have originally read, "You expiate largely upon helping to roll on the great work in the track of our fathers if you mean by this that I must support Brighamism [?] spiritual wifery and the other institutions which have been instituted since their deaths (for you very well know that they never upheld such doctrines in public or practised them in private) I most assuredly shall be your most inveterate adversary."
38. John Smith to Joseph Smith III, April 3, 1860, as cited in Buddy Youngreen, "Sons of the Martyrs' Nauvoo Reunion—1860," *BYU Studies* 20, no. 4 (Summer 1980): 355.
39. Youngreen, "Sons of the Martyrs' Nauvoo Reunion—1860," 356.
40. John Smith to Joseph F. Smith, March 14, 1863; see also letters dated December 27, 1862; February 10, 1863; June 8, 1863, in the John Smith Papers, Vault MSS 803, box 1, folder 30, L. Tom Perry Special Collections.
41. John Smith to Joseph F. Smith, March 14, 1863, December 27, 1862; see also letters dated February 10, 1863 and June 8, 1863, in the John Smith Papers, Vault MSS 803, box 1, folder 30, L. Tom Perry Special Collections.
42. John Smith mission diary, March 22, 1864, in John Smith Papers, Vault MSS 803, box 1, folder 3, L. Tom Perry Special Collections.
43. John Smith to Joseph F. Smith, December 27, 1862; spelling in original.
44. Bates and Smith, *Lost Legacy,* 124.
45. Quoted in Bates and Smith, *Lost Legacy,* 135.
46. This November 3, 1856, letter to Joseph F. Smith is cited in Bates and Smith, *Lost Legacy,* 127, as well as in an important article that gives insight into the strong relationship shared by John

and Hellen Smith; see Irene M. Bates, "The Wives of the Patriarchs," *Journal of Mormon History* 34, no. 3 (Summer 2008): 100.

47. The correspondence is quoted in Bates and Smith, *Lost Legacy,* 127, 129, and in Bates, "The Wives of the Patriarchs," 100–101.

48. See Bates, "Wives of the Patriarchs," 100, and Bates and Smith, *Lost Legacy,* 136. John admitted that he only infrequently wrote to Melissa while he was serving his mission in Denmark; in the 1880s he even apparently considered divorcing Melissa (which did not happen)—see Quinn, *The Mormon Hierarchy: Extensions of Power,* 121. John Smith's *Deseret News* obituary mentioned that he was "survived by his wife, Mrs. Melissa L. Smith"; Hellen had died four years earlier. Bates, "Wives of the Patriarchs," 103.

49. For a helpful overview, see Thomas G. Alexander, "The Adoption of a New Interpretation of the Word of Wisdom," in *Mormonism in Transition: A History of the Latter-day Saints, 1890–1930,* Illini Books edition, with a foreword by Stephen J. Stein (Urbana and Chicago: University of Illinois Press, 1996), 258–71. In writing about attitudes among Church leaders in the late 1890s, Alexander notes, "Though it seems clear that some church leaders like Heber J. Grant and Joseph F. Smith insisted upon complete abstinence from tea, coffee, liquor, and tobacco, all general authorities did not agree"—and Alexander then lists examples of those who did not practice or advocate such strict abstinence (*Mormonism in Transition,* 260). See also Bates and Smith, *Lost Legacy,* 139.

50. Joseph F. Smith, diary, August 15, 1872, Joseph F. Smith Papers, MS 1325, Box 3, Folder 2, LDS Church Archives; included on the *Selected Collections* DVDs. One year earlier, Joseph F. Smith had written that he "bought a coffee mill" for one dollar. Joseph F. Smith, diary, September 17, 1871, in Joseph F. Smith Papers, MS 1325, box 3, folder 1, Church History Library; included in the *Selected Collections* DVDs.

51. See Alexander, *Mormonism in Transition,* 261: "The death of Lorenzo Snow brought to the presidency Joseph F. Smith, whose views on the Word of Wisdom were close to those of Heber J. Grant. The path to the current interpretation of the Word of Wisdom leads from Smith's administration."

52. Wilford Woodruff, in an October 1894 general conference address, as quoted in Bates and Smith, *Lost Legacy,* 139. For public knowledge of John Smith's Word of Wisdom troubles, as well as his efforts to overcome such, see Bates and Smith, *Lost Legacy,* 129, 135, 139–40. See also Quinn, *The Mormon Hierarchy: Extensions of Power,* 121, 123.

53. Alexander, *Mormonism in Transition,* 261. See also Larson, *Ministry of Meetings,* 578–79, for this entry from 1903: "Pres. Lund [of the First Presidency] said that saints should be instructed that it is not right to move from place to place without counsel. Tobacco users should not be recommended to the temple, but cases might arise where a little leniency should be shown in regard to this matter." The growing attention to, yet persistent ambiguity around, Word of Wisdom adherence in the specific case of a *local* patriarch is illustrated in Elder Clawson's record of a later 1903 discussion. Following the recommendation by a member of the Twelve that a "former bishop of Wellsville be ordained a patriarch," the proposal was tabled since "it was known that [the man] had been addicted more or less to the use of liquor and tobacco, and it became a question of worthiness on his part to receive the patriarchal office. The matter was laid over for the present." Larson, *Ministry of Meetings,* 620.

54. See Alexander, *Mormonism in Transition*, 264: "In 1921 the church leadership made adherence to the Word of Wisdom a requirement for admission to the temple. Prior to this time, as indicated, stake presidents and bishops had been encouraged in this matter, but exceptions had been made." Alexander also quotes passages from the 1928 and 1933 editions of the Church's *General Handbook of Instructions* to illustrate the new inclusion of a passage about the Word of Wisdom as a strict temple recommend rule (Alexander, *Mormonism in Transition*, 265).
55. Bates and Smith, *Lost Legacy*, 135.
56. See John Smith to Joseph F. Smith, June 6, 1887, quoted in Bates and Smith, *Lost Legacy*, 136.
57. Heber J. Grant, diary, October 4, 1894, 143, as transcribed in the Kenney Collection, box 5, folder 1; emphasis added.
58. See Bates and Smith, *Lost Legacy*, 127.
59. Joseph F. Smith, diary, September 17, 1871.
60. See Quinn, *Mormon Hierarchy: Extensions of Power*, 121.
61. Quinn, *Mormon Hierarchy: Extensions of Power*, 121: "Four church presidents and the apostles encouraged him to become the Presiding Patriarch in the full sense of the term. Whereas William Smith had expected too much of the office, John Smith expected too little." For a discussion of "Uncle" John Smith, see Quinn, *Mormon Hierarchy: Extensions of Power*, 117; Bates and Smith, *Lost Legacy*, 104–22; and Lawrence R. Flake, *Prophets and Apostles of the Last Dispensation* (Provo, UT: Religious Studies Center, Brigham Young University, 2001), 311–12.
62. See the comments of President Joseph F. Smith at the November 10, 1901 "Special Conference" called by the First Presidency, in Conference Report, October 1901, 71; emphasis added. See another example of this attention to order cited in D. Michael Quinn, *The Mormon Hierarchy: Origins of Power* (Salt Lake City: Signature Books, 1994), 253, where Joseph F. Smith approved of the decision to "set apart" Lorenzo Snow as president of the Church whereas his predecessors had apparently not been set apart; in Joseph F. Smith's view, "[they] had failed to do something which he felt should have been done."
63. One additional important factor to consider is another of Joseph F. Smith's hallmarks: unfailing devotion to family. The intensity of this feeling was evident in so much of his personal and public life, but perhaps one case in point will suffice here. As President of the Church, Joseph F. Smith nominated two of his sons (Hyrum Mack and Joseph Fielding) and one of his cousins (George Albert Smith—his Uncle John Smith's grandson) to fill vacancies in the Quorum of the Twelve. While the Twelve Apostles unanimously sustained those appointments, they also discussed the reality that there would be inevitable criticism. Notwithstanding that criticism, it seems apparent that President Smith felt such appointments were appropriate and warranted—and he wished he could do more to honor family ties. On the occasion of nominating Hyrum Mack to fill the vacancy occasioned by the death of President Lorenzo Snow, he said, "I would be glad if we all had sons worthy of the apostleship, for I would like to see the sons of the apostles brought forward as far as possible. I feel that this is right." Larson, *Ministry of Meetings*, 341. Three years later, when he presented the name of George Albert Smith, he said that "he had made it a subject of prayer, for he desired the mind of the Lord respecting the matter. Many names of prominent families—such as Geo. Q. Cannon's, Daniel H. Wells', Wilford Woodruff's, Jno. Taylor's, Heber C. Kimball's, Parley P. Pratt's, Lorenzo Snow's, and others . . . had occurred to him." Larson, *Ministry of Meetings*, 660. It would be difficult, it seems, to ask where service to the family ended and service to the Church began in Joseph F. Smith's mind—and maybe that

would be asking the wrong question in any case. A fair analog might be found in Lucy Mack Smith, Joseph F.'s grandmother, who wrote about early Church history as the story of her family's ultimate sacrifices. See Richard Lyman Bushman, *Joseph Smith: Rough Stone Rolling* (New York: Alfred A. Knopf, 2005), 8–9. In that way it would only be natural to honor such sacrifice by recognizing the loyalty and leadership of these founding families—especially in honoring a position (Church Patriarch) that was hereditary and centered in the Smith family line.

64. There are good reasons to believe that John Smith did make efforts to conform to the rising Church standards—and that Joseph F. Smith's stance toward his brother's position reflected that. Irene Bates and Gary Smith frame the issue this way: "Despite the earlier criticism, . . . complaints about the Church Patriarch declined in the following years [after Joseph F. Smith's and Wilford Woodruff's reprimands]. Whether John Smith modified his behavior as a result of these criticisms is not apparent, although his grandson Ralph Smith claimed that he did" (Bates and Smith, *Lost Legacy*, 140). See also Quinn, *Mormon Hierarchy: Extensions of Power*, 123. Significantly, an interesting statement made by John Smith's nephew, Church apostle Hyrum Mack Smith, can be read in support of Ralph Smith's assertion. Elder Hyrum Mack Smith's statement was made in the context of the Apostles' discussion about Joseph F. Smith's (and John Smith's) proposal that a correct reading of what is now Doctrine and Covenants 124 would mean that the Church Patriarch should be sustained *after* the First Presidency, but *before* the Quorum of the Twelve (using their father Hyrum Smith as the precedent). As mentioned above, some of the apostles worried about the potential import of this change. Carried to its extreme, they saw this order of sustaining as leading to a misunderstanding by the Church's membership that the Patriarch would supersede the apostles in the order of succession. All agreed that this was not the intention, and apparently President Smith did not push the issue further; the only change made to the sustaining was to include the Patriarch in the list of the Church's "prophets, seers, and revelators." Yet in the course of the discussion concerning the reason for even considering such a change, Hyrum Mack Smith, the newest apostle, "took a little different view," as Elder Rudger Clawson characterized it, "to some of the brethren. He [Hyrum Mack Smith] understood that Brother John Smith lost his place in the line of presentation because of a failure to magnify his calling. If that be true, *and he repents, should he not be brought back into line*?" Larson, *Ministry of Meetings*, 457; emphasis added; the diary entry is for June 25, 1902. It does not seem unreasonable to suggest that Hyrum Mack Smith was here representing the view of his father, Joseph F. Smith, that the proposed change in sustaining order was motivated not by the question of succession, but (in addition to the prime issue of proper Church order) as a recognition of, or motivation toward, John Smith's reformation.

65. See evidence of that, for example, in Larson, *Ministry of Meetings*, 358, 461–63; Quinn, *Mormon Hierarchy: Extensions of Power*, 122–23.

66. On the double exclamation points, see Joseph F. Smith to John Smith, April 19, 1857, in John Smith Papers, Vault MSS 803, box 2, folder 46. On Joseph Fielding Smith's patriarchal blessing, see Joseph F. McConkie, *True and Faithful: The Life Story of Joseph Fielding Smith* (Salt Lake City: Bookcraft, 1971), 20.

67. Bushman, *Rough Stone Rolling*, 262–63. See also D. Michael Quinn, "The Mormon Succession Crisis of 1844," *BYU Studies* 16, no. 2 (Winter 1976): 202: "Determining what Joseph meant by his description of this office [Patriarch] as the highest in the Church is problematic, because the documents and history of the LDS Church from 1833 to 1844 unquestionably

refute the concept that the Presiding Patriarch's office was superior in authority either to the President of the Church or to the Quorum of the Twelve. . . . Perhaps the Prophet described that office as the 'highest' in honor, rather than in priesthood keys, due to the completely revelatory nature of its operation."

68. Bushman, *Rough Stone Rolling*, 262.
69. Elder Quentin L. Cook, "Selected Principles from the New Handbooks," *Worldwide Leadership Training Meeting* (2010); http://www.lds.org/broadcasts/article/print/worldwide-leadership-training/2010/11/selected-principles-from-the-new-handbooks?lang=eng.
70. Joseph F. Smith, *Gospel Doctrine*, 287.
71. Quoted in Church Educational System, *Presidents of the Church Student Manual: Religion 345* (Salt Lake City: The Church of Jesus Christ of Latter-day Saints, 2003), 146; quoting Jeanette McKay Morrell, *Highlights in the Life of President David O. McKay* (1966), 26. See also Gregory A. Prince and Wm. Robert Wright, *David O. McKay and the Rise of Modern Mormonism* (Salt Lake City: University of Utah Press, 2005), 5, for a description of President McKay's son's reaction to the prophetic promises in both David O. McKay's blessing and that of President McKay's younger brother, Thomas.
72. James E. Talmage, quoted in the *Deseret News*, November 13, 1911, as found in Journal History of The Church of Jesus Christ of Latter-day Saints, November 12, 1911, 15.
73. Cited in Journal History, November 6, 1911.

Personal Glimpses of Joseph F. Smith:

Adolescent to Prophet

Carole Call King, the great-granddaughter of Martha Ann Smith Harris, did not realize the treasure she inherited when her father passed away. Busy with the funeral and other family demands, she had overlooked the contents of one box. Left unnoticed on a closet shelf for a time, it finally caught her attention one day as she put away the vacuum. She discovered in the box, beneath her mother's chiffon wedding dress, three small, narrow boxes neatly wrapped in tissue paper. On them, her grandmother, Sarah Lovina Harris Call (1883–1961), had written with her own hand the words "Letters to mother." Inside she found nearly one hundred original letters written by Joseph F. Smith to his sister Martha Ann Smith Harris. Joseph F. and Martha Ann, the only children of Mary Fielding and Hyrum Smith, had written each other for nearly sixty years.

In the months that followed, Richard Neitzel Holzapfel, a professor from Brigham Young University, invited me to join the project of transcribing the letters of Joseph F. and Martha Ann. Additional letters written by Joseph F. to his sister were located in the Church History Library of The Church of Jesus Christ of Latter-day Saints, Salt Lake City, Utah (CHL). During the search to find Joseph F.

David M. Whitchurch is an associate professor in the Department of Ancient Scripture at Brigham Young University.

Envelope of a letter written from Martha Ann Harris to Joseph F. Smith on February 1, 1856. Courtesy of David M. Whitchurch.

Smith letters, a number of Martha Ann Smith Harris letters were discovered. The collection now comprises 180 letters written by Joseph F. Smith with 48 corresponding letters from Martha Ann Smith Harris.[1] This collection provides a rare glimpse into the personal life of adolescent Joseph F. whose circumstances prematurely thrust him into the responsibilities of adulthood in preparation to become prophet and President of The Church of Jesus Christ of Latter-day Saints.

Transcription Process

All letters between Joseph F. and Martha Ann were carefully transcribed to follow a systematized process to ensure reliability and accuracy of the transcription. The letters retain the original spelling, punctuation, superscripts, underlines, and strike-throughs. The transcribers have edited as little as possible, although some punctuation was altered for clarity. The following table provides a summary of the symbols used throughout the Joseph F. and Martha Ann Letter Collection.

Symbol		Description
[*italics*]	Square brackets	Italics within a square bracket used to describe missing words, partially missing words, or missing letters due to holes, tears, or cuts in the paper. Also used to describe illegible erasures from strike-through or illegible erasures
< >	Angle brackets	Readable strike-through, insertion, or correction
[...]	Bolded ellipsis in brackets	Used to indicate an omission in content from the original letter

Death of Mary Fielding Smith

After arriving in the Salt Lake Valley in 1848, Mary Fielding Smith purchased a forty-acre lot in the Mill Creek area, six miles southeast of the central Salt Lake settlement, where she and her family constructed a two-room adobe house.[2] Four years after she arrived in the Valley, while on a visit to Salt Lake, she came down with a debilitating illness, probably pneumonia, and died in the home of Heber C. Kimball on September 21–22, 1852.[3] She was just fifty-one years old. She left behind the children from the previous marriage of her deceased husband, Hyrum Smith, and her own son and daughter, Joseph F. and Martha Ann.[4]

Joseph F. and Martha Ann were devastated at the loss of their mother. Martha Ann wrote, "To lose my dear mother at the tender age of eleven was a severe trial in my life. I felt I did not care to live longer. My heart seemed crushed. I was not old enough at my father's death to fully realize it as I did the loss of my mother. I felt that the world was a blank. It was a sore bereavement which I felt I could never wear out with time."[5] Thirteen-year-old Joseph F. took his mother's death equally hard, turning deathly pale and fainting. It took considerable effort from those around to revive him.[6]

After their mother's death, Joseph F. and Martha Ann were cared for by Hannah Grinnels, a close family friend who had boarded with the Hyrum Smith family before Mary Fielding became Hyrum's second wife. Hannah remained with the family until she died at age fifty-eight, a little more than a year after Mary's passing.[7] Recalling this time, Joseph F. wrote, "After my mother's death there followed eighteen months . . . of perilous times for me. I was almost like a comet or fiery meteor, without attraction or gravitation to keep me balanced or guide me within reasonable bounds."[8] Evidence of this can be found in the account of a run-in he had with a schoolmaster. According to his own recollection, he and Martha Ann were in class when D. M. Merrick pulled out a leather strap to punish Martha Ann. When he told the girl to hold out her hand, Joseph F. shouted, "Don't whip her with that!" The schoolmaster turned on the young man, but the apparently stronger frontier boy "licked him good and plenty."[9] His actions resulted in his being expelled from school.[10]

The incident with his schoolmaster may also have influenced Brigham Young to send Joseph F. on a proselytizing mission.[11] During the April 1854 general conference, President Brigham Young read the names over the pulpit of those called to serve missions. A total of ten missionaries were called to the Pacific Isles, Joseph F. being the youngest one called. As reported in the *Deseret News,* these included Orson Whitney (age twenty-four), John Young (son of Lorenzo, age seventeen), Washington B. Rodgers (age twenty-eight), Simpson M. Molen (age twenty-two), George Spiers (age eighteen), Joseph Smith (son of Hyrum, age fifteen), Silas S. Smith (son of Silas, age twenty-three), Silas Smith (son of Asahel, age thirty-two), Sextus [Sixtus] Johnson (age twenty-four), and John T. Cain (age twenty-five).[12] Within a few months, Joseph F. had been ordained to the Melchizedek Priesthood, received his endowment, been set apart as a missionary and making his way with other missionaries to the Pacific Isles.[13] Traveling first to San Francisco by way of San Bernardino, the missionaries worked to pay for their travel expenses. Joseph F. and eight other missionaries finally left for the Sandwich Islands, arriving in Honolulu on September 27, 1854.[14]

It was there in the Sandwich Isles that Joseph F. Smith as a young missionary learning a new language in the middle of a new culture, began writing his sister. Pen and paper strengthened the bond between these two siblings throughout their lives. Several themes are evident through their sixty years of correspondence of which three will be addressed in this article: Joseph F.'s counsel to Martha Ann on the importance of education, Joseph F.'s dedication to missionary work in spite of the many hardships he faced, and Joseph F.'s perspectives on marriage and family.

Joseph F. Smith's Counsel to Martha Ann on the Importance of Education

Three weeks after Joseph F. arrived in the Sandwich Islands, he wrote his first letter to Martha Ann. Once in the mission, Joseph F. quickly realized the importance of education, because he lacked formal education of his own, as this letter vividly demonstrates. "My dear Sister," he wrote, "it is with pleasure and with very peculiar feeling that I take my peen in hand to write a fuw lines to you. [. . .] you must not git angery with me because I that I did not write to you before this time and this is what I call quite a present I came acrost this invelope which this letter is sent to you in. martha ann take good cair of this letter when you cut it. remember who sent it to you. [. . .] you must remember me in your prars day and night whare ever you are or what ever sircumstances you may be placed in."[15]

Aware of his lack own of education, in a letter written June 9, 1855, the fifteen-year-old Joseph F. Smith told his sister, "Go to school, as much as you can,

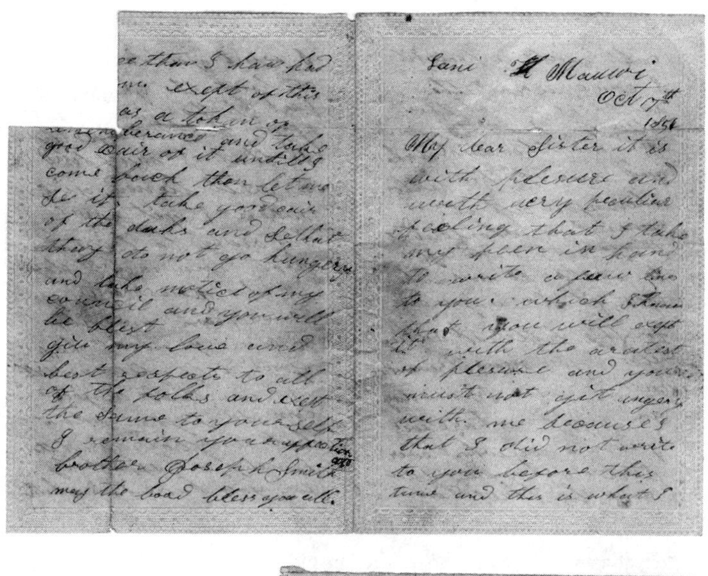

Lani [illegible] Mauwi
Oct 17th
1854

My dear sister it is with plesure and with very peculiar feeling that I take my pen in hand to write a few lines to you which I know that you will except it with the greatest of plesure and you must not git angry with me because that I did not write to you before this time and this is what I

...than I have had ... except of this as a token of rememberance and take good care of it untill I come back then let me see it take good care of the ducks and se that they do not go hungry and take notice of my council and you will be blest give my love and best respects to all of the folks and except the same to your self I remain your affection brother Joseph F Smith may the Lord bless you all.

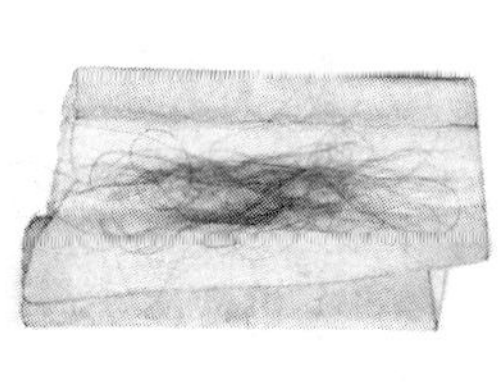

The first letter in the collection written by Joseph F. Smith to his sister Martha Ann was written on October 17, 1854. Courtesy of David M. Whitchurch.

and be attentive to study, for I know what it is to be without it, and you donot, at the Presant but will, when you are cast out into the woarld like I have been."[16]

Following the death of their mother, Joseph F. felt responsible for Martha Ann. He was not only her older brother but had in many ways assumed the role of a surrogate father and teacher. This relationship continued throughout their lives. Joseph F.'s first letter encouraged her to study her books "diligently so that I may find a well lirned girl when I git home in order to lirn your book you must stop in the house and go to school and stop running about keep your self jest as still and composed as you can se if you cannot bete enyboddy in the famely me espeshely for you have had a better [*text missing*] then I hav had."[17] In the very next letter to Martha Ann, Joseph F. again told her to "study your Book with diligence."[18]

Joseph F. also taught his sister about the need to make prayer part of the learning process, as evidenced in a short lesson on letter writing that he wrote as a sixteen-year-old to Martha Ann:

> I want to see you improve in writing, and every thing els, when you write take pains and make the letters all plain and destinct, and be shure to spell all of the words right that you can, [. . .] therefore you must improve everry moment of time that you can, [. . .] seek for wisdome and it shall be given to you, by an allmighty pour if you cannot get it by your own power, do you not know that there is a God in heven, who has said he that asketh recievth and he that seeketh find'th and he that knocketh it shall be opened, unto him,[19] and again he said, If any one lacketh wisdome let him ask god who giveth liberally ~~upbra~~ abraideth none,[20] now I will worant that if you will go to school with a prayerful heart, and your mind on your studies, insted of being upon play and folly, that you will learn faster than ever you did in your life before.[21]

Beyond recognizing the inherent value of education, Joseph F. likely saw a practical need for Martha Ann to go school. Simply put, her poor penmanship, grammar, and spelling made Martha Ann's letters extremely difficult to read. The first letter in the letter collection written by Martha Ann is dated January 31, 1856. She was just fourteen years old. It is evident that in the letter she is responding to her brother's concerns about her schooling:

> I hav been going to school to months now and am learning midling fast and I intend to learn a good deal faster than I have [. . .] I hav got a d<i>ctionary and I am sorry that I hav made mistakes in writing to you and both<e>ring you in reading my letters but you must excuse me this <time> and I will try to do better [*illegible strike-through*] <this [*illegible strike-through*]> time. [. . .] I intend to obey all that you counciled me to do iff it is in my pour. thank you dear brother for your good advice and if come up to the mark as you wish me to I wll be good enough for enny thing and I shall indever ~~to~~ by the help of the lord to do as you <w>ish me to do.[22]

It appears the demanding nature of farm life and lack of money prevented Martha Ann from attending school as often as she would have liked. Her

G. S. L. County Sugar House ward U S Jan 31st 1856

My dear and affectionate Brother Joseph
it is with pleasure that I
set down to write afew lines to you to answer
your kind and affectionate letter. I received it
this evening with the gratest of pleasure and
hapiness. to hear from you. John told me
that you was sick and I was sorry to hear
that for it will put you back agood deal I am
affraid but I hope ere this letter reaches your
you will be as well and harty as you ever was.
thank the lord, that of helth is ablessing
that I enjoy I havnot been sick soas to be
confined to my bed aday since youleft home.
and I wish that it had been so with you but
the lord orders all things for the best. I hav
been going to school to 6months now and am learning
midling fast and I intend to learn agood
deal faster than I have, we have got one of
the finest school houses in salt lake valley
and brother Eldredge keeps school and he is a
good school master. I hav got adictionary and
I am sorry that I have made mistakes in writing
to you and bothering you in reading my letters
but you must excuse me this time and I will try to
do better this next time. there is planty of diction
ary about and if you hav goot agood one
I would advise you to keep it even if you cold
send it for I presume that it is an artical
that you need your self when you are writeing
I hab written one letter to you befor that I
gave to John to send and he sent another
that I had witten in the place of it I wrote
it when I received the books that you sent me
I hav got all of the things you sent me

Letter from Martha Ann Harris to Joseph F. Smith on January 31, 1856. Courtesy of David M. Whitchurch.

responsibilities at home kept her quite busy, as her daughter Sarah Harris Passey details in a family history: "[Martha Ann] did many chores, morning and night, before and after school. She herded sheep on the hills east of home, many time barefooted until her feet would bleed. She spun wool into yarn and wove the yarn into cloth, blankets, sheets, jeans for men's clothing and linen with cotton war[p] and woolen wool for women's clothing."[23] At times, it was her poor circumstances that kept Martha Ann from school. In one letter, written in 1856, she explained, "I also live to Johns[24] yet, and and expect to this winter and go to school. school commenced last monday and I did not go then for I did not have enny shoos and I intend to start next mnday."[25]

Martha Ann recognized her poor writing skills and frequently apologized for them in her letters. When Joseph F. counseled her to write to her cousins in California (Ina Coolbrith and Agnes Smith),[26] she never followed through, possibly from embarrassment for her writing ability. Joseph F., however, may have unknowingly added to Martha Ann's trepidation to correspond with their cousins. "I have received a letter lately from Cousin Josephine," he once wrote. "She said she had written to you but had received no letter in return tolde me to speak to you about it, I would advise you to write to her. do your best to spell and write correct, for she is a good writer, this is what I wish you to progress in, till you are also a <u>good</u> <u>writer</u>."[27]

Whereas Joseph F. insisted that Martha Ann work hard in school, he explained why he did not expect much improvement in his own writing ability. In a letter dated July 25,1857, he stated:

> I have often tolde you I never expect to be a good writter, I've worked <u>too</u> <u>much</u>, at hard labor. I suppose you remember a certain ocasion <u>on</u> <u>which</u> I was <u>lain</u> <u>up</u> with a <u>Broken</u> <u>Bone</u> in my right <u>hand</u>,[28] I have never fully regained my usual agility in that hand, nor do I ever expect to;—It cramps my hand to write—so I am allways compelled to write as fast as posible—hence many mistakes and a bad hand-write.—I am verey careless too in writing—as I do not take much pride in it,—you should be more careful,—in writing—just say what you have to say—and then quit![29]

While Joseph F.'s early letters clearly demonstrate his own inexperience in letter writing, he would, in fact, go on to become an excellent writer. Martha Ann, however, would struggle with grammar and spelling throughout her life. To her credit and despite her poor writing ability, it was Martha Ann's persistence in writing to her brother that provides us with this illuminating collection of letters that offers so many insights into the life of Joseph F. Smith—future prophet of the Church.

Joseph F. Smith would emphasize the importance of education throughout his life. When writing to Martha Ann in December 1894, he told of his own family "which now numbers 36 souls—including myself" and although he had limited financial resources at the time, he told Martha Ann that "many of them [were] going to school."[30]

Joseph F. Smith's Dedication to Missionary Work through Hardship and Trial

Another prevalent theme throughout Joseph F.'s life was missionary work. In total, he served seven missions: three in the Sandwich Islands, two in Great Britain, one as president over the Europe Mission, and one in the eastern United States. Not surprisingly, Joseph F.'s letters to Martha Ann include many stories and comments related to preaching the gospel and the love that he had for missionary work. For the purposes of this paper, only a small sampling of mission experiences will be shared, most from letters he wrote during his first mission to the Sandwich Isles.

When Joseph F. first arrived in the Sandwich Islands in 1854, the mission was only four years old.[31] Joseph F. spent the first months of his mission very ill, but once he recovered, his determination and passion to preach the gospel quickly became apparent.[32] Through hard work he became proficient in speaking the Hawaiian language. Joseph F. wrote, "I have . . . been greatly blessed in obtaining a portion of their language, and by the blessings of the Lord I have got so that I can chat quite freely with the natives in their own tongue."[33] John Thomas Caine, a fellow missionary in the Sandwich Isles, wrote of Joseph F.'s linguistic ability: "Some of the brethren who came here first (I mean of our company) have advanced considerably in the language, and are speaking publicly. Among these, the most forward in the language is Joseph F. Smith, son of Hyrum."[34] His success in learning the native language likely influenced other assignments he received as a missionary. In July 1855, at the age of sixteen, Joseph F. was called to preside over the Church on the island of Maui. He later presided over the Hilo Conference and the Kohala Conference on the island of Hawaii.[35]

Living conditions in the Sandwich Islands were, in general, quite difficult. Saints and missionaries alike were poor. "I have slept in places," Joseph F. wrote, "where should my hog sleep my stumiche would forbid me eating of it."[36] On June 9, 1855, he made reference to preaching the gospel and his own hardships as he encouraged Martha Ann to maintain an optimistic outlook in dealing with problems at home:

> if you have any triyals to put up with, you must remember that it is to try you and to see whether you are smith grit or not, but sho your smith. [. . .] have patiance, and long suffering, be a Mormon out, and out, and you will be pl blessed, I find that thare is nothing that will try a person so as to tell this world that he is a mormon, but I feel first rate. I am fat, and stout, I feel like I could through all the hays down that thare is in the valeys. [. . .] I am a Preaching (Marty) like a good one, (you had aught to here me) or (or my voys, (I suppose if you wase any whare nee the Islands you could) we had a good meeting this morning, and I was caled upon to Preach, I acordingly, made an attempt, I expect, to go on my third trip around the Island. and if you ask Bro Lawson[37] he will tell you, how fare it is, and how bad the roads is, and what kind of houses we have to sleep in, and what kind of food to eat, &co,[38] and what kind of horses we have to ride also for we have to rid shanks horses[39] most of the time [. . .] and through all these difficultyes I get along first rate, and feel well.[40]

Even when he was homesick, Joseph F. found ways to maintain a positive outlook. In one letter he told Martha Ann, "Once in a while I got rite down lonesome, and commence to think that I would like to see Marty and the (ducks). besides to see the (rest) of the folks, but it is little that my mind is trubled with these thoughts for I try and drive them away."[41]

In the spring of 1857, Joseph F. wrote to Martha Ann about a harrowing experience representative of his faith and trust in God and the assurance that he had been divinely called to preach the gospel:

> Eight of us started from the Island of Lanai on Wednesday, and on acount of contrary and high winds we ware compelled to return to port, [. . .] at moon rise in the morning, (1 o clock) we went on board of our little Boat and started for this Island. Martha it would make you wonder if you could see us being tossed and driven by the waves of the mighty Paciffic, when every wave seemed

> like it was the next moment going to engulf us in ~~the~~ its auful surge, yes, to see us in an open Boat, with a tract of Ocean before us of some 15 miles, and only a one fourth inch of pine boards between us and the tremenduous, dreadful, yawning grave of thousands of poor ill-fated beings, who ware not so fortunate as ourselves; when you get with in a quarter of an inch of death itself, then who can save you?[42] Marth, the arm on which we trusted is that which hath delivered, it is ever willing to deliver, and will deliver all who lean upon it, and put all their trust on it, therefore lets be faithful. [. . .] I do not believe, that man lives outside of the kingdom of God that would begin to endure to allmoste indurable trials and privations that seem to beset us on every hand, and that we have to pass thro' evry day of our lives on these degraded lands, yet it is all for the best. I feel to rejoice, Martha, all the day long. I feel buoyant & hopeful, and like pressing forward, notwithstanding the hardships I have to encounter, because I know what I am doing, and for whom I am laboring.[43]

Through it all, the young missionary developed a great and tender love for the Saints on the Islands. Joseph F. noted the "good spirit" that prevailed at their meetings where he preached. Though some meetings were poorly attended, the Saints did occasionally enjoy some that were well attended. Joseph F. reported to his sister, "Where the saints are alive to the work, it is a chearing in sted of a labourious task to address them."[44] Clearly his commitment to the Lord, the demands of the work, and his love for preaching the gospel of Jesus Christ overshadowed all daunting tasks. In a letter written on July 25, 1857, he said:

> Mormonism is the verry life of my soul—I love it—would die for it without a groan. when ever I bare my testimony to it—I feel as though I could sink the world—hurl the eternal Hills into perpetual space, or shake the verry heavens with my strength! by this I know that the Spirit of the Lord Bears record of the Latter Work, and I never can deny its truth unless I lie! [. . .] my soul burns with-in me, and I fear and tremble. but those who have the same thoughts will know that feelings of this kind are easier experiansed than expressed—O! that we may "live our Religion!"[45]

Joseph F.'s mission was cut short in October 1857, when Brigham Young requested that all missionaries "that could be spared" be released and return home. US President James Buchanan sent an army to Utah to stop what had been

Page 3 of a letter written by Joseph F. Smith to Martha Ann dated July 25, 1857. The first line of the page begins, "Mormonism is the verry life of my soul!" Courtesy of David M. Whitchurch.

reported in the eastern newspapers as a "Mormon Rebellion."[46] President Young, expecting "to have warm times here," entreated the missionaries, "Would you not come and help us? if so, hasten to our midst."[47] Accordingly, Joseph F. and twelve other missionaries were released and gave farewell addresses during a conference the following day. Joseph F. arrived home in the Salt Lake Valley on February 24, 1858, where he immediately reported to Brigham Young and was assigned guard duty to protect the Saints against the encroaching army.

Soon the crisis was averted, and the Utah War ended. Joseph F. helped resettle some of his relatives in into their homes, including his cousin and future wife Levira Annette Clark Smith.[48] Shortly after they were married, Joseph F. would be called to serve another mission, this time in the British Isles. By accepting the call to serve in Great Britain, Joseph F. Smith once again demonstrated his commitment to serve in whatever capacity he was needed, a pattern that would prevail throughout his life.

Joseph F. Smith's Perspectives on Marriage and Family

During the years 1856 and 1857, the Saints in Utah experienced a period of spiritual awakening that has come to be known as the Mormon Reformation, characterized by religious zeal, introspection, and soul-searching. Church leaders frequently spoke to the Saints about greater commitment to gospel principles and focused on increased devotion. Martha Ann noted her own focus on reformation in a letter to her brother: "I hav been looking at my self and noticeing my self and triiy to reform and I see that I need a good deal of tutuing before I can become perfect."[49]

One aspect of the Mormon Reformation that profoundly influenced both Martha Ann and Joseph F. was the anxiety and enthusiasm with which the men in the territory pursued potential brides. "There is great excitment among the young folks here about getting married," wrote William Harris, a friend of Martha Ann's. "There is from twenty to forty a getting married evry day."[50] Historians estimate a 65 percent increase in plural marriages alone during 1856 and 1857 throughout the Utah Territory.[51]

Both Martha Ann and Joseph F. spoke often of marriage in their letters. In one letter written from the Sandwich Islands in 1856, Joseph F. wrote his sister about the importance of marriage. He said, in a somewhat humorous tone, "I hear that all the young people of your countrey are geting marred off—and that counsel is that they should continue to marrey. I think it is a good plan, the young folks are becomeing mormons fast. I am glad to here of it. I think it will be my turn next,(!)"[52]

Joseph F. explained in his letters to Martha Ann the sacred nature of marriage. He wrote the following to his sister upon first hearing of his sister's marriage to William Jasper Harris:

> You will certainly leave off Girl-ism now. I hope you will remember your possition, and let your actions and conduct in all things, and at all times be such as will store up for you Respect, Esteem, and Friendship in the heart of every honest and good person. now, do you want me to tell you the way to attain to this desireable possition?—prayer—with faith, and hope on Jesus and his Gospel, will alone do it. a person that holdes your stateon in the True Kingdom of God, need never fear the face of "Clay". [. . .] "lean not upon the arm of flesh."[53] I can never save you, neither can I be saved by aught but my own good faith and works—now if you are sinceerly prayrful, the spirit of prayer is the spirit of God and it will lead you "into all truth"[54] & will never ~~urr~~ <err>. you will never yeald to temptations, and allurements, but will stand fast, and ever True to him with whome you have covenented to abide through all the vicissittudes of Life and death.[55]

While it is clear that Joseph F. saw the importance of marriage, he also expressed some concern about Martha Ann getting married too young. On June 14, 1857, he wrote, "I do not want you to make any vows, with any one if you can avoid it."[56] He warned that it would be better not to make such a promise without being sufficiently mature. Unbeknownst to him, however, Martha Ann had already married.

Two months earlier, fifteen-year-old Martha Ann had married William Jasper Harris.[57] The arrangement was rather sudden and unexpected. As William prepared to serve a mission in the British Isles, President Heber C. Kimball asked him if there was anyone he would consider marrying. When he gave the name of Martha Ann, President Heber C. Kimball instructed him to "go and get her right now and be married."[58] William went home, asked Martha Ann for her hand, and they returned to the Endowment House to be married. It was a short honeymoon; William left on his mission two days later.[59]

Martha Ann did not write her brother with the news for nearly a month, but finally, on May 3, 1857, she shared, "Dear b<rother> I have an itam of news to write to you and my hand trembles when I go to write it for my concence is gilty before my brother for I fear that he will think I have slited him but for give me dear brother if I say that I have [*illegible erasure*] but I fear that it will dampen your feelings but I can not help it now I must say it enny how I am married—to William harris."[60]

Joseph F. answered his sister's announcement in a letter dated July 25, 1857. His response demonstrated his sincere concern and love for his sister that offers a perspective on his deep understanding of marriage: "I was somwhat surprised on hearing of your marriage. but as I was not there to partisipate in the ~~in the~~ scene, I can only wish you much joy;—and happy life You have now taken the moste important step of your life—or existance—under the Bonds of the Gospel. upon the step you have just taken is pending all the social enjoyments—and happiness of your present existance—and the Blessings of a happy and chearful home. as well as an obediant and God-like posterity."[61]

Some years later, as Martha Ann began to have children, Joseph F. shared his thoughts on raising a righteous family: "Inspire their youthful hearts to love virtue and dispise vice. Encourage and succor every noble and Godly aspiration of their Souls, and check with a kind and motherly affection, but with a firm, unwavering hand every tendancy to disobedience, or wrong. [. . .] Never—No! Never!! Scold them.—It is the greatest folly in the world to Scold. if any thing needs to be said, it may be said calmly, and affectionatly, not in a passion. Scolding of any kind is usless, and worse, it is a folley, and a crime. reason, counsel, instruct, but never scold."[62]

Much later, in 1874, he discusses the great example that their mother, Mary Fielding Smith, had been in their own upbringing: "Indeed yours is a thorney path in this world as mothers was, your patience and endurence are almost if not quite equal to hers. I only wish you had her education and her bold and firm decision, from which when once the [. . .] aim was fixed, in truth & right—neither prayers, nor tears, nor sympathy could move it. I wish I had these qualities myself, as she had them. We would both be better off."[63]

Joseph F. clearly understood the important role that mothers played in teaching and raising children. He eventually had five wives and forty-eight children and was frequently absent from home. On June 18, 1890, worried about being arrested by federal marshals for practicing plural marriage, he wrote:

> God has blessed me with good wives, and my children with good mothers; and O, how I feel to bless them, and to thank God. How all hell would grin <with delight> and the Devils laugh to see me "go back" on them! And well they might! but I have not the remotest idea of gratifying them in that regard. Exilement for the remainder of my life, or imprisonment till death, would

Joseph F. Smith family portrait dated November 13, 1904. Courtesy of David M. Whitchurch.

> be meat and drink to my soul, if necessity compelled me to suffer it for their sakes. They have been true to me, by Gods help I will be true to them in time and throughout all eternity![64]

However, just as his family brought Joseph F. some of his greatest joys, it also brought him some of his greatest sorrows. In late May 1870, his family was dealt a devastating blow when their two-year-old Mercy Josephine fell ill. Joseph F. tenderly cared for his young daughter throughout her illness. In his journal he recorded the toll it took on him. "I have no apetite," he wrote. "My sympathy & solicitude for my darling little Josephine, has greatly bowed my spirit. . . . She is a sensitive, delicate, and tender little creature and loves her 'papa.'"[65] On June 6, Joseph F. attended to his duties at the Endowment House during the day. When he returned home later that afternoon, he found that little Josephine had passed away.[66] Two months later, to the day, he wrote the following to Martha Ann:

> The weather is very oppressive, and the atmosphere sultry and merky, as tho' impregnated with smoke. Much as it was on the days memorable as the 27th, of June 1844. And the 21st. and 22nd of Sept. 1852—the day of fathers death, and the death and burial of Mother,[67] I recollect them distinctly. It is two months to day since my own sweet babe joined her grand father and mother [. . .] I mourn

> the earthly loss of the brightest, purest, dearest, treasure God ever gave me. the one, I prized and cherished most, within the great circle of that greatest gift of God "Eternal Life," which is incomparable, being "All in All," and yet as if to compensate in some degree, for my bereavement, fresh sweetness and beauty, increasing inteligence, and love daily developes in my precious, cheerful, merry little "rose bud", left me to bloom and blossom in my cottage "alone." O! in the midst of sorrow, I can say, I thank God for my three sweet, perfect little gifts, "one on earth and two in heaven",[68] the centre of my love, my own sweet "Jode."[69]

Joseph F. would bury thirteen of his children before his own passing. According to Julina, he loved them all but never got over losing his firstborn.[70] "He never got to where he could talk of his 'Dodo'[71] without tears in his eyes."[72] Nearly twenty years later, after he had buried his eighth child (Ruth),[73] he wrote his sister in words reminiscent of so many other letters of sorrow: "You will no doubt remember our sweet little Ruth—to be loved—she needed only to be seen. To be admired she had but to be heard—for she was one of the brightest little Souls I ever saw. But O! my Soul, we have had to yield her spirit up to God who gave her, and her sweet little body to the grave. She was buried to day. I should have written you sooner but to tell the truth my poor heart has been in the icey chamber with the cherished lovely form of my darling babe! I could not write."[74]

Joseph's tender love for his family was apparent not only in letters throughout his life, but also in his teachings as a prophet. In 1915, President Joseph F. Smith encouraged the Saints of the Church to hold a "Home Evening" in which they could spend time together as a family. He said in introducing the program, "This 'Home Evening' should be devoted to prayer, singing hymns . . . scripture-reading, family topics and specific instruction on the principles of the Gospel. . . . Love at home and obedience to parents will increase. Faith will be developed in the hearts of the youth of Israel, and they will gain power to combat the evil influence and temptations which beset them."[75]

Conclusion

In a decisive move, Church president Brigham Young (1801–77) called fifteen-year-old Joseph F. on a mission to the Sandwich Islands (Hawaiian Islands) during the April 1854 general conference. Joseph F. left his young twelve-year old sister, Martha Ann, in Utah, and made his way to California and then on to Hawaii.

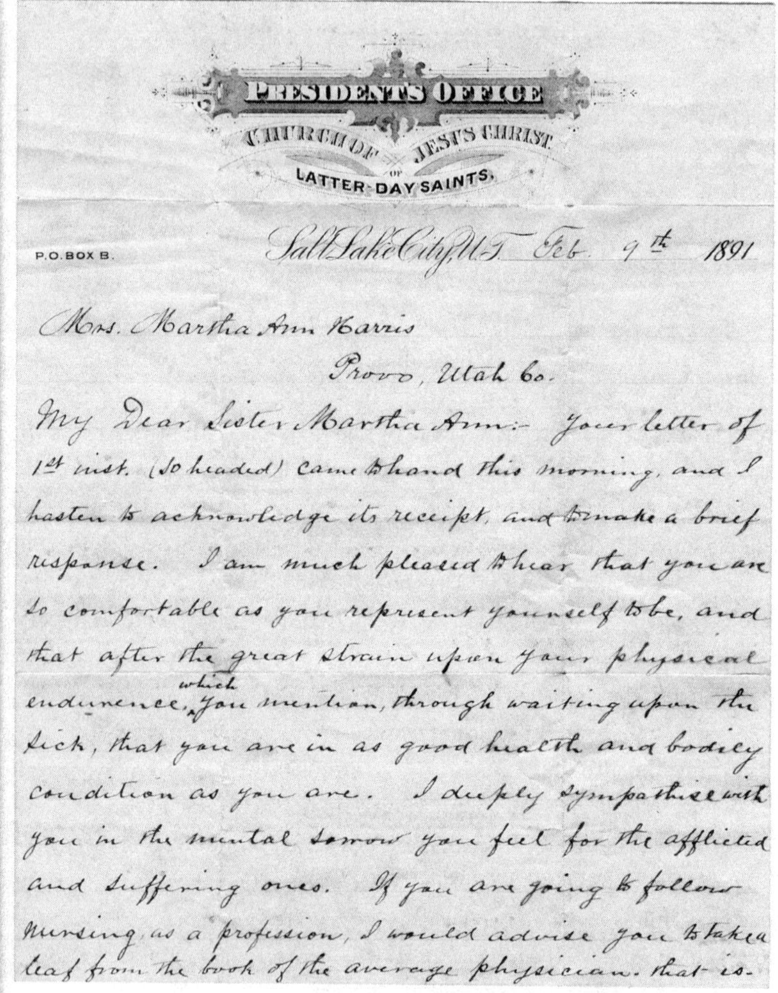

President's Office
Church of Jesus Christ of Latter-Day Saints.
P.O. Box B.
Salt Lake City, U.T. Feb. 9th 1891

Mrs. Martha Ann Harris
Provo, Utah Co.

My Dear Sister Martha Ann:- Your letter of 1st inst. (so headed) came to hand this morning, and I hasten to acknowledge its receipt, and to make a brief response. I am much pleased to hear that you are so comfortable as you represent yourself to be, and that after the great strain upon your physical endurence, which you mention, through waiting upon the sick, that you are in as good health and bodily condition as you are. I deeply sympathise with you in the mental sorrow you feel for the afflicted and suffering ones. If you are going to follow nursing, as a profession, I would advise you to take a leaf from the book of the average physician. that is.

Letter from Joseph F. Smith to Martha Ann Harris on February 9, 1891, written while he was serving as President of the Church. Courtesy of David M. Whitchurch.

It was during this three-year mission that Joseph F. began to correspond with his sister. They would continue to communicate through letters for six decades.

While only a few letters from Martha Ann have been included in this paper, her diligence and dedication in writing to her brother should not go unnoticed. Martha Ann's faithfulness, commitment to the gospel, and pioneering spirit reflect the heart and soul of a remarkable and courageous woman. Martha Ann often wrote to Joseph F. about the gratitude she had for him. An excerpt from Martha Ann's letter captures the heart and sensitivity of Joseph F. Smith, future prophet of the Church. "I am thankful to my father for giving me a brother that cears for mya. wefare," she wrote in one letter, "for I know that you care for my welfare more than enny boddy else can ~~feel~~ <care> fore upon this irth O Joseph would to god that I could expres feellings just as they are and [*illegible erasure*] I express my thanks to you for your kindness to me. I can never for git you for ever."[76]

The Joseph F. Smith and Martha Ann Smith Harris Letter Collection provides a rare glimpse into the personal life of Joseph F., the sixth President of The Church of Jesus Christ of Latter-day Saints, and his beloved sister. Their correspondence provides a rare view of the personal interaction between a brother and sister who were bound by blood and devotion to the cause of the Restoration. From the martyrdom of their father, Hyrum, in 1844, and the death of their mother, Mary, in 1852, they were strengthened in the furnace of affliction to confront the many trials that came their way. To Martha Ann, her brother was "my truest most faithfull friend,"[77] and to Joseph F., she would always be "My Dear beloved Sister Martha Ann."[78]

Notes

1. For the complete collection of letters between Joseph F. Smith and his sister, see David M. Whitchurch and Richard Neitzel Holzapfel, eds., *My Dear Sister: Letters between Joseph F. Smith and His Sister Martha Ann* (Provo, UT: Religious Studies Center, Brigham Young University; Salt Lake City: Deseret Book, forthcoming); original spelling preserved in all letters cited.
2. Leonard J. Arrington and Susan Arrington Madsen, *Mothers of the Prophets* (Salt Lake City: Deseret Book, 1987), 104–5.
3. Arrington and Madsen, *Mothers of the Prophets*, 105–6.
4. Joseph F. Smith (JFS) was born November 13, 1838, in Far West, Caldwell County, MO, to Hyrum Smith and Mary Fielding Smith. Martha Ann Harris (MHS) was born May 14, 1841, in Nauvoo, Hancock County, IL, to Hyrum Smith and Mary Fielding Smith.
5. Don Cecil Corbett, *Mary Fielding Smith: Daughter of Britain* (Salt Lake City: Deseret Book, 1966), 270.
6. Corbett, *Mary Fielding Smith*, 265.
7. When Hannah Grinnels died, a little more than a year later, it appears that Martha Ann lived with her half-brother, John, and his wife, Hellen Maria Fisher, in the family home and with her mother's sister, Mercy Rachel Fielding, who lived nearby. Following Martha Ann's marriage to William Jasper Harris, she lived with her mother-in-law, Emily Hill, a wife of Abraham Owen Smoot, while Martha Ann's husband served a mission in England. Upon his

return, they eventually settled in Provo, Utah, where she remained until her death in 1923. See Corbett, *Mary Fielding Smith*, 43, 273.

8. Joseph Fielding McConkie, ed., *Truth and Courage: Joseph F. Smith Letters* (unpublished manuscript, copy in possession of author, 1998), 6.
9. Joseph Fielding Smith, *Life of Joseph F. Smith, Sixth President of the Church of Jesus Christ of Latter-day Saints* (Salt Lake City: Deseret News, 1938), 229.
10. There is no record that explains why Merrick had chosen to discipline Martha Ann on this occasion. Later, B. D. Cummings reported that "President Smith speaks highly of him as a teacher . . . and states that under him made more rapid progress than any other teacher"; see B. F. Cummings, "Shining Lights: How They Acquired Brightness," *Contributor*, January 1895, 174.
11. Hyrum M. Smith and Scott G. Kenney, *From Prophet to Son: Advice of Joseph F. Smith to His Missionary Sons* (Salt Lake City: Deseret Book, 1981), 2.
12. See *Deseret News*, April 13, 1854, 2.
13. Smith, *Life of Joseph F. Smith*, 164–65.
14. Smith, *Life of Joseph F. Smith*, 168.
15. Holzapfel and Whitchurch, *My Dear Sister*, letter dated October 17, 1854.
16. Holzapfel and Whitchurch, *My Dear Sister*, letter dated June 9, 1855.
17. Holzapfel and Whitchurch, *My Dear Sister*, letter dated October 17, 1854.
18. Holzapfel and Whitchurch, *My Dear Sister*, letter dated November 1, 1854.
19. See Matthew 7:8; Luke 11:10; 3 Nephi 14:8.
20. See James 1:5–6.
21. Holzapfel and Whitchurch, *My Dear Sister*, letter dated October 18, 1855.
22. Holzapfel and Whitchurch, *My Dear Sister*, letter dated January 31, 1856.
23. Sarah Harris Passey, "Martha Ann Smith Harris," unpublished manuscript in possession of authors, courtesy of Carole Call King, granddaughter of Sarah Harris Passey.
24. John Smith, half brother of JFS and MSH. He was born September 22, 1832, in Kirtland, Geauga County, OH, to Hyrum Smith and Jerusha Barden. John married Hellen Maria Fisher on December 15, 1853, in Salt Lake City.
25. Holzapfel and Whitchurch, *My Dear Sister*, letter dated December 17, 1856.
26. Agnes Charlotte Smith and Josephine Donna Smith are the daughters of Don Carlos Smith and Agnes Moulton Coolbrith. Josephine Donna Smith would change her name to Ina Coolbrith and would be the first poet laureate of California. Ina's father, Don Carlos Smith, was the brother of Hyrum Smith and Joseph Smith Jr. See Roy B. Huff, "Don Carlos Smith," in *United by Faith: The Joseph Sr. and Lucy Mack Smith Family*, ed. Kyle R. Walker (American Fork, UT: Covenant Communications, 2005), 384–86. See also Josephine DeWitt Rhodehamel and Raymund Francis Wood, *Ina Coolbrith: Librarian and Laureate of California* (Provo, UT: Brigham Young University, 1973), 316–17.
27. Holzapfel and Whitchurch, *My Dear Sister*, letter dated June 14, 1857.
28. During his childhood, JFS broke a bone in his hand when he hit a hired farmhand who was chasing his older brother John with a pitchfork. See Blaine M. Yorgason, *From Orphaned Boy to Prophet of God: The Story of Joseph F. Smith* (Ogden, UT: Living Scriptures, 2001), 159.
29. Holzapfel and Whitchurch, *My Dear Sister*, letter dated July 25, 1857.
30. Holzapfel and Whitchurch, *My Dear Sister*, letter dated December 24, 1894.

31. George Q. Cannon, along with other missionaries, had visited the Islands in early December 1850. The mission had been dedicated on December 13, 1850. See R. Britsch, *Unto the Islands of the Sea: A History of the Latter-day Saints in the Pacific* (Salt Lake City: Deseret Book, 1986), 94–95.
32. Francis M. Gibbons, *Joseph F. Smith: Patriarch and Preacher, Prophet of God* (Salt Lake City: Deseret Book, 1984), 32.
33. JFS to George A. Smith, March 19, 1855, published in *Deseret News*, July 11, 1855, 7.
34. Smith, *Life of Joseph F. Smith*, 173.
35. The conference referred to was probably held in October 1856. At this conference JFS was transferred to preside over the Kohala Conference, still on Maui. See Smith, *Life of Joseph F. Smith*, 184.
36. Copied by JFS into his journal; letter dated July 4, 1856. Unless otherwise noted, all references to JFS's journal are taken from the document housed in the Church History Library in Salt Lake City.
37. James Lawson was a close friend of the Smith family. He was called on a mission to the Sandwich Islands in the fall of 1852, beginning his service there in 1853 and serving at least until the end of 1854. He appears to have been in Utah in 1855 but returned to the Sandwich Islands with his wife in 1856.
38. The abbreviation "&c." was commonly used for *et cetera* at this time. The abbreviation "& co." typically stood for "and company." JFS likely confused the two.
39. "Shanks' mare" or "shanks' horse" was an idiom referring to one's own legs, meaning here that the missionaries generally had to walk. See *Oxford English Dictionary*, 2nd ed. (Oxford: Clarendon Press, 1989), "shank."
40. Holzapfel and Whitchurch, *My Dear Sister*, letter dated June 9, 1855.
41. Holzapfel and Whitchurch, *My Dear Sister*, letter dated June 9, 1855.
42. JFS's experiences on the ocean may well have been part of his determination, during a later mission to the Sandwich Islands in 1864, to advise a group of his brethren not to attempt to land their smaller boat in a harbor under the conditions at that time. Their refusal to heed his counsel resulted in a capsized boat and the near drowning of Apostle Lorenzo Snow. See Smith, *Life of Joseph F. Smith*, 213–16.
43. Holzapfel and Whitchurch, *My Dear Sister*, letter dated April 17, 1857.
44. Holzapfel and Whitchurch, *My Dear Sister*, letter dated May 25, 1856.
45. Holzapfel and Whitchurch, *My Dear Sister*, letter dated July 25, 1857.
46. "The Mormon Rebellion," *New York Times*, February 16, 1858, 2.
47. JFS Journal, October 3, 1857. See also Smith, *Life of Joseph F. Smith*, 186–87.
48. Levira Annette Clark Smith was the daughter of Levira Clark and Samuel Harrison Smith, brother of Joseph Smith Jr. JFS and Levira married on April 4, 1859, and she filed for legal separation on June 10, 1867.
49. Holzapfel and Whitchurch, *My Dear Sister*, letter dated December 17, 1856.
50. Holzapfel and Whitchurch, *My Dear Sister*, letter dated February 3, 1857.
51. See Stanley S. Ivins, "Notes on Mormon Polygamy," *Western Humanities Review* 10 (1956): 231.
52. Holzapfel and Whitchurch, *My Dear Sister*, letter dated February 18, 1856.
53. See 2 Chronicles 32:8; 2 Nephi 4:34; Doctrine and Covenants 1:19.
54. See John 16:13.

55. Holzapfel and Whitchurch, *My Dear Sister,* letter dated July 25, 1857.
56. Holzapfel and Whitchurch, *My Dear Sister,* letter dated June 14, 1857.
57. William Jasper Harris was born October 25, 1836. He married Martha Ann Smith on April 21, 1857, at age twenty. Together they would have eleven children.
58. Richard P. Harris, "Martha Ann Smith Harris," *Relief Society Magazine,* January 1924, 15.
59. Harris, "Martha Ann Smith Harris," 15.
60. Holzapfel and Whitchurch, *My Dear Sister,* letter dated May 3, 1857.
61. Holzapfel and Whitchurch, *My Dear Sister,* letter dated July 25, 1857.
62. Holzapfel and Whitchurch, *My Dear Sister,* letter dated April 3, 1863. It is interesting to note that Joseph F. Smith was twenty-four years old when he wrote this letter and, at this point, still did not have children of his own.
63. Holzapfel and Whitchurch, *My Dear Sister,* letter dated August 5, 1874.
64. Holzapfel and Whitchurch, *My Dear Sister,* letter dated June 18, 1890.
65. JFS journal, June 5, 1870.
66. Smith, *Life of Joseph F. Smith,* 456–57.
67. Joseph Smith Jr. and Hyrum Smith were martyred at Carthage Jail on June 27, 1844; September 21 and 22, 1852, as JFS indicates, were the death and burial of JFS and MSH's mother, Mary Fielding Smith.
68. The two children in heaven that JFS makes reference to are Sarah Ella (born February 5, 1869; died February 11, 1869; daughter of JFS and Sarah Ellen Richards Smith) and Mercy Josephine (born August 14, 1867; died June 6, 1970; daughter of JFS and Julina Lambson Smith).
69. See Holzapfel and Whitchurch, *My Dear Sister,* letter dated August 6, 1870. The name "Jode" may be another nickname for Mercy Josephine Smith, JFS's recently deceased daughter, or it may be a simple spelling error. In other letters she is referred to as "Dode." Holzapfel and Whitchurch, *My Dear Sister,* letter dated June 25, 1870.
70. While all the deaths of JFS's children were hard on him, it seems that Mercy Josephine's death took a particular toll on JFS because she was his firstborn child.
71. Likely another pet name for his daughter Josephine.
72. Julina Lambson, journal, 1912, as cited in Smith, *Life of Joseph F. Smith,* 458–59.
73. Ruth Smith, Edna's daughter (born December 21, 1893), died on March 17, 1898. See *Deseret News,* March 18, 1898.
74. Holzapfel and Whitchurch, *My Dear Sister,* letter dated March 19, 1898.
75. Joseph F. Smith, Anthon H. Lund, Charles W. Penrose, First Presidency letter, April 27, 1915. See also "Home Evening," *Improvement Era,* June 1915, 733–34.
76. Holzapfel and Whitchurch, *My Dear Sister,* letter dated May 3, 1857.
77. Holzapfel and Whitchurch, *My Dear Sister,* letter dated May 31, 1874.
78. Holzapfel and Whitchurch, *My Dear Sister,* letter dated June 21, 1869.

Matthew C. Godfrey

10

"My Dear Charlie": The Friendship of Joseph F. Smith and Charles W. Nibley

In late June 1911, Joseph F. Smith, President of The Church of Jesus Christ of Latter-day Saints, sat in front of a special House of Representatives committee investigating the influence of the Sugar Trust in the nation's sugar industry. A subpoena had brought President Smith, who also served as president of the Utah-Idaho Sugar Company, to Washington, DC, and he was not in a talkative mood. Facing Representative Thomas W. Hardwick, chairman of the committee, President Smith, who just a few years earlier had had a less-than-pleasurable experience before the Senate committee investigating Reed Smoot's right to sit as a senator,[1] volunteered little information other than the bare minimum needed to answer Hardwick's questions. At one point during Smith's testimony, Hardwick, who was seeking information about the Lewiston Sugar Company in Utah, asked him, "Who is Charles W. Nibley?" The following exchange occurred:

> Mr. SMITH. I understand he is the president of that company [the Lewiston Sugar Company].

Matthew C. Godfrey is the managing historian of The Joseph Smith Papers *at the LDS Church History Department in Salt Lake City.*

The CHAIRMAN. He is also the business manager of the church, is he not—the bishop in charge of its temporal affairs?

Mr. SMITH. He is the presiding bishop of the church; yes.

The CHAIRMAN. Is he not the one man who is supposed to be the real business manager of the church's business affairs?

Mr. SMITH. Well, I presume so; yes.

The CHAIRMAN. Do you know whether he has any money of the church in that concern [i.e., the Lewiston Sugar Company] or not?

Mr. SMITH. I do not think he has.

The CHAIRMAN. You do not think he has?

Mr. SMITH. No, sir.[2]

The questioning then went in a different direction.

Taking Smith's terse responses to Hardwick at face value, one might think that he was only vaguely familiar with Nibley. In reality, Bishop Nibley and President Smith had been close friends, even best friends, for nearly thirty-five years and had made the journey to Washington, DC, together. The two regarded each other as brothers, traveling together frequently, corresponding, remembering each other's birthdays, and vacationing together with their families. "It is doubtful if Joseph F. Smith had at any time among his brethren a closer or more trusted friend" than Charles Nibley, Joseph Fielding Smith, son of Joseph F., explained, and "it is equally doubtful if Charles W. Nibley was ever drawn so near any other man as he was to Joseph F. Smith."[3] Correspondence between the two that began in 1877 and continued until Smith's death in 1918 provides insights into what attracted these two men to each other and why they maintained such a close friendship. Examining this close friendship provides a glimpse into the human side of both of these Church leaders. It also provides a window into the views of two men who were key leaders of the Church in the early 1900s, as well as key leaders of the Church's business enterprises.

Like many Latter-day Saints in Utah Territory in the mid-1800s, both Joseph F. Smith and Charles W. Nibley experienced childhoods filled with adversity and economic deprivation. Smith was born in 1838 in Far West, Missouri, just before the Saints were driven from that area by Missourians intent on fulfilling Governor Lilburn Boggs's extermination order. When Smith was five, his father, Hyrum, was killed in Carthage, Illinois, along with his uncle, Joseph Smith,

Joseph F. Smith shortly after his mission to the Hawaiian Islands, 1858. This copy print was probably based on an earlier daguerreotype. © Intellectual Reserve, Inc.

In 1846, Smith, together with his family, began the trek from Nauvoo, Illinois, to the Great Basin, arriving in what would become known as Utah in 1848. Although still young, Smith assumed many responsibilities on the trek, including driving a team of oxen. After arriving in the Salt Lake Valley, Smith and his

Left: Glass plate photo of Charles W. Nibley at age sixteen, ca. 1865. Courtesy of USU Special Collections and Archives; right: Charles W. Nibley, 1873.

family eked out a meager existence. According to one biography, Smith learned from his mother, Mary, the importance of hard work and thrift, as she was "the soul of thrift and economy, of industry and tireless energy." In September 1852, however, Mary died, leaving Smith an orphan at the age of thirteen. From that point on, he had to fend for himself, working as a "herd-boy."[4]

Nibley had similar difficulties in his upbringing. Born in 1849 in Scotland, Nibley and his family migrated to the United States in 1855 after his parents' conversion to Mormonism. Staying for a period of time in Rhode Island, the family moved to Utah Territory in 1860. There, they relocated to Cache Valley, an area in northern Utah still in the infancy of settlement. Residing in Wellsville, the family tried to make a living from the land, but it proved difficult. Nibley remembered living in "a little one-room, part dugout and part log house" for several years, as well as wearing clothing made from a tent. He and his family had only a paltry amount of food to eat. At the age of twelve, Nibley hired out as a sheep-hand "on the hills southeast of Wellsville," allowing him to help provide for his family. Those years were not easy for the young teenager. "It was a scramble of the severest kind for a mere existence," he later remembered. Yet, much like Smith, Nibley learned the value of hard work and thrift from his mother, who "was all energy and push and never seemed to tire of working and scheming to get on in the world."[5]

Their similar experiences, which were not unusual for Latter-day Saints trying to survive in the Great Basin, may have been one reason why Smith and Nibley formulated such a deep friendship. However, the two did not know each other until many of these hardships had passed. Nibley recalled that the first time he saw Joseph F. Smith was when the recently called Apostle preached in Cache Valley in the late 1860s. Nibley later remembered the Apostle as "a fine specimen of young manhood," blessed with "a beautiful voice, so full of sympathy and affection, so appealing in its tone." He regarded Smith as a "preacher of righteousness" without compare: "He was the greatest that I ever heard—strong, powerful, clear, appealing."[6]

In 1877, the two became better acquainted when both were called to serve in the European Mission: Smith as mission president and Nibley as a missionary.[7] According to Smith, the friendship blossomed after Nibley, who had never actually met the Apostle, approached Smith and asked whether he needed any kind of financial assistance to travel to Europe. The offer touched Smith, who reflected on it many times in later years, explaining that "the generosity of that act impressed me with the tenderness of heart and nobility of soul that prompted it." Smith stated that he "was thankful that [he] did not need to accept" Nibley's offer, but the gesture still provided "a grand lesson which my soul and sense approve and applaud."[8]

After traveling to England, Smith and Nibley worked closely together, as Nibley served in the mission office as financial manager. This enabled him to become acquainted with Smith's family. Evidently, one of Smith's young sons—Joseph Richards, who was four at the time—took a liking to Nibley and formed a close bond with him, calling him Uncle "Shawlie" and gaining a place in Nibley's heart.[9] Smith's wife Sarah, who accompanied him on the mission, also treated Nibley with kindness, especially during a bout of homesickness that Nibley experienced.[10] In addition, Nibley's financial prowess and administrative abilities gained Smith's trust. "I have the utmost confidence in you, that you will do all you can to save and use wisdom in the management of matters committed to you," Smith told Nibley on one occasion.[11] On another occasion, after reviewing financial records prepared by Nibley, Smith commented, "it is certainly a good showing, the credit of which is largely due to the 'chief clerk.'"[12]

After only a few months, Smith returned to Salt Lake City because of Brigham Young's death, remaining there indefinitely. He was not immediately released as president of the European Mission, though, and thus kept a close correspondence with Nibley relative to mission matters.[13] For example, Smith provided advice and counsel to his friend on the migration of Saints from Europe to the United States while also requesting that Nibley send him financial records. He instructed Nibley to chastise leaders of the conferences in Europe for a downturn in the payment of tithing, and advised him on potential leaders in the mission.[14] Engaging in such close counsel increased Smith's respect for the missionary. One example shows how Nibley's abilities and initiative impressed Smith.

In January 1878, Smith told Nibley that he had "full power to consummate any bargain for next year" in terms of rates for emigrants crossing the Atlantic Ocean.[15] Nibley thus executed a contract for such rates. Perhaps surprised at how quickly the missionary fulfilled his instructions, Smith expressed concern at what he regarded a premature action. The Church's agent had not yet closed on railroad rates in New York, Smith explained, and now might not be able to obtain "as favorable termes [*sic*] with the R. Roads" because of Nibley's contract. "What surprised me the most," Smith declared to Nibley, "was that you closed a bargain without first letting us know something of the terms." He hoped that the situation would "work out all right."[16] Smith's initial reservations, however, vanished after receiving the terms of the contract. "I was and am very much gratified with the bargain closed with Mr. Ramsden," he declared. "I think you did well." Smith was so pleased with the arrangement that he told Nibley that he had his "hearty approval in all [he] did."[17] Just two weeks later, Smith reinforced this trust, telling his friend that he was "leav[ing] matters of expediency entirely with [him] as to the emigration." Nibley could "do in every emergency just what you think for the best, and I will back you."[18] Nibley's business sense and efficiency had clearly earned Smith's respect.

Even after Smith was released as president of the European Mission in June 1878,[19] he continued to keep a close correspondence with Nibley. Smith also became acquainted with Nibley's young family in Utah, taking the opportunity whenever he was in Cache Valley to check on Nibley's wife Rebecca and his children. "We found your family in excellent health and spirits, prosperous and happy as they can be without you," Smith informed Nibley in May 1878. "'Alex' [who was two years old] wanted to come with me to 'yide on the T'ain,' but when I asked him to wait till tomorrow, he said 'All Yite.' and was happy."[20] Nibley reciprocated his correspondent's kindness by purchasing silk in England for Julina and Edna, two of Smith's wives, so they could make "coats or capes for themselves."[21] He also expressed sympathy when Smith's son Alfred passed away on April 6, 1878, the third of the Smith children to die at a young age.[22] Since Nibley had experienced the death of his own child—his first daughter at the age of one and a half in 1871[23]—he could empathize with his friend. "I appreciate your kind sympathy . . . in the temporal loss of my beloved little Alfred J.," Smith told Nibley. "I regard my present loss however as another strong link in the chain binding and drawing me closer to the other and better world."[24]

When Nibley returned from his mission in 1879, Smith met him at the train station and allowed him to stay at his home in Salt Lake City for a few days. The two then went their separate ways. Nibley moved back to Cache Valley, where he took a job as the manager of the United Order Lumber Company and served in the superintendency of the Cache Stake Sunday School, while Smith continued his service as an Apostle, worked in the Church Historian's Office, and became a counselor to President John Taylor in 1880. Both men experienced some difficulties in the 1880s because of their practice of plural marriage. In 1880, Nibley married Ellen Ricks, who joined Rebecca Neibauer as one of Nibley's wives. He then married Julia Budge in 1885 as his third wife. Smith had first entered plural marriage in 1866 when he married Julina Lambson as his second wife. Smith had also married Sarah Ellen Richards in 1868, Edna Lambson (Julina's sister) in 1871, Alice Ann Kimball in 1883, and Mary Taylor Schwartz in 1884.[25]

As the federal government increased its efforts under the Edmunds-Tucker Act of 1882 to prosecute those practicing plural marriage, both Nibley and Smith were forced into hiding to avoid arrest. Despite his efforts, Nibley was arrested in Idaho in 1885 for unlawful cohabitation, although he was never convicted.[26] Although plural marriage engendered hardships, both men believed strongly in the principle. According to Nibley, it was "a true principle revealed from God through the Prophet Joseph Smith for the salvation and blessing of all those who are worthy to receive it." The principle, he believed, had "greatly enlarged our souls and made us just a little more God-like in our lives."[27] Joseph F. Smith shared similar sentiments, calling plural marriage "a pure and holy principle" and one that could only be "practiced acceptably before God" by righteous individuals.[28]

It is unclear from extant records just how much interaction Nibley and Smith had in the 1880s, but in the 1890s, they became associated in business when Smith took some stock in the Oregon Lumber Company, a firm that Nibley started with David Eccles and John Stoddard in 1889.[29] Beginning this enterprise fit well with Smith's beliefs about the necessity of Church members engaging in industries that would benefit the Latter-day Saints as a whole. In 1878, he had discussed with Nibley the issue of the Union Pacific Railroad having a monopoly over rail transportation. "We are at the mercy of the U.P. for every ton of coal we use; and we pay them a royalty of from 2$ to 4$ pr. ton on the same." According to Smith, such a situation was problematic. "Why should we not own our Rail Roads when we have built them?" he asked. Or "why should we sell our coal mines when we need them for our own use, and can work them with our own labor?" In Smith's view, the Latter-day Saints were "shaping, it would seem, to become the 'hewers of wood and the drawers of water,' '[t]he tail and not the head.'" He hoped that, "with God's help," the Saints could build up their own industries, bringing in "millions" to Utah and allowing them "to weald [*sic*] a scepter of power, that would startle, and command the admiration of our nation and the world."[30] Although there is no evidence that Nibley was acting on Smith's concerns in establishing the Oregon Lumber Company with Eccles and Stoddard (both of whom were also Latter-day Saints), creating the business was a step in the direction that Smith wanted the Saints to go, as it provided lumber and other necessities to church members living in Utah, Idaho, and the Pacific Northwest.

Nibley's management of the company meant that he had to relocate to Baker City, Oregon, leading to a renewal of his correspondence with Smith. Letters between the two often touched on financial issues, as well as on the management of the Oregon Lumber Company. When the financial panic of 1893 hit, for example, Smith declared to Nibley that "no such close times as we are having now, have been experienced here since 1857"—the time when Albert Sidney Johnston led a contingent of federal troops to Utah Territory in response to accusations of rebellion among the Mormons.[31] "Our fears of Johnstons [*sic*] Army and the hard times were only as flea-bites compared to the bite of scorpions," Smith related, "in comparison to our fears of financial stringency and prospective hard times now."[32] Yet the Oregon Lumber Company continued to prosper despite the larger economic downturn, in part because of a contract it had concluded with the Union Pacific Railroad for favorable rates in lumber shipments—a contract that Nibley had a large hand in obtaining. Because of Nibley's role in securing the contract, he believed that he was entitled to a greater portion of compensation than David Eccles, the company's president, was allowing him. Although Smith was careful not to disparage Eccles, he agreed that Nibley had a right to the extra compensation. "As a stock-holder who had benefitted, in common with the rest, out of that transaction," he explained to Nibley, "I am willing, and feel that I ought to share a portion of such benefits or profits with <u>you</u> who secured, and to whom I am endebted [*sic*], for them."[33] The outcome of this particular situation is not clear from the historical record, although Nibley and Eccles would break off their business relations just a few years later.[34]

As he explained to his friend, Smith was grateful for the dividends that he received from Oregon Lumber—dividends that resulted from Nibley's capable management. "Surely kind Providence and the energetic managers of the O.L.C. deserve better than mere thanks from the Stockholders," Smith declared in 1895. "They are entitled to the highest of praise for their indefatigable labors and their skillful management of the business."[35] In making such statements, Smith hoped that Nibley understood that he did not "love money"; however, with "33 Souls, exclusive of myself, to feed, clothe, house and warm and school," he had "need of it." Therefore, whenever he received any kind of monetary sum, he "thank[ed] the Lord and my good friends who make it for me and supply me with it."[36]

While in Oregon, Nibley sometimes received visits from Smith and his family. In 1896, Smith traveled to Oregon, staying with Nibley in Baker City; in 1899, he made another visit, traveling with Nibley and his family to Portland and the Oregon coast. "How richly we enjoyed the precious season and sweet pleasure of our visit with you," Smith told Nibley.[37] These vacations led to a practice of frequent travel for the pair. After Smith was appointed President of the Church in 1901, he and Nibley took several trips together to Europe and Hawaii. In 1906, for example, when he had "a nice little bank account," Nibley paid for Smith and his wife Edna to travel to Europe with Nibley for a three-month visit. The group went to Great Britain, Germany, the Netherlands, Belgium, Switzerland, and France.[38] Although the group met with many Church members in these countries and President Smith gave several talks, he still found time to relax and later remembered the excursion as his "first real free-from-care trip" since becoming President and "an oasis in my sort of desert life."[39] Traveling together became a favorite pastime of the two and a way for Smith to relax from his responsibilities. By 1918, the two had taken four trips to Hawaii and two trips to Europe. "Surely it was a great favor and blessing to me to be thus privileged to associate with one whom I so dearly loved and who was always so companionable with me," Nibley declared.[40]

On these excursions, as well as at other times and in their correspondence, the two conversed about a variety of subjects, especially politics and economics. Both men were staunch Republicans at the time; after the 1900 election, for example, Smith exulted to Nibley about the Republicans' success, both in national and Utah politics.[41] Yet, in terms of Republican Reed Smoot's service as one of Utah's senators, the two friends disagreed. As the two returned from Europe in 1906, they discussed Smoot, a member of the Quorum of the Twelve Apostles, and his role as senator. "I took the position that it would be unwise for Reed Smoot to be re-elected to the United States Senate," Nibley recalled, in part because of the controversy congressional hearings into Smoot's right to sit as a senator had generated between 1904 and 1906. After listening to Nibley's "facts, arguments, and logic," Smith pounded the railing with his fist and declared, "If ever the Spirit of the Lord has manifested to me anything clear and plain and positive, it is this, that Reed Smoot should remain in the United States Senate. He can do more good there than he can anywhere else." The argument ended at that point; Nibley later explained that he "accepted from that hour [Smith's] view of the case and made it [his], too."[42] Indeed, Nibley became one of Smoot's strongest supporters and consulted with him frequently in the 1910s on matters affecting Nibley's business interests.[43]

The two friends also shared similar ideas about economics. Both men considered frugality to be a key aspect of economic life, in large part because of their meager upbringing. "I have learned to value even the small things, from necessity," Smith related to Nibley in 1877, while also declaring that he tried to steer clear from debt.[44] "I abhor debts," he informed Nibley at one point, "and so should every man."[45] Accordingly, whenever Nibley—who became a wealthy man in the 1890s and 1900s from his different business ventures—loaned Smith money or paid for some of his expenses, Smith tried to repay him promptly. "Please find herewith my cheque No. 4, of this date, for $1,319.50 for payment of my note of April 13th last," he wrote Nibley in 1916. This sum covered the original note plus interest for three months.[46] At other times, Smith was unable to repay his friend, something that weighed on his mind. "I dispair [*sic*] of ever getting even with you," he declared in 1903. "[I]t seems so far beyond my reach, but if ever I can requite you or yours in part, it will be a happy day for me."[47]

Smith's aversion to financial obligations extended to the Church as well, and he frequently counseled Church members and those responsible for Church finances to avoid debt. "By all means the Conferences must be clear from debts," Smith had instructed Nibley in 1877 in regard to the European Mission, "and none of them should be suffered to run behind."[48] When, in the late nineteenth century, the Church had considerable debt, Smith looked forward to the day when it could extricate itself from its obligations. "We hope soon to be able to return to the simple tithing of the people for the building of the temples, and for all other legitimate expenses of the church; . . . that Zion may prosper, and all be well," he had stated in 1877.[49] In the early twentieth century, after the Church had eliminated its debt, President Smith told his son David Smith, one of Nibley's counselors in the Presiding Bishopric, to tell Nibley, who by then was Presiding Bishop of the Church, to "see to it that I and no other man, in his time, shall ever suffer the Church again to get into debt."[50]

Nibley shared Smith's views of the necessity of living within one's means, but he also believed it worthwhile to contract some debt, especially when it led to more money down the road. In 1914, Nibley was presented with an opportunity to buy out the interest of the American Sugar Refining Company in the Utah-Idaho Sugar Company and the Amalgamated Sugar Company. According to his autobiography, Nibley "tried to induce President Smith to take more of the stock and still more, but he naturally shrinks from debt" and refused to purchase a large amount.[51] "The President," Nibley explained to Hyrum M. Smith, Joseph F.'s son, "dislikes to pay interest on borrowed money, and, of course, dislikes to borrow any money."[52] Nibley was able to convince Smith to allow him to purchase a large number of shares for the Church, but it was only after working with him "rather strenuously."[53] Soon after Nibley had concluded the transaction, the First World War broke out in Europe, disrupting sugar production there. The price of sugar soared, and Utah's sugar companies took advantage of the diminished production in Europe to expand their own operations. Because of this expansion and the elevated prices, the value of stock in the Utah-Idaho and Amalgamated Sugar companies increased tremendously; in 1915, Nibley estimated that he "could dispose of those same holdings and give the Church a profit of from $1,000,000.00 to $1,200,000.00 net profit."[54] He later recalled, "Never in the history of the west, I think, has such a large deal been turned out of which so much money has been made by everybody concerned."[55]

Nibley's willingness to borrow money, however, eventually led to difficulties in his personal life, indicating to him the wisdom of Smith's views. In 1911, Bishop Nibley noted to another associate that he had been "much worried" because of the large personal debts that he held. Explaining that President Smith had "counseled and advised" him "for a long time back" to pay off his obligations, Nibley expressed his desire to "make a strenuous effort to free myself."[56] Although Nibley made strides towards this, he also assumed additional obligations by agreeing to serve as security for notes contracted by friends and family. When the stock market collapsed in 1929, those obligations were called in, and Nibley had to sell much of his holdings to pay off his debts. He successfully did so, but at a significant reduction in his net worth.[57]

The two friends at times did not see eye to eye on other matters. For example, in the early 1900s, Nibley served as a director in the Amalgamated Sugar Company, which had factories in Ogden and Logan, Utah, among other places. However, by 1903, Nibley was anxious to begin his own sugar factory independent of Amalgamated and found financial backing from Henry Havemeyer, an eastern cane sugar magnate. Nibley thus proposed constructing an independent factory in Lewiston, Utah, controlled by him. When word got out about Nibley's proposal, Smith, who was serving as a director of Amalgamated Sugar, and other Amalgamated officials were not pleased, especially because of the financial backing of Havemeyer. David Eccles, president of the company, declared the proposed factory a menace to the Amalgamated's interest and Smith traveled to Oregon in the summer of 1903 to try to dissuade Nibley from undertaking the enterprise. Nibley told Smith that he would continue with his plans to build a Lewiston factory "unless, he, as president of the Church . . . would counsel against it." Smith informed Nibley that "it was out of the question" for him to provide counsel either for or against the concern in his official role as President of the Church, so Nibley decided to proceed.[58] Amalgamated Sugar eventually absorbed the Lewiston sugar factory, but the situation showed that Nibley was not above taking a financial position adverse to Smith.

Despite their sometimes differing views, Smith greatly admired Nibley's financial abilities and trusted his friend's advice. When Smith's wife Edna "c[a]me into a 'fortune'" of $500 in 1907, for example, Smith asked Nibley where to invest it.[59] Probably in part because of his confidence in Nibley's financial acumen, Smith appointed him Presiding Bishop, and thus responsible for the Church's temporal affairs, in December 1907. According to Smith, the call came from God and was not a result of his friendship with Nibley. In Bishop Nibley's words, Smith told him that "more than once or twice in my life I have heard the voice which has given revelation to me, and never in my life did I hear it more plainly or clearly than when this man was called to be Bishop of the Church."[60]

As Presiding Bishop, Nibley worked closely with President Smith in administering the Church's temporal affairs until Smith's death in 1918. During Nibley's tenure as Presiding Bishop, the Church constructed a new administration building, as well as temples in Alberta, Canada, and Hawaii. Working with Smith and his counselors, Bishop Nibley was able to get the Church to pay its employees in cash, rather than in tithing scrip. He also convinced his friend—"with great difficulty"—to discontinue the Church's butcher shop on the tithing block. In addition, Nibley became intimately involved in the management of the Utah-Idaho Sugar Company, assuming the position of general manager of the company in 1917 and directing an unprecedented expansion of the company's holdings. As both largest stockholder and general manager, he worked closely with Smith, who served as the company's president. Looking back on his tenure as Presiding Bishop under Smith, the Bishop declared, "The Church has never been so prospered, either in a material way or spiritual way."[61]

Even though they worked closely together on ecclesiastical issues, most of the two friends' personal correspondence focused on family and friendship, things which both men valued greatly. Whenever Smith had a birthday, for example, Nibley would send him a short note wishing him a happy birthday and expressing his love for him. Smith generally did the same. "I thank you, my best earthly friend, for <u>your purest</u> friendship for me," Smith wrote after receiving one such birthday note from his friend. "My soul overflows with gratitude for such a brother and such a friend."[62] In a similar vein, the Bishop wrote to President Smith on his birthday in 1918 (just shortly before Smith's death), calling him "my best and dearest Friend" and exclaiming, "My life has been bound up in yours for more than forty years. How much, O how much I owe to you."[63]

In these declining years of President Smith's life, the two friends took up the game of golf, becoming members of the Salt Lake City Country Club and the Brentwood Country Club in Santa Monica, California, a vacation spot for both men. "Although our game was usually not of the best," Nibley explained, "we have enjoyed many happy days together on the golf field."[64] Even though Nibley was a novice at the game, he served as his playing partner's instructor. "Just a line or two to remind you of my obedience to your commands," Smith wrote Nibley in 1916. "I am bold to inform you that I have so far made good, each time cutting down my score over the track from one to four points, last play coming down to 58 for the nine holes."[65] Just a couple of years later, the Bishop stated that both he and Smith could play nine holes in forty-five strokes. "On the whole," Nibley declared, "I believe I could beat him at golf more than I could beat him at checkers."[66] Indeed, checkers was another pastime that both enjoyed. On their trips to Europe and Hawaii, the two often played checkers. Nibley admitted that President Smith was a "much better" player than him and "could beat me four times out of five, but once in a while, when I played more cautiously, and no doubt when he was more careless, I could beat him." If Smith was winning, he rarely objected if Nibley drew back a misplaced checker, but if the Bishop had won a few games, Smith was less merciful. "No you don't, leave it right there," Nibley remembered Smith saying "in that positive way of his" on several occasions. According to Nibley, "it is in these little incidents that we show the human side of our natures."[67]

On November 19, 1918, at the age of eighty, President Smith passed away, succumbing to a bout of pleurisy that had developed into pneumonia. Because he considered the President to be his dearest friend, Bishop Nibley took the death hard. "The whole world is changed now, to me," Nibley declared to Reed Smoot.[68] Likewise, Nibley told his son Nathan, who was serving a mission in Tennessee, "It has been a sad time with us owing to the death of President Smith and we are just recovering a little from the blow; just trying to gather ourselves so to speak."[69] Three years later, the pain was still there, and Nibley confided in his reminiscences that the death of his friend "brought the greatest sorrow into my life, for to me he was my ideal."[70]

That Nibley would feel such sorrow at the death of his friend was not surprising, for they considered each other more as brothers than friends. Such a bond existed for various reasons. Both men came from childhoods fraught with hardships and poverty, and both had experiences that taught them the value of money and hard work—lessons reinforced by their mothers, whom they both loved and deeply admired. Both men had similar views on economics and politics, and both were, as the Bishop described President Smith, "hard-headed, successful business m[e]n."[71] Both men valued loyalty, friendship, and family, traits which helped cement their friendship. Both also had characteristics that the other admired. President Smith's spirituality and ability to preach impressed Nibley, while Smith appreciated the Bishop's business prowess and administrative capabilities. Nibley's generosity, exhibited on numerous occasions through gifts and loans to Smith, also strengthened their friendship. As the two men aged together, they found pleasure in leisure, traveling together, playing checkers, and learning the game of golf. All of these experiences created strong bonds of friendship that were hard to break, even when the two did not see eye to eye on financial or other matters. "With this little scrap of paper; and grateful memories reaching back a long, long way," President Smith wrote Bishop Nibley in 1917, "I simply remind you, that true friendship will always live in true hearts."[72] Such true friendship characterized Nibley and Smith's lengthy association.

Notes

1. See Michael H. Paulos, "Under the Gun at the Smoot Hearings: Joseph F. Smith's Testimony," *Journal of Mormon History* 34 (Fall 2008): 181–225.
2. "Testimony of Mr. Joseph F. Smith," June 27, 1911, *Hearings Held Before the Special Committee on the Investigation of the American Sugar Refining Co. and Others*, 62nd Cong. 1038 (1911), 1st session. See also Matthew C. Godfrey, *Religion, Politics, and Sugar: The Mormon Church, the Federal Government, and the Utah-Idaho Sugar Company* (Logan: Utah State University Press, 2007), 60–61.
3. Joseph Fielding Smith, *The Life of Joseph F. Smith* (Salt Lake City: Deseret News, 1938), 235.
4. Smith, *The Life of Joseph F. Smith*, 117–124, 129–130, 147–155, 157–158, 160, 162–163.
5. Charles W. Nibley, *Reminiscences, 1849–1931* (Salt Lake City: Stevens & Wallis, 1933), 5, 7–8, 14–23, 25, 28–33.
6. Charles W. Nibley, "Reminiscences of President Joseph F. Smith," *Improvement Era*, January 1919, 191, 195. Ironically, in later years, Smith would compliment Nibley on his speaking abilities, insisting that he would never be able to preach as well as Nibley. Joseph F. Smith (hereafter referred to as JFS) to Charles W. Nibley, July 23, 1907 correspondence; JFS to Nibley, November 16, 1907, correspondence, both in Charles W. Nibley Papers, box 3, folder 12, MS 1287, Church History Library, Salt Lake City; hereafter referred to as Nibley Papers. All sources quoted from Nibley Papers herein come from boxes 1, 2, 3, 4, or 10; and from folders 1, 2, 3, 4, 7, 8, 9, 10, 11, 12, or 15.
7. Nibley, *Reminiscences*, 72–73.
8. JFS to Nibley, June 27, 1894, in Nibley Papers.
9. See JFS to Nibley, December 11, 1877; JFS to Nibley, February 17, 1879; Nibley to JFS, December 20, 1877, in Nibley Papers.
10. Nibley to JFS, December 6, 1877, in Nibley Papers.
11. JFS to Nibley, October 22, 1877, in Nibley Papers.
12. JFS to Nibley, February 17, 1879, in Nibley Papers.
13. JFS to Nibley, September 21, 1877; JFS to Nibley, October 9, 1877, in Nibley Papers; Nibley, *Reminiscences*, 74.
14. JFS to Nibley, December 6, 1877; JFS to Nibley, January 5, 1878; JFS to Nibley, February 15, 1878, in Nibley Papers.
15. JFS to Nibley, January 25, 1878, in Nibley Papers.
16. JFS to Nibley, March 6, 1878, in Nibley Papers.
17. JFS to Nibley, April 30, 1878, in Nibley Papers.
18. JFS to Nibley, May 14, 1878, in Nibley Papers.

19. JFS to Nibley, May 27, 1878; JFS to Nibley, July 23, 1878, in Nibley Papers.
20. JFS to Nibley, May 6, 1878, in Nibley Papers; emphasis in original.
21. JFS to Nibley, May 24, 1878; see also JFS to Nibley, July 16, 1878, in Nibley Papers.
22. Smith, *Life of Joseph F. Smith*, 487–90. Mercy Josephine, born on August 14, 1867, to Joseph and Julina Lambson Smith, died on June 6, 1870, while Sarah Ella, born on February 5, 1869, to Joseph and Sarah Richards Smith, died six days after her birth.
23. Nibley, *Reminiscences*, 64.
24. JFS to Nibley, May 14, 1878, in Nibley Papers.
25. Nibley, *Reminiscences*, 78–79, 81, 84; Michael Elvin Christensen, "The Making of a Leader: A Biography of Charles W. Nibley to 1890" (PhD diss., University of Utah, 1978), 115–116; Smith, *Life of Joseph F. Smith*, 252, 487–90.
26. The arrest warrant was issued in Utah, but Nibley was arrested in Idaho. When he was brought to court in Salt Lake City, the judge released him because of this technicality. Before a new warrant could be issued, Nibley left Salt Lake City and went to Paris, Idaho. "This ended my escapade of arrest and slipping away as successfully as I did," he later recalled. Nibley, *Reminiscences*, 86–95.
27. Nibley, *Reminiscences*, 81.
28. Joseph F. Smith, in *Journal of Discourses* (London: Latter-day Saints' Book Depot, 1854–86), 20:26–27.
29. Nibley, *Reminiscences*, 100–101.
30. JFS to Nibley, February 19, 1878, in Nibley Papers.
31. For more information on Johnston and what was known as the Utah War, see Donald R. Moorman with Gene A. Sessions, *Camp Floyd and the Mormons: The Utah War* (Salt Lake City: University of Utah, 1992); Norman F. Furniss, *The Mormon Conflict, 1850–1859* (New Haven, CT: Yale University, 1960); William P. MacKinnon, ed., *At Sword's Point* (Norman, OK: Arthur H. Clark, 2008); David L. Bigler and Will Bagley, *The Mormon Rebellion: America's First Civil War, 1857–1858* (Norman: University of Oklahoma, 2011).
32. JFS to Nibley, June 30, 1893, in Nibley Papers.
33. JFS to Nibley, June 30, 1893, in Nibley Papers; emphasis in original.
34. Nibley, *Reminiscences*, 109–12.
35. JFS to Nibley, November 25, 1895, in Nibley Papers.
36. JFS to Nibley, February 20, 1893, in Nibley Papers; emphasis in original.
37. Unsigned letter to Nibley, October 24, 1896; see also JFS to Nibley, September 27, 1899; JFS to Nibley, September 11, 1899, in Nibley Papers.
38. Nibley, *Reminiscences*, 114; Smith, *The Life of Joseph F. Smith*, 396–398.
39. JFS to Nibley, July 23, 1907, in Nibley Papers; Smith, *The Life of Joseph F. Smith*, 396–98.
40. Nibley, *Reminiscences*, 122–23.
41. JFS to Nibley, November 8, 1900, in Nibley Papers.
42. Nibley, "Reminiscences of President Joseph F. Smith," 195; see also Nibley, *Reminiscences*, 125–26.
43. See, for example, Nibley to Reed Smoot, October 27, 1915, correspondence, in Reed Smoot Papers, MS 1187, box 41, folder 2, L. Tom Perry Special Collections, Harold B. Lee Library, Brigham Young University, Provo, UT; hereafter referred to as Smoot Papers.
44. JFS to Nibley, December 6, 1877, in Nibley Papers.
45. JFS to Nibley, December 11, 1877, in Nibley Papers.

46. JFS to Nibley, July 3, 1916, in Nibley Papers.
47. JFS to Nibley, June 23, 1903, in Nibley Papers.
48. JFS to Nibley, December 11, 1877, in Nibley Papers.
49. JFS to Nibley, November 21, 1877, in Nibley Papers.
50. JFS to David Smith, July 14, 1914, in Nibley Papers.
51. Nibley, *Reminiscences*, 127–128; see also Godfrey, *Religion, Politics, and Sugar*, 94–96.
52. Nibley to Hyrum M. Smith, December 14, 1914, in Nibley Papers.
53. Nibley to Hyrum M. Smith, December 6, 1915, in Nibley Papers.
54. Nibley to Hyrum M. Smith, December 6, 1915, in Nibley Papers; see also Nibley, *Reminiscences*, 127–28; Godfrey, *Religion, Politics, and Sugar*, 94–96.
55. Nibley, *Reminiscences*, 127–128.
56. Nibley to George Stoddard, November 4, 1911, in Nibley Papers.
57. Nibley, *Reminiscences*, 153.
58. Leonard J. Arrington, "Notes on Minutes of the Utah Sugar Company, Dec. 1902 to July 1907," 2–3, Leonard J. Arrington Papers, Series 12, box 10, folder 1, Manuscript Collection 1, Leonard J. Arrington Historical Archives, Special Collections and Archives, Utah State University, Logan, Utah; Nibley, *Reminiscences*, 110–11; Godfrey, *Religion, Politics, and Sugar*, 66–67; J. R. Bachman, *Story of The Amalgamated Sugar Company, 1897–1961* (Ogden, UT: The Amalgamated Sugar Company, 1962), 17–18, 21–23.
59. JFS to Nibley, July 23, 1907, in Nibley Papers.
60. Nibley, *Reminiscences*, 117–121.
61. Nibley, *Reminiscences*, 126–127; see also Godfrey, *Religion, Politics, and Sugar*, 95–96, 100.
62. JFS to Nibley, November 16, 1907, in Nibley Papers; emphasis in original.
63. Nibley to JFS, November 13, 1918, in Nibley Papers.
64. Nibley, *Reminiscences*, 115.
65. JFS to Nibley, August 24, 1916, in Nibley Papers.
66. Nibley, *Reminiscences*, 116.
67. Nibley, "Reminiscences of President Joseph F. Smith," 194.
68. Nibley to Reed Smoot, November 20, 1918, Smoot Papers, box 41, folder 4.
69. Nibley to Nathan Nibley, November 30, 1918, in Nibley Papers.
70. Nibley, *Reminiscences*, 138–39.
71. Nibley, "Reminiscences of President Joseph F. Smith," 197.
72. JFS to Nibley, June 1, 1917, in Nibley Papers.

Theology

Craig James Ostler

11

Joseph F. Smith on Priesthood and Church Government

As "the Presiding High Priest" (D&C 107:66) of The Church of Jesus Christ of Latter-day Saints, President Joseph F. Smith assured that the order, doctrinal principles, and practices of the priesthood were understood and observed. Biographer Francis M. Gibbons noted, "So frequently did President Smith return to the theme of the priesthood, and so detailed and explicit were his remarks on the subject, that this aspect of his public speaking overshadows all others. Indeed, his whole ministry was characterized by a deliberate effort to strengthen and magnify the priesthood, which he recognized as the key factor in the effective administration of Church affairs."[1] President Smith taught and clarified principles regarding priesthood authority, keys, offices, and presiding officers. In addition, his 1918 vision of the spirit world (D&C 138) made it clear that these principles operated on both sides of the veil. President Smith's instructions, explanations, and clarifications continue to guide the Saints in their understanding of principles of the priesthood and Church government up to the present day.

Craig James Ostler is a professor of Church history and doctrine at Brigham Young University.

Historical Context: Need for Instruction on Priesthood and Church Government

The decades preceding President Smith's administration had provided little opportunity for Church leaders to teach the Saints correct principles regarding the priesthood and Church government, and even less opportunity to observe priesthood leadership in action. During the era immediately following the martyrdom of the Prophet Joseph Smith, the organization of the Church appeared to emphasize leaders of pioneer companies under the direction of the Twelve Apostles as much as bishops and stake presidents presiding over local congregations (see D&C 136:1–3). During the 1880s, many general and local Church leaders were in hiding previous to the issuing of the Manifesto, which ended the practice of plural marriage, while other leaders had been committed to prison for their support of plural marriage. Visible Church government was veiled, and even the location of the President of the Church was often not known during that era. Thomas G. Alexander noted that President John Taylor "died in Kaysville, a small town north of Salt Lake City, while hiding from United States marshals bent on taking him to trial for practicing plural marriage."[2]

In addition, unlike today, prior to President Smith's administration, ward and stake priesthood leadership opportunities had been minimal. Each county served as the boundary for a stake and each town was a ward. "After the move to Utah in 1847, local units grew rather haphazardly until 1877, when Brigham Young supervised their reorganization. . . . Under the 1877 reorganization, most counties with large Mormon populations were designated as stakes, supervised by a stake presidency and high council. Wards were presided over by a bishop and two counselors, who were subordinate to stake officers. In the smaller settlements, each town constituted a ward. In the cities, wards corresponded to geographical subdivisions."[3] Even with President Joseph F. Smith's efforts to educate them, understanding of general priesthood principles appeared to be shallow among the Church membership. For example, Bill Hartley noted, "By 1913 the Church leaders felt it necessary to remind the Church that bishops were to be the presiding high priests over all local priesthood matters, and that all quorum loyalties therefore were subordinate to his local needs and directives."[4]

As President of the Church, Joseph F. Smith did not require new revelations to understand and explain priesthood and Church government. From the beginning of his prophetic ministry to the end of his life, President Joseph F. Smith built upon the foundation the Lord revealed to the Prophet Joseph Smith. In the special general conference at which Joseph F. Smith first presided as the President of the Church, he indicated he would be emphasizing priesthood principles—not teaching something new, but clarifying the previously revealed doctrinal principles of the priesthood. He explained:

> It is our privilege to live nearer to the Lord, if we will, than we have ever done, that we may enjoy a greater outpouring of His Spirit than we have ever enjoyed, and that we may advance faster, grow in the knowledge of truth more rapidly, and become more thoroughly established in the faith. . . .
>
> We can make no advancement only upon the principles of eternal truth. In proportion as we become established upon the foundation of these principles, which have been revealed from the heavens in the latter days, and determine to accomplish the purposes of the Lord, we will progress, and the Lord will all the more exalt and magnify us before the world and make us to assume our real position and standing in the midst of the earth. . . .
>
> We cannot deny the fact that the Lord has effected one of the most perfect organizations in this Church that ever existed upon the earth. I do not know of any more perfect organization than exists in the Church of Jesus Christ of Latter-day Saints today. We have not always carried out strictly the order of the Priesthood; we have varied from it to some extent; but we hope in due time that, by the promptings of the Holy Spirit, we will be led up into the exact channel and course that the Lord has marked out for us to pursue, and adhere strictly to the order that He has established.[5]

This theme of teachings upon the priesthood and Church government continued for nearly two decades. On September 13, 1917, a little more than a year before his death, President Smith delivered a message to the Parowan Stake in southern Utah entitled "Principles of Government in the Church." He declared, "I do not profess to be able to teach you anything that the Lord has not revealed. I have nothing that is not found written in the word of the Lord as it has come to us through the instrumentality of the chosen of God, Joseph the Prophet, and his associates who have succeeded in the presiding authority of the Church since the day of the Prophet Joseph Smith."[6]

Priesthood Authority, Offices, and Keys

President Smith taught by example and instruction the distinction between principles of priesthood authority, priesthood offices, and priesthood keys. At times these exemplary and clarifying teachings were so apparent that they offered startling reflection. All men who receive the priesthood have authority to act in the name of Jesus Christ. Those who have the authority of the priesthood are ordained to specific offices within the priesthood. In addition, keys are conferred upon those that preside and direct the labors of priesthood bearers.

At the death of President Lorenzo Snow, when Joseph F. Smith became the senior Apostle on the earth, he helped to answer an important question: In sustaining, then setting apart the senior member of the Quorum of the Twelve Apostles as a new President of the Church, does anyone on earth have higher authority, office, or keys to give to him that would make him the President of the Church? If, as occasionally is misunderstood today, some believed that each of the members of the Quorum of the Twelve Apostles holds authority or keys to bestow upon the future President of the Church that he does not already possess, President Joseph F. Smith quickly dismissed such a notion by means of the procedure he directed in being set apart as the President of the Church. "On October 17, 1901, the Twelve sustained Joseph F. Smith as president of the church." Following the unanimous sustaining by the presiding authorities,[7] Brigham Young Jr., next in apostolic seniority to President Smith, recorded, "Pres. Smith was set apart by all present, his brother Patriarch Jno. [John] S.[mith] being Mouth by his request."[8] Note that in requesting his brother John to be mouth in the setting apart rather than a member of the Quorum of the Twelve it was not thought that as Patriarch to the Church, John Smith held higher authority, office, or keys than did members of the Quorum of the Twelve Apostles; nor was it asserted that he had higher authority, office, or keys than his brother, Joseph F. Smith. Rather, this request demonstrated that an individual who already has been given the keys of the kingdom is set apart to the office the President of the Church by the authority of the Melchizedek Priesthood.[9] This specific procedure of being set apart as President of the Church illustrated the distinction between priesthood authority, priesthood keys, and priesthood offices. Joseph F. Smith had received the authority of the priesthood to act in the name of Jesus Christ when the Melchizedek Priesthood was conferred

President Joseph F. Smith requested that he be set apart as President of the Church by Patriarch John Smith, his brother. Members of the Quorum of the Twelve Apostles stood in the circle. Photo by Charles R. Savage, 1895, Church History Library.

upon him as a young man. Years later he had received priesthood keys to preside over the Church on October 8, 1867, when he was set apart as a member of the Quorum of the Twelve Apostles.[10]

Thus, in requesting his patriarch brother to set him apart to the office of President of the Church, Joseph F. Smith explicitly taught that he already held the authority and the keys to preside over the Church and that he could direct priesthood bearers in ordaining others to offices in the priesthood. In addition, this action emphasized the fact that all holders of the Melchizedek Priesthood are equal in authority, regardless of the particular office to which they are ordained. Thus, that which is true of the President of the Church, the Twelve Apostles, and the Patriarch to the Church is also true of other priesthood holders. All hold the same priesthood authority—the Melchizedek Priesthood; however, they differ in their rights and responsibilities according to their office. Those who receive keys preside and direct the labors of priesthood bearers. A few months prior to becoming the President of the Church, Joseph F. Smith clarified:

> The Priesthood in general is the authority given to man to act for God. Every man ordained to any degree of the Priesthood, had this authority delegated to him. But it is necessary that every act performed under this authority, shall be done at the proper time and place, in the proper way, and after the proper order. The power of directing these labors constitutes the *keys* of the Priesthood. . . . Thus, the president of a temple, the president of a stake, the bishop of a ward, the president of a mission, the president of a quorum, each holds the keys of the labors performed in that particular body or locality. His Priesthood is not increased by this special appointment, for a seventy who presides over a mission has no more Priesthood than a seventy who labors under his direction; and the president of the elders' quorum, for example, has no more Priesthood than any members of that quorum. But he holds the power of directing the official labors performed in the mission or the quorum, or in other words, *the keys* of that division of that work. So it is throughout all the ramifications of the Priesthood—a distinction must be carefully made between the general authority, and the directing of the labors performed by that authority.[11]

As aforementioned, President Smith already had the keys to preside over the priesthood and the Church before being set apart to the office of President. When President Lorenzo Snow died, as President of the Quorum of the Twelve Apostles, Joseph F. Smith became the presiding high priest on the earth. This apostolic authority had been transmitted from the hands of heavenly messengers upon the heads of Joseph Smith and Oliver Cowdery. In 1829 Peter, James, and

John restored the Melchizedek Priesthood and the apostolic keys of the kingdom (see D&C 27:12–13; Joseph Smith—History 1:72). Seven years later, on April 3, 1836, Moses, Elias, and Elijah committed additional keys for the gathering of Israel, the dispensation of the gospel of Abraham, and the sealing power (see D&C 110:11–15). The Prophet Joseph Smith conferred all of the keys and authorities of the priesthood upon members of the Quorum of the Twelve. President Joseph F. Smith's son Joseph Fielding Smith explained:

> Now mark! The Lord . . . in the winter of 1843–4, commanded the prophet to confer upon the heads of the Twelve Apostles, every key, power, and principle, that the Lord had sealed upon his head. The Prophet declared that he knew not why, but the Lord commanded him to endow the Twelve with these keys and priesthood, and after it was done, he rejoiced very much, saying in substance, "Now if they kill me, you have all the keys and all the ordinances and you can confer them upon others, and the powers of Satan will not be able to tear down the kingdom as fast as you will be able to build it up, and upon your shoulders will the responsibility of leading this people rest.[12]

He further clarified:

> The Prophet, in anticipation of his death, conferred upon the Twelve all the keys and authorities which he held. He did not bestow the keys on any one member, but upon them *all*, so that *each held the keys* and authorities. All members of the Council of the Twelve since that day have also been given all of these keys and powers. But these powers cannot be exercised by any one of them *until*, if the occasion arises, he is called to be the *presiding officer* of the Church. The Twelve, therefore, in the setting apart of the President do not give him any additional priesthood, but *confirm* upon him that which he already received; they *set him apart* to the office, which it is their right to do.[13]

Three Presiding High Priests: Calling Counselors in the First Presidency.

The Prophet Joseph Smith instructed the original members of the Quorum of the Twelve Apostles that the First Presidency of the Church consists of "three Presiding High Priests" (D&C 107:22). In his choice of counselors in the First Presidency, President Joseph F. Smith emphasized that members of the First Presidency preside as high priests who have keys bestowed upon them, rather than the often-held notion that their presiding authority devolves upon them because they have been ordained to the office of Apostle. This principle of Church government was clarified in President Smith's choice of John R. Winder as First Counselor and Anthon H. Lund as Second Counselor in the First Presidency. John R. Winder, a British immigrant, had been serving as Second Counselor in the Presiding Bishopric prior to his call to serve in the First Presidency.[14] President Winder was a high priest but not a member of the Quorum of the Twelve Apostles. His call to the First Presidency without ever being ordained to the office of an Apostle caused some concern among the Saints.

The First Presidency felt it necessary to clarify the principles of the priesthood and to cite past instances in which members of the First Presidency had not been ordained Apostles. They wrote:

> In the *Era* [the official Church magazine] for February [1902], it was stated that several persons who had acted as counselors in the First Presidency had never been ordained apostles. Several correspondents have objected to the statement that Sidney Rigdon, Jedediah M. Grant, Daniel H. Wells, John R. Winder, and

First Presidency, 1901: John R. Winder, Joseph F. Smith, Anthon H. Lund. President Joseph F. Smith called John R. Winder as his First Counselor. President Winder had been serving as Second Counselor in the Presiding Bishopric. He was a high priest but was never ordained an Apostle. Photo by C. R. Savage, circa 1905, courtesy of Church History Library.

> others, were not ordained apostles. We still maintain, upon lack of convincing evidence to the contrary that none of these brethren was ever ordained an apostle. We do know positively that John R. Winder, Sidney Rigdon, Wm. Law and Hyrum Smith, all of whom were members in the First Presidency of the Church, were never ordained apostles.[15]

Joseph F. Smith had previously addressed this principle in Church government during the special conference held on November 10, 1901, in which the newly organized First Presidency was sustained by the membership of the Church. He stated:

> I will call your attention to the fact that the Lord in the beginning of this work revealed that there should be three High Priests to preside over the High Priesthood of His Church and over the whole Church (D&C 107:22, 64–67, 91–92). He conferred upon them all the authority necessary to preside over all the affairs of the Church. They hold the keys of the house of God, and of the ordinances of the Gospel, and of every blessing which has been restored to the earth in this dispensation. The authority is vested in a Presidency of three High Priests. They are three Presidents. The Lord himself so calls them. But there is one presiding President, and his counselors are Presidents also. I propose that my counselors and fellow Presidents in the First Presidency shall share with me in the responsibility of every act which I shall perform in this capacity. I do not propose to take reins in my own hands to do as I please; but I propose to do as my brethren and I agree upon and as the Spirit of the Lord manifests to us. I have always held, and do hold, and trust I always shall hold, that it is wrong for one man to exercise all the authority and power of presidency in the Church of Jesus Christ of Latter-day Saints. I dare not assume such a responsibility, and I will not, so long as I can have men like these [pointing to Presidents Winder and Lund] to stand by and counsel with me in the labors we have to perform and in doing all those things that shall tend to the peace, advancement and happiness of the people of God and the building up of Zion.[16]

Some of the confusion which President Smith wished to correct may have arisen from misunderstandings regarding the office of high priest, the High Priesthood, and the Melchizedek Priesthood. Although there may be occasions when the term "High Priesthood" has been used to refer to the Melchizedek Priesthood, it more properly refers to those who have been ordained to the office of high priest within the Melchizedek Priesthood. In one of the early revelations on the priesthood, the Lord clarified that there are to be presiding officers to preside over those who are of the offices of an elder (within the Melchizedek Priesthood), priest, teacher, and deacon (within the Aaronic Priesthood). "Then comes the High Priesthood," the Prophet Joseph Smith explained, "which is the greatest of all . . . Wherefore, it must needs be that one be appointed of the High Priesthood to preside over the priesthood, and he shall be called President of the High Priesthood of the Church; or, in other words, the Presiding High Priest over the High Priesthood of the Church" (D&C 107:64–66).[17]

In the later 1902 article in the *Improvement Era*, the First Presidency continued to clarify and elucidate the revelation on the First Presidency:

> The main point we wish to make is this, that it was not necessary that they should be so ordained apostles in order to hold the position of counselor in the First Presidency. The leading fact to be remembered is that the Priesthood is greater than any of its offices; and that any man holding the Melchizedek Priesthood may, by virtue of its possession, perform any ordinance pertaining thereto, or connected therewith, when called upon to do so by one holding the proper authority, which proper authority is vested in the President of the Church, or in any whom he may designate.[18]

Authority and Keys of the Melchizedek Priesthood

President Smith and his counselors in the First Presidency also referred to the principle of priesthood authority and keys to clarify why an individual who had never been ordained to a specific office of the priesthood could still ordain other individuals to that office. For example, under the direction of the President of the Church, a high priest could ordain an individual to the office of an Apostle. However, only those that have received keys to preside may confer those keys upon others. Citing the ordination of the original members of the Quorum of the Twelve Apostles, President Smith explained:

> Every man holding the Holy Melchizedek Priesthood may act in any capacity and do all things that such Priesthood authorizes, it makes no difference what

> office in that Priesthood he holds, providing he is called upon by proper authority to so officiate . . .
>
> Witness the calling on Feb. 14, 1835, of David Whitmer and Martin Harris, both High Priests, by the Prophet Joseph, in conformity with prior revelation from God (see Doctrine and Covenants, section 18) to "search out the Twelve." They chose the Twelve, ordained, and set them apart for their exalted callings, because they were called upon by the prophet of God who had been instructed of the Lord, and also because these men held the necessary authority of the Priesthood, which authority was exercised, in this case as it should be in all cases, upon proper calling. The Doctrine and Covenants makes it very clear that while each officer in the Church has a right to officiate in his own standing, "The Melchizedek Priesthood holds the right of Presidency, and has power and authority over all the offices of the Church in all ages of the world to administer in spiritual things." (Doctrine and Covenants, section 107:8)[19]

At another time President Smith clarified the greater importance of priesthood authority above that of priesthood offices:

> There is no office growing out of this Priesthood that is or can be greater than the Priesthood itself. It is from the Priesthood that the office derives its authority and power. No office gives authority to the Priesthood. No office adds to the power of the Priesthood. But all offices in the Church derive their power, their virtue, their authority, from the Priesthood . . . If it were necessary, the Seventy, holding the Melchisedek Priesthood, as he does, I say IF IT WERE NECESSARY—he could ordain a High Priest; and if it were necessary for a High Priest to ordain a Seventy, he could do that. Why? Because both of them hold the Melchisedek Priesthood.[20]

The principle directing President Smith's teachings was again that of the distinction between priesthood authority, priesthood offices, and priesthood keys. Individuals do not preside because of any particular office to which they have been ordained, Apostles not excepted. Indeed, an individual could be ordained to the office of Apostle and not receive keys to preside. On the other hand, an individual could have keys conferred upon them without being ordained to the office of Apostle. The First Presidency further explained:

> When an Apostle presides, he, like the High Priest, the Seventy, the Elder, or the Bishop, presides because of the High Priesthood which has been conferred upon him; and furthermore, because he has been called upon so to do by the acknowledged head of the Church. (D&C 107:24) And so with the High Priest who has been called to officiate in the First Presidency, in which case he is "accounted equal" with the President of the Church in holding the keys of the Presidency (section 90:6), as long as the President remains. When he dies, the calling of his counselors ends, and the responsibility of Presidency falls upon the quorum of the Twelve Apostles, because they hold the Holy Melchizedek Priesthood and are the next quorum in authority. (D&C 107:24) It is not the apostleship, but the Priesthood and the calling by power and authority which enables any person to preside.[21]

Preparing the Church for Worldwide Expansion

The principles of priesthood authority, offices, and keys guide Church government from the highest quorums of General Authorities to the most immediate local priesthood leaders. As the Church grows, the order of the priesthood is repeated in each area in which congregations are established. That is, priesthood authority is conferred upon individuals—all being equal in authority according to the priesthood order, Aaronic or Melchizedek. Those that receive priesthood authority are then ordained to various offices within the priesthood, each office devolving specific rights and responsibilities. From those ordained to specific offices, individuals are given keys to preside over their respective quorums. Thus, the order of the priesthood is perfect in its organization and able to expand infinitely across the globe with the growth of the Church. This expansion requires that greater numbers of individuals be given and understand priesthood authority, offices, and keys.

Francis M. Gibbons noted, "The Church over which Joseph F. Smith was called to preside had grown from a membership of six in 1830 to a membership of almost two hundred eighty thousand in October 1901, divided into fifty stakes and twenty-one missions. Over one-sixth of the membership resided in the Salt Lake Valley, and until just a year before Joseph became president, the large concentration of Latter-day Saints was included in a single stake and fifty wards."[22] In order to meet the needs of a growing Church membership, President Smith focused on giving local priesthood leadership greater responsibilities and duties rather than emphasizing a greater role for central Church leadership. In so doing, Joseph F. Smith continued to emphasize the responsibilities of local priesthood leadership as he had done previously while serving as a counselor in the First Presidency to President Lorenzo Snow. Historian Thomas G. Alexander noted, "President Snow insisted that the local officials 'assume the burden of their charges and not expect the apostles to do their work.' As counselor in the First Presidency, Joseph F. Smith believed that the lowest possible level ought to deal with any problems."[23] From the beginning of his administration as President of the Church, Joseph F. Smith instructed the priesthood holders, "We want every man to learn his duty, and we expect every man will do his duty as faithfully as he knows how, and carry off his portion of the responsibility of building up Zion in the latter days."[24]

President Smith prophetically anticipated the day when the Church would be governed by priesthood councils and the auxiliaries of the Church would not be needed to support the latter-day work. In the general conference of April 1906, he described that future day in the Church:

> We expect to see the day, if we live long enough (and if some of us do not live long enough to see it, there are others who will), when every council of the Priesthood in the Church of Jesus Christ of Latter-day Saints will understand its duty, will assume its own responsibility, will magnify its calling, and fill its place in the Church, to the uttermost, according to the intelligence and ability possessed by it. When that day shall come, there will not be so much necessity for work that is now being done by the auxiliary organizations, because it will be done by the regular quorums of the Priesthood. The Lord designed and comprehended it from the beginning, and He has made provision in the Church whereby every need may be met and satisfied through the regular organizations of the Priesthood.[25]

Rights and Privileges of Offices in the Priesthood

During his ministry, Joseph F. Smith taught repeatedly regarding the rights and privileges belonging to the various priesthood offices.[26] He emphasized the fact that "all the quorums or councils are organized in the Church, each with special duties and special callings; not clashing with each another, but all harmonious and united."[27] Among his instructions he addressed the duties of each office of the Melchizedek and Aaronic Priesthoods. Regarding his own office and keys as President of the Church, he explained:

> I have the right to bless. I hold the keys of the Melchizedek Priesthood and of the office and power of patriarch. It is my right to bless; for all the keys and authority and power pertaining to the government of the Church and to the Melchizedek and Aaronic Priesthood are centered in the presiding officers of the Church. There is no business, nor office, within the Church that the President of the Church may not fill, and may not do, if it is necessary, or if it is required of him to do it. He holds the office of patriarch; he holds the office of high priest and of apostle, of seventy, of elder, of bishop, and of priest, teacher and deacon in the Church; all these belong to the Presidency of the Church of Jesus Christ of Latter-day Saints, and they can officiate in any and in all of these callings when occasion requires.[28]

"The duty of the twelve apostles," he explained, "is to preach the gospel to the world, to send it to the inhabitants of the earth and to bear testimony of Jesus Christ, the Son of God, as living witnesses of His divine mission."[29] Regarding the privileges afforded, as well as the responsibilities of the Twelve, President Smith admonished them thus:

> Be eye and ear witnesses of the divine mission of Jesus Christ. It is not permissible for them to say, I believe, simply; I have accepted it simply because I believe it. Read the revelation, the Lord informs us they must *know*, they must get the knowledge for themselves. It must be with them as though they had seen with their eyes and heard with their ears and they know the truth. That is their mission, to testify of Jesus Christ and Him crucified and risen from the dead and clothed now with almighty power at the right hand of God, the Savior of the world. That is their mission, and their duty, and that is the doctrine and the truth that it is their duty to preach to the world and see that it is preached to the world.[30]

Regarding the Seventy he taught:

> The Seventies are called to be assistants to the Twelve Apostles; indeed they *are* apostles of the Lord Jesus Christ, subject to the direction of the Twelve, and it is their duty to respond to the call of the Twelve, under the direction of

> the First Presidency of the Church, to preach the Gospel to every creature, to every tongue and people under the heavens to whom they may be sent. Hence they should understand the gospel. . . . They should take up the study of the Gospel, the study of the scriptures and the history of the dealings of God with the people of the earth.[31]

President Smith taught that the responsibility of the Presiding Bishopric is that of "temporal custodians of the means of the Church and whose duty it is to account for the receipt and disbursement of these funds."[32]

He described the role of patriarchs, indicating that this was their responsibility:

> To bestow blessings upon the heads of those who seek blessings at their hands. . . . It is their business and right to bestow blessings upon the people, to make promises unto them in the name of the Lord, as it may be given them by the inspiration of the Holy Spirit, to comfort them in the hours of sorrow and trouble, to strengthen their faith by the promises that shall be made to them through the Spirit of God, and to be fathers indeed of the people, leading them into all truth."[33]

He taught concerning the high priest:

> It is his bounden duty to set an example before the old and young worthy of emulation, and to place himself in a position to be a teacher of righteousness, not only by precept but more particularly by example—giving the younger ones the benefit of experience of age, and thus becoming individually a power in the midst of the communities in which they dwell. . . . From among those who hold this office are chosen the presidents of stakes and their counselors, and the High Councils, . . . and from this office are chosen the bishops, and the bishop's counselors, in every ward in Zion. . . . Those holding this office are, as a rule, men of advanced years, and varied experience, men who have filled missions abroad, who have preached the Gospel to the nations of the earth, and who have had experience not only abroad but at home. Their experience and wisdom is the ripened fruit of years of labor in the Church, and they should exercise that wisdom for the benefit of all with whom they are associated.[34]

President Smith explained regarding those ordained as elders:

> It is the duty of this body of men to be standing ministers at home; to be ready at the call of the presiding officers of the Church and the stakes, to labor in the ministry at home, and to officiate in any calling that may be required of them, whether it be to work in the temples, or to labor in the ministry at home, or whether it be to go out into the world, along with the Seventies, to preach the Gospel to the world.[35]

Concerning the bishopric he taught:

> It is expected that the Bishop of a ward and his counselors will understand the necessities of every member of his ward. . . . It devolves upon the Bishopric of the ward to look after the poor, to minister unto the sick and the afflicted and to see that there is no want nor suffering among the people in these organized divisions of the Church. It is also the duty of these presiding officers in the Church to look after the spiritual welfare of the people, to see that they are living moral, pure and upright lives, that they are faithful in the discharge of their duties as Latter-day Saints, that they are honest in their dealings with one another, and with all the world.[36]

President Smith summarized the duties of the Aaronic Priesthood, "which attends to the different temporal matters of the Church, consisting of Priests, Teachers, and Deacons, who labor under the direction of the Bishopric in the various wards in which they dwell."[37]

Under Joseph F. Smith's direction, the ages at which young men were ordained to the various offices in the Aaronic Priesthood were formalized. The Quorum of the Twelve was given the responsibility to oversee the instructions regarding regularizing the Aaronic Priesthood. In addition, President Smith established a General Priesthood Committee on Outlines to oversee unified selection and writing of material to be used in instruction for Aaronic Priesthood quorum members throughout the Church. Their counsel followed President Brigham Young's directions in 1877 that young men were to be ordained deacons when they were twelve years old. To facilitate regular advancement in the Aaronic Priesthood offices, it was determined that ordinations should occur at three-year intervals until they received the Melchizedek Priesthood and were ordained elders. Thus each deacon would be ordained at age twelve and then to the office of teacher at age fifteen. After another three years they should be ordained to the office of priest at age eighteen. Ordination to elder would follow when they were twenty-one years old.[38]

Priesthood Authority and Keys in the Postmortal Spirit World

Joseph F. Smith's culminating contribution, both doctrinally and regarding the priesthood, is his vision on the redemption of the dead (D&C 138). Among other important concepts, this vision emphasized the acts of the Savior in authorizing and sending forth individuals, including elders from this dispensation. Regarding the work of preaching the gospel in the spirit world President Smith wrote, "From among the righteous, he [Jesus Christ] organized his forces and appointed messengers, clothed with power and authority, and commissioned them to go forth and carry the light of the gospel to them that were in darkness, even to all the spirits of men; and thus was the gospel preached to the dead" (D&C 138:30).

President Smith posed at writing table, circa 1916. "So frequently did President Smith return to the theme of the priesthood, and so detailed and explicit were his remarks on the subject, that this aspect of his public speaking overshadowed all others." (Francis M. Gibbons, Joseph F. Smith: Patriarch and Preacher, Prophet of God, *269), Church History Library.*

President Smith chronicled seeing priesthood leaders from past dispensations such as Adam, Abel, Noah, Shem the great high priest, Abraham, Isaac, Jacob, Moses, Isaiah, Ezekiel, Daniel, Elias, Malachi (see D&C 138:38–46), "all these prophets and many more, even the prophets who dwelt among the Nephites and testified of the coming of the Son of God" (D&C 138:49). Concerning these individuals, President Smith testified, "our Redeemer spent his time during his sojourn in the world of spirits, instructing and preparing the faithful spirits of the prophets who had testified of him in the flesh; that they might carry the message of redemption unto all the dead, unto whom he could not go personally, because of transgression, that they through the ministration of his servants might hear his words" (D&C 138:36–37). In addition, President Smith witnessed regarding these prophets that "the Lord taught, and gave them power to come forth, after his resurrection from the dead, to enter into his Father's kingdom, there to be crowned with immortality and eternal life" (D&C 138:51).

President Smith also saw prophets from this dispensation that had departed to the world of spirits. He recorded that he saw "the Prophet Joseph Smith, and my father, Hyrum Smith, Brigham Young, John Taylor, Wilford Woodruff, and other choice spirits who were reserved to come forth in the fulness of times to take part in laying the foundations of the great latter-day work" (D&C 138:53). All of these he saw continued the work of salvation over which they presided in mortality. The Lord revealed to the Prophet Joseph Smith "the keys of this kingdom shall never be taken from you, while thou art in the world, neither in the world to come" (D&C 90:3). Thus the keys of the priesthood given to the Prophet Joseph Smith in mortality continued with him through the veil into the world of spirits, and he continues to direct the priesthood of this dispensation in that sphere. It is also evident that others that have held the keys continue to exercise those keys under the Prophet Joseph Smith's direction.

At the M. I. A. Conference on June 5, 1910, President Smith taught:

> This gospel revealed to the Prophet Joseph is already being preached to the spirits in prison, to those who have passed away from this stage of action into the spirit world without the knowledge of the gospel. Joseph Smith is preaching that gospel to them. So is Hyrum Smith. So is Brigham Young and so are all the faithful apostles that lived in this dispensation under the administration of the Prophet Joseph. They are there, having carried with them from here the Holy Priesthood that they received under the hands and by the authority of the Prophet Joseph Smith and with that authority conferred upon them in the flesh they are preaching the gospel to the spirits in prison. . . . Not only are these engaged in that work but hundreds and thousands of others; the Elders that have died in the mission field have not finished their missions, but they are continuing them in the spirit world.[39]

The following year he again emphasized the continuation of priesthood authority after death, "Those who are authorized to preach the gospel here and are appointed here to do that work will not be idle after they have passed away, but will continue to exercise the rights that they obtained here under the priesthood of the Son of God to minister for the salvation of those who have died without a knowledge of the truth."[40]

In the later 1918 revelation, President Smith saw in vision those individuals of whom he had testified concerning their work in the postmortal spirit world. "I beheld that the faithful elders of this dispensation," he testified, "when they depart from mortal life, continue their labors in the preaching of the gospel of repentance and redemption, through the sacrifice of the Only Begotten Son of God, among those who are in darkness and under the bondage of sin in the great world of the spirits of the dead" (D&C 138:57).

Conclusion

President Smith's teachings on priesthood authority, keys, offices, and presiding officers continue to guide our understandings today.[41] His clarifications and explanations were founded on the revelations of God to the Prophet Joseph Smith. Yet the direct and clear manner in which he taught expounded the doctrinal principles of priesthood and Church government in such a way that all might see application in their lives and Church experience. Personally, his explanations have become part of who I am as a priesthood holder and leader in the Church. That is, the authority of the Melchizedek Priesthood enables me to administer and perform all that I am called upon to do; the offices of the priesthood I have held provide me instruction as to my duties and privileges, and, when I was given keys to preside over quorums of the priesthood and as a bishop, I was authorized to direct others in their priesthood labors. As President Smith taught, the principles of the priesthood and Church government provide a perfect organization to carry forth the work of the Lord in complete harmony among the many priesthood bearers.

Notes

1. Francis M. Gibbons, *Joseph F. Smith: Patriarch and Preacher, Prophet of God* (Salt Lake City: Deseret Book, 1984), 269.
2. Thomas G. Alexander, *Mormonism in Transition: A History of the Latter-day Saints, 1890–1930* (Urbana: University of Illinois, 1986), 4.
3. Alexander, *Mormonism in Transition,* 94.
4. William G. Hartley, "The Priesthood Reform Movement, 1908–1922," *BYU Studies* 13, no. 2 (Winter 1973): 143–44.
5. Joseph F. Smith, in Special Conference Report, November 1901, 69–71.

6. James R. Clark, comp., *Messages of the First Presidency of the Church of Jesus Christ of Latter-day Saints* (Salt Lake City: Bookcraft, 1971), 5:80.
7. Alexander, *Mormonism in Transition*, 97.
8. Vera Jean Cassel, ed., *Diary of Brigham Young Jr., 1900–1902* (1931), L. Tom Perry Special Collections, Harold B. Lee Library, Brigham Young University, Provo, UT; manuscript contained in the New York City Library, New York; entry date of October 17, 1901, 87. Marriner W. Merrill, also a member of the Quorum of the Twelve at that time, recorded in his diary regarding the reorganization of the First Presidency, "Joseph F. Smith was unanimously sustained as the President and was set apart as such by his brother, Patriarch John Smith." Melvin Clarence Merrill, ed., *Utah Pioneer and Apostle: Marriner Wood Merrill and His Family* (n.p., 1937), 270.
9. Contrary to Irene Bates and E. Gary Smith's assertion that "Joseph F. Smith unsettled the other apostles at the very beginning of his tenure as president by requesting that his brother, the Patriarch, ordain him" (*Lost Legacy: The Mormon Office of Presiding Patriarch* [Urbana: University of Illinois, 1996], 142), there is no indication in the previously cited diaries that any of the members of the Quorum of the Twelve Apostles had any concerns with Patriarch John Smith setting apart his brother Joseph F. Smith as President of the Church and of the High Priesthood. Further, both Young and Merrill use the term "setting apart" rather than "ordain" as appropriate for the ordinance.
10. As shall be further explained in the discussions that follow, there is also a distinction between priesthood offices and priesthood keys. Joseph F. Smith had been ordained to the office of an Apostle more than a year before being set apart as a member of the Quorum of the Twelve. However, he did not receive the keys of the kingdom at that time. President Brigham Young ordained Joseph F. Smith to the priesthood office of an Apostle on July 1, 1866, at the time he called him to serve as a counselor to those serving in the First Presidency. Nevertheless, to repeat, ordination to a priesthood office or setting apart as a counselor to the First Presidency is distinct from receiving keys to preside over the kingdom of God.
11. Joseph F. Smith and Edward H. Anderson, "The Meeting of the Centuries," *Improvement Era*, January 1901, 230; emphasis in original; also cited in *Gospel Doctrine: Selections from the Sermons and Writings of Joseph F. Smith*, comp. John A. Widtsoe (Salt Lake City: Deseret Book, 1975), 136.
12. Joseph Fielding Smith, *Doctrines of Salvation*, comp. Bruce R. McConkie (Salt Lake City: Bookcraft, 1954–56), 1:259.
13. Joseph Fielding Smith, *Doctrines of Salvation*, 3:155.
14. Alexander, *Mormonism in Transition*, 97.
15. Joseph F. Smith, John R. Winder, and Anthon H. Lund, *Improvement Era*, May 1902, 549; also cited in Clark, *Messages of the First Presidency*, 4:42–43.
16. Joseph F. Smith, in Conference Report [Special Conference], November 1901, 82; brackets in original.
17. George Q. Cannon clarified that "an Elder is not a High Priest until he is ordained to the 'High Priesthood,' that is, is made a High Priest." *Gospel Truth*, comp. Jerreld L. Newquist. (Salt Lake City: Deseret Book, 1974), 1:243. For a discussion on the office of high priest and the High Priesthood please see the author's explanation in Joseph Fielding McConkie and Craig J. Ostler, *Revelations of the Restoration: A Commentary on the Doctrine and Covenants and Other Modern Revelations* (Salt Lake City: Deseret Book, 2000), 597–602.

18. Joseph F. Smith, John R. Winder, and Anthon H. Lund, "The Priesthood and Its Offices," *Improvement Era,* May 1902, 549; also cited in Clark, *Messages,* 4:42; *Gospel Doctrine,* 136.
19. Smith, Winder, and Lund, "The Priesthood and Its Offices," 550–51; also cited in Clark, *Messages of the First Presidency,* 4:43–42. As noted in this article, the Prophet Joseph Smith conferred all of the keys that he possessed upon the Twelve Apostles a few months prior to his death.
20. Joseph F. Smith, in Conference Report, October 1903, 87; emphasis and spelling in the original; also cited in *Gospel Doctrine,* 148; emphasis and spelling in original.
21. *Improvement Era,* April 1902, 550. Also note that this statement is an example wherein the term "High Priesthood," as used, appears to refer to the Melchizedek Priesthood and not to the office of high priest.
22. Gibbons, *Joseph F. Smith,* 215.
23. Alexander, *Mormonism in Transition,* 97.
24. Joseph F. Smith, in Conference Report [Special Conference], November 1901, 82.
25. Joseph F. Smith, in Conference Report, April 1906, 3.
26. Many of President Joseph F. Smith's teachings are compiled in the volume *Gospel Doctrine,* 136–200, in the chapter on priesthood. An abbreviated collection of his teachings was compiled for instruction in Relief Society and Melchizedek Priesthood quorums in *Teachings of the Presidents of the Church: Joseph F. Smith* (Salt Lake City: The Church of Jesus Christ of Latter-day Saints, 1998), 137–45. In addition, Francis M. Gibbons masterfully researched and organized President Joseph F. Smith's teachings on the responsibilities and rights of the various priesthood offices. I am indebted to him for the references and citations in this section on President Smith's teachings regarding specific offices in the priesthood and have liberally utilized his study and work. See Gibbons, *Joseph F. Smith,* 264–69.
27. *Improvement Era,* July 1903, 704–8; also cited in *Gospel Doctrine,* 144.
28. Joseph F. Smith, in Conference Report, October 1915, 7; see also D&C 107:65–67, 91–92.
29. Joseph F. Smith, in Conference Report, October 1915, 4; see also D&C 107:23, 33.
30. Joseph F. Smith, in Conference Report, October 1915, 6; emphasis in original; see also D&C 18:26–33.
31. Joseph F. Smith, in Conference Report, October 1915, 5–6; emphasis in original; see also D&C 107:25–26, 34.
32. Joseph F. Smith, in Conference Report, October 1915, 6; see also D&C 107:15–17; 119:1–2; 120:1.
33. Joseph F. Smith, in Conference Report, October 1915, 4; see also D&C 124:91–92.
34. Joseph F. Smith, in Conference Report, October 1915, 5–6; see also D&C 107:10–12.
35. Joseph F. Smith, in Conference Report, October 1915, 4; see also D&C 20:38–45.
36. Joseph F. Smith, in Conference Report, October 1915, 2–3; see also D&C 42:30–36; 72:9–18; 107:68–76.
37. Joseph F. Smith, in Conference Report, October 1915, 4; see also D&C 20:46–59.
38. Alexander, *Mormonism in Transition,* 111–12; see also William G. Hartley, "The Priesthood Reform Movement, 1909–1922," *BYU Studies* 13, no. 2, 137–56.
39. Joseph F. Smith, *Young Woman's Journal,* August 1910, 456–60; cited in Joseph F. Smith, *Gospel Doctrine,* 471–72.
40. Smith, *Young Woman's Journal,* March 1912, 128–32; also cited in *Gospel Doctrine,* 461.

41. President Joseph F. Smith's teachings on the priesthood have been cited by both President Thomas S. Monson and President Boyd K. Packer in instructing members of the Church. Thomas S. Monson, "Willing and Worthy to Serve," *Ensign*, May 2012, 66; Boyd K. Packer, "What Every Elder Should Know—And Every Sister As Well," in *The Things of the Soul* (Salt Lake City: Bookcraft, 1996), 147–60.

Joseph Stuart

12

Development of the Understanding of the Postmortal Spirit World

The 138th section of the Doctrine and Covenants holds the distinction of being the newest canonized section in the Doctrine and Covenants, and is accepted as a revelation by The Church of Jesus Christ of Latter-day Saints. Received by President Joseph F. Smith in October 1918, the revelation concerns the state of the spirits of those who have passed from mortality. Several important pieces have been written on the historical setting in which President Smith received the revelation, but little has been said on the doctrinal precedent of the spirit world in which D&C 138 was received by President Smith.[1]

In this chapter, I seek to demonstrate not only how President Smith's revelation differed from the theological, doctrinal, and developmental understanding of the spirit world prior to its reception but also how his vision crystallized existing understandings of the postmortal spirit world. I also suggest how President Smith was uniquely prepared to receive the revelation. To accomplish this, I will weave the story of President Smith's life into the narration of the doctrinal unfolding of this topic by previous Presidents of the Church.

Joseph Stuart is a graduate student at the University of Virginia.

Teachings of Joseph Smith

The understanding of the doctrine of the spirit world, the location of the soul between death and the judgment of God, developed subtly from the time of the formal organizing of The Church of Jesus Christ of Latter-day Saints until the time of President Joseph F. Smith's revelation found in section 138. The Church's founder, Joseph Smith, had much to say on the subject of the spirit world, but his understanding would have been shaped by his translation of the Book of Mormon. The separation of the just and the unjust described in Alma 40 of the Book of Mormon suggests that there is a separation between the righteous and the unrighteous in the spirit world. In addition to the writings of the Book of Mormon, Joseph Smith further taught, "Jesus Christ became a ministering spirit (while His body was lying in the sepulchre) to the spirits in prison, to fulfill an important part of His mission."[2] Joseph also taught, "Peter, also, in speaking concerning our Savior, says that, 'He went and preached unto the spirits in prison, which sometimes were disobedient, when once the long suffering of God waited in the days of Noah,' (1 Peter 3:19, 20). Here then we have an account of our Savior preaching to the spirits in prison, to spirits that had been imprisoned from the days of Noah; and what did He preach to them? That they were to stay there? Certainly not!"[3]

Joseph Smith's understanding of the postmortal spirit world likely came from what he had been taught by his parents, from the religious culture in which he lived, and from his personal and family study of the Bible. He understood 1 Peter 3:19–20 in a literal sense, and it is easy to understand why; the scripture doesn't seem to hint at any sort of dualism or secondary meaning. Joseph's unique theological teachings on salvation for the dead were reinforced by Peter's words, and also Paul's: "Else what shall they do which are baptized for the dead, if the dead rise not at all? Why are they then baptized for the dead?" (1 Corinthians 15:29). The Prophet said that "all those who die in the faith go to the prison of spirits to preach to the dead in body but they are alive in spirit; . . . they are made happy by these means."[4] These remarks proved Smith's central doctrinal tenet of organization, that God is a God of order, and not of confusion (see D&C 132:8).

Illustration of Jesus Christ teaching in the spirit world. © 1985, Robert Barrett.

Joseph F. Smith's Experiences with Death during Joseph Smith's Administration

Joseph F. Smith was haunted by the shadow of death nearly his entire life. He often shared Church sermons about the Missouri exodus, when the Latter-day Saints, including young Joseph F. and his mother, were forced from the state. At the time of the exodus, his father was imprisoned in Liberty Jail. From 1839 to 1844, his grandfather Joseph Smith Sr. and uncle Don Carlos Smith passed away, but the death that had the greatest effect on young Joseph F. was the murder of his father, Hyrum the Patriarch. What President Smith later called a "ruthless mob" martyred Hyrum alongside Smith's uncle the Prophet Joseph Smith.[5] He first heard the news of his father's death when a messenger rapped on the window and told his mother the news. That was a night of prayer and panic.[6] Later, Joseph F. participated in the family funeral, where someone lifted him up to see his father's mangled face in the funerary box. The sight of his father's face, which had been shot through the nose and under the jaw, remained permanently in his memory.[7]

Teachings of Brigham Young

The doctrinal foundation that the Prophet Joseph had set was expanded upon by his prophetic successor, Brigham Young. The basis for this expansion of understanding was President Young's teachings that faithful Latter-day Saints went on to preach in the spirit world after their mortal lives were over. Brigham's down-to-earth style and practical theology promised hard work even beyond the grave. He and the other men who presided over the Church from 1847 to 1877 focused on the help that mortals could contribute to the Savior's work of salvation after their time in mortality.

Parley P. Pratt taught that Jesus went to spirit prison, saying, "How many other places Jesus might have visited while in the spirit world is not for me to say, but there was a moment in which the poor, uncultivated, ignorant thief was with him in that world."[8] This major understanding, developed during the time Brigham Young led the Church, focused on what work would be done and how it would be organized in the spirit world. Wilford Woodruff expounded at the funeral of President Jedediah M. Grant, saying, "The same Priesthood exists on the other side of the v[e]il. . . . Every Apostle, every Seventy, every Elder, etc., who has died in the faith as soon as he passes to the other side of the v[e]il, enters into the work of the ministry."[9]

Brigham Young's teachings sum up the understanding of Saints in his administration with these words: "Jesus was the first man that ever went to preach to the spirits in prison, holding the keys of the Gospel of salvation to them. Those keys were delivered to him in the day and hour that he went into the spirit world, and with them he opened the door of salvation to the spirits in prison."[10] He further taught that he couldn't say it "any better than what the ancient Apostle has told it; he says he went to preach to the spirits in prison. Who are they to whom he went to preach? The people who lived in the antediluvian world." In a final summation, President Young taught, "When any of the Latter-day Elders or Apostles die, and leave this world, suffice it to say, that their spirits go to that prison, and preach the Gospel to those who have died without hearing it; . . . the spirits of good men like Joseph and the Elders, who have left this Church on earth for a season to operate in another sphere, are rallying all their powers and going from place to place preaching the Gospel, and Joseph is directing them."[11]

Joseph F. Smith's Experiences with Death, 1847–77

Joseph F. Smith escaped the agony of additional deaths in his immediate family for only eight more years before his mother, Mary, died of apparent pneumonia in 1852. Her death appeared to have had just as much of an impact on Smith as his father's death. When Joseph F. received the news of his mother's death, he is reported to have passed out.[12] A year and a half later, he still felt "like a comet or fiery meteor, without attraction or gravitation to keep me balanced or guide me within reasonable bounds."[13] Clearly, Mary's death unhinged her son emotionally.[14]

Death first struck Smith's own posterity with the death of his first child, Mercy Josephine (whom he called Dodo) in 1870.[15] Smith was thirty years old at the time, still a very young father, and busily engaged in civic and Church responsibilities. Despite his schedule, he was an attentive and loving father and husband to his wives and children. His journal is poignant in his description of his feelings about Mercy's death. Of the tragic events, Smith wrote:

> I scarcely dare to trust myself to write, even now my heart aches, and my mind is all chaos; if I should murmur, may God forgive me, my soul has been and is tried with poignant grief, my heart is bruised and wrenched almost asunder. I am desolate, my home seems desolate and almost dreary, yet here are my family and my little babe; yet I cannot help but feel that the tenderest, sweetest and

> yet the strongest cord that bound me to home and earth is severed, my babe, my own sweet Dodo is gone! . . . I am almost wild, and O God only knows how much I loved my girl, and she the light and the joy of my heart. . . . The image of heaven graven in my soul was almost departed. . . . The star of my life and happiness seemed to have shone its last on earth, and my soul bowed into the dust. Oh! my Dodo, my heart is almost broken for the loss of thee![16]

Joseph's wife Julina Lambson Smith said that her husband "never got over losing his firstborn" and that when a second daughter was born, "he [would take her in] his arms, walk the floor and cry. . . . He never got where he could talk of [Mercy Josephine] without tears in his eyes."[17]

Teachings of John Taylor, Wilford Woodruff, and Lorenzo Snow

Joseph F. Smith was selected as a counselor to John Taylor on October 10, 1880. During President Smith's first sojourn in the First Presidency, Church leaders discussed the spirit world at length in Church conferences, public meetings, and funerals. President John Taylor remarked, "It is also true that the same Savior who is our Savior, when he was put to death in the flesh, was quickened by the spirit, and that he visited those spirits in prison, opening up the door of salvation to them that they might be redeemed and come forth and accomplish certain purposes which God had designed; . . . the priesthood behind the veil is operating and preaching to the spirits that are in prison that have been there from the different ages."[18]

Other leaders chimed in, agreeing with President Taylor, saying that "[Jesus] entered the abode of the doomed"[19] and that "Jesus descended into hell. He certainly did, and visited those spirits that were in prison."[20] President Smith's teachings on the spirit world during the presidencies of John Taylor, Wilford Woodruff, and Lorenzo Snow showcase and highlight the teachings of the Church over his lifetime. He preached:

> The Priesthood that we hold is perfect, because it is of God. It is the authority which God has revealed and restored to the children of men for their government and guidance in the building up of Zion and in the proclamation of the Gospel to the nations of the earth, until every son and daughter of Adam shall have the privilege of hearing the sound of the Gospel, and of being brought to the knowledge of the truth, not only upon this earth, but in the spirit world. The

> millions and millions that have lived upon this earth and have passed away without the knowledge of the Gospel here, will have to be taught them there, by virtue of the authority of this holy priesthood that you and I hold. The Church of God will be organized among them by the authority of this priesthood.[21]

Joseph F. Smith's Presidency, 1901–18

On October 17, 1901, Joseph F. Smith was ordained as the President of the Church of Jesus Christ of Latter-day Saints. The teaching of the doctrine of the spirit world during the presidency of Joseph F. Smith offers excellent insight into the doctrinal climate in which President Smith received his vision of the redemption of the dead. Leaders spoke on varied points of emphasis, but their rhetoric can be grouped into two main themes: Christ visiting the spirit world, and the missionary work that takes place in the spirit world.[22]

Jesus Christ visited the spirit world. Church leaders told the world in general conference that Jesus "went into the spirit world and preached to that people the same principles that had been taught by Noah."[23] The conference congregations were told that "Scripture . . . bear[s] witness that Christ, before He arose from the grave and broke the shackles of death, went into the prison house and preached to the spirits which were in prison."[24] The scriptures affirm that Jesus opened the prison doors and descended into spirit prison and that he did so for the purpose of allowing faithful Latter-day Saints to do missionary work to those who "sometime were disobedient" in their earthly sojourn (1 Peter 3:20).

Missionary work. Missionary work for those in the spirit world was heavily emphasized during the presidency of Joseph F. Smith. Church members were reminded that a postmortal mission field was open on the other side of the veil. Those who had been faithful before Jesus' crucifixion and had followed in his footsteps went and preached to the spirits that were in the spirit world, which needed enlightenment and teaching. Faithful Church members would "mount up to the spirit world, and . . . carry the Gospel to countless millions of the once inhabitants of the earth, and in the footsteps of our Lord Jesus Christ we will walk always until the resurrection day shall dawn."[25] A "mighty work is going on [in the spirit world]" and was operated under the direction of Christ, and through those "brethren [of the priesthood who] depart hence and their places are taken up by their posterity, they will carry on this work in the spirit world."[26] There was to be priesthood organization after mortality, just as there was when their bodies tarried on earth. Part of the larger part of the Atonement was that Jesus' death had opened up the spirit world for missionary work[27] and that Latter-day Saints could begin helping now by "labor[ing] for the salvation of our ancestors by attending to ordinances for them which they could not now perform, being in the spirit world."[28] Missionary work, whether in mortality or the life beyond, always requires work by those who are willing.

President Smith himself spoke publicly about death and the spirit world, beginning only two months after his ordination as President of the Church. Smith preached to the Saints that "Jesus went to preach to their spirits in prison, and proclaimed liberty and deliverance to them"[29] and that "such men as Peter and James and the twelve disciples chosen of the Savior . . . [are] proclaiming liberty to the captives in the spirit world and in opening their prison doors. I do not believe that they could be employed in any greater work."[30]

Joseph F. Smith's Experiences with Death, 1901–18

In January of 1918, President Smith's son Hyrum Mack Smith died suddenly at age forty-five, from a burst appendix. His death was shocking and unnerving to President Smith, leaving him physically weak and melancholy. He had "prayed and pleaded with the Lord, but his soul was filled with foreboding anxiety." He expressed his feelings at the death of Hyrum M. Smith thus: "My soul is rent asunder. My heart is broken, and flutters for life! . . . He is my firstborn son; the first to bring me the joy and hope of an endless, honorable, name among men. . . . I needed him more than I can express. . . . He was most useful to the Church. . . . O God, help me!"[31] Smith had lost thirteen children to the persistent hand of death during a span of fifty years, but Hyrum's death must have been particularly painful because of his promising ministry as an Apostle.[32]

President Smith reportedly withdrew from the public following the death of his son. The time away from the public eye, in the midst of the Spanish flu pandemic and World War I, provided time for pondering, praying, and studying the scriptures. His musings on death and the spirit world do not seem to have immediately resulted in a new doctrinal understanding. This is evidenced by the last reference to Smith's understanding of the spirit world before the reception of his vision for the redemption of the dead. In July 1918, when asked by a Church member what happened between death and the Resurrection, President

Smith replied that "Jesus bridged over the 'great gulf' that divided the two divisions of the spirit world, and 'went and preached to the spirits in prison.'"[33] It is clear to see that President Smith, though he had been grieving over the loss of his son Hyrum, had not yet reached or shared the doctrinal understanding that he would reveal to the Church in less than a month.

On October 4, 1918, President Smith spoke at general conference. Those in attendance noted that his feet and voice trembled while he spoke but that his spirit remained strong.[34] He wanted the congregation to know that he had not been negligent in his duty as prophet, seer, and revelator and President of the Church despite his advanced age, grief, and physical fatigue. He continued, vaguely referencing his vision of the redemption of the dead, saying: "I will not, I dare not, attempt to enter upon many things that are resting upon my mind this morning, and I shall postpone until some future time, the Lord being willing, my attempt to tell you some of the things that are in my mind, and that dwell in my heart. I have not lived alone these five months. I have dwelt in the spirit of prayer, of supplication, of faith and of determination; and I have had my communication with the Spirit of the Lord continuously."[35]

President Smith had received a revelation, but he did not feel it appropriate to share at that time. He told the congregation, "When the Lord reveals something to me, I will consider the matter with my brethren, and when it becomes proper, I will let it be known to the people, and not otherwise."[36]

The Vision of the Redemption of the Dead

President Smith was contemplating, studying, and praying about the spirit world under these circumstances. The monster of death was all encompassing: the Spanish flu, World War I, and deaths in his own family caused President Smith to ponder on the "wonderful love" of the Father and the Son, perhaps in gratitude for the Atonement and Resurrection of Jesus Christ (see D&C 138:3–4).

President Smith's vision of the redemption of the dead is largely an affirmation of the previous ninety years of its doctrinal teaching in the Church. President Smith saw that Jesus went to the righteous in prison, where he "preached . . . the everlasting gospel, the doctrine of the resurrection and the redemption of mankind from the fall, and from individual sins on conditions of repentance" (D&C 138:19). The spirit world was described as a place of learning, a place of joy, and a place of eternal hope through Jesus Christ (see Alma 40:11–12).

One of the most significant doctrinal developments of President Smith's vision is that Jesus did not go to the wicked, the rebellious, or those that had rejected the gospel while in mortality. Darkness reigned where the Light of the World was not (see D&C 138:20–22). No public discussion of 1 Peter 3 and 4 in the Church from 1829 to September 1918 mentioned that Jesus sent messengers to the wicked, rather than visiting them himself. This is the most significant addition to the Latter-day Saint understanding of the spirit world that was made known through President Smith's vision.

Pondering upon the pragmatic problem of Jesus preaching to the unrepentant spirits in prison, Joseph F. had wondered how Jesus had been able to teach the millions—possibly billions—in spirit prison (see D&C 138:27). In his vision, President Smith saw that, although Jesus didn't descend into hell himself, he "organized . . . forces and appointed messengers, clothed with power and authority, and commissioned them to go forth and carry the light of the gospel to them that were in darkness, even to all the spirits of men" (D&C 138:29–30). President Smith saw that in this manner the gospel was preached to the dead.

These messengers were not just those who had qualified for spirit paradise. They were chosen messengers, sent to proclaim "liberty to the captives" (D&C 138:31). The messengers still operated under the priesthood hierarchy that they had lived in during their sojourn on earth. President Smith saw "the Prophet Joseph Smith, and [Joseph F.'s] father, Hyrum Smith, Brigham Young, John Taylor, Wilford Woodruff, and other choice spirits who were reserved to come forth in the fullness of times to take part in laying the foundations of the great latter-day work" busy directing and encouraging the work of preaching to the spirits in prison (D&C 138:57). This part of the vision confirms what Brigham Young and other Church leaders had taught—that priesthood responsibility for preaching the gospel extended beyond the grave.

Joseph F. also affirmed what Joseph Smith had taught about preaching to the dead: those that had passed on without acceptation or opportunity to hear the gospel must have their work done by faithful members of the Church in temples (see D&C 138:54).

President Smith saw death as a melancholy event—one to be looked at with mourning and sorrow. He had the empathy to weep and grieve at death, and identified with others' sorrow because of many life experiences with outliving his parents, parent figures, and many of his children. Nevertheless, despite the loss of his father, uncles, grandfather, mother, siblings, wife, and children, he never stepped away from his optimism that he would meet them again on the other side of the veil. That thought carried him through the darkest times in his life. Through his faith in Jesus Christ, and also through the vicissitudes he had faced in losing so many friends and family, he was *uniquely prepared* to receive this vision of the redemption of the dead. Perhaps the knowledge that he and his loved ones would continue to serve in Christ's Church even after mortality would have been of special solace to him, as one among the leaders of the Church who had served the Church for so long and seen so many deaths. Although section 138 largely reaffirms ideas that had been taught for generations in the Church, President Smith's unique life experiences opened his mind to further questions, thus also opening his mind to receive additional enlightenment to those questions he had on the subject of the spirit world.

Notes

1. George S. Tate, "The Great World of the Spirits of the Dead," *BYU Studies* 46, no. 1 (2007): 5–40. One other article touches on the development of the idea, though not in as much depth or with the background of Joseph F. Smith's life. See Charles R. Harrell, *This Is My Doctrine: The Development of Mormong Theology* (Draper, UT: Greg Kofford Books, 2011), 348–66. The pages listed cover the chapter on salvation for the dead.
2. *History of the Church of Jesus Christ of Latter-day Saints*, ed. B. H. Roberts, 2nd ed. rev. (Salt Lake City: Deseret Book, 1932), 4:425.
3. *History of the Church*, 4:596.
4. George Laub, autobiography, in *Writings of Early Latter-day Saints*, 326, L. Tom Perry Special Collections, Harold B. Lee Library, Brigham Young University, Provo, UT.
5. In Scott G. Kenney Research Collection, MS 2022, box 5, folder 1, L. Tom Perry Special Collections.
6. Joseph Fielding Smith, *The Life of Joseph F. Smith, Sixth President of the Church of Jesus Christ of Latter-day Saints* (Salt Lake City: Deseret News, 1938), 129–30.
7. Scott G. Kenney Research Collection, MSS 2022, box 5, folder 11, L. Tom Perry Special Collections; Smith, *Life of Joseph F. Smith*, 128.
8. Parley P. Pratt, in *Journal of Discourses* (London: Latter-day Saints' Book Depot, 1854–86), 1:9. The "ignorant thief" refers to one of the men who was crucified alongside Jesus Christ. Jesus promised him that he would be with the thief "in paradise." See Luke 23:43.
9. Wilford Woodruff, in *Journal of Discourses*, 22:333–34.
10. Brigham Young, *Discourses of Brigham Young*, ed. G. Homer Durham (Salt Lake City: Deseret Book, 1954), 378.
11. Brigham Young, in *Journal of Discourses*, 3:96, 372.
12. See Scott G. Kenney, "Before the Beard: Trials of the Young Joseph F. Smith," *Sunstone* 120 (November 2001): 23n20.
13. Kenney, "Before the Beard," 23n24.

14. For a full treatment of Joseph F. Smith's mental state, please consult Scott G. Kenney, "Before the Beard."
15. Due to space limitations, this essay will highlight only the first and last deaths in President Smith's family, although he ultimately lost thirteen children before he died.
16. Smith, *Life of Joseph F. Smith*, 455–56.
17. Julina Lambson Smith, journal, 1912, as cited in Joseph Fielding Smith, *Life of Joseph F. Smith*, 458–59.
18. John Taylor, in *Journal of Discourses*, 21:97.
19. Charles W. Penrose, in *Journal of Discourses*, 22:165.
20. George Q. Cannon, in *Journal of Discourses*, 25:173.
21. Joseph F. Smith, "Rights and Order of the Priesthood," in *Collected Discourses, 1892–1893* (Salt Lake City: Deseret Book, 2013), 3:99.
22. I repeat that President Smith taught and supported the teachings of his time on the spirit world to highlight the changes in the revelation now known as Doctrine and Covenants 138.
23. George Teasdale, in Conference Report, October 1901, 36.
24. Joseph E. Robinson, in Conference Report, April 1915, 75.
25. Charles W. Penrose, in Conference Report, October 1914, 43.
26. Charles W. Penrose, in Conference Report, April 1904, 72.
27. James E. Talmage, in Conference Report, April 1912, 126–27.
28. Charles W. Penrose, in Conference Report, October 1918, 12.
29. Joseph F. Smith, "Editor's Table," *Improvement Era*, December 1901, 146.
30. Joseph F. Smith, "Address of President Joseph F. Smith: Delivered at the Funeral Services of Sister Mary A. Freeze," *Young Woman's Journal*, March 1912, 130.
31. Smith, *Life of Joseph Smith*, 474.
32. There are several possibilities as to why this particular death took such a physical and emotional toll on President Smith. Perhaps the most obvious reason is that at age seventy-nine, President Smith was considerably older than he had been at the previous loss of a child (at which point he had been sixty). President Smith said this of his son Hyrum: "His mind was quick and bright and correct. His judgment was not excelled, and he saw and comprehended things in their true light and meaning. When he spoke, men listened and felt the weight of his thoughts and words. . . . We all needed him. . . . He has thrilled my soul by his power of speech, as no other man ever did. Perhaps this was because he was my son, and he was filled with the fire of the Holy Ghost. And now, what can I do! O what can I do!" First Presidency Reel 7/29/1918, MS 2022, box 2, folder 15, L. Tom Perry Special Collections.
33. *Gospel Doctrine: Selections from the Sermons and Writings of Joseph F. Smith*, 5th ed. (Salt Lake City: Deseret Book, 1939), 472–76.
34. Anthony W. Ivins, journal, October 4, 1918, Anthony W. Ivins Papers, Special Collections, J. Willard Marriott Library, University of Utah, Salt Lake City.
35. Joseph F. Smith, "Editor's Table," *Improvement Era*, November 1918, 81.
36. Joseph F. Smith, "Spurious Revelations and Visions," *Improvement Era*, December 1918, 106.

Jonathan A. Stapley

13

"The Last of the Old School": Joseph F. Smith and Latter-day Saint Liturgy

When the Committee on Courses of Study for the Priesthood published a compilation of Joseph F. Smith's teachings one year after his death, they appended the volume with several tributes and biographical sketches. Edward H. Anderson, President Smith's coeditor at the *Improvement Era*, penned the final piece, declaring that Smith was "the last of the old school of veteran leaders."[1] This statement certainly relates to many aspects of Smith's life and service. In this paper, however, I will focus on how this pithy description from the first edition of *Gospel Doctrine* is particularly cogent to Smith's role in the development and transmission of liturgy within the LDS Church.

During the nineteenth century, Latter-day Saint liturgy existed in an uncodified and dynamic state. New rituals emerged and the Saints adapted older rituals to address unmet needs. Generally transmitted through folk channels of instruction, Mormons learned ritual performance and worship patterns through proximate example and from oral texts. There were no Church handbooks or manuals from which to learn, no written formulae. Consequently, as Church members looked for authoritative performance, they looked to those individuals

---

Jonathan A. Stapley is an independent scholar living in Bellevue, Washington.

closest to Joseph Smith or his inner circle as authoritative examples. And while these authoritative examples were often members of the high quorums of the Church, they were not always so.

As a member of the Smith family with a childhood in Nauvoo, and due to his extensive experience associating in the highest quorums of the Church, Joseph F. Smith occupied an important and unparalleled position during the first decades of the twentieth century. He was a living receptacle of liturgical history when no written liturgical histories or instructions existed. And as leaders modernized Church bureaucracy and liturgy, he wielded tremendous influence over the patterns, forms, and rituals of Church life.

After discussing several examples which highlight features of this liturgical authority within nineteenth-century Mormonism, I will review Joseph F. Smith's interactions with three ritual systems: female healing, baptism for health, and baby blessing. Though limited in scope, this chapter will show how Smith held on to practices that were confusing to younger Church leaders who lacked his historical memory. In other cases Smith was also innovative, changing worship and ritual, and leaving an imprint on the Church to this day.[2] However, the cases described in this chapter elucidate the evolution in Mormon liturgy by focusing on Joseph F. Smith's deeply conservative approach to aspects of it.

Authority and Nineteenth-Century Mormon Liturgy

Current Latter-day Saints are accustomed to formal channels of authority, generally structured through priesthood quorums, ordination, and delegation. Questions about Church praxis are answered either by reference to handbooks of instruction created by general priesthood leaders which serve as Church law, or by appeal to one's closest priesthood leader in the authoritative bureaucracy. Both of these modes of clarification are largely products of the twentieth century. In the nineteenth century, Mormons generally lacked formal codified instruction. Instead, Church leaders relied on oral instructions, either through personal conversations or public sermons, though in some cases, instructional letters are extant, with general circular letters being particularly rare.

For example, as Joseph Smith participated in the development of the Mormon healing liturgy, he introduced many different rituals to the Latter-day Saints. By the time he died, Mormon men and women variously laid on hands, anointed the body or the head, drank consecrated oil, baptized for health, washed and anointed for health, and administered in conjunction with temple prayers.[3] There is no record of Joseph Smith's justification for the ritual diversity within this healing liturgy, nor did he ever leave concrete instructions for ritual performance.[4] Moreover, the Doctrine and Covenants mentions only laying on hands, whereas the Bible mentions anointing. Instead, Latter-day Saints relied on each other to learn how to participate in the healing liturgy. They learned by example and by oral instruction. When a question arose over what was to be done, or why it was to be done, members viewed those closest to Joseph Smith and later Church leaders as being most authoritative.

This dynamic played out in sometimes surprising ways. In the case of female ritual healing, perhaps the most authoritative voice in the late-nineteenth century was not a member of a priesthood quorum, but the general Relief Society president. Women had been authorized to perform healing rituals from the early Kirtland period, and Joseph Smith delivered instructions, which he said were by revelation, to the Female Relief Society of Nauvoo affirming their right to participate in the healing liturgy. By the time the Latter-day Saints arrived in Utah, lay Church members and leaders both recognized women as regular healers in the Church.[5]

In 1884, however, Eliza R. Snow, the recently set apart general Relief Society president, instituted a new policy with regard to female healing. Whereas Mormon women previously had the authority to administer healing rituals "in the name of Jesus Christ" by virtue of their Church membership alone, Snow declared that only those women who had participated in the temple liturgy were to be authorized to heal. The reason for this shift is not clear; however, it was a dramatic departure from previous practice. Immediately after Snow's death, acting Church President Wilford Woodruff reverted the policy back and reauthorized all female Church members to heal. While Church leaders continued to preach that all women could heal for the next several decades, many people remembered Snow's instructions and were confused. Even members of the First Presidency deferred to Snow on this position while she lived and for a few years after.[6] The reason for this confusion lay in Eliza R. Snow's role as chief interpreter of Joseph Smith's teachings to the Female Relief Society of Nauvoo.[7] She was widely recognized as one of Smith's plural wives, even taking his last name during the latter years of her life. She was the secretary who inscribed Smith's words to the Society in Nauvoo, and she kept the minute book with her to preach from until she died. In relation to

Lewis A. Ramsey, oil portrait of Eliza R. Snow, 1909, courtesy of Church History Museum, Salt Lake City.

female healing, people accepted that she knew what to do and how to do it because no one surpassed her access to Joseph Smith on the topic.

Another example of this empirical basis for authority relates to the temple liturgy. In 1887, Logan Temple Recorder Samuel Roskelley wrote Wilford Woodruff, then President of the Quorum of the Twelve Apostles, with several questions relating to ritual performance in the temple. In response, Woodruff stated:

> I consider that if there ever was any man who thoroughly understood the principle of the Endowments it was Brigham Young. He had been with Joseph Smith from the beginning of the Endowments to the end; and he understood it if any man did.... Brother Roskelley, I have given Endowments in Salt Lake City for twenty years, and I received my Endowments under the hands of the Prophet Joseph Smith. I directed the fixing up of the Temple in St. George for giving Endowments under the direction of President Young.... You say, "we are told here so and so concerning sealings and adoptions." Who is it that has told you these things and given these instructions? I don't think it can be President Taylor, for neither he nor I have ever received such teachings from either Joseph Smith or Brigham Young. But I have been taught right the reverse by President Young.

At the end of the letter, Woodruff concluded, "Now anything I have said in this letter in giving my views in relation to what you have asked need not be treated as a private matter, as you suggest. You may make whatever use of them you please."[8] Though Woodruff's ecclesiastical position was likely sufficient to dictate temple policy, in responding to Roskelley and clarifying that policy, Woodruff justified his responses by appealing to the authority he gained not from Church office, but from his experience having been personally instructed by Joseph Smith and Brigham Young.

Joseph F. Smith and the Twentieth-Century Mormon Liturgy

In the twentieth century, virtually all Church leaders had been born after the Latter-day Saint arrival in the Great Basin. Many had learned how to participate in the Latter-day Saint liturgy from those who knew Joseph Smith, but they themselves were not immediately connected to the context in which many rituals arose. With very few details regarding Church liturgy described in the canon and no written liturgical histories, as these foundational examples passed away, an explicative vacuum led many to question the nature of Mormon ritual and worship. Joseph F. Smith stood as a pillar against this stress on the structure of Mormonism's lived religion.

Baptism for Health

Though many Saints had been healed through baptism when they joined the Church, Joseph Smith and the Twelve introduced a specific ritual of baptism for health in Nauvoo. This healing ritual became common both in and out of the temples into the 1920s, with the first baptisms performed in several of the temples being for the health of the recipients. Temples documented every baptism for health performed as part of their regular records. For several years it was the most common ritual performed in the temples. However, in the first decades of the twentieth century, many Church leaders were confused by the practice.[9]

On November 19, 1912, Joseph F. Smith's son Alvin, a prominent Salt Lake Temple sealer, spoke to patrons and "said he thought it was not good to be baptized for health."[10] Anthon Lund, the president of the Salt Lake Temple and a member of the First Presidency, spoke to him afterward, trying to defend the practice with a Utah-era theological argument. Though a proponent of the practice, Lund most likely lacked knowledge of its history. The following year, at the regular meeting of the First Presidency, Quorum of the Twelve, and Presiding Patriarch, Hyrum Mack Smith, an Apostle and another of Joseph F. Smith's sons, asked about "the origin of Baptism for health, . . . seeking information on this subject." Without any mention of the ritual in the scriptural canon, it is no surprise that many were curious about baptism for health. In response, President Smith simply stated "that it had been customary to baptize for health from the early rise of the Church." In other words, baptism for health was something that he had learned from experience in Nauvoo. Both he and Anthon Lund then recounted specific examples of the ritual's efficacy.[11]

Baptism for health was an integral feature of the early Mormon healing liturgy, and Joseph F. Smith experienced its introduction in Nauvoo by Joseph Smith and the Twelve,[12] as well as the spread of the ritual throughout the world to wherever Church members were located. This experience anchored his support for it, and it was not until both he and his loyal counselor, Anthon Lund, passed away that the First Presidency of Heber J. Grant ended the practice of baptism for health in the Church. Grant's First Presidency, along with the new

Salt Lake Temple president, Apostle George F. Richards, initiated broad liturgical reforms in the Church, and specifically modernized the temple ceremonies.[13] As part of this process, the First Presidency wrote a circular letter that ended baptism for health: "We feel constrained to call your attention to the custom prevailing to some extent in our temples of baptizing for health, and to remind you that baptism for health is not part of our temple work, and therefore to permit it to become a practice would be an innovation detrimental to temple work, and a departure as well from the provision instituted of the Lord for the care and healing of the sick of His Church."[14] The younger Church leaders did not have the same anchoring experiences as Joseph F. Smith, and without historical context, baptism for health became superfluous. Moreover, there were few, if any, living obstacles to its removal from the Church liturgy.

Female Ritual Healing

Another example of Joseph F. Smith's strong conservative influence over the healing liturgy of the Church is the performance of healing rituals by women. In this case, however, his role in the development of the liturgy also included an instance of innovation, which pitted his authority against other strong examples outside of the priesthood hierarchy. As discussed earlier, women regularly administered healing rituals in the nineteenth-century Church. Joseph F. Smith regularly participated in healing blessings with women and received blessings from one of his wives.[15] Moreover, he explicitly taught that women "can seal their blessings in the name of the Lord Jesus."[16] At the turn of the twentieth century, many Church members and leaders experienced a sort of crisis in authority with the rise of non-Mormon Christian healing ritual performance. This, perhaps coupled with other shifts in the post-Manifesto organization of the Church, resulted in Joseph F. Smith's recommendation in 1900 to Church President Lorenzo Snow to bifurcate the healing liturgy, with only men being allowed to seal anointings.

The First Presidency maintained the right of women to continue administering healing rituals; however, they were to "confirm" anointings, not to "seal" them. This was an important development, and many women were confused by the change, as the policy was announced by a newspaper editorial and was not at first circulated under the imprimatur of the First Presidency. The former editor of the *Woman's Exponent* wrote incredulously to the editor of the newspaper and confronted him with the then-common understanding that Eliza R. Snow was instructed "from the Prophet Joseph Smith" to always seal the anointings.[17] At one meeting of the General Young Ladies' Mutual Improvement Association, Helen Woodruff, wife of young Apostle Owen Woodruff, testified that "Aunt Zina & Aunt Bathsheba" had sealed a healing anointing on her and that "she took them as very good authority."[18] These women had in the past been the ultimate authorities on female ritual healing performance.

However, Eliza R. Snow was dead, and her successor Zina D. H. Young had also just passed away. Joseph F. Smith was then one of the most experienced Church leaders with regards to female healing, and as such, his support did not deviate. Despite his alteration of the female ritual, he was the most prolific Church President on the topic. He explicitly and repeatedly sustained the right of women in the Church to administer healing rituals, both by performatively participating in such rituals with his wife and by writing letters from the office of the First Presidency. In fact, in 1914 the First Presidency wrote a general circular letter to all Church leaders in support of female healing the same day that Joseph F. Smith spoke in the general Relief Society conference in support of the same.[19]

Female participation in the healing liturgy was not addressed in the Grant administration's liturgical reforms mentioned above. Instead, it was left uncodified. While other aspects of Church liturgy were increasingly being formalized, written down, and taught in Church settings, only those who were taught by example maintained experience with female healing. Consequently, after Joseph F. Smith, it was only those Church leaders with the most experience with female healing, such as Joseph Fielding Smith and Bruce R. McConkie, that continued to support the practice. It was otherwise left to be forgotten.

Baby Blessing

In the days immediately after the organization of the LDS Church on April 6, 1830, Joseph Smith dictated the "Articles and Covenants" of the Church. Included in this instructional document was a commandment that "every member of the church of Christ having children is to bring them unto the elders before the Church, who are to lay their hands upon them in the name of Jesus Christ,and bless them in his name" (D&C 20:70).[20] Thus the blessing of children was one of the earliest rituals revealed to the Church. However, the short exhortation included in the "Articles and Covenants" lacked any detail. At the time it was written, the office of elder was the highest office in the Church, but there was no mention of when or how

Zina D. H. Young. © Intellectual Reserve, Inc., courtesy of Church History Museum.

the blessing was to be delivered, beyond the necessity of it being before the body of the Church.

As was common in Mormonism's liturgy, details like precisely how and when to bless children was a matter clarified by folk instruction. Giving blessings to children eight days after birth is documented by 1832.[21] It is unclear when the idea of children being named as part of this ritual developed. Though it is not universally attested, documentation for it exists from the time the Saints left Nauvoo.[22] It is likely that a specific eighth-day blessing was evocative of the Jewish practice of circumcision.[23] Baby blessings were common; however, written blessing texts are rare. Nevertheless, all of the early blessing texts of which I am aware are for eighth-day blessings.[24] Moreover, documentation for eighth-day blessings in the nineteenth century is commonplace.[25]

Whereas many post-Nauvoo baby blessings were commonly performed by presiding authorities in public meetings, and sometimes called "bishop's blessings,"[26] eighth-day blessings appear to be more commonly performed privately by fathers or relatives. These two practices were consequently in tension, as Quorum of the Twelve President John Taylor acknowledged when addressing the issue in 1878. Writing for the governing body of the Church (there was no First Presidency at this time), Taylor wrote, "some of the Elders have been teaching ideas concerning the blessing of children that we deem to be incorrect. If we are not misinformed it has been taught that there was no need of parents bringing their infants before the Church to be blessed by the Elders, but it were better for the father to attend to this rite at home, for if he did not, he lost a very great privilege as well as a right to, and power over his children that he might otherwise retain." Taylor indicated that fathers do indeed have the right to bless their children, and Church leaders did not object to "the father taking his babe on the eighth day and giving it a father's blessing"; however, he also indicated that the practice should not "interfere with our obedience to that law of the Lord." He then quoted the Articles and Covenants of the Church, stating that having the Church elders bless the child in public was "a direct command of Jehovah." Taylor then explained the virtues of having Church leaders bless the baby with the congregation present.[27] The pattern of double blessings thus introduced by Taylor became standard practice moving forward, as one non-Mormon observer of Utah described in 1894: "According to the Mormon customs, when the child is eight days old its father ought to bless and name it. Then on a fast day,—they come on the first Thursday of every month,—the baby is blessed and named by the Elders, with laying on of hands."[28]

After Taylor's statement, stakes, conferences (the organizational Church unit where stakes were not organized), and individual missionaries began regularly recording instances of baby blessings and reporting them on statistical reports. It appears that with this institutional support eighth-day blessings began to have something of a diminished character.[29] Joseph F. Smith, however, approached the subject of baby blessings with a memory of only performing one blessing, as was common before John Taylor's proclamation, and had given many of his children eighth-day blessings.[30] Smith, being concerned about ritual repetition more generally in 1903, wrote that it was common for parents to bring their children to fast meetings to be blessed, where the bishopric would typically allow the father, if an elder, to participate in the blessing circle. However, Smith also noted that "many Elders desire to perform this ordinance within the circle of their own families on or about the eighth day of the child's life. This also is proper, for the father, if he be worthy of his Priesthood, has certain rights and authority within his family, comparable to those of the Bishop with relation to the ward." He then encouraged all worthy men to bless their children, magnifying their role as fathers. He noted that the question had been asked, "If an Elder performs the ordinance of naming and blessing his own child at home, is it necessary that the ordinance be repeated in the ward meeting?" He responded, "We answer, No; the father's blessing is authoritative, proper, and sufficient."[31]

It appears that Joseph F. Smith's comments regarding double baby blessings did not have immediate impact, and they continued regularly after Smith's statement.[32] Fourteen years later, the *Improvement Era*, of which Smith was a coeditor, printed an unsigned editorial responding to a question of whether babies who had received eighth-day blessings at home needed to still be blessed at Church. The editorial stated the following: "We believe that it is not only the privilege but the duty of the father to so bless his child, also to record the blessing in his family record." However, the editorial further clarified, "the blessing of which the Church takes cognizance is the blessing that is given when the child is brought 'unto the elders before the Church.' It becomes the blessing of public record."[33] If Smith was not the author of this editorial, he was likely cognizant of its content.

Though discussion of repeat baby blessings occurred after Joseph F. Smith's death, I am unaware of any further discussion of the "eighth-day" blessing.[34] Though Joseph F. Smith may have vacillated over the necessity of repeating baby blessings, he consistently affirmed the value of eighth-day blessings. Neither blessing on the eighth day nor the naming function of baby blessings was delineated in extant revelation text. As later Church leaders evaluated the practice and focused solely on public baby blessings, naming was easily conserved and incorporated into the formal liturgy, whereas the eighth-day blessing was not. Though eighth-day blessings persisted for some time,[35] they lost their last documented public supporter in Joseph F. Smith.

Conclusion

That Joseph F. Smith naturally supported baptism for health, female ritual healing and eighth day blessings is entirely consistent with his experience having been trained in the early days of the Church by the example of Joseph Smith and his trusted associates. It is perhaps also natural that as he, the last of these "old school" leaders, passed away, younger leaders without access to that history were less constrained in their approach to that liturgy. Both Smith's tenure as Church

President and his role as living receptacle of liturgical history mark a transition point in Latter-day Saint rituals and worship.

Notes

1. Committee on Courses of Study for the Priesthood, *Gospel Doctrine: Selections from the Sermons and Writings of Joseph F. Smith, Sixth President of the Church of Jesus Christ of Latter-day Saints* (Salt Lake City: Deseret News, 1919), 683–85.
2. Examples include ordination and healing anointing. On the latter, see Jonathan A. Stapley, "'Pouring in Oil': The Development of the Modern Mormon Healing Ritual," in *By Our Rites of Worship: Latter-day Saint Views on Ritual in History, Scripture, and Practice*, ed. Daniel Belnap (Provo, UT: Religious Studies Center; Salt Lake City: Deseret Book, 2013): 283–316.
3. Jonathan A. Stapley and Kristine Wright, "The Forms and the Power: The Development of Mormon Ritual Healing to 1847," *Journal of Mormon History* 35 (Summer 2009): 42–87. Reprinted with revisions in Stephen C. Taysom, ed., *Dimensions of Faith: A Mormon Studies Reader* (Salt Lake City: Signature Books, 2011).
4. Joseph Smith's complete rejection of Church rule books is perhaps relevant. On December 14, 1834, Smith "preached three hours, . . . during which he exposed the Methodist Dicipline in its black deformity and called upon the Elders in the power of the spirit of God to expose the creeds & confessions of men." Jan Shipps and John W. Welch, eds., *The Journals of William E. McLellin, 1831–1836* (Provo, Urbana and Chicago: BYU Studies and University of Illinois, 1994), 152. The Methodist *Discipline* was the published rule book of the Methodist Episcopal Church. On popular anti-creedalism, see Nathan O. Hatch, *The Democratization of American Christianity* (New Haven, CT: Yale University, 1989).
5. Jonathan A. Stapley and Kristine Wright, "Female Ritual Healing in Mormonism," *Journal of Mormon History* 37, no. 1 (Winter 2011): 1–85. Joseph Smith's revelation to the Relief Society is documented in Female Relief Society of Nauvoo, Minutes, April 28, 1842, in Richard E. Turley Jr., ed., *Selected Collections from the Archives of The Church of Jesus Christ of Latter-day Saints*, 2 vols., DVD (Provo, UT: Brigham Young University, 2002), 1:19.
6. See discussion in Stapley and Wright, "Female Ritual Healing in Mormonism," 37–40.
7. Jill Mulvay Derr and Carol Cornwall Madsen, "Preserving the Record and Memory of the Female Relief Society of Nauvoo, 1842–1892," *Journal of Mormon History* 35, no. 3 (Summer 2009): 89–117.
8. Wilford Woodruff to Samuel Roskelley, June 8, 1887, typescript, Samuel Roskelley Collection, MS 65, Box 2, Book 4, Merrill-Cazier Library, Utah State University, Logan (hereafter Merrill-Cazier Library).
9. For a complete history of baptism for health, see Jonathan A. Stapley and Kristine Wright, "'They Shall Be Made Whole': A History of Baptism for Health," *Journal of Mormon History* 34 (Fall 2008): 69–112.
10. John P. Hatch, ed., *Danish Apostle: The Diaries of Anthon Lund, 1890–1921* (Salt Lake City: Signature Books, 2006), 490.
11. Minutes of the regular meeting of the First Presidency, Twelve Apostles and Patriarch, September 11, 1913, in Journal History of The Church of Jesus Christ of Latter-day Saints

(chronological scrapbook of typed entries and newspaper clippings, 1830–present), September 11, 1913, 6–7, *Selected Collections*, 2:31.

12. Though Smith was young while living in Nauvoo, baptism for health was ubiquitous and his siblings were documented to have been baptized with people who were baptized for their health. Dean C. Jessee, "The John Taylor Nauvoo Journal," *BYU Studies* 23, no. 3 (Summer 1983): 238.
13. See discussion in Stapley and Wright, "Female Ritual Healing in Mormonism," 64–74; Jonathan A. Stapley, "Last Rites and the Dynamics of Mormon Liturgy," *BYU Studies* 50, no. 2 (2011): 114–16.
14. First Presidency to Stake Presidents, December 15, 1922, Salt Lake City, quoted in James R. Clark, comp., *Messages of the First Presidency of the Church of Jesus Christ of Latter-day Saints*, 6 vols. (Salt Lake City: Bookcraft, 1965–75), 5:224.
15. Stapley and Wright, "Female Ritual Healing in Mormonism," 51–52; Susa Young Gates to Joseph F. Smith, correspondence, December 11, 1888, Joseph F. Smith Papers, MS 1325, box 15, folder 7, Church History Library, Salt Lake City; Joseph F. Smith to Susa Young Gates, correspondence, January 8, 1889, Joseph F. Smith Papers, MS 1325, box 31, folder 4, LDS Church History Library.
16. Joseph F. Smith to Susa Young Gates, January 8, 1889, correspondence, Joseph F. Smith Papers, MS 1325, box 31, folder 4, Church History Library.
17. Stapley and Wright, "Female Ritual Healing in Mormonism," 48–50.
18. Young Women, General Board minutes, September 16, 1901, microfilm of typescript, CR 13 6; see also Stapley and Wright, "Female Ritual Healing in Mormonism," 48.
19. Stapley and Wright, "Female Ritual Healing in Mormonism," 53–64.
20. See Robin Scott Jensen, Robert J. Woodford, and Steven C. Harper, eds., *Revelations and Translations: Manuscript Revelation Books*, in *The Joseph Smith Papers*, ed. Dean C. Jessee, Ronald K. Esplin, and Richard Lyman Bushman (Salt Lake City: Church Historian's Press, 2009), 83–84. Note that Oliver Cowdery's antecedent revelation does not include instructions on baby blessing. Scott H. Faulring, "An Examination of the 1829 'Articles of the Church of Christ' in Relation to section 20 of the Doctrine and Covenants," *BYU Studies* 43, no. 4 (2004), 75–79. For a broader history of baby blessings, see my forthcoming history. For a few early examples of baby blessings, see Gregory A. Prince, *Power from on High: The Development of Mormon Priesthood* (Salt Lake City: Signature Books, 1995), 97–98.
21. Joseph Smith Sr. blessed a grandchild on "the 8th Day," September 30, 1832. Hyrum Smith, diary, digital copy of holograph, 45–46, Digital Collections, L. Tom Perry Special Collections, Harold B. Lee Library, Brigham Young University, Provo, UT; hereafter Lee Digital Collections.
22. Joseph Smith Sr. blessed his grandchild Susannah Baily Smith and perhaps named her on November 3, 1835, as part of an eighth-day blessing. Dean C. Jessee, Mark Ashurst-McGee, and Richard L. Jensen, eds., *Journals, Volume 1: 1832–1839*, in *The Joseph Smith Papers* (Salt Lake City: Church Historian's Press, 2008), 84. Note that in the early years, the Saints typically counted the day the children were born as day one.
23. This position was later made explicit by Hannah T. King, "The Three Eras," *Juvenile Instructor*, October 15, 1879, 230. Eighth-day blessings may also be evocative of a revelation indicating

that John the Baptist was ordained to the priesthood at eight days old. Revelation, September 22–23, 1832, Joseph Smith Papers Online, id:1542 (D&C 84:28).

24. See, for example Wilford Woodruff, blessing on Joseph Woodruff, in Scott G. Kenney, ed., *Wilford Woodruff's Journal, 1833–1898*, 9 vols. (Midvale, UT: Signature Books, 1983–85), 2:584–86; Heber C. Kimball, Blessing on Moroni Young, Brigham Young Office Files, CR 1234 1, box 170, folder 27, reel 136, LDS Church History Library, Salt Lake City; Brigham Young, Blessing on Solomon Farnham Kimball, February 2, 1847, in S. F. Kimball, "A Brand Plucked from the Burning," *Improvement Era*, July 1906, 686; Harrison Burgess, blessing on Benjamin Hammond Burgess, June 21, 1851, facsimile of holograph in Delbert E. Roach and Barbara B. Roach, *A Heritage of Faith and Courage: William and Violate Burgess and Their Family* (Murray, UT: Family Heritage Publishers, 2006), 205.

25. See, for example, Kenney, *Wilford Woodruff's Journal*, 6:136; Stan Larson, ed., *A Ministry of Meetings: The Apostolic Diaries of Rudger Clawson* (Salt Lake City: Signature Books, 1993), 556. Elijah Funk Sheets, journal, April 20, 1848, September 10, 1858, June 29, 1860, May 3, 1861, March 13, 1862, December 27, 1863, October 14, 1867, June 20, 1872, April 1, 1874, microfilm of holograph, MS 1314, LDS Church History Library. Note that sometimes babies were also blessed on the day of their birth and not on the eighth day. For example, see Donald G. Godfrey and Rebecca S. Martineau-McCarty, eds., *An Uncommon Common Pioneer: The Journals of James Henry Martineau, 1828–1918* (Provo, UT: Religious Studies Center, Brigham Young University, 2008), 19, 75, 99, 133, 135.

26. Charles Kelly, ed., *The Journal of John D. Lee, 1846–47 and 1859* (Salt Lake City: University of Utah, 1984), 181; James Farmer, diary, vol. 1, 1851–1853, August 25, 1853, 438, digital copy of holograph, Lee Digital Collections; Spanish Fork Ward, Record, 45–53, microfilm of manuscript, LR 8611 29, LDS Church History Library, cf., Craig L. Dalton, ed., "Autobiography and Journal of Albert King Thurber," 33–34, 35, 38–39, and 41, digital typescript, in DVD-ROM included with William G. Hartley, *Another Kind of Gold: The Life of Albert King Thurber* (Troy, ID: C. L. Dalton Enterprises, 2011). For examples of "bishop's blessings," see Spanish Fork Ward, Utah Stake, Bishop's Blessing Records, microfilm of manuscript, LR 8611 26, LDS Church History Library.

27. John Taylor, "The Blessing of Children," in Clark, *Messages of the First Presidency*, 2:311–13. For an example of a Church elder stating that eight-day blessings were the standard ritual for children without anything else, see A. Milton Musser, *The Fruits of "Mormonism"* (Salt Lake City: Deseret News, 1878), 31.

28. Florence A. Merriam, *My Summer in a Mormon Village* (Boston and New York: Houghton, Mifflin, 1894), 117. For official statements indicating the same, see [George Q. Cannon], "Editorial Thoughts," *Juvenile Instructor*, March 1, 1895, 151; Albert Jones, "At Fast Meeting," *Young Women's Journal*, February 5, 1896, 238; "Lesson II: Blessing Children," *Children's Friend*, January 1902, 9–10; see also Hubert Howe Bancroft, *History of Utah, 1540–1886* (San Francisco: The History Company, 1889), 343n7. For examples of the practice of double blessings, see Eugene M. Cannon, diary, vol. 6, 193–94, Lee Digital Collections; Charles M. Hatch and Todd M. Compton, eds., *A Widow's Tale: The 1884–1896 Diary of Helen Mar Kimball Whitney* (Logan: Utah State University, 2003), 273, 298; Emma H. Adams, *George Mason Adams and Martha Louise Devey, Descendants and Ancestors* (Mesa, AZ: Hogue Printing, 1972), 85. Note as well that single blessings were also common during this time.

29. For example, see "Women's Sphere: Our Children. Christening Babies," *Deseret Weekly,* January 21, 1893, 12.
30. For examples of Joseph F. Smith performing eighth-day blessings for his own children, see Joseph F. Smith, diary, February 6, 1871, March 28, 1872, September 25, 1872, March 2, 1873, May 8, 1880, in *Selected Collections,* 1:26.
31. Joseph F. Smith, "The Repetition of Sacred Ordinances," *Juvenile Instructor,* January 1, 1903, 19.
32. Susa Young Gates, *Surname and Racial History: A Compilation and Arrangement of Genealogical and Historical Data for Use by the Students and Members of the Relief Society of the Church of Jesus Christ of Latter-day Saints* (Salt Lake City: General Board of the Relief Society, 1918), 68. The first General Handbook of Instructions to discuss baby blessings was issued in 1913. The instructions noted that people should have their babies blessed in their own wards, but that when taken to other wards, these bishops were authorized to bless them as well. *Circular of Instructions: To Presidents of Stakes and Counselors, Presidents of Missions, Bishops and Counselors, Stake, Mission and Ward Clerks and All Church Authorities, 1913* (Salt Lake City: The Church of Jesus Christ of Latter-day Saints, 1913), 26.
33. "Editor's Table: The Blessing of Children," *Improvement Era,* March 1917, 451–52.
34. The 1928 and 1934 General Handbooks of Instruction made provisions for baby blessings at church under the direction of the bishop and also blessings at home under the direction of the parents. However, the 1940 General Handbook removed the provision for a home blessing under the parent's direction, noting that any home blessings were to be performed only "under exceptional circumstances." *Handbook of Instructions for Bishops and Counselors, Stake and Ward Clerks* (Salt Lake City: Church of Jesus Christ of Latter-day Saints, 1928), 70; *Handbook of Instructions for Stake Presidencies, Bishops and Counselors, Stake and Ward Clerks* (Salt Lake City: The Church of Jesus Christ of Latter-day Saints, 1934), 90; *Handbook of Instructions for Stake Presidencies, Bishops and Counselors, Stake and Ward Clerks and Other Church Officers* (Salt Lake City: The Church of Jesus Christ of Latter-day Saints, 1940), 116. See also George S. Romney, *The Missionary Guide: A Key to Effective Missionary Work* (Independence: Press of Zion's Printing and Pub., [1931?]), 97.
35. For example, Spencer W. Kimball gave his youngest son an eighth-day blessing in 1930. Edward L. Kimball and Andrew E. Kimball, *Spencer W. Kimball: Twelfth President of the Church of Jesus Christ of Latter-day Saints* (Salt Lake City: Bookcraft, 1977), 122.

Church Administration

Patrick A. Bishop

14

The Apostolic Succession of Joseph F. Smith

The ordination to the office of Apostle and his subsequent placement as a counselor in the First Presidency would set Joseph F. Smith on a path as the longest-serving Apostle in the First Presidency.[1] (See appendix A for a timeline of his service.) However, because of his ordination as an Apostle and placement in the First Presidency before he was placed in the Quorum of the Twelve, many questions have been raised about Joseph F. Smith's seniority in the presiding quorums of the Church. A sequential narrative studying these questions—including his ordination to Apostle, call to the Twelve, service in the First Presidency, call as President, and sustaining in a special general conference—will guide this paper. The decisions reached during Joseph F. Smith's lifetime regarding seniority have solidified the Church's policies regarding succession to the presidency.

Ordination to Apostle

Upon returning home from his second mission to the Sandwich Islands, or present-day Hawaii, Joseph F. Smith was called by Brigham Young as a clerk in the Church Historian's Office. Consequently, Joseph F. was present at many of the council

---

Patrick A. Bishop is a coordinator of Seminaries and Institutes of Religion for the Casper and Gillette Wyoming Stakes and Rapid City and Pierre South Dakota Stakes.

meetings of the presiding officers of the Church. On July 1, 1866, Joseph F. recorded, "Pres. Brigham Young, Elders John Taylor, W Woodruff, Geo. A Smith, Geo. Q. Cannon and Joseph F. Smith met and prayed."[2] Although this entry is vague as to what happened during this meeting, it was one of the most sacred experiences in Joseph F. Smith's life. The Church Historian's Office's Journal History of the Church gives a more complete account of this sacred meeting:

> On ~~Saturday~~ Sunday afternoon July 1, 1866, Pres. Brigham Young of the First Presidency and Elders John Taylor, Wilford Woodruff, Geo. A. Smith and Geo. Q. Cannon of the Twelve Apostles and Elder Jos. F. Smith, son of Hyrum Smith, met as usual in the upper room of the Historian's Office in the prayer circle. After we were dressed . . . Elder John Taylor offered up the opening prayer and Pres. Brigham Young was mouth in the Circle and offered up a prayer with great spirit and power. When we had finished Pres. Brigham Young arose from his knees . . . [and started] undressing. Of a sudden he stopped and exclaimed: "Hold on, shall I do as I feel led?" I always feel well to do as the spirit constrains me. It is in my mind to ordain Bro. Jos. F. Smith to the Apostleship and to be one of my counselors. He then called on each one of us for an expression of our feelings, and we, individually, responded that it met our hearty approval, . . . after which Jos. F. Smith knelt upon the altar and . . . we laid our hands upon him, Bro. Brigham being mouth and we repeating after him in the usual form. He said: "Bro. Joseph F. Smith. We lay our hands upon your head in the name of Jesus Christ, and by virtue of the Holy Priesthood we ordain you to be an Apostle in the Church of Jesus Christ of Latter-day Saints, and to be a special witness to the nations of the Earth. We seal upon your head all the authority, power and keys of this Holy Apostleship, and we ordain you to be a counselor unto the First Presidency of the Church and Kingdom of God upon the Earth. These blessings we seal upon you in the name of Jesus Christ and by the authority of the Holy Priesthood Amen."
>
> After the ordination Bro. Brigham said: "This is the first time that any person has been ordained in this manner, and, though right, I do not wish in recording it that it should be written in a way to lead others to think that this mode is essential or the only way in which such ordinations can be performed." He suggested to us that it would be wisdom for us to keep the fact of this ordination to ourselves, but to be sure and record it.[3]

This was not the only private and undisclosed ordination that Brigham Young had administered. Brigham Young Jr. was ordained an Apostle by his father on February 4, 1864, in a private ordination that was not made known until two months later in another private setting. On April 17, 1864, "Pres. Brigham Young, John Taylor, and Geo. A. Smith met and prayed."[4] Wilford Woodruff, Church Historian at the time, indicates that much more took place at this prayer meeting. President Young said: "I am going to tell you [John Taylor and George A. Smith] something that I have never before mentioned to any other person. I have ordained my sons, Joseph A., Brigham, and John W., apostles and my counsellors, have you any objections? Brother Taylor, George A. Smith said that they had not that it was his own affair and they considered it under his own direction. . . . Signed John Taylor, and George A. Smith."[5]

Although Brigham Young Jr. and Joseph F. Smith had both been ordained to the office of Apostle, they were not part of the Quorum of the Twelve. These two brethren were not the only ones ordained to this office but placed outside of the Quorum. Many were ordained as Apostles who never served as members of the Quorum of the Twelve Apostles. Those in Joseph F. Smith's lifetime who were ordained to the apostleship either before they were made members of the Quorum of the Twelve or never became members of the Twelve include Jedediah Grant, John W. Young, Daniel H. Wells, and Joseph A. Young.

Called to the Quorum of the Twelve

Almost eighteen months after Joseph F.'s ordination to the office of Apostle, on October 6, 1867, Amasa Lyman of the Twelve was excommunicated and released from his position in the Quorum. Wilford Woodruff wrote of this action:

> The Presidency & Twelve held a Council at Noon & Cut off Amasa Lyman from the Quorum of the Twelve & Set apart Joseph Fielding Smith as one of the Twelve Apostles. He had been ordained an Apostle before. President Young said He did not wish to Ordain Joseph F Smith to take Amasas Place or to take his Crown But He ordain him an Apostle to take his own Crown & his own place. He viewed all the Apostles in the Same light. Presidet Young was mouth in setting Joseph F Smith Apart as one of the Twelve & as a Special witness to all Nations.[6]

Early 1869 photograph of the First Presidency and the Quorum of the Twelve Apostles. Notice that they are seated by seniority, and on the far right Joseph F. Smith sits behind Brigham Young Jr. Included are Orson Hyde, Orson Pratt, John Taylor, Wilford Woodruff, George A. Smith, Ezra T. Benson, Charles C. Rich, Brigham Young, Lorenzo Snow, Daniel H. Wells, Erastus Snow, Franklin D. Richards, George Q. Cannon, Brigham Young, Jr., and Joseph F. Smith. Courtesy of Church History Library.

In 1868, Heber C. Kimball, who had been serving as First Counselor in the First Presidency, passed away. George A. Smith was called to serve as First Counselor in the First Presidency. George A. Smith's vacancy in the Twelve was filled by Brigham Young Jr. This set of circumstances raised another question: Was Brigham Young Jr. or Joseph F. Smith the senior Apostle in the Quorum of the Twelve? Brigham had been ordained an Apostle first, but Joseph was a member of the Quorum of the Twelve first.

At the October conference in 1868, Brigham Young Jr. was sustained as the junior member of the Quorum of the Twelve, right behind Joseph F. Smith. However, at the following conference in April of 1869, his name was placed ahead of Joseph F. Smith's. This probably was done on the basis of the earlier ordination to the office of an Apostle that Brigham Jr. had received. Brigham Young Jr. later wrote that this question of seniority plagued his mind for a time:

> I submitted this matter to father one day and he said rather severely, "It is just right the way it is, and you let it alone." I never had courage to tackle [the] question again; still I am of the opinion that when a man is ordained an apostle and seeks to magnify that office, no new man can rank him in being

> set apart to fill a vacancy in [the] Quorum of the Twelve. I am anxious for God through my brethren to decide this question and I yield my views to theirs with all my heart.[7]

It was not until April 5, 1900, that the question of date of ordination or the date of entrance into the quorum was resolved. In a meeting of the First Presidency and the Twelve, this issue was brought up. It was decided that the date of entrance into the Quorum of the Twelve Apostles rather than the date of ordination to the office of Apostle determined seniority.

The minutes of the meeting reveal some of the logic and inspiration behind the decision:

> Bro. John Henry Smith said that he regarded this as a very important question from the fact that he understood there had been quite a number of men ordained apostles who had never been voted upon as such by the church. His kinsman, for instance, Joseph Smith, who stood at the head of the Re-organized Church, claims he was ordained an apostle by his father. . . . On this phase of the proposition, the question of man was simply this: Has a father—himself being an apostle—a right to ordain his son to the apostleship, and that son to preside without the action of the church, his ordination antedating that of the man chosen and acted upon by the church? The speaker said, to his mind there was but one view to be taken to safeguard the church and this council, and to the maintenance of their dignity in the world, such ordinations were dependent upon joint action, first, on the presentation by the First Presidency to the Council of the Apostles for their acceptance, and then to the people for their approval, and then he must be ordained in the proper way. . . . His view therefore was that the safety of the organization of the church must be based on the action of the people, the action of the Presidency and Apostles, and the final action of ordination after having been passed upon legitimate lines.[8]

This could be interpreted as a change in policy, but a more accurate observation is that this step in the succession debate harmonized several revealed gospel principles. Private ordinations had often been problematic when they affected public administration. The Lord revealed in 1831 the pattern for officers that publicly administer in the Church: "Again I say unto you, that it shall not be given to any one to go forth to preach my gospel, or to build up my church, except he be ordained by some one who has authority, and it is known to the church that he has authority and has been regularly ordained by the heads of the church" (D&C 42:11). In other words, Brigham Young Jr.'s and Joseph F. Smith's private ordinations were not made "known to the church that [they had] authority," and Brigham Young Jr. was only ordained by the head and not "ordained by the *heads* of the church." Furthermore, Joseph F. Smith was ordained by the "heads of the church" and was the first of the two to become "known to the church" in October of 1867. This shows the significance of turning to the revealed word of the Lord to answer questions of this nature. Up to this date, a practical application of this scriptural text regarding succession was not realized. Since 1900, however, seniority has been based on the date one becomes a member of the Quorum of the Twelve and not on a prior ordination to the office of Apostle.

Joseph F. Smith's own words describe his reaction to the decision:

> It was unanimously decided that the acceptance of a member into the council or quorum of the Twelve fixed his rank or position in the Apostleship. That the Apostles took precedence from the date they entered the quorum. Thus today, President Snow is the senior Apostle. President George Q. Cannon next, myself next, Brigham Young next, Francis M. Lyman next, and so on to the last one received into the quorum. In the case of the death of President Snow, President Cannon surviving him, would succeed to the Presidency, and so on according to seniority in the Apostleship of the Twelve; that ordination to the Apostleship under the hands of any Apostle other than to fill a vacancy in the quorum, and authorized by the General Authorities of the Church did not count in precedence; that if the First Presidency were dissolved by the death of the President, his counselors having been ordained Apostles in the Quorum of the Twelve would resume their places in the quorum, according to the seniority of their ordinations into that quorum. This important ruling settles a long unsettled point, and is most timely.[9]

If the date of ordination to the apostleship was the determining factor in seniority in the Twelve, when Brigham Young Jr. and Joseph F. Smith were placed in the Twelve, Brigham Young Jr. would have become President of the Twelve before Joseph F. Smith. In this case, Brigham Young Jr. would have been President of the Church for three years prior to Joseph F. Smith.

Call to Become President

On January 23, 1881, some of the leading brethren were attending a stake conference in Ogden, Utah. Wilford Woodruff recorded, "Joseph F Smith spoke in much power for one hour and 35 M. . . . W. Woodruff then Spoke One hour . . . said Joseph F Smith was One of the first Presidency and would be President of the Church of Jesus Christ of Latter Day Saints in his DAY."[10]

This prophecy was misinterpreted by some that Joseph F. Smith would be the next President of the Church after John Taylor. This caused some stir in the Church that the tradition of the senior Apostle succeeding would need to be altered if Joseph F. Smith should become the next President of the Church. Elder Woodruff responded to the spin on his prophecy thus,

> It was said that that prophecy was recorded. I will also make a statement, that I Wilford Woodruff, heard Heber C. Kimball and Joseph Young say that they heard Joseph Smith say in their presence and in the presence of others in 1832, the first time that Joseph Smith ever had an interview with Brigham Young he said Brigham Young would yet be President of the Church, and that was four years before there was any Twelve Apostles chosen, and no man knew that Brigham Young would ever be an Apostle (unless God revealed it to the Prophet). And still, after sixteen years of revelation and change, Brigham Young was president of the Church, without turning to the right or left from the path marked out to be the revelation of God. And that prophecy was also recorded. And there was not one chance in ten for that to be fulfilled that there is for Joseph F. Smith to be president of the Church in the regular channel of the order of God.[11]

Wilford Woodruff would obviously not live to see this prophecy fulfilled, but Joseph F. would later become the President of the Church following the "path marked out to be the revelation of God." Wilford Woodruff was not the only man to make the prediction that Joseph F. would become President of the Church. Lorenzo Snow told Joseph F. personally, "You will live to be the President of the Church of Jesus Christ of Latter-day Saints, and when that time comes you should proceed at once and reorganize the Presidency of the Church."[12] It should be noted that George Q. Cannon and Brigham Young Jr. still held seniority over Joseph F. at that time.

In keeping with the instruction received by President Snow—namely, that the First Presidency should be immediately reorganized—the Council of the Twelve met on October 17, 1901. Elders Joseph Merrill and John Henry Smith, two members of the Twelve at the time, wrote that President Smith was "set apart" as President of the Church on that day. Elder Merrill's journal states, "We organized the First Presidency again. Joseph F. Smith was unanimously sustained as the President and was set apart as such by his brother, Patriarch John Smith. He chose his Counselors, John R. Winder and Anthon H. Lund."[13] This action of the Patriarch to the Church setting apart the new President of the Church had never been done before. The question has been raised, did the Patriarch have the authority to "set apart" the President of the Church?

The phrase "set apart" used in Elder Merrill's journal is of great interest. Note that the terms "ordain," "appoint," "anoint," and "bless" were not used in the account. Just two years earlier, the First Presidency and Twelve had had a lengthy discussion on this subject, a discussion which filled nearly six full pages in the Journal History of the Church dated April 13, 1899. The minutes of this meeting state, "A question as to the proper use of the terms 'ordain' and 'set apart' came up and was discussed at length."[14] Elder Anthon Lund was the member of the Quorum that brought the question up after "setting apart" a member of the Presidency of the Seventy and not using the word "ordain." The brethren in the meeting had many differing views on this subject. Some were of the view that prominent offices in the Church should use the word "ordain" instead of "set apart." However, Joseph F. Smith was of the view that

> the Presidency of the Church is a prominent office, but the First Presidency are not ordained. . . . The words "set apart" used in the case of a President of Seventies were just as proper and appropriate as in the case of the Presidency of the Church, or in that of a Stake President, since it conferred no higher Priesthood upon either of them to call them to act in the Presidency of these several organizations.[15]

The latter reasoning is probably why Joseph F. Smith felt it proper to have his brother, the Patriarch to the Church, set him apart as President of the Church. Hoyt Brewster offers his own interpretation of this action:

> While the patriarch [John Smith] did not hold the apostolic keys, one must understand that this setting apart was not a conferral of keys; for . . . President

Joseph F. Smith already possessed the keys of the priesthood in their fulness by virtue of his apostolic office. This setting apart was simply the conferral of a priesthood blessing, which the patriarch, by virtue of his holding the Melchizedek Priesthood and having been invited by the senior apostle to do so, had a right to bestow.[16]

Joseph F. and John Smith, President of The Church of Jesus Christ of Latter-day Saints and Patriarch to the Church, respectively. Photo by Charles R. Savage, 1895, Church History Library.

With this reasoning, there still seem to be questions regarding the terms "set apart" and "ordain" in connection with the President of the Church. Current publications state that the President of the Church is ordained and set apart. The official Church publications have used this language from David O. McKay to the present. The standard works even seem to suggest that ordination should be part of the call of the President of the Church: "Of the Melchizedek Priesthood, three Presiding High Priests, chosen by the body, appointed and ordained to that office, and upheld by the confidence, faith, and prayer of the church, form a quorum of the Presidency of the Church" (D&C 107:22). Note the words "appoint" and "ordain" to a "quorum." Typically a quorum is a collection of multiple men that are ordained to an office in the priesthood. However, the Lord does state in this revelation that the minimum office needed to function in the "quorum of the Presidency of the Church" is high priest and not some other office in the priesthood. Thus the word "ordain" in the context of this 1835 revelation would have been appropriate, as the men called to the First Presidency would have also needed to be ordained to the appropriate office of high priest. Just as there seems to be no final consensus on this topic today, so it was on April 13, 1899, as the brethren were discussing it. Toward the end of the meeting, "President Snow expressed the belief that no further light would be obtained by discussing the question any longer,"[17] and the topic was tabled.

Perhaps Joseph F. Smith's final thought on this topic is the one we can all apply. He said that "he did not think, even if we failed to confine ourselves strictly to those prescribed forms, that it would vitiate our actions, if the intent was pure; as authority and intent would govern in such cases."[18]

Special Conference

In the 1901 semiannual general conference of the Church, held the first weekend of October, Lorenzo Snow addressed the people, but within a week President Snow had crossed the veil of death. With the immediate reorganization of the First Presidency, a special conference was held on November 10, 1901, for the purpose of sustaining the new General Authorities of the Church. Joseph F. Smith was the first speaker. He talked of the need for a complete organization of the priesthood, hence the calling of this conference to sustain the new First Presidency. This was not the only area of priesthood organization he addressed, however. It seems that the office of patriarch was weighing heavily on his mind from the time that his brother set him apart until this address. He said:

> We have not always carried out strictly the order of the Priesthood; we have varied from it to some extent; but we hope in due time that, by the promptings of the Holy Spirit, we will be led up into the exact channel and course that the Lord has marked out for us to pursue, and adhere strictly to the order that He has established. I will read from a revelation that was given to the Prophet Joseph Smith, at Nauvoo, Hancock Co., Illinois, January 19, 1841, which stands as the law of the Church in relation to the presentation of the authorities of the Holy Priesthood as they were established in the Church, and from which I feel that we have no right to depart. The Lord says:
>
> "First, I give unto you Hyrum Smith, to be a Patriarch unto you, to hold sealing blessings of my Church, even the Holy Spirit of promise, whereby ye are sealed up unto the day of redemption, that ye may not fall, notwithstanding the hour of temptation that may come upon you."
>
> It may be considered strange that the Lord should give first of all the Patriarch; yet I do not know any law, any revelation or any commandment from God to the contrary, that has ever been given through any of the Prophets or Presidents of the Church. At the same time we well know that this order has not been strictly followed from the day we came into these valleys until now—and we will not make any change at present. But we will first take it into consideration; we will pray over it, we will get the mind of the Spirit of God upon it, as upon other subjects, and be united before we take any action different to that which has been done.[19]

It appears from the previous quotation that President Smith's desire was to sustain the Patriarch of the Church before all other General Authorities. However, he was cautious not to make this change until the "mind of the Spirit of God" directed him to do so. It appears that this direction never came during President Smith's administration, and it is unlikely that it will come, with the office of Church Patriarch now retired.[20] What was the purpose for naming Hyrum Smith first in the officers of the Church? Many connected it to the office of Church Patriarch, which he held. But it must be remembered that Hyrum held two offices jointly, Assistant President of the Church and Church Patriarch. Section 124:91–95 makes this clear:

> Hyrum may take the office of Priesthood and Patriarch, which was appointed unto him by his father, by blessing and also by right;

> That from henceforth he shall hold the keys of the patriarchal blessings upon the heads of all my people,
>
> That whosoever he blesses shall be blessed, and whosoever he curses shall be cursed; that whatsoever he shall bind on earth shall be bound in heaven; and whatsoever he shall loose on earth shall be loosed in heaven.
>
> And from this time forth I appoint unto him that he may be a prophet, and a seer, and a revelator unto my church, as well as my servant Joseph;
>
> That he may act in concert also with my servant Joseph; and that he shall receive counsel from my servant Joseph, who shall show unto him the keys whereby he may ask and receive, and be crowned with the same blessing, and glory, and honor, and priesthood, and gifts of the priesthood, that once were put upon him that was my servant Oliver Cowdery.

The possible chiastic structure of these verses seems to connect the keys of blessing and sealing powers that Hyrum was given with the office of patriarch, but the titles prophet, seer, and revelator, along with other keys, were in connection to his office as Assistant President, the same office that Oliver Cowdery once held (see appendix B). It seems that the Lord in section 124:124–25 was doing what had been done on the first day that the Church was organized, namely, sustaining the first and second elders of the Church, or President and Assistant President. Why Hyrum was named first in section 124 has not been explained. Perhaps it was because he was older and also had the honor of holding the office of Church Patriarch. Although there was some deliberation on the role of a Church Patriarch in the succession question, time has shown that the Quorum of the Twelve is led by the senior Apostle and is the governing body of the Church when the First Presidency is dissolved. "They form a quorum, equal in authority and power to the three presidents" (D&C 107:24).

Conclusion

During the service of Joseph F. Smith in the presiding councils of the Church, many questions regarding succession and seniority were answered. Apostles received seniority based on entrance into the Quorum of the Twelve and not by ordination to the office. The importance of public announcement of ordination and common consent also came to light during this time. The need to reorganize the First Presidency immediately was highlighted. The question of the "setting apart" versus "ordaining" the President of the Church was discussed. And the question of the place of the patriarch in succession dissolved. The smooth process of succession in the Church today can be traced to the apostolic succession of Joseph F. Smith.

Appendix A

Timeline of Service

July 1, 1866–Oct. 8, 1867, as additional counselor to Brigham Young (464 days)

Oct. 8, 1867–Oct. 10, 1880, as member of the Quorum of the Twelve (4,751 days)

Oct. 10, 1880–July 25, 1887, as Second Counselor to John Taylor (2,479 days)

July 25, 1887–April 7, 1889, as member of the Quorum of the Twelve (622 days)

April 7, 1889–Sept. 2, 1898, as Second Counselor to Wilford Woodruff (3,435 days)

Sept. 2, 1898–Sept. 13, 1898, as member of the Quorum of Twelve (11 days)

Sept. 13, 1898–April 12, 1901, as Second Counselor to Lorenzo Snow (941 days)

April 12, 1901–Oct. 10, 1901, as First Counselor to Lorenzo Snow (never set apart) (181 days)

Oct. 10, 1901–Oct. 17, 1901, as President of the Quorum of the Twelve (7 days)

Oct. 17, 1901–Nov. 19, 1918, as President of the Church (6,242 days)

For a total of 19,133 days served in First Presidencies of the Church

Appendix B

Chiastic Structure of Doctrine and Covenants 124:91–97

91 And again, verily I say unto you, let **my servant William** be appointed, ordained, and anointed, as counselor unto my servant Joseph, in the room of my servant Hyrum, that **my servant Hyrum** may take the office of **Priesthood** and Patriarch, which was appointed unto him by his father, by **blessing** and also by right;

92 That from henceforth he shall hold the **keys** of the patriarchal blessings upon the heads of all my people,

93 That whoever he blesses shall be blessed, and whoever he curses shall be cursed; that whatsoever he shall **bind on earth shall be bound in heaven;** and whatsoever he shall loose on earth shall be loosed in heaven.

94 And from this time forth I appoint unto him that he may be a **prophet, and a seer, and a revelator** unto my church, as well as my servant Joseph;

95 That he may act in concert also with my servant Joseph; and that he shall receive counsel from my servant Joseph, who shall show unto him the **keys** whereby he may ask and receive, and be crowned with the same **blessing**, and glory, and honor, and **priesthood**, and gifts of the priesthood, that once were put upon him that was my servant Oliver Cowdery;

96 That **my servant Hyrum** may bear record of the things which I shall show unto him, that his name may be had in honorable remembrance from generation to generation, forever and ever.

97 Let **my servant William Law** also receive the keys by which he may ask and receive blessings; let him be humble before me, and be without guile, and he shall receive of my Spirit, even the Comforter, which shall manifest unto him the truth of all things, and shall give him, in the very hour, what he shall say.

A—my servant William
(counselor to Joseph Smith)

B—my servant Hyrum
(Patriarch to the Church)

C—priesthood
(patriarchal)

D—blessing
(by right)

E—keys
(of office of patriarch)

F—bind
(authority of patriarch)

G—Point of change

F¹—prophet, seer, revelator
(authority of Associate President)

E¹—keys
(of call as Associate President)

D¹—blessing
(by honor and glory)

C¹—priesthood
(Associate President calling)

B¹—my servant Hyrum
(Associate Church President)

A¹—my servant William
(counselor to Joseph Smith)

Notes

1. Joseph F. Smith has gone down in history as the man who served the longest period of time in a First Presidency. He served as counselor to Brigham Young, John Taylor, Wilford Woodruff, and Lorenzo Snow. His time as a counselor to these Presidents totaled twenty and a half years. He then became President of the Church, making the total time of his service in a First Presidency just over thirty-seven and a half years. This mark will probably never be reached by any other man.
2. Joseph F. Smith, in Church Historian's Office Journal, vol. 28, July 1, 1866, Church History Library, The Church of Jesus Christ of Latter-day Saints, Salt Lake City.

3. Journal History of The Church of Jesus Christ of Latter-day Saints, July 1, 1866, Church History Library. The manner or mode of this ordination as Brigham Young described it deserves noting. Previous to this, all other ordinations to a priesthood office were done simply by a group of brethren forming a circle and laying hands on the one to whom the power was being conferred. It appears from the record that the members dressed in sacred clothing, formed a sacred prayer circle, and repeated the words of the prayer. Brigham Young said that this was "the first time that any person has been ordained in this manner, and, though right, [he did] not wish in recording it that it should be written in a way to lead others to think that this mode is essential or the only way in which such ordinations can be performed."
4. Church Historian's Office Journal, 1844–1879, 252, Church History Library.
5. Eugene E. Campbell, *Establishing Zion: The Mormon Church in the American West, 1847–1869* (Salt Lake City: Signature Books, 1988), 154. See also Wilford Woodruff, Historian's Private Journal, 1858–78, April 17, 1864, as cited by D. Michael Quinn, *The Mormon Hierarchy: Extensions of Powers* (Salt Lake City: Signature Books, 1997), 164.
6. *Wilford Woodruff's Journal, 1833–1898 Typescript*, vol. 6, *1 January 1862 to 31 December 1870*, ed. Scott G. Kenney (Midvale, UT: Signature Books, 1983–84), 6:367.
7. Brigham Young Jr., diary, *1874–1899*, September 9, 1898, Church History Library.
8. Minutes of the First Presidency and Quorum of the Twelve, April 5, 1900, Church History Library; see also Steven H. Heath, "Notes on Apostolic Succession," *Dialogue: A Journal of Mormon Thought* 20, no. 2 (Summer 1987): 49–50.
9. Joseph Fielding Smith, *Life of Joseph F. Smith, Sixth President of the Church of Jesus Christ of Latter-day Saints* (Salt Lake City: Deseret News, 1938), 311.
10. *Wilford Woodruff's Journal*, vol. 8, *1 January 1881 to 31 December 1888*, 8.
11. Heath, "Notes on Apostolic Succession," 46–47.
12. Lorenzo Snow, quoted by Joseph F. Smith, in Conference Report, November 1901, 71.
13. Marriner Wood Merrill, *Notes from the Miscellaneous Record Book, 1886–1906*, Church History Library. See also *Church, State, and Politics: The Diaries of John Henry Smith*, ed. Jean Bickmore White (Salt Lake City: Signature Books, 1990), 496.
14. Journal History of the Church, April 13, 1899.
15. Journal History of the Church, April 13, 1899.
16. Hoyt W. Brewster Jr., *Prophets, Priesthood Keys, and Succession* (Salt Lake City: Deseret Book, 1991), 90.
17. Journal History of the Church, April 13, 1899.
18. Journal History of the Church, April 13, 1899.
19. Joseph F. Smith, in Conference Report, November 1901, 71.
20. At the October 1979 semiannual general conference, Elder Eldred G. Smith was given emeritus status and the office of Patriarch to the Church was eliminated.

Dennis B. Horne

15

Joseph F. Smith's Succession to the Presidency

Joseph F. Smith was the first person born in the Church to become its President. Yet a child when his father, Hyrum, and his uncle Joseph Smith were martyred, as the years passed and he grew in prominence and good works, his name became linked with prophecies of his eventual succession. Further, authoritative decisions solidifying the succession process placed him in a position to fulfill these inspired predictions, causing him to become the prophet, seer, revelator, and senior Apostle of God on the earth.

Joseph F.'s Succession Predicted

In 1864, Joseph F. Smith was sent to the Sandwich (Hawaiian) Islands along with Elders Ezra T. Benson, Lorenzo Snow, and a few others in order to remove from office an apostate who had usurped authority in the mission for self-aggrandizement.

Their sailing vessel dropped anchor outside the Lahaina Harbor at Maui, and the elders prepared to navigate a smaller boat ashore. With a storm causing high seas, Joseph F. emphatically refused to join the others and sought to

---

Dennis Horne is a technical writer for the Materials Management Department of The Church of Jesus Christ of Latter-day Saints, Salt Lake City. He is also an independent researcher and author.

dissuade them from leaving until the waves calmed. The other brethren, feeling he acted insubordinately, left him behind and started for shore. Soon, however, Joseph F.'s fears were realized, and a large wave capsized their craft. All passengers were thrown into the ocean, and Elder Snow soon drowned beneath sixty feet of water. Some native islanders managed to find and retrieve his body, and the brethren present initiated life-saving measures. Miraculously, about an hour later, he returned to life and fully recovered.

Evidently, during this near-death experience, Elder Snow received a revelation concerning Joseph F.'s future. Snow declared that "the Lord revealed to him that this young man, Joseph F. Smith, . . . would someday be the prophet of God upon the earth."[1]

President Heber J. Grant commented further on this dramatic experience: "Lorenzo Snow was drowned . . . , and it took some hours to bring him to life again. At that particular time the Lord revealed to him the fact that the young man, Joseph F. Smith, . . . would some day be the Prophet of God. . . . It was revealed to him then and there, that the boy, with the courage of his convictions . . . who stayed on that vessel, would yet be the Prophet of God. Lorenzo Snow told me this upon more than one occasion, long years before Joseph F. Smith came to the presidency of the Church."[2]

Charles W. Penrose, managing editor of the *Deseret News* in 1901, witnessed another such prophetic occasion. Of Joseph F.'s succession he wrote: "It also fulfills a prediction made many years ago in the Tabernacle in Ogden city by Apostle Wilford Woodruff. In a public meeting, that venerable Church leader prophesied that Joseph F. Smith would one day occupy the position formerly held by his uncle the Prophet Joseph. We were present on that occasion and made a mental note of the prediction, which was very forcible and impressed itself strongly upon the minds of many persons in the congregation, and particularly of prominent men who were on the stand at that time."[3]

Further, Joseph F.'s cousin and fellow Apostle, Elder John Henry Smith, testified in an October 1901 meeting in Lehi, Utah, of receiving a personal revelation or vision of the same nature. An associate reported that John Henry Smith said, "I saw the man who now presides over the Church in the very place he now occupies. At the same time I saw the Plates and sacred things given to Joseph, and my testimony was as clear as it could be."[4]

Apostolic Ordination and Setting Apart as a Member of the Quorum of the Twelve

Two years after the resolution of the Hawaiian Mission matter, on July 1, 1866, President Brigham Young felt a distinct impression while meeting with some of the presiding Brethren. He said: "Hold on, shall I do as I feel led? I always feel well to do as the Spirit constrains me. It is my mind to ordain Brother Joseph F. Smith to the Apostleship, and to be one of my counselors." President Young then ordained Joseph F. as an Apostle and as an Assistant Counselor to the First Presidency. He also asked that the ordination be kept confidential until a vacancy arose in the Quorum of the Twelve and Joseph F. could be publicly sustained.[5]

This sustaining and subsequent entry into the Quorum of the Twelve occurred over a year later at the October 1867 general conference. In this order of events it is important to recognize that Joseph F. was ordained an Apostle after Elder Brigham Young Jr., but he was set apart as a member of the Quorum of the Twelve Apostles before Elder Young. The timing of these actions would become an important succession question in later years.

Quorum Disunity in the Late 1880s

By the time President John Taylor died in July of 1887, the Quorum of the Twelve had not been able to meet and function as a complete unified council for some three years and had suffered from various internal conflicts. Some of the younger members of the Twelve had resented the administrative styles of President Taylor and his First Counselor, George Q. Cannon. They therefore emphatically resisted reorganizing the First Presidency without assurance that they would have greater influence on major decisions, especially those related to Church finances and their own position as a presiding Quorum in the Church. Despite all that President Woodruff (the quorum president) and others could do, they were unsuccessful in attaining a united consensus within the quorum for two years. President Woodruff had not hesitated to seek for reorganization himself, but in consequence of the quorum's disharmony, he had been forced to delay until 1889.[6]

This struggle for unification weighed heavily on President Woodruff even after he became Church President, and he determined, under inspiration, to forestall future similar troubles. Thus, in December of 1892, President Woodruff called

Lorenzo Snow into a sitting room by his office for a private interview. Elder Snow later related:

> He said, and spoke with much feeling and energy, "I have an important request to make of you which I want you to fulfill. A few months ago while on a visit to St. George I came near dying. I have no lease of my life, and know not how soon I may be called away, and when I go I want you, Brother Snow, not to delay, but organize the First Presidency. Take George Q. Cannon and Joseph F. Smith for your counselors; they are good, wise men of experience."
>
> Of course I was much surprised, and said, "President Woodruff, am I to receive this as a revelation?" I do not call to mind the words of his answer, but they were such as gave me the impression that he wished me to regard it as such. Without thought or considering of the impropriety of such questions, I continued: "President Woodruff, is this the place I am to occupy?" He hesitated a moment, then replied, "It is according to the order." I asked if he had mentioned this matter to his counselors. He said, "No, not to anyone." I told him I wished he would; I understood from his answer that he would do so.
>
> The interview was brief, I think not over five or six minutes. As we arose to return to the President's office he said, "Brother Snow, now do not neglect to organize as I have told you, *it may prevent much trouble.*"[7]

President Snow's greatest success as President of the Twelve was to unify the Council of the Twelve in spirit and purpose. President Woodruff did as Elder Snow asked and informed his counselors of the need to reorganize immediately upon his death.[8]

A Succession Question Is Settled

When President Woodruff died in 1898 and the First Presidency was consequently dissolved, Elder Brigham Young Jr. took a seat in the council room senior to that of Joseph F. Smith, feeling that because he was ordained an Apostle before Joseph F., he was naturally the senior of the two. This seniority arrangement had not gone unquestioned, but the issue had remained unaddressed while Joseph F. Smith was in the First Presidency and Brigham Young Jr. was not yet a senior Apostle, as the point was largely moot.[9]

As instructed by President Woodruff, and under the unifying and sustaining influence of the Holy Spirit upon the Quorum of the Twelve, President Snow reorganized the First Presidency quickly and without the troubles and delays of the past. Also at this time, President Snow spoke to Joseph F. of spiritual impressions that he had received: "At the time of the organization of the First Presidency after the death of President Woodruff, President Snow said to Joseph F. Smith that the Spirit whispered to him that Joseph F. Smith would succeed him as President of the Church. This statement President Smith recorded in his journal at that time."[10] At general conference three years later, President Smith himself remembered:

> As soon as the news reached us of the death of President Woodruff, who was in California at the time, President Lorenzo Snow said to me, "it will be our duty to proceed as soon as possible to reorganize the Presidency of the Church." As you are aware, after the burial of the remains of President Woodruff, he proceeded at once to do this. In this connection I may tell you another thing. President Snow said to me, "you will live to be the President of the Church of Jesus Christ of Latter-day Saints, and when that time comes you should proceed at once and reorganize the Presidency of the Church." This was his counsel to me, and the same was given to the Twelve Apostles. In accordance with this principle and with the injunction of President Snow, within one week after his death the Apostles proceeded to designate the new Presidency of the Church, and we did it strictly in accordance with the pattern that the Lord has established in His Church, unanimously.[11]

By March of 1900, with Presidents Snow and Cannon noticeably aging and with Franklin D. Richards, President of the Twelve, having passed away, the issues of dates of ordination and setting apart to the Quorum of the Twelve regained significance and needed settling. Joseph F. recorded:

> Presidents Snow, Cannon and I had a confidential talk together, introduced by President Cannon, relative to the choosing of a President of the Twelve. President Snow said: "It is President Cannon's right to stand at the head of the Twelve, but if he did he would have to resign his counselorship in the Presidency," and plainly intimated that he could do so if he chose. He then said to President Cannon: "If you and I were not here it would be the right of Brother Joseph F. Smith to stand where I am now, and if I were not here, it would be yours right now." President Cannon expressed his desire to possess and enjoy every right that belonged to

> him but suggested that matters go along for the present as they are and that the Presidency meet with the Twelve and take the lead.[12]

(As yet there was no provision established for an Acting President of the Twelve.) Joseph F. further wrote of this discussion: "Brigham's (Brigham Young Jr.) position in the quorum was talked over and President Snow favored and practically decided that Brigham Young—ranked next to [after] me in the council of Apostles. This decided the question, as it was decided by President John Taylor."[13]

Although the First Presidency had decided among themselves that date of entrance into the Quorum of the Twelve Apostles determined apostolic seniority, their decision still needed the unified acceptance of the Quorum of the Twelve—including Elder Young himself. This ratification took place shortly thereafter, on April 5. Joseph F. again recorded:

> We [the First Presidency] met with the eleven Apostles [in the temple]. . . . It was unanimously decided that the acceptance of a member into the council or quorum of the Twelve fixed his rank or position in the Apostleship. That the Apostles took precedence from the date they entered the quorum. Thus today, President Snow is the senior Apostle. President George Q. Cannon next, myself next, Brigham Young next, Francis M. Lyman next, and so on to the last one received into the quorum. In the case of the death of President Snow, President Cannon surviving him, would succeed to the Presidency, and so on according to seniority in the Apostleship of the Twelve; that ordination to the Apostleship under the hands of any Apostle other than to fill a vacancy in the quorum, and authorized by the General Authorities of the Church did not count in precedence; that if the First Presidency were dissolved by the death of the President, his counselors having been ordained Apostles in the Quorum of the Twelve would resume their places in the quorum, according to the seniority of their ordinations into that quorum. This important ruling settles a long unsettled point, and is most timely.[14]

Over the summer of 1900, President Snow became seriously ill, prompting him (despite his poor health) to further solidify the decision reached in the April temple meeting. On July 12, "President Cannon informed the council [of the Twelve] that President Snow came into the office yesterday, and in chatting with him desired the minutes of the Council of April 5th last passed upon, he having heard of them and approved of them himself. The minutes referred to the succession in the presidency and seniority of the Apostles quorum; and on motion of President Joseph F. Smith, and seconded by Elder Brigham Young, the minutes were unanimously approved."[15]

Joseph F. Smith Becomes the Senior Apostle after the Prophet

It did not take long for another major event to change Joseph F. Smith's position in the Twelve. President George Q. Cannon died in April of 1901, leaving Joseph F. second only to the prophet in seniority. The Journal History of the Church relates that "President Snow was deeply impressed [moved] when the information of President Cannon's death was communicated to him as was also President Joseph F. Smith."[16] While both were grieved, this news doubtless caused Joseph F. to reflect deeply on his new position as the senior Apostle on earth after President Snow.

President Snow did not move to replace President Cannon with a new counselor for six months. Over the summer and fall of 1901, President Snow became ill, first with symptoms of heat stroke and then with a severe cold that confined him to bed when October general conference arrived. Since his illness prevented him from attending all sessions himself, "he requested that word be sent to President Joseph F. Smith to the effect that he would not be at the opening session of the General Conference and for President Smith to take charge."[17] President Snow spoke once at the last session, and then requested that Joseph F. present the names of the General Authorities for a sustaining vote, with his own name as First Counselor and Elder Rudger Clawson's name as Second.[18] President Clawson served in the First Presidency for only four days and was never set apart. (President Smith did not reselect him as a counselor.)[19]

President Snow's Passing

After the conference, President Snow continued to spend most of his time in bed. By October 9, his condition had become alarmingly serious. Joseph F. described the events as they unfolded:

> On the morning of Wednesday, October the 9th, the directors of the Salt Lake and Los Angeles Railway Corporation, of which I was one, met with [President Snow] in the Beehive House instead of the President's Office, as we had been wont to do, and after the meeting, by his request we administered to him. We then thought, with him, that he was suffering from an ordinary cold on the

> lungs, and of course looked for his speedy recovery. At five o'clock the same day Sister Snow came into the office bearing the request that some of the brethren come and administer to President Snow, who was just reviving from a sinking spell. Myself, Brother John Henry Smith and others went immediately to his bedside, and it was apparent then that he was seriously and dangerously sick. After administering to him we urged the calling in of a physician. . . . [They] pronounced the President's ailment to be pneumonia, and their opinion was to the effect that unless there was a decided change for the better, hope for recovery could not be consistently entertained."[20]

Neither the doctor's care nor the priesthood administrations seemed to convey hope of recovery, for the Lord's will was otherwise. The Journal History continues the story:

> Presidents Smith and Clawson were at the office early this morning, and learned that President Snow's condition had not improved and had been quite serious at intervals during the night.
>
> President Smith presided at the meeting of the brethren in the Temple today. President Snow was the subject of most earnest prayer, all the brethren feeling alarmed over his condition.
>
> During the services, and while a letter . . . was being read, Elder Arthur Winter [an office clerk] came into the room where the council was, with a message from Sister Snow who asked that the brethren come to the Bee Hive house at once as it was feared that President Snow was dying. Brother L. John Nuttall [another employee in the President's Office] also came bearing the same message. The brethren immediately arose, closed the meeting. . . and then repaired to the bedside of President Snow, which was in the reception room, being the southwest room of the house which was for the time being turned into his bedroom. Although quite conscious, it was clearly seen that President Snow was rapidly sinking. A great number of his family was at the bedside. Prayer was offered at the instance of President Smith, with Brother Clawson mouth [speaking]. . . . What few words were spoken by [President Snow] after this were addressed to members of his family in answer to questions by them. He made no attempt to speak to President Smith or any of the Brethren. Soon, however, his speech became unintelligible and when he attempted to speak he was not understood. At about 1:15 he began to sink rapidly and passed away at 3:35 pm.[21]

With President Snow's death, Joseph F. Smith became the senior Apostle on the earth; from this perspective the prophet's demise affected no one else more than him. Yet even with this profound spiritual and emotional weight resting on him, practical considerations demanded prompt attention. After the undertaker had removed President Snow's body, President Smith met with the deceased prophet's sons to make funeral arrangements.[22]

The Journal History notes that the following day,

> A meeting of the Apostles was arranged for this morning at 10 o'clock at the office. . . . The object of this meeting was chiefly to arrange for the pallbearers and speakers at the funeral services. It was decided that no special speakers be named, but that the time be occupied by several of the older Apostles who should make brief remarks. . . . President Smith sought the mind of the brethren as to whether it would be proper for the Apostles to now act as the presiding quorum of the Church, or the counselors, until after the burial. The brethren generally accorded to the counselors the right to act until after the funeral services, and this according to precedent.[23]

Joseph F. Smith Becomes the President of the Church

On October 17, four days after President Snow's funeral, the following took place during the regularly scheduled temple meeting of the Quorum of the Twelve:

> Elder John Henry Smith moved that the question of reorganizing the First Presidency be considered, seconded by Elder Brigham Young, and carried.
>
> President Joseph F. Smith speaking to the motion, said that he would deplore very much anything that would look like premature haste in a step to reorganize the First Presidency, and he would not do it for all the world if he thought for a moment there was division of sentiment in relation to it. He then went on to show reason why a reorganization should take place because of business matters pending and requiring the attention of the Trustee-in-Trust, and a special conference would have to be called to ratify the appointment of a Trustee-in-Trust.
>
> Elder Brigham Young stated that his mind was clear that the First Presidency ought to be organized, and he nominated Joseph F. Smith as President of the Church of Jesus Christ of Latter-day Saints. This motion was

> seconded by the entire Council, all speaking in concert. Brother Young put the motion, and it was carried unanimously. President Smith expressed his gratitude for the unanimous feeling of the brethren. He named Elder Brigham Young as President of the Twelve Apostles, and also said that he would select John R. Winder and Anthon H. Lund as his first and second counselors, and recommended them for the consideration of the council. Elder John Henry Smith moved that these brethren be sustained as counselors to the President. Motion seconded by Brother Clawson and carried.[24]

President Smith's selection of John R. Winder, who had been serving as a counselor in the Presiding Bishopric, rather than Rudger Clawson, caused some mild surprise since the choice had not been anticipated. "Unexpected to him and to the public," the *Deseret News* editorialized, explaining that while such a decision was by no means unprecedented, it had been viewed as customary for many years to choose members of the Twelve for counselors in the First Presidency.[25] Bishop Winder served as First Counselor until his death but was never ordained an Apostle.

Continuing from the Journal History: "The work of setting apart was then attended to. President Joseph F. Smith, in accordance with his own wish, was ordained by Patriarch John Smith, . . . all the brethren present laying their hands on these brethren and assisting."[26] There are two items mentioned herein worth further notice: (1) the mention of both "setting apart" and being "ordained," and (2) the unusual but legitimate step of inviting John Smith, the Church Patriarch and Joseph F.'s half brother, to act as voice for the blessing. The terms *setting apart* and *ordained* as used here were interchangeable and simply meant that Joseph F. became the President of the high priesthood of the Church and the one man holding the right to exercise and direct all priesthood keys on the earth; *the* prophet, seer, and revelator.[27] John Smith, the Church Patriarch, did not hold apostolic authority, but by acting as voice with the Twelve helped give Joseph F. the blessing by the power of the Melchizedek Priesthood. President Smith had already been given all apostolic keys, rights, and powers at the time of his ordination by President Young.[28]

These Brethren further decided to call a special general conference on November 10 for the purpose of sustaining the new First Presidency and other newly called leaders.

A week later at the regular temple meeting of the First Presidency and Twelve on October 24, President Smith felt to nominate a new Apostle to fill the place vacated by Anthon H. Lund's advancement to the First Presidency. After some preliminary business,

> President Smith arose and said, I believe in being frank with my brethren. I am going to make a suggestion and leave the result in your hands. I would be glad if we all had sons worthy of the apostleship, for I would like to see the sons of the apostles brought forward as far as possible. I feel that this is right. I now nominate, as it is my privilege so to do, my son, Hyrum M. Smith, to fill the vacancy in the quorum of Apostles and will leave the matter entirely with the brethren. All present spoke, one by one, and endorsed the nomination. Apostle [John] H. Smith said that while he heartily endorsed the nomination, he felt that doubtless some fault would be found with our action, but at the same time he realized that there would be some to find fault with any action that might be taken in the premises. Pres. Smith made brief remarks. Was profoundly thankful to the brethren for the unanimity that had been manifested. No doubt some might find fault with the action of today, but faultfinders will always be in evidence among the people. He felt that it was his right to do as he had done. Hyrum is a good, honest, faithful, virtuous boy, and he had no doubt but that he would magnify the apostleship.[29]

Joseph F.'s son Hyrum was sent for and "having arrived he was informed of his selection by the council to become a member of the Quorum of Twelve Apostles. After several of the brethren had spoken of the duties that would be expected of him as an Apostle [the apostolic charge], Brother Hyrum expressed his willingness to accept, and he was set apart, all of the brethren laying their hands on his head, and President Smith officiating [voicing the ordination]."[30]

The day before the conference, the order of announcing names for sustaining was discussed:

> The Presidency met at the office this morning at 9:30 to discuss arrangements for the general conference. They had a talk in private yesterday afternoon in the office regarding the manner in which the authorities should be sustained, more particularly referring to the place the Patriarch of the Church should occupy in the presentation of the general authorities. Of late year it has been the custom to present his name after those of the Apostles, whereas in the early conferences of the Church his name followed those of the First Presidency, and President

> Smith remarked now that he was perfectly clear on this point that this was the place the Patriarch should occupy in the presentation of the authorities. However, after some discussion and consideration this question was left open for the present and it was decided not to make any change at present."[31]

President Smith's Second Counselor, President Lund, concerned with the troubling questions of succession such name positioning might raise, had persuaded the new prophet not to make the change.[32]

In his talks given at the special conference, President Smith spent time reviewing the inspiration received by the prophets related to the timing of the reorganization of the First Presidency and committed to rely heavily on his counselors, saying he would do nothing of importance without their support. Those spiritually attuned Latter-day Saints present felt the solemnity of the occasion. One wrote: "A special general conference of the Church was held in the Tabernacle; a most imposing, impressive scene was witnessed in the afternoon when the officers were voted in [sustained]. . . . The spirit and teachings of the conference were excellent."[33]

President Smith now moved forward magnifying the sacred office of President of The Church of Jesus Christ of Latter-day Saints and prophet of God on earth, with each day bringing a growing awareness of the weighty responsibilities placed upon him. Some three weeks after the general conference in which he was sustained as President of the Church, he shared his feelings with a close associate. Among other things, Joseph F. wrote:

> When confronted by the stern reality of the situation, I hardly know how to express the feelings of appreciation which well up in my heart; for I now keenly realize, as others have before me, that the eyes of the Lord, and those whom we have been wont to look up to, who are now on the other side of the veil, as well as my associate brethren in the flesh, are now directed towards me, as they have been towards my predecessors. But in contemplating the seriousness of the responsibility imposed upon me by the Lord and my brethren, its burden is at once comparatively lightened in the realization of the fact that you and I are the servants, servants of Him whom we have listed to obey; that the kingdom is the Lord's, and that it is for Him to guide and direct, and us to follow. . . . My mind naturally runs backward at times; and the men who have figured prominently in their time now appear to be nearer and stand out more clearly and conspicuously, perhaps, than ever before; and I cannot help but wonder at

the things which have been accomplished through them when the conditions surrounding them are considered.[34]

Thus began the Joseph F. Smith administrative era of Church history.

Notes

1. Summary and quotation found in Joseph Fielding Smith, *Life of Joseph F. Smith, Sixth President of the Church of Jesus Christ of Latter-day Saints* (Salt Lake City: Deseret Book, 1969), 212–16; see also Eliza R. Snow Smith, *Biography and Family Record of Lorenzo Snow* (Salt Lake City: Deseret News, 1884), 276–84.
2. Heber J. Grant, "Inspiration and Integrity of the Prophets," *Improvement Era*, August 1919, 847–48.
3. Editorial, *Deseret News*, October 18, 1901 (Charles Penrose was hired by President Snow as managing editor in December 1898 and later became a counselor in the First Presidency to Joseph F.); and Journal History of the Church of Jesus Christ of Latter-day Saints, October 18, 1901; hereafter cited as JH; see also *A Ministry of Meetings: The Apostolic Diaries of Rudger Clawson*, ed. Stan Larson (Salt Lake City: Signature Books, 1993), 339; hereafter cited as Rudger Clawson journal; and Smith, *Life of Joseph F. Smith*, 324.
4. As quoted in Anthon H. Lund, *Danish Apostle: The Diaries of Anthon H. Lund, 1890–1921*, ed. John P. Hatch (Salt Lake City: Signature Books, 2006), 159; hereafter cited as Anthon Lund journal.
5. Smith, *Life of Joseph F. Smith*, 227. At the same time, President Young "also admonished the brethren to keep the fact of this ordination to themselves, for it was wisdom that it should not be revealed at that time, although it should be recorded."
6. For a detailed review of these circumstances, see Ronald W. Walker, *Qualities That Count: Heber J. Grant as Businessman, Missionary, and Apostle* (Provo, UT: BYU Studies, 2004), 43:1, 195–229; and Dennis B. Horne, *Latter Leaves in the Life of Lorenzo Snow* (Springville, UT: Cedar Fort, 2012), 201–7, 224–28, 237, 240–59, 266.
7. Lorenzo Snow interview, December 3, 1892, interviewed by Wilford Woodruff, MS 3558, Church History Library, The Church of Jesus Christ of Latter-day Saints; emphasis added; see also Horne, *Latter Leaves in the Life of Lorenzo Snow*, 227–28.
8. See Joseph F. Smith, in Conference Report [Special Conference], November 10, 1901, 71; see also Smith, *Life of Joseph F. Smith*, 319.
9. See Travis Q. Mecham, "Changes in Seniority to the Quorum of the Twelve Apostles of The Church of Jesus Christ of Latter-day Saints" (master's thesis, Utah State University, 2009), 45–57, esp. 48.
10. Smith, *Life of Joseph F. Smith*, 324.
11. Joseph F. Smith, in Conference Report [Special Conference], November 10, 1901, 71.
12. Smith, *Life of Joseph F. Smith*, 310.
13. Smith, *Life of Joseph F. Smith*, 310.
14. As quoted in Smith, *Life of Joseph F. Smith*, 310–11 (April 5, 1900); see also JH, April 5, 1900, and Rudger Clawson journal, April 5, 1900.

15. JH, July 12, 1900. Elder Young's seconding of the motion affirms his willingness to abide by the decision of the First Presidency and Twelve with no reservations, especially in connection with his formal motion during the later meeting of October 17, 1901, that Joseph F. Smith be sustained as Church President.
16. JH, April 12, 1901.
17. JH, October 4, 1901.
18. See LeRoi C. Snow, "A Matter of History," *Improvement Era,* March 1937, 149.
19. See James R. Clark, *Messages of the First Presidency* (Salt Lake City: Bookcraft, 1966), 3:343; see also B. H. Roberts, comp., *A Comprehensive History of the Church of Jesus Christ of Latter-day Saints* (Salt Lake City: Deseret News, 1957), 6:362.
20. Joseph F. Smith, "The Last Days of President Snow," *Juvenile Instructor,* November 15, 1901, 688; see also Clark, *Messages,* 3:6; and JH, October 9, 1901.
21. JH, October 10, 1901; see also Joseph F. Smith, "The Last Days of President Snow," *Juvenile Instructor,* November 15, 1901, 688–91, also found in Clark, *Messages,* 3:6–10.
22. See JH, October 10, 1901.
23. JH, October 11, 1901.
24. JH, October 17, 1901. Further, "Brother Marriner W. Merrill moved that President Joseph F. Smith be Trustee-in-Trust for the Church of Jesus Christ of Latter-day Saints. The motion was seconded and carried unanimously. It was also moved that President Smith be made president of the Salt Lake Temple, with Brother John R. Winder as his assistant."
25. Editorial, *Deseret News,* October 18, 1901, 1.
26. JH, October 17, 1901.
27. When Lorenzo Snow was blessed by George Q. Cannon on becoming Church President, the term *set apart* was used, not *ordain.* See JH, October 10, 1898.
28. See Smith, *Life of Joseph F. Smith,* 227, where Joseph F. Smith was given "all the authority, power, and keys of this holy apostleship" by President Brigham Young; see also Hoyt W. Brewster Jr., *Prophets, Priesthood Keys, and Succession* (Salt Lake City: Deseret Book, 1991), 87–90.
29. Rudger Clawson journal, 341.
30. JH, October 24, 1901; see also Rudger Clawson journal, 341. Hyrum Smith died at age forty-five after serving less than seventeen years as a member of the Quorum of the Twelve.
31. JH, November 10, 1901.
32. "I had a private talk with the President and told him that I hesitated somewhat in making this change. While John Smith was a humble man there might come a man who was ambitious and might cause us trouble. In case of the First Presidency being disorganized and the Apostles presiding he might have to take a place behind them, and when the counselors and apostles are put up for Prophets, Seers, and Revelators he would be passed" (Anthon Lund journal, 164).
33. Journal of Richard S. Horne, unpublished, November 10, 1901; copy in author's possession.
34. President Joseph F. Smith to President F. M. Lyman, December 2, 1901, correspondence, MS 1325, box 33, folder 3, Church History Library; available in Richard E. Turley Jr., ed., *Selected Collections of The Church of Jesus Christ of Latter-day Saints* (DVD), vol. 1, under date.

Richard J. Dowse

16

Joseph F. Smith and the Hawaiian Temple

On June 11, 1843, to a large assembly of Saints at the Nauvoo Temple, the Prophet Joseph Smith delivered a sermon on the doctrine of the gathering. He taught the purpose of gathering "the people of God in any age of the world," saying, "The main object was to build unto the Lord an house whereby he could reveal unto his people the ordinances of his house and glories of his kingdom & teach the peopl the ways of salvation for their are certain ordinances & principles that when they are taught and practized, must be done in a place or house built for that purpose."[1]

The Prophet practiced what he preached by establishing the pattern of gathering Latter-day Saints to designated locations and then building temples. Subsequent Presidents of the Church continued to follow this pattern in their respective eras. Joseph Smith's own nephew, Joseph F. Smith, not only embraced this precedent but expanded it. As the sixth President of the Church, he enlarged the previous pattern's potential by introducing a model capable of accommodating the needs of a rapidly growing modern Church.

Richard J. Dowse is a teacher at Lone Peak Seminary in Highland, Utah.

The seventeen-year administration of President Joseph F. Smith began in the dawn of the twentieth century, a period of development and increased prosperity for the Church. One significant milestone during his tenure was the Church's becoming fiscally solvent. Despite such a monumental material achievement, however, Joseph Fielding Smith later recalled that his father's "administration was noted, perhaps above all else, in the spiritual progress which had been made."[2] The building of new temples in Canada and Hawaii was perhaps the most fitting symbol of the Church's temporal and spiritual success in that era.

Joseph F. Smith led the Church through a pivotal time of transition in Latter-day Saint history. The genesis of one transformational change can be seen in the conception and building of these two temples outside the continental United States. Indeed, the first Church President from the second generation of Latter-day Saints introduced the next generation of temple architecture and construction.

Under President Smith's direction, and due to his unique life experience, the Church was well-suited to embrace its increasing international presence in a paradigm-altering way. Evidence of this evolution is particularly manifest by President Smith's singular role in the construction of the Laie Hawaii Temple. The purpose of this essay is to explore how President Joseph F. Smith's integral involvement in the building of the Latter-day Saint temple in Hawaii resulted in the first temple "away from the traditional centers of Mormon colonization in Utah."[3] This is significant because with the temple comes the introduction of Laie as an early prototype of gathering, which did not really take hold Churchwide until the mid-twentieth century.

In examining this topic, a series of questions will be addressed. First, what connections did Joseph F. Smith have with the Hawaiian Islands that led to the building of a temple there? Second, why and how was Laie selected as the location for the temple? Third, what events led to President Smith's decision to build a temple in Laie, Hawaii, at that time in Church history? And lastly, what impact did the building of the Hawaiian Temple, as it was known, have on the Church today—nearly one hundred years later?

Aloha: Joseph F. Smith and His Connection to Hawaii

"It was on [the Hawaiian Islands] that President Joseph F. Smith began his missionary work," eulogized Apostle Reed Smoot, speaking in a general conference several years after President Smith's death. He continued, "Talk about people loving a man! I do not believe it is possible for human beings to love a man more than did the natives of the islands love President Joseph F. Smith."[4] It is abundantly clear that the love, or *aloha,* felt by the Hawaiian Saints for their former missionary and prophet was mutual. This deep and abiding love began to take root early in Joseph F.'s life, when he was called to serve a mission in the Pacific Isles.

Much has been said and written concerning this first mission. In short, it was a foundational experience during Joseph F.'s formative years. Looking back, he said this mission changed him into "a man, although only a boy."[5] Others sensed innate nobility and foresaw great potential in the young missionary with the impressive pedigree. Within his first few days in Hawaii, his mission president, Francis A. Hammond, recorded, "He is not yet 16 years old, but bids fain to make a mighty man in this Kingdom."[6]

Another prediction concerning the potential of young Joseph F. was made during his less-heralded second mission to Hawaii. Just six months after he returned home from a three-year mission to Great Britain, a call came to go back to Hawaii, or the Sandwich Islands as they were called at the time. On January 24, 1864, he nonchalantly recorded in his address book, which doubled as a makeshift diary: "I was called to take a mission to the Sandwich Islands, in company with E.T. Benson & L. Snow of the Twelve & W.W. Cluff and A.L. Smith."[7] Elder Lorenzo Snow reported that while he was in Hawaii, the Lord revealed to him that Joseph F. Smith "would someday be the Prophet of God."[8]

Indeed, the young elder eventually became the prophet of God, and interestingly, it was following Lorenzo Snow's own tenure as prophet. In fact, thirty-five years after Elder Snow's prophecy, Joseph F. became President Snow's counselor in the First Presidency. President Smith served in that capacity with President Snow for three years before succeeding him as Church President.[9]

The purpose of Joseph F. Smith's second mission to the Islands was to rectify the problems resulting from Walter Murray Gibson usurping Church leadership in Hawaii. The Sandwich Islands Mission was vacated by all Utah missionaries in 1858 following a largely unsuccessful attempt to create a Hawaiian gathering place on the island of Lanai.[10] The catalyst for the mass exodus of missionaries is historically reported to be the tensions that existed in the Utah Territory between the Latter-day Saints and the US government during the Utah War.[11]

Gibson took control of the Church on the islands several years after Church leadership was placed solely in the hands of Hawaiian members. Apparently on his way to Japan to spread the gospel, Gibson stopped in Hawaii and must have become interested in the prospects of the Sandwich Islands.[12] Upon introducing himself to the Hawaiian Saints, Gibson claimed that "he had been sent by President [Brigham] Young, not only to take charge of the mission on those islands, but to preside over all the churches that might be raised up on any of the Pacific islands." Gibson further purported to be "equal to, and entirely independent of President Young."[13]

He settled upon the title and office of "Chief President of the Islands of the Sea and of the Hawaiian Islands, for the Church of Latter Day Saints." As "Chief President," Gibson reconstructed the Church, sold Church membership and priesthood offices, reintroduced native superstitions, and defrauded the Saints out of personal and Church property. Gibson used the funds he procured through simony and extortion to purchase land upon which to build his own "little kingdom."[14] In time he raised "sufficient means for the purchase of one half of the island of Lanai."[15]

Gibson's story is likely the most chronicled episode in the history of the Church in the Pacific.[16] In late December 1863, several of the Hawaiian elders wrote letters to their former missionary friends in Utah, detailing all of Gibson's actions and seeking advice on how to proceed. The letters were translated and given to the First Presidency, who immediately dispatched the aforementioned delegation to go to Lanai and investigate the claims made against Gibson.[17]

On April 8, 1864, an obstinate and unrepentant Gibson was officially excommunicated from the Church. After mitigating the situation, Elders Benson and Snow returned home. Responsibility for the mission was left in the hands of the mission president they had just appointed: twenty-five-year-old Joseph F. Smith.[18]

Gibson refused to deed the Lanai property back over to the Church, so the Saints were counseled to return to their home islands and wait for their respective branches to be reorganized.

Meanwhile, President Smith and his remaining companions commenced a tour of the islands. They went to work reorganizing branches, rebuilding the Church, and inciting a "reformation" among the Hawaiian members.[19] As one historian explained, "Even though discouraged, [Joseph F. Smith] still loved the Hawaiian people and hoped for their success as Latter-day Saints. Out of this hope he developed the idea of establishing a new gathering place somewhere in the islands where the Saints could be taught manual skills and how to live according to gospel principles."[20]

The young mission president shared this idea with the prophet Brigham Young, and apparently the prophet approved.[21] Later that year, President Young deemed it time to release President Smith from his duties and assigned two men to replace him. These men were Francis A. Hammond, a former missionary to Hawaii, and George Nebeker, a seasoned Church man with colonization experience. They were sent to the Islands with specific instructions from the prophet to purchase land as a gathering place for the Hawaiian Saints.[22] After scouting for various possible locations themselves, the new co-presidents ultimately decided to acquire the plantation recommended by President Smith and his companions as the most suitable place for colonization. The plantation was on the island of Oahu, at Laie.[23]

On his second mission to Hawaii, Joseph F. Smith salvaged a church on the brink, reformed it, and formulated a plan to gather the Saints. Then, during the 1880s, on what has been called his third mission to Hawaii, President Smith, at the time an Apostle and the Second Counselor in the First Presidency of the Church, used his spiritual stature and administrative prowess to prepare Laie and its Saints for a temple.

At the height of the federally sponsored antipolygamy crusade, President Smith was forced into exile. US marshals had a keen interest in detaining him due to his experience as a recorder in the Endowment House. More particularly, they desired to obtain the records of the Endowment House in his possession, which would undoubtedly be key evidence in prosecuting many Church leaders.[24] Anxious that neither fall into the hands of their enemies, President John Taylor was persuaded to send his counselor on a "mission" to Hawaii in late 1884.

Accompanied by his wife Julina and their infant daughter, President Smith would make Hawaii his home for the next two and a half years. It was undoubtedly an incredible burden to be so far away from family for such a long time. Julina left behind five children, the youngest of whom had just turned three. Joseph was separated from four other wives and seventeen children.[25] Despite their personal difficulties, the Smiths' contributions provided a tremendous boon to the struggling settlement in Laie.

As expected, the Church's efficiency in Laie increased in many areas thanks to the leadership supplied by the extended presence of a member of the First Presidency.[26] A surprising example of his servant-leadership approach is reflected in the minutes of a council meeting held at Laie in September of 1885. According to the record, President Joseph F. Smith "suggested the propriety of giving Laie a separate branch organization" and the motion passed unanimously. Enoch Farr, who was serving as mission president, was appointed president of the new Laie Branch. The record continues, "[Farr] chose Joseph F. Smith and Albert W. Davis as his counselors, and Van R. Miller was appointed clerk of the Branch."[27] Having the second counselor in the First Presidency simultaneously serving as the first counselor in a branch presidency is perhaps the best example of the uniqueness of the privilege provided to the people of Laie at that time.

President Smith's hands-on service was not limited solely to ecclesiastical matters, however. "Besides these duties, he was constantly assisting in the building of fences, cultivating fields, shingling houses, making sugar, mending wagons, and otherwise laboring with his hands."[28] Occasionally, the scope of President Smith's duties expanded even further, adding to the already unconventional work for a member of the Church's First Presidency. For example, President Smith's wife Julina had assumed the responsibility of being the colony's midwife. When the time came for her to have her own baby, however, midwifery duties fell upon her husband. On April 21, 1886, she gave birth to a baby boy, Elias Wesley, who was delivered by his father.[29] Interestingly, Wesley, as he was called, would return to his birthplace nineteen years later to serve as a missionary, and later still to serve as the area's mission president on two occasions.[30]

When President Taylor's severe illness demanded Joseph F. Smith's return to Utah, he left Hawaii on July 1, 1887.[31] He undoubtedly left Laie in a better position temporally and spiritually. Under President Smith's tutelage, "the church was fully organized and functioning, including all the auxiliaries," and the work of the Hawaiian Mission was streamlined and expanded.[32] But perhaps the most significant impact of Joseph F. Smith's time in Laie is that it may arguably have been one of the greatest contributing factors for building a temple there.

The Hawaiian Saints and the Gathering

During his first mission to the Sandwich Islands in 1854–57, Elder Smith and his fellow missionaries clearly taught the doctrine of gathering to a centralized Zion. This was consistent with the direction of the day. Their native converts were taught that the purpose of gathering was to receive temple ordinances necessary for salvation. At that point in time, these essential blessings were only available in Salt Lake City.[33]

A longing to heed the call to "come to Zion"[34] compelled converts the world over to brave the arduous trip to Utah. Many faithful Saints in the South Pacific felt that same desire, yet relatively few were able to make the journey to Salt Lake to obtain the spiritual blessings they desperately wanted. Those who were able to emigrate, however, began visiting the Utah Territory as early as 1869.[35]

One contemporary missionary, Castle Murphy, noted how "handicapped the saints . . . were without having a Temple nearby." He explained the extent to which many Hawaiian Saints were willing to sacrifice in order to "come to Utah to receive their endowments and sealings." "Some," he wrote, "used their life's savings to make the trip and returned home in debt."[36]

Others who traveled to Utah for the temple, however, never made the return trip. By the late 1880s, a portion of northwest Salt Lake City was home to a small community of about seventy-five Hawaiians.[37] This gathering led to the August 1889 founding of a Hawaiian colony at Skull Valley. It was located west of Salt Lake City in Tooele County. Fittingly, the community was named *Iosepa* (pronounced *yoh-seh-pa*), which means "Joseph" in Hawaiian. It was a tribute to their beloved missionary and Apostle, Joseph F. Smith.[38]

"The Hawaiian Saints desired to obtain their endowments and be sealed together as families," observed one historian. "Endowment work," he continued, "was undoubtedly the major motivation for gathering to Zion."[39] Other scholars agree that the reason behind the Hawaiian pioneers' settling in desolate Skull Valley rather than a more agronomically favorable location was that such available locations were "far from a temple, and that was the reason that Hawaiians wanted to be in Utah."[40]

The agricultural village was supervised by several former Hawaiian missionaries. It was partially modeled after, and managed much like, the plantation in Laie. The colony lasted for twenty-eight years and, in 1915, was a profitable, thriving community with 228 inhabitants. Even though Iosepa was a successful community with satisfied residents, and the only home many of its younger residents had ever known, by early 1917 the last group of Hawaiians had left. The ranch was sold shortly thereafter, and until fairly recently, there was little recognition or remaining evidence that the largely forgotten colony ever existed.[41]

A historic announcement in the 86th Semiannual General Conference of 1915 incited the exodus from Iosepa. Shortly after ten in the morning on Sunday, October 3, the prophet and President of the Church stood to address the congregation seated in the Salt Lake Tabernacle. Near the end of his sermon, Joseph F. Smith explained:

> Now, away off in the Pacific Ocean are various groups of islands, from the Sandwich Islands down to Tahiti, Samoa, Tonga, and New Zealand. On them are thousands of good people . . . of the blood of Israel. When you carry the Gospel to them they receive it with open hearts. They need the same privileges that we do, and that we enjoy, but these are out of their power. They are poor, and they can't gather means to come up here to be endowed, and sealed for time and eternity, for their living and their dead, and to be baptized for their dead. What shall we do with them? Heretofore, we have suffered the conditions that exist there. . . .
>
> Now, I say to my brethren and sisters this morning that we have come to the conclusion that it would be a good thing to build a temple that shall be dedicated to the ordinances of the house of God, down upon one of the Sandwich Islands, so that the good people of those islands may reach the blessing of the House of God within their own borders, and that the people from New Zealand, if they do not become strong enough to require a house to be built there also, by and by, can come to Laie, where they can get their blessings and return home and live in peace, having fulfilled all the requirements of the Gospel the same as we have the privilege of doing here.

President Smith then proposed to "build a temple at Laie, Oahu, Territory of Hawaii." All present manifested their approval by raising their right hand, to which the prophet noted, "I do not see a contrary vote."[42]

In the announcement of a temple in Laie, the Hawaiians living in Iosepa also heard a call to return to their homeland. They felt the need to help build Zion there, complete with its temple. Temple blessings led to the formation of the colony at Iosepa, but it was the blessing of having a temple in their native land that caused the Hawaiian Saints to abandon it.[43] The establishment and eventual disbandment of Iosepa can be valuably viewed as a microcosm for the purpose and evolution of the doctrine of gathering Zion.

Furthermore, the establishment and building up of Laie, and the construction and dedication of a temple there, marked the genesis of a shift in gathering and temple building for the Church. This temple, in the middle of the Pacific Ocean, became the first realization of the long-foreseen direction of the gathering of scattered Israel on the "isles of the sea" (2 Nephi 10:8). It was a forerunner to the future method of building Zion in the dispensation of the fulness of times.

Ground Dedicated for a Temple in Hawaii

It is no secret that Joseph F. Smith loved Hawaii—the place, the poi, the pace, and especially the people.[44] He prized these sites that had had such personal significance from the formative years of his life and faith. Tellingly, he visited the islands more throughout his life than any other destination outside of the American West. In fact, President Smith traveled to Hawaii four times during his administration as Church President alone.[45]

President Smith was continually impressed by the progress he observed in Hawaii, and among the members there, during his visits from January 1899 to May of 1915. Observations from his 1915 trip were summarized in a letter written from Laie to his son Hyrum M. Smith. After detailing infrastructure improvements and other modern advancements, he reported, "In brief, I may say our saints in Hawaii, especially those of this little colony and those of Honolulu, are apparently in vastly better temporal conditions than I have ever seen them in before. Every indication points to the belief that they have made excellent spiritual progress also."[46]

This must have been gratifying to the prophet who was known to have "kept a careful eye on Hawaii." The number of missionaries sent there increased during his presidency (at one point by more than 50 percent), as did the membership of the church in Hawaii. This included the significant addition of over a thousand new members from 1910 to 1915.[47] President Smith's announcement to build a temple in Hawaii was made just over three months after returning home from that momentous visit. His experiences from his 1915 trip to Hawaii were crucial in his determination to see a temple built there.

Apostle Reed Smoot, a United States senator at the time, was invited to visit the Islands as a guest of the Hawaii Legislature. Senator Smoot then asked President Smith and his wife, Julina, to accompany him as his guests on the trip, set for early May.[48] The Smiths' departure was delayed due to a family illness, but along with Presiding Bishop Charles W. Nibley and his wife, they finally met up with the Smoots upon their May 21 arrival.[49]

The vacation was filled with the typical fanfare expected during the stay of a beloved prophet, especially one so highly esteemed as Joseph F. Smith. It was also filled with the anticipated ministerial duties and—as is the lot of nearly

Top: On board the SS Manchuria *in Honolulu Harbor, Julina Smith and President Joseph F. Smith pose with Rebecca Nibley and Presiding Bishop Charles W. Nibley prior to disembarking on May 21, 1915. Courtesy of Church History Library. Bottom: Welcome celebration for President Smith and his party held in Laie, Oahu, Hawaii, on May 22, 1915. Standing on the porch of the Laie Social Hall are (left to right): President Joseph F. Smith, Julina Smith, Elder Reed Smoot, Allie Smoot, Bishop Charles W. Nibley, Rebecca Nibley, and Samuel E. Woolley. Courtesy of Church History Library.*

Apostle and senator Reed Smoot invited President Joseph F. Smith and his wife Julina on a trip to Hawaii May 21–June 5, 1919. While in Laie, President Smith dedicated ground for the Laie Hawaii Temple on June 1, 1919. This photo was taken during their stay. President Smith (front row, center right) and Julina are seated next to Bishop Charles W. Nibley and his wife Rebecca. Elder Smoot (back row, center) and his wife, Allie, are pictured along with missionaries from the Hawaiian Mission (from left to right) Elders Robert Smith, Dick Wells, and Wilford J. Cole, and Hawaiian Mission president Samuel E. Woolley. Courtesy of Church History Library.

all priesthood leaders—some unanticipated ones, too. On Saturday, May 29, President Smith presided and spoke at the funeral of a faithful Hawaiian brother, and it may be that this Saint's sudden passing was instrumental in prompting the inspiration the prophet needed to dedicate ground for the long-awaited temple in Hawaii.

Mission records reported, "Peter Kealakaihonua, an aged Hawaiian Elder, . . . died suddenly in Honolulu."[50] Not a great deal is known about this man. He lived in Honolulu for many years with perhaps the most prominent Latter-day Saint couple in Hawaii, Abraham and Minerva Fernandez.[51] The fact that President Smith and Elder Smoot attended his funeral was mentioned in an article printed in the *Liahona*, the Church's missionary publication of the day. The article provides the following information about "Elder Kealakaihonua." It states that he was "one of the oldest and most respected members of the Church in the islands. He had been a member of the Church for many years and had been the means of converting a large number of the islanders."[52] In his journal, Elder Smoot noted

Peter's unexpected passing, adding this intriguing insight: "The old man has been to Utah and received his endowments."[53]

Available records do not indicate the extent of this event's impact on President Smith specifically, but a later journal entry confirms that Peter's death certainly had made an impression on Elder Smoot. Elder Smoot wrote, "After the funeral services of Peter last Saturday I told Sister Smith and Sister Nibley as we were going to the grave yard [*sic*] that the church ought to erect an Endowment House or Temple at Laie so the islanders could secure their endowments and do temple work for the living and the dead."[54]

Elder Smoot made this timely comment just three days before, as one biographer put it, "an ecclesiastical event of historic significance."[55] On the well-documented evening of Tuesday, June 1, 1915, President Smith requested that Bishop Nibley and Elder Smoot accompany him on a walk. They strolled through their beautiful surroundings about four hundred yards up a small hill to the chapel called *I Hemolele,* which in Hawaiian suitably means "Holiness to the Lord." According to President Smith, the men then "had some conversation on the subject of recommending that a small temple or endowment house be erected [there] at Laie."[56]

In his account of the evening's events, Elder Smoot adds several noteworthy details: "President Smith said [Bishop] Nibley had suggested to him that as the Mission was in a financial condition that [if] it could build a small Endowment House or Temple it should do so." According to Elder Smoot, Nibley also suggested that the temple be built on that very spot where the chapel stood, which would necessitate moving the *I Hemolele* meeting house. President Smith then stated, "If that met with approval of all three of us he felt impressed to consecrate and dedicate the ground for that purpose."[57]

In a later telling of the experience, Elder Smoot included this description of President Smith's pre-dedicatory words: "I feel impressed to dedicate this ground for the erection of a temple to God, for a place where the peoples of the Pacific Isles can come and do their temple work. I have not presented this to the Council of the Twelve or to my counselors; but if you think there would be no objection to it, I think now is the time to dedicate the ground."[58]

Elder Smoot is clear that the notion "met with [his] hearty approval." While recording the evening's events in his journal, he added his conviction that the event was "the first step towards the erection of a small temple here in Laie wherein the Hawaiian Saints as well as the saints of other Islands of the Pacific can have their temple ordinations, sealings, baptisms, etc attended to." Then, as if to acknowledge the magnitude of this milestone, Elder Smoot proclaimed, "This can be considered a blessed day for members of the church living on the islands of the Pacific."[59]

There is no question as to the significance of the step taken on that "blessed day." Elder Smoot's records supply rich contextual information about the circumstances surrounding this monumental event, especially the connection and timing of the funeral just a few days prior to the dedication of the temple site. Peter's death was noteworthy enough to have been reported in a newspaper article on the mainland that highlighted President Smith's trip to Hawaii. Was his passing poignant enough to cause the prophet to reflect upon the state of those Hawaiians who, unlike Peter, had not had the opportunity to go to the temple in Utah?

Regardless of the impetus of the inspiration, the important fact remains: Joseph F. Smith, in his role as the prophet of God, dedicated the ground in Laie, Hawaii for the building of a house of the Lord. Thus, the evening of Tuesday, June 1, 1915, marked the dawning of a new era of temple construction and expansion in Church history—it would be the first temple outside of North America.

Temple Built in Hawaii

Following the dedicatory prayer, Elder Smoot noted that "the very ground seemed to be sacred."[60] The trio then returned to the mission home, and each of them spoke to a group of Saints gathered there. While nothing was mentioned regarding the sacred experience they had just come from, President Smith makes it clear that at some point that day they "talked the matter over with President S. E. Woolley," the president of the Hawaiian Mission.[61]

President Smith and President Woolley continued regular correspondence in connection to the progress of the temple. At the end of a letter written to Woolley soon after his return home, Joseph F. Smith included a status update following the heading "<u>Private</u>" (emphasis in original). The news read, "The matter of building a sacred place at Laie was presented to the Council last Thursday, at our first meeting, and was joyfully accepted and approved by all present. While it is not time to make it public, I will soon give you further information as the first steps which will be taken."[62] A few months later President Smith apprised President Woolley further, saying, "We expect to make public announcement of the Sacred building . . . during our October conference. In the meantime it will not be necessary to make any positive declarations of it to the public."[63]

Following its announcement in October 1915, mission records state that "Work commenced for the erection of the new Temple" on January 12, 1916. The first major undertaking was moving the meetinghouse from the temple site. Relocating the hundred-ton chapel "was quite a task" and took an entire month.

The frequent correspondence Joseph F. maintained with Hawaiian Mission president Samuel E. Woolley was one sign of the prophet's keen interest in the temple. His interest was demonstrated more overtly, however, by his efforts to monitor its progress personally. Twice he made trips to Hawaii to oversee work on the temple.

President Smith arrived for his first visit on March 1, 1916, the day the chapel was installed in its new location. That very day, "a special meeting, was held at Laie," over which President Smith presided. During the meeting "the proposition was discussed as to the advisability of entering into a contract with the Spaulding [*sic*] Construction Company of Honolulu to build the L.D.S. Temple at Laie." At length a resolution was unanimously passed to contract with Walter Spalding, after which the prophet said, "I am mighty well pleased with this arrangement, for I must admit that it has been somewhat of a worry to me, but now I feel perfectly easy about the matter. I feel that my trip has been a success now."[64]

While plans were being solidified for the temple in Hawaii, construction on the temple in Alberta, Canada, was already under way. Pleased with the plans and progress of the temple in Canada, President Smith turned again to the temple's architects, Hyrum C. Pope and Harold Burton, to prepare plans for the new temple in Laie. They were directed to continue with a similar design, only smaller.

The Hawaiian Temple was significant to the Church, but it was especially so to President Joseph F. Smith. He was intimately involved in the details of its construction—even to the point of ordering the correction of the color schemes in a mural's water scene.[65] His concern and desire to ensure that the project was progressing brought him again to the temple site a year later in May of 1917. His biographer, Francis Gibbons, reflected President Smith's feelings: "The day after reaching Oahu, Joseph made his way to Laie and immediately delved into the matter that was uppermost in his thoughts: 'We visited the temple & found the workmen all around.'"[66]

Plans originally called for the completion and dedication of the temple by the first of June 1917.[67] As work on the temple advanced, however, it became clear that the temple would not be ready. Gibbons underscored the prophet's anxious desire for the temple's completion when he wrote, "a combined sense of urgency and irritation may be inferred from [Joseph's] entry of the fourteenth [of May]: 'Visited the temple this morning. Workmen still busy and to all human appearance the finish is by no means nearby.'"[68]

The thinly-veiled disappointment in President Smith's progress report is evidence of his excitement for the temple's dedication. From a later entry, however, there is an indication that a portion of his frustration may have been caused by his fear that he may not have lived to see its completion. At the conclusion of his 1917 trip, while en route to the mainland, Joseph F. pensively reminisced in this telling journal entry: "We boarded the ship and bid good by [*sic*] to our friends and Honolulu, perhaps for the <u>last time.</u>".[69]

Sadly, the prophet's entry turned out to be prophetic, and a dedication of the temple by President Smith was not to be. With the exception of landscaping, construction on the temple itself was completed on April 18, 1918. The worldwide influenza pandemic of 1918, however, reached the United States and Hawaii by summertime, causing the dedication to be postponed.[70] That summer and fall found Joseph F. Smith battling his own illnesses until he finally succumbed to a bout of pleurisy that developed into pleuropneumonia. He passed away Tuesday morning, November 19, 1918.[71]

"Great regret [was] felt by the Hawaiian people that their dearly beloved leader, the late President Joseph F. Smith, [would] not be with them at dedication time." Reported reaction to the news of President Smith's passing continued as follows: "During his three missions to the islands he became loved and reverenced by all. His honest, gentle, fearless and sympathetic character drew the confidence, respect and boundless love of this naturally trusting people."[72]

The mission history for that fateful day records, "The sad news of the death of President Joseph F. Smith reached Laie, which sent a gloom over mission headquarters. The schools were closed half a day and the flag set at half mast in honor of the beloved president." Though deeply saddened, the Hawaiian Saints still had much to look forward to. The dedication of the sacred structure that would forever stand as a token of President Smith's undying *aloha* for the Hawaiian Saints approached.

Memorial service for the late President Joseph F. Smith held in the Laie Chapel on Sunday, November 24, 1918. The meeting was well attended, with 245 Hawaiian Saints present. Courtesy of Joseph F. Smith Library Archives, Brigham Young University–Hawaii.

The new prophet, President Heber J. Grant, was also compelled to delay the dedication until the ongoing "Spanish flu" pandemic subsided. Harold Burton, one of the temple's architects, later recalled that the dedication was also delayed "owing to the First World War."[73] In the meantime, labor continued on the landscape architecture, and all was said to be completely finished by July 15, 1919.[74] With the dedication of the temple imminent, the temple needed to be prepared for public display. This was done, and for more than two months before its dedication "the Laie Temple [was] opened to visitors, and many had visited the Temple."[75] At last, on Thursday, November 13, 1919, a telegram arrived in Hawaii with word that the temple dedication was set for the end of that month.[76]

Although Joseph F. Smith did not live to see the temple in Hawaii completed, his memory lived on in the dedication services. Presiding Bishop Charles W. Nibley was one of Joseph F. Smith's dearest friends and spoke in one of the dedicatory sessions. Nibley was with President Smith when he dedicated the temple site, and his first remarks referenced that special occasion. President Clawson recorded, "With deep emotion [Bishop Nibley] expressed his sorrow that President Smith had not lived to attend [the] dedication but reminded the Saints that the authority which he held was still [there] and . . . [rested] upon President Grant."

When it was President Heber J. Grant's opportunity to offer his concluding remarks, a major portion of his words were centered on his late predecessor. He "expressed a keen regret that President Joseph F. Smith had not lived to come here

Members at the dedication of the Laie Hawaii Temple, November 27, 1919. The temple was dedicated by President Heber J. Grant almost exactly a year after President Smith's death. President Grant keenly regretted that President Smith had not lived to dedicate the temple. He reportedly said it was "the saddest assignment of his life. He knew how much President Smith would have enjoyed being there." Courtesy of Joseph F. Smith Library Archives, Brigham Young University–Hawaii.

and dedicate this temple." It seems as though President Smith's earthly absence from this singular event had a powerful effect on President Grant. An associate claimed that President Grant later confided in him that "going to Hawaii to dedicate the Temple was the saddest assignment of his life. He knew how President Smith would have enjoyed being there to dedicate the Temple."[77] Nevertheless, on November 27, 1919, President Grant presided over the dedication of the temple in Laie, Hawaii, the Church's fifth operating temple.[78]

A Shift in Gathering and Temple Building

The establishment and building up of Laie and the construction and dedication of a temple there marked the genesis of a shift in gathering and temple building for the Church. This temple, in the middle of the Pacific Ocean, became the first realization of the long-foreseen direction of the gathering of scattered Israel and a foreshadowing of the future of building Zion in the dispensation of the fullness of times.

Joseph F. Smith long recognized the Church's need for temples in distant areas of the world. While serving as the Second Counselor to Church President Lorenzo Snow in 1901, he said, "I foresee the necessity arising for other temples or other places consecrated to the Lord for the performance of the ordinances of God's house, so that the people may have the benefit of the House of the Lord without having to travel hundreds of miles for that purpose."[79]

President Smith not only saw the need for such temples, but on several occasions he prophesied that someday there would be multiple temples built in many diverse countries throughout the world.[80] The Laie Hawaii Temple was the first temple dedicated in one of the missions of the Church. It was also the first to begin to fulfill Joseph F. Smith's prophecies. It is unlikely that nearly twenty years before its existence, President Smith would have known that a temple in Hawaii would hold this distinction in Church history. Nor would he likely have dreamed he would play such a vital role in the realization of this temple that was so personally significant to him.

The Latter-day Saint temple in Laie, Oahu, Hawaii, became the first temple "away from the traditional centers of Mormon colonization in Utah."[81] This is significant because with the temple came the introduction of Laie as an early prototype for the method of gathering, which did not appear to begin taking hold Churchwide until the mid-twentieth century.

In a 1972 area conference in Mexico City, Elder Bruce R. McConkie clearly identified this new chapter in the gathering saga when he declared that "the place of gathering for the Mexican Saints is in Mexico; the place of gathering for the Guatemalan Saints is in Guatemala; . . . and so it goes throughout the length and breadth of the whole earth. . . . Every nation is the gathering place for its own people."[82] At the general conference the following October, the President of the Church, Harold B. Lee, referred to and endorsed Elder McConkie's significant statement.[83] In 1992, Elder Boyd K. Packer referred to President Lee's quoting Elder McConkie and declared that, "in effect, [this] announced that the pioneering phase of gathering was now over. The gathering is now to be out of the world into the Church in every nation."[84] Nowhere is this mid-twentieth-century shift in the Latter-day Saint conception of "gathering" more evident than in recent temple expansion.

Near the end of the Hawaiian Temple's first year in operation, Elder Reed Smoot looked back at the foundational events of this magnificent structure, of which he was a part. He then looked forward, prophesying, "Temple building, temple work, salvation for our dead and salvation for ourselves have just begun. . . . I look to see the time when temples will be erected in all parts of the world."[85]

Latter-day Saints today are witnessing the fruition of Elder Smoot's vision. Presently, the Church has one hundred and forty operating temples with several in every inhabited continent of the world, and another twenty-eight under construction or announced.[86] President Thomas S. Monson illustrated the vastness of this expansion in the April 2011 general conference by pointing out that "eighty-five percent of the membership of the Church now live within 200 miles (320 km) of a temple, and for a great many of us, that distance is much shorter."[87]

Fortuitously, in the same talk, President Monson recognized a man whose foresight and efforts have proved to be instrumental in our prolific modern temple program. "During the October general conference in 1902," he said, "Church President Joseph F. Smith expressed in his opening address the hope that one day we would 'have temples built in the various parts of the [world] where they are needed for the convenience of the people.'" After detailing further examples of the swiftness at which this work is progressing, President Monson vowed, "These numbers will continue to grow." He then continued, "The goal President Joseph F. Smith hoped for in 1902 is becoming a reality. Our desire is to make the temple as accessible as possible to our members."

Joseph F. Smith and the Laie Hawaii Temple

According to President Smith, "not many years" before the announcement of the Hawaiian Temple, the Brethren wanted to build a temple in Northern Mexico, but it could not be done.[88] The temple in Alberta, Canada, was already under construction in October 1915, but would take nearly a decade to complete. And so, as destiny would have it and as history would record it, the Laie Hawaii Temple became the fifth temple completed after the Saints settled in the Rocky Mountains. In addition, this significant structure was the first temple built in one of the missions of the Church, and the first temple dedicated outside of Utah and the continental United States.

We do not know what the Church would look like today if not for the leadership of its forward-thinking sixth President with his compelling life experience. In considering this, however, one thing may be safely suggested: without Joseph F. Smith there would be no Laie Hawaii Temple—at least not as we know it.

Just as it seems Joseph F. Smith's life was destined to intertwine with Hawaii and the Saints who lived there, so it seems the temple in Laie was destined to play its singular role in Church history as the forebear of the modern temple building movement. This temple is a premier pioneering example of the Church's current focus of bringing temples to the people by spreading the gospel and gathering and strengthening the believers in preparation for a temple. In short, the Laie Hawaii Temple is the culmination of a prophetic prototype for building Zion in a new era of Church history.

Thus, when considering this impressive monument to the dedication and faith of the Hawaiian Saints, it feels appropriate to acknowledge the contributions of the missionary and prophet they so deeply loved. How fitting indeed it was when, in November of 2011, in the temple's most recent rededicatory prayer, President Monson expressed gratitude "for the insight and inspiration of President Smith, . . . who served faithfully and tirelessly so that a House of the Lord could be built here."[89]

Notes

1. *Words of Joseph Smith,* ed. Andrew F. Ehat and Lyndon W. Cook (Provo, UT: Religious Studies Center, Brigham Young University, 1980), 212; original spelling preserved.
2. Joseph Fielding Smith, *Life of Joseph F. Smith* (Salt Lake City: Deseret Book, 1938), 420.
3. Richard O. Cowan, *Temples to Dot the Earth,* 1st ed. (Salt Lake City: Bookcraft, 1989), 120.
4. Elder Reed Smoot, in Conference Report, October 1920, 137.
5. Joseph F. Smith, *Gospel Doctrine: Selections from the Sermons and Writings of Joseph F. Smith,* 12th ed. (Salt Lake City: Deseret Book, 1919), 43.
6. Scott Kenney, "Joseph F. Smith," in *The Presidents of the Church,* ed. Leonard J. Arrington (Salt Lake City: Deseret Book), 186.
7. Joseph F. Smith, journal, Sunday, Jan 24, 1864, from *Selected Collections from the Archives of The Church of Jesus Christ of Latter-day Saints,* ed. Richard E. Turley Jr., 2 vols., DVD (Provo, UT: BYU Press, 2002).
8. Heber J. Grant, "Inspiration and Integrity of the Prophets," *Improvement Era,* August 1919, 848.
9. President Lorenzo Snow died on Thursday, October 10, 1901. His Second Counselor, Joseph F. Smith, was set apart as the sixth President of the Church on Thursday, October 17. He was later sustained as the prophet and President of the Church at a special conference held on Sunday, November 10, 1901.
10. A more recent article on the efforts to gather the Hawaiian Saints on the island of Lanai is Fred E. Woods, "The Palawai Pioneers on the Island of Lanai: The First Hawaiian Latter-day Saint Gathering Place (1854–1864)," *Mormon Historical Studies* 5, no. 2 (Fall 2004): 3–35. R. Lanier Britsch wrote "The Lanai Colony: A Hawaiian Extension of the Mormon Colonial Idea," *Hawaiian Journal of History* 12 (1978): 68–83. He also has sections dedicated to Lanai in his books *Unto the Islands of the Sea: A History of the Latter-day Saints in the Pacific* (Salt Lake City: Deseret Book, 1986), and in *Moramona: The Mormons in Hawaii* (Laie, HI: Institute for Polynesian Studies, 1989). Raymond Clyde Beck, "Palawai Basin: Hawaii's Mormon Zion," (master's thesis, University of Hawaii, 1972) is the most comprehensive work on the subject.
11. "In 1858, in consequence of disturbed conditions in Utah, the missionaries on Hawaii were called home by Pres. Brigham Young and the mission was left in charge of native Elders."

Andrew Jenson, "Hawaiian Mission," in *Encyclopedic History of the Church of Jesus Christ of Latter-day Saints* (Salt Lake City: Deseret News, 1941), 324.

12. Britsch, *Moramona*, 53.
13. William W. Cluff, *My Last Mission to the Sandwich Islands*, ed. George Q. Cannon (Salt Lake City: Juvenile Instructor Office, 1882), 61.
14. Walter Murray Gibson, diary, November 5, 1861 and January 31, 1862, as cited in *Moromona*, 54–55.
15. Cluff, *My Last Mission*, 62.
16. Britsch, "The Lanai Colony," 80. Britsch also gives an exhaustive list of the most frequently cited book, articles, and theses on Gibson's Mormon years in *Moromona*, 217.
17. Cluff, *My Last Mission*, 63. See also B. H. Roberts, *A Comprehensive History of the Church of Jesus Christ of Latter-day Saints*, 6 vols. (Salt Lake City: Deseret News, 1965), 5:99–100.
18. William W. Cluff, "Acts of Special Providence in Missionary Experience," *Improvement Era*, March 1899.
19. *Manuscript History of the Hawaiian Mission*, October 1–4, 1864, comp. Andrew Jenson, Church History Library, The Church of Jesus Christ of Latter-day Saint, Salt Lake City; hereafter CHL. See also Britsch, *Moramona*, 61–62.
20. Britsch, *Moramona*, 61–62.
21. Joseph F. Smith to Brigham Young, July 5, 1864, correspondence, Manuscript History of Brigham Young, as quoted in Britsch, *Moramona*, 61–62.
22. Britsch, *Moramona*, 63. See also Cluff, *My Last Mission*, 74–75.
23. Cluff, "Acts of Special Providence in Missionary Experience." See also Francis M. Gibbons, *Joseph F. Smith: Patriarch and Preacher, Prophet of God* (Salt Lake City: Deseret Book Company, 1938), 79; Joseph Fielding Smith, *Life of Joseph F. Smith*, 224; R. Lanier Britsch, *Moramona* 61–63; and Riley M. Moffat, Fred E. Woods, and Jeffrey N. Walker, *Gathering to Laie* (Laie, HI: The Jonathan Napela Center for Hawaiian and Pacific Island Studies, 2011), 23–24.
24. Joseph Fielding Smith, *Life of Joseph F. Smith*, 262. See also Gibbons, *Joseph F. Smith: Patriarch and Preacher, Prophet of God*, 136.
25. The author derived the figure of seventeen children from Joseph Fielding Smith, *Life of Joseph F. Smith*, 487–90.
26. R. Lanier Britsch reports the following benefits of President Smith's leadership in Laie: "He regularly taught the missionaries and their president concerning the organization of the Church and correct procedures. He encouraged better record keeping and stricter attention to statistical matters. His ability to use the Hawaiian language had diminished little since his last mission in 1864. He frequently spoke in Sunday meetings and also in every conference session while in the islands." *Moramona*, 100–101.
27. Manuscript History of the Laie Ward, Oahu Stake, Wednesday, September 30, 1885, CHL.
28. Joseph Fielding Smith, *Life of Joseph F. Smith*, 279.
29. Joseph Fielding Smith, *Life of Joseph F. Smith*, 279. See also Russell T. Clement, "Apostle in Exile: Joseph F. Smith's Mission to Hawaii, 1885–1887" (Mormon Pacific Historical Society Proceedings, 1986), 57.
30. Clement, "Apostle in Exile," 57. Wesley Smith's first mission was from 1907 to 1910. He served as mission president from 1919 to 1922 and again from 1947 to 1950. He died in 1970.

31. Joseph Fielding Smith, *Life of Joseph F. Smith*, 286. See also Gibbons, *Joseph F. Smith: Patriarch and Preacher, Prophet of God*, 154–55.
32. Moffat, Woods and Walker, *Gathering to Laie*, 47.
33. The St. George Temple was dedicated in April 1877. It was the first temple in operation after the forced abandonment of the Nauvoo Temple. Prior to its completion, members generally received temple ordinances in the Endowment House in Salt Lake City. The Endowment House functioned from 1855 through 1889.
34. Richard Smyth, "Israel, Israel, God Is Calling," *Hymns* (Salt Lake City: The Church of Jesus Christ of Latter-day Saints), no. 7; see also D&C 133:7–9.
35. Fred Woods, "An Islander's View of a Desert Kingdom: Jonathan Napela Recounts His 1869 Visit to Salt Lake City," *BYU Studies* 45, no. 1 (2006): 28–29.
36. Castle Murphy to Hawaiian Temple Jubilee, November 14, 1969, Castle H. Murphy papers, L. Tom Perry Special Collections, Harold B. Lee Library, Brigham Young University. Castle Murphy and his wife, Verna, were missionaries in Hawaii for ten years before the temple was dedicated (from 1909 to 1913). They returned less than twenty years later, and from 1930 to 1936, the Murphys served as president and matron of both the Hawaiian Mission and the Hawaiian Temple. They would return in 1938 for another stint as temple president and matron. In January 1944, they were called back a fourth time to preside over the Hawaiian and Central Pacific Missions. By June of that year, they were assigned to again oversee the Laie Hawaii Temple. The Murphys were released from their final mission in May 1947. Jeffrey S. Hardy, Digital Collections, L. Tom Perry Special Collections, 2012.
37. Britsch, *Mormona*, 123. The most recent and thorough study on Iosepa is James Matt Kester, "Remembering Iosepa: History, Place, and Religion in the American West" (PhD diss., University of California, Santa Barbara, 2008). An earlier, more general, and less technical work on Iosepa is found in Dennis Atkin, "A History of Iosepa, the Utah Polynesian Colony" (master's thesis, Brigham Young University, 1958).
38. Britsch, *Mormona*, 124.
39. Britsch, *Mormona*, 123.
40. Moffat, *Gathering to Laie*, 49.
41. Britsch, *Mormona*, 122–26, 135. See also Moffat, *Gathering to Laie*, 48–50, and Richard H. Jackson and Mark W. Jackson, "Iosepa: The Hawaiian Experience in Settling the Mormon West," *Utah Historical Quarterly* 76, no. 4 (2008): 334.
42. Joseph F. Smith, in Conference Report, October 1915, 9.
43. Jackson, "Iosepa: The Hawaiian Experience in Settling the Mormon West," 330–33. See also Britsch, *Mormona*, 123; Comfort Margaret Bock, "The Church of Jesus Christ of Latter-day Saints in the Hawaiian Islands" (master's thesis, University of Hawaii, 1941), 77.
44. Gibbons, *Joseph F. Smith: Patriarch and Preacher, Prophet of God*, 198.
45. Joseph Fielding Smith noted, "Four times [President Smith] made trips to the Hawaiian Islands, in March, 1909, May, 1915, February, 1916, and the last time in May, 1917. It was while on his visit in 1915, that he selected and dedicated a site for a Temple at Laie." *Life of Joseph F. Smith*, 421.
46. "Far Away Hawaii," *Millennial Star*, July 8, 1915.
47. Britsch, *Moramona*, 120.
48. Reed Smoot to Joseph F. Smith, March 15, 1915, Church History Library, hereafter CHL.

49. Harvard S. Heath, ed., *In the World: The Diaries of Reed Smoot* (Salt Lake City: Signature Books, 1997), 268.
50. *Manuscript History of the Hawaiian Mission*, May 27, 1915. In the manuscript history, Peter's last name is spelled Kealakaihomua. The spelling used by the author was decided on by consulting several other sources.
51. Reed Smoot, diary, May 27, 1915, Reed Smoot Papers, L. Tom Perry Special Collections.
52. "President Smith and Party Return," *Liahona*, July 6, 1915.
53. Smoot, diary, May 27, 1915.
54. Smoot, diary, June 1, 1915.
55. Gibbons, *Joseph F. Smith: Patriarch and Preacher, Prophet of God*, 310.
56. Gibbons, *Joseph F. Smith: Patriarch and Preacher, Prophet of God*, 310.
57. Heath, *In the World: The Diaries of Reed Smoot*, 273.
58. Reed Smoot, in Conference Report, October 1920, 137.
59. Heath, *In the World: The Diaries of Reed Smoot*, 273.
60. Reed Smoot, in Conference Report, October 1920, 137.
61. See *Manuscript History of the Hawaiian Mission*, October 3, 1915.
62. Joseph F. Smith to Samuel Woolley, June 23, 1915.
63. Joseph F. Smith to Samuel Woolley, August 17, 1915.
64. *Manuscript History of the Hawaiian Mission*, January 12; February 1; March 1, 1916. This reference to Walter Spalding and his construction company in the mission history is significant. It is important because in the majority of existing literature Ralph Woolley is given sole credit for the building of the temple in Hawaii. In fact, it wasn't until 2011 that a recorded interview of Walter Spalding was discovered, fully examined and reported on by a professor at BYU–Hawaii. Dr. Riley Moffat prepared a paper for the Mormon Pacific Historical Society titled "The Spalding Construction Company and the Building of the Laie Temple." Moffat's contribution constitutes the most comprehensive understanding of the subject to date. As a result of its late exposure, unfortunately, Walter T. Spalding and his company, the Spalding Construction Company, are rarely acknowledged in available literature for their role in constructing the temple. See Riley M. Moffat, "The Spalding Construction Company and the Building of the Laie Temple" In *Mormon Pacific Historical Society* 32 (2011).
65. Zipporah L. Stewart, *Hawaiian Temple*, 3, CHL. See also Lewis A. Ramsey correspondence; May 7, 1917, CHL; and Gibbons, *Joseph F. Smith: Patriarch and Preacher, Prophet of God*, 320.
66. Gibbons, *Joseph F. Smith: Patriarch and Preacher, Prophet of God*, 320.
67. Ramsey, entries for January 10, 13, and March 5, 1917. See also *Liahona*, May 30, 1916, vol. 13:778 (*Manuscript History of the Hawaiian Mission*, April 9, 1916).
68. Gibbons, *Joseph F. Smith: Patriarch and Preacher, Prophet of God*, 320; emphasis in original.
69. Gibbons, *Joseph F. Smith: Patriarch and Preacher, Prophet of God*, 320.
70. Moffat, *Gathering to Laie*, 116–118.
71. Joseph Fielding Smith, *Life of Joseph F. Smith*, 475, 479.
72. Edwin S. Bliss, "Hawaiians Prepare to Entertain Prest. Grant," *Deseret News*, November 11, 1919.
73. N. B. Lundwall, ed. *Temples of the Most High*, 16th ed. (Salt Lake City: Bookcraft, 1940), 151.
74. Rudger Clawson, "The Hawaiian Temple," *Millennial Star*, November 1919.
75. Manuscript History of the Hawaiian Mission, November 5, 1919.
76. Manuscript History of the Hawaiian Mission, November 13, 1919.

77. Castle Murphy letter for Hawaiian Temple Jubilee, November 14, 1969, Castle H. Murphy Papers, L. Tom Perry Special Collections.
78. *Manuscript History of the Hawaiian Mission*, Wednesday, November 5; Thursday, November 13; and Thursday, November 27, 1918.
79. Joseph F. Smith, in Conference Report, April 1901, 69; as cited in Cowan, *Temples to Dot the Earth*, 119–20.
80. In 1955, President David O. McKay reported that Joseph F. Smith had "prophesied forty-nine years ago in the city of Bern that "temples would be built in divers [*sic*] countries of the world" (David O. McKay, in Conference Report, October 1959, 35). Over a span of fifty years several general authorities of the Church referenced prophecies Joseph F. Smith had made regarding a coming day when there would be multiple temples. A majority of the prophecies pertained specifically to Europe being "dotted with temples." Serge F. Ballif, in Conference Report, October 1920, 9. The following addresses (listed in order by date) contain similar accounts of predictions made by Joseph F. Smith: Charles W. Nibley, in Conference Report, October 1924, 97; LeGrand Richards, in Conference Report, April 1944, 44; Charles A. Callis, in Conference Report, October 1945, 82; Clifford E. Young, in Conference Report, October 1955, 126; LeGrand Richards, in Conference Report, October 1959, 35; LeGrand Richards, in Conference Report, October 1970, 62.
81. Cowan, *Temples to Dot the Earth*, 120.
82. Bruce R. McConkie, Mexico and Central America Area Conference, August 26, 1972, 45.
83. Harold B. Lee, in Conference Report, April 1973, 7.
84. Boyd K. Packer, "'To Be Learned Is Good If . . .'" *Ensign*, November 1992, 71.
85. Reed Smoot, in Conference Report, October 1920, 137.
86. The Church of Jesus Christ of Latter-day Saints, "Temple Statistics"; http://www.lds.org/church/temples/find-a-temple?lang=eng.
87. Thomas S. Monson, "The Holy Temple—A Beacon to the World," *Ensign*, May 2011, 90–91.
88. Joseph F. Smith., in Conference Report, October 1915, 9.
89. "Laie Hawaii Temple Rededicatory Prayer," *Church News*, November 27, 2010, 6.

Gary L. Boatright Jr.

17

"We Shall Have Temples Built":

Joseph F. Smith and a New Era of Temple Building

On July 26, 1847, two days following his arrival in the valley of the Great Salt Lake, Brigham Young designated the location where the Saints would build a temple.[1] Young explained to the Saints, "We must be situated in local circumstances wherein we can efficiently administer in those ordinances of the house of God that cannot be administered to a people while they are scattered abroad among the nations of the wicked."[2] To accomplish this, Church leaders encouraged the Saints around the world to come to the Great Basin. But notwithstanding this call to gather, Church leaders anticipated the day that the Church would build temples around the world.[3]

In 1877, thirty years following the arrival of the first Saints to the Salt Lake Valley, Brigham Young dedicated the St. George Temple. In 1884, the Church celebrated the completion of the Logan Temple in northern Utah, and four years later the dedication of the Manti Temple, completed in 1888. Then, after forty years of construction, President Wilford Woodruff dedicated the Salt Lake Temple, which was built on the location selected by Brigham Young forty-six years before. These temples, along with the Endowment House, provided the

---

Gary L. Boatright Jr. is a historic sites curator for the Church History Department, The Church of Jesus Christ of Latter-day Saints, Salt Lake City.

gathered Saints with the opportunity to receive the ordinances of the temple, yet they also had to serve those living in areas outside of the Mormon core.

The call to gather to the Intermountain West slowly faded in the waning years of the nineteenth century, and leaders began to encourage Saints to build up the Church in the areas where they lived. As this philosophy gained momentum, pockets of Church membership began to grow around the world. Among these were strong communities of Latter-day Saints in southern Alberta, the Pacific Isles, Arizona, and northern Mexico. The members living in these areas had long desired to have temples constructed closer to their homes.

Building on the doctrinal foundation of early leaders and on the push for financial stability led by Lorenzo Snow, President Joseph F. Smith guided the Church into a new era of temple construction. Recognizing the need to provide all members, not just those living in Utah, with the ordinances of the temple, Smith directed an effort to build temples in southern Alberta and Hawaii. He also hoped for a temple for the Latter-day Saint colonies in Mexico, but when those were abandoned, his attention shifted to the possibility of a temple in Arizona.

Additionally, the architectural designs of these sacred structures strikingly announced the Church's departure from the pioneer era of temple construction and its entrance into the twentieth century. Architects took the best building elements of the four pioneer-era temples, improved upon them, and eliminated other components that came to be considered unnecessary.

As Church membership grew around the world and the call to gather diminished, those members living great distances from the four Utah temples hoped for the day when other temples would be built closer to them. This hope became a reality as the Church emerged from the constricting shackles of debt and improved its financial stability. With resources now available, Joseph F. Smith led the Church into a new era of temple construction. The concepts developed in the site selection and construction of the three temples discussed in this chapter have influenced temple construction ever since.[4]

Looking Forward to a Temple

For many years, Latter-day Saints living in the outlying communities of southern Alberta, Hawaii, and Arizona had hoped for, made reference to, and even prophesied of the building of temples in their areas. In June 1887, just days following the arrival of Saints in the area that is now Cardston, Alberta, Jonathan E. Layne addressed a congregation of Saints gathered for Sunday services and predicted that "temples would yet be built in this country. . . . I could see it as plain as if it already was here."[5] A year later, Elder John W. Taylor, an Apostle, stated while in Cardston, "I now speak by the power of prophecy and say that upon this very spot shall be erected a temple to the name of Israel's God."[6] As the Latter-day Saint communities in southern Alberta grew, local Church leaders reserved two possible locations in the towns of Cardston and Raymond for a future temple.

Hawaiian Latter-day Saints, like their counterparts in southern Alberta, also anticipated the day when a temple would be built. In April 1853, the *Deseret News* published a letter from Henry W. Bigler, who was in the Hawaiian Islands, to George A. Smith. Bigler asked, "Do you think these Saints [in Hawaii] will ever be gathered to California or in the Valley of the Mountains? or will they gather on these Islands, and have Temples built, &c."[7] Sixty-four years later, after visiting the temple construction site at Laie in 1916, John A. Widtsoe wrote, "Many persons have foreseen the coming of the temple at Laie." He continued by explaining that George Q. Cannon, during a visit to the islands in 1900, had "declared that he believed the time was near at hand when the temple ordinances would be enjoyed by the people of the Hawaiian Islands."[8]

As early as 1870, Church members in Arizona had hoped for a temple in their area. More than twenty years before the formal announcement of the construction of the Mesa Arizona Temple, Helena Roseberry, a widow residing in Pima, Arizona, gave five dollars to Apostle Moses Thatcher for the construction of a temple in her area.[9] Additionally, according to tradition, Elias S. Kimball, then the president of the Southern States Mission, prophesied during a visit to the Mesa area in 1897 that the Church would build a temple there.[10]

Just before the turn of the twentieth century, Joseph F. Smith toured the Latter-day Saint settlements in Hawaii, southern Alberta, Arizona, and Mexico.[11] During these trips it is likely that he heard firsthand the desires of local leaders and members to construct a temple closer to their communities. Speaking at a ward meeting in Stirling, Alberta (approximately forty-five miles northeast of Cardston), Smith went so far as to say that "temples would be built here."[12] Into his presidency, Smith continued to visit the Saints around the world and became the first sitting Church President to visit the Saints in Europe. Wherever he went, Smith counseled Church members not to gather with the Saints in the American West but to stay and build up the Church in their native lands, despite not being able to benefit from all the programs of the Church, including participating in temple work.[13]

Despite the hope that the Church would build temples in outlying Latter-day Saint communities, the reality remained: there were only four temples, and they were all in Utah. For those outside of Utah, traveling to and from one of these temples was difficult, expensive, and time-consuming. In April 1901, Joseph F. Smith addressed this issue in general conference:

> There never was a time, until within the last few years, when the Latter-day Saints had access to four temples [Logan, Salt Lake, Manti, and St. George] in which to administer the ordinances of the Gospel for the living and the dead; and those four are becoming too distant—at least, the people are becoming so numerous in distant parts of the country that even though we have four temples in which to administer the ordinances of the Gospel, there are thousands of our people who are practically deprived of the privilege of enjoying them, because they are so far removed from them. Under these circumstances, I foresee the necessity arising for other temples or places consecrated to the Lord for the performance of the ordinances of God's house, so that the people may have the benefits of the house of the Lord without having to travel hundreds of miles for that purpose.[14]

But despite the need and the desire to build more temples, the Church simply lacked the resources to do so.

Heavily in debt at the turn of the century, Church leaders made a number of moves to ground the Church on more stable financial footing.[15] Initially, Church leaders began focusing their efforts on encouraging members to live the principle of tithing. During meetings throughout southern Utah in 1899, President Lorenzo Snow pleaded with Latter-day Saints to pay a full tithe. Payment of tithing became a constant theme in discourses given by Church leaders in general conference and other meetings over the next few years.[16] In a 1901 discourse, Joseph F. Smith addressed the topic. He stated, "I hope to see the day when . . . non-tithe payers will add their mite to the tithes and offerings of the Church, in order that there may be more substance in the storehouse of God with which to meet the necessities of the work, and give the servants of the Lord an opportunity to do far more good than they have means to do with today."[17] And in addition to the increased emphasis on tithing, the Church also purchased interest in a number of businesses whose profits helped to fill Church coffers, providing the Church with additional resources to fund its operations.[18]

Church leaders succeeded in securing Church finances. Historian Thomas G. Alexander has determined that the Church gained a 5 percent increase in revenue between 1900 and 1907.[19] This allowed Joseph F. Smith, speaking as President of the Church, to announce in 1907, "Today the Church of Jesus Christ of Latter-day Saints owes not a dollar that it cannot pay at once. At last we are in a position that we can pay as we go. We do not have to borrow any more, and we wont [*sic*] have to if the Latter-day Saints continue to live their religion and observe this law of tithing."[20] With the finances of the Church solidified, the possibility of funding the construction of more temples became a reality.

Between 1899 and the 1907 announcement that the Church was free from debt, Smith continued to address the need to take temples to distant members. In the opening address of the October 1902 general conference, Smith stated:

> We also feel that when the time shall come and our hands shall be free from the obligations that now rest upon us, other places should be prepared for the convenience of the Latter-day Saints in more distant stakes, in order that those who are living at great distances from the center may have the privilege of receiving the ordinances of the Gospel without being put to the great expense and loss of time that is necessary now in journeying from 500 to 1,000 miles in order to reach the houses of God. We hope to see the day when we shall have temples built in the various parts of the land where they are needed for the convenience of the people.[21]

However, despite the importance of temple work and the desire to build temples closer to the people, the demand to fund many other Church projects substantially multiplied. Higher-priority projects, possibly including those slated for Church headquarters (the Hotel Utah and the Church Administration Building), delayed other plans that leaders considered important.[22] As a result of this and other construction and investment projects (meetinghouses, tabernacles, business ventures, and so forth), it would be another ten years before Smith's desire to build temples closer to the people came to fruition.

The Alberta Temple

Edward J. Wood, president of the Alberta Stake, was in Salt Lake City attending the October 1912 general conference. "To the surprise of us all," Wood recorded, "[President Joseph F. Smith] announced that the Church would build a Temple in Canada and took a vote on it which received the especial support of all present."[23] Elder Benjamin Goddard reported that the announcement came "in response to the pleas of the people" and that it "indicate[d] how the people are craving for blessings, for the true path of life and salvation."[24] The following day, the *Deseret News* announced, "The temple will be built . . . just as soon as possible, and at a point within the province of Alberta, Canada, to be decided upon later, and of such a character as to meet the needs of the people of the section in which it will be constructed." Continuing, the paper reported that President Smith said, "The proposition to build a temple for the benefit of the Latter-day Saints who live at remote points had been under consideration by the Church authorities for some time." Smith gave "assurances . . . that the structure would be of sufficient size to amply take care of all the requirements of the people in the section where it is to be built."[25]

Shortly following the announcement, the First Presidency authorized the Presiding Bishopric to invite architects to submit drawings as part of a competition to select the design of the temple. The invitations included guidelines regarding architectural elements that were required and some that were not needed (for example, a large assembly room or towers) for the new temple. These instructions significantly contrasted with the temples built during the pioneer era, all of which had a large assembly room and at least one tower. By excluding these building elements, which were unnecessary for the completion of vital ordinances, the Church could reduce overall construction costs. In all, seven firms responded to the invitation to submit designs for the temple and sent their proposals to Church headquarters by the December 24, 1912, deadline.[26]

After reviewing the submissions, Church leaders selected the design of Hyrum C. Pope and Harold W. Burton of Salt Lake City. Their design radically differed from anything the Church had previously built. The *Deseret News* stated that Pope and Burton's aim was to "conform to the peculiar requirements of such a building rather than to imitate any style."[27] The chosen architects meticulously kept to the guidelines established by the Church and even met with

As part of a design competition Hyrum C. Pope and Harold W. Burton submitted this winning design for the Alberta Temple. In 1992 the Historic Sites and Monuments Board of Canada listed the temple as a National Historic Site. Courtesy of Church History Library.

Church leaders to better understand what the leaders envisioned for the new temple. Anthon H. Lund recorded that Hyrum Pope met with him, President Joseph F. Smith, and Presiding Bishop Charles W. Nibley on October 28, 1912, in the Manti Temple. "We went through all the rooms," Lund wrote, "and estimated the size of the rooms needed in the Canada Temple."[28]

Pope and Burton's design, inspired by the works of renowned American architect Frank Lloyd Wright and pre-Colombian architecture found in Central and South America, challenged any preconceived notions of what a temple should look like. The drawings of the fortress-like structure, with no towers, must have surprised many readers of the *Deseret News,* which printed the drawings on January 1, 1913. But despite the influences on their work, Pope and Burton's drawings exhibited an architectural uniqueness. Architectural historian Paul L. Anderson wrote, "To say that the temple was influenced by the work of other architects does not imply that it was lacking in originality. Indeed, Pope's and Burton's great achievement was their ability to use the newest and best design ideas in a way that was particularly appropriate for a Latter-day Saint temple."[29] Writing of the architecture of the temple in 1923, the year of its dedication, Joseph Young Card described the temple thus: "Impressive and unique, it occupies a distinctive place of its own in the historic field of architecture. It has the Grecian massiveness, a Peruvian touch,

President Joseph F. Smith dedicated sites for the Cardston Alberta and Laie Hawaii Temples. This photo shows him in Cardston, Alberta, Canada, on July 27, 1913. Courtesy of Church History Library.

and is similar only to the ancient temples of the Aztecs." He went on to say that of all the "temples erected by the Latter-day Saints, there is no other of similar exterior design."[30]

The floor plan also represented a significant change in temple design. Because Church leaders had determined that a large assembly room was not needed, interior space could be more efficiently utilized for the presentation of ordinances. The architects wrapped ordinance rooms around the center of the structure, with each room slightly elevated above the other and the celestial room in the center and highest point of the building. This design reflected the "perfectly logical and simple" thought of the architects while adding a symbolic undertone of progression as patrons would steadily move upward toward the celestial room.[31]

The architects also incorporated artwork throughout the new temple. As had been done in the four Utah temples, the Church commissioned artists to paint elaborate murals in the ordinance rooms and in other areas of the temple. This work brought together the best painters in the Church, bringing their own styles and adding artistic diversity throughout the temple. The Church also looked to emphasize beautification of the exterior of the building and commissioned Torleif S. Knaphus to create a frieze for the temple entitled *The Samaritan Woman at the Well*. Originally located outside the temple walls, the frieze was visible to all in front of the temple. Over time, additions to the structure have enclosed it, and the frieze now stands in the entrance lobby of the building.

The Hawaii Temple

As work progressed on the temple in Cardston, President Joseph F. Smith explained the Church's decision to build a temple in Alberta. He shared with the congregation of the October 1915 general conference the story of a young man from northern British Columbia who had recently returned from a mission and who was penniless. Shortly after his return, he found a good woman to marry, but he lacked the means to travel to a temple to be sealed. In a situation like this, President Smith stated, "All we could do was say to him: 'Go to the nearest bishop or elder of the Church that you can find, and with our permission and approval ask him to unite you in marriage for time, and as soon as you are able to reach a temple . . . go.'" Smith continued, "Those who are in these circumstances will not be

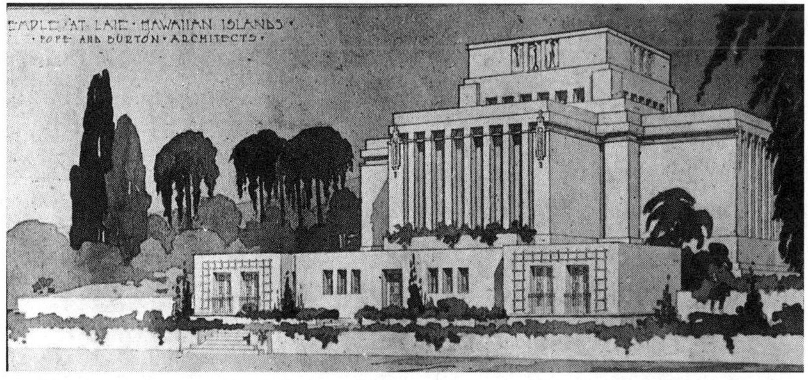

The Church once again looked to Hyrum C. Pope and Harold W. Burton to design the Laie Hawaii Temple. The influence of Frank Lloyd Wright is clearly seen in this early rendering of the temple. Courtesy of Church History Library.

Designed by renowned American architect Frank Lloyd Wright, the Unity Temple in Oak Park, Illinois, served as inspiration to Latter-day Saint architects Hyrum C. Pope and Harold W. Burton. Design elements from the Unity Temple are seen in both the Cardston Alberta and Laie Hawaii Temples. Photo 1967, courtesy of Library of Congress.

compelled to waste all their substance in travel to come to a temple here [in Utah]." Smith then briefly alluded to his desire to build a temple in Mexico. He then spoke of Church members "away off in the Pacific Ocean" who lacked the means to travel to Utah, and then announced the following: "We have come to the conclusion that it would be a good thing to build a temple that shall be dedicated to the ordinances of the house of God, down upon one of the Sandwich [Hawaiian] Islands, so that the good people of those islands may reach the blessing of the House of God within their own borders."[32] The congregation unanimously supported the decision to build the temple in Laie on the island of Oahu.

Unknown to most of the congregation, President Smith had selected and dedicated the site of the temple on June 1, 1915, four months before the announcement in conference. To the small group gathered at the site that day, Smith stated, "I feel impressed to dedicate this ground for the erection of a Temple of God, for a place where the peoples of the Pacific Isles can come and do their temple work."[33] He explained further that he had not discussed this with any members of the Quorum of the Twelve, nor his counselors in the First Presidency, and then proceeded to dedicate the site for a temple on the Church-owned plantation in Laie. Elder Reed Smoot, who accompanied Smith on this visit, recorded, "I am positive it is the first step towards the erection of a small temple here in Laie wherein the Hawaiian Saints as well as the saints of other Islands of the Pacific can have their temple ordinations, sealings, baptisms, etc attended to."[34] Considered by Hawaiians "as their local Zion" and as "the spiritual center of the Church," Laie proved to be an ideal location for a small temple.[35]

The Church again turned to architects Pope and Burton to design the temple. They were tasked to design a temple similar to that done for Alberta (without a spire or assembly room, and so forth), except that the temple for Hawaii should be smaller, reflecting the size of the population it would serve. Rather than simply create a smaller version of the Alberta Temple, Pope and Burton designed a structure to complement the landscape of the site.

Like the Alberta Temple and other structures designed by Pope and Burton, the design for the Hawaii Temple was heavily influenced by the work of Frank Lloyd Wright and closely resembles his Unity Temple in Oak Park, Illinois. Pope and Burton drew additional inspiration from the ancient ruins of Central and South America and later compared the finished temple to the ancient temple in the Holy Land. "If the now generally accepted equivalent for the cubit, the ancient unit of measure, is correct," Pope wrote in 1919, "then the principal portion of this famous edifice of antiquity [Solomon's temple] had about the same cubical contents as the Temple in Hawaii."[36]

Like the Alberta Temple, sculpture was used to beautify the exterior of the building. Joseph F. Smith asked sculptors J. Leo and Avard Fairbanks to create sculptures "representing the Four Great Gospel Dispensations," which together would "not only tell a story but also . . . adorn or decorate the upper part of the temple."[37] Painters were also commissioned to decorate and beautify the interior of the temple, providing an artistic setting for temple patrons participating in ordinance work.

The Arizona Temple

As previously discussed, Joseph F. Smith desired to have a temple built in the Latter-day Saint colonies in Mexico. But a number of events led to the eventual abandonment of the colonies in the early twentieth century, thus eliminating the need—for the time being—for a temple in northern Mexico. Concurrently,

For the design of the Mesa Arizona Temple, the Church again held a competition. Latter-day Saint architects Don Carlos Young Jr. and Ramm Hansen looked to other buildings designed and built during the early part of the twentieth century for inspiration. Courtesy of Church History Library.

the reality of building a temple in Arizona gained momentum as Church membership grew in the area. Shortly following his call as the Maricopa Stake president in March 1912, James W. Lesueur remembered, "I was in Salt Lake City in April 1912, asking that a Temple be erected in Mesa, Arizona. . . . A year later, [the First Presidency] expressed willingness to have a temple built and said they would come down and look over sites" in Mesa.[38] In the fall of 1913, Smith and other Church leaders traveled to the Mesa area to tour potential sites for a temple, but with resources devoted to the temples in Alberta and Hawaii as well as other projects, and with the outbreak of World War I, the temple for Arizona had to be postponed.[39]

Seven years later, on October 1, 1919, Heber J. Grant announced that the Church would at last construct a temple in Mesa, Arizona. The Church again held a design competition and selected that of Don Carlos Young Jr. and Ramm Hansen. The design, as described by Paul L. Anderson, "was an essay in dignified and restrained classical style." He noted that the architects drew much of their inspiration "from monumental public buildings of the previous two decades."[40] Included in the design were many of the features found in the Alberta and Hawaii Temples, one of which was the efficient design of the interior floor plan. Regarding this, Anderson stated that the design was "based on the classical principle of strict symmetry and circulation paths and major rooms arranged along a central axis"—nearly mirroring that of its immediate predecessors.[41]

Like the temples in Cardston and Laie, sculpture also decorates the exterior of the Mesa Arizona Temple. Latter-day Saint artist A. B. Wright sketched four panels which Torleif Knaphus sculpted in plaster of paris. The four pieces, located at the corners of the temple near the top, were "intended to portray the gathering of Israel from the four corners of the earth in the last dispensation of the fullness of time."[42]

Conclusion

The Hawaii Temple, the second temple announced by President Joseph F. Smith, was the first temple completed in the twentieth century. President Heber J. Grant offered the dedicatory prayer on November 27, 1919, just over a year following the death of Joseph F. Smith, which occurred on November 19, 1918.

Following ten years of construction, and four years after the Laie dedication, Grant dedicated the Alberta Temple on August 26, 1923. Its completion had been delayed by a number of things, including World War I.

The Arizona Temple took just over five years to complete and was dedicated on October 23, 1927, also by Grant. Two years following its completion, with the United States entering the Great Depression, the Church's temple-building efforts paused out of necessity and were not renewed until the announcement of the Idaho Falls Temple in 1937.

In the one hundred years since the announcement of the Alberta Temple, the successors of Joseph F. Smith have expanded upon the principles of temple construction exemplified during the early twentieth century. President David O. McKay, during his nearly two decades of leadership, significantly expanded temple building efforts around the world and oversaw a change in their design in order to increase efficiency, which is reflected in the temples built in Ogden and Provo, Utah.[43] Temple construction continued to expand modestly around the world during the 1980s and early 1990s, with varying designs of temples. And, in 1997, under the direction of President Gordon B. Hinckley, the Church announced that it would once again build a number of small temples in "areas of the Church that are remote, where the membership is small and not likely to grow very much in the near future."[44] This led to many more temples being erected in various locations around the world.

Today the Cardston, Laie, and Mesa Temples stand as monuments to the vision held by President Joseph F. Smith of taking the temple to faithful Latter-day Saints wherever they may be. The enduring designs of these three temples stand unique as timeless examples of Latter-day Saint architecture and are celebrated by the communities they serve and by all Church members everywhere.[45]

Notes

1. See Randall Dixon, "Wilford Woodruff and the Site of the Salt Lake Temple," unpublished paper presented at the Mormon History Association Conference in Provo, Utah, in 2004.
2. Brigham Young, in *Journal of Discourses* (London: Latter-day Saints' Book Depot, 1854–86), 12:162.
3. Brigham Young stated, "To accomplish this work there will have to be not only one temple but thousands of them, and thousands and tens of thousands of men and women will go into those temples and officiate for people who have lived as far back as the Lord shall reveal." *Journal of Discourses,* 3:372. Wilford Woodruff declared that temples would be built across "North and South America—and also in Europe and elsewhere" around the world. *Journal of Discourses,* 19:229–30.
4. Historians have long written about the history of the temples in Cardston, Laie, and Mesa separately, without looking at the common influences leading to their locations and designs. For example, each was built in an area with a large, faithful population of Church members, and each temple's design was based on the efficient use of both space and funds. For publications regarding the Cardston Alberta Temple, see Paul L. Anderson, "First of the Modern Temples," *Ensign,* July 1977, 6–11; Richard O. Cowan, "The Alberta Temple: Seventy-five Years of Service," in *Regional Studies in LDS Church History: Western Canada,* ed. Dennis A. Wright and others (Provo, UT: Department of Church History and Doctrine, 2000), 239–50; V. A. Wood, *The Alberta Temple: Centre and Symbol of Faith* (Calgary, AB: Detselig Enterprises, 1989). For publications regarding the Laie Hawaii Temple, see Paul L. Anderson, "A Jewel in the Gardens of Paradise: The Art and Architecture of the Hawaii Temple," in *Voyages of Faith: Explorations in Mormon Pacific History,* ed. Grant Underwood (Provo, UT: BYU Press, 2000), 147–63; Mormon Pacific Historical Society, *Proceedings, Ninth Annual Conference Mormon History in the Pacific, May 21, 1988*; Joseph H. Spurrier, "The Hawaii Temple: A Special Place in a Special Land," in Mormon Pacific Historical Society, *Proceedings, Seventh Annual Conference Mormon History in the Pacific,* March 1, 1986, 28–40; George Whisenand, "An Architect's View of the Mormon Temple at Laie," *Hawaii Architect,* May 1978, 10–11, 18–19. For publications regarding the Mesa Arizona Temple, see Paul L. Anderson, "Desert Imagery and Sacred Symbolism: The Design of the Arizona Temple," *Journal of Mormon History* 31, no. 1 (Spring 2005): 71–98; Richard O. Cowan, "The Historic Arizona Temple," *Journal of Mormon History* 31, no. 1 (Spring 2005): 99–118; Evan Tye Peterson, comp., *The Ninth Temple: A Light in the Deseret* (Orem, UT: Granite, 2002). Moreover, scholarship addressing the larger scope of temple construction during and immediately after the Joseph F. Smith era is limited. In his work *Mormonism in Transition: A History of the Latter-day Saints, 1890–1930,* Thomas G. Alexander discusses a number of changes the Church made as it entered the twentieth century, including giving attention to the

Church building program. However, he glosses over the importance of the construction of the temples built in Alberta, Hawaii, and Arizona. In the epilogue, Alexander states that the three new temples, along with the many meetinghouses and tabernacles built by the Church during this period, "were the signs of stability and prosperity . . . constructed through the efforts and sacrifice of church members over three decades." See Thomas G. Alexander, *Mormonism in Transition: A History of the Latter-day Saints, 1890–1930* (Urbana and Chicago: University of Illinois Press, 1986), 307. In his 1997 publication *Temples to Dot the Earth,* historian Richard G. Cowan shares the Church's history of temple building and highlights Joseph F. Smith's influence on the Alberta and Hawaii Temples, but groups the construction of the Mesa Temple with the building of the Idaho Falls Temple, ignoring its connections to the Joseph F. Smith era. See Richard G. Cowan, *Temples to Dot the Earth* (Springville, UT: Cedar Fort, 1996), 119–46. Leonard J. Arrington and Davis Bitton group the Cardston, Laie, and Mesa Temples together: "The greatest skill and most generous funding which the church afforded was put into that [the Salt Lake Temple] and subsequent temples, each representing its period and, in some way the feelings and concerns of the members at that time: . . . the early twentieth-century temples in prairie style, with motifs reminiscent of Central American Indian architecture, in Cardston, Alberta, Mesa, Arizona, and Laie, Hawaii." See Leonard J. Arrington and Davis Bitton, *The Mormon Experience: A History of the Latter-day Saints,* 2nd ed. (Urbana and Chicago, IL: University of Illinois Press, 1992), 266.

5. Quoted in Lethbridge Stake, *A History of the Mormon Church in Canada* (Lethbridge, Alberta: Lethbridge Herald, 1968), 47.
6. Quoted in V. A. Wood, *The Alberta Temple: Centre and Symbol of Faith* (Calgary, Alberta: Detselig Enterprises, 1989), 27.
7. Henry W. Bigler to George A. Smith, October 3, 1852, in "Foreign Correspondence," *Deseret News,* April 2, 1853.
8. John A. Widtsoe, "The Temple in Hawaii: A Remarkable Fulfillment of Prophecy," *Improvement Era,* September 1916, 955–56.
9. Harry T. Payne, "History of the Arizona Temple," Church History Library, 1992, 11. The author does not provide source information for his statements.
10. "Temples of Our Lord: Ancient and Modern," *Genealogical and Historical Magazine of the Arizona Temple District* 2, no. 2 (1925): 38.
11. Joseph Fielding Smith, *The Life of Joseph F. Smith* (Salt Lake City: Deseret Book, 1938), 305–7, 311–13.
12. Stirling Ward Historical Record, Book A, November 8, 1899, Church History Library, Salt Lake City, 5.
13. James B. Allen and Glen M. Leonard, *The Story of the Latter-day Saints,* rev. ed. (Salt Lake City: Deseret Book, 1992), 471.
14. Joseph F. Smith, in Conference Report, April 1901, 69.
15. Alexander, *Mormonism in Transition,* 99–100.
16. Allen and Leonard, *The Story of the Latter-day Saints,* 453–55.
17. Joseph F. Smith, in Conference Report, April 1901, 71.
18. See Alexander, *Mormonism in Transition,* 74–92; Richard O. Cowan, *The Latter-day Saint Century, 1901–2000* (Salt Lake City: Bookcraft, 1999), 38.
19. Alexander, *Mormonism in Transition,* 100.

20. Joseph F. Smith, in Conference Report, April 1907, 7.
21. Joseph F. Smith, in Conference Report, October 1902, 3.
22. The Church built the Hotel Utah between 1909 and 1911 and the Church Administration Building between 1914 and 1917. It is probable that the Church expended funds on these projects prior to the start of actual construction. It is important to note that the Hotel Utah also provided income for the Church. See Alexander, *Mormonism in Transition*, 100.
23. Edward J. Wood, journal, October 4, 1912, holograph, Edward J. Wood Collection, 1884–1982, Church History Library, Salt Lake City.
24. Benjamin Goddard, in Conference Report, October 1912, 102.
25. "Church Will Build Temple in Alberta, Canada," *Deseret News*, October 5, 1912.
26. "Approved Design for Temple in Alberta Province," *Deseret News*, January 1, 1913.
27. "Approved Design for Temple in Alberta Province." The design of the Alberta Temple is generally regarded as that of the Prairie style influenced by Frank Lloyd Wright.
28. John P. Hatch, ed., *Danish Apostles: The Diaries of Anthon H. Lund, 1890–1921* (Salt Lake City: Signature Books, 2006), 489.
29. Paul L. Anderson, "First of the Modern Temples," *Ensign*, July 1977, 10.
30. "Alberta Temple Is Masterpiece of Construction and Finish," *Lethbridge Daily Herald*, August 27, 1823.
31. Paul L. Anderson, "A Jewel in the Gardens of Paradise: The Art and Architecture of the Hawai'i Temple," in *Voyages of Faith*, 150.
32. Joseph F. Smith, in Conference Report, October 1915, 8.
33. Smith, *Life of Joseph F. Smith*, 421; see also Harvard S. Heath, ed., *In the World: The Diaries of Reed Smoot* (Salt Lake City: Signature Books, 1997), 273–74.
34. Heath, *Diaries of Reed Smoot*, 273. Smoot recorded that Bishop Charles W. Nibley felt the Church should "erect an Endowment House or Temple in Laie." He believed that Joseph F. Smith's dedicating the site for the Hawaii Temple was the "first step towards the erection of a small temple here in Laie." See Heath, *In the World: The Diaries of Reed Smoot*, 273.
35. R. Lanier Britsch, "The Conception of the Hawaii Temple," in *Proceedings, Ninth Annual Conference: 21 May 1998* (Provo, UT: Mormon Pacific Historical Society, 1988), 21.
36. Hyrum C. Pope, "The Temple in Hawaii," *Juvenile Instructor*, November 1919, 576.
37. J. Leo Fairbanks, "The Sculpture of the Hawaiian Temple," *Juvenile Instructor*, November 1921, 575. Of the four temples originally built with exterior friezes, Harold Burton was involved in the design of three of them: Cardston, Laie, and Oakland.
38. James W. Lesueur, "Autobiographical Notes of My Life," 1939, Church History Library, 59–60.
39. James W. Lesueur, "The Arizona Temple," *Improvement Era*, October 1927, 1064.
40. Paul L. Anderson, "Desert Imagery and Sacred Symbolism: The Design of the Arizona Temple," *Journal of Mormon History*, 6, no. 1 (Spring 2005), 84.
41. Anderson, "The Design of the Arizona Temple," 86.
42. "Arizona Temple: Architect's Description," *Genealogical and Historical Magazine of the Arizona Temple District*, January 1924, 15.
43. See Gregory A. Prince and Wm. Robert Wright, *David O. McKay and the Rise of Modern Mormonism* (Salt Lake City: University of Utah Press, 2005), 256–78.
44. Gordon B. Hinckley, "Some Thoughts on Temples, Retention of Converts, and Missionary Service," *Ensign*, November 1997, 49.

45. In 1992, the Historic Sites and Monuments Board of Canada listed the Cardston Alberta Temple as a National Historic Site of Canada. The Mesa Arizona Temple is the anchor of the Temple Historic District, which has been listed on the National Register of Historic Places since the year 2000. The Laie Hawaii Temple, though not listed on any national or local historic registers, is cherished as an important architectural and historic building of the Church.

W. Ray Luce

18

Joseph F. Smith and the Great Mormon Building Boom

Joseph F. Smith's presidency of The Church of Jesus Christ of Latter-day Saints (1901–18) produced a veritable explosion of Latter-day Saint buildings. His presidency was pivotal in the change from a pioneering, colonizing, gathering concept of Zion to a larger view allowing for the expansion to a worldwide Church. Church priorities are evident in buildings constructed during his presidency. These buildings completed Joseph Smith's plan for the City of Zion—as constructed in Nauvoo, Illinois, and extended the plan with additional structures. Temples expanded the "official" boundaries of Zion—in a major way. Period schools and meetinghouses show Church efforts to provide education at all levels after Utah education was secularized and no longer centered in ward schools. Basic design changes in temples and a redefinition of ward meetinghouses are fundamental to current Church buildings. A new system of Church aid to local building projects continued for the next seven decades. Finally, Church leaders and architects searching for a "Mormon style" of architecture raise questions about what style is appropriate for Church structures.

W. Ray Luce is an adjunct professor in the Heritage Preservation program at Georgia State University. He previously headed the State Historic Preservation Offices in Ohio and Georgia.

The magnitude of the new construction is impressive. Two temples—the first two since Brigham Young, and the first outside Utah—were started in Cardston, Alberta, Canada, and in Laie, Hawaii. A major expansion took place in tabernacles, with the construction of thirty-four new buildings—almost 40 percent of all the tabernacles identified by Richard Jackson.[1] An even greater explosion of meetinghouse construction also took place. A 1915 report noted that building projects had been undertaken in 58 percent of the wards in the Church.[2] Not all of these projects were for new structures; some involved new furnaces or other major improvements, but both the breadth of the projects and the number of new buildings during this seventeen-year period is remarkable. The magnitude of the buildings can be seen by noting that in Provo, projects (almost all new buildings) were built in the Provo First, Second, Third, Fourth, Fifth, and Sixth Wards—all the numbered wards. Similarly, in Ogden projects—mostly new buildings—were done in the Ogden First, Second, Third, Fourth, Fifth, Sixth, Seventh, Eighth, Ninth, Tenth, Eleventh, and Twelfth Wards. Similar projects also took place in smaller communities. New buildings or remodels were done in the American Fork First, Second, Third, and Fourth Wards; the Brigham City First, Second, Third, and Fourth Wards; and the Oakley Idaho First, Second, Third, and Fourth Wards. Salt Lake City is more difficult to evaluate because of numbered wards in individual stakes, but many wards had projects during this period, including the Twenty-First, Twenty-Second, Twenty-Third, Twenty-Fourth, Twenty-Fifth, Twenty-Sixth, Twenty-Seventh, Twenty-Eighth, Twenty-Ninth, Thirtieth, Thirty-First, and Thirty-Third Wards.[3] One of the most dramatic moments in this building boom was the dedication of new buildings for all three Heber wards on the same day—December 26, 1915—with dedications by Apostles Joseph F. Smith Jr., Francis W. Lyman, and George F. Richards.[4]

Major Salt Lake buildings constructed during this period included the Hotel Utah, the Bishop's Building, the Deseret News Building, the Deseret Gymnasium, LDS Hospital, a new campus for LDS University, the Temple Square Bureau of Information, and the first seminary building.

The First Presidency of the Church included these accomplishments in their 1913 Christmas message: "More Church edifices have been erected and such property acquired than ever before in our history."[5]

This impressive building spurt reflected both pent-up demand and increased Church financial resources. New buildings were greatly needed. The

Church had grown—the number of stakes, for example, more than doubled between statehood in 1896 and the end of Smith's presidency in 1918. Most Latter-day Saint meetinghouses existing in 1901 were single room multipurpose buildings. Expanding Church programs in Sunday School, Primary, Mutual, weekday religion classes, priesthood quorums, and Relief Societies—when they did not have their own buildings—needed additional space and classrooms to effectively carry out their programs.

Two additional factors increased the need for additional ward structures. Conflicts between the United States government and the Church over polygamy culminated in the Federal Edmunds-Tucker Act of 1887, disincorporating the Church and confiscating its property. The struggle finally ended with Utah statehood in 1896 following the 1890 Manifesto ending plural marriage. The aftermath of the prolonged dispute was deep and long lasting. The Church was deeply in debt and its members out of the habit of paying tithing. The Church thus faced a growing membership with limited structures because of the conflict with Washington.

Finally, meetinghouses needed to be constructed to replace ward buildings in numerous communities now operating as school buildings owned by local governments. Local congregations or wards met, in all but the most urban areas, in one-room multipurpose buildings which served as schools as well as churches. These multipurpose buildings lost the ability to serve both functions when, as part of agreements for Utah statehood, free public schools replaced Church ward schools.[6] Following the 1890 Free School Act in Utah, "many of these meetinghouses passed into the hands of the city and county governments."[7] Local wards now had to build meetinghouses or rent buildings they no longer owned. Continued use of these former structures became increasingly difficult. The Jameston Idaho Ward said they met "under many difficulties."[8] The Fredonia Arizona Ward could not hold Primary because there was no place in the schoolhouse to meet.[9] The Granite Ward in Salt Lake County noted that part of the ward was outside the school district and "some 'outsiders' are making strong objections" to Church use of the school.[10] The Garden Creek and Holden Wards reported that they could no longer use their former buildings because they had been partitioned for a graded school, making them useless for general meetings.[11]

Similar needs existed for other buildings. During the Latter-day Saint building construction hiatus, Salt Lake City had grown and developed into a major city—perhaps not yet the "crossroads of the West," but a thriving regional center. However, Church buildings did not reflect those changes. The Church's President's Office was still housed in the small buildings Brigham Young constructed between his two residences, the Beehive and Lion Houses. Church financial operations were still housed in the Tithing Office, a complex constructed to deal with farm produce given as tithing in kind, when the economy was now largely cash based.

Utah statehood was granted in 1896, five years before Smith became Church President, symbolically marking the end to a long period of conflict. This not only removed many impediments to building, but allowed the Church to receive needed funding. Church President Wilford Woodruff completed the Salt Lake Temple after forty years of construction, and his successor, Lorenzo Snow, placed additional stress on paying tithing, both of which helped provide needed Church funds. By 1897, the effects of the Panic of 1893 were lessening and greater prosperity was returning. This combination of forces meant that needed funding was or would soon be available. Finally, building materials and expertise were increasingly available. The completion of the transcontinental railroad in 1869 made eastern building materials available at a fraction of the cost of transporting them cross-country by ox cart. Architects and contractors were also increasingly available. In 1888, only six architects were listed in the Utah territorial directory. The number of architects in the state directory increased almost tenfold during the next thirty years—increasing to fifty-seven in 1918.[12] Increased funding and available workforce were soon at work to meet the building backlog.

Buildings constructed during Joseph F. Smith's presidency show basic changes that facilitated the Church's change from a gathered Zion concept to a worldwide Zion with members living successfully in a secular world. The gathering concept envisioned a supportive community as the ideal for individual growth. Such a community would provide educational, social, and spiritual activities while limiting the outside world's temptations. Such an ideal was undermined both by the increasing secularization of Mormon communities, as shown by the switch from Church to secular schools, and was not applicable for the increasing number of Church members living outside LDS communities. Adding classrooms to ward meetinghouses and the introduction of new building types for education proved to be fundamental to this change. The first change was the development of ward meetinghouses. Specifics will be discussed later, but the decision that every ward would have an amusement hall and enough classrooms ensured that the buildings could provide social and educational instruction for all age groups. In addition, two innovations in Church education allowed similar support outside the Intermountain West. The first was the start of the seminary program and, second, the foreshadowing of the institute program, discussed in more detail later. These changes were fundamental in the transition from gathering to providing support for members living throughout the world.

Many new Salt Lake City buildings completed the plan of Zion, as established in Nauvoo, or expanded upon the Nauvoo plan to meet new opportunities. Joseph Smith formulated several plans for the City of Zion, but the plan's physical execution in Nauvoo was the most powerful model for Church leaders and members. Joseph F. Smith was the last Church President to have personally experienced that model. Several structures were new replacement buildings for earlier buildings. The Deseret News Building, home to the Church-owned newspaper and printing office, continued a long line of Church printing offices that had started in Kirtland, Ohio, as well as consolidated company operations. Two new buildings—a building for the Presiding Bishop (commonly referred to as the Bishop's Building) and the new Church Administration Building—similarly continued functions that had originally been housed in a variety of locations, including the Kirtland and Nauvoo temple attics. The Bishop's Building consolidated and oversaw Church financial operations on the same land where the Tithing Office had earlier managed these functions. The structure also provided office space for the Seventies Quorum, Church Board of Education, the Relief Society, and the other Church auxiliaries. The new Administration Building was built near the earlier Church's Presidents Office, but on the other side of the Lion House. The classical building, which might have been mistaken for a bank, projected dignity and security while housing the Church's General Authorities as well as the historical library and archive. A final group of buildings continuing the Nauvoo pattern were school structures in Salt Lake City. Five new Salt Lake buildings behind the Hotel Utah created a new campus for the LDS University. These buildings were used for many years and ultimately became the LDS Business College.

The Hotel Utah's construction was the most visible element in completing the plan of Zion. The Nauvoo House was to be a major hotel for visitors to the Illinois city; the Hotel Utah served a similar function in Salt Lake City. It is somehow fitting that Joseph F. Smith completed in Salt Lake City a building with a similar function to the uncompleted one in which, as a five-year-old, he saw his father's

The Hotel Utah served the same function envisioned for the Nauvoo House in Nauvoo—a fine hotel for visitors. Its construction symbolized the completion of the public and Church buildings in Joseph Smith's plan for Zion—as constructed in Nauvoo, Illinois. Souvenir Novelty Company, postcard no. 720, courtesy of W. Ray Luce.

and uncle's bodies after they had been retrieved from Carthage. The new Hotel Utah, designed by major California architectural firm Parkinson and Bergstrom, was located on one of the city's most prominent lots—part of the former Tithing Lot, which adjoins the Temple Block. Festive and clad in terra cotta, the building was fine enough that it was listed as one of the five unexpectedly best hotels in America in John Günter's *Inside USA*.[13]

These buildings completed the Nauvoo pattern—although additional buildings were constructed to serve additional functions for an expanding Church and community. Salt Lake hospitals were run by churches, and the Church followed suit when the LDS Hospital opened in 1905. The Salt Lake hospital expanded to include a nursing college. It became the flagship for a string of fifteen Church-owned hospitals in the Intermountain West before the Church divested them in 1975. The Deseret Gymnasium is the second building which expanded the plan of Zion. It was originally planned as part of the LDS University, but was opened to the public to provide physical activity for city dwellers that no longer had farm work to keep them in shape. It should be noted that ward amusement halls had not yet become

Deseret Gymnasium provided a wide range of recreational opportunities as Salt Lake City became more urbanized. The building was constructed to meet new needs; it was not just a continuation of Joseph Smith's Nauvoo plan. Souvenir Novelty Company, postcard no. 714, courtesy of W. Ray Luce.

ward gymnasiums where basketball and other sports were enthroned.[14] The local halls were used primarily for dances, theatrical productions, and similar activities. While the Deseret Gymnasium's full service gymnasium with swimming pool, track, and bowling alleys did not become a model for Church buildings in other western cities, the Church did construct several large multistake free-standing gymnasiums during the 1950s—although their main focus was basketball. The Temple Square Bureau of Information was a final addition to Salt Lake City's Plan of Zion during Smith's presidency. The bureau was an opportunistic building. Two factors spurred its construction. Church leaders recognized that thousands of tourists were coming to Salt Lake City to see Temple Square and learn about the Church and its history while the Church was sending missionaries around the world. Here was an opportunity to tell their story to people who were coming to them. The second factor came as Church members heard what local tour guides were telling visitors. The stories were good and some were correct. Church leaders decided that they should tell the story, and in 1902 a small octagonal kiosk was constructed on the temple grounds. It quickly proved to be too small, and in 1904 a permanent Bureau of Information was constructed next to the south entrance to Temple Square. That building was doubled in size in 1910 and doubled again in 1915 when a second story was added to the building.[15] The enterprise proved successful and the Church's First Presidency noted in their 1909 Christmas message that 300,000 tourists had passed through the Tabernacle grounds that year.[16]

Church buildings constructed during Smith's presidency dramatically illustrate the physical expansion of Zion. Access to temples, the Church's most sacred buildings, was perhaps the most cherished blessings of living in Zion. Temples provided earthly ordinances such as the endowment and eternal marriage. All operating temples were located in Utah—which clearly defined the limits of the gathered Zion. President Smith's most dramatic building announcement was the Cardston Alberta Temple in 1912. The building is unusual in many ways. It was the first temple planned since the presidency of Brigham Young, who had died more than thirty-five years before. Its location was not only outside Utah, but outside the United States. It clearly indicated that Zion had been dramatically expanded to include the Mormon colonies in Canada and Mexico. President Smith wanted to announce two temples at the same time—one in Canada and one in the Mormon colonies in Mexico—but Pancho Villa's raids delayed the Mexican temple for almost one hundred years.[17]

The second temple outside of Utah was equally innovative. Its location in Hawaii expanded the concept of Zion even further. The location bore visible record that Joseph F. Smith knew of island Saints' needs from his long association with them, and that, indeed, the members from the isles of the sea—at least the Polynesian islands—would not be asked to gather to the Great Basin to fully avail themselves of temple blessings. It was designed by the same architectural firm in the same revolutionary Prairie School style. Smith strongly hinted at additional temples in the South Pacific, saying that New Zealand Saints would use the Hawaiian temple unless they "become strong enough to require a house to be built there also"—indicating that the islands of the South Pacific, not just Hawaii, were now included in "Zion."[18]

The physical definition of Zion was also expanded by tabernacle and meetinghouse construction in new areas outside the Mormon Corridor. Tabernacles—large assembly buildings constructed for stakes, rather than wards—were built in Cardston, Alberta, and in La Grande, Oregon. The Union Stake Tabernacle in La Grande has been described as "the best building in Eastern Oregon."[19] These tabernacles defined Zion, but proved too large to be sustained in areas with relatively few Church members. Meetinghouses were constructed in Gridley, California; New Zealand; and Samoa. These buildings, unlike most earlier meetinghouses in outlying areas, were planned for use by established local wards and branches rather than missions and missionaries.

These new facilities, which expanded Zion, contrast with a series of more traditional structures built to house missionary activities. A series of rather spectacular new mission facilities were constructed during Smith's presidency. Pope and Burton, architects for the Cardston and Hawaiian Temples, designed new mission headquarters—with Prairie School meetinghouses—for three missions: the Northwestern States Mission in Portland, the Western States Mission in Denver, and the Eastern States Mission in New York City. Two of these survive: the Brooklyn, New York, building as the Morning Star Baptist Church, and the Portland meetinghouse as a Zen Temple. Similar complexes in other architectural styles were constructed in Chicago, Illinois, for the Northern States Mission; Independence, Missouri, for the Central States Mission; later in Atlanta, Georgia, for the Southern States Mission; and Los Angeles for the California Mission. A similar complex was constructed in Christiania (now Oslo), Norway, in 1903.[20] This building replaced one constructed by President Anthon L. Skanchy in the late 1880s.[21]

Education was one of President Smith's highest priorities. Education had also been the primary vehicle used by many Protestant and Catholic missionaries in the nineteenth century who believed that if they educated the deluded Mormons they would see the errors of their ways. The United States government demanded that a free public education system be set up, replacing the ward schools, before Utah could be a state. The Free School Act of 1890 set up such a system, but contests for control of the local school districts occurred, especially in urban school districts. The Salt Lake City School Board quickly had a majority of nonmembers. Church officials feared that some public schools might mirror previous denominational schools in trying to question faith as well as teach the ABCs. They responded by introducing ward after-school programs in religious education for grade school and high school students. Such programs were held in the ward meetinghouses, often requiring additional classrooms. In addition, President Wilford Woodruff requested that every stake establish a stake academy or high school.[22] Smith's presidency was the high point of academy construction, with buildings completed throughout the Intermountain West: Murdock Academy, Emery Academy, Dixie Academy, and Snow Academy in Utah; Oneida Academy and Ricks Academy in Idaho; Snowflake

Academy and St. Joseph Academy in Arizona; Big Horn Academy in Wyoming; and San Louis Academy in Colorado.[23] Additional academies ranged as far as Colonia Juárez, Mexico, and the Maori Agricultural College in New Zealand.

The after-school program and academy construction did not prove to be viable, long-term answers to secular education. Three other initiatives during Smith's presidency did provide a long-term solution. First was the decision to provide greater Church college opportunities, exemplified by the construction of the Maeser Building, the first building on BYU's "upper campus." Second was the construction of the Granite Stake Seminary Building in 1912. Rather than providing religious education after school in ward meetinghouses, the Granite Seminary moved the building close to the school and taught religious classes throughout the day—the beginning of a now worldwide program. The seeds of a similar institute program for college students were introduced in the Logan Fifth Ward Annex. The annex was larger than the chapel, and was designed to provide greater room capacity for classes and social activities for college students at Utah State Agricultural College. Elder John A. Widtsoe wrote that "there is probably no meeting house in the Church that has more meeting rooms for the various quorums and organizations of the ward than had the Logan Fifth Ward."[24]

Temples, tabernacles, and ward meetinghouses were all changed during Smith's presidency—temples and meetinghouses dramatically. The Cardston Temple's design is every bit as revolutionary as the design of the new small temples at the end of the twentieth century. Because there was no Church architect, a competition was held for the building's design. The selected plan was modern, unlike any temple yet constructed. In keeping with the design guidelines, the structure did not have a large assembly room or towers, features of every previous temple. It was the first temple and the second building (the Endowment House being the first) to be designed primarily around the ceremonial endowment rooms. It is the model for later temples. The leading book on Canadian churches calls the Cardston Temple "surprising" and "altogether unforgettable." The "innovative structure in Wright's idiom is hardly indebted at all to typical church structures and, rather daringly, they included Aztec and Mayan overtones in the decorative touches."[25] The architect's achievement is even more remarkable when it is realized that the structure was designed only five years after the completion of Frank Lloyd Wright's Unity Temple in Oak Park, Illinois—the Cardston Temple's inspiration—and one of America's greatest buildings.

Tabernacles were on a very different long-term trajectory, as the Smith years were almost the last gasp for tabernacle building. A great number were constructed, but the basic design for most tabernacles remained very similar. Their main function was to provide an assembly space large enough for stake conferences four times a year. The buildings were often also the site for civic functions because many of these Church buildings were the town's largest halls. Many tabernacles are impressive. Architecturally they range from the delicate first Granite Tabernacle, designed by Richard K. A. Kletting, who designed the Utah State Capitol and Saltair, to the Alpine Stake Tabernacle in American Fork with its understated exterior and unexpected, wonderful interior. Some were very utilitarian, like the Teton Stake Tabernacle in Driggs, Idaho, while others were on the cutting edge of American architecture. The Montpelier Idaho Tabernacle, designed by Pope and Burton, for example, is extraordinary, inspired by Louis Sullivan's landmark St. Paul's Church in Cedar Rapids, Iowa, that was constructed only four years earlier. During Smith's presidency an unusual phenomenon occurred as a single stake had multiple tabernacles. The Alpine Stake had tabernacles in Lehi and Pleasant Grove as well as the "official" stake tabernacle in American Fork. Similarly, the Bear Lake Stake had tabernacles in Montpelier and Paris, Idaho. The cost of construction and maintenance limited the construction of new tabernacles. In California and other outlying areas, most tabernacles constructed after Smith's presidency housed one or two wards as well as a stake. After World War II, when public address systems allowed greater flexibility, stake houses and large meetinghouses took over tabernacle functions. Those functions were further reduced when stake conferences were cut from four times a year to two and from two Sunday sessions to one.

Ward meetinghouses changed greatly during Smith's presidency. In fact, ward meetinghouses were the most numerous structures built and changed more during this period than at any other period in Church history. Changes in ward programs found a response in ward buildings. Sunday School, Primary, and weekday religious education classes were increasingly important since schools were now secular and did not include theology along with the three R's. Fast and testimony meetings were changed from Thursday morning to Sunday, and weekly priesthood meetings were instituted; a 1914 Joseph F. Smith Jr. *Improvement Era* article outlines current practices for ward buildings. These new meetinghouses were so new that there was no agreement on what to call them. Smith reported that they were called meetinghouses, chapels, or churches[26] and that each ward has its own meetinghouse.[27]

"Modern buildings" included both a chapel—worship space—and an amusement hall. The amusement hall was used for dances, "under proper regulation and restrictions," as well as for production of dramas, opera, friendly debates, declarations, and musical, oratorical, and other contests. Classrooms were these structures' third component. Smith outlined the Church's scheduled meetings. Sunday: priesthood quorums from 9:00 to 10:30; Sunday School from 10:30 to noon; sacrament meetings in the afternoon or evening as local circumstances determine—usually determined by how many members had cows to milk before coming to evening services. School-age children had two meetings: smaller children in the Primary Association met one day a week, and other religious classes were held on the other days. As has been mentioned, these classes provided religious education no longer available in the public schools. The women's organization, the Relief Society, also used the meetinghouse unless they had their own hall. Many Relief Societies continued to own or build their own halls until the Presiding Bishop asked them to stop in 1924, while at the same time directing ward bishops to provide well for the sisters in their meetinghouses. Smith claimed these new Church meetinghouses were "equal to the best of the kind to be found in any land."[28]

These new modern meetinghouses were a drastic change from the multipurpose buildings that had been built through the nineteenth century. The new buildings had many advantages: sacred space—the chapel—could be divided from the recreational use of the amusement hall. The bishop of the Franklin Ward emphasized the point in the ward's application for funding assistance: "As our meeting house has been used for all purposes and could not be kept in fit condition for a house of worship, its sacredness being destroyed by the uses to which it was put."[29] The separate chapels could now have permanent pews, a permanent stand with seats for ward leaders, the ward choir, ward clerk, and a sacrament table—often centered under the pulpit. The chapel often had a small balcony at the back to provide additional seating. Some ward buildings began incorporating baptismal fonts, including the Morgan Second Ward, whose building had a unique combination of a swimming pool and a baptismal font.[30] One of the most fundamental changes occurred in a few buildings, such as the Miller and Thirty-First Wards in Salt Lake City, which included a chapel with overflow capacity in the amusement hall. Additional chapel seating could be provided by opening doors between these two areas. Both buildings were constructed in 1909, but the new plan did not become dominant until much later when it became a fundamental feature of meetinghouse design.[31] In

The Salt Lake Thirty-First Ward constructed in 1909 was among the first Church buildings built with an overflow from the chapel into the amusement hall. The doors on the right open into the chapel. Photo by W. Ray Luce.

addition to design changes, this period also saw many meetinghouses first acquire gas or electrical lighting, indoor plumbing, and steam or forced air heating.

While an increasing number of American churches had social halls, few embraced the concept of amusement halls with the same vigor as the LDS Church. These halls applied the concept of a gathered Zion to the ward. Every ward had an amusement hall to provide "wholesome recreation," while classrooms and the chapel provided religious education. Some of the bishoprics' most earnest pleadings in their building applications concern amusement halls. Ward leaders took very seriously their responsibility to provide their youth "proper" recreation in an increasingly threatening environment. Clearfield Ward leaders "keenly" felt "the responsibility of our calling . . . as watchmen on the tower and . . . do not wish to spare time or means to guard, advise, and protect our people against that which would lead to the downfall of our Sons and Daughters." They said they were at a critical point as to "whether the priesthood shall control our amusements or whether we will submit to an outside element." The outside threat, in this case, was someone not from the ward who wanted to build a local amusement hall.[32] The threat to the Burton Ward was not theoretical: "For the past six years our young people had been frequenting a Hall of Questionable character a few miles south of our ward. And we came to the conclusion that in order to hold our young people in the proper environment, it was necessary that we should build a Hall that would be under our own supervision."[33] Similar sentiments were expressed by many wards, including St. Johns, Arizona: "We are surrounded on every side by mining camps, smelter towns etc. and our sons and daughters have formed the habit of patronizing these places for their amusement."[34] The Elwood Ward bishopric described in detail their concern. Most people in the area were not members, "and last fall they erected a Dancing Hall there and close by opend [*sic*] up a Saloon. They have tried their utmost to get our young People to go there but so far have not succeeded very well."[35] Clearly amusement halls were viewed as more than a nice place for ward socials.

The Churchwide funding process started during Smith's presidency for constructing meetinghouses and tabernacles provided the basic outline for a process which later became standardized. Funding was overseen by the Church's First Presidency and almost always signed personally by Smith. A ward or stake submitted an application form seeking funding. The form provided the ward bishopric space to outline their request and a section for the stake presidency to support or suggest modifications to the request. The bishopric often outlined the need for the building, the support the ward had given, and local conditions to support their request. These ranged from the impact of a bad harvest to ward members' struggles colonizing a new area with the attendant costs for land, homes, and irrigation systems. The section was often used to provide information on ward members' economic status or the congregation's large number of widows. Stake presidencies commented on the request, usually fully supporting a ward's request, but they might suggest modifications or note the needs of other wards in the stake. A series of fill-in-the-blank questions asked about the building itself, as well as the financial condition and tithing record of the ward. Building questions included size, materials, seating capacity, classrooms, the building's designer or architect, and who held title to the land—usually the local bishop or a ward corporation. The financial section asked for the estimated cost of the building, how much had been raised, and how much expended. Questions about the ward included how many members, how many families, and the cost of the building per member and per family. A tithing section requested information on how much tithing had been paid the year before and how much cash and produce were currently on hand. These questions were important because some wards asked to use tithing on hand or tithing to be collected for their building project. Although plan submittal was not required, it is clear that many wards submitted plans, or had their architect submit plans. Several applications note that plans have been sent in, and in some cases—like that for the Holbrook Idaho Ward—they followed a suggestion to provide a basement for classrooms.[36] Local authorities often noted previous discussions with President Smith or other General Authorities about the building, while others suggested that any questions could be answered by a specific Apostle who had recently visited the community. In some cases these visits prompted changes in building plans. The Hyrum First Ward's building site was moved after the foundation excavation had already started in response to Apostle Teasdale's recommendations.[37] Apostle Hyrum M. Smith suggested that the Farr West Ward building be improved and used for a few more years rather than be replaced. The ward complied and requested a lesser amount.[38]

Applications were reviewed personally by Joseph F. Smith, who balanced individual merit with money available. Some projects were already under way, while others were finished and needed money to complete the building or pay off debts. Smith signed each application personally as the Church's Trustee-in-Trust and wrote the amount allowed and any conditions. Awards ranged from a few hundred dollars to four or five thousand dollars. Although there were not rigid regulations, certain guidelines were usually used. First, the ward could expect no more than one-third of the money needed for the building—although on rare occasions, that amount might rise to almost one-half. Local units were almost always admonished to avoid debt, and money was usually given with the stipulation that it would be received only after the ward raised any required match without going into debt. Many buildings were the subject of more than one funding request because the building cost had been underestimated, or because of hard times or additional costs. The Hyrum Third Ward, for example, claimed that the architect misled them about the building's real cost.[39]

Ward leaders oversaw the construction process, including fund-raising, selection of the architect and contractor, and oversight of construction. Constructing a new meetinghouse could be a daunting task, especially in a rural area where ward members did much of the work. The Rockville Ward worked on their building for twelve to fifteen years, and it was still not finished.[40] Similarly, the Goshen Second Ward met in their building's basement for four years before they submitted an application for Church funds to continue construction.[41] The Circleville Ward met for a time in the Relief Society hall, and the Enterprise Ward was forced to hold Primary outdoors.[42] Several wards purchased other buildings and remodeled them for Church use. The Center Ward, Wasatch Stake, bought the Heber Methodist Church building and moved it, while the Corinne Ward bought the local opera hall for a meetinghouse.[43] Several wards purchased schools and remodeled them either as chapels or amusement halls.

The system initiated by President Smith, served the Church for many years after system modifications were made. Wards continued to apply for a percentage of building costs after meeting requirements for size and contributions. Changes to the system were modifications rather than wholesale replacement. The Church first supplied plans at no cost, hoping wards would select them, and later oversaw design for all Church buildings; buildings were owned by the Corporation of the President after it was established in 1923 rather than ward bishops or ward corporations.

These new meetinghouses were much more concerned with style than earlier ones. In fact, the majority of the earlier structures were vernacular buildings without pretense of a style. Many applications for funding mentioned that the new building would be a credit to the Church. This concern came from a desire for credible Church buildings, but in a few applications there are hints of competition with other denominations. Rigby Ward leaders, for example, said they were "confronted" with "the building of a church by our Presbyterian friends. This building is nearing completion, and it is their boast that when finished our children will be enticed to their services; this we do not desire, and we believe that if our own building can be nicely finished, that this difficulty can be overcome."[44] The bishop of the Harrisville Ward wrote that their meetinghouse would be worthy of the Church. He continued that one reason it was so expensive was that they were completely surrounded by "the People of the World," adding that "the best was none too good for the Saints."[45]

New Latter-day Saint meetinghouses utilized many architectural styles, but Gothic Revival was the most used style, and Prairie School the most unexpected. During the first two decades of the twentieth century, Gothic Revival was the most popular style for American churches, including Latter-day Saint meetinghouses.

Top: The Malad Idaho Second Ward is a good example of the many Gothic Revival meetinghouses built during Joseph F. Smith's presidency. Photo by W. Ray Luce. Bottom: Malad Second Ward interior. The stand has an oval enclosure to help project a speaker's voice. Note that the sacrament table is in the center—just below the pulpit—to emphasize the importance of the sacrament. Photo by W. Ray Luce.

Stained glass window, Salt Lake Second Ward meetinghouse. Joseph Smith's First Vision was a favorite subject for stained glass windows constructed during Smith's presidency. Photo by W. Ray Luce.

Some claimed Gothic Revival was the "only Proper style."[46] Gothic Revival originated in Gothic cathedrals, and Gothic structures looked like churches. Many well-designed Gothic buildings graced towns throughout the Mormon Corridor. They were well designed, if not always fully accessible, and contain some of the Church's best stained glass windows. Several Gothic Revival structures survive, including the buildings for the Salt Lake Second Ward, the Salt Lake Tenth Ward's new chapel, the Liberty Ward, the Brigham City Third, and the Malad Second Wards. Unfortunately, some of the best buildings constructed during this period have been sold or demolished, including that of the Salt Lake Seventeenth Ward.

Prairie School–style Church buildings are unusual and unprecedented. Prairie-style architecture was developed in Chicago, Illinois, principally by Frank Lloyd Wright. It was primarily used for houses, but religious, governmental, and commercial structures also would use the design. The style emphasized horizontal lines and geometric patterns, while creating new, nontraditional,

The Blackfoot Idaho Tabernacle is one of several Church buildings designed by Pope and Burton, architects in the Prairie School style. The building, constructed just after Smith's presidency, is now a funeral home. Photo by W. Ray Luce.

decorative motifs for capitals and cornices. While there are a few other American Prairie School church buildings, the style was embraced by the Church as by no other denomination. The Cardston and Hawaiian Temples obviously spurred the movement, but at least sixty other Mormon Prairie School buildings were constructed.[47] The Salt Lake First Ward's building (built in 1913 and demolished in 1978), was one of the finest Prairie-style meetinghouses. This building was not only architecturally important as one of the Church's finest Prairie School–style buildings, but it was historically significant as well; in fact, former Church President Gordon B. Hinckley and his wife grew up in the ward, and President Hinckley's father served in the Liberty Stake as stake president.[48] The style was prevalent enough to be called "Mormon Style."[49] Today only a handful of these buildings are left, including the Parowan Third Ward building and the Ogden Deaf Branch building. It is interesting to speculate on the apparent strong symbolic relationship between Prairie School, this new American architectural style that had never existed anywhere before, and a religion restored in America. Perhaps Gothic Revival, the prevailing Church style, represented traditional Christianity better than it did the new, restored gospel.

Joseph F. Smith's presidency produced an amazing legacy in the number of buildings, their styles, and plans. Understanding this building heritage can help us understand the transformation of the Church from an isolated organization in the western United States to a modern organization expanding into the world. Only a few of these buildings remain, and we need to understand and cherish them so that they can tell their story to future generations of Church members.

Notes

1. Richard W. Jackson, *Places of Worship: 150 Years of Latter-day Saint Architecture* (Provo, UT: Religious Studies Center, Brigham Young University, 2003), appendix 5. Thirty-four of the ninety-two buildings he identified as tabernacles were constructed during Smith's presidency (38 percent).
2. Specifically, 465 wards out of 797. See *Improvement Era*, May 1916, 653.
3. See Joseph F. Smith local unit appropriation files in Church History Library, The Church of Jesus Christ of Latter-day Saints, Salt Lake City, for the noted buildings.
4. *Deseret Evening News*, December 28, 1915, quoted in Journal History of The Church of Jesus Christ of Latter-day Saints, Church History Library, December 26, 1915.
5. "A Christmas Salutation from the First Presidency," *Deseret News*, December 20, 1915.
6. For information on the school changes, see Frederick S. Buchanan, *Culture Clash and Accommodation: Public Schooling in Salt Lake City*, 1890–1994 (San Francisco: Smith Research Association in association with Signature Books, 1996).
7. Joseph F. Smith Jr., "Uses and Maintenance of the Churches by the Latter-day Saints," *Improvement Era*, June 1914, 727.
8. Smith Local Appropriations, Jameston Idaho Ward.
9. Smith Local Appropriations, Fredonia Arizona Ward.
10. Smith Local Appropriations, Granite Ward.
11. Smith Local Appropriations, Garden Creek and Holden Wards.
12. *Utah Gazetteer and Directory of Salt Lake, Ogden, Provo and Logan Cities for 1888* (Salt Lake City, 1888), 45, 90, 115, 327; *Utah State Gazetteer and Business Directory, 1918–1919* (Salt Lake City: R. L. Polk & Co., 1918), 618.
13. John Gunther, *Inside U.S.A.* (New York: Harper & Brothers, 1947), 910. He added that the Hotel Utah "is to Salt Lake City what the Waldorf is to New York" (190).
14. See discussion of gymnasium uses of amusement halls in *Improvement Era*, April 1908, 477–79.
15. Joseph S. Peery, "The Bureau of Information," *Improvement Era*, June 1914, 688–94.
16. "Greetings from the First Presidency, Review of Year's History of the Church, *Deseret Evening News*, December 18, 1909, 7.
17. Joseph F. Smith, "Editors' Table," *Improvement Era*, November 1915, 79.
18. Smith, "Editor's Table," 79.
19. Richard Oman, interview by the author, July 2000.
20. A. B. Larsen, "The Christiania Conference House," *Improvement Era*, July 1909, 734–36.
21. See "Anthon L. Skanchy: A Brief Autobiographical Sketch of the Missionary Labors of a Valiant Soldier for Christ," *Improvement Era*, December 1914, 119–26; January 1915, 236–42; February 1915, 326–31; March 1915, 417–24; April 1915, 500–506; May 1915, 593–96.
22. See Scott C. Esplin, "Wilford Woodruff: A Founding Father of the Mormon Academies," in *Banner of the Gospel: Wilford Woodruff*, ed. Alexander L. Baugh and Susan Easton Black

(Provo, UT: Religious Studies Center, Brigham Young University; Salt Lake City: Deseret Book, 2010), 205–32.

23. There may have been additional buildings constructed as well. For general background on the Church stake academies, see Horace H. Cummings, "The Church Schools," *Improvement Era*, July 1913, 929–40; William E. Berrett, *A Miracle in Weekday Religious Education* (Salt Lake City: Salt Lake Printing Center, 1988), 33–39; Harold R. Laycock, "Academies," *Encyclopedia of Mormonism*, ed. Daniel H. Ludlow (New York: Macmillan, 1992), 11–13.
24. John A. Widtsoe quoted in Joel E. Ricks, "Logan Fifth Ward History," *1950 Utah State University Special Collections and Archives*; http://digitalcommons.usu.edu.joel_ricks/4. Widtsoe was in a good position to know. He had been president of the Utah State Agricultural College before being ordained an Apostle in 1921.
25. Peter Richardson and Douglas Richardson, *Canadian Churches: An Architectural History* (Richmond Hill, Ontario: Firefly Books, 2007), 340–42.
26. This same uncertainty about what to call these buildings is found in the signs on the structures. Church buildings from the period are identified as "meeting house," "chapel," "house of worship," and "assembly hall." This paper will use the term *meetinghouse* to refer to ward buildings and chapel for the worship space or sanctuary. Smith was still using the name Joseph F. Smith Jr., rather than Joseph Fielding Smith, which he used later.
27. This practice continued until after World War II.
28. Smith, "Uses and Maintenance of the Churches by the Latter-day Saints," 727.
29. Smith Local Appropriations, Franklin Ward.
30. Lewis T. Cannon, "Architecture of Church Buildings," *Improvement Era*, June 1914, 800. Previously, most baptisms took place in streams or lakes or in temple baptismal fonts. The scarcity of baptismal fonts is shown by the fact that Gordon B. Hinckley was the first President of the Church baptized in a baptismal font. See Michael D. Taylor, "The Baptisms of Latter-day Prophets," *Religious Educator* 3, no. 3 (2002): 61–64.
31. In 1923, for example, Bishop LeGrand Richards wanted the plans for the Sugarhouse Ward in Salt Lake City to allow overflow seating, but the Church Architects Office under Willard and Don Carlos Young successfully pushed a plan which separated the chapel and the amusement hall. Lucile C. Tate, *LeGrand Richards: Beloved Apostle* (Salt Lake City: Bookcraft, 1982): 117.
32. Smith Local Appropriations, Clearfield Ward.
33. Smith Local Appropriations, Burton Ward.
34. Smith Local Appropriations, St. Johns Arizona Ward.
35. Smith Local Appropriations, Elwood Ward.
36. Smith Local Appropriations, Holbrook Idaho Ward.
37. Smith Local Appropriations, Hyrum First Ward.
38. Smith Local Appropriations, Farr West Ward.
39. Smith Local Appropriations, Hyrum Third Ward.
40. Smith Local Appropriations, Rockville Ward.
41. Smith Local Appropriations, Goshen Second Ward.
42. Smith Local Appropriations, Circleville and Enterprise Wards.
43. Smith Local Appropriations, Center and Corinne Wards.
44. Smith Local Appropriations, Rigby Ward.
45. Smith Local Appropriations, Harrisville Ward.

46. See Calder Loth and Julius Trousdale Sadler, *The Only Proper Style: Gothic Architecture in America* (New York: New York Graphic Society, 1975).
47. See Jackson, *Places of Worship*, app. 4.
48. See Sheri L. Dew, *Go Forward with Faith: The Biography of Gordon B. Hinckley* (Salt Lake City: Deseret Book, 1996), 33, 41.
49. "New $10,000 L.D.S. Mission Home; William E. Barr House," *Deseret News*, December 19, 1914, 22.

Jennifer L. Lund

19

Joseph F. Smith and the Origins of the Church Historic Sites Program

When Joseph F. Smith became President of The Church of Jesus Christ of Latter-day Saints on October 17, 1901, the Church owned one historic site—an acre of ground and a small monument in a cemetery at Mount Pisgah, Iowa. At his death seventeen years later, the Church boasted more than 550 acres over six Church history sites stretching from Sharon, Vermont, to Salt Lake City, Utah. This major foray into the ownership, preservation, and interpretation of historic places formed the foundation of a Church historic sites program that has expanded to include, as of 2012, approximately twenty-five key sites, dozens of markers and monuments, and nearly one hundred historic temples, tabernacles, and meetinghouses. At first glance, it appears that the acquisition of historic sites during the Joseph F. Smith administration was a calculated effort to memorialize the Church's past. On closer examination, however, it is a much more complicated story—one in which opportunity and serendipity play prominent roles.

For most of the nineteenth century, the places where significant events in Church history occurred received only limited attention from Church leaders. In

---

Jennifer L. Lund is director of the Historic Sites Division of the Church History Department, The Church of Jesus Christ of Latter-day Saints, Salt Lake City.

fact, historic sites held little importance for both Latter-day Saints and Americans in general. This indifference toward history and toward historic sites in particular began to change midcentury, a permutation that intensified and accelerated in the wake of the Civil War.[1] The most prominent expression of this shifting attitude was the proliferation of monuments on the landscape. In his important *Mystic Chords of Memory,* cultural historian Michael Kammen referred to the decades between 1870 and 1910 as "the most notable period in all of American history for erecting monuments in honor" of great men and "great deeds."[2] This was also an era when a growing appreciation for the nation's historical and architectural heritage spawned efforts to preserve and protect, as well as celebrate, important sites of cultural significance. The quintessential example of this populist movement is the effort to preserve Mount Vernon. In 1853, when pleas to Congress were ignored, activists formed the Mount Vernon Ladies Association of the Union and rallied women throughout the country to purchase and preserve the home of George and Martha Washington. By 1889, the federal government had begun to embrace the idea of historic preservation, and efforts to secure federal funding for the repair of Casa Grande Ruins in southern Arizona were successful. Three years later the site was designated as the first archaeological and cultural reserve in the country, becoming the first National Monument and formally receiving that title in 1918.[3]

In an era when the national attention turned to the past and railroads linked even remote places, historic sites became prominent travel destinations.[4] For Latter-day Saints, visits to locations associated with the events of the Restoration were not solely motivated by curiosity; rather, they were religious pilgrimages wherein the faithful sought to experience firsthand the places of sacred events. The impetus to visit the sites of the Restoration may have begun as early as the 1830s. It was further established following the deaths of Joseph and Hyrum Smith in 1844, when a few Latter-day Saints traveled the mournful road to Carthage to witness for themselves the scene of the Martyrdom.[5] Following the westward trek, missionaries and others journeying east frequently stopped at Nauvoo or Kirtland. Some actually constructed itineraries around Latter-day Saint historic sites, such as the important 1888 tour that Andrew Jenson, Edward Stevenson, and Joseph S. Black made in Missouri, New York, Ohio, Illinois, and Iowa, to gather historical material for the Church Historian's Office. These Saints also made a point of seeing all the major places of interest along their itinerary and documenting the historic sites in precise detail, interviewing local residents, measuring dimensions and distances, and in one case, commissioning a photograph. The letters the trio wrote to the *Deseret News* recounting their experiences, and particularly their descriptions of places, were influential in popularizing an interest in Latter-day Saint historic sites.[6] For those who could not travel, pilgrimages could also be taken from one's parlor via the stereoscope. In 1904, the prominent stereograph company Underwood & Underwood took advantage of the national interest in historic sites and focused their lenses on the Church. They published thirty-eight views of Latter-day Saint sites in their series *The Latter-day Saints Tour from Palmyra, New York, to Salt Lake City Through the Stereoscope.*[7]

It was in this climate of burgeoning interest in national and regional history, and particularly in the preservation of historic sites, that Joseph F. Smith began his administration as President of the Church. The fiftieth anniversary of the pioneer trek to the Great Basin in 1897 and the centennials of the births of Brigham Young in 1901 and Joseph Smith in 1905 initiated a series of anniversaries—each being marked and celebrated—which would keep history at the forefront in the approaching decades. With his early years as a clerk in the Church Historian's Office and a mission in 1878 with Orson Pratt to gather records, President Smith was particularly attuned to the cause of history—a cause which for him, as a son of Hyrum Smith and a nephew of the Prophet Joseph, was very personal.[8] He was certainly also cognizant of the fact that he was one of the last Church leaders to have personally known the Prophet Joseph Smith. As a counselor to John Taylor, President Joseph F. Smith had also been involved in the decision to acquire the Church's first historic site fifteen years earlier, thus introducing him to the concept of honoring the past through ownership, preservation, and interpretation.

In the mid-1880s, A. C. White, a farmer from Afton, Iowa, wrote to John Taylor about the small burial mound in the center of his farm that he and his father had carefully maintained. His inquiry had been sparked by a letter from his sister in Montana who described a conversation with Hannah S. Lapish, a Latter-day Saint visiting the area. Lapish discovered that her hostess's family owned the farm where the Mount Pisgah cemetery was located and encouraged them to write to President Taylor, who she felt confident would buy the burial site to preserve it. White duly inquired, "What do the people want to do with the remains of their friends who were buried here?" President Taylor's answer was to purchase one acre in the middle of the "old burial ground of the Saints" at Mount Pisgah.[9] He then assigned Oliver B. Huntington, the son of former branch president William

Huntington, to finalize the purchase and plan a fitting memorial. Motivated by a commitment to honor his father who was buried in the cemetery, Oliver B. Huntington solicited donations from relatives and friends of the interred to fence the property and erect a fitting tribute. Since 1888, an obelisk has marked the spot telling visitors about the Latter-day Saints who, driven out of their homes in Nauvoo, stopped there for a season to prepare for their final journey west.[10] It became the first historical site purchased and preserved by the Church.

This first purchase of a historic site is an interesting case study for the acquisition of sites during the Joseph F. Smith administration. The site and its availability first came to the attention of Church leaders through an unsolicited letter from a source outside the Church, albeit suggested by a member. Once the site was in the Church's ownership, minor improvements were made and a monument erected, in this case under the sponsorship of a committee. Of the historic sites considered by the Church between 1901 and 1918, all but one were initially contemplated in response to proposals by either lay members or outsiders.[11] Some proposals were turned down at first but later reconsidered.[12] Other sites were rejected outright, while a few were investigated seriously before being dropped.[13] A few additional sites not owned by the Church were memorialized with markers.[14] None of these cases reveals an overarching plan or strategy. I have surveyed conference addresses, publications, and the correspondence and diaries of Church leaders, and there is no hint of a deliberate, calculated attempt to celebrate Church history on the landscape. Indeed, once the Church acquired these sites, leaders were not quite sure what to do with them. While they talked about the opportunities to distribute religious literature, there was little effort to do so. It appears that the Church's historic sites program began as a series of opportunities, presented at a time when the Church was emerging from significant debt. They cultivated a new public image in a climate where the celebration of history—particularly through the avenue of historic preservation and monuments—was on the rise. It was also a moment when significant anniversaries—the fiftieth anniversary of the pioneer trek and the centennials of the births of Church leaders—inspired a commemoration of the Church's past. The historic sites designated or acquired during the administration of Joseph F. Smith are listed in order as follows: Temple Square (1902); Carthage Jail (1903); the Independence, Missouri, Temple Lot (1904); Joseph Smith's birthplace (1905); the Smith farm and the Sacred Grove (1907); and the Far West Temple site (1909).

The first of these sites, Temple Square, does not always appear on lists of historic sites, but there can be no doubt that it encompasses the most historically and theologically significant space in Salt Lake City and perhaps in the entire Church.[15] While the Church did not acquire this site during the Smith administration, it did transform it into a visitor destination for the purpose of explaining the Church's beliefs, as well as interpreting its historical roots. Charles J. Thomas, Salt Lake Temple custodian during its construction, officially hosted visitors in the Temple Block beginning in 1875. James Dwyer, a local bookseller, spent an hour or two each day on the square during the 1880s–90s, explaining Church history and doctrine and handing out Articles of Faith cards. However, when the Bureau of Information—under the direction of the First Presidency—opened in 1902, more than a hundred local missionaries were assigned to serve as guides, which heralded a significant shift in approach.[16] No longer was the goal simply to welcome visitors, but rather to present those visitors with an accurate, positive portrayal of the Church in an effort to alter public perception. Building upon the model used at the 1893 Chicago World's Fair, Temple Square represented the first foray into creating a permanent location for telling the Church's story.[17] In *Exhibiting Mormonism: The Latter-day Saints and the 1893 Chicago World's Fair,* Reid L. Neilson characterized the fair as "the catalyst of Mormonism's emerging transformation from a nineteenth-century missionary-minded people to a twentieth-century evangelistic *and* public relations juggernaut."[18] Indeed, Temple Square became the faith's primary public relations venue. However, since the Square also included three important buildings—the Salt Lake Temple, Tabernacle, and Assembly Hall—history was a central part of the site's message. In fact, other than a new bureau building in 1904 and an expansion six years later, all of the major elements added to the Square over the next three decades memorialized the Church's past: the statues of Joseph and Hyrum Smith, first conceived in 1904, realized and placed in the sculpture niches of the Salt Lake Temple in 1909 and finally placed on Temple Square in 1911; the *Seagull Monument* by Mahonri Young erected in 1913; the major 1919 expansion of the Bureau of Information to house the collection of the Deseret Museum and the installation of the Deuel log cabin in a memorial bowery; and the monument to the Three Witnesses by Avard Fairbanks erected in 1927.[19]

Of all the historic sites acquired during this era, Temple Square is the only one that had a built-in audience. By 1902, Salt Lake City was a prominent tourist destination. Easily accessed by railroad, visitors came to see the sites of Latter-day

Opened in 1902, the Bureau of Information at Temple Square and its hundreds of local missionaries who served as guides marked a significant change in showcasing Church sites as a destination place.

Saints, particularly the magnificent temple completed and dedicated in 1893, as well as the natural wonders of the West. Thus efforts to beautify the square, develop public relations kiosks, conduct tours, present organ recitals, erect monuments, and distribute literature met an already existing demand from both LDS and non-LDS tourists. Today, Temple Square remains Salt Lake City's most visited historic site.

The first historic site actually acquired during the Joseph F. Smith administration was also the site of the murder of President Smith's father and uncle. Carthage Jail seems to be an odd place to begin an effort to memorialize the Mormon landscape. Indeed, when the matter was presented to Church leaders, John Smith, then the Patriarch to the Church and also a son of Hyrum Smith, remarked that "if some one would put dynamite under it and blow it to atoms it would suit him." President Smith, on the other hand, felt that it could be used to distribute literature and "enlighten the many Tourists."[20] The owner of the property, Elizabeth M. Browning, approached the Church through an agent in May 1903, offering to sell the old jail where she and her late husband had resided for many years.[21] This was apparently

President Joseph F. Smith saw the Carthage Jail, purchased by the Church in 1903, as a place to distribute literature and enlighten those who visited the site. Photo 1907 by George Edward Anderson.

not, however, the Browning's first attempt. President Smith reported that several years earlier the jail had been "offered for sale . . . and was considered favorably with a view to opening up in the building a bureau of information and keeping on sale the church works and gospel tracts, but for some reason the matter dropped through."[22] After serious discussion, on this occasion the council concluded to purchase the jail, as Rudger Clawson noted, for its "great historic interest to the Latter-day Saints and in fact to the world."[23] The purchase was finalized in November. Although an Iowa newspaper reported that a "memorial museum" would soon open on the property, the Church continued to lease the building to tenants.[24] Asahel H. Woodruff, president of the Northern States Mission, investigated the possibility of finding a Latter-day Saint to rent the property or possibly using it as conference headquarters.[25] These options did not come to fruition and the building continued to be a residence with the tenants conducting occasional tours.[26]

On the very day that the Quorum of the Twelve reorganized the First Presidency following the death of Lorenzo Snow, they also determined to explore the purchase of a tiny portion of the Temple Lot in Independence, Missouri. A. L. Hartley of the Church of Christ Temple Lot, or the Hedrickite Church as it is commonly known, wrote to inform the Church in Utah that less than an acre of ground was available for sale.[27] James G. Duffin, president of the Southwestern States Mission, investigated on behalf of the First Presidency. He discovered that the lot was extremely small, the title was not clear, there would be hefty expenses for curb and gutter, and the city was unsure how that section of Independence would be developed. Duffin recommended that the Church not pursue the purchase at the time. However, he also learned that another twenty-five acres of the Temple Lot was also for sale.[28] After several fits and starts and much negotiation over three years, President Duffin finalized the acquisition on April 14, 1904, adding additional acreage the following year.[29]

The purchase of a portion of the Temple Lot was not motivated by historical sentiment, but rather by theology. From the time the Saints were evicted from Jackson County in 1833, they had intended to return to redeem Zion and build a temple in the "center place." In 1900, representatives of the Hedrickites visited Salt Lake City to persuade Church leaders to join them, along with a delegation from the Reorganized Church of Jesus Christ of Latter Day Saints (now known as Community of Christ), in meetings to consider jointly building the temple in Zion. Leaders of the Church declined to participate, yet they renewed their commitment to one day build a temple in Independence. President Lorenzo Snow stated that "the time was fast approaching, in his opinion, when the Lord would require the building of the Temple at Jackson county."[30] He also outlined a plan whereby the Church, once it was out of debt, could quietly purchase land in Independence—including portions of the Temple Lot.[31] Thus, when an opportunity presented itself, Church leaders were prepared to act swiftly. They even had a fund for that purpose at their disposal.[32]

While the Temple Lot was purchased with the intent of building a temple, the construction was a dream far in the future. Instead, President Duffin often found himself leading tours across the fields which were rented to a local farmer. Church leaders and members thought of the site as one of primarily historical significance, including it on the pilgrimage circuit when visiting Independence. It

Purchased for theological rather than historical purposes, the temple lot site in Independence still served as a gathering place for Saints, as in this 1907 photo by George Edward Anderson.

was also the site to which missionaries and members retreated to celebrate events such as the Fourth of July and Pioneer Day.[33]

The most prominent and influential site acquired during this period was the birthplace of Joseph Smith in Sharon, Vermont. When he first visited the site in 1894, Junius F. Wells, editor of the *Contributor,* thought that a monument ought to be erected there someday. As the centennial of Joseph Smith's birth neared in 1905, Wells recalled his impression and approached the First Presidency with a proposal. He was assigned to investigate the authenticity of the farm, purchase the property in behalf of the Church, and oversee the placement of an impressive granite shaft, all in time to mark the anniversary of the Prophet's birth in December.[34] More than just a simple marker, the monument is highly symbolic, celebrating Joseph Smith as both a son of Vermont and a prophet of God. Together, the monument, the nearby Memorial Cottage[35] or visitors' center, and the formal landscaping combine in a complex and very sophisticated interpretive program

The monument, Memorial Cottage, and formal landscaping of the Joseph Smith Birthplace Memorial combine in a complex and very sophisticated interpretive program that has served as a model for other Church historic sites. Here, members of the Smith family gather at the Joseph Smith Birthplace Memorial, December 23, 1905.

that has long served as a model for other Church historic sites. The dedication and unveiling of the monument was a grand affair, with local dignitaries and a large contingent of visiting Church leaders in attendance. President Joseph F. Smith offered the dedicatory prayer. The Utah delegation, having witnessed firsthand the public relations success in Vermont, embarked on a brief tour of Smith family and Latter-day Saint historic sites in Massachusetts, New York, and Ohio, before returning home.[36]

The company arrived in Palmyra, New York, on December 26, 1905, and went immediately to the Smith farm and Hill Cumorah which they toured with much interest, holding a brief devotional at each location. While the visitors waited for the train that evening, William Avery Chapman, the owner of the Smith farm, came to the hotel and met privately with President Joseph F. Smith. According to Edith Ann Smith, who kept a detailed journal, "it is supposed" that Chapman "offered to sell the church his farm." There are no documents that confirm the topic of conversation between the two men; however, Sister Smith expressed the sentiment of the company thus: "We all hope some day the church will own the Home—the grove and the Hill, but whether it will be secured within a short space of time or in the future we cannot tell. The thought was expressed that some day it would be done."[37] Fifteen months later, shortly after President Smith had announced that the Church's debt had been retired, Church leaders decided to buy the Smith farm and the Hill Cumorah.[38] George Albert Smith, who was sent to negotiate the purchases, was met with only partial success. Pliny T. Sexton declined to sell his portion of the property encompassing the Hill Cumorah, whereas Chapman agreed to the deal as long as he would be allowed to continue to live on the property as a tenant. Thus the Church made its first self-initiated acquisition of a historic site in 1907.

One last property, the Far West Temple site, also came into Church ownership during these years. The land, which was then owned by Jacob Whitmer, a son of John Whitmer, had first been offered to the Church in 1888 when Andrew Jenson, Edward Stevenson, and Joseph S. Black visited.[39] Twelve years later, in 1900, Whitmer renewed the offer. President Snow tersely instructed a clerk to inform Whitmer, "Not buying land at present & don't expect to."[40] Nine years later, priorities and interests had changed along with the Church's financial status. Samuel O. Bennion, president of the Central States Mission, purchased approximately eighty acres at Far West in behalf of the Church, including the temple site.[41]

In 1904 the stereograph company Underwood & Underwood produced The Latter-day Saints' Tour from Palmyra, New York, to Salt Lake City. *This set of thirty-eight stereographs allowed people to travel to the sites in the comfort of their parlor.*

These acquisitions represent a major new initiative for the Church during the Joseph F. Smith administration—the ownership of sites that are significant primarily for their historical character. Each of the sites was foundational, directly connected to major events in the life and ministry of the Prophet Joseph Smith or to the establishment of Church headquarters in Salt Lake City. There were also several additional sites that were considered and declined or else ignored. While the reasons for such decisions are not always evident, these latter sites were perhaps not as central to the Church's history as those previously purchased. These sites included the Winter Quarters cemetery in Florence, Nebraska, Lucy Mack Smith's birthplace in Gilsum, New Hampshire, and the Nauvoo House in Nauvoo, Illinois. Although it is clear that Church leaders had some interest in returning to Nauvoo, they likely did not want another point of potential conflict with the Reorganized Church. The theological distinctions between the two churches had already played out on the historic site landscape when the Reorganized Church initiated lawsuits to establish ownership of the Kirtland Temple and Independence Temple Lot, and publicly voiced their objections to the Latter-day Saint–sponsored monument at Sharon, Vermont.[42] When Charles Bidamon wrote announcing the Nauvoo House was for sale, the First Presidency did not respond. They may have been particularly wary since Bidamon confided that he was in negotiation with Heman C. Smith, Apostle and Church Historian of the Reorganized Church, for the same property and may have been hoping for a bidding war to his advantage.[43]

During this initial era of historic site ownership, the Church rented the sites primarily to non-Latter-day Saint tenants who gave occasional tours or at least tolerated visitors. The main exceptions are Temple Square and Joseph Smith's birthplace. In both cases, the Church created a public venue where it could reach out to people, fostering understanding of Latter-day Saint history and beliefs, thereby improving the Church's public image. Both sites deliberately used history to that end. A third exception, the Smith Farm in New York, had Latter-day Saint tenants beginning in 1915 who provided tours to visitors. While the primary rationale for these sites looked outward, there was also an imperative to teach the membership as well. When President John R. Winder, a counselor to President Joseph F. Smith, first proposed erecting a memorial "to perpetuate the memory of the Prophet and Patriarch" on Temple Square in 1904, he reasoned that such a monument would communicate the significance of these men and their contributions and sacrifices to two distinct audiences—first, the youth of the Church for generations to come, and second, "the thousands of people who visit us."[44]

The historic sites program which developed under President Joseph F. Smith's direction revolved around three principles: first, ownership of the land in order to protect the site from desecration, destruction, or development; second, preservation of key elements of the site as a record of the past; and third, interpretation of the site through tours, monuments, statuary, formal landscaping, and publications. Although no one at the time refers to this as a "program," the hallmarks of multiple acquisitions and guiding principles are present. As President of the Church, Joseph F. Smith led the way. He recognized the value of historic sites and committed resources to both their acquisition and memorialization. Perhaps of equal importance, however, was the continuing legacy he inspired. President Smith assigned Apostle George Albert Smith to acquire two of the most important sites, the Smith Farm and the Hill Cumorah, in New York. That assignment, which was not completed until 1928, cultivated a deep and abiding interest in historic places in the young Apostle. In 1930, Elder Smith became the founding president of the Utah Pioneer Trails and Landmarks Association, which marked 120 sites during his presidency. He also played a key role in the centennial celebrations in 1930 and 1947 and converted several sites from rental property to tourist attractions with missionary-led tours.[45]

During his presidency, Joseph F. Smith faced a rabid anti-Mormon press and the challenge of leading a people in the throes of transforming a peculiar sect isolated in the west to a religious faith more in tune with American values. As Kathleen Flake suggests in her book *The Politics of Religious Identity*, President Joseph F. Smith and other Church leaders may have championed the Church's past as a vehicle to preserve a unique Latter-day Saint identity while at the same time giving up the distinctive social, economic, and political attributes of the Church's kingdom.[46] Whatever the motives, Joseph F. Smith made a major commitment to preserving Church history through the acquisition, preservation, and interpretation of historic sites. Now more than one hundred years later, we are the beneficiaries of his foresight.

Notes

1. Michael Kammen, *Mystic Chords of Memory: The Transformation of Tradition in American Culture* (New York: Knopf, 1991), 52–61.
2. Kammen, *Mystic Chords of Memory*, 115.
3. Norman Tyler, Ted J. Ligibel, and Ilene R. Tyler, *Historic Preservation: An Introduction to its History, Principles, and Practice*, 2nd ed. (New York: W. W. Norton, 2009), 30–31; National Park Service, "History and Culture," Casa Grande Ruins National Monument; http://www.nps.gov/cagr/historyculture/index.htm.

4. Kammen, *Mystic Chords of Memory*, 106, 201–2.
5. Davis Bitton, "The Ritualization of Mormon History," *Utah Historical Quarterly* 43, no. 1 (Winter 1975): 76; Brian Q. Cannon, "'Long Shall His Blood . . . Stain Illinois': Carthage Jail in Mormon Memory," *Mormon Historical Studies* 10, no. 1 (Spring 2009): 3.
6. The letters were later issued in a special supplement issue to Jenson's *Historical Record* and as a pamphlet titled *Infancy of the Church*. Andrew Jenson, *Autobiography of Andrew Jenson* (Salt Lake City: Deseret News, 1938), 150–84; Andrew Jenson and Edward Stevenson, *Infancy of the Church* (Salt Lake City: n.p., 1889).
7. Underwood & Underwood published two boxed sets, one with twenty-nine views and one with thirty-eight views. James Ricalton and Henry A. Strohmeyer, *The Latter-day Saints' Tour from Palmyra, New York, to Salt Lake City Through the Stereoscope* (Ottawa, KS: Underwood & Underwood, 1904); B. H. Roberts, *The Latter-day Saints' Tour* (Ottawa, KS: Underwood & Underwood, 1905); see Richard Neitzel Holzapfel, "Stereographs and Stereotypes: A 1904 View of Mormonism," *Journal of Mormon History* 18, no. 2 (Fall 1992): 155–76.
8. Richard Neitzel Holzapfel & R. Q. Shupe, *Joseph F. Smith: Portrait of a Prophet* (Salt Lake City: Deseret Book, 2000), 33–36, 61–62.
9. A. C. White to John Taylor, ca. 1885, as cited in O. B. Huntington, "Pisgah Burying Ground," *Deseret Evening News*, January 7, 1888, 5; Hannah Settle Lapish, "The 'Mormon' Burial Ground at Mt. Pisgah, Iowa," *Improvement Era*, May 1914, 662–66.
10. White to Taylor, *Deseret Evening News*, 5.
11. The lone exception was the Smith farm in Manchester, New York.
12. Carthage Jail in Carthage, Illinois, and the Far West Temple Lot, Caldwell County, Missouri.
13. Lucy Mack Smith's birthplace in Gilsum, New Hampshire; Winter Quarters Cemetery in Florence, Nebraska; Nauvoo Cemetery and Nauvoo House in Nauvoo, Illinois.
14. Three Witnesses Monument at Richmond, Missouri, and the Hyrum Smith Monument in the Salt Lake City Cemetery are two examples of monuments erected during this era.
15. B. H. Roberts, *A Comprehensive History of the Church of Jesus Christ of Latter-day Saints* (1957; repr., Provo, UT: Brigham Young University, 1965), 6:426–31; Steven L. Olsen, "Museums and Historic Sites of Mormonism," in *Mormon Americana: A Guide to Sources and Collections in the United States*, ed. David J. Whitaker (Provo, UT: BYU Studies, 1995), 523–37. Temple Square does appear on lists of historic sites in the following: Richard H. Jackson, "Historical Sites," in *Encyclopedia of Mormonism*, ed. Daniel H. Ludlow (New York: Macmillan, 1992), 2:592–95; T. Jeffery Cottle and Richard Neitzel Holzapfel, "Historical Sites," in *Encyclopedia of Latter-day Saint History*, ed. Arnold K. Garr, Donald Q. Cannon, and Richard O. Cowan (Salt Lake City: Deseret Book, 2000), 502–4.
16. "Bureau of Information and Church Literature," *Improvement Era*, September 1902, 899–901; Levi Edgar Young, "The Temple Block Mission," *Relief Society Magazine*, November 1922, 559–63; Church Educational System, *Church History in the Fulness of Times*, 2nd ed. (Salt Lake City: The Church of Jesus Christ of Latter-day Saints, 2000), 474–75.
17. The strategy employed at the Chicago World's Fair represented a shift from "private evangelization" to "public education." The new model emphasized the physical and cultural accomplishments of the Saints over doctrine, celebrated the Mormon Tabernacle Choir, and utilized exhibits, artwork, and tour guides to communicate with visitors. See Reid L. Neilson, *Exhibiting*

Mormonism: The Latter-day Saints and the 1893 Chicago World's Fair (New York: Oxford University, 2011), 47, 178.

18. Neilson, *Exhibiting Mormonism*, 7.
19. "Bronzed Statues Placed. Figures of the Prophet and Hyrum Smith Adorn Temple Doors," *Deseret Evening News*, November 5, 1909, 8; Edward H. Anderson, "The Prophet and Patriarch," *Improvement Era*, July 1911, unpaginated insert; Journal History of The Church of Jesus Christ of Latter-day Saints, October 1, 1913, 3–9, Church History Library, The Church of Jesus Christ of Latter-day Saints, Salt Lake City, "Mormons Open New Museum in Temple Square," *Salt Lake Herald*, May 14, 1919, 7; "Log Abode of Sturdy Pioneer is Re-erected," *Salt Lake Herald*, November 3, 1918, 36; "First Log Cabin Preserved Intact," *Salt Lake Herald*, April 13, 1919, 21; "Monument to the Three Witnesses of the Book of Mormon," *Improvement Era*, May 1927, [624].
20. *Danish Apostle: The Diaries of Anthon H. Lund, 1890–1921*, ed. John P. Hatch (Salt Lake City: Signature Books, 2006), 247.
21. Stan Larson, ed., *A Ministry of Meetings: The Apostolic Diaries of Rudger Clawson* (Salt Lake City: Signature Books, 1993), 602; George F. Gibbs to G. Edmunds, May 8, 1903, correspondence.
22. Larson, *A Ministry of Meetings*, 602.
23. Larson, *A Ministry of Meetings*, 602.
24. *Keokuk Constitution Democrat*, as republished in "Church Now Owns Old Carthage Jail," *Lehi Banner*, December 3, 1903, 1, 3; Cannon, "'Long Shall His Blood,'" 6.
25. Asahel H. Woodruff to Joseph F. Smith, January 25, 1904, correspondence, Letterpress Copybooks, 1901–12, Northern States Mission, Church History Library
26. Cannon, "'Long Shall His Blood,'" 6–7.
27. Clawson, *Ministry of Meetings*, 338.
28. James G. Duffin to Joseph F. Smith, December 19, 1901, correspondence as recorded in James G. Duffin, diary, December 31, 1901, holograph, Mormon Missionary Diaries; http://contentdm.lib.byu.edu/cdm/compoundobject/collection/MMD/id/66169/rec1.
29. Duffin to Smith, April 14, 1904; August 24, 1904; October 3, 1905.
30. Journal History, February 10, 1900, 4. For background, see R. Jean Addams, *Upon the Temple Lot: The Church of Christ's Quest to Build the House of the Lord* (Independence: John Whitmer Books, 2010), 31–40.
31. Journal History, February 21, 1900, 14.
32. Journal History, February 21, 1900, 13; "Redemption of Zion," *Improvement Era*, May 1904, 547.
33. Duffin, diary, April 27, 1904; July 4, 1904; July 22, 1904; July 25, 1904; August 23, 1904; George Albert Smith, diary, September 6, 1904, microfilm of holograph, Church History Library.
34. Keith A. Erekson, "American Prophet, New England Town: The Memory of Joseph Smith in Vermont" (master's thesis, Brigham Young University, 2002), 60.
35. A small cottage for a caretaker and guests was constructed on the site of the birthplace home and served to host visitors until 1959, when it was demolished to be replaced by a modern visitors' center dedicated in 1961. Gary L. Boatright Jr., "Historical Landscape of the Joseph Smith Birthplace Memorial," *Mormon Historical Studies* 11, no. 1 (Spring 2010): 101, 108.
36. Richard Neitzel Holzapfel and Paul H. Peterson, "New Photographs of Joseph F. Smith's Centennial Memorial Trip to Vermont, 1905," *BYU Studies* 39, no. 4 (2000): 107–14.
37. Edith Ann Smith, journal, December 26, 1905, holograph, Church History Library.

38. G. A. Smith, diary, March 28, 1907.
39. Alexander L. Baugh, "The Mormon Temple Site at Far West, Caldwell County, Missouri," in *The Missouri Mormon Experience*, ed. Thomas M. Spencer (Columbia: University of Missouri, 2010), 86.
40. Undated note on letter from J. D. Whitmer to Bishop Black, November 30, 1900, correspondence, Lorenzo Snow General Correspondence Files, 1898–1901, Church History Library.
41. Max H. Parkin, *Sacred Places*, vol. 4: *Missouri*, ed. LaMar C. Berrett (Salt Lake City: Deseret Book, 2004), 314.
42. Kim L. Loving, "Ownership of the Kirtland Temple: Legends, Lies, and Misunderstandings," *Journal of Mormon History* 30, no. 2 (Fall 2004): 45–71; Adams, *Upon the Temple Lot*, 26–31; Benjamin C. Pykles, *Excavating Nauvoo: The Mormons and the Rise of Historical Archaeology in America* (Lincoln: University of Nebraska, 2010), 23–25.
43. Mrs. M. J. Beaty to Joseph F. Smith, October 13, 1906, correspondence; John Bliss to Joseph F. Smith, June 16, 1906, correspondence; Charles E. Bidamon to Joseph F. Smith, May 26, 1909, correspondence, Joseph F. Smith General Correspondence. Bidamon offered Smith family furniture two years later, noting that he was in negotiation with the State of Iowa, which suggests he may have been hoping for a bidding war. Charles E. Bidamon to Joseph F. Smith, November 6, 1911, correspondence, Joseph F. Smith General Correspondence.
44. John R. Winder, "Joseph and Hyrum Memorial," in Conference Report, April 1904, 77.
45. Glen R. Stubbs, "A Biography of George Albert Smith, 1870 to 1951" (PhD diss., Brigham Young University, 1971), 250–55, 334–35, 338–91.
46. Kathleen Flake, *The Politics of American Religious Identity: The Seating of Senator Reed Smoot, Mormon Apostle* (Chapel Hill & London: University of North Carolina, 2004), 109–17.

Reid L. Neilson and Mitchell K. Schaefer

20

Excavating Early Mormon History:

The 1878 History Fact-Finding Mission of Apostles Joseph F. Smith and Orson Pratt

On October 7, 1878, Mormon Apostles Joseph F. Smith and Orson Pratt addressed their fellow Latter-day Saints during a general conference session of The Church of Jesus Christ of Latter-day Saints (hereafter referred to as the Church) in the Salt Lake Tabernacle. Elders Smith and Pratt reported on their recent Church history fact-finding mission to the Midwest and New England regions of the United States on behalf of the First Presidency. Elder Smith related to the packed congregation, "The chief object of their mission east, was to obtain, if possible, some dates and facts that pertained to the early history of the Church."[1] Both men shared their experiences meeting with early Mormon luminaries, who included William E. McLellin and David Whitmer, and visiting sacred sites while touring Missouri, Illinois, Ohio, and New York. Neither Elder Smith nor Elder Pratt, however, divulged many details during the general conference session about their month-long mission. Perhaps their reticence stemmed from their own initial evaluation of their journey. Elder Smith related to the gathered Latter-day Saints that he and Pratt had "found no one who could give them any information, or who knew as much as ourselves on these matters."[2] In hindsight, the Apostles'

Reid L. Neilson is the managing director of the Church History Department, The Church of Jesus Christ of Latter-day Saints, Salt Lake City. Mitchell K. Schaefer is a researcher for the Church History Department.

tentative self-deprecating assessment obscures the important contributions of their history-gathering mission, as described in this essay.

Joseph Fielding Smith (known as Joseph F. Smith to Latter-day Saints) was born on November 13, 1838, in Far West, Missouri, just weeks after his father, Hyrum Smith, and uncle Joseph Smith were taken as prisoners by the Missouri militia. "He commenced life in the midst of tribulation and dark persecution," one biographer described.[3] When he was just five years old, Joseph F.'s father and prophet-uncle were murdered by an anti-Mormon mob in Carthage, Illinois. A few years later Joseph F. trekked west to Utah with his mother, Mary Fielding Smith, while a large portion of his extended Smith family remained in the Midwest. These Smith family members eventually affiliated themselves with the RLDS Church, which was led by his first cousin Joseph Smith III. While living in Utah as a young man, Joseph F. served two missions to the Hawaiian Islands and afterward labored in the Church Historian's Office in downtown Salt Lake City with his cousin George A. Smith, who was then serving as an Apostle and Church Historian. In July 1866, President Brigham Young privately ordained Joseph F. to the apostleship, and during the April 1877 general conference he called him to preside over the European Mission. But the young Apostle returned from Great Britain that September when he learned of President Young's death.

John Taylor, Brigham Young's successor as President of the Church, called Joseph F. to join Elder Orson Pratt, then serving as Church Historian, on a history fact-finding mission to the cradles of the Restoration in the Midwest and New England. Orson Pratt, born in 1811, was Joseph F.'s senior by twenty-seven years. Parley P. Pratt baptized Orson, his younger brother, on September 19, 1830, just eighteen days after he himself was baptized by Oliver Cowdery. In December 1831, Orson moved to Hiram, Ohio, and was ordained a member of the Quorum of the Twelve Apostles in April 1835. He served various missions for the Church throughout his life. Orson even participated in the Camp of Israel (Zion's Camp) in 1834. In 1842, while living in Nauvoo, Illinois, he became disaffected from the Church and was excommunicated in August. But not much time passed before he was rebaptized in January 1843 and reinstated to the apostleship. In 1847 Orson migrated west to Utah, and in 1848 he presided over the LDS mission in Great Britain. In 1874 he succeeded George A. Smith as Church Historian.[4]

On Monday, September 2, 1878, LDS leaders John Taylor, Wilford Woodruff, George Q. Cannon, and Albert Carrington set apart Elders Smith and Pratt "to take a mission to the States, to gather up records and data relative to the early history of the Church."[5] Church leaders were seemingly interested in having these two Apostles, both working in the Church Historian's Office, view the original manuscripts of Latter-day scripture then in the hands of the former Latter-day Saints and their families who did not come to Utah. This was during the time that the Church was preparing new editions of the Doctrine and Covenants, Book of Mormon, and Pearl of Great Price. The following day the two Apostles departed by railroad from Salt Lake City on their fact-finding mission, joined by Mormon emigration agent William C. Staines, who accompanied them as far east as Kansas City, Missouri. Over the next four weeks, they would travel the breadth of the United States and tour early Mormon history sites in Missouri, Illinois, Ohio, and New York, with Elder Smith returning to Utah on September 28 and Elder Pratt on October 3.

Visiting Church History Sites in Missouri

Three days after leaving Salt Lake City by train, Elders Smith and Pratt arrived in Independence, Missouri. That Saturday morning, after washing and eating breakfast, the two Apostles walked to view the temple site, near where the Independence courthouse then stood.[6] Nearly five decades earlier, in July 1831, Elder Smith's uncle, the Prophet Joseph Smith, traveled to the frontier lands of Missouri and there dictated a revelation that designated the location for the future temple in the region: "Behold, the place which is now called Independence is the center place; and a spot for the temple is lying westward, upon a lot which is not far from the courthouse" (Doctrine and Covenants 57:3). Although the fledgling Latter-day Saints were eager to establish a Zion community, the local Missourians did not share the Saints' religious vision of communalism and overcoming individual poverty, so they became antagonistic toward the Mormon emigrants. In July 1833, just two years after the first Latter-day Saints arrived in the area, mobs destroyed the Mormon printing press and tarred and feathered the local leader, Bishop Edward Partridge. By November 12, 1833, armed mobs forced the Mormons to depart from Jackson County, Missouri. The Latter-day Saints and their leaders remained hopeful for decades that they would be able to return and build the prophesied Zion in Jackson County, but they were unable to gather in large numbers in Missouri until the mid-twentieth century.[7]

Accordingly, Latter-day Saints had viewed their experiences in Jackson County with sadness and frustration since the 1830s. As Elders Smith and Pratt looked upon the abandoned temple site that September, their perspective was a dreary one. "In 1831, or about 47 years ago, when Elder O[rson] Pratt visited the ground, it was covered with trees, but now there is not a tree nor even a stump standing, except on the portions surrounding the immediate Temple site, which are occupied by dwellings and orchards. The ground, at the time of our visit, was exceedingly dry and dusty, the season having been a very dry one," they later described to LDS leaders.[8] That afternoon the two Apostles met William Eaton, who lived on the Temple Lot with his family. As it turned out, Eaton's wife was the widow of John E. Page, a former Mormon Apostle and the man who had ordained Granville Hendrick as prophet of the Temple Lot church in July 1863. Eaton's wife remembered Pratt from their earlier Church association in Missouri. Although Mrs. Eaton treated the Utah Apostles "cordially," she struggled with "great difficulty to restrain the expression of her bitterness towards polygamy." Even though Elders Smith and Pratt were both practicing plural marriage at this time, their visit ended on a friendly note. After visiting the Eatons, the two men "plucked a few sprigs struggling for existence on the dry parched, dusty summit" on the Temple Lot and then offered "an earnest prayer that God would hasten his work in its time."[9]

Elders Smith and Pratt next visited William E. McLellin, an original member of the Quorum of the Twelve Apostles, who had served with Pratt. Born in Tennessee in the winter of 1806, McLellin initially received the message of the Restoration from Harvey Whitlock and David Whitmer in July 1831. It was on that occasion that McLellin first heard Whitmer's testimony of the Book of Mormon, including his account of a "Holy Angel [Moroni] who had made known the truth of [the Book of Mormon] record to him." Professing his early faith in Joseph Smith Jr. as God's prophet, McLellin wrote the following to his family in the summer of 1832: "I can truely [*sic*] say I believe him to be a man of God. A Prophet, a Seer and Revelater to the church of christ."[10] The Three Witnesses to the Book of Mormon—Oliver Cowdery, David Whitmer, and Martin Harris—ordained McLellin an Apostle in February 1835. Eventually, despite his apostolic calling, McLellin expressed distrust in Joseph Smith Jr. and other Mormon leaders. By May 1838, his testimony had faltered. During a Church disciplinary court called to discuss his transgressions, McLellin confessed that "he had no confidence in the heads of the Church" and claimed that he had learned, from some unstated source, that "they had transgressed," so he "went his own way, and indulged himself in his lustfull [*sic*] desires." Thereafter,

McLellin and the Church parted ways since he was apparently "cut off . . . for unbelief and aposta[s]y."[11]

Between 1838 and 1878, just before Elders Smith and Pratt arrived at his doorstep, McLellin had floated between several Mormon schismatic groups, eventually settling down in Independence, Missouri. During those four decades, he put his spiritual thoughts to paper and produced several doctrinal treatises and personal reflections on his religious experiences. In 1872 McLellin prepared a lengthy manuscript discussing his beliefs and disbeliefs in "Mormonism," including an unwavering affirmation of the truthfulness of the Book of Mormon and a pronounced ambivalence toward its translator, Joseph Smith Jr.[12] Elder Smith noted of their interview with McLellin that "while he claimed to hold to his faith in the Book of Mormon and its inspired translation by the Prophet Joseph, with the pertinacity of absolute knowledge, he denounced in toto, all the revelations in the Doctrine and Covenants and the idea of the restoration of the priesthood of Melchisedek or of . . . Aaron to man, but believes in the Apostleship, which he thinks comprises everything, although he had no faith in the ordination of the first Twelve." Smith observed of McLellin, "With one breath he would extol and reverence the memory of the prophet and with the next fling at him some slanderous accusation in the most spiteful manner, as if mentally writhing under some real or fancied wrongs."[13] Though McLellin's ideologies likely seem awkward to historians and some of the Mormon faithful, at times he was not alone. Some of his theories resemble those of David Whitmer, with whom McLellin remained in close contact for most of the latter portion of his life.

During the course of their interview with McLellin, Elders Smith and Pratt came to learn a number of McLellin's spiritual feelings and religious beliefs. The three men also discussed a variety of issues, including Emma Smith's knowledge of her husband Joseph's practice of plural marriage during the Nauvoo period. According to McLellin, "Emma Smith told him that Joseph was both a polygamist and an adulterer and what was most strange to him [was] that she should joine [*sic*] in with her Son Joseph in his theory of Religion which holds up the Prophet as the founder of their faith."[14] Interestingly, Emma publicly denied her husband's involvement in plural marriage following his assassination in June 1844, instead blaming the alternative marriage system on Brigham Young, her husband's prophetic successor. McLellin also shared his doubts about the revelation concerning the Canadian Book of Mormon copyright. "Joseph had given a false revelation in

1829, ordering O[liver] Cowdery to go to Canada and get out the copy right of the Book of Mormon, and after wards acknowledge it was false," McLellin complained.[15] After the interview with McLellin came to an end, "it was with unmistakable regret" that he parted from Elders Smith and Pratt at the railroad station as they boarded the train bound for Richmond, Missouri.[16]

The two Mormon Apostles arrived in Richmond late in the evening of Friday, September 6.[17] Richmond was settled in 1827 as the seat of Clay County, Missouri. For a time it became a center of Mormon population growth and religious freedom. But when the Missouri militia captured Joseph Smith Jr. and other Mormon leaders in October 1838, General John B. Clark incarcerated them for a time in the Richmond Jail. After a good night's rest, Elders Smith and Pratt surveyed the damage that a tornado had inflicted upon Richmond earlier that May. A local newspaper reported that "the havoc and desolation which then ensued are beyond our abilities to describe. Not a house is left to mark that once beautiful portion of the town. . . . Nor is there a single foundation that was not swept away."[18] Accordingly, Elder Smith dedicated nearly six pages of his journal to describe the wreckage that he and Pratt witnessed.

After observing the tornado destruction, the Utah Mormon representatives sought out David Whitmer, who "seemed somewhat surprised and delighted at seeing his old acquaintance Orson Pratt."[19] Whitmer was born in January 1805 near Harrisburg, Pennsylvania. In his early childhood, his family moved to Ontario County, New York, where his family encountered the Restoration. Whitmer and his family learned of the Book of Mormon and Joseph Smith Jr. through a mutual acquaintance, Oliver Cowdery. During the translation process of the golden plates, Smith and Cowdery invited Whitmer to come to Harmony, Pennsylvania, to pick them up and take them to the Whitmer farm so they could finish the translation. Whitmer and his family believed in Joseph Smith's message and prophetic gifts, and they were baptized in early 1829. Whitmer then became one of the Three Witnesses of the Book of Mormon and eventually held a number of important Church callings, including being named as the president of the fledgling church in Missouri in 1834. Four years later, Church leaders excommunicated Whitmer and his brother John, along with a number of other Missouri Church leaders, for apostasy. Owing to threats by the Mormon paramilitary organization known as the Danites, the Whitmer families and a number of other former Latter-day Saints moved to Richmond, where many of them remained for the rest of their lives. Not surprisingly, they had little desire to migrate west with Brigham Young's Mormon movement, and they harbored great animosity toward their Utah brothers and sisters.[20]

David Whitmer was willing to meet with the Utah Apostles, but he required that a friend remain near his side so that their ensuing conversation could be verified later. At one point, Whitmer turned to his colleague for advice on how to answer a particular question, indicating that distrust still ran high between the two Mormon groups. Although Elders Smith and Pratt felt uncomfortable not being able to meet with Whitmer in private, there was nothing they could do about the arrangement. So they began asking a series of questions about the foundational events of the Restoration, including Whitmer's role in what had transpired in those early days. During their interviews, Whitmer reaffirmed his earlier testimony of the coming forth of the Book of Mormon, including the reality of the physical plates. "I heard the voice of the Lord as distinctly as I ever heard anything in my life, declaring that they were translated by the gift and power of God," Whitmer declared. He also claimed to possess the *original* manuscript of the Book of Mormon translation, and he allowed the Apostles to view his copy. But they would not be taking it back to Utah with them, as they hoped. When Elder Pratt tried to buy the manuscript on behalf of the Utah church, Whitmer rebuffed him, "No, Oliver [Cowdery] charged me to keep it and Joseph [Smith] said my Father's house should keep the records. . . . I consider these things sacred and would not barter them for money." Smith was likewise disappointed, noting in his journal: "What we most desired we have failed for the present to accomplish, to obtain the M.S.S. [manuscript] of the Book of Mormon and I must say I regret it."[21]

David Whitmer, however, was mistaken about which version of the Book of Mormon manuscript he had. He actually possessed the *printer's*—not the *original*—copy of the golden plates translation.[22] After establishing the terms of publication for the Book of Mormon with printer Egbert B. Grandin in Palmyra, New York, Joseph Smith Jr. instructed Oliver Cowdery to prepare a backup, or *printer's*, copy, lest the *original* manuscript be lost or stolen, as was the case with the 116 pages. Whitmer was clearly unaware of the existence of the primary transcription. Unbeknownst to Whitmer, Joseph Smith had deposited the *original* Book of Mormon manuscript in the cornerstone of the Nauvoo House in October 1841. Lewis Bidamon, the widower of the late Emma Hale Smith, would not open the cornerstone and reveal the water-damaged manuscript until 1882, four years after this visit.[23] But Elder Smith was aware of the existence of the *printer's* copy: "Before the [Book of Mormon manuscript] was sent to the printers an exact copy was made and it is my belief that this [Whitmer's manuscript] is that copy and not the original or if it is the original then there is another copy." The Utah Apostle evinced some uncertainty when he wrote in his journal, "There is another copy, or was, and with that no doubt are the actual signatures of the eleven witnesses to their respective testimonies."[24]

Elder Smith's and Pratt's two-day visit with David Whitmer in Richmond came to a close on friendly terms. "There he stands," Smith wrote of Whitmer, "the one lone monument of the first myraculous [*sic*] manifestations of over 49 years ago at the rise of this church." Between interviews, the two men were led by some of Whitmer's associates to the location where the Richmond Jail once stood. "It was there," Smith noted, that Parley P. Pratt and other Church leaders "were so long and cruelly confined on account of their religion" while they waited for Judge Austin King's decision whether there was sufficient evidence to try the Prophet and his companions for treason. After several weeks in November 1838, the leaders were transferred to Liberty Jail in Clay County, where they arrived in early December. Before parting with his longtime friend, Whitmer told Elder Pratt, "I may never meet you again (in the flesh) so farewell."[25]

The following morning, Monday, September 9, Elders Smith and Pratt awoke, ate breakfast, paid the hotel bill, and began their travels to Far West, Missouri.[26] Decades earlier, Church members William W. Phelps and John Whitmer purchased portions of what became Far West in 1836, as a location for the Latter-day Saints to gather and settle within the newly created Caldwell County. But Church leaders were unable to make Far West their headquarters for very long. In late October 1838, Missouri governor Lilburn W. Boggs signed an "extermination order" ordering the removal of all Mormons from the state of Missouri. On October 31, a Missouri militia group, under the command of General Samuel Lucas, arrested Joseph and Hyrum Smith, along with a number of other Mormon leaders, and incarcerated them in the Richmond Jail, as noted above. Within weeks, Missouri militia members and mobs drove the Latter-day Saints from the state of Missouri altogether. Joseph F. Smith was born during the Missouri Mormon War on November 13, 1838. "In the midst of tribulation, sorrow and distress, when the dark clouds of persecution hung low over the members of the Church with a pall of menacing hate of overwhelming proportions," his son Joseph Fielding Smith wrote, "there was born in the village of Far West, Caldwell County, Missouri, a man-child." His birth occurred while his father, Hyrum, was incarcerated in Richmond.[27] Since being driven out of Missouri as an infant, Elder Smith had never returned to his birthplace in Far West.

Fresh from their pleasant visit with David Whitmer in Richmond, Elders Smith and Pratt arrived in Far West and called upon Jacob Whitmer and Sarah Johnson, two adult children of the late John Whitmer (David's brother), who was one of the Eight Witnesses of the Book of Mormon plates and the second Church Historian. Elder Smith asked if Whitmer and Johnson would host him and Elder Pratt for an evening, to which they consented until they learned that the two visitors officially represented the Utah-based Church. Taken aback by their sudden coldness, Elder Smith still asked them if they might show him and Elder Pratt around town, in hopes of discovering his 1838 birthplace. But the Whitmer children again denied his request. As their conversation continued to deteriorate, Elder Pratt asked to see and purchase their father's manuscript history, which Joseph Smith Jr. commanded John Whitmer to keep in March 1831 (Doctrine and Covenants 47). "We have got no history here, all Father's papers have gone to Richmond long ago," Jacob Whitmer replied. Elders Smith and Pratt were unaware that, when John Whitmer passed away earlier that July, his papers were given to his brother David, while his children inherited his Far West home. Elder Pratt responded that he and Elder Smith had just enjoyed two days of interviews and conversations with their uncle David but that he had "said nothing about having any other papers" but the Book of Mormon manuscript. "We've got no papers here," Jacob Whitmer countered, ending the meeting. "At this point we concluded it was no use to try any further, the Spirit of the man was most contemp[t]ible and low, neither trying to Show us common courtecy [*sic*] or to conceal his disrespect and bigotry," Elder Smith noted.[28]

Rejected, Elders Smith and Pratt bid John Whitmer's children good-bye and made their way to the abandoned Mormon temple site in Far West. "I stood on the S[outh] E[ast] Cor[ner] Stone where Geo[rge] A. Smith and W[ilford] Woodruff were ordained Apostles 39 years ago," Elder Smith related. Decades before, on July 8, 1838, Joseph Smith Jr. had dictated a revelation calling members of the Quorum of the Twelve Apostles to evangelize in Great Britain. That same commandment directed the Apostles to leave for their European mission "on the twenty-sixth day of April next [1839],"[29] starting from the Far West Temple site. The revelation also called four men to fill vacancies in the Quorum of the Twelve (see Doctrine and Covenants 118:4–6). Recall that in October 1838 the Latter-day Saints were forced from Missouri to neighboring Illinois. For the Apostles, fulfilling the revelation and commencing their overseas missions from Far West in 1839 seemed difficult at best. Nevertheless, these men returned to the specified temple site on April 26 as directed and ordained Wilford Woodruff and George A. Smith to the apostleship that evening.[30] After surveying the four cornerstones, the Elders Smith and Pratt continued their journey to Cameron, Missouri, where they planned to board a train headed to Plano, Illinois. They slept that evening at the Western House, eager to meet with Smith family members the following day.

Visiting Smith Family Members in Illinois

The Mormon Apostles next traveled from Cameron, Missouri, to the homes of Smith family members in Illinois. On Wednesday, September 11, they passed through Cholchester, Illinois, where they visited Joseph F. Smith's paternal aunt and uncle, Lucy and Arthur Millikin. Lucy was the youngest sister of Hyrum and Joseph Smith Jr. Excited by their nephew's arrival from faraway Utah, they gathered their children and enjoyed "quite a family gathering." This spontaneous Smith family reunion brought great pleasure to Elder Smith, since most of his extended family had remained in the Midwest when he and his family crossed the plains in 1848 as part of the great Mormon westward migration. The extended Smith relatives happily discussed "family matters" for several hours until the two Utahns had to catch a train to Plano, Illinois.[31]

When the two Mormon Apostles arrived in Plano, they paid a visit to the home of Joseph Smith III, president of the Reorganized Church of Jesus Christ of Latter Day Saints and Joseph F. Smith's first cousin. They were disappointed, however, to learn that President Smith was away attending the semiannual RLDS conference in Galland's Grove, Iowa.[32] Years earlier, on April 6, 1860, Joseph Smith III and his mother, Emma Hale Smith Bidamon, met with other Mormons who had remained in the Midwest rather than follow Brigham Young to Utah after Joseph Smith Jr.'s death. On this occasion he accepted the leadership of what became the RLDS Church. But Joseph III made it clear he would not take the role of prophet-president "to amass wealth out of it," nor did he plan to accept the Mormon practice of plural marriage. "There is but one principle taught by the leaders of any faction of this people that I hold in utter abhorrence; that is a principle taught by

Brigham Young and those believing in him," he declared. "I have been told that my father taught such doctrines. I have never believed it and never can believe it. If such things were done, then I believe they never were done by divine authority."[33] Joseph III would lead the RLDS Church until his death in December 1914.

On Thursday, September 12, Elders Smith and Pratt again called on President Smith's family and met with his wife, Bertha, and their children.[34] The Mormon Apostles then made their way to the Herald Office, where RLDS editors prepared the *True Latter Day Saints' Herald,* their church's official periodical. There they met with John Scott, Mr. Cooper, and Harvey Dillie and discussed the extant manuscript of Joseph Smith Jr.'s New Translation of the Bible, or the Joseph Smith Translation (JST) as LDS Church membership would come to call it. Beginning in 1831, Joseph Smith Jr. began his inspired revisions of the Old and New Testaments. He considered this undertaking a "branch" of his prophetic calling. Although the Mormon founder did seemingly complete his corrections to the biblical texts, he was murdered before its publication. His New Translation manuscripts, together with his marked-up Phinney Bible, remained in the possession of his widow Emma.[35]

Two decades later, Emma granted an RLDS scripture committee access to both the manuscripts and Bible as they prepared an edition of the translation at the request of her son, Joseph Smith III. It was published as the Inspired Version (IV) in 1867. A year later, President Joseph Smith III sent a copy of this scriptural edition to Elder Orson Pratt in Utah.[36] His gift, on behalf of the RLDS Church, would have an impact on LDS scripture. In 1878 Orson Pratt was preparing the first American edition of Elder Franklin D. Richards's British edition of the Pearl of Great Price (1851), a selected compilation of Joseph Smith Jr.'s dictated revelations and translated ancient texts, for publication in Salt Lake City.[37] It is important to note that Elder Pratt based the biblical texts of his American edition on his gifted copy of the 1867 RLDS Inspired Version and not on Elder Richards's 1851 LDS text.[38]

Elders Smith and Pratt were understandably eager to see the original manuscripts and the Phinney Bible while visiting Plano, so they sent the still-absent President Smith a telegram of explanation: "Jos[eph] F. Smith and Orson Pratt here, wish to examine M.S.S. [manuscript] new translation, when can you return, is M.S.S. here[?] answer."[39] President Smith promptly sent a telegram in response, but it was delayed.[40] Disappointed that a response was not forthcoming, Elders

Smith and Pratt purchased a few RLDS missionary tracts and departed from the Herald House. They returned a few hours later but were again disheartened to learn that no telegram had arrived from President Smith.

That same afternoon, Mr. Cooper invited the Mormon Apostles to attend an RLDS prayer meeting that evening. Both men were uncomfortable but finally accepted the offer. When they arrived at the meeting, the presiding RLDS leader, Harvey Dille, asked them to address the congregation. Elder Smith hesitated, but Elder Pratt took the podium and discoursed on the doctrine and history of plural marriage, the most contested difference between the two Mormon factions and a huge concern for the United States government. Elder Pratt testified that "Joseph Smith the Prophet revealed the principle of plural marriage and practiced it before B[righam] Young . . . and gave facts in proof." He also related an experience that Lyman Johnson, a former member of the Quorum of the Twelve Apostles, had related to him when they served together as Apostles. "Joseph [Smith] had told [Lyman Johnson] that God had revealed to him that plural marriage was a divine and correct principle and would be again practiced but the time had not yet come. This was as early as 1832 or 1831." Elder Smith then made a few remarks of his own. He reported that by the end of the meeting, the entire RLDS congregation was discussing plural marriage, a doctrine that Joseph Smith III claimed his father never implemented. He also recorded that several members in attendance acknowledged that they were aware that Joseph Smith Jr. actually had practiced plural marriage. Others allegedly contended that "the polygamy revelation [Doctrine and Covenants 132] and the Book of Mormon could not both be true." Still others expressed ignorance on the subject and wished not to discuss it further.[41]

Visiting Church History Sites in Ohio and New York

By Friday, September 13, Elders Smith and Pratt had yet to hear from President Smith, so they traveled by train through Chicago and Cleveland en route to Kirtland, Ohio.[42] In September 1830, while living in upstate New York, Joseph Smith Jr. had dictated a revelation to Oliver Cowdery that called him on a mission "unto the Lamanites" and commanded him to "preach my gospel unto them" (Doctrine and Covenants 28:8). Interpreting "Lamanites" to mean the American Indians then living on the western frontier of the United States, Cowdery and three missionary companions set off to share the Restoration message with the natives that October. Cowdery and Parley P. Pratt stopped in Mentor, Ohio, on

October 29, 1830, and gave a Book of Mormon to Sidney Rigdon. Before leaving the area weeks later, the Mormon elders had baptized over thirty individuals in and around Mentor and Kirtland. That December, Joseph Smith Jr. received a revelation directing the Church to "assemble together at the Ohio" (Doctrine and Covenants 37:3). From February 1831, when the Prophet arrived in Kirtland, to January 1838, when dissenters forced him from town, Kirtland served as one of the headquarters of the Church; a second headquarters was in Missouri. During the Kirtland period, Joseph Smith Jr. received thirty-seven revelations—more than he received in any other locale during his life—that were later canonized in the Doctrine and Covenants. Many of those revelations served as key doctrinal and theological guides for the growing church. Additionally, it was in Kirtland that early Mormons built their first temple.

On September 14, 1878, Elders Smith and Pratt arrived in Kirtland and immediately made their way to the landmark Kirtland Temple. Elder Smith devoted five pages of his journal to a description of the sacred edifice. He made a careful comparison to its earlier state in the 1830s, obviously relying on the memory of his traveling companion, since he was not born until 1838, months after the Latter-day Saints had abandoned Kirtland as their Church headquarters. While touring the "House of the Lord," Elders Smith and Pratt met former Latter-day Saint James McDowell, who shared his opinion that "Hyrum Smith was a good man," expressed regret that the early Church had splintered following the Martyrdom, and lamented that the various Mormon factions could not come to a unity of the faith. The two Apostles also encountered Electra Stratton, an elderly woman who had joined the Church when Joseph and Hyrum Smith lived in Kirtland but who remained in the area while the majority of the Latter-day Saints moved to the West. She noted that the tone of Joseph F. Smith's voice matched his father's but that he looked more like his mother, Mary Fielding. Following their temple experience, Elders Smith and Pratt visited a number of other Mormon historical sites in Kirtland, including the store of Newel K. Whitney and A. Sidney Gilbert. They then traveled on to Painesville, Ohio, where they purchased rail tickets to Buffalo, New York.[43]

The two Apostles arrived in Buffalo and noted that it seemed to be a center of spiritual activity. "I judge this must be a religious place by the [number] of church goers," Elder Smith recorded in his journal. Before leaving Buffalo en route to Rochester and Palmyra, New York, he sent a telegram home to Utah and another to William Staines, who had accompanied them on the first leg of their trip to Kansas City, Missouri, notifying him that they would "be in New York city Tuesday or Wednesday." The two men passed through Rochester and finally arrived in Palmyra on the evening of September 15. Palmyra is recognized as the birthplace of the Mormon faith. It was here that Joseph Smith Sr. and Lucy Mack Smith settled with their children in 1816 after a few years of crop failure in Vermont and New England. When their son Joseph Jr. discussed a "war of words and tumult of opinions" in his 1838 history, he was referring to the conditions of the religious excitement in Palmyra and other nearby villages and townships. It was on his father's farm a mile or so south of Palmyra that Joseph experienced his first theophany in the spring of 1820. Just a few miles farther south lay the hill that Latter-day Saints today commonly call Cumorah. Elders Smith and Pratt were highly aware of such history, and they were not about to let the opportunity of seeing these sites go to waste.

Of the churches in this area, Elder Smith's uncle Joseph wrote: "There was in the place where we lived an unusual excitement on the subject of religion. It commenced with the Methodists, but soon became general among all the sects in that region of country. Indeed, the whole district of country seemed affected by it, and great multitudes united themselves to the different religious parties, which created no small stir and division amongst the people" (Joseph Smith—History 1:5). Elder Smith described in his journal a visit he and Elder Pratt made to this area: "The point where the Cananda[i]gua Road crosses the main street at right angles, the main street running east & west, are 4 protestant churches at each corner. On the South west corner the Baptists, on the north west the Methodists, on the north east the Presbyterians, and on the South east the Episcopalians. Just north of these is the Catholic Church."[44]

The following day (September 16), Elders Smith and Pratt made their way to the south end of the Hill Cumorah, which was then owned by a man named Parker, and which still had many trees. It was on this hill that Joseph Smith Jr. met once a year for four years with the angel Moroni, and received the plates from which he translated the Book of Mormon in 1827. Elder Smith commented on the physical condition of the hill, including a mention of the lack of trees, since previous owners had cleared the hillside for agricultural use. Near the southern end, where the hill flattens and widens a bit, the two Apostles knelt down in prayer. Elder Pratt prayed "long and fervently for all Israel and for all the interests of Zion for the hastening of the time when the records now concealed in this hill shall come forth." Elder

Smith followed, offering his solemn prayer by "thanking, praising and beseeching God." Elder Pratt next laid his hands on Elder Smith and blessed him, "pronouncing many provisions and asking for great gifts to rest upon me." In return, Elder Smith pronounced a blessing on Elder Pratt and "blessed him the Spirit of the Lord giving me utterance." The two men then continued to explore the hill and took a few sticks as keepsakes for the experience. They also "spent several hours meditating and praising God," and Elder Smith recorded that his "heart was filled even to tears, and [he] rejoiced." Such an experience must have been enlightening, and it seemed to spiritually strengthen the two Apostles.[45]

Return to Utah via Illinois

On Tuesday morning, September 17, after "another sleepless night" for Elder Smith, the two Apostles awoke and departed for New York City. While in the city, they decided to spend some time on their own attending to personal business. That Wednesday, however, they drafted their report of their fact-finding mission to the Quorum of the Twelve Apostles. The report was subsequently published in the *Deseret News* in Utah and was reprinted in the *Millennial Star* in England.[46] At this point, Mormon emigration agent William Staines purchased railroad tickets for Elder Smith's return to Utah, since Elder Pratt chose to remain in New York City a few days longer. "This makes me a free pass clear home, for which I am very thankful," Elder Smith noted.[47] On Friday, September 20, Elder Smith sent a final telegram to President Joseph Smith III in Illinois: "Start home tomorrow evening, can I see manuscripts? Answer. Stevens House N.Y." The next day, Elder Smith received the following reply from his RLDS cousin: "Cannot tell till I see you," to which he vented in his journal, "This leaves me where I was before." Unsure if a return trip to the RLDS headquarters warranted his effort, Smith consulted with his LDS brethren, who encouraged him to shoulder the risk in hopes of seeing the manuscript of Joseph Smith Jr.'s New Translation of the Bible. After much vacillation, Smith finally agreed with Staines and made preparations to return to Plano: "I feel as tho[ugh] it was my duty as Pres. [John] Taylor seemed particularly anxious about this matter."[48]

Three days later, on Tuesday, September 24, Elder Smith arrived in Plano to finally visit with President Smith face-to-face. After breakfast and conversation with Smith family members, the two cousins made their way to President Smith's office, where Elder Smith eagerly asked to see the JST manuscripts, which he assumed were housed in Plano. President Smith informed him, however, that the manuscripts had been returned to the care of his mother, Emma Hale Smith Bidamon, but that during her recent illness they had been entrusted to her other son, Alexander Smith, who was then living in Nauvoo. Anticipating Elder Smith's return visit, President Smith had written a letter to his brother Alexander asking that the manuscripts be brought to Plano, but Alexander did not want to ship their father's translation papers until they were certain that Elder Smith would be coming back. So by the time Elder Smith was passing through Plano for the second time, the papers had not yet arrived. Moreover, it is unclear if Elder Smith would have been permitted to see the manuscript even if the papers were in Plano.[49]

President Smith informed Elder Smith that he required a signed written request from the President of the LDS Church, John Taylor, before he would let any Latter-day Saint, including members of the Quorum of the Twelve Apostles, view the JST papers. "The manuscripts can be seen whenever a duly authorized commission possessing proper credentials shall come and sit down with a commission duly appointed by the Reorganized church to examine [the materials] and not till then," a dejected Elder Smith noted. There was seemingly more at stake than he was aware. His cousin was worried about the image of the RLDS Church, over which he presided. "We are perfectly willing," President Smith clarified, according to Elder Smith, that "the [manuscript] and the bible should be compared, but the decision will be for or against us, and our credit is involved in the matter."[50]

Recall that the RLDS Church published the Inspired Version of the Bible in 1867. President Smith and his fellow leaders were concerned that an LDS representative, if left alone with the original manuscripts, might attempt to discredit the RLDS publication committee's work and thereby discredit the RLDS Church in general. By requesting "duly authorized" representatives from both Mormon churches to be present to view the manuscripts, President Smith was safeguarding the reputation and image of his faith and followers. Pressed for time, Elder Smith felt this arrangement was unnecessary and should be sidestepped. This proved to be a moot point, however, since the manuscripts were still not in Plano and Elder Smith needed to continue his return trip to Utah. President Smith gave Elder Smith a copy of the Inspired Version of the Bible as a parting gift.[51]

Conclusion

Rebuffed by his RLDS cousin in his attempt to see the JST, Elder Smith left Plano, Illinois, and on September 24 traveled to Chicago, where he made preparations to return to Utah by railcar. He finally arrived in Salt Lake City on Saturday, September 28. Two days later he met alone with President John Taylor and shared the report that he and Elder Pratt had drafted while in New York City.[52] Elder Pratt did not return to Utah until October 3.[53] The following week, Elders Smith and Pratt reported on their fact-finding mission to the membership of the Church during October general conference in the Tabernacle on Temple Square.

While speaking at the Tabernacle, Elder Smith said he "was well satisfied that the [Inspired Version] so published [by the RLDS Church] is only a partial translation by the Prophet, and merely contains the translation of King James, with some changes in the first chapter of Genesis and the 24th chapter of Matthew, which had been published by this Church, in the Pearl of Great Price, many years ago."[54] He made no mention according to the report published in the *Deseret News*, which stated that the Inspired Version's Matthew 24 differed from the version published in the Pearl of Great Price in 1851. This may have been an attempt on Elder Smith's part to downplay the importance of the Inspired Version. By stating this, Elder Smith may have also been trying to make the point that the Pearl of Great Price was all that would be needed in order to understand Joseph Smith's translation of the Bible.

All in all, Elders Smith's and Pratt's month-long journey to the East enriched the historical record because of the Elders' efforts to interview multiple individuals and learn more about extant manuscripts containing historical information about the Church. The personal and corporate records they kept about this trip have become an important source in sorting out some of the evidences and episodes of early Mormon history. Elder Pratt, an adult member of the LDS Church since 1831, knew much of this history. The journey was more formative for Elder Smith's historical consciousness, however. Smith eventually served as Church President and was a driving force behind the beginnings of the Church's historical sites program, including initiating and overseeing the construction of the 1905 monument at the birthplace of Joseph Smith Jr. in Sharon, Vermont.

Notes

1. Joseph F. Smith, "Semi-Annual Conference," *Deseret News*, October 9, 1878, 572. Their conference report was reprinted in the *Latter-day Saints' Millennial Star*, October 28, 1878, 676–77.
2. Smith, "Semi-Annual Conference," 572.
3. Joseph Fielding Smith, *Life of Joseph F. Smith: Sixth President of The Church of Jesus Christ of Latter-day Saints* (Salt Lake City: Deseret News Press, 1938), 3.
4. See Breck England, *The Life and Thought of Orson Pratt* (Salt Lake City: University of Utah, 1985).
5. Joseph F. Smith, journal, September 2, 1878, Church History Library, The Church of Jesus Christ of Latter-day Saints, Salt Lake City.
6. Smith, journal, September 6, 1878.
7. For a history of the Temple Lot, see R. Jean Addams, "The Church of Christ (Temple Lot) and the Reorganized Church of Jesus Christ of Latter Day Saints: 130 Years of Crossroads and Controversies," *Journal of Mormon History* 36, no. 2 (2010): 54–127.
8. "Report of Elders Orson Pratt and Joseph F. Smith," *Deseret News*, November 27, 1878, 674. Elders Pratt and Smith wrote this report in New York City on September 17, 1878, prior to their return to Salt Lake City.
9. Smith, journal, September 6, 1878.
10. Jan Shipps and John W. Welch, eds., *The Journals of William E. McLellin, 1831–1836* (Provo, UT: BYU Studies, Brigham Young University; Urbana and Chicago and University of Illinois Press, 1994), 29, 82; original spelling and capitalization preserved throughout this paper.
11. Dean C. Jessee, Mark Ashurst-McGee, and Richard Jensen, eds., *Journals, Volume 1: 1832–1839*, vol. 1 of the Journals series of *The Joseph Smith Papers*, ed. Dean C. Jessee, Ronald K. Esplin, and Richard Lyman Bushman (Salt Lake City: Church Historian's Press, 2008), 268; spelling in original. "History of William E. McLellin," *Deseret News*, May 12, 1858, 49.
12. Mitchell Schaefer, ed., *William E. McLellin's Lost Manuscript* (Salt Lake City: Eborn Books, 2012). See also Mitchell Schaefer, "'The Testimony of Men': William E. McLellin and the Book of Mormon Witnesses," *BYU Studies* 50, no. 1 (2011): 101. Accounts from people like McLellin who were present in early Church history, some of whom even witnessed the miraculous events that now stand as spiritual pillars to adherents of the Church, add color and variety to the historical record.
13. "Report of Elders," 674.
14. Smith, journal, September 6, 1878.
15. Smith, journal, September 6, 1878; spelling in original. For a more complete explanation of the Canadian Book of Mormon copyright, see Stephen Ehat, "'Securing' the Prophet's Copyright in the Book of Mormon: Historical and Legal Context for the So-Called Canadian Copyright Revelation," *BYU Studies* 50, no. 2 (2011): 5–70.
16. "Report of Elders," 674.
17. Smith, journal, September 6, 1878.
18. "The Town of Richmond, Mo., visited by a Tornado," *Phelps County New Era*, June 8, 1878.
19. Smith, journal, September 7, 1878.
20. See Erin B. Jennings, "Whitmer Family Beliefs and Their Church of Christ," in *Scattering of the Saints: Schism within Mormonism*, ed. Newell G. Bringhurst and John C. Hamer (Independence, MO: John Whitmer Books, 2007), 25–45.

21. Smith, journal, September 7, 1878. For descriptions and transcripts of the Smith-Pratt-Whitmer interview, see Lyndon W. Cook, ed., *David Whitmer Interviews: A Restoration Witness* (Orem, UT: Grandin Book, 1991); and "Report of Elders Orson Pratt and Joseph F. Smith," *Deseret News*, November 27, 1878, 674. Pratt seemingly did not keep a journal during the 1878 mission, but he did draft an account of the interview in a letter to his wife. See Orson Pratt to Marian Pratt, September 18, 1878, correspondence, Church History Library, The Church of Jesus Christ of Latter-day Saints, Salt Lake City.
22. Smith, journal, September 7, 1878. David Whitmer later gave the printer's manuscript to his grandson George W. Schweich, who sold it to the RLDS Church (Community of Christ since 2001) in 1903. Today it is housed in the Community of Christ Archives in Independence, Missouri. See Royal Skousen, ed., *The Printer's Manuscript of the Book of Mormon* (Provo, UT: FARMS at Brigham Young University, 2001), 4.
23. "Relics of the Old Nauvoo House," *Deseret News*, October 4, 1882, 577. Lewis Bidamon gifted portions of the original manuscript to visitors, and today most, if not all, of the extant document is housed at the LDS Church History Library in Salt Lake City, Utah. See Dean C. Jessee, "The Original Book of Mormon Manuscript," *BYU Studies* 10, no. 3 (1970): 1–15.
24. Smith, journal, September 8, 1878.
25. Smith, journal, September 8, 1878.
26. Smith, journal, September 9, 1878.
27. Smith, *Life of Joseph F. Smith*, 117.
28. Smith, journal, September 9, 1878. See also Scott C. Esplin, "'A History of All the Important Things' (D&C 69:3): John Whitmer's Record of Church History," in *Preserving the History of the Latter-day Saints*, ed. Richard E. Turley Jr. and Steven C. Harper (Provo, UT: Religious Studies Center, Brigham Young University, 2010), 57.
29. Smith, journal, September 9, 1878.
30. The Apostles' courage remained a staple in the Mormon lore, making it understandable that Elders Smith and Pratt were eager to see the site.
31. Smith, journal, September 11, 1878.
32. Smith, journal, September 11, 1878; see also "General Conference Minutes," *Saints' Herald*, October 1, 1878, 289.
33. Joseph Smith III, *The Memoirs of President Joseph Smith III (1832–1914)*, ed. Richard Howard (Independence, MO: Herald Publishing House, 1979), 463.
34. Smith, journal, September 12, 1878.
35. See Robert J. Matthews, "Joseph Smith's Efforts to Publish His Bible 'Translation,'" *Ensign*, January 1983, 57–64.
36. Joseph Smith III traveled through Salt Lake City after Elder Orson Pratt's death and held a brief interview with Sarah Pratt, Orson's first wife and then widow. According to his recollection of the event, during the interview he asked Mrs. Pratt "if she remembered her husband's having received a copy of the *New Inspired Translation* of the Scriptures." She replied in the affirmative and said that when Orson finally had an opportunity to sit down and read through the book "he laid the book aside with a sigh, and said: 'Sarah, these men have done their work honestly! This translation is just as it was left by the Prophet Joseph in 1833. I could quickly have detected it had they tampered with or altered what he wrote. I am delighted with it, and I thank God that I have received this copy!'" Smith III, *Memoirs of President Joseph Smith III*, 32–33.

37. His resulting 1878 version was canonized as LDS Church scripture in October 1880.
38. Robert J. Matthews, *"A Plainer Translation:" Joseph Smith's Translation of the Bible: A History and Commentary* (Provo, UT: Brigham Young University Press, 1975), 225–29; Kent P. Jackson, *The Book of Moses and the Joseph Smith Translation Manuscripts* (Provo, UT: Religious Studies Center, Brigham Young University, 2005), 21, 34.
39. Smith, journal, September 12, 1878.
40. Shortly thereafter, he wrote his cousin Joseph F. Smith, who was now in New York City, a note of explanation: "I received the telegram sent me apprising me of your visit to Plano, and sent a reply to the Telegram Office; but through the thoughtlessness of the messenger it was delayed too long, and so failed to reach you. . . . I left Conference ground as soon as feasible and reached home Tuesday at 2.15 P.M; and expect to remain at home for some time. Any communication you may wish to make will receive consideration." Joseph Smith III to Joseph F. Smith, September 19, 1878, correspondence, Joseph F. Smith Papers, Salt Lake City, Church History Library.
41. Smith, journal, September 12, 1878.
42. Smith, journal, September 13–14, 1878.
43. Smith, journal, September 14, 1878.
44. Smith, journal, September 15, 1878. It is possible that Elder Smith was mistaken about the location of two of the churches. Today the Western Presbyterian Church sits on the northwest corner of the intersection, and the First Methodist Church resides on the northeast corner. Otherwise, according to his account, the congregations mentioned by Elder Smith still own edifices dedicated to regular worship services in those respective locations today. But it is important to note that none of these churches were there at the time of Joseph Smith's First Vision in 1820.
45. Smith, journal, September 16, 1878.
46. "Report of Elders," 674–75; and December 4, 1878, 690; "Report of Elders Orson Pratt and Joseph F. Smith," *Latter-day Saints' Millennial Star*, December 9, 1878, 769–74, and December 16, 1878, 785–89.
47. Smith, journal, September 18, 1878.
48. Smith, journal, September 21, 1878.
49. Smith, journal, September 24, 1878.
50. Smith, journal, September 24, 1878.
51. Smith, journal, September 24, 1878.
52. Smith, journal, September 30, 1878.
53. Smith, journal, October 3, 1878.
54. Smith, "Semi-Annual Conference," 572.

Brett D. Dowdle and Casey Paul Griffiths

21

"A Godsend for the Salvation of Modern Israel":

The Creation of the Seminary Program

One constant throughout the history of the Restoration is the Lord's concern for the spiritual welfare of the younger members of the Church. Just as in our day, the rapid pace of societal change and moral decay at the start of the twentieth century alarmed the leaders of the Church. In the midst of these challenges, President Joseph F. Smith and the other leaders of his era found new and innovative ways to provide for the spiritual welfare of the youth of the Church, developing the methods which are the foundation of the worldwide Church Educational System (CES) of our day. Faced with the task of helping young Latter-day Saints gain testimonies of their own, Church leaders during the Joseph F. Smith era found new ways to teach the gospel. Just as important, these innovations helped gospel study remain a part of the education of the youth without infringing on the boundaries of church and state.

Joseph F. Smith and Education

Education was at the heart of Joseph F. Smith's concerns over the future of the Church. In 1914 he wrote, "There are at least three dangers that threaten the

---

Brett D. Dowdle is a PhD student in American history at Texas Christian University. Casey Paul Griffiths is a seminary teacher and a member of the curriculum staff for Seminaries and Institutes of Religion.

Church within, and the authorities need to awaken to the fact that the people should be warned unceasingly against them. As I see these, they are the flattery of prominent men of the world, *false educational ideals*, and sexual impurity."[1] Specifying the false educational ideals he was concerned with, President Smith continued, "Incorrect educational ideals are implanted in the hearts of our young people, often at home, and nearly always abroad. We have hundreds of young men, and young women, too, for that matter, who go abroad to receive their higher education, who partake to a great extent of the teachings of the world in these institutions."[2] Continuing, President Smith made it clear that his concerns rested not in learning itself, but in the philosophies which could undermine a person's faith in God. He worried that many of the Church's youth who embarked into higher education returned "filled with the so-called 'higher criticism' which not only tends to disbelief in the inspiration of the Holy Scriptures, but disbelief in God, and in the saving mission and divinity of Jesus Christ our Lord, upon which Christianity and the faith of the Latter-day Saints are founded."[3]

President Smith's warnings still resonate in our time, and they only become more meaningful when the historical circumstances of his presidency are examined. First, he acknowledged that many of the dangerous educational ideals he spoke of were creeping in at home but also came from students going abroad to receive training. During his presidency, Mormonism as a religion continued to move away from the relative isolation enjoyed in the West and closer toward the American mainstream. Many young Latter-day Saints left the Mormon strongholds of the West to gain training in the eastern United States.[4] When they returned, new ideas relating to higher biblical criticism and the scriptures came with them and stirred controversy among the Saints. One of the most pointed illustrations of these circumstances came at Brigham Young University in 1911, when several professors were dismissed for the teaching of evolution and higher biblical criticism.[5] During Joseph F. Smith's tenure, the First Presidency issued doctrinal statements clarifying Church positions on the origin of man, the relationship of the Father and the Son, and a number of other critical doctrines. All of these moves were devoted to combating the false educational ideals filtering in among the Saints.

The first effort to organize a unified system of education throughout the Church began in the 1870s, resulting in a loose confederation of Church-sponsored high schools spread through the Intermountain West. At these schools, formally referred to as "academies," Latter-day Saint youth received instruction in a wide range of subjects, including religion. Church academies functioned with varying degrees of success throughout the remainder of the nineteenth century, but by the time Joseph F. Smith became President, some problems within the academy system began to become more evident.[6]

One of the most serious concerns with the academy system was the geographical limitations of the Church schools. During Joseph F. Smith's term as President, the increasing size of the Church membership, combined with the spreading of Church members into areas outside the Intermountain West, made it increasingly difficult for the Church to provide education to all of the youth of the Church. Still recovering from the antipolygamy crusades of the late 1800s, the Church lacked the financial resources to provide enough schools for all of its members. In addition, members began to gravitate towards the increasing number of public schools providing free education. As more LDS students moved toward the state-sponsored schools, Church leaders began to fear for the spiritual well-being of their youth. At Church-sponsored academies, students could be taught the scriptures alongside secular subjects, but in the public schools, no provision for spiritual education existed. As the number of state-sponsored schools grew in Utah, enrollments at the Church academies leveled off and then began to decline. By 1911, public school enrollment in Utah passed the academies, and it kept on growing. The pressures of supporting dual systems of education, combined with the limited resources of the Church, all but ensured the rise of public schools as the main vehicle for education in areas where Church members lived. All of these developments begged the question, Was there a way to provide a daily spiritual education for students attending public schools?

The answer to the dilemma lay in a different approach towards education. The Church could not duplicate what the public schools offered on the same scale, but it was possible for the Church to *supplement* the education of its youth with spiritual training. Instead of serving as the primary provider of education and reaching only a few students, state-sponsored educational systems could provide secular education to the youth of the Church, while the Church could work in concert to do what it did best—namely, teach the spiritual truths of the gospel. This philosophy, which came to dominate the educational plan of the Church, was woven with many different historical threads, each eventually coming together to create the seminary program. The seminary model was flexible enough to allow the Church to provide religious instruction in a wide variety of settings. These practices became the foundation for a system adaptive enough to meet the needs of Church membership as Mormonism moved outside of the American West and on to a global stage. This new system grew gradually out of earlier efforts, most importantly what was known as the Religion Class program.

Forerunner of the Seminaries: The Religion Class Program

The first seminary opened in 1912, but the shift toward supplementary religious education began over two decades earlier. The Church's first experiment with supplementary religious education began in 1890, when the Church Board of Education established the Religion Class program at the suggestion of Elder Anthon H. Lund.[7] President Smith did not have direct responsibility for the Religion Classes during the first eleven years of the program's existence, but his position in the First Presidency kept him apprised of the program's growth, development, and struggles during this period. During the early years of President Smith's administration, the Religion Class program raised a number of important questions about the nature of Church auxiliaries and Church education. These issues would ultimately play an important role in organizing the seminary program, making the Religion Classes a trial run for the seminary program.

The founding of the Religion Class program came in response to the various challenges plaguing Mormonism during the late 1800s. With the end of Reconstruction in the mid-1870s, the federal government began to focus significant attention on what the nation viewed to be the theocratic government of Utah and Mormonism's peculiar institution of polygamy. The government used a variety of measures aimed at quelling polygamy and eliminating Mormonism's less democratic features, such as its hierarchical government and the practice of block voting.

In an effort to respond to the "Mormon Question," the government attempted to utilize the territory's schools to curb the religious commitment of Latter-day Saint youth. Americans had long understood and used the power of education to assimilate immigrants and other social, religious, and racial outsiders into American democracy.[8] Utah's public schools became an important part of the government's effort to undermine Mormonism. In 1890, Jacob S. Boseman, the federal commissioner of schools in Utah, reported to the secretary of interior that Mormon leaders were "unfriendly to the district schools" and that the development of a public school system would "work in Utah a wonderful change in a very few years."[9] Such attitudes culminated in the passage of the territory's Free Schools Act on February 18, 1890. The law provided for the establishment of tax-supported schools throughout Utah and mandated school attendance for children who were not otherwise enrolled in private schools. The act also expressly forbid the teaching of any "atheistic, infidel, sectarian, or denominational doctrine" in the territory's schools.[10]

While the wording of the law seems innocuous to readers today, Church officials at the time viewed the Free Schools Act as a direct affront to the Church and their children. The First Presidency worried that the new law would create a system of "Godless education"[11] that would cause many Mormon youth to "lose all liking for religious principles and become alienated in their feelings toward the gospel."[12] Church superintendent of education Karl G. Maeser worried that the territory's educational laws would enable the spread of agnosticism, "the common enemy of all religion."[13]

Noting the significant problems posed by the Free Schools Act, the Church Board of Education began discussing measures to protect the faith of the rising generations from the dangers posed by free schools. Maeser and others suggested that the Church establish primary schools to complement its growing number of secondary academies. The economic conditions of the Church during the 1890s, however, rendered Maeser's proposal entirely unfeasible and compelled Church officials to consider establishing programs that would supplement rather than replace the public schools.[14] At the urging of President George Q. Cannon, Elder Anthon H. Lund proposed an alternative to Maeser's plan for primary schools. Elder Lund suggested that the Board establish a series of classes where Mormon children could receive a half hour of religious instruction after school each day. For the sake of convenience, wherever possible, Elder Lund advised leaders to hold classes in the schoolhouses, led by the local teachers.[15]

Although Elder Lund's idea showed promise, the members of the Board of Education expressed a number of reservations about the program. First, they questioned the propriety of using the schoolhouses and territorial teachers for a religious education program. Second, they feared that the program would violate the separation of church and state by introducing sectarian doctrine into the schools, thus creating additional problems with the government. Finally, some board members worried that the parents of the youth would resist the program because of the time it would keep their children away from their homes and their assigned chores.

Even as Elder Lund acknowledged each of these potential problems, however, he continued to argue for the program's importance, maintaining, "We can not afford to lose our childrens [*sic*] souls."[16] Time would ultimately validate each of these initial concerns about the Religion Class program. However, each of these questions and the associated challenges they created proved instrumental in providing the Church with a template from which the more efficient seminary program was finally created.

Despite their initial concerns, the members of the Church Board of Education voted to establish the Religion Class program on October 8, 1890, providing for "daily theological classes in those settlements where church schools could not be established."[17] The board appointed Karl G. Maeser to serve as superintendent of the program and charged him with developing an appropriate curriculum for the classes. Although he initially favored building additional private schools, Maeser became an instant convert to supplementary religious education. He later wrote that supplementary religious education, with its capacity to provide programs for each denomination, was the only answer to the "great defect in [the] public school system."[18] After prayer and significant thought, Maeser developed a plan and curriculum for the classes. Elder Lund described Maeser's plan in the April 1916 general conference:

> The classes are opened by singing, led by the teacher or by one of the children, as he or she may direct. . . . After the children have sung a hymn, their hearts are attuned for the second step, which is prayer. Here one of the boys or girls will volunteer to offer the prayer . . . and the boy or girl chosen to lead will utter a short sentence or a short phrase, which all repeat in concert, and then the next sentence will be given and repeated, and so on until the prayer is ended. . . . The third step is to learn a memory gem or good thought. . . . Then comes the fourth step, which is the real lesson, and takes the longest time. . . . The fifth step is testimony bearing. . . . The sixth step is singing and prayer, conducted as were the opening exercises.[19]

Negotiating Church and State Problems

Although the Religion Class program was well intentioned and experienced varying measures of success throughout the 1890s, it suffered from a number of organizational flaws. These problems challenged both the program's legal standing and its relationship with the other auxiliaries and organizations of the Church. These deficiencies became a source of increasing discussion during President Smith's tenure as Church President and led to a number of important policy changes eventually affecting the whole population of the Church.[20]

As anticipated, the Religion Class program raised significant questions about the nature of religious education in the public schools and the relationship of the Church to the state. Wards throughout Utah frequently held Religion Classes in public school buildings. Utah laws permitted school buildings to be used "for any purpose which [would] not interfere with the seating or other furniture or property,"[21] providing that rent was paid for the use of the building. Under these terms, Church officials felt they had "a perfect right to ask for the use of these buildings" for Religion Class purposes.[22] Further, the Church leaders declared that they were "perfectly willing for the Catholics, Presbyterians, or any other religious denomination" to also use the buildings for religious purposes. Such statements, however, did little to pacify the members of Utah's non-Mormon community, which argued that the practice violated the separation of church and state.[23]

During the first five years of the twentieth century, the use of school buildings for religion classes continued to cause contention in Utah. The practice was even discussed in the US Senate during the Reed Smoot senate confirmation hearings, making it a part of the larger national issues and questions about Mormonism.[24] The Smoot hearings uncovered the fact that Religion Classes made extensive use of school buildings throughout Utah with the classes frequently being taught by "the regularly employed teacher of the school." State Superintendent of Public Instruction A. C. Nelson suggested that the practice likely led "a large percentage of the children" to view the Religion Classes as a part of their school activities, regardless of the amount of time separating the classes from the regular school day. He accordingly deemed these practices a "violation of the spirit of the constitution and the statutes of the State of Utah."[25]

As a result of these discussions, General Authorities began to question the propriety of continuing to use public school buildings to house Religion Classes. In 1904, B. H. Roberts expressed his concerns that the classes were "needlessly irritating people not of our faith by the use of public school buildings for imparting religious instruction" and urged the Brethren to consider alternate locations for the classes. According to one report, Elder Roberts's opinion reflected "the sentiments of most of the brethren," signaling an important shift in Church relations with the state and federal governments.[26] Following the series of questions about the program during the Smoot hearings, President Smith and the First Presidency issued a circular advising ward and stake leaders to remove Religion Classes "from the public school buildings." While the First Presidency maintained that the classes had not violated the separation of church and state and had done nothing to endanger the public schools, they noted a desire "to be in harmony with the statutes of our state and nation," and to maintain cordial relationships with citizens of other faiths.[27] Although some wards and stakes apparently ignored this counsel, leading to a few complaints, the controversy over public buildings did not generate as much animosity or as many problems for the Church after 1905 as it had during the early years of the Religion Class program.[28]

Church Relationships and the Need for a Better System

While church and state questions plagued the Religion Class program throughout much of its history, the most significant complaints about the program ironically came from within the Church rather than from outside of it. Almost from its inception, several ward and stake officials throughout the Church questioned the necessity of the Religion Class program. Commenting on this rocky beginning, Karl G. Maeser stated that during the early years of the program, "Religion Classes were either not started at all, or ceased after a feeble existence." To remedy this problem, Maeser publicized and praised the program in wards and stakes from 1891 until his death in 1901. He also wrote circulars pleading with stake presidents throughout the Church for their "earnest co-operation in the establishment of these classes."[29] Further, in 1900 the Church organized a presidency and board to oversee the Religion Class program.[30] These efforts to bolster the classes yielded a modest amount of success, but participation in the Religion Classes fluctuated throughout the program's history. Extant documents reveal high enrollment statistics for the program during many years but also demonstrate frequent discrepancies with regard to attendance. At its height in 1919, attendance was roughly 70 percent of enrollment, while attendance in earlier years was often little more than 50 percent of the program's enrollment.

Several complaints about the program came from stake presidents and bishops who noted the program's tendency to overlap with and duplicate the duties and responsibilities of the other auxiliaries. Its similarities with the other organizations caused some local leaders to see it as "a superfluous burden" and a "fifth wheel"

The Salt Lake Twenty-Ninth Ward religion class, 1905. Courtesy of Church History Library.

rather than a critical component of the Church's auxiliary system.[31] This problem is most visible when examining the program's complicated relationship with the Primary Association. Primary leaders believed that the "original purpose for organizing the Religion Class was to gather boys and girls between the ages of twelve and fourteen who would not attend Primary," rather than the elementary-aged children that the Religion Classes most frequently served. Accordingly, the two organizations quickly found themselves competing with each other for the patronage of children as well as for the services of the same capable teachers to instruct them.[32]

In an effort to resolve these problems, the First Presidency began encouraging the auxiliaries to correlate their efforts to avoid unnecessary overlap and develop greater cooperation with the priesthood quorums.[33] In 1906, President Smith authorized the organization of a committee with representatives from each of the auxiliaries, except the Relief Society, to investigate the possibility of a "correlation and adjustment of the work pertaining to the several auxiliary organizations of the Church," establishing the beginning of a movement which would eventually lead to the Church's correlation program.[34] Among the committee's suggestions was that the Primary Association and the Religion Class program be combined into "one organization whose field shall be the teaching of manners, morals, and religion." Additionally, the committee suggested that the Church reinforce the importance of the home as the place that was "most valuable for the instruction of the youth in religion, morals, polite deportment, and patriotism."[35] This suggestion countered the occasional criticisms of parents that the Church auxiliaries had kept children away from their homes too frequently, making it difficult for parents to adequately teach the gospel to their children. Among the foremost critics of this problem was Granite Stake President Frank Y. Taylor, who in 1909 initiated the family home evening program to give parents more time to teach the gospel to their children at home.[36]

While no immediate actions were taken to implement this original correlation committee's suggestions, many of the ideas were later implemented. Despite its many deficiencies, however, the Religion Class program had helped to change the entire trajectory of Mormonism's educational programs. Troubled though it had been, the Religion Class program had outlined many of the key issues that any successful supplementary religious education program would have to deal with in order to succeed. In this sense, the Religion Class program became a necessary precursor and guide for the more successful seminary and institute programs established in later years.

The Creation of the Seminary Program

The ups and downs of the Religion Class program made it clear that a more efficient system was needed to meet the needs of the Church. The matter became more urgent as the enrollment in Church academies continued to decline steeply. In 1910 the number of high school students enrolled in public schools in Utah surpassed the academies for the first time and kept on climbing.[37] In this environment came the creation of the first released-time seminary program. Though similar in many ways to the Religion Class program, the seminaries emerged in a much different way. The Religion Classes began as a Churchwide initiative, created at the highest levels of Church government and implemented simultaneously in all the wards and branches of the Church. Seminary, on the other hand, began as a grassroots program, started as an experiment by one stake and then gradually introduced to the rest of the Church. Religion classes began in the highest councils of the Church government, while seminary was inspired by a meeting of the most basic unit of the Church, a single family.

The seminary program came about as the efforts of many different people, but the individual perhaps most responsible for its creation was Joseph F. Merrill.

In many ways, Merrill fit the mold spoken of by President Smith as a young man who went abroad to receive his education and was exposed to the teachings of the world. The son of Apostle Marriner W. Merrill, Joseph Merrill left Utah as a young man to attend school in the eastern United States, first at the University of Michigan, and later at Johns Hopkins University and the University of Chicago. Navigating the often treacherous waters of faith and academia, Merrill was aware of the concerns other Church members might hold over his pursuit of higher education. He wrote his fiancée back in Utah about the concerned letters he received from his mother, "Ever since I first left for Ann Arbor there have been busy tongues always telling her that I would deny the faith—for college education in the east always 'ruins our boys.'"[38]

Merrill's experiences in the East deeply affected his religious development. Thrust into a sea of secularism, he often longed for the fellowship of other Latter-day Saints or just a simple place to be taught the tenets of the gospel. He later reflected, "I usually attended one non-Mormon church service, sometimes two services, every Sunday. For a considerable number of years I was out of intimate contact with my own Church so I went to all the churches in the communities where I lived .. . . I listened to many eloquent sermons, but never once did I hear the preacher use the word 'know' with the meaning we give it in our testimony bearing."[39]

When Merrill returned to Utah, he married, started a family of his own, and began teaching at the University of Utah. In 1911 he was called as a member of the Granite Stake presidency and given responsibility over the education of the youth in the stake. Many of the younger members of the Granite Stake were attending public schools without access to the religious instruction offered at the Church academies. Recognizing this, Merrill began to search for some way to allow them to receive religious training. The initial inspiration for the seminary program struck Merrill during a family home evening where his wife, Laura, acted as the teacher.[40] During the family meeting, Merrill was enraptured by his wife's ability to tell stories from the Bible and Book of Mormon to his own children. He later remarked, "Her list of these stories was so long that her husband often marveled at their number, and frequently sat as spellbound as were the children as she skillfully related them, preparatory to the children's going to bed."[41] When Merrill asked his wife where she had learned these stories, she replied they had come from James E. Talmage's Bible class when she was a student at the Salt Lake

Joesph and Annie Merrill family, 1914. Courtesy of Annie Whitton.

Stake Academy. Merrill concluded, "If Bible study in school could thus make one girl an effective religious teacher of her children at home, it could do the same for other girls."[42] Inspired by his wife's example, Merrill became possessed by the idea of bringing the same kind of opportunity his wife had experienced at the Church academy to the students in his stake attending public schools.

Influenced by religious seminaries he had seen in Chicago during his education,[43] Merrill worked out a plan to teach religion courses to students at Granite High School who would be released from their studies for one period a day. The teaching would take place in a building constructed by the stake adjacent to the high school. Merrill's plan included some aspects of the earlier Religion Class program while improving on it in other ways. The new plan took advantage of the fact that the students were already gathered together at the high school during the day, and made religion course work a part of their regular studies. Holding the classes in a completely separate building from the high school solved many of the tricky issues of church and state which had troubled the Religion Class program. In the months leading up to the 1912–13 school year Merrill worked enthusiastically on the new program, meeting with the Granite Stake presidency, the Church Board of Education, the Granite School

District Board, and even the Utah State Board of Education to ensure the legality and acceptance of the new venture.[44]

The First Seminary Teacher

With the support of the school administration, the next task facing Joseph Merrill was the selection of the right teacher for the venture. In a letter outlining the qualities he wanted for the position, he wrote: May I suggest it is the desire of the presidency of the stake to have a strong young man who is properly qualified to do the work in a most satisfactory manner. By young we do not necessarily mean a teacher who is young in years, but a man who is young in his feelings, who loves young people, who delights in their company, who can command their respect and admiration and exercise a great influence over them. . . . We want a man who is a thorough student, one who will not teach in a perfunctory way, but who will enliven his instructions by a strong, winning personality and give evidence of a thorough understanding of and scholarship in the things he teaches. . . . A teacher is wanted who is a leader and who will be universally regarded as the inferior of no teacher in the high school.[45]

The man ultimately selected for the task was Thomas J. Yates, a member of the Granite Stake high council.[46] He held no specific expertise in religion, nor was he a career educator. His only experience in teaching had come twenty years earlier during a one-year stint at the Church academies in Millard County, Utah. A graduate of Cornell University, at the time of his call Brother Yates was working as an engineer on the construction of the nearby Murray power plant. Yates did not fit the traditional mold of a teacher, but he did excel as a disciple. He served faithfully on the stake high council and in a number of important missionary assignments. Frank Taylor, the president of the Granite Stake, once commented, "Brother Yates always reminds me of Joseph who was sold into Egypt; he is a tower of purity and strength."[47]

With the right teacher selected, Brother Merrill and Brother Yates set about working out the details of the new venture. They made the vital decision to center the class around the scriptures, with two courses for credit—a class on the Old Testament and another on the New Testament—and a third course, offered without credit, combining the study of the Book of Mormon and Church history.[48] Brother Yates met with the faculty of Granite High School several times to secure full cooperation. During the same time,

Granite Seminary. Courtesy of Church History Library.

President Frank Y. Taylor secured a $2,500 loan from Zion's Savings Bank for the construction of a building near the high school. Construction on the first seminary building began just a few weeks before school started. The finished structure consisted of three rooms: an office, a cloak room, and a classroom. The classroom itself had a blackboard, armrest seats, and a furnace for heat. There were no lights, and the only textbooks were the Bible and the Book of Mormon. In fact, the seminary's entire library consisted of a Bible dictionary belonging to Brother Yates. Students made their own maps of the Holy Land, North America, Mesopotamia, and Arabia.[49]

The first class in the fall of 1912 consisted of about seventy young men and women.[50] Many students were unable to take seminary the first year because the building wasn't finished until three weeks into the school year.[51] For the entire first year, Thomas Yates spent the morning working at the Murray power plant, then he rode his horse to the seminary to teach during the last two periods of the day.[52] In a 1950 interview he described how the class operated that first year: "Students were asked to prepare a whole chapter in the Bible and then report to the class. Then the class would discuss it. No textbooks were used. The students did not have any form of recreation, there were no parties, no dances, no class affairs or anything in recreation to deviate from the regular pattern of things."[53]

Thomas Yates taught for only one year. President Taylor asked him to return for the second year, but the strain of traveling back and forth from the Murray power plant proved to be too much, and he declined. As his replacement, Brother Yates recommended Guy C. Wilson, a professional educator who had recently moved to Salt Lake City after completing a year of studies at Columbia University. Wilson's assignment to the Granite Seminary demonstrated the deep commitment of Church leaders to the fledgling program. He was the former head of the Church academy in Colonia Juárez.[54] A gifted teacher, Wilson was informed by Church leaders after his arrival from Columbia that he could "take [his] choice" of any of the Church schools, but he chose the new seminary in the Granite Stake.[55] During his tenure Wilson began urging bishops and stake presidents to let his students speak to their congregations about the virtues of the seminary program. At the same time, he had a profound effect on his students, even baptizing several non-members attending the seminary classes.[56]

Brother Wilson later commented that he generally felt that the lack of funding and facilities had prevented Brother Yates from giving the work a longer trial.[57] Despite the difficulties, the new venture had already begun to bless the lives of the students in ways still felt in our day. Nearly a century later, President Henry B. Eyring of the First Presidency commented on the impact of the first class at Granite Seminary. Feeling overwhelmed as the newly appointed deputy commissioner of the Church Educational System, President Eyring recalled:

> My assignment to help such a vast number of teachers seemed overwhelming until someone handed me a small roll book. It was for the first class of seminary taught in the Church. It was for the school year 1912–13. . . .
>
> In that roll book was the name of Mildred Bennion. She was 16 years old that year. Thirty-one years later she would become my mother. She was the daughter of a man we would today call "less active." Her mother was left a widow the fall of the year after that first seminary class began. She raised and supported my mother and five other children alone on a small farm. Somehow that one seminary teacher cared enough about her and prayed fervently enough over that young girl that the Spirit put the gospel down into her heart.

That one teacher blessed tens of thousands because he taught just one girl in a crowd of 70.[58]

"No Better Illustration of Prophetic Preparation"

Granite remained the only seminary in the Church until 1915, when the Box Elder Seminary in Brigham City, Utah, opened with Abel S. Rich as the teacher.[59] Throughout the remainder of the decade the seminary system began to pick up momentum, with more and more seminaries being established throughout the Church.[60] The basic pattern started in the Granite Stake was repeated in different areas throughout the Church.[61] By the end of Joseph F. Smith's presidency, twelve more seminaries had been established at different locations throughout the Church.[62] In 1920 the Church Board of Education proposed the closure or transfer to state control of nearly all the remaining Church academies and called for a major expansion of the seminary program to meet the needs of the youth in the Church.[63] In the years after the organization of the academy system, Church members grew more comfortable with public education, and now seminary accorded students a chance to study the scriptures alongside the secular subjects taught in the high schools. With the closure of most of the academies, the Church focused its efforts on the kind of education only the Church could provide—religious training. With the majority of the academies closing, the number of seminaries grew at an explosive rate during the 1920s. The number of operating seminaries nearly quadrupled from twenty to eighty-one by the end of the decade.[64]

As the seminary program became the preferred model used by the Church, it even grew to overshadow and replace its forerunner, the Religion Classes. Seminary used almost the same curriculum as the Religion Class program, but with superior organization. These two sister programs operated in conjunction, sharing resources, teachers, and methodology.[65] Seminaries and Religion Classes operated side by side until 1929, when after a turbulent forty-year history, the Religion Class program was combined with the Primary Association, bringing an end to the Church's first program of supplementary religious education.[66] Even though the Religion Class program ended, its methodology continued through the seminaries. As Church leaders looked for ways to adapt the seminary program to areas where smaller numbers of Latter-day Saints lived, the methods used in the Religion Classes received new life. Early-morning seminary programs fused the positive aspects of released-time seminary and the old religion classes, operating outside the regular school day, and utilizing a wide number of buildings, ranging from Church meetinghouses to the homes of local members.[67]

The seminary program continued to expand to meet the growth of the Church. Church leaders adapted seminary methods to bring religious education to the collegiate level. The first Institute of Religion opened in Moscow, Idaho, in 1928.[68] When the Salt Lake School District refused to allow released-time seminary, early-morning seminary classes began in the area during the 1920s. Harold B. Lee and a young returned missionary named Gordon B. Hinckley both served for a time as teachers in these early-morning programs.[69] In 1950, the first early-morning seminary classes outside of Utah began in Los Angeles, designed as an effort to bring religious education to areas with smaller and more scattered populations of Latter-day Saint youth. During the 1960s further efforts brought seminary to the global membership of the Church through the utilization of home study seminary.[70]

Today over 700,000 students are enrolled in seminary and institute programs, taught by a dedicated force of nearly 50,000 full-time and volunteer teachers. Speaking on the critical role these programs have played in the last century of the Church, President Boyd K. Packer, a veteran seminary teacher, commented:

> The seminaries were an outgrowth of the old religion classes, and the institutes of religion were an outgrowth of the seminaries and were originally called college seminaries. In the history of the Church there is no better illustration of the prophetic preparation of this people than the beginnings of the seminary institute program. These programs were started when they were nice but not critically needed. They were granted a season to flourish and to grow into a bulwark for the Church. They now become a godsend for the salvation of modern Israel in a most challenging hour.[71]

With the benefit of over a century of hindsight, the inspiration of the leaders of the Church during Joseph F. Smith's era is clear. Hundreds of thousands of youth throughout the Church are blessed in our time because of the innovations made during this period. Through the religion classes and other programs, the modern seminaries and institutes trace their pedigree back to Karl Maeser, Anthon Lund, and the earliest educational pioneers of Mormonism. The revelations which sparked the programs represent the best of the highest and the lowest levels of Church government. From ideas received in the meetings of Joseph F.

Smith and his fellow leaders, combined with spiritual whisperings given in the simple meetings of Joseph F. Merrill's family, all came together to show the way to bring the knowledge of the gospel to the youth of the Church.

Notes

1. Joseph F. Smith, "Three Threatening Dangers," *Improvement Era*, March 1914, 476–77; emphasis added.
2. Smith, "Three Threatening Dangers," 477.
3. Smith, "Three Threatening Dangers," 477.
4. See Thomas Wendell Simpson, "Mormons Study 'Abroad': Latter-day Saints in American Higher Education, 1870–1940" (PhD diss., University of Virginia, August 2005).
5. See Gary James Bergera, "The 1911 Evolution Controversy at Brigham Young University," in *The Search for Harmony*, ed. Gene A. Sessions and Craig J. Oberg (Salt Lake City: Signature Books, 1993).
6. For an excellent study on the Church academies, see Scott C. Esplin, "Education in Transition: Church and State Relationships in Utah Education, 1888–1933" (PhD diss., Brigham Young University, 2006).
7. The standard history of the Religion Class program is D. Michael Quinn, "Utah's Educational Innovation: LDS Religion Classes, 1890–1929," *Utah Historical Quarterly* 43, no. 4 (Fall 1975): 379–89.
8. David B. Tyack, *The One Best System: Public Schools in a Diverse Society* (Cambridge: Harvard University Press, 2003), 22; David Wallace Adams, *Education for Extinction: American Indians and the Boarding School Experience, 1875–1928* (Lawrence: University of Kansas Press, 1995), 8–9; Lawrence A. Cremin, *The Transformation of the School: Progressivism in American Education, 1876–1957* (New York: Vintage Books, 1964), 66–67; Michael McGerr, *A Fierce Discontent: The Rise and Fall of the Progressive Movement in America* (New York: Oxford University Press, 2003), 292; Margaret D. Jacobs, *White Mothers to a Dark Race: Settler Colonialism, Maternalism, and the Removal of Indigenous Children in the American West and Australia, 1880–1940* (Lincoln: University of Nebraska Press, 2009).
9. Congress, "Letter from the Secretary of the Interior, transmitting a letter of the Governor of Utah and a report of the Commissioner of Public Schools," 51st Cong., 1st sess., 1890, S. Exec. Doc 27, Serial 2682, page 5.
10. *An Act to Provide for a Uniform System of Free Schools Throughout Utah Territory Passed at the Twenty-ninth Session of the Legislative Assembly of the Territory of Utah, 1890*, L. Tom Perry Special Collections, Harold B. Lee Library, Brigham Young University, Provo, UT.
11. First Presidency, circular letter, October 25, 1890, in James R. Clark, comp., *Messages of the First Presidency of the Church of Jesus Christ of Latter-day Saints, 1833–1964*, 6 vols. (Salt Lake City: Bookcraft, 1966), 3:196.
12. George Q. Cannon, quoted in Karl G. Maeser, "Church School Papers—No. 16," *Juvenile Instructor*, October 1, 1892, 607–8.
13. Karl G. Maeser, *School and Fireside* (Salt Lake City: Skelton & Co, 1898), 130.
14. Quinn, "Utah's Educational Innovation," 380–81; Church Board of Education Minutes, June 2, 1890, General Church Board of Education Meeting Minutes, 1888–1902, UA 1376,

box 1, L. Tom Perry Special Collections. For a discussion of economics in Utah during the 1890s, see Leonard J. Arrington, "Utah and the Depression of the 1890s," *Utah Historical Quarterly* 29, no. 1 (January 1961): 3–18.

15. *Program of Lund Day Exercises in Religion Classes*, 1912, Church History Library, The Church of Jesus Christ of Latter-day Saints, Salt Lake City, (hereafter cited as CHL); Anthon H. Lund, diary, June 2, 1890, in *Danish Apostle: The Diaries of Anthon H. Lund, 1890–1921*, ed. John P. Hatch (Salt Lake City: Signature Books, 2006), 7.
16. Lund, diary, June 2, 1890, in *Danish Apostle*, 7–8.
17. Church Board of Education Minutes, October 8, 1890, D. Michael Quinn Papers, Beinecke Rare Book and Manuscript Library, Yale University, New Haven, CT; Alma P. Burton, "Karl G. Maeser, Mormon Educator" (master's thesis, Brigham Young University, 1950), 106.
18. Maeser, *School and Fireside*, 131.
19. Anthon H. Lund, in Conference Report, April 1916, 10–11.
20. For a discussion of the successes and failures of the Religion Class program during the 1890s, see: Brett D. Dowdle, "'A New Policy in Church School Work': The Founding of the Mormon Supplementary Religious Education Movement" (master's thesis, Brigham Young University, 2011), 60–103.
21. Revised Statutes, Sec. 1822, quoted in "Laws and Religion Classes," Journal History of the Church of Jesus Christ of Latter-day Saints, October 19, 1904, CHL.
22. Joseph W. McMurrin, in Conference Report, April 1902, 57.
23. McMurrin, in Conference Report, April 1902, 57.
24. *Proceedings Before the Committee on Privileges and Elections of the United States in the Matter of the Protests Against the Hon. Reed Smoot, a Senator from the State of Utah, to Hold His Seat*, 5 vols. (Washington, DC: Government Printing Office, 1904), 2:105–38, 366–74; 3:77–78, 201–3, 263
25. *Proceedings Before the Committee on Privileges and Elections*, 2:369–70, 372–73.
26. Journal History, December 1, 1904, CHL.
27. First Presidency, circular letter, February 1905, in Clark, *Messages of the First Presidency*, 4:101–2.
28. In 1912, Adolf Merz, president of the North Sanpete Stake, reported to the General Board of Religion Classes that "the best reports of [Religion Class] attendance were from the Wards in which the schoolhouses are used for holding the classes." General Board of Religion Class Minutes, November 6, 1912, Quinn Papers, Beinecke Library, Yale University, New Haven, Connecticut. In 1914, Carl R. Marcusen, superintendent of the Carbon County schools complained that Religion Classes were being held in a number of schools throughout Carbon County, with the district schoolteacher often teaching the classes as well. Carl R. Marcusen to School Boards of Carbon County, January 21, 1914, in General Board of Religion Class Minutes, June 3, 1914, Quinn Papers, Beinecke Library, Yale University, New Haven, Connecticut.
29. Karl G. Maeser to Presidents of Stakes and the Stake Boards of Education, September 12, 1893, Salt Lake Stake Board of Education Files 1893–1896, CHL.
30. General Board of Religion Class Minutes, January 19, 1900, Quinn Papers, Beinecke Library, Yale University, New Haven, Connecticut.
31. Karl G. Maeser, "Church School Papers—Series II, No. 2," *Juvenile Instructor*, November 15, 1895, 695; "Religion Class Department," *Juvenile Instructor*, January 1, 1907, 13–14; L. John

Nuttall, diary, August 5, 12, and 14, 1899, L. Tom Perry Special Collections; Karl G. Maeser, "Church School Department," *Juvenile Instructor*, February 15, 1901, 117–18.

32. General Board of the Primary Association Minutes, April 6, 1901, quoted in Conrad A. Harward, "A History of the Growth and Development of the Primary Association of the LDS Church from 1878 to 1928" (master's thesis, Brigham Young University, 1976), 131.
33. Dale C. Mouritsen, "Efforts to Correlate Mormon Church Agencies in the Twentieth Century: A Review," CHL.
34. First Presidency to Deseret Sunday School Union Board, November 15, 1906, quoted in James E. Talmage and Mae T. Nystrom to First Presidency, July 29, 1907, Scott G. Kenney Research Collection, L. Tom Perry Special Collections.
35. Talmage and Nystrom to First Presidency, June 29, 1907, L. Tom Perry Special Collections.
36. President Taylor had consistently pled for "fathers and mothers . . . to be more careful in regard to the rearing of our youth," taking time "to sit down by the fireside with them and explain unto them the Gospel." He wanted Latter-day Saints to make the home "the center of attraction" and "the most pleasant place that a boy or girl can find in this world." Frank Y. Taylor, discourse, October 5, 1902, in Conference Report, October 1902, 59. As a corollary to such sentiments, President Taylor later opined, "I sometimes think that many of our parents leave entirely too much to [the auxiliaries] to educate their boys and girls in the fear of the Lord, and it does not seem that is right." Frank Y. Taylor, in Conference Report, April 1913, 50.
37. Milton L. Bennion, *Mormonism and Education* (Salt Lake City: Department of Education of the Church of Jesus Christ of Latter-day Saints, 1939), 175.
38. Joseph F. Merrill to Annie Hyde, March 11, 1896, Joseph F. Merrill papers, MSS 1540, box 14, folder 1, L. Tom Perry Special Collections.
39. Joseph F. Merrill, "Some Fundamentals of Mormonism," *Church News*, December 7, 1946.
40. The two most complete accounts of the circumstances surrounding this meeting are Joseph F. Merrill, "A New Institution in Religious Education," *Improvement Era*, January 1938, 55–56, and A. Theodore Tuttle, "Released Time Religious Education Program of the Church of Jesus Christ of Latter-day Saints" (master's thesis, Stanford University, 1949). The first account was written by Merrill himself; the second draws from an interview conducted by A. Theodore Tuttle with Joseph F. Merrill.
41. Merrill, "A New Institution," 55.
42. Merrill, "A New Institution," 55.
43. Thomas G. Alexander, *Mormonism in Transition* (Urbana & Chicago: University of Illinois Press, 1986), 168. Alexander cites an interview with Merrill's daughter as the source for his inspiration being the religious seminaries he saw during his time in Chicago. An interview conducted by one of the authors with two of Merrill's grandchildren confirmed this story as common knowledge within the Merrill family. Annie Whitton and Joseph Ballantyne, interview by Casey Paul Griffiths, November 17, 2011; notes in author's possession.
44. Tuttle, "Released Time Religious Education Program," 57–59.
45. Merrill, "A New Institution," 55.
46. See Casey Paul Griffiths, "The First Seminary Teacher," *Religious Educator* 9, no. 3 (2008): 115–30.
47. Thomas J. Yates, "Autobiography and Biography of Thomas Jarvis Yates," 42, CHL.

48. See Merrill, "A New Institution," 55. The Book of Mormon was covered as part of the Church History year. Interestingly, the Book of Mormon did not receive its own year as permanent part of the seminary curriculum until the 1970s. See Joe J. Christensen, "Abiding by Its Precepts," in *Living the Book of Mormon: Abiding by Its Precepts,* ed. Gaye Strathearn and Charles L. Swift (Provo, UT: Religious Studies Center; Salt Lake City: Deseret Book, 2007), 1–24.
49. See Coleman and Jones, "History of Granite Seminary, 1933," 6–7.
50. See Coleman and Jones, "History of Granite Seminary, 1933," 7.
51. See Yates, "Autobiography," 80.
52. See "New Building Dedicated at Granite, the Oldest Seminary in the Church"; www.ldsChurchNews.com/articles/24154/New-building-dedicated-at-Granite-the-oldest-Seminary-in-the-Church.html (accessed September 10, 2012).
53. Ward H. Magleby, "Granite Seminary 1912," *Impact: Weekday Religious Education Quarterly,* Winter 1968, 15.
54. See Coleman and Jones, "History of Granite Seminary," 8; Yates, "Autobiography," 81.
55. Anna Lowrie Ivins Wilson to Guy C. Wilson, March 8, 1913, Wilson Correspondence, CHL.
56. See Dowdle, "A New Policy in Church School Work," 146–47.
57. Coleman and Jones, "History of Granite Seminary, 1933," 32.
58. Henry B. Eyring, "To Know and to Love God," An Evening with President Henry B. Eyring, February 26, 2010, 5.
59. See Tuttle, "Released Time Religious Education," 69–70. As an illustration of historic continuity, it should be noted that Abel S. Rich stayed at Box Elder Seminary for nearly forty years after it opened, eventually training another young seminary teacher, Boyd K. Packer. See Lucille C. Tate, *Boyd K. Packer: A Watchman on the Tower* (Salt Lake City: Bookcraft, 1995), 98.
60. The Religion Class program continued to function until 1929, when it officially ended by Joseph F. Merrill, who by then was serving as the Church commissioner of education. See Clark, *Messages of the First Presidency,* 5:267–68.
61. It should be noted that released-time religious education was not only a Latter-day Saint movement. During the 1910–30 period specifically, similar programs spread throughout the nation. One historian has argued that the Religion Class program represents the first American attempt at supplemental religious education (see Quinn); however, most released-time programs trace their beginnings to the a program established in Gary, Indiana, in 1914 that came to be known as the "Gary Plan." Granite Seminary was in operation three years prior to the opening of the Indiana program, and the Religion Class program existed more than twenty years prior to that! Officials from Indiana even contacted LDS leaders requesting "literature in relation to the Religion Class work of the Church of Jesus Christ of Latter-day Saints." See Joseph W. McMurrin, in Conference Report, October 1914, 119.
62. See Tuttle, "Released Time Religious Education," 71–74.
63. See Bell, "Adam Samuel Bennion," 51–54. While the majority of the academies closed, several schools were retained and even upgraded to serve as junior colleges for the training of teachers. Among the schools retained were Dixie College, Snow College, Weber College, LDS University in Salt Lake City, Brigham Young College in Logan, Gila College in Arizona, and Ricks College in Idaho. The Juárez Academy in Mexico was retained and remains open

even today. See Scott C. Esplin, "Education in Transition: Church and State Relationships in Utah Education, 1888–1933" (PhD diss., Brigham Young University, 2006), 164–65.

64. See Tuttle, "Released Time Religious Education," 71–73.
65. From 1912 to 1919, Church seminaries actually operated under the direction of the General Board of Religion Classes rather than the Church Board of Education. See Brett Dowdle, "'A New Policy in Church School Work': The Founding of the Mormon Supplementary Religious Education Movement" (master's thesis, Brigham Young University, 127).
66. First Presidency to Presidencies of Stakes, May 29, 1929, in Clark, *Messages of the First Presidency*, 5:267.
67. See David B. Rimington, *Vistas on Visions: A Golden Anniversary History of Church Education in Southern California*, (Anaheim, CA: Shumway Family History Services, 1988), also Dennis C. Wright, "Good Morning Los Angeles: The Beginning of the Early Morning Seminary Program," in *Regional Studies in Latter-day Saint History: California*, ed. David F. Boone and others (Provo, UT: Department of Church History and Doctrine, 1998), 224.
68. See Dennis A. Wright, "The Beginnings of the First LDS Institute of Religion at Moscow, Idaho," *Mormon Historical Studies* 10, no. 1 (Spring 2009): 72; also, Casey Paul Griffiths, "The First Institute Teacher," *Mormon Historical Studies* 11, no. 2 (2010): 175–201.
69. Harold B. Lee taught an early-morning seminary class at South High in Salt Lake from 1931 to 1933. He later described his experience as "the most enjoyable teaching I ever did." L. Brent Goates, *Harold B. Lee: Prophet and Seer* (Salt Lake City: Deseret Book, 1985), 90. In 1935, Gordon B. Hinckley was to teach a seminary class at South High School in Salt Lake City at a salary of thirty-five dollars a month. See Sheri L. Dew, *Go Forward with Faith: The Biography of Gordon B. Hinckley* (Salt Lake City: Deseret Book, 1996), 85.
70. See Jon Thomas, "The Worldwide Expansion of Seminaries and Institutes to English-Speaking Countries During the Administration of William E. Berrett" (master's thesis, Brigham Young University, 2011).
71. *Mine Errand from the Lord: Selections from the Sermons and Writings of Boyd K. Packer*, ed. Clyde J. Williams (Salt Lake City: Deseret Book, 2008), 358–59.

Scott C. Esplin

22

Joseph F. Smith and the Shaping of the Modern Church Educational System

From 1901 to 1918, President Joseph F. Smith presided over one of the most expansive eras in the history of Latter-day Saint education, when the Church operated a series of after-school religion classes, private secondary academies, normal colleges, and a university. "The course of the church educational system from 1900 to 1930," noted historian Thomas G. Alexander, "resembled nothing quite so much as a balloon. Expanding during the period to 1920, it shrank rapidly during the 1920s."[1] Interestingly, though President Smith chaired the Church Board of Education during an era of explosive educational growth, near the end of his presidency he remarked, "I believe that we are running education mad."[2] Responding to this concern, the policy decisions made by President Smith during his administration set the stage for the Church's drastic reduction of the academy system following his death. Ultimately, it was his presidency that supported the creation of the released-time seminary program, the innovation that reshaped Church education, guiding it toward the supplementary education model it employs today. This paper analyzes the educational background, philosophy, and legacy of Joseph F. Smith and his impact on Church education. Beginning with

---

Scott C. Esplin is an associate professor of Church history and doctrine at Brigham Young University.

his own limited education, it traces the role President Smith played in expanding the academies as a counselor in the First Presidency and later facilitating the formation of the seminary system as Church President. It places these changes within the context of the dramatic growth in public education that occurred in the West during the Smith era, demonstrating the transformative role he played in the formation of the modern Church Educational System.

Joseph F. Smith's Educational Background and Philosophy

While little is known about Joseph F. Smith's formal education, it seems apparent that his early life experiences heavily influenced his later educational philosophy. Though he grew up in frontier settlements, education was a hallmark of the communities where Smith was raised. Nauvoo, where he lived until he was nearly eight years old, enjoyed a robust educational system. Joseph F. Smith's uncle Don Carlos Smith editorialized in the *Times and Seasons* in 1841, lamenting that "from the unsettled state of the Saints, in consequence of being driven from their inheritances, and their sudden transitions from affluence to poverty; the education of their children has consequently been neglected." "But," he continued, "we hope the night of darkness has passed away, and that we behold the dawning of a refulgent morn, which shall shine upon our youthful city."[3] Encouraged by this educational zeal, each of the city's four wards operated a school, overseen by the Board of Regents of the University of the City of Nauvoo. These common schools were augmented by numerous private schools throughout the city.[4] However, while schools were available in Nauvoo, we know only that Joseph F. Smith frequented school one winter in the City of Joseph, attending Merilla Johnson's class in the basement of the *Nauvoo Neighbor* print building.[5]

Smith had what one of his biographers later termed an abbreviated childhood, brought about by the death of his father five months before the boy turned six.[6] For what should have been his common school years, his widowed mother, Mary Fielding Smith, tutored Joseph. "Well-educated, in her own right, and properly reared," Mary Fielding Smith received an education in her native Britain, reared in "the home of a pious, refined, intellectual and educated family."[7] In Kirtland, Ohio, she taught school and tutored pupils privately for a brief time in the fall of 1837 before marrying Hyrum Smith later that December.[8] The influence she had on her son Joseph left a deep impression. Later in life, he declared, "To her I owe my very existence as also my success in life, coupled with the favor and mercy of God."[9] His son Joseph Fielding Smith similarly observed, "Most of his education up to the time of his mother's death had been obtained from her. Busy as she was with the many cares and tribulations, she nevertheless found time to teach her children some of the fundamentals of education, she being a well educated woman."[10]

Though Nauvoo was different for the Church and for Joseph F. Smith following the death of his father and uncle, the drive to educate the children of the Church was not extinguished. At a conference in October 1845, the Church and its leaders discussed various business items preparatory to their westward exodus the following winter. Addressing the congregation, Heber C. Kimball declared, "There is yet another piece of business of great importance to all who have families; that is, to have some school books printed for the education of our children, which will not be according to the Gentile order." Answering the call, it was moved that "W. W. Phelps write some school books for the use of children."[11] Joseph F. Smith, however, seemed not to have benefited much from these educational endeavors. Rather, leaving Nauvoo for the West prior to his eighth birthday, Smith's education became a practical one as he forsook formal education for the rigors of riding herd and leading oxen.

Education continued to be stressed in the Utah territory of Smith's boyhood. The first schoolhouse in the Salt Lake Valley sprung up in an old military tent just three months after the arrival of Brigham Young and his pioneer company. By 1850, the *Deseret News* reported, "Common schools were beginning in all parts of the city for the winter; and plans for the construction of school houses in every ward were being made, with a view for a general system of school houses throughout the city."[12] While conditions varied throughout the territory, historian Leonard Arrington later summarized, school "was held wherever a place could be found."[13]

Arriving in the valley in September 1848, Joseph F. Smith settled with his mother and siblings in the Mill Creek area, where they built a small cabin. While schools were being established around him, Smith continued his practical learning. "My principal occupation from 1848 to 1854," he later recalled, "was that of a herd-boy, although I made a hand always in the harvest field and at threshings, and in the canyons cutting and hauling wood."[14] His son later wrote, "After the family was settled in the Salt Lake Valley, the children found time to attend school a portion of the time, but the many cares and labors of those early days did not permit of any extended course of schooling." The lack of formal education seems not to have deterred Joseph F. Smith's learning. His son continued, "However, being of a studious mind, Joseph F. Smith never let an opportunity to gain knowledge escape him. The early records which he kept all bear strong evidence of this great desire, and it can truthfully be said, that in later life he stood preeminently among his fellows for the extensive knowledge and wide understanding which he possessed."[15] Smith's youth was further affected when his mother died and he lost his guiding light. "It was in 1852 that my blessed Mother passed away," he later recalled, "leaving me fatherless & motherless, but not altogether friendless at the early age of 13 years. . . . After my mother's death there followed 18 months—from Sept 21st, 1852 to April, 1854 of perilous time for me. I was almost like a comet or fiery meteor, without attraction or gravitation to keep me balanced or guide me within reasonable bounds."[16]

While it is unclear what formal schooling Smith received in Utah prior to his mother's death, one known reference to his education comes from the era of imbalance that followed her passing. Speaking of the influence Church leaders had on Joseph F. Smith, George A. Smith recalled, "His father and mother left him when he was a child, and we have been looking after him to try and help him along. We first sent him to school, but it was not long before he licked the schoolmaster, and could not go to school. Then we sent him on a mission." Years later, President Smith himself elaborated on the incident:

> The reason [I] had trouble with the schoolmaster was that the schoolmaster had a leather strap with which he used to chastise the children. He was a rather hard-hearted schoolmaster, one of the olden type that believed in inflicting bodily punishment. My little sister [Martha Ann] was called up to be punished. I saw the school-master bring out the leather strap, and he told the child to hold out her hand. I just spoke up loudly and said, "Don't whip her with that!" and at that he came at me and was going to whip me, and instead of him whipping me, I licked him good and plenty.[17]

Ending his limited formal education, Smith began informal education at the hand of the Lord and his servants. In addition to his several missions, where he learned to preach the gospel and administer its ordinances, Smith worked in the Church's Historian's Office, learning from Elder George A. Smith and other leading brethren about the history of the Church as well as about gospel principles and Church organization. "This contact in the Historian's Office," his son later wrote, "was also a wonderful school for the young man who had spent so much time in the mission field." In addition to his work in the Historian's Office, Smith "also engaged in the ordinance work and recording in the Endowment House under the direction of Presidents Brigham Young, Heber C. Kimball, and the Apostles, who were trained in this labor under the Prophet Joseph Smith," further expanding his knowledge of the gospel.[18]

The shaping influence of Smith's lack of formal education coupled with his practical training by Church leadership is reflected in his later statements regarding education. Acknowledging that truth could come from many sources, Smith argued as Church President that ignorance was inexcusable. "Search out the truth of the written word; listen for and receive the truth declared by living prophets and teachers; enrich your minds with the best of knowledge and facts. Of those who speak in his name, the Lord requires humility, not ignorance. Intelligence is the glory of God; and no man can be saved in ignorance."[19] While encouraging the acquisition of "knowledge and fact," Smith also reflected his upbringing, placing a primacy on the spiritual over the secular. "Educate yourself not only for time, but also for eternity. The latter of the two is the more important. Therefore, when we shall have completed the studies of time, and enter upon the commencement ceremonies of the great hereafter, we will find our work is not finished, but just begun."[20]

While emphasizing the significance of spiritual education, Smith also drew upon his experiences learning from his mother to shape his educational philosophy. As Church President, he challenged parents, "Let [your children] see that you are earnest, and practice what you preach. Do not let your children out to specialists in these things, but teach them by your own precept and example, by your own fireside. Be a specialist yourself in the truth. Let our meetings, schools and organizations, instead of being our only or leading teachers, be supplements to our teachings and training in the home."[21] He later declared, "Schools are instituted to help the home, not to domineer and direct it."[22] The value of education in the home was reflected in Smith's later support for the "Home Evening" program, which he instituted in 1915.

Emphasizing more than mere book learning, Joseph F. Smith also reflected the influence of his own practical education in the rural society in which he was raised. "We need manual training schools instead of so much book-learning and the stuffing of fairy tales and fables which are contained in many of our school books of today," Smith counseled. "If we would devote more money and time, more energy and attention to teaching our children manual labor in our schools than we do, it would be a better thing for the rising generation."[23] Though he allowed educational diversity in Church schools, Smith editorialized in 1903, "None can deny that there is too great a tendency among the young men, especially in our larger cities, to seek the lighter employments. Politics, law, medicine, trade, clerking, banking are all needful and good in their place, but we need builders, mechanics, farmers, and men who can use their powers to produce something for the use of man."[24]

The Championing of Educational Expansion

Armed with an educational philosophy emphasizing both the spiritual and the temporal, Joseph F. Smith was called to Church leadership at a young age. At the age of twenty-seven he was ordained an Apostle and called as a counselor to Brigham Young. He continued to serve as a counselor in the First Presidency to Church Presidents John Taylor, Wilford Woodruff, and Lorenzo Snow until his call as President of the Church in October 1901. Educationally, these callings placed him on the Church Board of Education, giving him influence during a time of significant educational change. In fact, some of the First Presidency statements issued during Smith's years as counselor heavily directed Church education into the path it took during his own presidency.

At the height of the antipolygamy opposition, in March 1886, John Taylor's First Presidency issued a lengthy epistle to the Saints. In part, it decried efforts in the Idaho Territory to revoke teaching licenses for Church members. Fearing "placing . . . our children, by the help of our taxes, under the tuition of those who would gladly eradicate from their minds all love and respect for the faith of their fathers," the Presidency declared, "The duty of our people under these circumstances is clear; it is to keep their children away from the influence of the sophisms of infidelity and the vagaries of the sects. Let them, though it may possibly be at some pecuniary sacrifice, establish schools taught by those of our faith, where, being free from the trammels of State aid, they can unhesitatingly teach the doctrines of true religion combined with the various branches of a general education."[25] Six months later, another First Presidency epistle praised the work of the Brigham Young Academy in Provo and the Brigham Young College in Logan, declaring, "We would like to see schools of this character, independent of the District School system, started in all places where it is possible."[26] The call for Church schools came to fruition when, following the death of President John Taylor, Wilford Woodruff

The First Presidency, 1880–87 (left to right: George Q. Cannon, John Taylor, and Joseph F. Smith). As a counselor in the First Presidency, Joseph F. Smith participated in the dramatic expansion of the Church academy system by Presidents John Taylor and Wilford Woodruff.

announced in 1888, "We feel that the time has arrived when the proper education of our children should be taken in hand by us as a people." Woodruff formed the Church Board of Education, and stakes were instructed to organize their own local boards and create a stake academy "as soon as practicable."[27]

As a counselor to President Woodruff and his successor, Lorenzo Snow, Joseph F. Smith witnessed the Church's enthusiastic response to the call for separate education. From 1888 through President Smith's presidency, the Church operated as many as fifty-seven separate schools.[28] For those unable to attend one of the Church academies, Smith and others championed the formation of the Religion Class program, an after-school supplement to the secular education prevalent in public schools. In 1890, Wilford Woodruff, George Q. Cannon, and Joseph F. Smith wrote to local leaders, lamenting "training which our youth receive in the district schools," noting that it did not "increase their feelings of devotion to God and love for His cause, for, as is well-known, all teachings of a religious character are rigorously excluded from the studies permitted in these institutions." Their remedy was "that in every ward where a Church school is not established, that some brother or sister or brethren and sisters well adapted for such a responsible position by their intelligence and devotion, as well as their love

Brigham Young Academy, circa January 4, 1892. Joseph F. Smith rode in the buggy being pulled by white horses, accompanied by Karl G. Maeser and George A. Brimhall. Greatly concerned by the expenses necessary to operate Church academies, President Smith set in motion the policy decisions that led to the replacement of most Church schools with seminary and institute alternatives.

for the young, be called, as on a mission . . . to take charge of a school wherein the first principles of the Gospel, Church history and kindred subjects shall be taught. This school is to meet for a short time each afternoon after the close of the district school."[29] As Church President, Smith oversaw a boom in Religion Class enrollment as well as further expansion to the educational system, including the creation of the St. George Stake Academy, Snowflake Stake Academy, Big Horn Stake Academy, San Luis Stake Academy, Millard Academy, and the Knight Academy, all under his watch.

As Church school alternatives expanded early in Joseph F. Smith's presidency, public school options likewise blossomed. At the beginning of the twentieth century, only six high schools existed in the entire state of Utah. Of the six schools, only the schools in Salt Lake City and Ogden boasted student populations of more than sixty-five.[30] By 1902, the second year of Smith's presidency, the State Superintendent's report counted nineteen public high schools in Utah; only three years later, there were thirty-three.[31] In 1914, during the height of Smith's presidency, State Superintendent of Public Instruction A. C. Matheson summarized, "No other branch of the public school system has developed so rapidly during recent years. In a little more than a decade the number of high schools has increased from four to forty and the enrollment of students from one thousand to eight thousand." Matheson boasted that the state of Utah constructed twenty-five high school buildings in a six-year period from 1908 to 1914, ranging from "substantial modern structures costing $40,000 each to the East Side High School, Salt Lake City, which represents an expenditure of $600,000." Jordan High School in Sandy, Matheson continued, "is declared by leading educators to be the finest and best equipped rural high school in the west."[32]

A System "Run Mad": Reining in Educational Exuberance

The expansion of public high schools in the West during the early twentieth century led to a dramatic educational shift during the Smith presidency. During the early years of his presidency, the Church moved toward supporting public schools, in spite of rhetoric by Smith's predecessors against taxation for secular curriculum. The softened position towards public education came, in part, because of the realization that many members were unable to send their children to Church schools. In fact, if the Church and the public school systems were in competition, the Church's program was clearly losing, at least from a statistical perspective. In 1890, for example, public high schools in Utah enrolled only 5 percent of the state's secondary student population. By the decade after President Smith's death, 90 percent of all students attended public schools.[33]

In February 1905, President Smith and his counselors endorsed the growing public school system. Interestingly, they also expressed support for its secular curriculum. "We wish it distinctly understood that we are not in favor of, but are emphatically opposed to, denominational teachings in our public schools. We are proud of that splendid system of schools, and do not desire that they should be interfered with in any way whatever. For religious and devotional training, other institutions are provided, by our Church as well as by other churches, and we cannot too strongly urge that the two systems continue to be kept entirely separate and apart."[34] Two years later, Smith and his counselors further clarified,

"It has been charged that 'Mormonism' is opposed to education. The history of the Church and the precepts of its leaders are a sufficient answer to that accusation." Summarizing the Church educational legacy from its founding to the present, Smith concluded, "The State of Utah, now dotted with free schools, academies, colleges, and universities, institutions which have given her marked educational prominence, furnishes indisputable evidence that her people—mostly 'Mormons'—are friends and promoters of education."[35]

Not only did President Smith openly support public schools, he sought to get Latter-day Saint teachers employed in them. In May 1911, Smith wrote to the State Board of Education, requesting "recognition of the normal work in our Church schools, so that the graduates from our normal courses may be regarded in the same class as State normal graduates, and be granted certificates to teach in the public schools without examination."[36] This was done to satisfy the growing need for public school teachers in the region while providing employment opportunities for Church school graduates.

Though he appeared supportive, President Smith's endorsement of public education may have been a practical response to the realization that Church members were flooding public school classrooms. In fact, though the state superintendent of public instruction claimed "the rapid growth of high schools in the state is a matter of congratulation," the expense of the burgeoning public and private educational system eventually worried Joseph F. Smith, a man whose education came from the home and the herd.[37] Knowing he would be "criticized by professional 'lovers of education' for expressing [his] idea in relation to this matter," Smith voiced his concern about escalating costs to support the new programs in his opening address of the October 1915 general conference. "I hope that I may be pardoned for giving expression to my real conviction with reference to the question of education in the State of Utah," Smith declared. "I believe that we are running education mad. I believe that we are taxing the people more for education than they should be taxed. This is my sentiment."[38] During his presidency, Smith founded educational alternatives and issued cautions regarding expansion, setting the stage for the rise of the modern Church Educational System.

Finding a way to provide religious instruction for the children of Church members attending public schools led to the creation of the most significant educational legacy of President Smith's administration, the formation of the modern released-time seminary program. Formed by the Granite Stake Presidency as an alternative for Latter-day Saint students attending Salt Lake City's Granite High School instead of one of the Church's academies, with Smith's support the program quickly blossomed from one program in 1912 to thirteen by his death in 1918.[39] Enrollment jumped from 70 students the first year to 1,528 students in 1918.[40] At the same time, high school enrollment at Church academies remained steady, ranging between four and five thousand students from 1912 to 1918.[41]

Spiritual and Temporal Concerns within Church Education

While the seminary program flourished, Church academies caused problems for President Smith during his presidency. In particular, controversial teachings relating to evolution and biblical interpretation shaped Smith's educational legacy. Reflecting on one of the most divisive religious issues of their era, in 1909 President Smith and his First Presidency published a statement entitled, "The Origin of Man." The following year, one of his biographers noted, "President Smith's conservative approach toward education collided with the competing desires of some of the faculty and students on the Provo campus [of Brigham Young University]."[42] Perpetuating modernist critiques on the authenticity of the Bible and the origin of man, three Brigham Young University professors, Ralph Chamberlain, Joseph Peterson, and Henry Peterson, were eventually let go from the faculty.[43]

The flare-up elicited several comments by President Smith and ultimately a warning regarding the dangers false educational ideas could pose. At the Church's general conference in April 1911, he defended sources of eternal truth: "I believe that the Latter-day Saints, and especially the leading men in Israel, have sufficient knowledge and understanding of the principles of the gospel that they know the truth, and they are made free by its possession—free from sin, free from error, free from darkness, from the traditions of men, from vain philosophy, and from the untried, unproven theories of scientists, that need demonstration beyond the possibility of a doubt." Reflecting the supremacy he placed on revealed truth and the skepticism he shared for unproven ideas, Smith continued, "We have had science and philosophy through all the ages, and they have undergone change after change. Scarcely a century has passed but they have introduced new theories of science and of philosophy that supersede the old traditions and the old faith and the old doctrines entertained by philosophers and scientists. These things may undergo continuous changes, but the word of God is always true, is always right."[44] He later warned of the influence of false ideas in a caution to the Church, "There are at least three dangers that threaten the Church within, and the authorities need to awaken to the fact that the people should be warned unceasingly against them. As I see these, they are flattery of prominent men in the world, false educational ideas, and sexual impurity."[45]

Concerns about false teachings at Church schools were coupled with rising costs to maintain the schools. In a 1909 letter to Brigham Young College, President Smith voiced his concern about escalating expenses at Church schools, "Within less than a decade the annual appropriation for maintaining the Church schools has increased almost ten fold, so rapid has been the growth of the schools. This is altogether out of proportion to the increase of the revenues of the Church; a ratio that cannot longer be maintained."[46] In general conference in 1916, he further lamented Church school costs. Summarizing Church expenditures for the fifteen-year period from 1901 to 1915, he reported spending $3,714,455 for schools, the largest expenditure in the entire Church budget for the time period. By comparison, $3,279,900 had been spent through all Church channels aiding the poor during the same era. Slightly over $2,000,000 was spent building meetinghouses and only $1,169,499 was spent on maintenance and repair of temples.[47] Of concern to President Smith, Church schools were receiving the lion's share of the faith's funds and requesting more at an alarming rate.

Church Board of Education minutes for April 28, 1915, reflect Smith's growing apprehension regarding educational expenses. Responding to Weber Academy's request for funding to add a normal course, the minutes record:

> President Smith explained to the brethren the condition of the Church finances and clearly pointed out that the trustee-in-trust is in no position at present to promise an increase of funds for educational purposes. While he was heartily in favor of the idea of our turning attention to the making of teachers and would be very glad if some of the smaller schools could be turned into public high schools, to have the means thus saved expended for normal work, he did not see how he could undertake at present to branch out and incur more expense; we should simply have to trim our educational sails to the financial winds.[48]

While the minutes report President Smith's concern, they also hint at his solution. By transforming smaller schools into public high schools, focusing on teacher training in the remaining institutions, and augmenting religious instruction with the seminary system, President Smith saw a way out of the fiscal dilemma Church schools presented.[49] Ultimately, it was this approach that his successor—President Heber J. Grant—adopted, concluding the educational transformation begun by Joseph F. Smith by closing or transferring to the state nearly all of the Church academies during the 1920s and early 1930s, replacing them with an expanded seminary and institute program.[50] President Smith's plan, implemented by President Grant, charted the course of the Church Educational System across the remainder of the twentieth century.

Summary and Conclusion

Ezra Taft Benson taught, "Each President has been uniquely selected for the time and situation which the world and Church needed. All were 'men of the hour.'"[51] President Joseph F. Smith's life and administration witness to the Lord's preparing him for his particular mission. The last Church President to have known Joseph Smith personally, Joseph F. Smith was a transitional figure, leading the faith from its pioneer founding into its modern era, turning Church attention beyond the Intermountain West.[52] His legacy continues to impact Church teachings and practice today.

The shaping of Church education was one of Smith's most important legacies. The least formally educated Church President of the twentieth century, Joseph F. Smith marked the faith's educational trajectory for the century. He presided over the formation of the Church's seminary program, laying the groundwork for the transition to supplementary religious education. Nurtured at his own mother's knee, he encouraged the beginnings of the modern family home evening program, counseling parents to "gather their boys and girls about them in the home and teach them the word of the Lord."[53] His fiscal restraint reined in excess, curtailing Church academy growth. Educationally, he placed a primacy on spiritual learning and his teachings continue to guide understanding of eternal things.[54] Indeed, much of the doctrinal understanding and educational practice of The Church of Jesus Christ of Latter-day Saints today are an outgrowth of the life and ministry of Joseph F. Smith.

Notes

A longer version of this piece appeared in *BYU Studies Quarterly* 52, no. 3 (2013): 39–62.

1. Thomas G. Alexander, *Mormonism in Transition* (Urbana: University of Illinois, 1986), 157–58.
2. Joseph F. Smith, in Conference Report, October 1915, 4.
3. "The City Council, and General Bennett's Inaugural Address," *Times and Seasons,* February 15, 1841, 319.
4. Paul Thomas Smith, "A Historical Study of the Nauvoo, Illinois, Public School System, 1841–1845" (master's thesis, Brigham Young University, 1969), 80–81.
5. Joseph Fielding Smith, *Life of Joseph F. Smith: Sixth President of The Church of Jesus Christ of Latter-day Saints* (Salt Lake City: Deseret Book, 1969), 225–26.
6. Francis M. Gibbons, *Joseph F. Smith: Patriarch and Preacher, Prophet of God* (Salt Lake City: Deseret Book, 1984), 7–9.
7. Don Cecil Corbett, *Mary Fielding Smith: Daughter of Britain* (Salt Lake City: Deseret Book, 1966), 13; Susa Y. Gates, "Mothers in Israel," *Relief Society Magazine,* March 1916, 123.
8. Kenneth W. Godfrey, Audrey M. Godfrey, and Jill Mulvay Derr, eds., *Women's Voices: An Untold History of the Latter-day Saints, 1830–1900* (Salt Lake City: Deseret Book, 1982), 58–68.
9. Smith, *Life of Joseph F. Smith,* 4.
10. Smith, *Life of Joseph F. Smith,* 225. Mary reared the five surviving children of Hyrum Smith and his first wife Jerusha Barden, who died in 1837. A seven-year-old son died in September 1841. The oldest daughter, Lovina, married Lorin Walker in June 1844, shortly before her father's martyrdom. Mary also gave birth to Hyrum's two youngest children, Joseph Fielding and Martha Ann.
11. "Conference Minutes," *Times and Seasons,* November 1, 1845, 1015.
12. *Deseret News,* November 27, 1850, cited in Levi Edgar Young, "Education in Utah," *Improvement Era,* July 1913, 879.
13. Leonard J. Arrington, "The Latter-day Saints and Public Education," *Southwestern Journal of Social Education* 7, no. 9 (Spring–Summer 1977): 11.
14. Smith, *Life of Joseph F. Smith,* 163.
15. Smith, *Life of Joseph F. Smith,* 226.
16. Joseph F. Smith to Samuel L. Adams, May 11, 1888, cited in Richard Neitzel Holzapfel and R. Q. Shupe, *Joseph F. Smith: Portrait of a Prophet* (Salt Lake City: Deseret Book, 2000), 20.
17. Smith, *Life of Joseph F. Smith,* 229.
18. Smith, *Life of Joseph F. Smith,* 225–26.
19. Joseph F. Smith, "Testimony Bearing," *Juvenile Instructor,* August 1906, 466.
20. *Gospel Doctrine: Sermons and Writings of President Joseph F. Smith* (Salt Lake City: Deseret Book, 1939), 269.
21. Joseph F. Smith, "Worship in the Home," *Improvement Era,* December 1903, 138.
22. Joseph F. Smith, "Dress and Social Practices," *Improvement Era,* December 1916, 173.
23. Joseph F. Smith, in Conference Report, April 1903, 3.
24. Joseph F. Smith, "Looking for Easy Work," *Improvement Era,* January 1903, 229.
25. John Taylor and George Q. Cannon, in James R. Clark, comp., *Messages of the First Presidency of The Church of Jesus Christ of Latter-day Saints, 1833–1964* (Salt Lake City: Bookcraft,

1966), 3:58–59. Joseph F. Smith did not sign the epistle because he was serving a mission in Hawaii at the time.

26. John Taylor and George Q. Cannon, in Clark, *Messages of the First Presidency*, 3:86–87.
27. Wilford Woodruff, in Clark, *Messages of the First Presidency*, 3:168.
28. Because of some short operational lives, enumerating the exact number of Church schools is problematic. Researchers for Brigham Young University's Education in Zion exhibit found that the Church operated as many as thirty-five stake academies and twenty-two other schools, called seminaries because a corresponding stake academy already existed in the stake. These twenty-two seminaries are not to be confused with the present Church education endeavor of the same name that was also begun during Smith's presidency at Granite High School in Salt Lake City in 1912. C. Terry Warner and Brett D. Dowdle to Scott C. Esplin, e-mail, June 5, 2008; see also Scott C. Esplin and Arnold K. Garr, "Church Academies: 1875–1933," in *Mapping Mormonism: An Atlas of Latter-day Saint History*, ed. Brandon S. Plewe, S. Kent Brown, Donald Q. Cannon, and Richard H. Jackson (Provo, UT: BYU Press, 2012), 126–27.
29. Wilford Woodruff, George Q. Cannon, and Joseph F. Smith, in Clark, *Messages of the First Presidency*, 3:196–97.
30. Public high schools operated in the communities of Salt Lake, Ogden, Park City, Brigham City, Nephi, and Richfield at the dawn of the twentieth century. *Third Report of the Superintendent of Public Instruction of the State of Utah for the Biennial Period Ending June 30, 1900* (Salt Lake City: State of Utah, Department of Public Instruction, 1901), 25–26.
31. *Fourth Report of the Superintendent of Public Instruction of the State of Utah for the Biennial Period Ending June 30, 1902* (Salt Lake City: Star Printing, 1903), 22; William E. Berrett and Alma P. Burton, eds., *Readings in LDS Church History* (Salt Lake City: Deseret Book, 1958), 3:338.
32. *Tenth Report of the Superintendent of Public Instruction of the State of Utah for the Biennial Period Ending June 30, 1914* (Salt Lake City: Arrow Press, 1915), 24.
33. William E. Berrett and Alma P. Burton, eds., *Readings in LDS Church History* (Salt Lake City: Deseret Book, 1958), 3:338.
34. Joseph F. Smith, John R. Winder, and Anthon H. Lund, "Religion Classes and School Buildings," *Improvement Era*, February 1905, 302.
35. Joseph F. Smith, John R. Winder, and Anthon H. Lund, "An Address. The Church of Jesus Christ of Latter-day Saints to the World," *Improvement Era*, May 1907, 485.
36. Joseph F. Smith to the State Board of Education, May 5, 1911, in William Peter Miller, Weber College—1888 to 1933, Church History Library, Salt Lake City.
37. *Tenth Report of the Superintendent of Public Instruction*, 24.
38. Joseph F. Smith, in Conference Report, October 1915, 4.
39. Seminary programs formed during Smith's presidency include Granite (1912), Box Elder (1915), Mount Pleasant (1916), American Fork (1917), Lehi (1917), Huntington (1918), Mesa, AZ (1918), Sandy (1918), Blanding (1918), Roosevelt (1918), Richfield (1918), Pleasant Grove (1918), and Heber (1918). Historical Resource File, 1891–1989, Church Educational System (1970–), Church History Library.
40. Historical Resource File, 1891–1989, Church Educational System (1970–), Church History Library. For a brief history of the first seminary and its teacher, Thomas J. Yates, see Casey Paul Griffiths, "The First Seminary Teacher," *Religious Educator* 9, no. 3 (2008): 115–30.

41. Seminary and Institute Statistical Reports, 1919–53, Unified Church School System (1953–70), Church History Library.
42. Francis M. Gibbons, *Joseph F. Smith: Patriarch and Preacher, Prophet of God*, 254–55.
43. For additional information about the modernism controversy at BYU, see Ernest L. Wilkinson, ed., *Brigham Young University: The First One Hundred Years* (Provo, UT: Brigham Young University Press, 1975), 1:412–33.
44. Joseph F. Smith, in Conference Report, April 1911, 7–8.
45. Joseph F. Smith, "Three Threatening Dangers," *Improvement Era*, March 1914, 476–77.
46. Minutes of the General Church Board of Education, June 30, 1909, cited in Centennial History Project Papers, L. Tom Perry Special Collections, Harold B. Lee Library, Brigham Young University, Provo, UT.
47. Joseph F. Smith, in Conference Report, April 1916, 7.
48. General Church Board of Education minutes, April 28, 1915, in Miller, Weber College—1888 to 1933.
49. Minutes from the Church Board of Education on June 30, 1909, reflect support for limiting the number of Church schools and emphasizing teacher training:

> This recommendation was also unanimously adopted by the General Board of Education.
>
> It is not the feeling of either of the committees, nor is it thought a wise policy by this Board to use from the limited money available the large sums that would be needed in giving college education to the comparatively few who are able to take it; but it is thought that this portion of the tithes of the people should be spent in making many Latter-day Saints of our children in high schools rather than a comparative few in colleges.
>
> Though desirable, the Church cannot maintain a complete system of schools from the primary grade to the college work and has, therefore, concentrated its efforts in maintaining a system of high schools to best meet the needs of the young people.
>
> Nevertheless, the need for teachers, not only for our own schools, but for the many other organizations of the Church, make it necessary to have a teachers' college; but neither the money at our disposal nor the number of college students in the Church at present who desire to become teachers, is sufficient to warrant maintaining properly more than one such college.
>
> Therefore the General Board of Education has decided to discontinue all college work in the Church schools except what is really necessary to prepare teachers; and we feel that when the people understand this matter they will see the wisdom of the decision and feel satisfied with it.
>
> We would be pleased if you would furnish copies of this communication to all the Presidents of Stakes included in the Brigham Young College district that it may be read at their conferences or priesthood meetings or ward meetings.
>
> Your brethren and fellow laborers in the gospel,
> The General Church Board of Education,
> Joseph F. Smith, President.

Minutes of the General Church Board of Education, June 30, 1909, cited in Centennial History Project Papers, L. Tom Perry Special Collections.

50. Of the more than thirty Church academies, only four (Brigham Young University, Ricks College, LDS Business College, and the Juárez Academy) survived as Church-sponsored institutions after 1933. Meanwhile, seminary enrollment grew exponentially from nearly three thousand students in 1920 to thirty-four thousand students in 1933. For additional information regarding the discontinuance of Church academies and the growth of the seminary and institute program, see Scott C. Esplin, "Education in Transition: Church and State Relationships in Utah Education, 1888–1933" (PhD diss., Brigham Young University, 2006).
51. *The Teachings of Ezra Taft Benson* (Salt Lake City: Bookcraft, 1988), 142.
52. During his administration, the first temple outside the continental United States (Laie, Hawaii) and the first temple outside the United States itself (Cardston, Alberta, Canada) were announced. Historically, he also guided Church efforts in acquiring and developing significant historic sites including the Carthage Jail, the Joseph Smith farm, the Sacred Grove, the Joseph Smith birthplace, and the Hill Cumorah.
53. Joseph F. Smith, Anthon H. Lund, and Charles W. Penrose, in Clark, *Messages of the First Presidency*, 4:338.
54. Of Joseph F. Smith's teachings, Harold B. Lee observed, "When I want to seek for a more clear definition of doctrinal subjects, I have usually turned to the writings and sermons of President Joseph F. Smith" (in Conference Report, October 1972, 18).

Richard O. Cowan

23

Church Programs in Transition

The basic priesthood and auxiliary organizations of the Church had their origins in the nineteenth century. Priesthood quorums as well as the basic local units—stakes and wards—were established by the Prophet Joseph Smith. However, most auxiliary organizations—the Relief Society, the Sunday School, the Young Men's Mutual Improvement Association (YMMIA), the Young Ladies' Mutual Improvement Association (YLMIA),[1] and the Primary—were added or reemphasized during the era of Brigham Young. Although the Sunday School and Relief Society traced their beginnings back to Joseph Smith's era, each of these organizations received expanded emphasis and became a regular part of local units Churchwide under the leadership of Brigham Young. A lesser known auxiliary, the Religion Class, had its beginning in 1890, when a Utah law prohibited religious instruction in public schools and the Church provided gospel classes for elementary-school children one afternoon each week. Many programs sponsored by these organizations, now familiar to Latter-day Saints, experienced such significant development during the era of President Joseph F. Smith that a person who had been active in the Church prior to 1890 would scarcely be able to recognize

---

Richard O. Cowan is a professor of Church history and doctrine at Brigham Young University.

its programs a quarter century later. Historian Thomas G. Alexander has referred to this period in Church history as an era of "transition."[2] These changes not only affected the work of the priesthood and the auxiliaries but had an impact on the Saints' basic meeting pattern as well.

Developments in Sacrament and Fast Meetings

The scriptures have directed that members of the Church meet together often to instruct and strengthen one another and to partake of the sacrament (see Moroni 6:5–6; D&C 20:75; 43:8–9; 59:9–10). Although the basic objectives have remained constant, the pattern of these meetings has changed over the years to meet varying needs and conditions.

In 1852, Brigham Young directed the Saints to meet "each sabbath at 10 a.m., and 2 p.m.," and indicated that "in the evening, the several quorums of the priesthood would assemble to receive instructions." Each Thursday, they were to meet at 2:00 p.m. "for prayer and supplication." In addition, a special fast meeting was to convene at 10:00 a.m. on the first Thursday of each month.[3] On this occasion, the Saints were asked to bring offerings to the bishop for the relief of the poor. This meeting pattern would characterize the Saints' activities through the next several decades.

By the 1890s, in some of the larger centers, such as Salt Lake City and Provo, the custom was to hold just one worship service at a central location on Sunday afternoons, and the sacrament was administered in these community-wide meetings rather than in the separate wards. Speaking at general conference in 1894, however, President George Q. Cannon directed that the administration of the sacrament should be moved to the regular Sunday-evening services held in each ward. In this way, "the Bishops of the wards . . . could carry out the requirement which forbids that the unworthy shall partake of the sacred emblems" as is set out in 3 Nephi 18.[4] Thus, just prior to the administration of Joseph F. Smith, the ward sacrament meeting finally became the standard Churchwide practice.

By 1896, new patterns of life made a shift in the fast day advisable. During pioneer times, the Saints generally had lived in agricultural communities where most people were of the same faith, making a midweek fast meeting possible. By the end of the century, however, an increasing number lived in urban centers and worked for non-Mormon employers, making it awkward to disrupt their workday to attend a fast meeting. The First Presidency, in which Joseph F. Smith was

Second Counselor, observed that attendance at these meetings "dwindled to such an extent that comparatively few have the opportunity of attending them." They therefore concluded that "Thursday as a day of fasting and prayer in the Church no longer serves the object for which it was intended." Consequently, the monthly fast day was shifted to the first Sunday of each month. Afternoon fast meetings were to include the administration of the sacrament, the bearing of testimonies, the blessing of children, and the confirming of those who had been baptized. The First Presidency indicated, "We feel assured that excellent results will follow the giving of members of the Church an opportunity to bear their testimony to each other and to seek for the gifts which the Lord has promised to those who keep His commandments." The First Presidency cautioned that "care should also be taken on such occasions to see that the wants of the poor are relieved by the contributions of the Saints in their behalf, that no cry of the indigent or suffering shall arise from our land in the ears of the Lord of Sabaoth." The First Presidency also discouraged Sunday-afternoon meetings in the Tabernacle, as well as stakewide fast meetings elsewhere, so that "all the members of the ward, including the aged and infirm, and others who are unable to go to the Tabernacle, [have] an opportunity to participate in the fast meeting and share in the blessings of the occasion."[5]

The Auxiliaries Expand

The opening years of the twentieth century witnessed rapid expansion of both the priesthood organizations and the auxiliaries. Joseph F. Smith not only served as President of the Church but also presided as superintendent over the Sunday School and the Young Men's Mutual Improvement Association. The pattern of having the President of the Church also be the executive of these organizations had developed just a few years earlier. Wilford Woodruff was already serving as superintendent of the YMMIA when he became President of the Church in 1887. When the Sunday School became a Churchwide organization in the 1860s, Brigham Young called George Q. Cannon to be superintendent, a position in which he served until his death in 1901. At that time, Lorenzo Snow, in the last year of his administration as President of the Church, also became superintendent of the Deseret Sunday School Union. This same dual role undoubtedly gave President Joseph F. Smith a keener awareness of and greater involvement in the work of the auxiliaries, which in turn probably contributed to his favorable view on expanding the scope of their work.

From its beginnings on March 17, 1842, the Relief Society's prime objective was charitable or compassionate service. Throughout the nineteenth century, its meetings emphasized sewing or other projects directly related to assisting the needy. In 1902, however, Relief Society leaders felt a need to provide expanded educational opportunities for the sisters, and the "mother's class" became a regular part of the society's program.

At first, local Relief Societies provided their own study materials, but in 1914, the Relief Society general board began providing uniform lessons for these weekly classes. A pattern soon developed: the lessons would feature theology in the first week of the month, and then the Relief Society would study homemaking, literature, and social science, respectively, during the other weeks.[6]

President Joseph F. Smith was interested in the Relief Society's work and was convinced of its divine origin. He asserted that worldly organizations "are men-made, or women-made," but he was convinced that the Relief Society "is divinely made, divinely authorized, divinely instituted, divinely ordained of God to minister for the salvation of the souls of women and of men."[7]

The Sunday School also expanded the scope of its work under President Smith's leadership. Richard Ballantyne's objective in 1849 for establishing the first Latter-day Saint Sunday School in the Rocky Mountains had been to carry the gospel message to the children in the Church. The Sunday School remained a children's organization throughout the nineteenth century and into the early years of President Joseph F. Smith's administration. Its focus on children is reflected in hymns still sung today over one hundred years later: "List! the merry children singing! / What a pleasing, joyful sound! . . . From the books of revelation / We are taught while yet in youth. . . . Here we meet with friends and neighbors; / Parents too are in the throng."[8] "Oh, blessed hour! communion sweet! / When children, friends, and teachers meet."[9] Note that the adults in these hymns were identified from the point of view of the children, as either teachers or parents. The first Sunday School class for adults was not inaugurated Churchwide until 1906. Significantly, it was called the "parents' class."[10]

David O. McKay had a profound impact on Sunday School development. As a young returned missionary at the turn of the century, he was called to be a member of the Weber Stake Sunday School superintendency in Ogden and to give particular attention to instruction. He introduced refinements in teaching methods, such as defining lesson goals, outlining materials, using teaching aids, and applying of the lesson to daily life. Students were sorted into "grades" according to age, and a specific course was developed for each group throughout the stake. As general superintendent of the Sunday School, President Joseph F. Smith was undoubtedly well aware of these improvements in nearby Ogden. In 1906, when Elder McKay was called to the Council of the Twelve, President Smith asked him to become one of his assistants in the Sunday School general superintendency. In this latter position, Elder McKay was able to promote the Ogden improvements throughout the entire Church.

During the following years, a "clear-cut departmentalization"[11] of Sunday School work into classes for specific age groups was accompanied by an improvement of published lesson materials.[12] Following George Q. Cannon's death in 1901, the Sunday School purchased the *Juvenile Instructor* from the Cannon family. Originally, the magazine itself had been the instructor of the youth; the Sunday School now transformed it into a resource for teachers, the group with whom the magazine's title increasingly came to be identified.

The Primary program continued relatively unchanged. Children met one afternoon each week for religious activities. The new Religion Class began meeting during these years, involving many of the children in Primary; students attending public elementary schools met at their ward chapel on a different afternoon each week, with the program focusing on instruction rather than activity.

The Priesthood Reform Movement

At the height of this rapid auxiliary expansion, President Joseph F. Smith looked forward to a time when the priesthood organizations would again occupy a position of preeminence. At the April general conference in 1906, he declared:

> We expect to see the day, if we live long enough (and if some of us do not live long enough to see it, there are others who will), when every council of the Priesthood in the Church of Jesus Christ of Latter-day Saints will understand its duty, will assume its own responsibility, will magnify its calling, and fill its place in the Church, to the uttermost, according to the intelligence and ability possessed by it. When that day shall come, there will not be so much necessity for work that is now being done by the auxiliary organizations, because it will be done by the regular quorums of the Priesthood. The Lord designed and comprehended it from the beginning, and He has made provision in the Church whereby

> every need may be met and satisfied through the regular organizations of the Priesthood. It has truly been said that the Church is perfectly organized. The only trouble is that these organizations are not fully alive to the obligations that rest upon them. When they become thoroughly awakened to the requirements made of them, they will fulfill their duties more faithfully, and the work of the Lord will be all the stronger and more powerful and influential in the world.[13]

Interestingly, David O. McKay, who would figure prominently in the fulfillment of this prophecy, was sustained as a member of the Council of the Twelve at this same conference.

Records indicate that during the later nineteenth century, priesthood meetings had been held at varying intervals. Most quorums met monthly, and Melchizedek Priesthood meetings were not necessarily connected to any particular ward. Customarily, these meetings were held on different weeknights rather than Sunday. In many rural areas, the quorums did not meet at all during the farming season. With such infrequent and often irregular meetings, the priesthood quorums' effectiveness declined.

Under President Joseph F. Smith's leadership, the Quorum of the Twelve, the Presiding Bishopric, and especially the First Council of the Seventy took steps to remedy these deficiencies and to revitalize the priesthood organizations. This "priesthood reform movement" was to have a far-reaching effect on the priesthood quorums as well as the auxiliaries.[14]

At the general conference held April 4–6, 1908, President Joseph F. Smith reported, "Several very important movements have been inaugurated of late among us for the advantage of the Saints, and especially for the benefit and advancement of those who are associated with the various quorums of the Priesthood. I desire to mention the effort that is being made by our Seventies in their organization of classes and schools for the instruction of the members of their quorums, that they might be qualified for the great work of the ministry to which they are dedicated." Nevertheless, President Smith also expressed concern over some other aspects of the priesthood program. "The Elders' quorums should also be looked after, and those who preside in them [should be] vigilant and faithful in looking after those entrusted to their care, and are subject to their direction and counsel." And concerning the Aaronic Priesthood, he noted, "Efforts are also being made to organize and put to usefulness the quorums of the Lesser Priesthood." He then added, "We should look after our boys who have been ordained Deacons, Teachers, and Priests in the Church. We should find something for them to do in their callings."[15]

Responding to President Smith's charge, the Presiding Bishopric wrote to the First Presidency two days after the conference closed, proposing that a general board be called to assist the Bishopric in preparing lesson outlines for the Aaronic Priesthood quorums.[16] That same day (April 8, 1908), the First Presidency and the Twelve met and appointed a committee, including Elder David O. McKay and others, to prepare lesson materials for the Aaronic and Melchizedek Priesthood organizations.[17] In reference to the suggestion that a special board be formed for the Aaronic Priesthood quorums, President Joseph F. Smith observed that the Twelve Apostles themselves "constitute the priesthood board."[18]

At an important meeting of the Priesthood Committee on Outlines held June 5, 1908, Elder David O. McKay was named committee chairman. He submitted several recommendations which were to have a profound impact on subsequent priesthood developments. Although the practice of ordaining young men to the Aaronic Priesthood had become increasingly common since 1877, there was not yet a fixed schedule for moving from one office to another.[19] In order to facilitate the committee's work in developing meaningful lessons, Elder McKay suggested that the Aaronic Priesthood be divided into grades (as had been done in the Sunday School and MIA) by ordaining young men as deacons at twelve, teachers at fifteen, priests at eighteen, and elders at twenty-one years of age. At that time, individuals officially became adults at age twenty-one. In subsequent years, these ages were modified from time to time.

One of the committee's most far-reaching recommendations was for the inauguration of weekly ward priesthood meetings. They were to be held Monday evenings for at least one hour and forty-five minutes. All groups would meet in an opening session before separating for individual quorum activities. A minimum of one hour should be spent in separate quorum sessions, with the lesson occupying thirty-five minutes and the balance of the time being devoted to "practical work," including the assigning of duties. These plans recognized the importance of learning of the duty and then acting in performance of duty (see D&C 107:99–100). The committee supplied a detailed agenda for the weekly sessions in the wards as well as for monthly stake priesthood meetings.[20]

The new program went into effect at the beginning of 1909. In their New Year's greeting to the Church, the First Presidency observed: "Special attention is called to the weekly meetings of the priesthood quorums in all the wards. We believe this movement will not only increase the proficiency of the priesthood by reason of its educative features, but by bringing all the brethren together once a week they will acquire the habit of regular activity as servants of the Lord. It has the additional advantage of putting the bishop in communication with every home once a week. We like the idea of these weekly reunions of the fathers of the ward with their sons and associates."[21]

The inauguration of weekly ward priesthood "classes" did not do away with the long-standing pattern of monthly quorum meetings. The *Improvement Era* explained, "For the convenience of men who belong to quorums that are widely scattered, and who could not come together frequently for instruction, owing to the distance to be traveled, a system of ward priesthood meetings has been introduced by the presiding authorities of the Church which divides quorums that are located in more than one ward into ward classes; but this arrangement does not contemplate excusing men from coming together in quorums as the Lord has commanded."[22] This system, with two kinds of meetings, couldn't help but be confusing.

Inertia needs to be overcome in getting any new program moving. By 1913, only 76 percent of the priesthood bearers were even enrolled in the weekly ward classes, and only 22 percent attended. The specific figures for each office were as follows: high priests, 34 percent; Seventies, 26 percent; elders, 15 percent; priests, 17 percent; teachers, 14 percent; and deacons, 23 percent.[23] Monday evenings interfered with evening chores, especially in farming areas, so Sunday morning gradually became the preferred time for ward priesthood meetings.[24] "The shift of priesthood meeting from Monday night to Sunday morning," one historian noted, "not only helped priesthood attendance but had also boosted activity in Sunday School. In fact, in light of the results, the MIA considered shifting its meeting to Sunday as well."[25]

New Emphasis for the MIA

The Young Men's and Young Ladies' Mutual Improvement Associations followed similar but generally separate courses of development during the nineteenth century. Unlike today's Young Men and Young Women organizations, the MIAs included adults as well as youth. Brigham Young's goal in establishing these organizations was to develop faith through promoting public speaking and testimony bearing. As their programs developed, four areas of emphasis emerged: theology, science, history, and literature. The pattern of regular weekly meetings was established by the late 1880s, and by 1890, class discussion had replaced lectures. With this new format came the half-hour "preliminary program," featuring musical numbers, short talks, and other contributions by members of the associations. Until the early twentieth century, all ages met in a single class, but by 1903, most MIAs had been graded into "juniors" and "seniors." In 1911, the YMMIA adopted the Boy Scout program for its younger group, and shortly thereafter the YLMIA developed its own Beehive Girls program.[26]

At first, the local associations met on various evenings, although Tuesday was most common. In some areas, especially in the country, where it was difficult to get good attendance on a weeknight, the MIA met on Sunday evenings. In 1898, the two general boards officially recommended Tuesday evening.[27]

Originally, the two MIAs met separately. This was consistent with the wishes of Brigham Young, who, interestingly, did not want the sessions to degenerate into "courting meetings."[28] Within a short time, however, in some areas, the Young Men's and Young Ladies' Associations began meeting together, and "the very evil that the President said would ensue, from admitting the young ladies as members [of the Young Men's Associations], is to be observed in many places," noted the *Contributor*. "The boys go to meeting to take the girls home, and the girls go to be taken."[29] Following the turn of the century, the move to unite the two associations gained impetus: "Bishops and young men pleaded . . . for the assistance and presence of the girls to help their own associations, and to draw out the boys. As ever, the girls consented, though not always convinced that they were gainers in the new arrangement."[30] By 1914, the practice of both MIAs meeting together had become the rule.

As early as 1891, the YMMIA and YLMIA sponsored a monthly "conjoint" meeting in addition to their regular weekly sessions. Normally held on fast-Sunday evenings, these meetings featured the best materials from the previous month's work in each organization. These were "the one means of letting parents see what their children [were] learning in the associations." Therefore, the young people themselves were to take the lead in planning and conducting the sessions and were to be prepared at a moment's notice to speak, perform a musical number, and so on.[31]

The advent of regular priesthood meetings had a direct impact on the Mutual Improvement Associations. As noted earlier, theological study was one of the areas regularly stressed in MIA work. In 1908, however, when lessons began to be prepared for the priesthood quorums, the MIA's emphasis on theology no longer seemed necessary. Thus the YMMIA general board resolved, "Owing to the fact that the priesthood quorums have formally taken up a study of theology, the YMMIA should take up educational, literary and recreative studies permeated by religious thought. That music and art be encouraged and that social culture and refinement of manners constitute an important part of our endeavor, . . . that athletic work be encouraged and established wherever practicable."[32]

The YLMIA followed a similar course. Thus the MIAs were redirected into an emphasis on cultural and social programs, which would be a prime characteristic of their work during the twentieth century.

Meeting Special Needs

The Progressive Era of the early twentieth century was a time when many churches and other organizations were beginning to respond to newly felt social and educational needs. In this spirit, the Relief Society organized its Social Services Department in 1919. Beginning in 1904, the Church addressed the needs of one specific group. In that year, under the direction of President Joseph F. Smith, the Church created the Society of the Aid of the Sightless. The Church charged it with the responsibility of publishing literature for the blind, "aiding in their education, endeavoring to improve their condition, becoming interested in all that pertains to their welfare," and cooperating with others to accomplish these ends through education and legislation.[33]

The lack of braille scriptures, hymns, or lesson materials was a substantial obstacle to blind Latter-day Saints' becoming fully involved in Church activities. Largely through the efforts of Albert M. Talmage (a blind brother of Elder James E. Talmage) and his wife, Sarah, the society worked to fill this void. Beginning in 1912, a monthly braille periodical, the *Messenger to the Sightless*, published religious and general-interest materials.

Publishing the Book of Mormon in braille was an important project for Albert and Sarah. They had to prepare the metal printing plates by hand. They thoroughly moistened the special braille paper before embossing the dots with their hand-operated press. They then hung completed pages to dry on clotheslines that had been strung all around their home. These pages were distributed piecemeal to eagerly waiting readers.

Seminaries

With the growth of free, tax-supported high schools, enrollment declined in the Church's own academies, where students were required to pay tuition. By 1911, there were more Latter-day Saint youth attending public schools than were attending Church schools. President Joseph F. Smith was quite concerned about this trend. He explained that the Church continued to spend a substantial share of its tithing funds to maintain Church schools so that "true religion, . . . undefiled before God the Father, may be inculcated in the minds and hearts of our children while they are getting an education, to enable the heart, the soul and the spirit of our children to develop with proper teaching, in connection with the secular training."[34]

The Church therefore inaugurated a part-time religious education program similar to the Religion Classes but directed to high school students. The first "seminary" was opened in 1912 at Granite High School near Salt Lake City. The start of the first seminary was done on recommendation by the presidency of the Granite Stake. Joseph F. Merrill, the member of the stake presidency in charge of education (and future member of the Quorum of the Twelve Apostles), had based his ideas for the new program on "religious seminaries he had seen in Chicago."[35] The new program quickly proved to be an effective way to supplement the secular education students were receiving in public high schools, and within a few years, several more seminaries were opened, primarily in Utah. Thus, in the early twentieth century, the Church was conducting two distinct types of educational programs: full-time schools—the academies—providing secular as well as religious instruction, and part-time religious education—the Religion Classes and seminaries—which supplemented secular instruction in public schools on the elementary and secondary levels, respectively.

Local Initiative

Individual stakes sometimes made refinements or launched programs that were subsequently adopted Churchwide. For example, David O. McKay's improvements in Ogden Sunday Schools and Stake President Merrill's idea for a seminary have blessed Latter-day Saints worldwide.

In 1909, the Granite Stake in Salt Lake Valley inaugurated a "home night." President Joseph F. Smith became acquainted with this stake program and gave his wholehearted support as he accepted the invitation to speak at a Granite

Stake gathering in which this new program was being introduced. Six years later, President Smith and his counselors launched the program churchwide. The First Presidency directed, "We advise and urge the inauguration of a 'Home Evening' throughout the Church, at which time fathers and mothers may gather their boys and girls about them in the home and teach them the word of the Lord." These gatherings could include music, prayer, scripture reading, discussions of gospel principles and family issues, activities, and refreshments. The Presidency promised, "If the Saints obey this counsel, we promise that great blessings will result. Love at home and obedience to parents will increase. Faith will be developed in the hearts of the youth of Israel, and they will gain power to combat the evil influence and temptations which beset them."[36]

Reflections

During Joseph F. Smith's era, there were significant developments in Church meetings and activities.

Regular Church Meetings before 1890

	Sunday	Weekdays	
Morning	Sunday School for children only	Relief Society work meetings	Fast meeting (first Thursday)
Afternoon	Sacrament meeting on community basis	-	Primary
Evening	-	Young Men's MIA	Young Ladies' MIA
	Individual quorum meetings (at various times and on various days)		

Regular Church Meetings after 1920

	Sunday	Weekdays	
Morning	Ward priesthood meetings Sunday School (including adults) Fast meeting (first Sundays)	Relief Society with lessons	-
Afternoon	Ward sacrament meeting	Religion classes	Primary
Evening	MIA conjoint meeting (fast days)	Mutual Young Men's and Young Women's	Genealogy meeting

The rapid expansions of priesthood, auxiliary, and other programs heightened the need for coordination among them. Unwanted duplication needed to be avoided and gaps in their collective programs filled. By 1907, representatives from the Religion Class, Primary, Sunday School, and the Young Ladies' and Young Men's Mutual Improvement Associations (no representative of Relief Society was mentioned) formed a Committee of Correlation and Adjustments. This body sought to define the relative roles of the priesthood and auxiliaries. They considered the priesthood quorums best adapted to formal theological study, while religious instruction in the Sunday School would be less rigorous and would emphasize moral training. The MIAs should promote "religious feeling and sentiment" and cultivate social qualities and cultural refinement, giving attention to recreation for the youth. The committee recognized the home as being best suited to the teaching of the gospel and encouraged the other organizations to support the home in this role.[37] The committee's recommendation that the programs of the Religion Class and the Primary be combined would be carried out in 1929. Similarly, their proposal that the *Improvement Era* (published by the YMMIA), the *Young Women's Journal* (magazine of the YLMIA), and the *Instructor* (the Sunday School's periodical) be combined would not be fully accomplished until 1971. The recommendation that the home be placed at the center of the Church was reemphasized in a statement by the First Presidency in 1940, and this idea would become a major focus of Priesthood Correlation beginning in the 1960s.

The restructuring of Church programs during and just before the administration of President Joseph F. Smith set the basic pattern for Church organization that would remain mostly unchanged for more than half a century. These meetings, activities, organizations, and publications have been a significant source of blessings to the Latter-day Saints as they look forward to the Second Coming of the Lord Jesus Christ.

Timeline

1830 Church organized

1842 Relief Society organized in Nauvoo

1866 *Juvenile Instructor* first published by George Q. Cannon

1890 Religion Classes organized

1894	Sacrament shifted from communitywide to ward meetings
1896	Fast day shifted from Thursday to Sunday
1897	Conference reports and *Improvement Era* inaugurated
1901	*Juvenile Instructor* becomes official organ of the Sunday School
1902	*Children's Friend* first published by the Primary; Mothers' Classes added to Relief Society
1904	Society for the Aid of the Sightless organized
1906	Class for adults added to Sunday School; President Smith anticipates emphasis on priesthood
1907	Committee on Adjustments recommends consolidations
1908	General Priesthood Committee called; David O. McKay recommends ordination to Aaronic Priesthood offices at specific ages
1909	Weekly ward priesthood meetings commence; MIAs shift emphasis to cultural and other activities
1910	*Utah Genealogical and Historical Magazine* inaugurated
1911	YMMIA adopts Boy Scout program
1912	First seminary opened in Salt Lake City
1914	YM and YLMIA start meeting together
1915	*Relief Society Magazine* instituted; First Presidency urges regular family home evenings

Notes

1. This organization was originally known as the Young Ladies' Department of the Cooperative Retrenchment Association; after other changes, it was finally named Young Women's Mutual Improvement Association in 1934.
2. Thomas G. Alexander, *Mormonism in Transition: A History of the Latter-day Saints, 1890–1930*, 3rd ed. (Salt Lake City: Greg Kofford Books, 2012).

3. Thomas Bullock, "Minutes of the General Conference of the Church of Jesus Christ of Latter-day Saints Held at New Tabernacle, Great Salt Lake City, April 6, 1852, 10 a.m. President Brigham Young Presiding," *Deseret News*, April 17, 1852, 2.
4. "Morning Session," *Deseret Evening News*, April 9, 1894, 4.
5. James R. Clark, comp., *Messages of the First Presidency* (Salt Lake City: Bookcraft, 1965–75), 3:282–83.
6. Relief Society general board, *History of Relief Society, 1842–1966* (Salt Lake City: Deseret News, 1966), 34–49.
7. Quoted in *Daughters in My Kingdom: The History and Work of Relief Society* (Salt Lake City: The Church of Jesus Christ of Latter-day Saints, 2011), 65–66.
8. Robert B. Baird, "Welcome, Welcome, Sabbath Morning," *Hymns* (Salt Lake City: The Church of Jesus Christ of Latter-day Saints, 1985), no. 280.
9. George A. Manwaring, "'Tis Sweet to Sing the Matchless Love," *Hymns*, no. 177.
10. George R. Hill, "Deseret Sunday School Union," *Improvement Era*, November 1956, 800–801, 849–50.
11. Hill, "Deseret Sunday School Union," 850.
12. Hill, "Deseret Sunday School Union," 800ff.
13. Joseph F. Smith, in Conference Report, April 1906, 3.
14. See William Hartley, "The Priesthood Reform Movement, 1908–1922," *BYU Studies* 13, no. 2 (Winter 1973): 137–56. See also Alexander, *Mormonism in Transition*, chapters 6–8.
15. Joseph F. Smith, in Conference Report, April 1908, 5–6.
16. Presiding Bishopric to the First Presidency, April 8, 1908.
17. First Presidency to Presiding Bishopric, April 8, 1908.
18. Quoted by Harold B. Lee, in Conference Report, April 1963, 85.
19. See Lee A. Palmer, *Aaronic Priesthood through the Centuries* (Salt Lake City: Deseret Book, 1964), 391–95.
20. Report from the General Priesthood Committee on Outlines to the First Presidency and Twelve, September 29, 1908.
21. Clark, *Messages of the First Presidency*, 4:195.
22. "Priesthood Quorums' Table," *Improvement Era*, May 1911, 841.
23. "Priesthood Quorums' Table," *Improvement Era*, May 1913, 737.
24. Hartley, "Priesthood Reform," 144–45.
25. Alexander, *Mormonism in Transition*, 118.
26. Marba C. Josephson, *History of the YWMIA* (Salt Lake City: The Young Women's Mutual Improvement Association, 1955), 174–210; Leon M. Strong, "A History of the Young Men's Mutual Improvement Association, 1875–1938" (master's thesis, Brigham Young University, Provo, UT, 1939), 21–120; Bertha S. Reeder, "The Growth of the Young Women's Mutual Improvement Association," *Improvement Era*, November 1956, 804ff.
27. Susa Young Gates, *History of the YLMIA* (Salt Lake City: YLMIA General Board, 1911), 137–38.
28. "The General Superintendency," *Contributor*, May 1880, 181, quoted in Strong, "YMMIA," 174–75.
29. "Membership and System," *Contributor*, October 1880, 28, quoted in Josephson, *YWMIA*, 175.
30. Gates, *YLMIA*, 138.

31. Jeanette Petterson, "Officers' Notes: Convention Topics," *Young Woman's Journal*, February 1908, 79, quoted in Josephson, *YWMIA*, 178, 188–89; Strong, "YMMIA," 82–84.
32. YMMIA general board minutes, 1908, quoted in Strong, "YMMIA," 79; see also Hartley, "Priesthood Reform," 147.
33. Society for the Aid of the Sightless, minutes, 1–2, Church History Library, The Church of Jesus Christ of Latter-day Saints, Salt Lake City.
34. Joseph F. Smith, in Conference Report, October 1915, 4.
35. Alexander, *Mormonism in Transition*, 177.
36. Clark, *Messages of the First Presidency*, 4:338–39.
37. Quoted in Josephson, *YWMIA*, 182–84.

Kenneth L. Alford

24

Joseph F. Smith and the First World War:

Eventual Support and Latter-day Saint Chaplains

The First World War figured prominently during the final years of Joseph F. Smith's Church presidency. After decades of rising international tension fueled by European imperialism and an increasingly complex network of treaty obligations, the first truly modern war was triggered on June 28, 1914, when Francis Ferdinand, archduke of the Hapsburg imperial dynasty, was assassinated in Sarajevo, Serbia. One month later, on July 28, the Austro-Hungarian Empire declared war on Serbia and, in rapid succession, numerous countries followed suit, turning the regional conflict into a world war.[1] Before the war ended, over fifty-nine million men had been mobilized, and tens of millions of soldiers and civilians had died.[2] This essay considers the increasing role that President Joseph F. Smith played in supporting the American war effort, with an emphasis on his selection of three Latter-day Saint chaplains and their wartime service.

The United States declared its neutrality on August 4, 1914, and during the next three years endured a series of challenges to that position—such as the sinking of the *Lusitania* in 1915 and the *Sussex* in 1916, which resulted in the loss of hundreds of American lives; the January 1917 Zimmermann telegram, in

---

Kenneth L. Alford is an associate professor of Church history and doctrine at Brigham Young University.

which Germany proposed an alliance with Mexico against the United States; and Germany's January 1917 declaration that it would conduct unrestricted submarine warfare on the open seas.[3] In 1916, Woodrow Wilson won reelection as president based in large measure on the fact that "he kept us out of war."[4] America's neutrality ended on April 6, 1917, when the United States declared war on Germany. As the Latter-day Saint historian Elder B. H. Roberts wrote, "The high plane on which the United States entered the war made it easy for even the saints to sustain the relationship of service to it without violence to their consciences."[5] The nation widely accepted support for the war as a patriotic duty.

Joseph F. Smith's Wartime Leadership

Church President Joseph F. Smith set the tone and led the way in formulating the Church's response and reaction to the world war. In a general conference address on October 5, 1914, a few months after the beginning of the war, President Smith noted reluctantly that in the world, "nations are arrayed against nations. . . . Each [nation] is praying to his God for wrath upon and victory over his enemies. . . . God has [not] designed or willed that war [should] come among the people of the world, that the nations of the world should be divided against each other in war."[6]

While a proponent of peace, President Smith was not a pacifist. Speaking of patriotism and individual responsibility, he taught that "a good Latter-day Saint is a good citizen in every way."[7] He believed "patriotism should be sought for and will be found in right living, not in high sounding phrases or words. True patriotism is part of the solemn obligation that belongs both to the nation and to the individual and to the home. Our nation's reputation should be guarded as sacredly as our family's good name. That reputation should be defended by every citizen."[8]

The Church withdrew American missionaries from Europe as an early consequence of the war.[9] By the October 1914 general conference, President Smith told Church members that "every precaution has been taken that could be taken for the protection of our elders in those foreign missions where war exists. In Germany, France, Austria, and portions of other countries so dreadfully involved in war, our elders have all been invited to withdraw, to come away from those parts of the country, and so far as we know our German missionaries have largely and almost entirely withdrawn from that country, and also from France."[10]

In April 1915, President Smith reported that "the Church of Jesus Christ of Latter-day Saints is at peace with itself, and it is at peace with all the world. We have no spirit of war in our hearts. . . . I am glad that we have kept out of war so far, and I hope and pray that we may not be under the necessity of sending our sons to war, or experience as a nation the distress, the anguish and sorrow that come from a condition such as exists upon the old continent. Oh God, have mercy upon thy poor children in Europe, and throughout the world, who are brought under the awful conditions that exist there because of the ambition and pride of men."[11] But as the war in Europe continued into 1916, President Smith's public attitude was clearly shifting. The following October he said bluntly, "I do not want war; but the Lord has said it shall be poured out upon all nations, and if we escape, it will be 'by the skin of our teeth.' I would rather the oppressors should be killed, or destroyed, than to allow the oppressors to kill the innocent."[12]

President Smith was kept apprised of America's movement toward a declaration of war by United States senator and Apostle Reed Smoot. The day after war was declared, Smoot wrote to President Smith and shared an experience that occurred on April 4, 1917, on the floor of the Senate as that body debated a resolution to declare war:

> I had my notes prepared to speak in favor of the resolution, but before asking recognition late in the evening, an impression came to me not to speak but to offer an appeal in the form of a prayer. Just before eleven o'clock I obtained recognition from the Vice President, the galleries were packed, I waited until you could hear a pin drop in the Chamber, and then said, "Mr. President, I rise to make this simple but earnest appeal: God bless and approve the action to be taken by the Senate this day. Oh, Father, preserve our government and hasten the day when liberty will be enjoyed by all the peoples of the earth." I do not believe that there has ever been a statement made to the Senate that had such an effect as this prayer had upon not only the Senators but everyone in the galleries. No further remarks were made on the resolution, and the vote was taken upon it.[13]

Although President Smith was "slow at first to recognize that the hour had struck for the United States to drop the neutral attitude and enter the World War on the side of the allies,"[14] he quickly joined with President Wilson and Congress in supporting the war. During the April 1917 general conference, which was held during the same week that the United States declared war on Germany, President Smith declared, "Let the soldiers that go out from Utah be and remain men of honor. And when they are called obey the call, and manfully meet the duty, the

PERTINENT FACTS ON
UTAH'S LOYALTY
AND WAR RECORD

SALT LAKE CITY, UTAH
1918

In 1918, Church leaders authorized the publication of this pamphlet, which documented Utah's active support of the war. Courtesy of Kenneth L. Alford.

dangers, or the labor, that may be required of them, or that they may be set to do; but do it with an eye single to the accomplishment of the good that is aimed to be accomplished, and not with the blood-thirsty desire to kill and to destroy."[15] As the United States changed from a peacetime to wartime footing, President Smith could agree with President Wilson when he said, "We have no selfish ends to serve. We desire no conquest, no dominion. . . . We are but one of the champions of the rights of mankind. We shall be satisfied when those rights have been made as secure as the faith and the freedom of the nations can make them."[16]

President Smith took a direct role in supporting the American war effort. Through a common consent vote during the October 1917 general conference, the Church (which itself had only recently paid off its debts and become solvent) authorized President Smith, as the trustee-in-trust, to purchase $150,000 in Liberty Bonds with Church funds. Six months later, in April 1918, President Smith proposed that the Church purchase another $250,000 in Liberty Loan Bonds, and his proposal was unanimously approved by conference attendees. Following the vote, President Smith said, "This Country gave us the right in its Constitution to believe religiously according to the dictates of our own conscience, and it is only right that we should stand by the Nation with our wealth in money, resources and spirit."[17] Between 1917 and 1919, the Church purchased a total of $850,000 in Liberty Bonds (about fifteen million dollars today), demonstrating that Joseph F. Smith meant what he said in April 1918: "There isn't a feeling in my soul nor in any fibre of my being that is disloyal to the Government of the United States."[18]

With President Smith's approval and encouragement, the Church took several other actions to support the war. The Relief Society gave more than 100,000 bushels of wheat, 42,000 quarts of canned fruit and jelly, and over sixteen tons of fruit and vegetables to the United States Food Administration.[19] With Church assistance, the Salt Lake City Red Cross prepared 250 million medical dressings for local and army hospitals.[20] President Woodrow Wilson issued a proclamation, sustained by the First Presidency, calling for Sunday, June 17, 1917, to be observed as Red Cross Sunday. Bishops and branch presidents across the United States were encouraged to "provide speakers, music and other exercises in harmony with the spirit of the occasion, the duty of the hour, and the lofty object of the cause." Over eight hundred wards participated.[21] With the support of state and Church leaders, "Utah did her part in the great war to the last man called and the last dollar required of her."[22]

In 1917, almost two-thirds of Utah's population consisted of Latter-day Saints. Utah's response to military recruiting and war bond drives reflected

Joseph F. Smith (1838–1918), pictured here with one of his wives, Edna, supported the cause of peace and hoped that the United States would be able to remain neutral, but he became an ardent supporter of the American war effort after war was officially declared on April 6, 1917. Courtesy of Utah State Historical Society.

directly upon the Church. Utah received initial enlistment quotas for 872 men. With the approval and encouragement of President Joseph F. Smith, almost five thousand men responded during 1917. In 1918 nearly twenty thousand additional Utah men volunteered to serve in the army, navy, and marines. By the end of the war, over 5 percent of Utah's population was serving in the military.[23]

Latter-day Saint Chaplains

One meaningful way to support both the nation and the soldiers who served was to provide chaplains for active duty military units.[24] General John J. Pershing, commander of the American Expeditionary Force, was quoted as saying that military chaplains "are very important influences in the highest efficiency of the army. The men need them for all kinds of help. They sustain the men especially at the most critical times."[25] The First World War was the first time that the United States military invited the Church to directly select active duty Latter-day Saint military chaplains, a practice that continues to this day.

Only one Latter-day Saint chaplain had served on active federal military duty prior to World War I. Elias S. Kimball, a younger brother of Elder J. Golden Kimball, was serving as president of the Southern States Mission when the Spanish-American War began. On June 14, 1898, Kimball received a letter from the First Presidency notifying him that the "Presidency had been invited by Col. Willard Young of the 2nd Regiment Volunteer Engineers to name the Chaplain for his regiment, and the question was considered at to-day's meeting. It was unanimously decided to recommend you for that position, and Col. Young was informed of this by telegram to-day. He is at present at Washington, D.C., and you are requested to report by letter to him, care of Senator F. J. Cannon, if you feel to accept of the appointment." Colonel Young could have selected his own chaplain, but he deferred to the First Presidency. President Kimball had mixed feelings regarding the request, confiding to his diary that "in the vernacular of the street, this is what would be called a 'corker.'"[26] The following day he wrote the First Presidency that he "would accept of the position of Chaplain"; he served in Cuba with great dedication.[27]

During the Church's October 1918 general conference, David A. Smith, a member of the Presiding Bishopric, noted that the Church had "nearly fifteen thousand of our young men" in the army and navy of the United States and observed that the Church had received only three chaplain positions. "According to the ruling of the government,' he said, "we should be entitled to the appointment of others."[28] In June 1919, President Heber J. Grant suggested that the Church should have been "entitled to twenty chaplains."[29]

With only three chaplain positions to fill, President Joseph F. Smith and other senior Church leaders wanted to ensure that each appointee would represent the Church well. The three chaplains selected—Calvin S. Smith, Herbert B. Maw, and Brigham H. (B. H.) Roberts—each had a unique relationship with the Church's First Presidency. Calvin Smith was one of Joseph F. Smith's sons. Herbert Maw's father was close friends with the brother of Charles W. Penrose, a counselor in the First Presidency. And B. H. Roberts served as a Church General Authority (one of the seven presidents in the First Council of the Seventy) and knew the First Presidency well. A brief summary of the service of these three Latter-day Saint chaplains follows.

Calvin Schwartz Smith

The second child of Joseph F. Smith's last wife (Mary Taylor Schwartz), Calvin S. Smith (May 29, 1890–June 15, 1966) was one of six sons of the prophet who served in the military during World War I.[30] Chaplain Smith was called in February 1918 to serve as an active duty army chaplain for the Ninety-First Infantry Division. He defined his assignment as serving as an "at-large" chaplain, meaning he was to "look after the [approximately 1,800] members of the LDS Church in the division as a whole." (A World War I division contained up to 28,000 men.) Regarding his call, he said, "If I'd have had my own choice of a position in the Army, it wouldn't have been chaplain." He was concerned that he "had no training whatever" and "didn't know what was expected of a chaplain," but his father had faith in his ability to serve.[31] After initial training in the United States, his division landed in France on July 22, 1918.[32]

Few people owe their life to a can of beef, but Chaplain Smith did. In September 1918, allied armed forces moved to occupy a position recently evacuated by German soldiers. After passing a graveyard for German soldiers, he walked into a nearby field and suddenly "became aware of the fact that somebody was shooting at [him]." He "flattened out on the ground" and waited while the enemy "shot two or three times and then quit." That evening at dinner, he discovered that a bullet had "gone through the top of the can" of beef he carried in his mess kit and "part way out of the back." As he started to eat, he reported,

"I nearly cracked my teeth because it was dark when . . . I bit down on the bullet. It was in the mess kit. It saved me from being wounded in the back."[33]

Chaplain Smith's final wartime letter to his father, President Joseph F. Smith, was written in France on November 15, 1918, four days after the armistice. In it, he shared several of his combat experiences. He wrote that he ministered to Latter-day Saint soldiers in the 346th Machine Gun Battalion, joined a medical detachment and "tried to be generally useful." At one point, he "put on a French uniform and helped the intelligence officer of the 362nd infantry [regiment] map out the trails which were to be cut through the forest to the front line trenches," and survived an aerial bombardment when a dud bomb dropped a few feet from him. Finding himself at the front lines, he "went over the top" with his unit to attack the enemy. Serving as part of a medical unit, Chaplain Smith said, "I went out with stretcher-bearers to find wounded. . . . [We] worked till nearly exhausted. . . . We tried to sleep, [but] we nearly froze." During the same offensive, the Germans launched a systematic artillery barrage on his location—shells "fell every dozen feet, and soon there were many cries for help. One shell lighted within a dozen feet . . . as I lay in the hole." Suddenly, he "felt as if someone had lashed [him] with a whip and blood began to run down [his] trousers." He recognized that he had been wounded. Although injured, he "got up many times during the night to help carry wounded [soldiers] to the automobiles." His colonel recommended him for a promotion, but, as he informed his father, "A chaplain serves seven years as a first lieutenant and then is automatically promoted," which led him to believe (correctly, as it turned out) that "this recommendation may never be acted on."[34] A few days later, his unit again marched to the front and was ordered into action at Ypres, where he was wounded again, this time in his right arm.

In his letter home, he acknowledged the armistice and wrote, "I am happy to say that peace seems to have come. . . . I felt happy to be alive and safe. . . . I hope I come home from this war more of a man than I went into it. If I don't I'll feel that I have not played my part." President Joseph F. Smith never had the opportunity to read his son's last letter; the prophet died November 19, 1918, just four days after the letter was written.[35]

The book *Utah in the World War,* a 1924 history of Utah's participation in World War I, observed that in the 362nd Infantry "there was no more popular man in the division than the chaplain, who never considered personal risk when he could serve his comrades."[36]

Chaplain Calvin Smith wrote to his father, President Joseph F. Smith, to share some of his war experiences just four days after the Armistice ending the war was signed in this railroad car on November 11, 1918; President Smith died before the letter reached Salt Lake City. Courtesy of Library of Congress.

Herbert Brown Maw

In 1916, prior to the American declaration of war, Herbert Maw (March 11, 1893–November 17, 1990) enjoyed a busy life as an aspiring lawyer and teacher at LDS High School in Salt Lake City. In July 1917, shortly after the United States declared war on Germany, he enlisted in the Army Air Service and was accepted for pilot training.[37] He graduated from ground school and found flying to be "a thrilling experience."[38]

Maw soon learned that "life . . . had other plans for [him] which did not include becoming a pilot in the army." His military service changed in a dramatic way when he received a long-distance telephone call in March 1918 from President Charles W. Penrose, one of Joseph F. Smith's counselors in the Church's First Presidency. President Penrose informed Maw that "the U.S. Army had authorized the appointment of three Mormon Chaplains to serve for the duration of the war; that they were to be selected by the First Presidency of the Church; and that this was the first time the Church had ever received such recognition from the military forces of our country." President Penrose notified Maw that he was to be one of the three chaplains. "I was flabbergasted! I thought at first that someone was kidding me, for I could not conceive of my being called by the First Presidency to such

First Presidency (from left: Anthon H. Lund, Joseph F. Smith, and Charles W. Penrose), circa 1911–12. President Penrose invited Herbert B. Maw (1893–1990), newly called to serve as an army chaplain, to meet with the First Presidency in 1918. © Intellectual Reserve, Inc.

an assignment," Maw later reflected. "The conversation," Maw recalled, "ended with my reluctantly accepting the call even though I much preferred continuing my training as a pilot." As their telephone conversation concluded, President Penrose invited Maw to visit him the next time he was in Salt Lake City.[39]

Newly commissioned as a first lieutenant, Chaplain Maw was assigned as a chaplain with the Eighty-Ninth Infantry Division stationed at Camp Funston, Kansas. A few weeks later, Maw found himself in Salt Lake City on furlough. Summoning his courage, he decided to visit Church headquarters to take advantage of President Penrose's invitation. When Maw asked "if there were any special instructions as to [his] official duties," President Penrose told him to "be a good example to the soldiers." He then took Chaplain Maw to the office of President Joseph F. Smith, where he also met President Smith's first counselor, Anthon H. Lund. The First Presidency asked Chaplain Maw if he would like to receive a priesthood blessing. Maw said, "Of course I did, so they all arose and placed their hands on my head as I sat in my chair." During the blessing, he was promised "every protection, guidance, and inspiration that a representative of the Church of Jesus Christ should have in a war"—a blessing that was soon fulfilled in combat.[40]

Chaplain Maw quickly learned that his division had very few Latter-day Saint soldiers but did contain numerous members of the Reorganized Church of Jesus Christ of Latter Day Saints from Missouri who were not very excited, initially, about being assigned a Mormon chaplain. Through continued patience and service, he "gained the confidence of the men and a wholesome religious spirit" developed. He ministered to soldiers at the front and was "exposed . . . to almost continuous enemy fire."[41]

Chaplain Herbert B. Maw served as the governor of Utah from 1941 to 1949. Courtesy of Utah State Historical Society.

On one occasion near Metz, France, he accompanied a balloonist aloft to observe and report on the effectiveness of an artillery barrage. After ascending to two thousand feet, they found themselves being attacked by an enemy airplane. The balloon was at risk of exploding, so both the observer and Chaplain Maw were forced to jump from the balloon and parachute to the ground. Noting that he had never jumped from a plane or balloon before, Maw commented wryly that events like that "added a considerable amount of interest and excitement to the routines of army life."[42]

Chaplain Maw later observed that "scores of times at the front, that pronouncement of protection, guidance, and inspiration [from the First Presidency] was fulfilled during months which followed, for I was repeatedly prompted to move from places of danger which would have resulted in disaster for me if I had not heeded those promptings."[43] He was mustered out of the service in June 1919.[44] In 1940 he was elected as the eighth governor of Utah and served with distinction; his reelection in 1944 remains the closest gubernatorial election in Utah history.

Brigham Henry Roberts

In the October 1914 general conference, Elder B. H. Roberts (March 13, 1857–September 27, 1933) described the developing world war as "inevitable."[45] When Utah launched a military recruitment effort, Governor Simon Bamberger appointed Roberts chaplain (and captain) of the First Utah Light Field Artillery (which was soon renamed the 145th Field Artillery Regiment). The governor shortly thereafter promoted Roberts to major.[46] According to a general order from March 1917, the unit included "B. H. Roberts appointed Major and Chaplain on [the] Governor's Staff."[47] To assist with Utah's recruiting efforts, Elder Roberts traveled around the state giving speeches encouraging young men to enlist. In fact, he spoke at a recruiting rally in Manti on the day that war was declared.[48] During a March 1917 rally in Ogden, Major Roberts said, "I want to tell the fathers and mothers of Utah that if their sons go to the trenches I will go with them." The audience reportedly cheered for three straight minutes.[49]

Although he was past sixty years of age, B. H. Roberts asked to serve as the unit's active duty chaplain. Not surprisingly, his initial request was rejected. He turned to Senator Reed Smoot of Utah to help obtain a chaplain's commission, telling him, "You must get me in!" Senator Smoot's appeal on Roberts's behalf was successful, but it came with two stipulations. First, Roberts must enter

Although over sixty years old, Elder B. H. Roberts served during World War I as an active duty chaplain for the 145th Field Artillery Regiment from Utah, 1918.

active duty several ranks lower as a lieutenant—the standard active duty rank for new chaplains—and second, he had to complete the standard chaplain's officer training program before he could join his unit. Elder Roberts promptly agreed to both conditions.[50]

Chaplain Roberts, now a lieutenant, and the 145th Field Artillery Regiment—"distinctively a Utah organization"—were mustered into service on August 5, 1917 when the Utah National Guard officially became part of the National Army.[51] Chaplain Roberts later wrote that with almost fifteen hundred Latter-day Saint soldiers, "one unique thing about this Utah regiment was that it was so nearly recruited from one religious body . . . that the 145th F.A. [Field Artillery] (1st Utah) came nearly to being a 'Mormon' regiment."[52]

Chaplain Roberts's unit was sent to Camp Kearny near San Diego. He reported to Officer and Chaplains School at Camp Zachary Taylor near Louisville,

Utah's Governor Simon Bamberger appointed Elder B. H. Roberts as a chaplain. Courtesy of Utah State Historical Society.

Kentucky, in April 1918.[53] The commandant offered to ease his program requirements, but Chaplain Roberts answered, "No, sir; I came here to take the full course."[54] He completed the entire training program—all of the course work, obstacle courses, marches, bivouacking, marksmanship, and physical fitness activities—without receiving any waivers. After successfully completing the course, he commented, "It was the most strenuous and anxious six weeks within my experience."[55] When Roberts returned to Camp Kearny in June, his unit was away on a road march. He was offered a car to visit them, but "he chose instead a spirited horse. . . . As he approached the regiment, he kept out of sight until he was at the head of the column. Then he galloped into view, reining his horse high on its haunches and lifting his hat to sweep the sky in a symbolic gesture that electrified the men."[56] The *Salt Lake Tribune* reported that "from every throat" of the sixteen hundred men in his regiment "there arose a mighty cheer. Discipline relaxed and there was a waving of arms and a tumult of shouting. . . . To these men, their chaplain was a heroic figure of a man, nothing less."[57] According to historian Truman G. Madsen, "then the chaplain left his mount, shouldered the standard sixty-pound pack, and joined his men in the hike on equal terms."[58]

In July, as the 145th Field Artillery Regiment was traveling from California to New York bound for Europe, they stopped in Salt Lake City. Chaplain Roberts arranged for the unit band to serenade President Joseph F. Smith at his residence, the Beehive House. President Smith watched from the window and invited Roberts to join him on the balcony, where "President Smith gave the men a kindly reception and reminisced in a touching manner about his associations with Chaplain Roberts."[59] Chaplain Roberts's regiment traveled to France and was sent to Camp DeSouge for training. They were ordered to the front on November 9, 1918, but the armistice was signed two days later; the war ended before they saw any combat.[60]

Perhaps the best known experience from Chaplain Roberts's military career occurred during an interdenominational worship service on Thanksgiving Day in 1918. Sitting at the rear of the review stand, Chaplain Roberts had not been invited to participate in the program. During the service he was surprised to hear the presiding chaplain announce, "Elder Roberts, the Mormon chaplain from Utah, will now step up and read the Thanksgiving Psalm"—a scriptural reference he did not know. Several "years later, he testified that during the long walk to the front, he distinctly heard an audible voice announce: 'The 100th Psalm.' It was as clear as though another person had spoken at his side." He reached the

This Christmas postcard was produced by Chaplain B. H. Roberts's unit, the 145th Field Artillery Regiment, in France the month after the war ended. Courtesy of Kenneth L. Alford.

podium, opened his Bible, and read the 100th Psalm. "After Brother Roberts had closed his Bible and was returning to his seat, he noticed that his fellow chaplains refused to look at him; their eyes were immovably fixed on the floor. It was then he realized that his part on the program had been a deliberate attempt to embarrass him, the Church and the priesthood."[61]

The *History of the 145th Field Artillery Regiment* records that Chaplain Roberts "was a fine chap and well liked by all, regardless of religion."[62] Unlike the wartime experiences of Chaplains Smith and Maw, Chaplain Roberts's unit never saw any action or lost a man.[63] He left the military in January 1919 and returned to Church service as a General Authority.[64]

During the June 1919 general conference, which had been postponed from April because of the Spanish flu epidemic and was the first conference after the armistice, President Heber J. Grant, newly sustained to replace Joseph F. Smith as Church President, commented on Elder Roberts's military service. "We are grateful to Brother B. H. Roberts, who also volunteered, notwithstanding he was beyond the age limit, and did splendid service in looking after our boys, as chaplain," he said. "He gained their love and their confidence and had an excellent influence over them for good."[65]

Summary

President Joseph F. Smith was deeply affected by World War I. While he was initially reticent to have the United States fight in Europe, he actively supported the nation's cause after war was declared. As Anthony V. Ivins (who served as a counselor to Heber J. Grant in the Church's First Presidency) noted, beginning in 1917 "the Church [was] brought into direct contact for the first time with a great world war.... Never before [had] the effect of war been so universally felt and the people put to a similar test."[66] During the Church's April 1920 general conference, President Grant read selections from speeches made in the United States Senate. Quoting Utah Senator Reed Smoot, President Grant read, "No one can examine the record made by [Latter-day Saints] during the World War without coming to the conclusion that no more loyal people live on this earth. No call was made upon them without an immediate response, and not only for the amount asked for but for nearly double the amount in most every case."[67]

In his father's biography, Church President Joseph Fielding Smith wrote that Joseph F. Smith "regretted the outbreak of war, and the necessity of the United States entering the conflict, yet he encouraged the members of the Church in the United States to be loyal to their country, feeling that their cause was just and would eventually prevail."[68] President Smith lived long enough to learn that an armistice ending the war was signed on November 11, 1918, but he died just eight days later.

In outlining Utah's role during the First World War, historian Noble Warrum observed that President Joseph F. Smith "placed at the service of his country the most efficient non-military organization in the United States [The Church of Jesus Christ of Latter-day Saints]."[69] The service rendered by President Smith included calling three faithful Latter-day Saint chaplains who served on active duty during the war with honor and distinction. They set a high standard for the Latter-day Saint chaplains who have followed them during the past century.

Notes

1. John Spencer Bassett, *A Short History of the United States, 1492–1920* (New York: Macmillan, 1921), 873–78.
2. Statistics regarding civilian and military death tolls from World War I vary widely. Some totals, for example, include deaths from the Russian Revolution and the Spanish influenza; others do not. Historian Martin Gilbert notes, "If each of the nine million military dead of the First World War were to have an individual page, the record of their deeds and suffering, their war-time hopes, their pre-war lives and loves, would fill twenty thousand books." Martin Gilbert,

The First World War: A Complete History, 2nd ed. (New York: Henry Holt, 1994), xxi. See also "Source List and Detailed Death Tolls for the Primary Megadeaths of the Twentieth Century"; http://necrometrics.com/20c5m.htm; B. H. Roberts, *A Comprehensive History of The Church of Jesus Christ of Latter-day Saints* (Provo, UT: Brigham Young University Press, 1965), 6:442.

3. Noble Warrum, *Utah in the World War: The Men Behind the Guns and the Men and Women Behind the Men Behind the Guns* (Salt Lake City: Arrow Press, 1924), 444.
4. On November 9, 1916, Joseph F. Smith wrote to his son Wesley and made several observations regarding the elections held earlier that month: "The substitution of the pretentious, pedantic, two-faced democratic infidel W.H.K. [William H. King] in the Senate of the U.S. for the scholarly, consistent capable and friendly Geo. Southernland is a blistering disgrace upon the majority voters of Utah in this election. But the whole Nation seems to have been crazed over the silliest of all silly things, that:—'Wilson has kept us out of war'!! The assalts [*sic*] made at Vera Cruz and by Gen. Pershing on Mexico, by order of Prest. Wilson, and the expenditure of three-hundred millions of money—to keep the army of the U.S. along the Southern Border of the Domain is not war!! Consistency is a Jewel! Mamma and all—Send love to all. Even Sincerely, Papa." Joseph F. Smith to Wesley Smith, November 9, 1916, *Joseph F. Smith Letterpress Copybooks, 1875–1917,* MS 1325, box 36, folder 1, 402–21, October 20, 1916–November 30, 1916, also available in *Selected Collections from the Archives of The Church of Jesus Christ of Latter-day Saints,* ed. Richard E. Turley Jr. (Provo, UT: Brigham Young University Press, 2002); http://ldsarch.lib.byu.edu.erl.lib.byu.edu/CD%20Volume%201/Disc30/b36/seg25.htm.
5. Roberts, *Comprehensive History,* 6:453.
6. Joseph F. Smith, in Conference Report, October 1914, 7.
7. Joseph F. Smith, "Congress and the Mormons," *Improvement Era,* April 1903, 469.
8. "National Patriotism," *Juvenile Instructor,* July 1912, 388–89.
9. One of the mission leaders involved in Europe was Hyrum M. Smith, the eldest son of President Joseph F. Smith and his third wife, Edna Lambson; he withdrew missionaries from the continent of Europe first to Great Britain and then to the United States.
10. Joseph F. Smith, in Conference Report, October 1914, 2.
11. Joseph F. Smith, in Conference Report, April 1915, 3, 6. Interestingly, during the October 1915 and April 1916 general conferences, President Smith did not mention the war once during his addresses to the Church.
12. Joseph F. Smith, in Conference Report, October 1916, 154.
13. Reed Smoot to Joseph F. Smith, April 7, 1917, quoted in Joseph F. Boone, "The Roles of The Church of Jesus Christ of Latter-day Saints in Relation to the United States Military, 1900–1975," vol. 1 (PhD diss., Brigham Young University, 1975), 160–61.
14. Roberts, *Comprehensive History,* 6:467.
15. Joseph F. Smith, in Conference Report, April 1917, 3–4.
16. Roberts, *Comprehensive History,* 6:454.
17. Benjamin Goddard, *Pertinent Facts on Utah's Loyalty and War Record* (Salt Lake City: The Church of Jesus Christ of Latter-day Saints, 1918), 22–23. This Church-produced promotional pamphlet appears to have been written after June 1918 but prior to the end of World War I.
18. Roberts, *Comprehensive History,* 6:467; Joseph F. Smith, in Conference Report, April 1918, 5.
19. Goddard, *Pertinent Facts,* 17–19.
20. Warrum, *Utah in the World War,* 61.

21. "Passing Events," *Improvement Era*, July 1917, 846–47.
22. Warrum, *Utah in the World War*, 33. The war had an increasing influence on the affairs of the Church. In an effort to honor Latter-day Saint service members during the October 1918 general conference, President Smith declared, "Bishops should enter every member of their ward who is in the military service of the United States or its allies on the tithing record." President Smith further announced that "in consequence of so many of our young men being drafted into the war, the activities of our quorums of the priesthood, especially of the Elders, Priests and Teachers quorums, are very much impaired. In some wards nearly every priest and teacher of draft age is in the war. The quorums have been seriously depleted, and a corresponding effect has also been felt in the Sunday School and Y.M.M.I.A. (Young Men's Mutual Improvement Association)." Joseph F. Smith, in Conference Report, October 1918, 3.
23. Roberts, *Comprehensive History*, 6:455–56.
24. Joseph F. Smith had served as a chaplain twice during his life—once in a military setting and once in a pioneer company. Called as a young missionary to serve in the Sandwich Islands (Hawaii) in 1854, Elder Smith was recalled to Utah by Brigham Young in 1857 at the beginning of the Utah War. Departing Hawaii in October, he arrived in Salt Lake City on February 24, 1858. The day after he arrived in Salt Lake City, he enlisted in the Utah militia prepared to defend Utah Territory against the advancing US army. Later he was called to serve as chaplain in a regiment of the Utah militia. During the Civil War, Elder George Q. Cannon, a Church Apostle, asked Joseph F. Smith to accompany him in the fall of 1862 on a Church conference tour in Denmark. Returning to the United States in July 1863, he landed at New York City shortly after the battle of Gettysburg occurred in neighboring Pennsylvania. Not having sufficient funds to pay for a return trip to Utah, he found employment and worked his way to Florence, Nebraska, where he waited until he could join a company of Latter-day Saint immigrants traveling to Utah. He joined the John W. Woolley pioneer company later that year, serving as both chaplain and physician. Joseph Fielding Smith, *Life of Joseph F. Smith* (Salt Lake City: Deseret Book, 1969), 204, 481.
25. "Chaplains Needed, Minister Cables," *Salt Lake Telegram*, July 12, 1918.
26. Elias Smith Kimball, journal, June 14, 1898, 3–4, MS 13348, Church History Library, The Church of Jesus Christ of Latter-day Saints, Salt Lake City. A "corker" is something "that is excellent or remarkable" (*Merriam Webster's Collegiate Dictionary*, 11th ed.) or something "that closes a discussion, or puts an end to any matter" (*Oxford English Dictionary*, s.v. "corker," definition 2a).
27. Elias Smith Kimball, journal, June 15, 1898, 7. See also James Mangum, "The Spanish-American and Philippine War," in *Nineteenth-Century Saints at War*, ed. Robert C. Freeman (Provo, UT: Religious Studies Center, 2006), 155–93.
28. David A. Smith, in Conference Report, October 1918, 153.
29. The determination that Latter-day Saints should have received up to twenty chaplain authorizations was apparently based on undisclosed Church calculations. See Heber J. Grant, in Conference Report, June 1919, 110. In July 1918 there were "approximately 900 regular chaplains in the army and navy, and the number is rapidly being increased." "What the Church is Doing for Uncle Sam's Soldiers," *Salt Lake Telegram*, July 20, 1918.
30. Roberts, *Comprehensive History*, 6:476.

31. Calvin S. Smith interview, December 29, 1965, MS 23095, Church History Library, The Church of Jesus Christ of Latter-day Saints, Salt Lake City. Chaplain Maw was also described as serving as an "at-large" chaplain. "Bishop Charges Discrimination," *Salt Lake Telegram*, July 27, 1918.
32. Warrum, *Utah in the World War*, 47.
33. Calvin S. Smith interview, December 29, 1965.
34. Calvin S. Smith to Joseph F. Smith, November 15, 1918, MS 1325, Church History Library.
35. Calvin S. Smith to Joseph F. Smith, November 15, 1918.
36. Warrum, *Utah in the World War*, 47.
37. Herbert B. Maw, *Adventures with Life* (Salt Lake City: n.p., 1978), 74–75.
38. Andrew Jenson, *Latter-day Saint Biographical Encyclopedia: A Compilation of Biographical Sketches of Prominent Men and Women in the Church of Jesus Christ of Latter-day Saints* (Salt Lake City: Western Epics, 1971), 4:217; Maw, *Adventures with Life*, 78.
39. Maw, *Adventures with Life*, 79–80.
40. Maw, *Adventures with Life*, 81.
41. Maw, *Adventures with Life*, 82–83, 85.
42. Maw, *Adventures with Life*, 87–88.
43. Maw, *Adventures with Life*, 80–81.
44. "Mormon Chaplain Returns from War," *Salt Lake Telegram*, June 13, 1919.
45. "Mormon Heads Sustained as Conference Closes," *Salt Lake Telegram*, October 6, 1914.
46. Robert H. Malan, *B. H. Roberts: A Biography* (Salt Lake City: Deseret Book, 1966), 103.
47. E. W. Crocker, ed., *History of the 145th Field Artillery Regiment of World War I: 8-5-1917 to 1-28-1919* (Provo, UT: J. Grant Stevenson, 1968), 3.
48. "Utah Guards Await Mobilization Call," *Salt Lake Tribune*, April 7, 1917, in Journal History of the Church, CR 100 137, Church History Library.
49. "B. H. Roberts Says He Will Go to the Trenches with Boys," *Deseret Evening News*, March 28, 1917.
50. Truman G. Madsen, *Defender of the Faith: The B. H. Roberts Story* (Salt Lake City, Bookcraft, 1980), 302.
51. Warrum, *Utah in the World War*, 56; Crocker, *History of the 145th Field Artillery Regiment*, 8.
52. Roberts, *Comprehensive History*, 6:460. The fact that it was primarily a Latter-day Saint unit was illustrated in a soldier's letter published in the *Vernal Express*; the soldier reported, "We haven't one venereal case in our whole regiment now. Pretty good for Utah, isn't it? Best record made by any regiment." "Letters from Our Boys with the Flag," *Vernal* (Utah) *Express*, March 1, 1918, 4.
53. "Utah Boys at Kearny Justify Pride of State," *Salt Lake Telegram*, April 16, 1918. The chaplain training school at Camp Taylor opened on April 20, 1918. "The course aim[ed] to teach a civilian how to minister in a military environment. Thirty chaplains appointed since America entered the war and sixty just appointed" as of May 1918 were scheduled to take the course. "School Opened to Train Chaplains," *Salt Lake Telegram*, May 6, 1918.
54. "Lieut. Roberts in His Missionary Days," *Deseret Evening News*, August 31, 1918.
55. B. H. Roberts, remarks to the general board of the MIA, as recalled by Axel A. Madsen, quoted in Madsen, *Defender of the Faith*, 306.
56. Madsen, *Defender of the Faith*, 307.

57. *Salt Lake Tribune*, October 2, 1933, 27, quoted in Malan, *B. H. Roberts, A Biography*, 107.
58. Madsen, *Defender of the Faith*, 307.
59. Madsen, *Defender of the Faith*, 307–8.
60. Madsen, *Defender of the Faith*, 311.
61. "Inspiration Key to Thanksgiving Psalm," *Church News*, November 22, 1975.
62. Crocker, *History of the 145th Field Artillery Regiment*, 47.
63. Crocker, *History of the 145th Field Artillery Regiment*, 105. Some soldiers from the 145th Field Artillery Regiment replaced losses in other units, and some of them were killed.
64. Madsen, *Defender of the Faith*, 313.
65. Heber J. Grant, in Conference Report, June 1919, 110.
66. Anthony W. Ivins, in Conference Report, June 1919, 81–82.
67. Heber J. Grant, in Conference Report, April 1920, 7.
68. Smith, *Life of Joseph F. Smith*, 419.
69. Warrum, *Utah in the World War*, 408 (image caption).

Public Perceptions

Justin R. Bray

25

Joseph F. Smith's Beard and the Public Image of the Latter-day Saints

Following the Civil War, it became common for American men to sport a "natural, dignified beard." These men's whiskers were rarely muttonchops or mustaches but rather long, bushy chin fur. Apparently this type of facial hair grew so popular during the American Gilded Age (1877–1893) that it became known as "the American beard." Yet, by the early 1900s—seemingly overnight—this trend turned old-fashioned and out of style. In fact, by the time Joseph F. Smith became President of The Church of Jesus Christ of Latter-day Saints in 1901, shaggy beards graced only the "cheeks and chins of rustic sages."[1]

At this time in early twentieth-century America, Latter-day Saints were already experiencing negative public opinion. Outsiders believed that the Mormon headmen unlawfully practiced plural marriage, swore themselves to secret allegiances, and unethically used their ecclesiastical influence over other members. Thus, to non-Mormons, long beards, which were noticeably outdated and unpopular in American culture, could be seen as another subtle expression of nonconformity with the rest of the United States and as a reflection of the Latter-day Saints' isolation in the Great Basin.

Justin R. Bray is an oral historian at the Church History Department in Salt Lake City.

This chapter is not intended to criticize, tease, or lampoon any former Latter-day Saint leaders. Rather, this chapter is an attempt to understand the rise and fall of bushy beards in American fashion during the latter half of the nineteenth century and to provide context to the negative public perception of Joseph F. Smith and other seasoned Latter-day Saint leaders' long beards when such facial hair was noticeably outmoded in the rest of the United States at the turn of the century. This chapter will also explore ways in which Reed Smoot and his clean-cut countenance helped improve the public image of the Latter-day Saints when the Church stood trial for the practice of plural marriage from 1903 to 1907.

Background

Between the tenures of Joseph Smith and Joseph F. Smith, the Latter-day Saints struggled to assimilate into the American mainstream. Like other religious movements, according to Armand L. Mauss, Mormons had to grapple over a predicament: maintaining their peculiarity while also adopting cultural traits in order to be acceptable to society.[2] Sometimes, however, the Latter-day Saints' uniqueness—whether it was culture, doctrine, or population—led to unintentional contention with their neighbors, and conflict followed them from upstate New York to Jackson County to the Salt Lake Valley.[3]

The Latter-day Saints' contested struggle for acceptability intensified toward the end of the nineteenth century. Non-Mormons across the country would hear outrageous rumors of the polygamous marriages in Utah and wonder how a people could uphold such a doctrine. The marriage system among the Latter-day Saints was only one of a number of distinguishing aspects of the Utah-based faith. Their dress and physical appearance were also depicted differently from mainstream Americans as well. A typical rank-and-file Mormon male, for example, was often portrayed in print culture as old, overweight, and out of style, wearing tattered clothing and surrounded by numberless women in ragged dresses or pantalets. There was an intentional look of otherness about them. Joseph F. Smith was similarly satirized in the press with frayed clothing and a long, exaggerated beard during his seventeen-year tenure as President of the Church.

Measuring Public Perception

Jan Shipps, one of the most noted scholars of Mormon studies, wrote about the difficulty historians have in determining "what the public said, thought, and felt about particular individuals." The remarkable rise of media and public opinion polls will facilitate future studies of historical figures, yet there still persist thorny problems with studying nonverbal messages from the early twentieth century. Consequently, many historians agree that the best way to reconstruct the public perception of a person who lived before radio and television is through the press and printed word.[4]

Newspapers, journals, and magazines were the most "important vehicles of information and opinion" in the early twentieth century, largely due to muckrakers and watchdog journalism. In fact, Americans probably learned more about Joseph F. Smith and the Latter-day Saints from nationally circulated newspapers than from any other information outlet. The LDS Church received coverage in scores of broadsheets and gazettes, but some of the printed publications most closely tied to Mormons were *Collier's, Salt Lake Tribune, McClure's, Harper's,* and *Saturday Evening Post.*[5]

These media sources covered not only news but also American society, heritage, culture, tradition, lifestyle, and even fashion trends. There were often special-interest sections in newspapers and magazines with inserts and advertisements indicating what styles were in vogue, making public print perhaps the greatest influence over the life and thought of the nation in terms of fashion and image. Thus, what columnists wrote about beards and facial hair could quickly elevate, or just as easily tarnish, a man's reputation depending on what graced his face at the time.

Beards in the United States

Prior to the Civil War, beards were uncommon in American culture. In fact, the first fifteen presidents of the United States remained clean-shaven while in office. According to Allan Peterkin, a "facial-hair historian," late eighteenth- and early nineteenth-century Americans seemed to follow the pattern of their trendsetting presidents. Beards were worn "only in isolated cases by the old, mad, or clueless."[6] Even Abraham Lincoln had never worn any facial hair until a young girl wrote him saying that he "would look better if he wore a beard,"[7] because his face was so thin.[8] Lincoln grew out his iconic beard, became the president of the United States, and ushered in what some have called the Golden Age of Beards.

Beards proved so popular throughout the country that American men began allowing their razors to "rust in disuse . . . in obedience to the prevalent fashion."[9] Beards became a sign of manliness and respectability. Of the next ten United States presidents after Lincoln, only two remained clean-shaven—Andrew Johnson and William McKinley. Some men became so desperate for a bushy beard that they would buy compositions and formulas claiming to produce "a luxuriant beard in from 5 to 8 weeks."[10] Many tried to shape the woolly shag into points, forks, and squares, but according to the newspapers, these men only robbed it of the "dignity which the full beard imparted." In fact, writers hoped that "if any form of beard survives the all-threatening razor, it will be the full beard."[11]

But by the 1890s, society began again to frown upon bewhiskered men. Although facial hair was once known for having "purified the air that entered the respiratory tracts," new progressive thought caused Americans to associate full beards with poor hygiene and disease. For example, newspapers spread the word that the full beard was "infected with the germs of tuberculosis, and is one of the deadliest agents for transmitting the disease to the lungs." Bristly whiskers even became known as "the Creator's mistake."[12] They were so unpopular at one point that men began buying new ointments and formulas, such as Modene, which "quickly dissolved and removed" hair on the face. Just a few drops of some of these mixtures destroyed men's facial hair forever.[13]

Like much of the rising generation of Americans at the time, many young Latter-day Saints expressed their displeasure with full beards, particularly in sacrament services. At this time in the 1890s, the sacramental water or wine was still distributed in a common cup, from which every member sipped regardless of age, health, gender, or social standing. Thus, many members detested partaking after "some of the full-bearded old men" whose whiskers would float atop the water after they drank from the cup.[14] After years of complaints and petitions to the General Authorities, the time-honored method of administering the sacramental water in a common goblet changed to a small, individual cup service.[15] Interestingly, this transition came under the direction of President Joseph F. Smith, who kept his beard despite outside opinions of fashion, hygiene, and grooming.

Religious Beards

Joseph F. Smith's beard meant something entirely different to him and other Latter-day Saints than it did to critical non-Mormons. Rather than an expression of defiance against outside American ideas, President Smith's patriarchal beard symbolically reflected a prophetic hue—something he shared with each of his post-Nauvoo predecessors, if we include John Taylor's chin curtain. Even Hugh B. Brown, a former member of the First Presidency and Quorum of the Twelve Apostles, believed that "Joseph F. Smith looked like a prophet" because "he had a long beard."[16]

Particularly during this time period, full, tufty beards were considered "a primary sign of masculinity, wisdom, and patriarchal authority and honor," but they had long held meaning within religious circles.[17] This idea was especially emphasized among ancient Israel, when priests were commanded to "not make baldness upon their head" nor "shave off the corner of their beard" (Leviticus 21:5). This was even the case during New Testament times. Tradition holds, for example, that Jesus' executioners pulled out the hair from his cheeks as a form of humiliation.[18] Having one's beard shaved was an utmost insult, not only in ancient times, but in nineteenth-century America as well. Lorenzo Snow's experience in the Utah Territorial Penitentiary illustrates this idea.

Snow, then a senior member of the Quorum of the Twelve Apostles, was incarcerated in early 1886 for unlawful cohabitation. Jailhouse rules required male prisoners' hair to be cut once a month and facial hair shaved once a week. This policy, according to historians Andrew H. Hedges and Richard NeitzelHolzapfel, "was considered a degrading personal affront." Facial hair was important among the Latter-day Saints and the repercussions of shaving the beards of the Church's highest authorities would be significant. It could very well have demeaned the Mormon leader in the eyes of the rank-and-file members. Fortunately for Snow, however, the warden was "often lenient with the 'brethren,'" and he approved doctors' recommendations to allow Lorenzo Snow "to retain his beard" over health concerns.[19]

Joseph F. Smith's Beard

The press that would give President Smith a hard time about his beard had already railed against several Latter-day Saint leaders in the past. For example, Daniel H. Wells, whose sight was impaired, was called the "one-eyed pirate of the Wasatch."[20] Other members of the First Presidency and Quorum of the Twelve Apostles were not as fortunate in their offensive nicknames.[21] Joseph F. Smith similarly received a number of insulting epithets, but his were centered around his long facial hair, not only because of its length, but also because he was known for frequently stroking his hand through it and even perfuming it.[22] He was called "graybeard," "scraggly," and "the man with the beard."[23]

President Smith attracted even more attention after being summoned to Washington, DC, to take part in the Reed Smoot hearings. These highly publicized

Top: Joseph F. Smith was known to frequently stroke his long beard. Photo by Clawson Film Co., circa 1915, courtesy of Church History Library. Bottom: Cartoonists were not afraid to exaggerate Joseph F. Smith's long beard. Political cartoon from the Saturday Globe, *March 12, 1904. Courtesy of L. Tom Perry Special Collections, Harold B. Lee Library, Brigham Young University, Provo, Utah.*

court cases against Mormon leaders for practicing plural marriage placed the Latter-day Saints on a platform to be widely judged and surveyed. The proceedings were so popular among the public that "spectators lined the halls, waiting for limited seats in the committee room, and filled the galleries to hear floor debates." And "for those who could not see for themselves, journalists and cartoonists depicted each day's admission and outrage."[24]

THE REAL OBJECTION TO SMOOT.

One of many political cartoons exaggerating Church leaders' long beards. Courtesy of Library of Congress Prints and Photographs Division.

These cartoonists generally exaggerated Joseph F. Smith's beard, his most distinguishable characteristic, drawing it so low that it reached "almost to his waist."[25] As a result, according to a member of the Senate committee, many Americans with little knowledge of the Utah-based faith began to "commonly associate an overgrown beard" with the general male population of Latter-day Saints.[26] Some cartoonists purposefully portrayed Mormons as physically different from typical American men, often sketching them as overweight and bearded in tattered garb. These caricatures, printed in newspapers and magazines across the country, were not so different from cartoon depictions of other segregated classes of society at the time, such as Asian and Irish immigrants, American Indians, and African Americans. The beards were a central part of this particular social stigma.

Many of these cartoons surfaced during the Reed Smoot hearings, including 600 in the *Salt Lake Tribune* alone between 1905 and 1909—three hundred of them depicting Joseph F. Smith and his beard.[27] The long beard was not the most highly discussed censure of President Smith or the Latter-day Saints, but critics identified the seemingly trivial trademark whiskers with what they believed to be a Mormon counterculture. A long beard, so noticeably untrendy in early twentieth-century America, signified in the public eye not only a fashion statement but also a social statement.[28]

Yet President Smith's beard, as mentioned above, was not necessarily a symbol of subversion. Instead, it typified the traditional profile of his predecessors—the Presidents of the Church since Brigham Young. Smith was a historically minded individual during a time of transition for the Church. Edward H. Andersen, an early-nineteenth-century editor of the *Improvement Era,* even called President Smith "the last of the old school of veteran leaders," a statement, as researcher Jonathan Stapley points out, that relates to a number of aspects of Smith's tenure as President of the Church.[29] A case can thus be made that Smith was "old-school" not only about Latter-day Saint procedures and doctrines but also about his physical appearance, and despite prevalent fashions and even pointed criticisms regarding his beard, he never shaved it off.[30]

Reed Smoot's Mustache

At the center of the extensive court cases in Washington, DC, sat Reed Smoot, a junior member of the Quorum of the Twelve Apostles. He was elected to the United States Senate only two and a half years after his ordination, and in many

Reed Smoot with a nicely trimmed mustache. Courtesy of Library of Congress.

ways he represented a younger generation of Latter-day Saints and members of the Quorum of the Twelve Apostles. Not only was Smoot the second-youngest member of the Twelve, but he also did not practice plural marriage and looked noticeably different from his fellow brethren. Non-Mormons, particularly members of the press, showed an interest in Smoot.

Several gazettes described Elder Smoot as "a normal character" and "decidedly human," a far cry from the bearded, behindhand, polygamist image that many of his contemporaries received in the news. Smoot's keenness, diplomacy, and earnest belief in Latter-day Saint teachings reflected a "likable and sincere" personality that "impresses an unprejudiced person on first meeting."[31] Furthermore, Elder Smoot's physical appearance seemed to appeal to average Americans and members of Congress alike, since "his prototype is found in cities and villages all over the United States."[32] He was "tall, well-knit, erect, with brown hair" and "steady blue eyes." Perhaps most importantly, however, he wore a "drooping brown mustache" and exhibited "clean-cut features," which may have helped him associate to a greater degree with the Senate committee.[33] Of the fifteen committee members at the hearings, eight wore mustaches similar to Elder Smoot's, six were bald-faced, while only one had a beard, which was almost incomparable to President Joseph F. Smith's lifelong, full-grown facial hair.[34]

This isn't to say that Elder Smoot's mustache was the primary factor in upholding his seat in the Senate, or that it alone helped the Latter-day Saints shed their obscure image. The clean-cut countenance and well-groomed mustache were, however, his most distinguishable characteristics and clarified misconceptions that all Mormons wore full beards. In a way, Smoot normalized the Latter-day Saints, as he became the *ex officio* poster child for the Utah-based faith, receiving unprecedented national spotlight as a "good, clean, progressive chap." One *Saturday Evening Post* article from January 1907 demonstrates how Smoot's appearance helped the Latter-day Saints' image.[35]

The author begins the article by describing the appearance of the New Testament Apostles, including their full beards as depicted in paintings, stained glass, and statues. He then compares the appearance of the ancient disciples of Jesus Christ with that of Joseph F. Smith, "head of the Mormon Church, with his rambling, gray hair, and his patriarchal beard." Smith could easily "be framed into a hazy picture of such a person [like the Apostles]; but not Smoot. He looks like a country merchant, which is what he is." The author continues, "Smoot is an undemonstrative, placid sort of a man. . . . He wears a mustache and plasters his hair down on his forehead in that semi-circular style the country barber gets."[36]

The article continues to praise Smoot for the way he weathered the storm and retained his seat in the United States Senate, but perhaps most importantly, the article—like many other contemporary newspaper articles—describes Smoot as a normal-looking American male. In fact, "there [was] nothing in Smoot's appearance to suggest the Mormon apostle, with whom [outsiders] commonly associate[d] an overgrown beard and the linen-duster habit."[37] Smoot's mustache was even noticeable enough among the public for it to make national headlines when he shaved it off in 1925.[38]

Conclusion

Beards began to disappear among the Church's highest authorities after President Smith and his contemporaries passed away. However, it was not until Richard L. Evans, a member of the Quorum of the Twelve Apostles, shaved his neatly trimmed mustache in the mid-1960s that facial hair finally faded away definitively among members of the First Presidency and Quorum of the Twelve. There is much more to be said of beards and their place in Latter-day Saint culture; however, the purpose of this paper was to understand the rise and fall of facial hair in America and to examine Joseph F. Smith's patriarchal beard, its portrayal in the media, and the public's perception. President Smith never did shave his beard, despite outside public opinion, while newer members of the Twelve, including Apostle Reed Smoot, preferred a more clean-cut look, which began to slowly set a new standard for the Latter-day Saint leaders.

Notes

1. "The Passing of the Beard," *Harper's Weekly*, January 17, 1903, 102.
2. See Armand L. Mauss, *The Angel and the Beehive: The Mormon Struggle with Assimilation* (Urbana: University of Illinois Press, 1994), 3–6.
3. See James B. Allen and Glen M. Leonard, *The Story of the Latter-day Saints* (Salt Lake City: Deseret Book, 1976).
4. Jan Shipps, "The Public Image of Senator Reed Smoot, 1902–1932," *Utah Historical Quarterly* 45, no. 4 (Fall 1977): 383–84.
5. Shipps, "The Public Image of Senator Reed Smoot, 1902–1932," 385.
6. Allan Peterkin, *One Thousand Beards: A Cultural History of Facial Hair* (Vancouver, British Columbia: Arsenal Pulp Press, 2001), 34.

7. As cited in Charles W. Moores, ed., *Lincoln Addresses and Letters* (New York: American Book, 1914), 136–37.
8. Grace Bedell to Abraham Lincoln, October 15, 1860, holograph letter, Detroit Public Library, Burton Historical Collection; http://myloc.gov/exhibitions/lincoln/vignettes/candidatelincoln/pages/objectlist.aspx.
9. "The Passing of the Beard," 102.
10. "Beard! Beard!" advertisement in *Harper's Weekly*, April 8, 1865, 223.
11. "The Passing of the Beard," 102.
12. "The Passing of the Beard," 102.
13. "Modene," advertisement in *Harper's Weekly*, June 27, 1891, 3.
14. James L. Jacobs, "Sacrament at Conference," *Saga of the Sanpitch* 15 (1983): 8.
15. Justin R. Bray, "The Lord's Supper During the Progressive Era," *Journal of Mormon History* 38, no. 4 (Fall 2012): 88–104.
16. As cited in Edward Brown Firmage, ed., *An Abundant Life: The Memoirs of Hugh B. Brown* (Salt Lake City: Signature Books, 1999), 10.
17. Andrew H. Hedges and Richard Neitzel Holzapfel, eds., *Within These Prison Walls: Lorenzo Snow's Record Book, 1886–1897* (Provo, UT: Religious Studies Center; Salt Lake City: Deseret Book, 2010), xxxvii.
18. A number of nineteenth-century biblical scholars wrote that Jesus had his beard shaved prior to the crucifixion. See, for example, *The Works of the Reverend John Newton* (New York: Williams and Whiting, 1810), 164.
19. Hedges and Holzapfel, *Within These Prison Walls*, xxxvii. See also Richard S. Van Wagoner, "To Beard or Not to Beard," *Sunstone* 8, no. 6 (November–December 1983), 10.
20. As quoted in Will Bagley, *Blood of the Prophets: Brigham Young and the Massacre at Mountain Meadows* (Norman: University of Oklahoma Press, 2002), 302.
21. See Richard E. Turley, "Recent Mountain Meadows Publications: A Sampling," *Journal of Mormon History* 32, no. 2 (Summer 2006): 223.
22. Richard Neitzel Holzapfel and R. Q. Shupe, *Joseph F. Smith: A Portrait of a Prophet* (Salt Lake City: Bookcraft, 2000), 206. See also "Some Recollections of Grandfather Joseph F. Smith"; http://www.josephfsmith.org/sites/default/files/recollections.pdf.
23. Philip Loring Allen, "The Mormon Church on Trial," *Harper's Weekly*, March 26, 1904, 469–71. Michael Paulos, ed., *The Mormon Church on Trial: Transcripts of the Reed Smoot Hearings* (Salt Lake City: Signature Books, 2008), 177n. Nelson B. Wadsworth, *Through Camera Eyes* (Provo, UT: Brigham Young University Press, 1975), 167.
24. Kathleen Flake, *The Politics of American Religious Identity: The Seating of Senator Reed Smoot, Mormon Apostle* (Chapel Hill: University of North Carolina Press, 2004), 5.
25. As cited in Samuel Woolley Taylor, *Rocky Mountain Empire: The Latter-day Saints Today* (New York: Macmillan, 1978), 74.
26. Tattler, "Notes From the Capital: Reed Smoot," *The Nation*, August 9, 1917, 158.
27. Holzapfel and Shupe, *Joseph F. Smith: A Portrait of a Prophet*, 6.
28. Richard Barry, "The Political Menace of the Mormon Church," *Pearson's Magazine*, July 1910, 320. Philip Loring Allen, "The Mormon Church on Trial," *Harper's Weekly*, March 1904, 469–71.

29. Edward H. Anderson, "Last of the Old School of Veteran Leaders," in *Gospel Doctrine: Selections from the Sermons and Writings of Joseph F. Smith* (Salt Lake City: Deseret News, 1919), 684.
30. For a progression of Joseph F. Smith's appearance, see Holzapfel and Shupe, *Joseph F. Smith: Portrait of a Prophet.*
31. "Church Is on Trial," *Daily Telegram,* March 3, 1904, 7.
32. "Church Is on Trial," 7.
33. "Church Is on Trial," 7.
34. Mustaches had become the new sign of masculinity, replacing the full beard from previous decades. A "mustache cup" was even invented to accommodate the growing trend. The cup had a half-circle ledge across its top, with a small opening that left just enough room on the rim for someone to sip the drink without wetting the fuzzy upper lip.
35. "Smooting—A New Senate Game," *Saturday Evening Post,* January 12, 1907, 20.
36. "Smooting—A New Senate Game," 20.
37. Tattler, "Notes From the Capital: Reed Smoot," *The Nation,* August 9, 1917, 158.
38. "Smoot of Utah Now Clean Shaven," *Bryan Democrat,* November 24, 1925, 8.

Matthew R. Davies

26

The Tongues of the Saints:

The Azusa Street Revival and the Changing Definition of Tongues

The Church of Jesus Christ of Latter-day Saints has always derived its identity from claiming to be Christ's restored church on earth, with which the apostolic gifts of the Spirit contemporaneously reside. The return of the gifts of the Spirit to the Church, namely contemporary revelation and speaking in tongues, lent legitimacy to the Church's claim of restoration. One must ask, then, how did the Church react to the rise of Pentecostalism, a movement which itself claimed to uniquely possess the apostolic gifts of the Spirit? By examining the teachings of President Joseph F. Smith and numerous Latter-day Saint journals during the rise of the Azusa Street Revival, we can discover how the Church responded to the rise of Pentecostalism by reexamining its own practice of tongues.

The Azusa Street Revival, which began in Los Angeles in 1906, is largely seen as the primary impetus for the promotion and spread of Pentecostalism. Numerous religious practices differentiated and marginalized Azusa Street from mainline American Protestantism, including its extemporaneous spiritual gifts, interracial worship, and an ecstatic worship style. Most notably, the Azusa Street Revival emphasized the speaking of tongues, a key component of Pentecostalism.

Matthew R. Davies is a professor of religion at Chemeketa Community College in Salem, Oregon.

It cannot be said that the rise of the Pentecostal movement necessitated the Church to modify its doctrine on *glossolalia,* the speaking of heavenly tongues, but it did cause the Church to reexamine and stress the redefined position of tongues among its members in an attempt to dismiss the Azusa Street claims of a modern-day Pentecost. Such an examination allows us to explore an example of the lengths to which ostracized religious groups go in order to gain acceptance in hegemonic American society. When confronted with a competing claim of apostolic restoration and while attempting to reenter society, the LDS Church emphasized a redefined practice of tongues rather than the Church's prototypical practice.

This reexamination of the Church's practice of glossolalia occurred as the Church was preparing to reenter American society after decades of isolation, both forced and self-imposed. Historian Thomas G. Alexander penned a study documenting this transition, which will be useful for this essay. Alexander argues that beginning in the 1890s, "Mormons began groping for a new paradigm that would save essential characteristics of their religious tradition, provide sufficient political stability to preserve the interests of the church, and allow them to live in peace with other Americans."[1] This led the Church to abandon, modify, or de-emphasize doctrines and practices the Church had previously held dear and essential; in this case, glossolalia proper was discouraged in favor of *xenoglossia,* or the ability to speak a foreign language previously unknown to the speaker. This de-emphasis was in part due to the diminishing need to view tongues as a necessary proof of the veracity of the Church; Mormons were gaining testimonies regarding the Church without relying solely on tongues and other gifts of the Spirit, save contemporary revelation. Terryl Givens largely agrees with Alexander's dating, arguing that following the Manifesto ending plural marriage that was issued by President Wilford Woodruff, the Church reexamined its doctrine and culture in an attempt for "accommodation and integration" into American society.[2] Neither of these authors, however, focused on the impact the transition had on glossolalia in the Church, previously a prominent divine gift. This paper helps close that gap, examining President Smith's completion of an effort to reclassify glossolalia as part of a larger effort to gain favorability for the Church in the larger American society.

Let us first (too) briefly examine how Azusa Street viewed glossolalia. Tongues were heavily emphasized on Azusa Street, and the Pentecostal newspaper, the *Apostolic Faith,* documented instances of tongues as the movement spread, first up the West Coast, then nationally, and eventually internationally. The *Apostolic Faith* carried the essential message of Azusa Street: "The wonderful sign in 1906 is the restoration of tongues, which foretells the preaching of the pure gospel to all nations, which must be done before the Gentile Times end."[3] The tongues signaled a return of the biblical apostolic age, the time Jesus' disciples received the gifts of tongues, evinced by tongues of fire appearing over their heads, as a precursor to spreading the gospel. In support of the return of the apostolic times, Pentecostals sometimes reported seeing "cloven tongues" above the heads of those practicing glossolalia, or bright lights filling rooms immediately before tongues were spoken.[4]

Similar to the Apostles' description in Acts, the contemporary Pentecostal tongues were gifted for a particular and specified purpose: "The gift of languages is given with the commission, 'Go ye into all the world and preach the Gospel to every creature.'"[5] This commission had influenced Pentecostal leader Charles Parham's belief that xenoglossia was the true apostolic gift, for even the unlearned could then spread the gospel to the world by speaking foreign languages through the Holy Spirit. The gift of xenoglossia allowed the Pentecostal movement to spread internationally; the *Apostolic Faith* reported a group of Pentecostal missionaries leaving for Africa on September 13, mere months after the Pentecost fell on Los Angeles. The missionaries had been given "the gift of the Uganda [*sic*] language, the language of the people to whom she [a missionary] is sent. . . . Her husband is with her and her niece, who also has been given the African language."[6] In its two years of publication, the *Apostolic Faith* reported missions to every habitable continent except South America.

The speaking of heavenly tongues, the classic definition of glossolalia, was also present alongside xenoglossia. "Many are speaking in new tongues, and some are on their way to the foreign fields, with the gift of language."[7] The Pentecostals on Azusa Street clearly differentiated between glossolalia and xenoglossia, indicating that both were present during the revival. Glossolalia was not confined to speaking alone, for instances of writing in "unknown languages" were also reported. Some experienced both types of tongues, receiving "many tongues, also the gift of prophecy, and writing in a number of foreign languages."[8] In this manner, Azusa Street could spread their message through either voice or print, making their missions more effective.

While the role of tongues on Azusa Street could be examined more in depth, let us now consider the role of tongues in the early LDS Church, for a reexamination of the Church's use of glossolalia occurred at the turn of the twentieth century, due in part to the Church's reaction to Pentecostalism. The role of glossolalia in the Church, especially while the Church was based in Nauvoo, has been the subject of some scholarly conversation. This paper contributes to that conversation by reconsidering the prominence of tongues in the post-Nauvoo Church, mainly by responding to the arguments of Dan Vogel and Scott C. Dunn presented in "'The Tongues of Angels': Glossolalia Among Mormonism's Founders." It is widely agreed that glossolalia was present and popular during the genesis of the Church. Glossolalia among the Saints and Church leaders was widespread, beginning in Ohio and quickly spreading through New York, Pennsylvania, and Missouri. Tongues flourished in the Church, most notably in Kirtland, and turned into a "widespread, persistent, and integral feature of early Mormon religious experience."[9] In the early Church, tongues were encouraged and practiced by both lay members and Church leaders, including Joseph Smith, Brigham Young, and Heber C. Kimball, among others. In fact, according to W. W. Phelps, one of Smith's scribes, nearly every early Saint spoke in tongues at some point.[10] Glossolalia was also manifested during conferences and official Church business. This included Smith speaking in glossolalia at a Church conference on January 22, 1833, and glossolalia spreading among the Church authorities when the Prophet, First Presidency, the Twelve, and the Seventy were gathered together in conference in January of 1836 and during the time surrounding the dedication of the Kirtland Temple.[11]

In the midst of widespread usage of tongues, Joseph Smith and Church leaders issued warnings about the proper place of tongues, although this does not appear to have stalled or eliminated the use of tongues. The warnings were not about speaking in tongues as such, but only about the doctrinal impact of the glossolalia spoken by the Saints. Joseph Smith informed the Relief Society in May of 1842, "You may speak in tongues for your own comfort but I lay this down for a rule that if anything is taught by the gift of tongues, it is not to be received for doctrine."[12] Smith is almost certainly mentioning glossolalia here rather than xenoglossia, for Saints were not previously claiming doctrinal revelation through xenoglossia. Previously, Smith had declared in 1834 that tongues were "not given for the government of the Church," but for teaching and preaching.[13] Importantly, glossolalia was not to be used by Saints for receiving revelation apart from the Church hierarchy. Such individual claims of divine revelation, no matter how accurate, challenged the charismatic and revelatory power of Joseph Smith. Other warnings were issued as well. Parley P. Pratt warned Saints in the *Millennial Star* in 1840 against the public use of tongues: "Never give out appointments for speaking in tongues; . . . .either speak in tongues to an assembly who have come together for the purpose of hearing you thus speak, . . . for this is not pleasing in the sight of heaven."[14] Pratt was indeed instructing the Saints not to publically display their tongues during mission appointments, nor to give appointments for the express purpose of speaking in tongues. Instead, glossolalia was to be used for personal edification and verification of the restored gospel. Furthermore, Saints were advised to always have interpreters present, lest the devil come and manipulate the teachings.[15]

Yet while the Church may have issued warnings about exuberant tongues, tongues were still prominent in the lived religion of the Saints. Vogel and Dunn cite numerous instances of both glossolalia and xenoglossia being spoken during the life of Joseph Smith, including occurrences under the approval of Church leaders.[16] And despite the claim that a renewed deemphasis of glossolalia by Joseph Smith beginning in 1839 "virtually removed [glossolalia] from Mormon worship," Vogel and Dunn recall times that tongues were present in the post-1839 performance of the Saints' religion. This includes an 1857 quote from Apostle Heber C. Kimball regarding his ability to speak in tongues and Hannah Savage speaking in "the tongue of Adam" with Medora Gardner translating during a Relief Society meeting in 1896, indicating that glossolalia was present as well.[17] We can draw from Vogel and Dunn that a redefinition of tongues may have been attempted during Joseph Smith's time, but glossolalia was not wholly removed from the lives of the Saints. Instead, the discouraging of glossolalia impacted only the doctrinal relevance of a Saint's glossolalia, not the practice of it. That is, glossolalia itself was not de-emphasized or banned among the Saints, but the Saints were reminded that tongues could not produce revelation apart from the Church authorities, solidifying Smith's role as the Church's revelator. Indeed, tongues continued to prevail among the Saints, acting as a personal devotion and testament to the restored gospel and apostolic gifts.[18]

Tongues continued to play a role in the Church during its migration west under Brigham Young, albeit a slightly different role. While in Nauvoo and during the exodus to Utah, women were heard singing in tongues. While in Winter Quarters, Brigham Young addressed the Saints in tongues and even "conversed" in tongues with Heber C. Kimball.[19] It is probably doubtful that Mormons used tongues as a conversational language, yet perhaps Young at one time envisioned such a possibility. According to John G. Turner's recent biography of Young,

"Young and other early Mormons understood speaking in tongues as a foretaste of the divine language of heaven, which Adam had spoken but which had then become a Babel of confusion." Young saw his creation of the new Deseret alphabet as "'a step and partial return to the pure language which has been promised unto us in the latter days.'"[20] While the routinization and structuring of glossolalia may have limited its mystical function, it would have allowed for expanded proselytization to non-English speakers, furthering the Church's mission and solidifying the role of tongues in the Church.

Under the presidency of Brigham Young, the presence of xenoglossia also increased, often without formal distinction from glossolalia. One such instance occurred during a meeting between Young and Ute band leaders in May 1850. One morning, Brigham Young required the use of a translator to converse with the natives. Following the singing of two hymns in the afternoon, however, the gift of tongues struck Young and he "proceeded to speak in tongues. When he asked the Utes if they had understood the mystical language, they all said yes." Jared Farmer cites that Young's physician also "performed glossolalia," which a band leader clarified as the doctor having spoken Sioux.[21] While the use of the terms *glossolalia* and *mystical* to refer to Young speaking the natives' language may be Farmer's own authorial prerogative, the accounts do make it clear that Young's xenoglossia appeared much as glossolalia did, through an outpouring of the Holy Spirit.

Alongside the xenoglossia spoken by Young, a renewed outpouring of glossolalia was seen in Utah. The Mormon Reformation of 1855–57 saw a similar increase of religious enthusiasm as the Saints had experienced in Kirtland. In the midst of a famine, a plague of grasshoppers, controversies with natives, and tensions with the federal government, religious faith was lukewarm, in the opinion of Church leaders. While the reformation was guided by strict preaching, rebaptisms, and monitored repentance, "it also produced an outpouring of spiritual gifts: 'Brethren generally confessing their Sins and wrong doings and receiving forgivness [*sic*] & testimonies to the Gospels power the presence of the Holy Spirits, Angels, and the Spirit of Joseph Smith. Angels singing; Tongues &c &c.'"[22]

Despite the claims by some scholars that glossolalia began to decrease toward the end of Joseph Smith's life and continued until near extinction at the beginning of the twentieth century, it appears that tongues continued in the lives of the Saints. Thomas G. Alexander cites myriad uses of tongues, writing that "at the turn of the [twentieth] century, such experience [of glossolalia] was still widespread in the church." This included tongues being used during healing rituals, being spoken in the Tabernacle by a missionary, and being expressed through song. Alexander posits that instead of tongues having been in decline since 1839, tongues did not begin declining until the early twentieth century. One reason for mistaking an early decline may be due to the fact that "glossolalia declined more rapidly among men than among women," according to Alexander. With men running the Church, writing the histories, and issuing doctrine, it is easy to write an androcentric history of glossolalia, and thereby to attribute a decline in tongues among men as a decline among all members. Yet the practice was clearly supported and sustained by Mormon women's religious experiences. In fact, at least six of the eight instances of tongues Alexander cites between 1899 and 1908 were women practicing the gift of tongues, while men recorded the majority of these cited events.[23]

The role and acceptability of tongues in the Church began to be reexamined at the turn of the twentieth century. Church leaders, led by President Joseph F. Smith, deemphasized glossolalia, the type of tongues seen on Azusa Street, by first cautioning about the potential danger of tongues without proper ecclesiastical limits. President Smith warned about the potential manipulation by the devil and apostates, stating, "There is perhaps no gift of the Spirit of God more easily imitated by the devil than the gift of tongues. Where two men or women exercise the gift of tongues by the inspiration of the Spirit of God, there are a dozen perhaps that do it by the inspiration of the devil. . . . Apostates [can even] speak in tongues." In fact, due to the importance of the gifts of the Spirit to the Church of Jesus Christ, the devil would specifically imitate such gifts in order to deceive the Saints. "The gifts of the Spirit and the powers of the holy Priesthood are of God, they are given for the blessing of the people, for their encouragement, and for the strengthening of their faith. This Satan knows full well, therefore he seeks by imitation-miracles to blind and deceive the children of God."[24] While these warnings against demonic influence had been issued by Joseph Smith as well, they took on a more pointed meaning with the rise of Pentecostalism.

Furthermore, the Church shifted the proper ecclesiastical sphere for tongues, declaring that tongues should be used only in missionary work, which essentially removed the power for all Saints to speak in tongues.[25] Even President Smith expressed his diminishing need for tongues. "I do not want the gift of tongues, except when I need it. I needed the gift of tongues once, and the Lord gave it to me. I was in a foreign land, sent to preach the gospel to a people whose language I could not understand. . . . [A] hundred days after landing upon those islands I could talk to the people in their language as I now talk to you in my native tongue."[26] President Smith demonstrated the completion of the change the Church experienced in the definition of tongues. Transitioning from frequent and early use of glossolalia, the "language of Adam," under Joseph Smith, traversing through Brigham Young's interchangeable and mixed use of both glossolalia and xenoglossia in Utah, the Church, in the early twentieth century, had arrived at a place where xenoglossia was seen as the proper definition of tongues over and against glossolalia.[27]

This transition in the use of tongues served a protective function for Mormons. As Spencer Fluhman explains, tongues were perhaps the most disturbing part of Mormon religiosity for non-Mormons, and indeed may have been a deciding factor in the anti-Mormon violence in Missouri. Missourians cited glossolalia as a main reason for labeling Mormons as delusional. Parley P. Pratt responded to a letter circulating in Missouri, one accusing that Mormons "openly blaspheme the most High God, and cast contempt upon His Holy Religion, by pretending to receive Revelations directly from Heaven—by pretending to speak in unknown tongues by direct inspiration."[28] They had, according to accusations, "pretended revelations from heaven—their personal intercourse with God and His angels— . . . and the contemptible gibberish with which they habitually profane the Sabbath, and which they dignify with the appellation of unknown tongues." This sort of religious enthusiasm was not seen in other denominations. While there were biblical precedents for tongues, there were no American precedents, according to anti-Mormons, making the Mormon's glossolalia suspect.[29] The Church utilized public scrutiny to reinterpret essential Latter-day Saint practices; in this case, xenoglossia was emphasized over and against glossolalia, thereby giving tongues a more pragmatic and "acceptable" function.

At the turn of the century, the Church was also in the midst of a conflict between science and tradition, as many religious organizations were. The Church therefore had a vested interest to routinize and regularize forms of worship in an attempt to diminish claims of extreme supernaturalism in the face of scientific discovery. Just as the reliance on scientific discovery and methodology rose in the early twentieth century, so also did the discomfort with overt displays of supernaturalism and gifts of the Spirit rise, not only among the general public but also among Saints themselves. Church officials began to discourage the gift of tongues in Church meetings, for emphasis was placed on an orderly and respectful worship experience instead of a prophetic and supernatural one. In Alexander's words, "The reconstruction of Latter-day Saint doctrine, ... while addressing the reconciliation of church doctrine with scientific theory, had brought supernaturalism into question. . . . The church leadership could tolerate and even encourage personal spiritual experiences. On the other hand, public displays of prophecy or glossolalia tended to the discomfort of some members and perhaps even to disharmony in the organization." To replace the supernatural gifts and glossolalia, the Church emphasized testimony meetings and temple ordinances for the dead, practices that were either publically acceptable or practiced behind closed, sacred doors.[30]

The de-emphasis on tongues by the Church leadership did not always match the lived religious experience of Church members. A letter appeared in the *Improvement Era* in 1904, just over a year before the first meeting on Azusa Street, recounting the former prominence of speaking in tongues in the LDS Church and lamenting the loss, as the author saw it, of this gift. In an article entitled "Passing of the Gift of Tongues," Dr. James X. Allen recounted his amazement that a returned missionary from Scandinavia had never heard anyone speak in tongues. The way Allen phrased his surprise is telling: "This same young brother was reared in Utah. His father and mother, as also he himself, are good Latter-day Saints. He has filled an honorable mission, and is today strong in the faith, and yet, he has never heard and experienced one of the most common gifts of the gospel, as enjoyed years ago."[31] For Allen, tongues were prominent enough in the lived religion of the Church to expect others to have experienced or to have at least witnessed them. In his telling, there should be no Mormon who had not yet experienced or witnessed this gift, let alone one from Utah and a good Latter-day Saint family. How tragic was this lack of glossolalic experience, a lack of experience in one of the most common gifts the Church had to offer!

Allen reiterated the common prevalence of tongues in the early Church, confirming the report of W. W. Phelps: "In the early days of the Church—where I was reared—there were so many of the Saints who enjoyed the gifts, and there were none among my acquaintances who had not heard the sweet sound of the gift of tongues. . . . In fact, we were wont to regard the speaking in tongues, [and] the interpretation of tongues . . . as an essential part of the latter-day gospel." From Allen's account, it appears that some Mormons became almost disillusioned with the Church after the de-emphasis of tongues. "If men now think they can get along without the gifts of the gospel, may not the time come when they may believe they can get along without its ordinances?"[32] The gift of tongues, among other things, had helped confirm the veracity of the restored gospel for Mormons. If the Church could redefine this gift of the Spirit, this gift that lent credence to that claim of restoration, what did it mean for the other Church doctrines?

After Allen's article, the Church periodically published articles affirming the new official role of xenoglossia over glossolalia proper. A question-answer style article appeared in the *Liahona* in 1907, asking about the nature of Peter's xenoglossia on the day of the apostolic Pentecost. The answer, presumably written by the editor, stressed that the original Pentecost featured xenoglossia, striking a similar tone to Charles Parham's belief on the nature of tongues at the biblical Pentecost. It then recounted the episode of "an experienced elder" who had practiced xenoglossia. By referring to an experienced elder, the Church could, in a way, adopt a different stance than Allen's. Allen, who was reared in the early days of the Church, claimed that glossolalia proper was common in the Church; this article countered that xenoglossia was more prevalent in the early church, which "confirms the view of President [Joseph F.] Smith."[33]

Perhaps due to the Church's de-emphasis on glossolalia, only one Latter-day Saint journal at the turn of the twentieth century made a direct, albeit somewhat implicit, reference to the speaking in tongues by the Pentecostal movement. It appears the Church, possibly because of the disillusionment of some members such as Allen, minimized its conversation on gifts of the Spirit, and tongues explicitly, save for the few references mentioned above. Yet the national and international attention gained by Azusa Street meant the Church could not fully ignore the movement.

Dated February 22, 1908, a letter was published in the *Liahona* at the height of the Azusa Street Revival. Confined to an editorial section, the letter manifests both the Latter-day Saint view of Pentecostal tongues and the change in the role for tongues as propagated by Joseph F. Smith:

> Benighted fanatics in heathen countries are not the only persons who are being deluded by a "gift of tongues" emanating from a wrong source. Here in the United States, during recent years, in the full blaze of a much boasted Christian enlightenment, scholarship and civilization, many pious and educated persons have been carried away by the same delusion. The persons here referred to, filled with missionary zeal, and claiming to be possessed of "the gift of tongues," by which they were able to "preach the gospel" to the inhabitants of

> such heathen countries as China, Japan, India, etc. have gone to those remote parts of the earth expecting to preach to the natives, without study or other effort to acquire the language, and dismal failure has been the result in every case, so far as we have yet learned.[34]

Pentecostalism is undoubtedly referenced here, despite its lack of explicit mention. The Church, completing its redefinition of tongues as xenoglossia rather than glossolalia proper, was already applying this redefinition in an attempt to "give an opinion as to whether this gift of tongues [of the Pentecostals] . . . comes from the Spirit of the Lord, or from some other source."[35] Clearly they originated from some other source, maintained the *Liahona*.

The editorial highlights two foreign Pentecostal missionaries for their purportedly unsuccessful attempts at xenoglossia. Despite mentioning the missionaries by name, their religious inclinations and association with Pentecostalism are not explicitly mentioned, leading us to believe that the Church did not want to explicitly mention Pentecostalism or Azusa Street, perhaps thinking it would lend credibility to the new movement. T. J. McIntosh was a Pentecostal preacher who traveled to China in 1907.[36] His mission, as described by the Latter-day Saint editorial, was an utter failure. "From the day of his arrival in China until now neither he nor his wife has been able to speak a single sentence in Chinese. I do not speak from rumor, but from personal knowledge, and the personal admission of failure by Mr. McIntosh himself." By claiming firsthand knowledge of this failure, the author attempts to lend legitimacy to the account. In fact, the author continued, McIntosh had to use a translator to even function daily in China, meaning his claim to xenoglossia failed in even the "simplest affairs of every-day life."[37]

A second missionary couple mentioned in the editorial traveled to Calcutta, India, where they experienced the same purported failure. Reverend Garr was a pastor in Los Angeles in 1906 when the Azusa Street Revival began. After being baptized by the Holy Spirit, Garr was endowed with the gift to speak Bengali, which had prompted his mission to India.[38] "Rev. A. G. Carr [Garr] and wife went there, also expecting to speak to the people in this supernatural way. But did they? . . . I have attended two of their services. Mr. Garr, in reply to a personal question of mine as to whether either he or his wife had been able to talk in the native language of India, said that they had been unable to do so."[39] There exist Pentecostal accounts, however, that dispute the failure reported by the *Liahona*. The Pentecostal newspaper, the *Apostolic Faith,* reported success in the words of Mrs. Garr herself, combating the LDS firsthand account. "God is spreading Pentecost here in Calcutta . . . . [and] the Spirit is giving the interpretation, song and writing in tongues, and other wonderful manifestations of His presence among us."[40] Mrs. Garr's definition of "tongues" is ambiguous here—she could have meant either glossolalia proper or xenoglossia. It is plausible that she deliberately left the word ambiguous in order to mask a failure to communicate in the native language. Regardless, there were certainly competing interpretations as to the exact work of tongues in Calcutta.

Although these accounts do not explicitly mention Azusa Street, or even speaking in tongues in America, the view of the Latter-day Saints would not have changed depending on the location of the tongues, especially when the nature of the criticisms are taken into account. The *Liahona* could not fault Pentecostalism for the sphere in which its tongues were spoken in these accounts, for they were in agreement with the Latter-day Saints' redesignated proper sphere for speaking in tongues only on missions. According to the First Presidency, tongues were given to the Church only for "'preaching among peoples whose language is not understood.'" Non-missionaries should "'let speaking in tongues alone and . . . confine [their] speech to [their] own language.'"[41] The Latter-day Saint editorial confirmed that the Pentecostal foreign missions utilized xenoglossia, according to the proper Latter-day Saint understanding, yet did not mention glossolalia proper, or the speaking in heavenly or unknown tongues, which was still common on Azusa Street.

Speaking tongues in the proper sphere does not guarantee success, however. In the eyes of the Church, the Pentecostal missionaries failed in their xenoglossia for a simple reason: they "ha[d] not the necessary 'key of knowledge' to do this, as have the elders of the Church of Jesus Christ of Latterday [*sic*] Saints."[42] The Latter-day Saint priesthood contained the "keys of the kingdom" and the ability to confer the Holy Ghost upon converts (see D&C 7:7; 68:15–21; 81:2; 107:1–100, *inter alia*). The Pentecostal tongues could not be successful simply because they did not have the keys of the priesthood, regardless of the Pentecostal accounts coming from the foreign mission fields. It is entirely plausible that the Church classified the Pentecostal tongues as failures in order to maintain its legitimacy and identity as the only true apostolic Church. The "complete failure" among the "sectarian zealots and missionaries or would-be missionaries" proved "the source of the wonder-exciting phenomenon to be evil.... No fiasco attends this gift when it emanates from the right source." In a final and curt dismissal, the *Liahona* made clear where it stood: "Why is it that such beneficent results flow from the exercise of the gift of tongues by missionaries of the Church of Jesus Christ of Latterday [*sic*] Saints, while failure, chagrin and distress attend attempts to employ it made by missionaries of other denominations? Because that Church is the only one in the world which possesses divine authority to confer upon converts the Holy Ghost, of which the genuine gift of tongues is at once a fruit and a proof."[43]

At the end of the Azusa Street Revival, the First Presidency issued another warning about those speaking tongues with messages not approved by the Church. As before, the Church did not refer to the Pentecostal movement by name. Addressed to the "officers and members" of the Church, the letter informed members how to gauge the veracity of tongues: "When... tongues, prophecy, impressions or any extraordinary gift or inspiration, convey something out of harmony with the accepted revelations of the Church or contrary to the decisions of its constituted authorities, Latter-day Saints may know that it is not of God, no matter how plausible it may appear." Since the Church receives direct revelations from God, and then communicates said revelations to the members, any gift of tongues purporting to be from God had to be consistent with the revelations of the Church, for "the Holy Ghost does not contradict its own revealings."[44] While the Church left open the option for members to receive personal revelation, that revelation could only affect the member receiving the revelation and the member's family, but no one else.

The recategorization of speaking in tongues, by which we mean the de-emphasis of glossolalia in favor of xenoglossia, by the Church coincided with the rise of the Pentecostal movement at Azusa Street in Los Angeles. While one cannot claim a cause-and-effect relation between the two, the rise of Pentecostalism did cause the Church to discreetly emphasize its reexamined position on tongues—that is, categorizing the legitimate role of xenoglossia in missions while de-emphasizing glossolalia proper—all while attempting to maintain its identity as the true restored church. With the rise of the Pentecostal movement, the Church avoided explicitly mentioning the Pentecostal movement and demonstrated caution when referring to the gifts of the Spirit as a whole, due largely to the disillusionment with the gifts some members felt. The Church, therefore, made deliberate attempts to link the new categorization of tongues back to the Prophet Joseph while warning about the dangers of those outside the Church speaking in tongues. It is not easy to say if the Church felt threatened by Pentecostalism's speaking in tongues, but Azusa Street did require the Church to delicately stress the changing role of tongues in the Church while maintaining the Church's identity as Christ's true restored apostolic church on earth.

Notes

1. See Thomas G. Alexander, *Mormonism in Transition: A History of the Latter-day Saints, 1890–1930* (Urbana: University of Illinois, 1986), 14.
2. Terryl L. Givens, *People of Paradox: A History of Mormon Culture* (Oxford: Oxford University, 2007), xiv–xvii, 191–93.
3. *Apostolic Faith* 1, no. 8 (May 1907).
4. *Apostolic Faith* 1, no. 1 (September 1906); no. 2 (October 1906).
5. *Apostolic Faith* 1, no. 1 (September 1906).
6. *Apostolic Faith* 1, no. 2 (October 1906).
7. *Apostolic Faith* 1, no. 1 (September 1906).
8. *Apostolic Faith* 1, no. 1 (September 1906).
9. Dan Vogel and Scott C. Dunn, "The Tongue of Angels: Glossolalia among *Mormonism's* Founders," *Journal of Mormon History* 19, no. 2 (1993). 10, Lee Copeland, "Speaking in Tongues in the Restoration Churches," *Dialogue: A Journal of Mormon Thought* 24, no. 1 (Spring 1991): 16–17; John G. Turner, *Brigham Young: Pioneer Prophet* (Cambridge: Harvard University, 2012), 26–33, 64, 131.
10. Vogel and Dunn, "The Tongue of Angels," 13.
11. Vogel and Dunn, "'The Tongue of Angels,'" 11; Copeland, "Speaking in Tongues in the Restoration Churches," 20; *History of the Church of Jesus Christ of Latter-day Saints*, ed. B. H. Roberts, 2nd ed. rev. (Salt Lake City: Deseret Book, 1978), 1:323, 2:376, 2:383; Dean C. Jessee, Mark Ashurst-McGee, and Richard L. Jensen, eds., *Journals, Volume 1: 1832–1839*, vol. 1 of the Journals series of *The Joseph Smith Papers*, ed. Dean C. Jessee, Ronald K. Esplin, and Richard Lyman Bushman (Salt Lake City: Church Historian's Press, 2008), 180–82, 213–16. See also Samuel Morris Brown, *In Heaven as It Is on Earth: Joseph Smith and the Early Mormon Conquest of Death* (New York: Oxford University, 2012), 158–63.
12. Andrew F. Ehat and Lyndon W. Cook, eds., *The Words of Joseph Smith* (Provo, UT: Religious Studies Center, Brigham Young University, 1980), 119; quoted in Copeland, "Speaking in Tongues in the Restoration Churches," 23.
13. *History, 1838-1856, Vol. B-1*, September 8, 1834, in The Joseph Smith Papers, http://josephsmithpapers.org/paperSummary/history-1838-1856-volume-b-1?p=8, p. 8. See also, *History of the Church* 2:162.
14. *Millennial Star*, September 1840; also quoted in Copeland, "Speaking in Tongues in the Restoration Churches," 23.
15. *History, 1838-1856, Vol. C-1*, added addendum to July 2, 1839, in The Joseph Smith Papers, http://josephsmithpapers.org/paperSummary/history-1838-1856-volume-c-1?p=547, p. 547.

16. Vogel and Dunn, "'The Tongue of Angels,'" 2-24.
17. Vogel and Dunn, "'The Tongue of Angels,'" 23-24.
18. Vogel and Dunn, "'The Tongue of Angels,'" 16–24.
19. Turner, *Brigham Young: Pioneer Prophet*, 131, 157.
20. Turner, *Brigham Young: Pioneer Prophet*, 249. It certainly is true that a main impetus for the creation of a new alphabet was to create a phonetic language easier to read and write, which would help the Mormons in their missions to non-English speakers. Yet the quote by Young makes it appear that this phonetic alphabet could accomplish the same function as glossolalia did before Babel; glossolalia, the language spoken by Adam and understood by all before Babel, would be reconstituted in this easily understood phonetic alphabet. See Turner, 249.
21. Jared Farmer, *On Zion's Mount: Mormons, Indians, and the American Landscape* (Cambridge: Harvard University, 2008), 78–80; Turner, *Brigham Young*, 214. It is interesting that the native heard Samuel Sprague, the physician, speak Sioux despite the fact that natives in the Great Basin mostly spoke Numic. See page 23. Farmer does not mention this discrepancy, leaving it unclear how precisely the tongues were manifested.
22. Turner, *Brigham Young*, 254–64; Farmer, *On Zion's Mount*, 92–96.
23. Alexander, *Mormonism in Transition*, 294-98. All quotes and examples of tongues are found on p. 294.
24. Smith made this comment at general conference in April of 1900. Joseph F. Smith, *Gospel Doctrine: Selections from the Sermons and Writings of Joseph F. Smith* (Salt Lake City: Bookcraft, 1998), 201, 376.
25. Copeland, "Speaking in Tongues," 24. See also Alexander, *Mormonism in Transition*, 294.
26. Smith, *Gospel Doctrine*, 201.
27. Copeland, "Speaking in Tongues," 20. This allows for most missionaries to claim the gift of tongues while studying in the Missionary Training Center (MTC) before their call to a foreign land. Bruce McConkie iterates such in his book *Mormon Doctrine*, "[T]he Lord's missionaries learn to speak and interpret foreign languages with ease, thus furthering the spread of the message of the restoration. When the elders of Israel, often in a matter of weeks, gain fluency in a foreign tongue, they have been blessed with the gift of tongues." *Mormon Doctrine*, 2nd ed. (Salt Lake City: Bookcraft, 1979), "Tongues." Perhaps tellingly, this transition in tongues seen in the Church from Joseph Smith to President Smith mirrored a transition seen in Brigham Young's personal use of tongues.
28. Parley P. Pratt, *History of the Late Persecution Inflicted by the State of Missouri Upon the Mormons* [1839], The Joseph Smith Papers, accessed December 3, 2012, http://josephsmithpapers.org/paperSummary/parley-p-pratt-history-of-the-late-persecution-1839, 9–10.
29. J. Spencer Fluhman, *"A Peculiar People:" Anti-Mormonism and the Making of Religion in Nineteenth-Century America* (Chapel Hill: University of North Carolina, 2012), 53–58. For another example, see Terryl Givens, *The Viper on the Hearth: Mormons, Myths, and the Construction of Heresy* (New York: Oxford University, 1997), 44.
30. Alexander, *Mormonism in Transition*, 293–98. Alexander states, "These public prophecies should be distinguished from personal religious experiences which continued into the new century and were not discouraged" (295). The speaking and interpretation of tongues, however, were among the discouraged personal experiences.
31. James X. Allen, "The Passing of the Gift of Tongues," *Improvement Era*, November 1904, 109.

32. Allen, "The Passing of the Gift of Tongues," 109, 111.
33. Editorial, "Gift of Tongues," *Liahona: The Elders' Journal,* July 1907, 120–21.
34. Editorial, "Speaking in Tongues," *Liahona: The Elders' Journal,* February 22, 1908, 955.
35. Editorial, "Speaking in Tongues," 955.
36. L. Grant McClung Jr., "Explosion, Motivation, and Consolidation: The Historical Anatomy of a Missionary Movement," in *Azusa Street and Beyond: Pentecostal Missions and Church Growth in the Twentieth Century,* ed. L. Grant McClung Jr. (South Plainfield, NJ: Bridge Publishing, 1986,) 18.
37. Editorial, "Speaking in Tongues," 955.
38. Maynard Ketcham and Wane Warner, "When the Pentecostal Fire Fell in Calcutta," in McClung, *Azusa Street and Beyond,* 27–28. See also Gary B. McGee, "'Latter Rain' Falling in the East: Early-Twentieth-Century Pentecostalism in India and the Debate over Speaking in Tongues," *American Society of Church History* 68, no. 3 (September 1999): 648–65.
39. Editorial, "Speaking in Tongues," 955–56.
40. Sister A. G. Garr, "In Calcutta, India," *Apostolic Faith,* April 1907, 1.
41. Alexander, *Mormonism in Transition,* 294.
42. Editorial, "Speaking in Tongues," 956.
43. Editorial, "Speaking in Tongues," 956, 958.
44. Joseph Fielding Smith, Anthon H. Lund, and Charles W. Penrose, "A Warning Voice," *Improvement Era,* September 1913, 1148–49.

Index

Aaronic Priesthood, 214–15, 423–24
academies
closure of, 394
constructed during building boom, 328–29
creation of, 408
enrollment in, 388, 428
false doctrine taught at, 23–24, 380, 411–12
maintenance costs for, 412–13
problems in, 380–81
Adam, 22, 26
Adams, Samuel L., 47
Administration Building, 324
after-school programs, 328–29
Allen, James, 478
Amalgamated Sugar Company, 192
American Sugar Refining Company, 191
amusement halls, in meetinghouses, 331, 332–33
Angell, Phoebe Morton, 35n42
anointings, 239–40
Apostle(s). *See also* Seventy, responsibilities and privileges of; Twelve Apostles
called to European mission, 367–68
First Presidency and, 206–7
Joseph F. Smith as senior, 271
Joseph F. Smith learns from, 404–5
Joseph F. Smith ordained as, 249–51, 264n3, 267, 406
priesthood keys and, 209–10
seniority among, 252–54, 268–71
auxiliary organizations
coordination of, 430
establishment and development of, 418–19
expansion of, 420–22
priesthood and, 211
Religion Class program and, 382, 384–85, 386–87
Azusa Street revival, 470–72, 479–82

baby blessings, 240–43, 247nn32,34
Bamberger, Simon, 446, 448
baptism. *See also* rebaptism
  for dead, 222
  for health, 238–39
  of Joseph F. Smith, 38
  locations for, 340n30
baptismal fonts, 331, 340n30
beards, 457–64, 467
beef, Calvin Smith saved by can of, 441–42
Bennion, Mildred, 393–94
Bible
  higher criticism and, 21, 23–24, 34n19, 380, 411
  Joseph Smith Translation of, 369, 373–74
Bidamon, Charles, 354
bishops and bishopric, 124, 214
bishop's blessings, 241–42
Bishop's Building, 324
blessings
  of bishops, 241–42
  given to babies, 240–43, 247nn32,34
  performed by fathers, 148–49
blind, Church literature for, 427
Book of Mormon
  David Whitmer on, 365
  given to Joseph Fielding Smith, 110–11
  printer's copy of, 365–66
  teachings on spirit world in, 222
  William E. McLellin on, 363
books, sent to Edward Arthur Smith, 116, 124
braille, Church literature in, 427
Brigham Young University, false doctrine taught at, 23–24, 380, 411
Brimhall, George H., 21–22
Browning, Elizabeth M., 347–48
building boom
  factors necessitating, 321–23
  funding, 323, 333–34
  gathering and, 323–24
  under Joseph F. Smith, 320
  magnitude of, 321
  and plan of Zion, 324–27
  schools built during, 328–29
  tabernacles and meetinghouses built during, 327, 330–38
  temples built during, 327, 329
Burton, Harold W., 292, 308–9, 313

Caldwell County, Missouri, 366–68
Cannon, George Q., 44, 269–70
Cardston Alberta Temple
  dedication of, 315
  design and construction of, 308–11, 329
  as historic site, 319n45
  prophecies concerning, 304–5
  unique aspects of, 327
Carthage Jail, 39, 347–48
chapels, in meetinghouses, 331
chaplain(s)
  B. H. Roberts as, 446–50
  Calvin Schwartz Smith as, 441–42
  Herbert Brown Maw as, 443–46
  Joseph F. Smith as, 453n24
  LDS, 440–41
Chapman, William Avery, 352
chastisement, 45–46
checkers, 44, 194
chiasmus, 262–63
children. *See also* youth
  blessing of, 240–43, 247nn32,34
  illness and death of, 105–6, 121–22

children (*cont.*)
impact of fathers on, 96
of Joseph F. Smith, 76
love for, 13–14, 48n8, 100–109
recreation with, 99–100
teaching, 12–13, 99, 109–11, 405
time for, 97, 99
Christians, Mormons as, 19–20
Christmas presents, 102
Church education. *See also* Religion Class program; seminary program
expansion of, 406–9
under Joseph F. Smith, 401–2, 413
separation of public education and, 409
spiritual and temporal concerns in, 411–13
Church government
and calling counselors in First Presidency, 205–8
need for instruction on, 200–201
priesthood authority, offices, and keys and, 202–5
Church meetings, developments in, 419–20, 429–31
Church of Jesus Christ of Latter-day Saints, The
as Christian church, 19–20
critics of, 32–33
defense of, 42–43
depictions of members of, 458
finances of, 190–91, 306–7, 323, 333–34
First World War and, 438, 451, 453n22
gift of tongues and, 470–77, 481–83
growth of, 304
John Smith's loyalty to, 142–44
Joseph F. Smith's impact on, 10
long beards' reflection on, 457–58
love for, 45–46
membership of, in Hawaii, 52, 60
public perceptions of, 458–59, 464, 466–67
worldwide expansion of, 210–11, 280
Clawson, Rudger, 271, 274
Cluff, Benjamin, 61
Cluff, William W., 54–55, 57, 60, 61
Committee of Correlation and Adjustments, 430
common sense, 25
continuing revelation, 19–20
Coolbrith, Ina, 166, 178n26
Cowdery, Oliver, 370–71
creation, spiritual and temporal, 22–23
Cummings, Horace, 23
Cumorah, 352, 372–73

Darwinism, 21, 23–24
dead
baptism for, 222
redemption of, 29–31, 122–23, 215–17, 229–31
death
Joseph F. Smith's experiences with, 224, 225–26, 228–29
Joseph F. Smith's views on, 230–31
debt, 190–92, 306–7, 334
Deseret Gymnasium, 325–26
Deseret News Building, 324
divorce, 90
doctrine
regarding discernment of truth, 24–25
regarding divinity of Jesus Christ, 27–28

regarding eternal progression, 26–27
regarding false doctrine, 23–24
regarding figurative and literal, 25–26
regarding Godhead, 28
regarding higher criticism and Darwinism, 21
regarding human origins, 21–23
in letters to Edward Arthur Smith, 123–26
regarding Mormons as Christians, 19–20
regarding redemption of dead, 29–31
dreams, 46–47
Duffin, James G., 349
Dwight, Gelston, 43
Dwyer, James, 346

early-morning seminary, 395
Eaton, William, 362
Eccles, David, 188–89
economics and economy, 118–21, 190–92. *See also* debt
education. *See also* Church education; Religion Class program; seminary program
building boom and, 328–29
counsel to Martha Ann Smith regarding, 162–67
encouraged for Edward Arthur Smith, 116–18, 124
of Joseph F. Smith, 116–17, 402–5
Joseph F. Smith's concerns regarding, 379–82
Joseph F. Smith's philosophy on, 405–6
through missionary work, 41–42
eighth-day blessings, 241–43
elders, responsibilities of, 214
emigration, Charles W. Nibley and, 186
endowment, 237
Endowment House, 283, 300n31
eternal progression, 26–27
European Mission, 185–87
evolution, doctrine regarding, 21, 23–24

facial hair. *See* beards; mustaches
fact-finding mission
calling to, 360–61
in Illinois, 368–70
in Missouri, 361–68
in Ohio and New York, 370–73
report concerning, 359–60
return from, 373–75
Fairbanks, Avard, 313
family
counsel regarding, 171–75
devotion and love for, 48n8, 74, 156–57n63
education in, 388, 398n36, 405, 428–29
gifts for, 102
influence of, 43–45
Joseph F. Smith's love for, 12–14
recreation with, 99–100
Relief Society Magazine's portrayal of, 74–76
teaching gospel to, 109–11
family home evening, 175
farm duties, 97, 118–19
Far West, Missouri, 366–68
Far West Temple site, 352
fasting, 124
fast meetings, 419–20
father(s)
influence of, 96

father(s) (*cont.*)
 ordinances and blessings performed by, 148–49, 242–43
 presiding authority of, 141
 showing affection as, 100–107
 surrogate, 107–9
 teaching gospel as, 109–11
 time management as, 97–100
female ritual healing, 235–37, 239–40
Fielding Joseph, 44
figurative, versus literal, 25–26
First Presidency
 calling counselors in, 205–8
 dissolution of, 254, 260
 Joseph F. Smith's service in, 249, 263n1, 406
 ordination to, 258
 reorganization of, 256, 258, 267–69, 273–74
First World War
 B. H. Roberts as chaplain during, 446–50
 Calvin Schwartz Smith as chaplain during, 441–42
 causes of and U.S. involvement in, 434–35
 Church's response to, 435–40
 death tolls of, 451n2
 Herbert Brown Maw as chaplain during, 443–46
 impact of, on Church, 453n22
 Joseph F. Smith's role in, 451
 LDS chaplains in, 440–41
Free Schools Act (1890), 383
French, Mary, 3
friend(s)
 Charles W. Nibley as, 181–82, 193–95
 influence of, 43–45
Garr, A. G., 480–81
gathering
 building boom and, 323–24
 Laie as prototype of, 280, 284–87
 purpose of, 279
 temples and, 295–97, 303–4
Gibson, Walter Murray
 actions of, in Hawaii, 52–54, 56–60, 63, 281–82
 followers of, 68n40, 71n74
 ordinations performed by, 65–66n8
gifts, showing love through, 102
glossolalia. *See* tongues, gift of
God
 Jesus Christ as Son of, 27–28
 man created in image of, 22–23
 titles for, 28
Godhead, 28
golf, 193–94
Gothic Revival architecture, 335–37
government, allegiance to, 20, 435. *See also* Church government
grandchildren, 107–8
Grant, Heber J., 238–39, 295
Grinnels, Hannah, 151–52n11, 161

Hammond, Francis A., 283
Hansen, Ramm, 314
Hardwick, Thomas W., 181–82
Harris, Martha Ann Smith
 counsel given to, 162–67, 171–75
 and death of Mary Fielding Smith, 161
 homes of, 177–78n7
 Joseph F. Smith defends, 9, 116–17, 161, 404
 letters to, 159–60, 175–77
Harris, Martin, 209
Harris, William Jasper, 171–72

Hawaii. *See also* Laie; Laie Temple
  Castle and Verna Murphy's missions to, 300n36
  correspondence from, 167–71
  gathering and, 284–87
  Joseph F. Smith's connection to, 280–84, 287
  missionary work in, 9–10, 52–65, 66–67nn9-11, 161–62
Hawaiian language, 167
healing, 235–40
health
  baptism for, 238–39
  in letters to Edward Arthur Smith, 121–23
higher criticism
  caution regarding, 21, 23–24
  taught at BYU, 380, 411
  Will Durrant on, 34n19
High Priesthood, 207–8
high priests, 205–7, 213
Hill Cumorah, 352, 372–73
Historian's Office, 404–5
historical sites. *See also* fact-finding mission
  acquisition of, under Joseph F. Smith, 342, 345, 353–55
  birthplace of Joseph Smith as, 350–52
  Carthage Jail as, 39, 347–48
  as educational experiences, 354
  Far West Temple site as, 352
  Independence Temple Lot as, 349–50
  interest in, 342–43
  in Missouri, 361–68
  Mount Pisgah cemetery as, 344–45
  Temple Square as, 346–47
  as travel destinations, 343–44, 346–47
home, Joseph F. Smith on, 12. *See also* family
Home Evening, 175
hospitals, 325
Hotel Utah, 318n22, 324–25
human origins, doctrine regarding, 21–23, 49n15, 380, 411
Huntington, Oliver B., 344–45

Illinois, fact-finding mission in, 368–70
Independence, Missouri, 361–64
Independence Temple Lot, 349–50, 361–62
Indians, 475
Inspired Version, 369, 374, 375, 377n36
institute program, 329, 395
Iosepa, 10
Iosepa, Utah, 285, 286

Jackson County, Missouri, 361–64
Jesus Christ
  divine sonship of, 27–28
  teaches in spirit world, 215–16, 222, 224–25, 226, 227, 229–30
  titles for, 28
Johnson, Lyman, 370
Johnson, Sarah, 367
Johnston, Albert Sidney, 188
Joseph Smith Translation, 369, 373–74
Juvenile Instructor, 422

Kealakaihonua, Peter, 289–90, 291
Kimball, Alice, 85–88, 91–92
Kimball, Andrew, 86
Kimball, Elias S., 440

Kimball, Heber C., 172
Kirtland, Ohio, 370–71
Kirtland Temple, 371
Knaphus, Torleif S., 311

Laie
  creation of branch in, 283–84
  land purchased in, 61, 283
  as prototype of gathering, 280, 284–87, 295–96
Laie Temple
  announcement regarding, 285–86, 311–13
  construction of, 291–93
  dedication of, 293–95, 315
  design of, 313
  ground dedicated for, 287–91
  prophecies concerning, 305
  role of, in Church history, 297–98
  significance of, 327
Lamanites, mission to, 370–71
Lambson, Edna, 82–85
Lambson, Julina. *See* Smith, Julina Lambson
Lanai, 52–53, 56–57, 59–60, 69nn48,49, 282
Lathrop, John, 4
Lemmon, Nancy Melissa, 144–45
Leo, J., 313
Liberty Bonds, 438
lightning, 103–4
Lincoln, Abraham, 459
literal, versus figurative, 25–26
liturgy
  baby blessings and, 240–43, 247nn32,34
  development of, 233–34, 237–38
  healing, 238–40
  priesthood authority and, 234–37
Logan Fifth Ward Annex, 329
Lund, Anthon H., 206, 238, 383–84
Lyman, Amasa, 251
Lyons, Tom, 127

Mack, Solomon, 143–44
Maeser, Karl G., 383, 384, 386
marriage, counsel regarding, 171–75. *See also* plural marriage
Martyrdom
  influence of, on Joseph F. Smith, 224
  reactions to, 7–8
  vengeance for, 39
Maw, Herbert Brown, 443–46
McDowell, James, 371
McIntosh, T. J., 480
McKay, David O., 150, 421–22, 424
McLellin, William E., 362–64
media
  depictions of Joseph F. Smith in, 461–64
  depictions of Reed Smoot in, 466–67
  public opinion and, 459
meetinghouses
  architectural styles of, 335–38
  changes to, 323–24
  constructed during building boom, 321, 327–28, 330–35
  increased need for, 322
Melchizedek Priesthood, 202–5, 207–10
Merrick, D. M., 161
Merrill, Joseph F., 388–91
Merrill, Laura, 389–90
Mesa Arizona Temple, 305, 313–15, 319n45
Millet, Robert L., 37
Millikin, Arthur, 368

Millikin, Lucy, 368
Mills, George, 151–52n11
missionary work
 among Lamanites, 370–71
 dedication to, 167–71
 First World War and, 435
 as foundational experience, 40–41
 gift of tongues and, 476–77, 478, 480–82
 in Hawaii, 9–10, 52–65, 66–67nn9–11, 161–62, 280–84
 intellectual development through, 41–42
 of John Smith, 138
 of Joseph F. Smith and Charles W. Nibley, 185–87
 and love for Saints, 45
 Pentecostalism and, 472
 and revelation of truth, 46
 in spirit world, 29–31, 215–17, 224–30
 through historic sites, 346
"Mormon Rebellion," 169–70
Mormon Reformation (1856–57), 62–63, 171, 475
motherhood
 Edna Lambson Smith and, 85
 Julina Smith's devotion to, 77–79
Mount Pisgah cemetery, 344–45
Mount Vernon, 343
Murphy, Castle, 300n36
Murphy, Verna, 300n36
mustaches, 464–67, 469n34
Mutual Improvement Associations, 420, 425–27

Native Americans, 475
Nauvoo, Illinois, 402
Nauvoo House, 354
Nebeker, George, 283
Nibley, Alex, 186
Nibley, Charles W.
 as business partner, 187–89
 childhoods of Joseph F. Smith and, 182–85
 economic views of, 190–92
 friendship with, 44, 181–82, 193–95
 Laie Temple and, 290, 294
 missionary work of, 185–87
 plural marriage and, 187
 political views of, 189–90
 as Presiding Bishop, 192–93
nicknames, for children, 101–2

optimism, through trials, 168–69
order, 147, 149
ordination
 method for, 264n3
 versus setting apart, 256–58, 274
Oregon Lumber Company, 187–89
"Origin of Man, The," 21–23, 411

Palmyra, New York, 371–73
patriarchal blessing(s)
 of David O. McKay, 150
 of Joseph F. Smith, 38–39
patriarchs, responsibilities of, 213
Patriarch(s) to the Church
 authority of, 256–57
 John Smith as, 133, 137, 146–48, 150, 153n24
 Joseph Smith Sr. as, 148
 list of, 137
 and organization of priesthood, 258–60
 succession of, 139–41, 152–53n23, 157n64
patriotism, 435
Pearl of Great Price, 369

Penrose, Charles W., 443–44
Pentecostalism, 470–72, 479–82. *See also* Azusa Street revival
persecution
  due to plural marriage, 89, 91–92, 120–21, 200, 283, 322
  gift of tongues and, 477
  in Missouri, 361
pilgrimages, 343–44
plural marriage
  Charles W. Nibley and, 187
  demise of, 93
  John Smith and, 144–45
  Joseph Smith and, 363, 370
  Joseph Smith III on, 368–69
  Julina Smith on, 79–80
  persecution due to, 89, 91–92, 120–21, 200, 283, 322
Pope, Hyrum C., 292, 308–9, 313
Prairie School architecture, 337–38
Pratt, Orson, 360, 369, 377n36. *See also* fact-finding mission
Pratt, Parley P., 370–71
prayer, 164
preparation of Joseph F. Smith
  and defense of Church, 42–43
  foundational experiences as, 38–41
  intellectual development and, 41–42
  and love for Saints, 45–46
  and revelation of truth, 46–47
  through family and friendship, 43–45
President of Church
  Joseph F. Smith called as, 255–58, 273–77
  prophecies regarding Joseph F. Smith as, 265–66, 269, 281
  responsibilities and privileges of, 212
presiding authority, 140–41
Presiding Bishop, 192–93, 213
priesthood
  authority, offices, and keys in, 202–5
  gift of tongues and, 481–82
  Joseph F. Smith's focus on, 199
  need for instruction on, 200–201
  organization of, 258–60
  in spirit world, 215–17, 224, 226–28, 230
  and worldwide expansion of Church, 210–11
priesthood authority
  First Presidency and, 206–7
  liturgy and, 234–37
  of Melchizedek Priesthood, 208–10
  of patriarchs, 256–57
  priesthood keys and offices and, 202–5
  in spirit world, 215–17
  and worldwide expansion of Church, 210–11
priesthood keys
  of Church President, 212
  of Melchizedek Priesthood, 208–10
  priesthood authority and offices and, 202–5, 218n10
  in spirit world, 215–17
priesthood offices
  priesthood authority and keys and, 202–5, 209–10, 218n10
  rights and privileges of, 211–15
priesthood reform movement, 422–25
Primary Association, 387, 422
progression, eternal, 26–27

public schools and education
after-school programs supplement, 328
distrust for secular, 118
enrollment in, 381, 388, 428
expansion of, 408–9
as means to undermine Mormonism, 382–83
religious education and, 385–86, 407–8
support for, 409–10, 416n49
versus ward schools, 322

railroads, 187–88
reading, 41
reason, 25
rebaptism, 62–63, 71n71
recreation, 97–100, 332–33. *See also* travel
Red Cross, 438
released-time religious education, 388, 399n61, 410–11
Relief Society
expansion of, 421
supports war effort, 438
religion
in letters to Edward Arthur Smith, 123–26
science versus, 24–25, 477–78
Religion Class program
Church and state problems regarding, 384–86
complaints regarding, 386–88
creation of, 382–84, 407–8
seminary program and, 394
Reorganized LDS Church, 125–26, 142–44, 354, 368–70, 373–74
repentance, 125
revelation(s)
canonized as scripture, 29
chiastic structure in, 262–63
continuing, 19–20
gift of tongues and, 474
received in Kirtland, 371
truth and, 25
Rich, Joseph C., 42
Richards, Sarah Ellen. *See* Smith, Sarah Ellen Richards
Richmond, Missouri, 364–66
RLDS Church, 125–26, 142–44, 354, 368–70, 373–74
Roberts, Brigham Henry, 446–50
Roskelley, Samuel, 237

sacrament, 124, 460
sacrament meeting, 419–20
St. George Temple, 300n31
Salt Lake First Ward meetinghouse, 338
Samaritan Woman at the Well, The (Knaphus), 311
Satan, gift of tongues and, 476
schoolmaster, Joseph F. Smith fights, 9, 116–17, 161, 404
schools. *See also* academies; education; public schools and education
built during building boom, 328–29
establishment of Church, 406–8
Martha Ann Smith's attendance at, 164–66
in Nauvoo, 402
Religion Classes held in, 385–86
in Salt Lake Valley, 403
secular, 118
Schwartz, Mary Taylor, 88–90, 91–92
science
evolution of word, 24
religion versus, 24–25, 477–78

scripture(s)
figurative and literal reading of, 25–26
revelations canonized as, 29
teaching children through, 104
seminary program
creation of, 388–91
emergence of, 379–82
expansion of, 394–95, 428
first teachers in, 391–94
released-time, 410–11
Religion Class program and, 382–84
setting apart, as Church President, 202–4, 256–57, 274
Seventy, responsibilities and privileges of, 212–13
sin, 125
Skull Valley, Hawaiian community in, 285, 286
Smith, Agnes Charlotte, 166, 178n26
Smith, Alexander, 126, 374
Smith, Alfred J., 186–87
Smith, Alice Kimball, 85–88, 91–92
Smith, Alma L., 60, 61
Smith, Alvin, 238
Smith, Asael, 4, 152n12
Smith, Calvin Schwartz, 441–42
Smith, Edith, 110
Smith, Edna Lambson, 82–85
Smith, Edward Arthur
adoption of, 129–30n5
biographical information concerning, 115–16
birth date of, 129n2
encouraged to learn, 116–18
encouraged to live righteously, 123–26
encouraged to work, 118–21
final years of, 127–28
health discussed with, 121–23
letters to, 114–15
love for, 128–29
Smith, Elias Wesley, 284
Smith, Ella, 115–16, 127–28
Smith, Emma, 363
Smith, Frederick, 126
Smith, George A., 100–101
Smith, George Albert, 156n63, 355
Smith, Hellen, 144
Smith, Hyrum
children of, 136
faith of, 4
mantle of, 39
martyrdom of, 7–8, 224
names Joseph F. Smith, 35n42
offices held by, 259–60
physical affection from, 103
vengeance for, 39
Smith, Hyrum Mack
as Apostle, 156n63, 275
baptism of, 100
death of, 84, 85, 228, 232n32
education of, 118
letter to, 107
Smith, John (1781-1854), 38–39
Smith, John (1855-1911)
anonymity of, 133–34
Joseph F. Smith's attitude toward, 134
life of, 135–38
as patriarch, 150, 153n24
prominence of, 139–41
sets apart Joseph F. Smith as Church President, 202–4, 256–57, 274
worthiness of, 141–48, 157n64
Smith, John Henry, 266
Smith, Joseph F.. *See also* succession of Joseph F. Smith

achievements of, 10
ancestors of, 3–5
death of, 14–15, 293–95
life of, 360
name of, 35n42
Smith, Joseph Fielding, 110–11, 118, 156n63
Smith, Joseph, III, 142–43, 368–69, 373–74
Smith, Josephine Donna, 166, 178n26
Smith, Joseph, Jr.
ancestors of, 3–5
birthplace of, 350–52, 354
confers priesthood keys upon Twelve, 205
foreordination of, 3
Joseph F. Smith on, 5
Joseph F. Smith's recollections of, 6
liturgical development and, 234–35
martyrdom of, 7–8
plural marriage and, 370
priesthood keys of, 216
teachings of, on spirit world, 222
William E. McLellin on, 363
Smith, Joseph Richards, 185
Smith, Joseph Sr., 4–5, 148, 152n12
Smith, Julina Lambson, 76–80, 90–92, 127–28, 283, 284
Smith, Lester Ray, 121–22
Smith, Levira, 90
Smith, Lucy Mack, 4–5, 8
Smith, Marjorie, 103–4
Smith, Martha Ann. *See* Harris, Martha Ann Smith
Smith, Mary Fielding
death of, 9, 38, 47, 136–37, 161, 225, 404
as example, 173
faith of, 4, 5–6
following Martyrdom, 7
as teacher, 402–3
Smith, Mary French, 3
Smith, Mary Sophronia, 106–7
Smith, Mary Taylor Schwartz, 88–90, 91–92
Smith, Mercy Josephine, 13, 122, 174–75, 225–26
Smith, Nancy Melissa Lemmon, 144–45
Smith, Robert, 3
Smith, Ruth, 121, 175
Smith, Samuel, 103
Smith, Sarah Ellen Richards, 79–82, 185
Smith, Willard, 104
Smith family reunion, 64
Smoot, Reed, 190, 287, 290–91, 436, 461–67
Snow, Eliza R., 235–37
Snow, Lorenzo
death of, 271–73
drowning of, 55
incarceration of, 461
Independence Temple Lot purchase and, 349
prophecy of, regarding Joseph F. Smith, 56, 255, 266, 281
and reorganization of First Presidency, 268–69
seniority issue and, 269–70
Society of the Aid of the Sightless, 427
Spalding, Walter, 292, 301n64
Spalding Construction Company, 292, 301n64
special conference, 258–60
special needs, accommodating Saints with, 427
spiritual education, 405

spirit world
  Brigham Young's teachings on, 224–25
  doctrine of, during Joseph F. Smith's presidency, 227–28
  Joseph Smith's teachings on, 222
  missionary work in, 29–31, 215–17, 224–27, 229–30
  priesthood authority and keys in, 215–17
stakes, reorganization of, 200
statehood, 323
stereoscope, 344
St. George Temple, 300n31
Stratton, Electra, 371
succession of Joseph F. Smith
  calling as Church President, 255–58, 273–77
  calling to Quorum of the Twelve, 249–51, 267
  ordination as Apostle, 249–51
  prophecies regarding, 265–66
  seniority issue and, 268–71
  timeline for, 261
sugar, 191
Sunday School, 420, 421–22

tabernacles, constructed during building boom, 321, 327–28, 330
Talmage, Albert M., 427
Talmage, James E., 21
Talmage, Sarah, 427
Taylor, Agnes, 89
Taylor, Frank Y., 388
Taylor, John, 200, 226, 344
temper, of Joseph F. Smith, 43
temple(s). *See also* Cardston Alberta Temple; Independence Temple Lot; Laie Temple; Mesa Arizona Temple
  anticipation for, 304–6
  baptism for health in, 238–39
  construction of, 306–7, 315, 321, 327, 329
  Edna Lambson Smith and, 84
  gathering and, 279, 284–85, 295–97, 303–4
  as historic sites, 319n45
  liturgy for, 237
  prophecies on, 302n80, 316n3
Temple Square, 346–47, 354
Temple Square Bureau of Information, 326–27, 346, *347*
Thanksgiving Psalm, 449–50
Thomas, Charles J., 346
Thompson, Mercy R., 44
Thorpe, Edward Arthur. *See* Smith, Edward Arthur
thunderstorm, comfort for child during, 103–4
tithing, 306, 307, 334
tongues, gift of
  Church's reexamination of, 471
  de-emphasis on, 475–79, 482–83
  in early Church, 472–76
  Pentecostalism and, 471–72, 479–81
travel
  with Charles W. Nibley, 189
  to Hawaii, 287
  historical sites and, 343–44, 346–47
trials, optimism through, 168–69
truth
  discernment of, 24–25, 55–56
  eternal, 411–12
  Joseph F. Smith as revealer of, 46–47
  opposing, 25–26
  seeking out, 405

Twelve Apostles
  Apostles outside of, 251
  called to European mission, 367–68
  disunity among, 267–68
  Hyrum M. Smith called to, 275
  Joseph F. Smith called to, 251–54, 267
  priesthood keys conferred upon, 205
  responsibilities and privileges of, 212
  seniority among, 252–54, 268–71

Union Pacific Railroad, 187–88
Utah, statehood for, 323
Utah-Idaho Sugar Company, 193
Utah War, 169–71, 453n24
Utes, 475

vision, of redemption of dead, 29–31, 122–23, 215–17, 229–31
vocational training, 117, 405–6

Walker, Lorin, 142
wards, reorganization of, 200
Wells, Junius F., 351
White, A. C., 344
Whitmer, David, 209, 364–66
Whitmer, Jacob, 352, 367
Whitmer, John, 367
Widtsoe, John A., 21
Wilson, Guy C., 393
Winder, John R., 206, 274, 354
wives of Joseph F. Smith
  Alice Kimball Smith, 85–88
  Edna Lambson Smith, 82–85
  gifts for, 102
  Julina Lambson Smith, 76–80
  Mary Taylor Schwartz Smith, 88–90
  relationship among, 90–92
  Relief Society Magazine's portrayal of, 74–76
  Sarah Ellen Richards Smith, 80–82
women, healing and, 235–37, 239–40
Woodruff, Wilford
  prophecy of, regarding Joseph F. Smith, 255, 266
  rebukes John Smith, 138
  and reorganization of First Presidency, 267–68
Woolley, Samuel E., 291–92
Word of Wisdom
  John Smith and, 145–46
  leniency in, 155–56nn53,54
work
  children and, 99
  encouraged for Edward Arthur Smith, 118–21
World War I. *See* First World War
worthiness
  of John Smith, 141–48, 157n64
  of Patriarchs, 141
Wright, A. B., 315
writing, 42, 166–67

xenoglossia
  under Brigham Young, 475
  glossolalia versus, 471, 472, 477, 479, 480
  under Joseph Smith, 474
  missionary work and, 480–82
  Pentecostalism and, 472
  revelation through, 473

Yates, Thomas J., 391–93
Young, Brigham
- auxiliary organizations under, 418
- calls Joseph F. Smith to preside over Hawaii, 54, 66–67n11
- calls missionaries home, 169–71
- dream of, 46
- gift of tongues and, 474–75
- John Smith and, 137, 146
- Joseph F. Smith defends, 64
- ordains Apostles, 250–51
- prophecy regarding, 255
- as surrogate father, 100–101
- teachings of, on spirit world, 224–25
- temple building and, 303
- Walter M. Gibson's letter to, 68–69n42

Young, Brigham, Jr.
- called as Twelve, 252–54
- ordained as Apostle, 251
- seniority issue and, 268, 270

Young, Don Carlos, Jr., 314
Young, John R., 61, 62, 70–71n64
Young Ladies' Mutual Improvement Association, 425–27
Young Men's Mutual Improvement Association, 420, 425–27
youth. *See also* children
- concerns regarding education and, 379–82
- recreation for, 332–33
- spiritual welfare of, 379

Zion
- expansion of, 327–28
- plan of, 324–27